# The
# Bed & Breakfast
# Directory

**Barbara Notarius**

WILEY

## John Wiley & Sons, Inc.

New York • Chichester • Brisbane • Toronto • Singapore

This publication is designed to provide accurate and authoritative information in regard to the subject matter covered. It is sold with the understanding that the publisher is not engaged in rendering professional services in the subject matter discussed. Due to the ever-changing marketplace, we suggest that you contact the addresses given to verify information.

**Library of Congress Cataloging-in-Publication Data**

Notarius, Barbara.
    The bed & breakfast directory.

    1. Bed and breakfast accommodations—Directories.
I. Title.  II. Title: Bed and breakfast directory.
TX907.N69  1987    647'.94    87-25325
ISBN 0-471-85302-X

Printed in the United States of America

88 89 10 9 8 7 6 5 4 3 2 1

# Acknowledgments

I wish to express my appreciation and sincere thanks to:

Marjorie and Bob Mausler who were responsible for untold hours of entering information on the computer, without whom this book would not have been possible.

Gary Craig, who inspired this book and helped bring it to fruition.

Katherine Schowalter, my editor, who has the patience of a saint.

All the members of Bed & Breakfast Reservation Services Worldwide who contributed diligent effort at compiling the B&Bs.

All the B&B hosts whose warmth and outgoing nature make the B&B industry what it is.

My husband, George Klein, and my daughter, Cydney Gael, who have supported me during the seemingly endless hours which were necessary to make this book a reality.

# Preface

Although bed and breakfast has been offered in Great Britain since the 1940s, the widespread availability of lodging in private homes in North America began only in the late 1970s and early 1980s. At first, they were frequented by foreign travelers and Americans who had experienced B&B overseas. As media attention and word of mouth spread through the United States, Americans have begun seeking out B&Bs in rapidly increasing numbers. To meet the growing demand, some 20,000 families across the United States and Canada have opened their homes to travelers. Most are not easy to find, however.

Unlike Great Britain, where B&Bs are governmentally regulated and permitted to hang signs, few B&Bs in North America can or wish to have strangers walk in without reservations. Many prefer to list their homes with reservation services in order to ensure that guests are screened. The administrative work and advertising is taken care of by the service. Hosts are left free to do what they do best: meet new people and offer gracious hospitality.

## WHY RESERVATION SERVICES?

The reservation service system is of greatest advantage to the traveler since they can be assured that the host home has been personally inspected and is subject to ongoing quality control. For a small fee or yearly membership dues, travelers can avail themselves of a variety of personal services offered by reservation services. Many services will help plan the trip, share their insiders' knowledge of the area, and even offer packages that include admissions to local attractions and restaurants.

## KEEPING UP WITH CHANGE

The B&B industry is a very dynamic one. The fact that each home is unique is what attracts travelers to B&Bs, yet it is this same fact that makes it difficult for travelers to choose where to stay and makes it important for the industry to provide accurate information from which travelers may select the B&B that best meets their needs. Successful B&Bs may be in business for a long time or close after a season or two. Many hosts have lived in fine homes and entertained family and friends graciously for years. Opening their home to travelers has involved few changes in their home, but considerable thought and a new focus. They continue to be available for guests while family considerations are favorable. Should an elderly parent become ill and need to move in, a job transfer necessitate moving, or some other situation occur, the B&B activity may naturally cease or be put on hold.

B&B reservation services keep current on these changes as well as more subtle ones such as the addition of family pets or changes in decor. This attention to detail assures travelers that they will get what they expect. Many a traveler has phoned a reservation service, after having made many long-distance phone calls to B&Bs listed in traditional guidebooks, only to find out that the B&B they had wanted was not available, no longer met the traveler's needs, or had stopped taking guests entirely. Calling a reservation service assures up-to-date information, prompt response, fewer calls, and courteous caring staff to understand a traveler's special requests.

## NOT YOUR ORDINARY GUIDEBOOK

This book is not just another B&B guide. It is unique in that all host homes described have been inspected and belong to a reservation service that is a member of Bed & Breakfast Reservation Services Worldwide—A Trade Association, the only nonprofit association in the B&B industry today. This group has set up guidelines for its member reservation services so that they can work together to provide you access to host homes both near and far and be assured of high-quality accommodations and warm, welcoming hosts.

## CHOOSE FROM A WIDE VARIETY OF B&BS

Until now the one drawback of the reservation service system has been that many travelers prefer to select from a wide variety of B&Bs, but it has been difficult for reservation agents to describe more than three choices over the phone before the information becomes confusing rather than helpful. Mailing out directories of their local region to travelers who plan their trips ahead has eased this problem, but no single reservation service is able to do this for more than their own local area. The demand for a more comprehensive directory is what has prompted reservation services to cooperate on this book.

BARBARA NOTARIUS
*January 1988*

# How to Use
# This Book

To make your planning easier, this directory has been geared to help you work with a B&B reservation service. All the B&Bs listed are members of a reservation service and all the reservation services are in turn members of the national B&B trade association, *Bed & Breakfast Reservation Services Worldwide*. This means that all the listed homes in this book are inspected regularly and must meet standards of quality control provided by the local reservation service, which is concerned with maintaining high standards. Each host home has been selected after personal inspection and lengthy interviews with the prospective host or hostess. Descriptions provided by the reservation service are also updated regularly.

Although there is a good cross section of North America, this first edition of *The Bed & Breakfast Directory* by no means includes every B&B. The reservation services are constantly adding to their lists and you may request updated listings from them for B&Bs that may not have been included.

## GEOGRAPHICAL ORGANIZATION

The guide has been organized according to geographic regions, then alphabetically by state, areas of state, cities, neighborhoods and in some cases down to specific streets. These are listed in the Table of Contents. Note that not every state has listings. There are a number of reasons for this. One is that not every state has inspected B&Bs that are members of the trade association. Another is that some services were not able to meet our publication deadline and we were forced to go ahead without their listings for this edition. If you want to go to Illinois, for example, you will find no listings. However, addresses and phone numbers for the local reservation services in Illinois are listed under this state's heading in the appendix and you can call them for local listings. Any state that has a reservation service but which no individual listing were provided for is listed in the Reservation Service Appendix (see section B of this appendix, which lists these states and their reservation services separately).

There might be times where you are looking for a B&B in a particular city and can't find it listed in the Table of Contents. For easy referencing a city index has been provided since you might not know the particular area in which a town or city is located. If you are looking for a city and can't find it in the index, try to determine from a map what area it is in and see if the B&B is listed in the surrounding area.

An effort has been made to give you as much information as possible for each B&B listed; for example, we have tried to include descriptions of the homes and any relevant information about the rooms and hosts, proximity to points of interest, types of accommodations, rates, and any other relevant information on pets, smoking, and the like. There is a key at the beginning of the listings that will explain how some of this information has been abbreviated. Before making a reservation, confirm these specifics with the reservation service since it is subject to change.

## USING THIS DIRECTORY TO MAKE RESERVATIONS

This book is a reference to use when booking B&B reservations with a reservation service. Any reservation service listed in this guide can book through other reservation services; therefore, if a particular B&B isn't in their local listing they can still make a reservation for you. Usually the only requirement is that you become a member of their service. Notice also that all the B&Bs listed in this book have the name of the local B&B reservation service and phone number at the end of the description. These are then listed alphabetically in the Reservation Service Appendix with corresponding address, contact's name (when available), and business hours. No individual phone numbers are listed for the B&Bs. Many of the B&B homes accept guests only by reservation service and do not promote themselves publicly. It is also easier for you to work with the reservation services. You can join the service closest to you and have them request your reservations from their affiliates or if you prefer call the service that represents the particular host home where you want to stay. There are small fees associated with using any reservation service and they each have their own policies. The nicest thing about working with a reservation service is that you don't have to make the phone calls to individual B&Bs and should one be booked the reservation service will follow up by calling your backup choices. Your reservation service will have to check availability and you should book as far in advance as possible. Although they will try, no reservation service can guarantee that they can reach a host for same day reservations.

**Key**

In writing the paragraph descriptions of the B&Bs you will notice that some words are capitalized, for example SMOKING or CHILDREN. This was done to make scanning easier. If smoking is not mentioned in a paragraph, you may assume it is permitted, the same for children. If smoking or children are prohibited or restricted in any way (for example No CHILDREN under 10), we have capitalized. We did include children welcome, since we feel that there is a difference between children accepted and encouraged. All capital letters were also used to make it easier to scan for special things. Since very few homes are handicapped accessible, this was also capitalized for easier scanning. The same applies to POOL and TENNIS courts on the property.

In general, guests' pets present problems in private homes. It is a rare place that will accept them, so we use the following guideline: If pets are not mentioned in a listing, they are not welcome. If pets are welcome, this is included along with any restriction about kind of pet, etc. For example: Cats welcome.

Although each home is placed according to area, you will notice that some areas or other geographical regions are described in paragraph form while others are not. The general rule of thumb was that if a geographic region contained five or more home listings, the reservation service could provide us an area description that would save our having to describe this area over and over again in each listing. There are a few services who did not choose to do this, so they too are described within each listing.

Many of the reservation services are in areas where B&B Inns are more prevalent than B&B homes to date. Because of this, B&B Inns are included. They generally have more rooms than private home B&Bs and it was too cumbersome to describe each room. Instead of labeling each room A, B, C, etc., accommodations are described in general, such as 10 rooms with choice of double, queen and twin beds. The rates are usually spelled out by room so that you can see them or the range given from most inexpensive to most expensive. For more detail, you can consult the reservation service representing this inn at time of booking.

Very few abbreviations have been used. Consistently you will see rates given with the following abbreviations: S single person in room, D two people in the room, T three people in the same room, Q four people in the same room. If a rate says S or D, it means that the price is the same whether occupied by one or two people.

## TIPS WHEN CALLING FOR RESERVATIONS

1. Before calling a reservation service, make sure you have the exact dates and places where you want to stay. Realize that changing dates once a reservation has been made incurs additional time and expense to the service and you may have to pay a small additional fee.

2. If you are traveling with others, find out if they smoke, have pet allergies, or other special needs (e.g., "can't walk steps" or "are over 6 feet tall").

3. Decide if you must have a private bath or if you are able to share your bath with another guest.

4. Always let your booking agent know your price range.

5. Let your agent know if you have alternative choices should your first pick be unavailable. Should she use her judgment to select an alternative? Which is more important, for instance, double bed or private bath if you have to give up one?

6. Call early! Have your credit card available to guarantee your stay.

7. Call during business hours. Reservation services are usually staffed for answering calls during specific days and hours only. At other times, you will most likely get an answering machine and have to call back or accept a collect phone call if you want to be called back.

8. Deposits are always required to hold a reservation. Make sure to send yours promptly.

These tips should make requesting your reservations easier, keep your calls shorter and reduce the need for extra calls.

## PLANNING SOMETHING SPECIAL

If you are planning a wedding or other large party with many out of town guests, make a chart so that you can indicate information about each guest requiring accommodation. You should know if they smoke, have pet allergies, type of bed required, or who needs a room of his own or who will be sharing a room. Find out who will have cars and indicate which people should be placed in the same home if the group has to be split between a few nearby places. Try to group smokers together and make sure that someone in each home will have a car if needed.

# Introduction

## WHAT TO EXPECT AT A B&B

Although B&Bs differ in style, amenities, and price, guests should expect: clean and pleasant surroundings, a private bedroom made up with fresh sheets and towels, and a clean bathroom that may be private or shared with other guests. Breakfast may be full or continental, but no one should leave the table hungry. Hosts are well versed on nearby attractions, convenient restaurants, local lore, and happy to share their insider's expertise with guests. They are sensitive to guests' needs and respect guests' privacy.

## DIFFERENT TYPES OF B&BS

Throughout this book you will see references to private home B&Bs, B&B inns, and unhosted B&Bs.

### Private Home B&Bs

In a private home B&B the host may live alone or with his family, but always resides there. Most private home B&Bs have no signs and although they have between one and six rooms, the hosts usually do not consider B&B their main occupation. They usually have rich, interesting lives, enjoy meeting people, and often travel themselves. Although they are very attentive to guests' needs, they do not rely on B&B for their livelihood and take guests only part time. You are generally welcome in most parts of their home, certainly not expected to hide in your bedroom, unless that's what you're in the mood for. You are not generally given kitchen privileges, however.

If a home is described as having a piano, a fireplace in the guest bedroom, a swimming pool or hot tub, you can assume that they are for your use. They may require some instruction from your hosts, however, so do check protocol before using anything unusual. There is seldom outside staff at a private home B&B. Although some hosts do provide daily maid service, it is not to be expected and guests who like to return to a neatly made bed after a day of sightseeing should make sure that they make their bed before setting off. Fresh towels are usually provided as needed, but many hosts expect guests to ask for them, since they are reluctant to violate guests' privacy by entering their room in the guests' absence. If you are staying long term, rest assured that your room will be thoroughly cleaned at least once a week and your bed will be changed with fresh sheets.

**Bathrooms**    A private bathroom may or may not be attached to your room since very few homes have more than one master suite. Make sure to bring a robe as you may well have to take a few steps into the hall to get to your bath. For those who stay at places with shared baths, understand that you will arrive to find a clean bathroom and your hostess will most likely look in to tidy it up whenever she passes by, but it is your responsibility to leave the bath as clean as you can so that the next guest finds the bathroom as clean as you did. Bathroom cleansers are always left in the bathroom so that they are easy to find.

**Breakfast**    Breakfast is usually served at a regular hour or adjusted to meet the needs of the guests. Different hosts have different rules about breakfast hours and it's a good policy to check with your host at arrival to determine when breakfast is served. It's a good idea, also, to let your host know ahead of time if anyone in your party has unusual food preferences or allergies so that he can stock up with the appropriate provisions.

Health department regulations vary from state to state. There are some states that do not permit B&Bs to prepare cooked food and in these states you will receive a continental breakfast only. If a full breakfast is important to you, always check with your host about what is served there. A continental breakfast may be juice, coffee, and rolls or may be more elaborate and include fresh fruits, cheeses, and homemade pastries. Full breakfasts are usually the equivalent of bacon, eggs, juice, coffee or tea, and bread. Many hosts, however, pride themselves on more gourmet fare and try to incorporate regional specialties in their breakfast menu.

## The B&B Inn

B&B inns many have a small sign outside and usually at least 4 rooms and sometimes as many as 10. They serve breakfast to their guests, but usually no other meals and the restaurant is not open to the public. Hosts at B&B inns usually expect a significant portion of their income to come from the inn and since they need to maintain a high occupancy rate will usually make sure that someone is there most of the time to take reservations and receive guests. It is unlike a full scale country inn in that there will probably be little if any staff. Guests are unlikely to find maid service, or TV and telephones in every room, nor are they likely to pay country inn prices.

## Unhosted B&Bs

Unhosted B&Bs are usually found in big cities, as cottages on large estates, or carriage houses to historic homes. The unhosted B&B usually means that the guest has a full apartment (a studio, a larger apartment, or a separate cottage). Sometimes the owner lives across the hall, on another floor, or in a main house on the property. In an unhosted B&B there is always a private entrance, private bath, and some cooking facility. Guests arrange their arrival with their host in advance so that someone will be there to greet the guest, turn over a key, and share the little idiosyncrasies of the B&B that the guest will need to know about. Unhosted B&Bs will often have the refrigerator stocked with breakfast food, but it is definitely self-served. Unhosted B&Bs are often popular with business travelers, skiers, families, and those in the relocation process.

## SAY YES TO BEING A GOOD GUEST!

### Arrange a Mutually Convenient Arrival Time!

It is very important to speak to your hosts at least a day or two before your arrival so that you can work out a mutually satisfactory arrival time. If you fail to do this, you may arrive to find that the family has gone to soccer practice and will be back in a few hours. Worse still, you may arrive to find a host who has had to stay home all day waiting for you to arrive and missed out on family activities for fear that you would arrive and find no one at home. It's unfair to expect gracious hospitality unless you have the consideration to think of your host as having other interests also.

## In Case of Delay

If delayed, always remember to phone your host as soon as possible with the change in your arrival time. Understand that once you arrive and get settled in, you will be able to come and go at will. Remember that unlike a hotel with 24 hour check-in, waiting up for you is likely to keep a host awake who has already put in a full day.

## Keys

You will most likely be given keys to your host home. This gives you freedom to come and go as you need. Don't forget to return them when leaving. Although each room should have a private lock on the inside so that you know that no one will disturb you, it is rare for bedroom doors to have their own keys.

## Book Early

B&B travel is best booked in advance to ensure that you get what you want. Reservation services have business hours. Make sure that you call during these hours. Services are seldom open on weekends. If you call when your service is closed, you will have to call again or let them know that you will accept a collect call.

Hosts are often difficult for a reservation service to reach at the last moment, since a host who has no guests due to arrive will take advantage of the time for himself and go out or make weekend plans that preclude having guests.

## Beds

Always indicate your preference about type of bed and let your reservation service know if anyone in your party is over 6 feet tall, since most antique beds have footboards that can cause considerable discomfort to tall sleepers.

## Respect Other Guests

If you come in late, remember that others are already asleep, and keep your voices down. Remember, these are the same folks you'll be sharing breakfast with in the morning.

## Deposits

Deposits are always necessary to reserve a B&B. Hosts often have only a few rooms and holding a room for you means turning others away. Your deposit shows that you are taking the reservation seriously, too. Once your booking is confirmed, deposits can often be made by credit card if you'd rather use it than send a check.

## Balance of Payment

Expect to pay any balance due in cash or travelers' checks on arrival. In most states, local sales tax and in some states an occupancy tax will also be due at this time.

## Cancellations

If circumstances force you to cancel a reservation, don't delay in informing the reservation service and your host. When booking, check to see how far in advance you must cancel before owing a cancellation fee. Most places will charge at least a day's stay for cancellations made after designated dates. Certain places have no-refund policies at special times of the year, (e.g., college graduation).

## Get to Know Your Hosts!

Your hosts are an important reason you've chosen B&B travel. You may find that you have a lot in common and may even become friends. And don't get so hurried getting from place to place that you forget to avail yourself of this wonderful resource.

## Tipping

I am often asked if tipping is expected. The answer depends on whether there are staff at the B&B. Where there are staff, it is appropriate to tip the maid. Most private home B&Bs don't have a staff. If your hosts do something for you that you feel is above and beyond what is normally expected, do what you would do for friends who have done something special for you, send a note or a small gift. I have often welcomed guests who arrived with a small regional token from their hometown, produce from their garden, a small bottle of homemade jam, a sample of their handiwork, or something for my little girl. These friendly gestures immediately make me want to do something special to make their trip more memorable. Recently, I stayed at a hotel in order to be close to my colleagues at a convention. The cost of tipping everyone from the doorman, the bell boy, the maid and the waiters absolutely raised the cost of my stay at least $20 for a three night stay for two.

**Send Back Your Evaluation Forms**

Reservation services value your feedback. Evaluation forms serve as ongoing quality control. Your reactions are appreciated. By spending a few minutes on this, you help the service to serve you better in the future.

**IN RETURN FOR BEING A GOOD GUEST:** Your hosts will extend a warm welcome, personal attention, and gracious hospitality at reasonable rates. They will help make your stay a memorable one and traveling once more an enriching experience.

# Contents

# The
# Bed & Breakfast
# Directory

# 1

---

# New England

☐ **Connecticut**

☐ **Maine**

☐ **Massachusetts**

☐ **Rhode Island**

☐ **Vermont**

# CONNECTICUT

## FAIRFIELD COUNTY

Dubbed the "Gold Coast" for its sophistication and high priced lifestyle, Fairfield County is where urban, suburban, and rural vistas dramatically converge. Here tucked away among the towns and the traffic are sophisticated inns, fine shops, and many top notch restaurants. Accessibility is one of Fairfield County's key virtues. Easily reached by the Merritt and I-95 and railroad lines.

### GREENWICH
### COS COB

A historic 1830 New England home less than an hour away from New York City. The furnishings and decor are as charming and warm as the hostess. Guests can walk from the train (50 minutes to NYC). Accommodations include two double bedrooms, one with private bath, one with shared. Full breakfast is served. One CAT resides here. Hostess is a social worker. Children welcome.
**Rates:** $67 DAILY.
**Reservations:** (203) 236-6698 MONDAY THROUGH FRIDAY 9 A.M. TO 5 P.M.

## HARTFORD COUNTY

In Hartford you will roam from the glittering glass facades of Constitution Plaza to the maze of shops and restaurants in the Civic Center. Visit the State Capitol, the Old State House, Wadsworth Athenaeum, and ride the carousel in Bushnell Park. Not far from there is the peerless Victorian mansion Mark Twain built to celebrate his arrival as a major author. Neighboring towns include Bloomfield, Avon, Simsbury, and Farmington. This area is home to the University of Connecticut Health Center, University of Connecticut Law School, University of Hartford, Trinity, Wesleyan, and many fine private schools.

### BLOOMFIELD

Located on 6 acres, this home has a 70 mile view of the Connecticut Valley. In the spring, 200 varieties of daffodils greet visitors. In the winter, cross-country skiing is right out the door. Jogging, hiking trails, POOL. In the barn 10 goats live, cut the grass, and answer to their names. These are some of the reasons why this is a popular spot. Accommodations include: A) king bed, private bath, working FIREPLACE; B) twin bedded double, private bath; C) 3/4 bed, shared bath in hall; D) twin bedded double with shared bath in hall. Your hostess is a crewel embroiderer. She has two CATS. DOGS and CATS ARE WELCOME with owners. Convenient to Trinity College, University of Connecticut

Law School, and University of Hartford. A full gourmet breakfast is served. Children welcome.
**Rates:** $50-$65 DAILY.
**Reservations:** (203) 236-6698 MONDAY THROUGH FRIDAY 9 A.M. TO 5 P.M.

## HARTFORD

A beautifully restored brownstone offers a canopied bed, bath, window seat, and working FIREPLACE. Your hosts are a retired physician and legal secretary who prefer NONSMOKERS, only. A furnished one bedroom apartment on the ground floor is also available for executive stays. Convenient to Trinity and Wesleyan Colleges and many businesses. In the main house a CAT is also in residence.
**Rates:** $65 DAILY.
**Reservations:** (203) 236-6698 MONDAY THROUGH FRIDAY 9 A.M. TO 5 P.M.

## LITCHFIELD COUNTY

Historic Colonial villages with solid homes and lofty church steeples, covered bridges, wooded uplands, and river valleys, all enhanced by the fiery splendor of autumn foliage, snow covered hills, perfect for skiing. An antique buff's delight. Many fine private schools in the area.

### NEW PRESTON
### LAKE WARAMAUG

A picture perfect setting for a lovely home right on Lake Waramaug with a spectacular view. Enjoy fall foliage, WATERFRONT sports (canoe available) and proximity to fine dining at nearby inns. Excellent location, close to a number of private schools (Kent, Gunnery, and Westover). Accommodations include two double rooms with private baths. Your hostess is a teacher who serves a continental breakfast. For NONSMOKERS, only.
**Rates:** $65 DAILY.
**Reservations:** (203) 236-6698 MONDAY THROUGH FRIDAY 9 A.M. TO 5 P.M.

## NEW HAVEN COUNTY

Yale University puts New Haven on any list of the world's cultural centers. New Haven is only 75 miles from New York City, but is typically New England. Its 340 year colorful history is built into the stones and timbers of the town. Excellent theater, museums, and fine dining make this a favorite stop.

## NEW HAVEN

Situated within walking distance of Yale, this 1902 Georgian Federalist Colonial is one of New Haven's most attractive homes. Spacious rooms and hospitable hosts add to the comfort of guests. This is a prime location for all New Haven activities. Accommodations include: A) king bed with private bath; B) queen bed with shared bath; C) twin bedded double. Accessible by public transportation. Hostess is a director of tourism in one of Connecticut's towns. A 20 year old daughter resides here. Children welcome.
**Rates:** $50-$60 DAILY.
**Reservations:** (203) 236-6698 MONDAY THROUGH FRIDAY 9 A.M. TO 5 P.M.

## STONEY CREEK

Your own log cabin with large bedroom, full bath, living room, and kitchen. Your host built this charming retreat and now lives next door. Enjoy the smell of fresh pine, woodstove, stereo, TV, and all the amenities you need for a perfect getaway weekend. It is 10 minutes from New Haven. HANDICAPPED ACCESSIBLE. Continental breakfast. Children of all ages welcome.
**Rates:** $75 DAILY.
**Reservations:** (203) 236-6698 MONDAY THROUGH FRIDAY 9 A.M. TO 5 P.M.

# MAINE

## MID COAST
## BATH

NEAR ROUTE 1 — Comfortable and newly renovated B&B on a quiet street 10 miles north of Brunswick. Short walk to the Maritime Museum. Guests are invited to enjoy the entire house, read, or watch TV in the library, relax in the parlor or use the grand PIANO in the music room. Hostess taught piano and enjoys music, theater, and gardening. Resident DOG says no pets. Hostess will direct you to the BEACHES and many festivals planned for July and August. Open year-round. Three comfortable guest rooms share a bath. Double accommodations available. Two DOGS reside here. For NONSMOKERS, only. No small CHILDREN.
**Rates:** A & B) S $35, D $40; C) S $30, D $35 DAILY.
**Reservations:** (207) 781-4528 EVENINGS AND WEEKENDS.

## BELFAST

OFF ROUTE 1 — This old fishing village which is not heavily tourist oriented is known for its stunning Greek Revival homes and gracious brick commercial district. You can spend one or more nights in one of the Greek Revival homes, circa 1840. While sitting back from the street behind a sprawling lawn a few blocks from the village, you will marvel at the ornate tin ceilings and cherrywood spiral staircase leading to the second floor in this house. It's a real step back in time. The week long Bay Festival is held here in July. Enjoy the sights of the working HARBOR or possibly a day cruise. Children are welcome and a babysitting service is offered for a small fee. No pets. Full country breakfast. Hosts will also pack a lunch if you like. Many of the bedrooms have their own marble sinks or an attached lavatory. All five rooms share several full baths. Double accommodations are available. Two boys and a girl live here. Host is interested in civic affairs; hostess in decorating. Cots are available.
**Rates:** S $30-$35, D $40-$45 DAILY.
**Reservations:** (207) 781-4528 EVENINGS AND WEEKENDS.

## BOOTHBAY

NEAR ROUTE 1 — A large historic home in a quiet area just a mile from all of the bustle of the HARBOR. This B&B borders a golf course which you are welcome to enjoy. Bike available. The 200 year old home has been transformed into a cozily inviting B&B with each guestroom having its own personality. Bountiful breakfast is prepared by the host who is a former chef. You may enjoy it in the dining room or overlooking the gardens. No pets. The ambiance here is one of delightfully old-fashioned charm and hospitality. Spacious and comfortable rooms, five with private baths, a few also have FIREPLACES. Two additional rooms

share a bath. Double accommodations available. Closed December through April. CHILDREN over 14 welcome.
**Rates:** D SHARED BATH $50, D PRIVATE BATH $60-$70 DAILY.
**Reservations:** (207) 781-4528 EVENINGS AND WEEKENDS.

## BRISTOL
## PEMAQUID PENINSULA

Just a mile from the main road, you will find this 1800 Federal period home at the end of a tree shaded lane surrounded by immaculately tended lawns and orchards. Thoroughbred horses romp in the rear; goats, sheep, and chickens greet you as you arrive (behind fences, of course). DOGS and CATS outside, but not allowed in house. Paddle a guest canoe on hosts' own lake just down the road from the house. This B&B exudes charm and native congeniality. Energetic hosts provide a full and hearty breakfast. Open year-round with reduced rates off-season. No pets. One room with queen bed, private bath. Three other rooms that share two baths. Cot available. For NONSMOKERS, only. CHILDREN over 14 welcome. HANDICAPPED ACCESSIBLE.
**Rates:** A & B) D $60, C-E) D $50 DAILY.
**Reservations:** (207) 781-4528 EVENINGS AND WEEKENDS.

## CUMBERLAND

NEAR ROUTE 1 — 100 year old Colonial home with cozy breakfast room, guest parlor, and porch overlooking Casco Bay, easy access to Portland and Freeport. Visit the nearby restaurant marina with a view of the sailboat races on the BAY. Continental breakfast. Open year-round. Three guestrooms share a bath. Hostess is a dental hygenist. CHILDREN over 14 welcome.
**Rates:** S $35, D $45 DAILY.
**Reservations:** (207) 781-4528 EVENINGS AND WEEKENDS.

## RURAL

NEAR I-95 — Spacious and attractive farmhouse set on 144 acres of rolling fields and woods. Watch the sheep graze in the meadows. Farm is actively at work with the care of Belgian draft horses. Dorset sheep and Hereford cattle are raised here. Family room contains two grand PIANOS which you are invited to use and your hostess will gladly share her interest in music with you. A large game room and outdoor patio are also available. Just 3 miles from Interstate 95, it is easy to find. Just 8 miles from Portland, 12 miles to Freeport. Full country breakfast. All four guestrooms have private baths. Double accommodations available. No pets. Children welcome but there are no cots. NO SMOKING.
**Rates:** S OR D $45 DAILY.
**Reservations:** (207) 781-4528 EVENINGS AND WEEKENDS.

## NEWCASTLE-DAMARISCOTIA

This lovely Victorian home has high ceilings and antiques throughout. A short stroll to the center of one of the prettiest village harbors on the coast. Front porch has view of the WATER. A rear patio is surrounded by gardens. Hostess is retired career person, now enjoying reading, gardening, and sharing her home with visitors. No pets, say the resident DOG and CAT. Airport limousine and bus from Portland serves this community. Full gourmet breakfast. Two spacious rooms share a bath, third has a private bath. A comfortable apartment with private entrance, double bedroom, and daybed in living room, has a kitchenette. Open all year. PIANO. FIREPLACE in bedroom. NO CHILDREN.
**Rates:** A & B) S $35, D $40; AND C) S $40, D $45 DAILY. $10 FOR EXTRA PERSON. TWO NIGHT MINIMUM.
**Reservations:** (207) 781-4528 EVENINGS AND WEEKENDS.

## SOUTH HARPSWELL

A special home overlooking a cove on the tip of the peninsula 13 miles southeast of Brunswick. Enjoy the downstairs housekeeping suite with twin beds, kitchenette with breakfast fixings, private bath, and sitting area. It is delightfully sunny with a view of the water. The area is quiet and very picturesque. Your genial host is a world traveler and might be convinced to play the ORGAN that stands in his living room. Open May through October. WATERFRONT. No pets or CHILDREN.
**Rates:** $45 DAILY. TWO NIGHT MINIMUM.
**Reservations:** (207) 781-4528 EVENINGS AND WEEKENDS.

## WALDOBORO

NEAR ROUTE 1 — Artists, photographers, antique buffs, and nature lovers will find this gracious home a perfect base from which to explore the COAST. Filled with antiques, this B&B is nestled in the heart of a quiet village. An art gallery in the barn features paintings and crafts of vintage Maine artists. A short drive will bring you to the Audubon Sanctuary. Or take a day trip on a ferry to one of the nearby islands. Relax in the common room and enjoy sherry or tea in the afternoon. Enjoy the deck overlooking the gardens. If you plan ahead, your hosts will even prepare a succulent lobster dinner for a fee. On Friday and Saturday candlelight dinners are always available with reservations. The complimentary gourmet breakfasts each morning will be one of the highlights of your trip. Four guestrooms share three baths. Open year-round. Double accommodations available. One DOG resides here. French is spoken here. Bikes are available. HANDICAPPED ACCESSIBLE.
**Rates:** S $30-$50, D $35-$55 DAILY. 20 PERCENT REDUCTION FOR MIDWEEK STAYS (SUNDAY THROUGH THURSDAY).
**Reservations:** (207) 781-4528 EVENINGS AND WEEKENDS.

## MID STATE
## WINTHROP

NEAR ROUTE 202 — A real farm. Watch the ducks and geese in the small pond, then take advantage of this delightfully hospitable home 10 miles from Augusta. Large LAKE for swimming. Help gather eggs for breakfast or watch the cows being milked in the evening or butter being made in the kitchen. The Shakespeare Theater is a 10 minute drive and has a varied program for young and old alike during the summer season. The Maine State Museum in Augusta is worth a visit. A day of shopping in Freeport (L.L. Bean country) is only a half hour away. The farmhouse dates back to 1811. All three rooms share a bath. Two CATS live here. A cot is available. 25 minutes to Colby College. Double accommodations available. Children welcome.
**Rates:** S $30, D $35 DAILY.
**Reservations:** (207) 781-4528 EVENINGS AND WEEKENDS.

## MOUNT DESERT ISLAND
## BASS HARBOR

Refurbished old sea captain's home sits on a knoll looking right at the OCEAN. Short stroll to the ferry landing where you can take a day trip to Swan's Island. Visit the Oceanarium or the Gilley Bird Museum. Hike the many nature trails or just enjoy an unforgettable sunset from the front porch. Host is a woodcarver and was born "downeast." Full breakfast. A DOG and CAT live here. No pets. One room with private bath. Five others with shared bath. Cot available. Checkout is 11 A.M. Double accommodations available. Hostess is interested in crafts, decorating, and travel. NO CHILDREN. SMOKING, outside only.
**Rates:** S $30, D $45 DAILY. EXTRA PERSON ON COT $10. TWO NIGHT MINIMUM.
**Reservations:** (207) 781-4528 EVENINGS AND WEEKENDS.

## SOUTHWEST HARBOR

Sitting on a ridge with a spectacular view of the harbor, this Contemporary home welcomes you to one of the prettiest spots on Mount Desert Island. Enjoy the view from the fully glassed family room or the several decks available to guests. Since the property borders the southern side of Acadia National Park, there is ample opportunity for hiking, biking, or jogging right out the back door. Cycle and canoe rentals in the village. A 20 minute ride to Bar Harbor. Most rooms have a view of the OCEAN. Resident POODLE. Your hostess is very active professionally, yet still finds time to prepare a hearty breakfast and visit awhile. Accommodations include: A) king bed, private bath; B) two twins, shared bath; C - E) queen beds, shared bath. Efficiency apartment with private entrance and private bath also available. No CHILDREN or pets.

**Rates:** D SHARED BATH $45, D PRIVATE BATH $60 DAILY.
**Reservations:** (207) 781-4528 EVENINGS AND WEEKENDS.

## SOUTHERN COAST
## ELIOT
## COUNTRY SETTING

A gracious old Colonial home situated high on a hill, circa 1736 and built by a sea captain. It now has all of the modern comforts without sacrificing the charm of the past. Located just 6 miles north of Portsmouth, New Hampshire, a coastal community with a renovated shopping district, fine restaurants, day cruises to offshore islands, flshing, or WHALE WATCHING. Also close to York. Friendly hosts serve a hearty breakfast on the porch or terrace when weather permits. Guest den and "party barn" for leisure enjoyment. Very attractive first floor guestroom with FIREPLACE, queen bed and private bath. Several other spacious rooms share a bath. Open May through November. Host is a professional; hostess is interested in travel and decorating. No pets or CHILDREN.
**Rates:** D SHARED BATH $50, QUADRUPLE PRIVATE BATH, FIREPLACE $65.
**Reservations:** (207) 781-4528 EVENINGS AND WEEKENDS.

## KENNEBUNK
## COUNTRY SETTING

NEAR ROUTE 1 — Contemporary Cape style home nestled under the pines has its own private guest wing. Located in a nice residential area a short walk to the RIVERBANK or a mile to the port village. This immaculate home is so comfortable that you'll surely want to extend your stay. Picnic under the pines. No pets. Friendly DOG in house. Full country breakfast. Guest suite has twin beds, private bath, and large sitting room with books, TV, and stereo. Sleep sofa will accommodate a third person. Hostess ls a professional. SMOKING downstairs, only. CHILDREN over 12 years of age welcome.
**Rates:** D $50 DAILY. EXTRA PERSON ON SLEEP SOFA $15.
**Reservations:** (207) 781-4528 EVENINGS AND WEEKENDS.

## KENNEBUNKPORT

ON ROUTE 9 — A turn of the century farmhouse now converted to B&B accommodations. The wraparound porch looks over a tidal brook and marsh. Old-fashioned rocking chairs provide guests' enjoyment. House is just one-half mile to the port village and one mile from sandy BEACHES. Several bikes available to guests. Picnic lunches also available for a fee with notice. Hostess, fluent in Spanish, served as a Peace Corps volunteer, enjoys art and travel. Resident CAT shares the house but never the bedrooms. Accommodations include: A) first floor double bed,

shared family bath; B) second floor, private entrance, queen bed, private bath; C) double bed. shared guest bath. Two night minimum stay required during July and August and all holiday weekends. A full gourmet breakfast is served. Open all year. Children welcome.
**Rates:** D SHARED BATH $50, D PRIVATE BATH $60 DAILY.
**Reservations:** (207) 781-4528 EVENINGS AND WEEKENDS.

Renovated early 1800s historic home. Located in the port village near the BEACH, marina, shops and galleries, restaurants, yet quietly hidden from the noise and bustle. An ideal location for a visit to this popular community. Enjoy rear deck overlooking the gardens. A large living room with woodstove for guests' use. Full breakfast served on closed-in porch. Two very comfortable guestrooms share a bath. Closed December to May. No pets and NO CHILDREN. For NONSMOKERS only.
**Rates:** S $36, D $48 DAILY.
**Reservations:** (207) 781-4528 EVENINGS AND WEEKENDS.

## CAPE PORPOISE

OFF ROUTE 9 — Rambling shingled home with a spectacular view of the OCEAN. Private rear terrace leads down to the dock. Watch lobster boats pass by or paint the picturesque fishing village across the harbor. Stroll to the end of the street to watch fishermen in action. Just 3 miles from the port village, the easy ambiance of this B&B is difficult to match. Hosts are interesting, hospitable, and well traveled. Hostess is an artist and sculptor. Full gourmet breakfast. No pets. Three guestrooms have private baths, one shares bath with hostess. Two night minimum on weekends during July and August as well as holidays. One small DOG lives here. Double accommodations available in guestrooms. Not suitable for CHILDREN. NONSMOKERS only.
**Rates:** D $80 DAILY.
**Reservations:** (207) 781-4528 EVENINGS AND WEEKENDS.

## CLOSE TO VILLAGE

OFF ROUTE 9 — Conveniently located in town, this Greek Revival home is within easy access to all attractions. Antique lovers' delight. Accommodations are sumptuous and full breakfast is elegantly served, as are afternoon tea and early morning coffee in the guest sitting room with balcony. Accommodations include: three guestrooms with private baths. Breakfast is served at 8:30 promptly. Host is a history professor; hostess now enjoys gardening and decorating. Two night minimum in July and August. FIREPLACE in bedroom. NO SMOKING. NO CHILDREN.
**Rates:** D $75 DAILY.
**Reservations:** (207) 781-4528 EVENINGS AND WEEKENDS.

## COUNTRY SETTING

NEAR ROUTE 1 — Large 100 year old farmhouse located on a quiet back road just 4 miles from the harbor. Hosts have enjoyed restoring this ancestral home with private guest quarters and guest sitting room. A continental breakfast is served in the dining room or on deck overlooking farm pond and 100 acres of natural woodlands. Four guestrooms share a large bath. Open June to September and on weekends in October. No pets. Cot available for extra person. Host is in the postal service; hostess is an English teacher. One DOG resides here. Children welcome.
**Rates:** S $30, D $40 DAILY.
**Reservations:** (207) 781-4528 EVENINGS AND WEEKENDS.

## SECLUDED ON RIVER

OFF ROUTE 35 — This hideaway B&B was named for the Buffalohead Duck that inhabits the area. Nestled under a grove of trees on the bank of a tidal river that empties into the sea a few miles away. The home, a Dutch Colonial, overlooks the port village. There are sundecks on several levels. A large guest living room is spacious and comfortable. Host is a commercial fisherman; hostess enjoys books, theater, jogging, and can speak Spanish. Resident DOG says no pets. Hearty breakfast served. Four rooms have private baths, two share a bath. Many antiques in home. Open April through December. WATERFRONT. Guestrooms have double accommodations. NO CHILDREN.
**Rates:** D WITH SHARED BATH $40-$50 DAILY. $10 FOR EXTRA PERSON. D PRIVATE BATH $60 DAILY.
**Reservations:** (207) 781-4528 EVENINGS AND WEEKENDS.

## OGUNQUIT
## ON BEACH

CLOSE TO ROUTE 1 — Two cozy inns centrally located, just a short walk over a footbridge to the sandy BEACH. There is something to interest everyone. Cruise to the lighthouse, walk on the beach, or take a trolley into town. Six bedrooms have private baths; four have shared baths. Continental breakfast is served on the veranda overlooking the sea. No pets. Checkout 11 A.M. Open May through October. Double accommodations available in guestrooms; there is also a kitchenette available. Both hosts enjoy antiquing. NO CHILDREN.
**Rates:** S SHARED BATH $47, D PRIVATE BATH $59, D KITCHENETTE $65 DAILY.
**Reservations:** (207) 781-4528 EVENINGS AND WEEKENDS.

## PORTLAND
### PEAKS ISLAND

Charming and affordable guesthouse situated on an island 17 minutes by ferry from intown Portland. The ferry leaves hourly and the B&B is located just 3/10s of a mile from the island landing. Cars are permitted but not recommended. Walking or cycling is the best way to see the island. Deck with view of the Portland harbor and steps leading to the BEACH. Continental breakfast. Open year-round. Cots and cribs available. Seven guestrooms share three baths. Double accommodations available in guestrooms. Children and smokers welcome.
**Rates:** S $38, D $43 DAILY.
**Reservations:** (207) 781-4528 EVENINGS AND WEEKENDS.

### WEST END

Interesting brownstone located in the west-end residential area of the city. Patio and gardens are hidden behind a city fence and guests may enjoy coffee in the morning or a cool drink in the afternoon there. Parking available, but you will find that with comfortable shoes you can see much of the city by foot. Host is a meteorologist; hostess is a garden consultant. Several resident CATS. Close to the airport and highways. Open April through December. Two comfortable guestrooms share a bath. NO CHILDREN.
**Rates:** S $35-$45, D $40-$50 DAILY.
**Reservations:** (207) 781-4528 EVENINGS AND WEEKENDS.

## SACO
### RURAL

NEAR INTERSTATE 95 — Looking for a farm vacation? Watch cows being milked or cheese being made as you enjoy the friendly hospitality of this farm family of several generations. Located on 165 acres of rolling hayfields and woods, this neat and trim farmhouse is only 20 miles south of Portland and 8 miles from the beaches and recreational activities of Old Orchard Beach. No pets. A shaggy ST. BERNARD lives here. Cots and crib available. Accommodations include: A) double bed; and B) two twins. Both share a guest bath. Fabulous and hearty farm breakfasts. Be adventurous, cross the creek and explore old Indian burial grounds. Farmhouse furnished with many antiques.
**Rates:** S $30, D $40 DAILY.
**Reservations:** (207) 781-4528 EVENINGS AND WEEKENDS.

# MASSACHUSETTS

## BERKSHIRES

The Berkshires area is famous for its beautiful mountain scenery, swimming, hiking, and fishing in the summer and skiing in the winter. It is the home of the Tanglewood music festival and Jacob's Pillow ballet festival.

## GREAT BARRINGTON

Once a coach stop on the Historic Register, this 1791 home has wide plank floors, four fireplaces, and paneled doors that are reminiscent of bygone times. Minutes to Tanglewood, Jacob's Pillow, Berkshire Theater, and Butternut ski basin. The 10 acres includes a babbling brook. Accommodations include A) double bed, shared bath; B) twin beds, shared bath; C) queen-sized bed, private bath; D) twin beds, private bath, FIREPLACE; and E) room on first floor with queen sofabed, private bath. Cots are available: TV and laundry facilities available. Full breakfast is served to guests. Available June, July, and August plus weekends and school vacations. Children of all ages are welcome. SMOKING downstairs only.
**Rates:** A-E) S $55-$65, D $65-$75 DAILY. ADDITIONAL PERSONS $10 EACH DAILY.
**Reservations:** (914) 271-6228 MONDAY - FRIDAY 10 A.M. TO 4 P.M. APRIL - OCTOBER. 9 A.M. - 3 P.M. NOVEMBER - MARCH.

## OTIS

ROUTE 23 (WEST) NEAR ROUTE 8 — An 1840 Colonial home in country setting, 3 hours from New York City, 2 hours from Boston, within walking distance to an unspoiled New England village. Guest sitting room has Franklin stove and antique furnishings. Large private bath has a great shower, bedroom has double bed with firm mattress, room for child on futon. An ideal three bedroom, two bath vacation home that host uses on weekends. This is available both hosted and unhosted, and it is perfect for ski season, fall foliage, or during the summer when the Boston Symphony Orchestra plays at Tanglewood or Jacob's Pillow dancers are in residence. Cultural attractions abound. Guests may keep snacks in refrigerator located in eat-in country kitchen which has woodstove. Breakfast available. Host also has two seasonal three bedroom lake cottages with all amenities including boats available weekly. Host is a teacher; hostess is a librarian. Japanese, German, and Spanish are spoken. No pets, NO SMOKING.
**Rates:** A) S $40 D $50; AND B) S $30, D $40 DAILY: ADDITIONAL CHILDREN $10 EACH DAILY. $250 HOSTED; $350-$500 UNHOSTED WEEKLY.

Reservations: (914) 271-6228 MONDAY - FRIDAY 10 A.M. TO 4 P.M. APRIL - OCTOBER. 9 A.M. - 3 P.M. NOVEMBER - MARCH.

## SHEFFIELD

MAPLE AVENUE — A beautiful 1840 New England house, operated as a guesthouse since 1888. Furnished with fabulous antiques, includes large living and dining rooms with two fireplaces and a woodstove as well as spacious screened-in porch. Nine bedrooms, one has a private bath, others share three baths. Seven acres on quiet road off Route 7. From New York City 2 1/2 hours. Many antique shops, covered bridges, Butternut, Catamount skiing, and Tanglewood nearby. Queen, double, and twin beds are available. One DOG resides here. TV. Large country breakfast is served. Children welcome. NO SMOKING.
Rates: 9 ROOMS S $35, D $45-$55 DAILY. S $245, D $315-$385 WEEKLY.
Reservations: (914) 271-6228 MONDAY - FRIDAY 10 A.M. TO 4 P.M. APRIL - OCTOBER. 9 A.M. - 3 P.M. NOVEMBER - MARCH.

A brand new 3,000 square foot log home nestled in pines at the foothills of Mt. Everett. Large lounge and dining area with fireplace-type woodstove, central air conditioning. Swimming, tennis, golf, and hiking nearby. Antique shops galore. Easy access to and from main highway. Located on scenic route 41. Very quiet and homey. Have fun in the gazebo surrounded by pine trees as you enjoy those quiet moments. Accommodations include: A) double bed, private bath; B) twin beds, private bath; C) double bed, private bath with private deck; and D) available at times double bed, private bath. Hosts speak some Italian and Spanish. TV. Host is a home renovator; hostess is a homemaker interested in interior decorating. NO SMOKING. CHILDREN over 13 welcome, but must occupy separate rooms.
Rates: A-D) D $70-$95 DAILY. D $535-$625 WEEKLY.
Reservations: (914) 271-6228 MONDAY - FRIDAY 10 A.M. TO 4 P.M. APRIL - OCTOBER. 9 A.M. - 3 P.M. NOVEMBER - MARCH.

## BOSTON AREA, ROUTE 128
## BURLINGTON

ROUTE 61 NEAR ROUTE 3 — Spacious 15 year old Ranch house, set back 300 feet from the road on a 4 acre wooded lot. This well-decorated home has five bedrooms, 3 1/2 baths, kitchen/family room with a fireplace wall, living room with beamed cathedral ceiling, and fireplace. A cellar pub with dartboard, game tables, and bar is available for guest use, as is a library. Guests are also welcome to join hostess, who is a nurse, and host, who is in marketing, in a friendly card game, discussing travel, or watching TV. Enjoy your continental breakfast on an oversized deck in a rustic setting. Boston, Concord, Lexington, Salem, Bedford, Gloucester,

and Rockport are all an easy drive. Within a half hour ride are 17 colleges and universities, as are Hanscom Field and many electronic firms. Air conditioned. CHILDREN over 8 welcome.
**Rates:** A & B) S $45, D $55; C) S $40, D $48, T $50 DAILY. S $250 D $280 WEEKLY. IN-LAW SUITE WITH KITCHEN $60 DAILY. $300 WEEKLY.
**Reservations:** (617) 921-1336 7:00 A.M. TO 9:00 A.M., 12:00 NOON TO 9:00 P.M., 7 DAYS A WEEK.

## GREATER BOSTON
### BOSTON

Overlooking a beautiful Boston park, this midtown apartment is UNHOSTED. In excellent location, the apartment has two bedrooms: one with two twin beds, the other a king. One full bathroom is shared between the two guestrooms. There is a large living room with loads of books and a kitchen that is stocked with everything from silverware to cookbooks. It has a dishwasher, freezer, refrigerator, and china, also. The butcher block table seats four. There is a 19 inch color TV, stereo, radio, and futon. This apartment is on the fifth floor of an elevator building and is fully air conditioned. Enough food is supplied for about three days of full breakfasts and then guests are on their own. Children welcome. No pets: Parking on the street with permit given by host.
**Rates:** S OR D $83, T OR Q $151 DAILY.
**Reservations:** (617) 277-5430 MONDAY THROUGH FRIDAY 9 A.M. TO 5 P.M.

### BACK BAY

Excellently located double-bed room with shared bath in brownstone apartment. Convenient by public transportation. Walking distance to many historic sites and fine restaurants and shops. Continental breakfast included.
**Rates:** S $52, D $54 DAILY.
**Reservations:** (617) 277-5430 MONDAY THROUGH FRIDAY 9 A.M. TO 5 P.M.

COMMONWEALTH AVENUE — A magnificent 1890 brownstone located in one of Boston's finest residential areas. Minutes from the Public Garden, fine shops, and elegant restaurants. Guests occupy one of two large understated rooms with 2 twin beds, 16 foot ceilings, fireplaces, eighteenth century furniture, and dark mahogany floors adorned with oriental rugs. Each has a private adjoining bath. TV, air conditioning, continental breakfast, and use of other rooms. Lunch and dinner available by reservation. Parking possibilities. HANDICAPPED ACCESSIBLE. POOL. Hungarian is spoken. ADULTS ONLY.
**Rates:** S $70, D $75 DAILY.

Reservations: (617) 277-5430 MONDAY THROUGH FRIDAY 9 A.M. TO 5 P.M.

## CHARLESTOWN

A registered historic home erected in 1799 by General Nathaniel Austin. This little gray stone house now opens its doors to guests. The guestroom has a double bed, private bath. Full breakfast is offered by your hostess who has a thorough knowledge of this fascinating house and its varied occupants. Walking distance to Faneuil Hall, Quincy Market, the waterfront, and the downtown financial district. FIREPLACE in bedroom. Children welcome. NONSMOKERS only.
Rates: S $73, D $75 DAILY.
Reservations: (617) 277-5430 MONDAY THROUGH FRIDAY 9 A.M. TO 5 P.M.

## BROOKLINE
### FISHER HILL

Conveniently located for driving in or out of Boston, near public transportation, this fine older brick Colonial offers two lovely guestrooms with shared guest bath on the B&B floor. This home is close to many colleges and businesses, too. Adjoining den for guests' use and patio off each bedroom. Your host and hostess are warm, relaxed, and witty. Very knowledgeable about things Bostonian. Guests share modern full bath (stall shower). Two beautiful guestrooms include: A) two twin beds and B) queen bed. Color TV in each room. Excellent breakfasts. CHILDREN over 18 are welcome. Parking included. SMOKING allowed in restricted areas.
Rates: S $50, D $55 DAILY.
Reservations: (617) 277-5430 MONDAY THROUGH FRIDAY 9 A.M. TO 5 P.M.

## LONGWOOD MEDICAL AREA

Beautiful, 40 year old center hall Colonial in a quiet residential neighborhood minutes to hospitals, Harvard Medical School, Harvard Dental School, the Museum of Fine Arts, and the Gardner Museum. Your hostess is an accomplished watercolorist who offers watercolor painting lessons at an extra fee. Accommodations include: A) large room with king bed, private bath, B) two twins, shared bath, and C) one twin, shared bath. A CAT resides here. Close to public transportation. ADULTS ONLY. Parking is included. For NONSMOKERS only.
Rates: S $43 SHARED BATH, $47 WITH PRIVATE BATH, D $45 WITH SHARED BATH, $47 WITH PRIVATE BATH DAILY.
Reservations: (617) 277-5430 MONDAY THROUGH FRIDAY 9 A.M. TO 5 P.M.

BEACON STREET — Huge, newly renovated brownstone and brick 1891 townhouse. Excellent location, serviced by three streetcar and subway transportation lines. Dramatic skylight overlooking stairwell balconies. There are 6 guestrooms and 3 1/2 baths offered. Comfortable family room for guests' use. Host is president of a software company; hostess renovates historic homes. Double rooms with private bath available, with queen-sized or twin beds. Full breakfast with family or continental plus left for you at your leisure. Convenient location for sightseeing without a car. Many restaurants within walking distance or short trolley ride. Parking $5 a day. NONSMOKERS, only.
**Rates:** S $55, D $60 DAILY.
**Reservations:** (617) 277-5430 MONDAY THROUGH FRIDAY 9 A.M. TO 5 P.M.

## CAMBRIDGE
## NORTH CAMBRIDGE

MASSACHUSETTS AVENUE — Enjoy a classic B&B experience! Treat yourself to a stay in this gorgeous Colonial Revival built by Hartwell & Richardson in 1892 and completely redecorated in period style by Ronald Peltier of New York in 1985. Four beautiful guestrooms with sinks, mirrors, and color TV in each room, one with working FIREPLACE. Plenty of bathrooms for guests' use. Full made to order breakfast cooked by professional chef and served in the formal wood paneled dining room with sideboard spread with lighter fare. Sitting area for guests' use. Fully air conditioned. Close to Harvard Square and Porter Square.
**Rates:** S $66, D $73 IN CARRIAGE HOUSE; S $76, D $83 IN MAIN HOUSE DAILY.
**Reservations:** (617) 277-5430 MONDAY THROUGH FRIDAY 9 A.M. TO 5 P.M.

## SCITUATE
## NEAR CENTER

Lovely room in attractive Cape Cod style home with queen bed and private adjoining bath. Located halfway between Boston and Cape Cod. A romantic South Shore town, it boasts many fine restaurants and shops and dates back to 1636. Visit Scituate's two lighthouses and four BEACHES. A great location for long walks along the rugged Atlantic Coast. Host is a computer scientist; hostess is a primary schoolteacher. For NONSMOKERS, only.
**Rates:** S $45, D $47 DAILY
**Reservations:** (617) 277-5430 MONDAY THROUGH FRIDAY 9 A.M. TO 5 P.M.

## NORTH SHORE

The towns on the North Shore of Massachusetts (running north of Boston) share a common heritage and seafaring influence. There are many beautifully restored seventeenth and eighteenth century homes and buildings, many of them B&Bs. Marblehead and Beverly rival in their claim to be the birthplace of the U.S. Navy. Salem is famed for the witchcraft hysteria and has some fascinating witchcraft museums. Also, Salem has the Peabody Museum with its wonderful whaling and clipper ship exhibits. If you're lucky you may attend a light orchestral concert in the Peabody Museum Auditorium surrounded by the figureheads of ships of bygone eras. These towns are within 30 minutes of Boston and Logan Airport, yet some have few or no hotels (only B&Bs) and retain the quaint atmosphere of earlier times.

A New England Cape Cod home with second floor for guests. Two oversized bedrooms: A) twin beds; and B) double and one twin. Guestrooms share full bath. Hostess teaches yoga and is interested in holistic living. Guests invited to use yoga and meditation room. Located: 1 block from tennis court, park, and conservation walking paths; 2 blocks from bus to Boston (18 miles); beach and restaurants (1 mile); town historic area and harbor, whale watching, harbor cruises, sailing, antique shops, and bird sanctuary (2 miles); Salem and Salem State College (3 miles); and Logan Airport (Boston, 15 miles). Continental breakfast served in dining room. CHILDREN over 8 welcome. No pets. No SMOKING in house.
**Rates:** S $48, D 54; OVER 2 $10 EACH NIGHT DAILY. S $250, D $300; OVER 2 $50 EACH NIGHT WEEKLY.
**Reservations:** (617) 921-1336 7:00 A.M. TO 9:00 A.M., 12:00 NOON TO 9:00 P.M., 7 DAYS A WEEK.

## BEVERLY

LOTHROP AT DANE — This Victorian home on the OCEAN in Beverly is elegantly furnished with antiques. It is a 5 minute drive from historic Salem. Beverly claims to be the "Birthplace of Washington's Navy." Here, the first four armed Continental vessels were fitted out by Washington during the Revolution. Three miles from Salem, Beverly has commuter rail and bus transportation to Boston and Gloucester. This home is a 5 minute walk to the Cabot Street Theater, home of Marco the Grand Magician Show, held every Sunday. Host is a dealer in estate jewelry and coins; hostess is a merchandising representative. Spanish and Hebrew are spoken. Two teenage sons reside here. One DOG also lives here. Children of any age welcome. NO SMOKING.
**Rates:** S $38-$40, D $45-$50 DAILY. S $125, D $200 WEEKLY.
**Reservations:** (617) 921-1336 7:00 A.M. TQ 9:00 A.M., 12:00 NOON TO 9:00 P.M., 7 DAYS A WEEK.

## BOXFORD

ROUTE 133 — Beautiful architect designed home in secluded country setting. Close to Interstate 95 on the way to New Hampshire and Maine ski country and seacoast. Near to Newburyport, Ipswich Audubon Sanctuary, and Myopia Hunt Club. Separate entrance, kitchenette, breakfast/sitting room, and swimming POOL. Large, double bedroom with FIREPLACE and air conditioning. Two twin bed rooms also available. The fireplace double bedroom with air conditioning and one of the twin bedrooms are also available as a suite with separate entrance at garden level, with sitting room, kitchenette, private half bath, and shared full bath. One DOG lives here. Prefer NONSMOKERS.
**Rates:** A) S $45, D $54; AND B & C) S $40, D $50 DAILY. ON SECOND AND SUBSEQUENT NIGHTS TAKE $5 OFF RATE.
**Reservations:** (617) 921-1336 7:00 A.M. TO 9:00 A.M., 12:00 NOON TO 9:00 P.M., 7 DAYS A WEEK.

## GLOUCESTER

Very attractive Colonial home close to Gloucester harbor and BEACHES. Hostess enjoys entertaining guests in her large home and sharing with them her interest in Gloucester and its many historical and maritime attractions. Accommodations include: A) double room, private bath in hall, double bed; B) double room, private bath in hall, two twin beds; C) double room shared bath, double bed; and D & E) double room, shared bath, two twin beds. Continental breakfast served. Children welcome. Cots available. NO SMOKING.
**Rates:** A) S $70, D $75; B) S $65, D $70; AND C-E) S $50, D $62 DAILY.
**Reservations:** (617) 921-1336 7:00 A.M. TO 9:00 A.M., 12:00 NOON TO 9:00 P.M., 7 DAYS A WEEK.

## LYNN
## NEAR SHORE

OCEAN STREET — Minutes to historical Marblehead and Salem, 20 minutes to Logan Airport and 35 minutes to downtown Boston. An 1870 two story Victorian home one street from ocean in what was once known as the "Gold Coast." This gracious nine room features high ceilings, fans throughout, hardwood floors, and decorative woodwork. Four FIREPLACES grace this home furnished with interesting period pieces. Host has his own CPA practice; hostess works with an airline; both enjoy investing in real estate and traveling. Host and hostess offer afternoon tea and host enjoys providing wood for fireplace. Accommodations: A) blue room features a large room with very comfortable double bed, working fireplace, cable TV, and furnished with period pieces; B) red room features cozy room with comfortable twin beds with a glimpse of the ocean. Second

floor full bath shared by all bedrooms; two half baths available on the first floor. Enjoy having a continental breakfast served outside on the large front porch on nice weekend days. Breakfast includes fluffy buttermilk biscuits, fresh muffins served with juice, freshly ground coffee, and tea. NO SMOKING.
Rates: A) S $50, D $60; AND B) S $40, D $50 DAILY.
Reservations: (617) 921-1336 7:00 A.M. TO 9:00 A.M., 12:00 NOON TO 9:00 P.M., 7 DAYS A WEEK.

## MANCHESTER
## ESTATE AREA

Beautiful seaside community with many large summer estates, sandy BEACHES, and scenic harbor. This lovely Victorian home is situated on private, wooded, and landscaped grounds, within sound of the sea, and is just a short walk to the beach. The home has been in the family for generations. Recently, it has been restored in loving detail and is beautifully furnished with many antiques. Three guestrooms with double accommodations, one with private bath and the other two with baths shared with other guests. One DOG lives here. Hostess is a real estate broker who enjoys skiing and golf. CHILDREN over 6 welcome. SMOKING only in common areas. JACUZZI. VCR.
Rates: A) S $70. D $75; AND B & C) S $60, D $70 DAILY.
Reservations: (617) 921-1336 7:00 A.M. TO 9:00 A.M., 12:00 NOON TO 9:00 P.M., 7 DAYS A WEEK.

## MARBLEHEAD

Romantic and charming, this early 1720 Colonial home is located among 150 historic homes in a beautiful, sheltered harbor. Elegantly appointed house has seven fireplaces and was originally owned by Captain Nathaniel Lindsey, who was granted a sword by Congress in the War of 1812. Watch magnificent yachts and Ted Hood's boat yard. Visit antique shops, art galleries, gourmet restaurants, and neighboring historic Salem. Marblehead is situated on the ocean, this historic old town was settled in 1629. A great many of its original buildings and homes are still intact and beautifully restored. With its beautiful harbor and wide beaches it is one of the country's yachting capitals. Only 15 miles north of Boston and 20 minutes from Boston's Logan Airport. Listen to the ocean and the sea birds. A brief walk to a sandy beach. Many specially selected homes in the English B&B tradition. The town offers turn of the century mansions on the ocean with spectacular views. Your lovely host and hostess know the area intimately and will be most helpful in giving good advice. Your spacious, separate air-conditioned guest quarters have a private entrance and overlook the harbor. It's a studio apartment with beamed cathedral ceiling, FIREPLACE, and a very comfortable queen-sized hide-a-bed. Guest deck just outside. Included is a completely modern kitchen area

with all major appliances, silverware, and dishes. Your refrigerator is fully stocked for breakfast. Full, private guest bathroom. Parking included.
**Rates:** $50 DAILY.
**Reservations:** (617) 277-5430 MONDAY THROUGH FRIDAY 9 A.M. TO 5 P.M.

## NAHANT

NAHANT STREET — This large, Victorian house built in 1842 recalls the grandeur of yesteryear. Your spacious accommodations in the remodeled attic are full of charm. The bedroom with an antique brass and iron bed has a picturesque OCEAN view. There is also a large, comfortable sitting room to relax in and a private bath. The sitting room can accommodate children. The host invites you to come sit by the fire any evening in the family's chestnut paneled grand living room. Nahant is a quaint seaside town jutting out into the Atlantic Ocean, only 15 minutes from Boston's Logan Airport, yet secluded. There are many large Victorian and Colonial homes with great ocean views. As a guest at this B&B in Nahant, you gain access to its beautiful, unspoilt beaches. Nahant is 10 minutes from historic Marblehead and Salem. A leisurely walk past the many old homes that abound is recommended as well as a stop at the town wharf and exploration of the many beaches. Three young boys live here. Two CATS reside here. PIANO. Children welcome.
**Rates:** S $48, D $60 DAILY. ON SECOND AND SUBSEQUENT DAYS, TAKE $5 OFF THE RATE.
**Reservations:** (617) 921-1336 7:00 A.M. TO 9:00 A.M., 12:00 NOON TO 9:00 P.M., 7 DAYS A WEEK.

## NEWBURYPORT

On the mouth of the Merrimac River, Newburyport was settled in 1640 and was originally a ship building town. It has a beautiful harbor, now full of sailboats. High Street still has many of the original buildings, with many beautiful shops and restaurants. Only 5 minutes from Plum Island Wildlife Reserve.

A large, very charming Colonial home in a historic area. Close to Plum Island Wildlife Reserve and Plum Island Airport (for light planes). Accommodations include: A) double room, private bath en suite, double bed; B) double room, private bath in hallway, double bed; C) double room, shared bath, double bed; D) double room, shared bath, two twin beds; and E) double room, shared bath, two twin beds. Continental breakfast served. Full breakfast by arrangement. Children welcome. NO SMOKERS welcome.
**Rates:** A) S $65, D $75; B) S $60, D $70; C & D) S $50, D $62, AND E) S $47. D $58 DAILY.

Reservations: (617) 921-1336 7:00 A.M. TO 9:00 A.M., 12:00 NOON TO 9:00 P.M., 7 DAYS A WEEK.

## ROCKPORT

Lovely home close to the OCEAN and Rockport's art galleries and attractive shops. Steps to the beach. Accommodations include: A) double room, private bath en suite, king-sized bed; B) double room, private bath in hall, double bed; C) double room, shared bath with one other guestroom, double bed; D) double room, shared bath with one other guestroom, two twin beds; and E) single room, shared bath, one twin bed. Continental breakfast served. Cots available. Children welcome. NO SMOKING.
Rates: A) S $70, D $75; B) S $65, D $70; C & D) S $55, D $65; AND E) S $50 DAILY.
Reservations: (617) 921-1336 7:00 A.M. TO 9:00 A.M., 12:00 NOON TO 9:00 P.M., 7 DAYS A WEEK.

## SALEM
## SALEM COMMON AREA

WINTER STREET — This home is one of Salem's finest examples of Greek Revival architecture. Elegantly restored and beautifully decorated, guests enjoy spacious accommodations located in the heart of Salem's Historic District. A 5 minute stroll finds downtown shopping, historic houses, and museums, or Pickering Wharf's waterfront dining. Salem State College is a 2 mile drive. A light buffet breakfast is served to help guests start their day and provides your hosts the opportunity to share with guests information about this wonderful city and all its witchcraft mystique. On the premises off-street parking is available. Salem was settled in 1626 and was once a hub of Oriental shipping and trading. Salem has many beautiful and very historic buildings. Once the center of witchcraft hysteria, it has "bewitching" Witch Museums. The Peabody Museum has fascinating whaling and seafaring exhibits. Visit Pickering Wharf and many other historical and tourist attractions. Plan a whale watch cruise from Salem. Convenient to Boston (16 miles), public transportation is available by bus or train. The North Shore Shuttle is available for door to door service to and from Logan Airport (Boston). PIANO. Children over toddler age welcome. Hosts are nonsmokers; SMOKING guests are asked to restrict smoking to a designated sitting room area.
Rates: S $40-$46, D $60-$75 DAILY. S $180, D $250-$300 WEEKLY.
Reservations: (617) 921-1336 7:00 A.M. TO 9:00 A.M., 12:00 NOON TO 9:00 P.M., 7 DAYS A WEEK.

## SWAMPSCOTT

This Victorian house is located in a beautiful seacoast town on the historic North Shore. A turn of the century home that glows with the warmth and charm of days gone by. The rooms are spacious and elegant, featuring handmade quilts and stenciling. The living room features a sitting area and a woodburning stove. Several BEACHES are just steps away from the sprawling old fashioned porch; two of the rooms have an ocean view. Each room has a TV and small refrigerator. Four rooms share two baths. The location is just 10 miles north of Boston and Logan International Airport, minutes from old Salem, Marblehead, and many other historic seacoast towns with an endless selection of boutiques, galleries, and shops. Restaurants are within walking distance, and for those enthusiastic about biking, two popular touring routes are nearby. Your hosts extend to you the comfort and tranquility of a fine Christian home. CHILDREN over 6 welcome. NONSMOKERS only.
**Rates:** S $46, D $56 DAILY. S $165, D $250 WEEKLY.
**Reservations:** (617) 921-1336 7:00 A.M. TO 9:00 A.M., 12:00 NOON TO 9:00 P.M., 7 DAYS A WEEK.

## LOWELL

DARTMOUTH STREET — This is an 1893 Queen Anne Victorian home. Many antiques, stained glass, a wraparound porch, many parlors with well-filled book shelves and perhaps a friendly ghost. Your host is a marketing manager for Wang Labs; your hostess has a masters in psychology. Breakfast on fine china in the formal dining room or casually on the porch according to your desire. Convenient to Route 3, Interstate 495, 30 minutes to Boston, and 15 miles to Concord. Accommodations include: A) twin beds, shared bath; B) double bed, shared bath. Children welcome. Fireplace in home, laundry facilities, and TV. SMOKING outside only.
**Rates:** A & B) S $40, D $45 DAILY.
**Reservations:** (914) 271-6228 MONDAY - FRIDAY 10 A.M. TO 4 P.M. APRIL - OCTOBER. 9 A.M. - 3 P.M. NOVEMBER - MARCH.

# RHODE ISLAND

## AQUIDNECK ISLAND
### NEWPORT
### THE POINT

ELM STREET — Gracious 1860s Colonial near center of attractions. Continental breakfast in cozy nook or on outdoor patio. Atmosphere of quiet elegance, tasteful antiques, art work, and Oriental rugs. Hostess is an elementary school teacher and movie buff. Co-hostess is a sales manager. Accommodations include: A) king or twin beds, shared bath; or B) queen bed, shared bath. Second floor guestrooms. One CAT in residence.
**Rates:** D $80-$90 DAILY.
**Reservations:** (401) 849-1298 IN SEASON MONDAY - FRIDAY 9 TO 5:30, SATURDAY 9 TO 12. OFF SEASON MONDAY - FRIDAY 9 TO 5:30.

## PORTSMOUTH

JOHNNY CAKE LANE — Contemporary house just 50 feet from WATER'S EDGE. Spiral oak staircase to second floor guestrooms. Sliding doors on sleeping rooms to balcony to catch the sunrise. Light continental breakfast offered. Inground POOL. Hostess is a gregarious, active senior citizen who worked in real estate. Accommodations include: A & B) twin beds, shared bath. CHILDREN over 8 welcome. SMOKING outside, only.
**Rates:** S $40-$45, D $55-$60 DAILY.
**Reservations:** (401) 849-1298 IN SEASON MONDAY - FRIDAY 9 TO 5:30, SATURDAY 9 TO 12. OFF SEASON MONDAY - FRIDAY 9 TO 5:30.

## ASHAWAY
### HOPKINTON

HIGH STREET — Set in a semirural area, this turn of the century home offers a retreat from life's hectic pace yet is close to area attractions, including golf and tennis. Just 7 miles from Watch Hill beach and less than a mile from Interstate 95, it is an easy drive for day trips to either Mystic Seaport or Newport. Guests enjoy the inground swimming POOL, screen house, and brick patio for outdoor fun, picnics, and just relaxing. The sleeping rooms are comfortably furnished with country style accents. Breakfast is served in the comfortable dining room, which overlooks the outdoor lounge area. Guests are always welcomed with wine and crackers. The hostess is a retired secretary who enjoys politics, gardening, and cooking. She formerly served on the town council and is now pursuing a

college degree at the University of Rhode Island. CHILDREN over 10 welcome.
**Rates:** S $40, D $45-50, $10 EXTRA ADULT, $5 CHILD IN ROOM DAILY.
**Reservations:** (401) 849-1298 IN SEASON MONDAY - FRIDAY 9 TO 5:30, SATURDAY 9 TO 12. OFF SEASON MONDAY - FRIDAY 9 TO 5:30.

## EAST PROVIDENCE

SEAVIEW AVENUE — Lovely Federal style home just across the street from the WATERFRONT. Within walking distance to four marinas and a private beach. Hearty continental breakfast in dining room, patio, or family room. Hostess enjoys crafts and gardening. Her 83 year old mother also resides here. Accommodations include: A) two twin beds, water view, shared bath; B) king bed, shared bath; and C) two twin beds, shared bath. Also small single room for extra guest. All guestrooms on second floor. DOG in residence. Small putt putt boat and bikes available. CHILDREN over 5 welcome. SMOKING not permitted in sleeping rooms.
**Rates:** S $50, D $55-$60; $10 EXTRA PERSON IN ROOM DAILY.
**Reservations:** (401) 849-1298 IN SEASON MONDAY - FRIDAY 9 TO 5:30, SATURDAY 9 TO 12. OFF SEASON MONDAY - FRIDAY 9 TO 5:30.

## EAST SIDE
## PROVIDENCE

MEETING STREET — An 1849 Greek Revival with interesting blend of contemporary and traditional decor. Continental breakfast in modern kitchen or on private terrace. Host is bank executive; hostess is homemaker and organizer of Providence Preservation Society's Annual Festival of Historic Houses. Two preschool children. Accommodations include: third floor room with two twin beds, private bath, plus separate room with daybed. Crib available. Walking distance to Brown University and Rhode Island School of Design. Air conditioned. Children welcome.
**Rates:** S $55, D $65, $15 EXTRA PERSON, $5 CHILD UNDER 3 DAILY.
**Reservations:** (401) 849-1298 IN SEASON MONDAY - FRIDAY 9 TO 5:30, SATURDAY 9 TO 12. OFF SEASON MONDAY - FRIDAY 9 TO 5:30.

## HOPKINTON

Built in 1763, this home is on the National Register of Historic Homes. Original beamed ceilings and antique furnishings give a sense of old world comfort. Proximity to Mystic Seaport makes this a most popular and

pleasing B&B. Accommodations include: A & B) two double beds, and C) two rooms with one twin bed. The four rooms share two baths. This home is HANDICAPPED ACCESSIBLE. There is a FIREPLACE in one bedroom. Children welcome. NONSMOKERS, only.
**Rates:** $50 DAILY. EACH ADDITIONAL PERSON $15 DAILY.
**Reservations:** (203) 236-6698 MONDAY THROUGH FRIDAY 9 A.M. TO 5 P.M.

# MISQUAMICUT
## WESTERLY

ROUTE 1A, SHORE ROAD — Turn of the century home with wraparound stone porch. Hilltop location affords panoramic view of ocean. Hearty continental breakfast on enclosed porch. Host is sportscaster; hostess is self-employed and a tennis enthusiast. Accommodations include: A) double bed, access to shared porch with water view, shared bath down the hall, second floor; B) twin beds, private porch with water view, adjoining shared bath, second floor; C) twin beds, private porch with water view and adjoining shared bath, second floor; D) double bed, water view, shared adjoining bath, second floor; E) twin beds, shared bath, third floor; F) twin beds, shared bath, third floor; G) double bed, shared bath, third floor. Outdoor DOG on premises. NO CHILDREN. SMOKING allowed on porches and in sitting room, only.
**Rates:** DOUBLE $60, $70, AND $80 DAILY.
**Reservations:** (401) 849-1298 IN SEASON MONDAY - FRIDAY 9 TO 5:30. SATURDAY 9 TO 12. OFF SEASON MONDAY - FRIDAY 9 TO 5:30.

# NARRANGANSETT

ROBINSON STREET — Sense the bygone era in this special Victorian home. Lots of lacey touches, tastefully selected wallpaper, and hand wall stenciling. Gourmet full breakfast served in lovely dining room. Host is self-employed; hostess is a kindergarten teacher. They have a 9 year old daughter. Accommodations: A) king or twin beds. private baths; B) king or twin beds, private bath; C) double bed, shared bath; and D) double bed, private bath. Second floor guestrooms. Children welcome, crib available. SMOKING allowed in parlor or on porch, only.
**Rates:** PRIVATE BATH $55-$60; SHARED BATH $44-$48; $10 FOR EXTRA PERSON IN ROOM DAILY. 6 NIGHTS 10% OFF.
**Reservations:** (401) 849-1298 IN SEASON MONDAY - FRIDAY 9 TO 5:30, SATURDAY 9 TO 12. OFF SEASON MONDAY - FRIDAY 9 TO 5:30.

# TIVERTON

EAST ROAD — Working 85 acre dairy farm offers taste of simpler lifestyle. Guests welcome to visit barn during chore time or walk paths through field and forest. Old fashioned 1875 Victorian farmhouse with mixed antiques, handcrafts, and stenciled walls. Continental breakfast served in country kitchen. Host is electronic technician and farmer; hostess is farmer, homemaker, and folk artist. Three teenage and young adult children. Accommodations include: A) double bed, shared bath; and B) double bed, shared bath, rollaway bed. Second floor guestrooms. CHILDREN over 12 welcome. SMOKING NOT PERMITTED.
**Rates:** D $50-$55 DAILY MEMORIAL DAY THROUGH COLUMBUS DAY; $40-$45 OFF-SEASON.
**Reservations:** (401) 849-1298 IN SEASON MONDAY - FRIDAY 9 TO 5:30, SATURDAY 9 TO 12. OFF SEASON MONDAY - FRIDAY 9 TO 5:30.

# WICKFORD
# NORTH KINGSTOWN

ANNAGUATUCKET ROAD — Nineteenth century Colonial farmhouse has been restored with love and care. It has country charm and period wall coverings and accessories. Restful 2 1/2 acres with gardens, stone walls, and flowers. Hearty continental breakfast served in dining room. Host is an oceanographer; hostess is former oceanographer who now designs children's clothes. They have one toddler daughter. Accommodations include: A) double bed, shared bath; B) twin beds, shared bath: and C) double bed, shared bath. Second floor guestrooms. Friendly black LABRADOR in residence. Well-behaved children welcome. SMOKING NOT PERMITTED.
**Rates:** $45-$55 DAILY.
**Reservations:** (401) 849-1298 IN SEASON MONDAY - FRIDAY 9 TO 5:30, SATURDAY 9 TO 12. OFF SEASON MONDAY - FRIDAY 9 TO 5:30.

PLEASANT STREET — Special care has been taken by the host couple in keeping the decor of this eighteenth century Georgian appropriate to its historical setting. The tastefully decorated second floor guest suite includes two spacious sleeping rooms, a comfortable sitting room, bathroom, and fully equipped kitchen. Guests revel in the gracious surroundings, which feature an Oriental rug, wide plank floors, fireplace mantles, and antiques. Anchored sailboats create a scenic backdrop in the salt cove just beyond the expansive backyard. Guests may sun themselves on the small private BEACH, stroll the grounds, or relax on the screened veranda. The home is located just a few minutes' walk to the town dock or the village center. The host is a business manager; the hostess is an interior decorator. Together they have created the setting for a truly unique B&B experience. One DOG lives here. Children of all ages welcome. NO SMOKING.

**Rates:** ROOM $60; SUITE $120 DAILY.

**Reservations:** (401) 849-1298 IN SEASON MONDAY - FRIDAY 9 TO 5:30, SATURDAY 9 TO 12. OFF SEASON MONDAY - FRIDAY 9 TO 5:30.

# VERMONT

## CENTRAL VERMONT
### ORWELL

This 1789 mansion has a 10,000 volume library, comfortable den, many fireplaces, and a large dining room where full country breakfasts are served. Close by is the Morgan Horse farm. On the 300 acres you may fish, cross-country ski, go hiking, skating, or running on the track. Everything is antique, even the Bosendorfer PIANO. Host is an orchestral leader and violinist. He speaks 10 languages fluently and enjoys archeology and traveling: the hostess speaks French and Spanish and enjoys cooking, music, and writing. Their son, 18, and daughter, 22, also live here. Middlebury College is 25 minutes away and the Burlington Airport is 1 hour. HANDICAPPED ACCESSIBLE. Accommodations include: A) doube and twin beds en suite, private bath; B) two twin beds, private bath; C & D) two twin beds; E) double bed; and F) two double and one twin beds. C-F share baths. Bikes available. Three DOGS reside here. Children of all ages welcome.
**Rates:** A) $50; B) $37.50; C-F) $25 DAILY PER PERSON.
**Reservations:** (802) 827-3827 MONDAY THROUGH FRIDAY 11 A.M. TO 7 P.M.

### READING

A graciously restored pre-1830 stone Colonial home, furnished with fine period antiques. Nearby are many sporting activities. Accommodations include: A) queen bed. shared bath; B) double bed Victorian suite, shared bath; and C) two twin beds (also sofabed), private bath. A continental breakfast is served, but guests may also use the kitchen. Host is in the automobile business and speaks fluent Italian; hostess is a photographer. Both enjoy antiques, cross-country skiing, and hiking. Thirty minutes to Dartmouth College and three downhill ski areas. Woodstock cross-country ski trails are within 15 minutes. The nearest airport is in Lebanon, New Hampshire, 25 minutes away. A small DOG also resides here. Children welcome. SMOKING not permitted in the bedrooms.
**Rates:** A & B) $60; AND C) $65 DAILY. ADDITIONAL PERSONS (OVER 2) $10 EACH.
**Reservations:** (802) 827-3827 MONDAY THROUGH FRIDAY 11 A.M. TO 7 P.M.

## NORTHWEST VERMONT
### EAST FAIRFIELD

UNHOSTED rental suites located across from the general store. Skiing, swimming, hiking, fishing, sightseeing, antiquing, auctions, covered dish suppers, interesting restaurants, and cultural activities provide day trip

activities and excursions. Each suite is fully furnished with linens and cooking implements. Each has two bedrooms, living room, kitchen/dining area, and bathroom. They are 20 minutes from Smuggler's Notch ski area and 45 minutes from Burlington Airport. Breakfast not provided, but provisions are available in nearby general store. Children of all ages are welcome. SMOKING not permitted in bedrooms.
**Rates:** $50 DAILY. $300 WEEKLY.
**Reservations:** (802) 827-3827 MONDAY THROUGH FRIDAY 11 A.M. TO 7 P.M.

UNHOSTED, this delightful guest cottage sits on the bank of a lovely brook and waterfall at the edge of the village. Skiing, swimming, hiking, fishing, sightseeing, antiquing, auctions, covered dish suppers, and interesting restaurants are nearby. This B&B has a woodstove fireplace; two bedrooms, one with double bed, the other with twin beds; the living room has a sofabed; kitchen; bath; and front porch. It is located 20 minutes from Smuggler's Notch ski area and 45 minutes from Burlington Airport. Breakfast is not provided, but provisions are available locally. Children are always WELCOME and PETS if well behaved. Smoking permitted.
**Rates:** $50 DAILY. $300 WEEKLY.
**Reservations:** (802) 827-3827 MONDAY THROUGH FRIDAY 11 A.M. TO 7 P.M.

## JEFFERSONVILLE

Over 150 year old brick, Cape farmhouse located conveniently between Johnson State College and Smuggler's Notch ski area. Host is a project manager for a commercial contracting company; hostess is in charge of the Smuggler's Notch horse riding, which both enjoy. Their two sons, 10 and 14, live here along with two DOGS and a CAT. Hostess serves a full breakfast. Many sports are closeby and hostess can offer you special rates for skiing at Smuggler's Notch. Burlington Airport is 35 minutes away. Accommodations include: A) two twin beds and a daybed, shared bath; B) double bed, private half bath; C) king bed, JACUZZI, private bath; and D) queen waterbed, shared bath. Snow mobiles can be rented nearby. Space available for bike storage. Children of all ages welcome. NONSMOKERS, only.
**Rates:** A) $35; B) $35; C) $40; AND D) $35 DAILY.
**Reservations:** (802) 827-3827 MONDAY THROUGH FRIDAY 11 A.M. TO 7 P.M.

## JERICHO

A wonderfully designed salt box home in Early American country style with PIANO and picnic area. Host is a state agency manager for a large insurance company; hostess makes sure your vacation runs smoothly and

starts your day with a full breakfast. She enjoys antiquing, quilting, and home decorating. Host likes to work in his garden, read, and attend church. Accommodations include: A) queen bed, private bath; and B & C) double bedded rooms which share a guest bath. All Burlington colleges are within 30 minutes. A crib and cot are also available. Children of all ages welcome. NO SMOKING.
**Rates:** A) $55; AND B & C) $40 DAILY S OR D. ADDITIONAL CHILDREN UNDER 12 $7, OVER 12 $10.
**Reservations:** (802) 827-3827 MONDAY THROUGH FRIDAY 11 A.M. TO 7 P.M.

A quiet spot on a 100 acre wooded property. Horses, sheep, pigs, ducks, chickens, and a donkey welcome you to their sprawling home full of European antiques and Vermont craftwork. Many sporting centers are closeby. Host is a physician and a retired college professor. He speaks German and enjoys skiing and gardening. Hostess enjoys horseback riding and sheep raising in her spare time. She serves a full breakfast. Two DOGs and two CATS also live here. Located 30 minutes from the Burlington colleges and Bolston ski area. Burlington Airport is 30 minutes away. Accommodations include: A, B, & C) double beds; and D) twin beds. All share family bath. Well-behaved children welcome. NO SMOKING.
**Rates:** S $30, D $40 DAILY. CRIB $5 DAILY.
**Reservations:** (802) 827-3827 MONDAY THROUGH FRIDAY 11 A.M. TO 7 P.M.

A gracious Victorian home conveniently located 20 minutes from Burlington, situated between Mount Mansfield and Lake Champlain. Many sports centers are closeby. Host is a hotel manager and enjoys sports; hostess is a choreographer who can speak French and Spanish. She enjoys sewing, playing PIANO, and her children, a son 3 and daughter 10. Their gentle DOG also lives here. Their home is located 30 minutes from the Burlington colleges and airport. The Catamount is 15 minutes away for cross-country skiing. Accommodations include: A & B) double bedded rooms, shared bath; and C) double bed suite with sofabed, private bath. Children of all ages welcome. NONSMOKERS, only.
**Rates:** A) $35; B) $35; AND C) $55 FOR S OR D DAILY. ADDITIONAL PERSONS IN ROOM $6 EACH.
**Reservations:** (802) 827-3827 MONDAY THROUGH FRIDAY 11 A.M. TO 7 P.M.

# SOUTHWEST VERMONT
## BENNINGTON

This Colonial home was built in 1774. It is the oldest in the village. Extras include: an exercise room, HOT TUB, PIANO, and many antiques, as well as TENNIS COURTS and a SWIMMING POOL next door that are available to guests. Host is a postal clerk; hostess is a homemaker. Both will make your visit a memorable one. They enjoy sports of all kinds, music, and reading. Babysitting by their 14 year old son is available. A 9 year old son also lives here. Accommodations include: A) double bed suite with twin beds, private bath; B) double bed, shared bath; C) double bed, shared bath; and D) queen bed, FIREPLACE, private bath. Full breakfast. Close to Bennington and Williamstown Colleges, Southern Vermont University, and North Adams State. There are five downhill skiing areas nearby. It is 15 minutes to Prospect cross-country skiing trails. Walking distance to restaurants and museums. Host smokes. Well-behaved PETS WELCOME. Hosts have a DOG. Bikes available.

**Rates:** A) $75 WITH TWINS $90; B & C) $48; AND D) $48 CRIB $5 DAILY.

**Reservations:** (802) 827-3827 MONDAY THROUGH FRIDAY 11 A.M. TO 7 P.M.

# 2

# Middle Atlantic

☐ New Jersey
☐ New York
☐ Pennsylvania

# NEW JERSEY

## ATLANTIC CITY

Casinos, big name entertainment, and beaches make Atlantic City and its environs a fabulous place to holiday. Clean beaches offer swimming, fishing, or just plain sunning. The 6 mile Boardwalk has marinas, tennis courts, shops, pools, and amusement areas. In nearby historic Gardiner's Basin, you will find a turn-of-the-century fishing village. It is complete with restaurants, aquarium, and museum. There is an eighteenth century clipper ship that you can board and hear the stories of yesteryear creak from the rigging. Following the waterways inland, you can track seasonal bird migrations from the 20,000 acre Brigantine Wildlife Refuge or tour the recreated town of Smithville and local wineries.

## ABSENCON

Hospitality abounds in the friendly atmosphere of this two story colonial. Your hosts are casino employees who will be happy to share their firsthand kmowledge of the Atlantic City area. As you will soon discover, one of the best treats will be a fabulous breakfast! Omelets, quiches, homemade breads and cakes, and fresh-squeezed juice are just a few of the many gourmet treats awaiting you. Guests share a bath and have a choice of comfortable air-conditioned twin or double rooms. The beach, golfing, casinos, a flea market, and many excellent restaurants are all close by and your outgoing hosts will make sure that you discover the Atlantic City area the locals love.
**Rates:** S $50, D $60 DAILY.
**Reservations:** (201) 444-7409 MONDAY THROUGH FRIDAY 9 A.M. TO 4 P.M.

## NORTHFIELD

You will be just 15 minutes from the casinos, but there is so much more to enjoy in this area. Smithville, Noyes Museum, Wheaton Village, Brigantine Wildlife Preserve, and the resorts of Ocean City or Wildwood are within a quick drive of this home. The young hosts love to entertain guests. In fact, the hostess taught and was active in mime and clowning, mostly for charitable causes! The hosts share their home with a friendly labrador retriever and their daughters who sometime visit on weekends. A bright and cheery guestroom has just been redecorated with twin beds. The bath is shared with the family. During the week, a continental breakfast can be served in the lovely backyard or a champagne breakfast is optional for weekends. Bikes for loan to use on the nearby bike paths or complimentary beach tags are available for Margate or Ventnor beaches. An added surprise is a complimentary travel gift basket filled with goodies to take home.
**Rates:** S $53, D $60 DAILY.

**Reservations:** (201) 444-7409 MONDAY THROUGH FRIDAY 9 A.M. TO 4 P.M.

## SOMERS POINT

Stay in this Spanish villa nestled within an impeccably landscaped golf course just outside of Atlantic City. The guestroom on the second floor is all carpeted and has an excellent view. This B&B offers very inviting accommodations that include a double bed and private bath. The adjacent sitting room has a color TV and lots of wonderful books. The entire villa is air conditioned. Walk to the beach (free passes) or perhaps you would like to use one of the bikes that are available for guests' use. It is a 10 mile drive to the casinos. Public transportation nearby. Your hosts are a professional couple who have traveled the world, but will be delighted to provide any local information you may need.
**Rates:** S $53, D $60 DAILY.
**Reservations:** (201) 444-7409 MONDAY THROUGH FRIDAY 9 A.M. TO 4 P.M.

## VENTNOR

This typical seashore house is one block from the beach, but the cool breezes and crisp salt air will make you believe you are right on the water's edge. The extra large master guestroom stretches across the front of the house on the second floor and includes two twin beds and a sofa. One additional guestroom is also available, a single. Two and one-half baths and an outside shower are shared. A large awning-covered porch will be especially welcome to those who spend the day on the beach (bikes. beach tags, and beach chairs are available). Casinos, jogging, tennis, fishing, and sailing are all nearby. Your hostess, a lifelong summer resident, can direct you to a wealth of activities. Infants and children over 6 years of age are welcome.
**Rates:** S $60, D $70 DAILY.
**Reservations:** (201) 444-7409 MONDAY THROUGH FRIDAY 9 A.M. TO 4 P.M.

## DELAWARE REGION

Upriver from the Delaware Bay and inland, those who enjoy walking the woods or wilderness canoeing will find the 1 million acres of the unusual New Jersey Pine Barrens. Accessible by many roads and highways, it occupies a good portion of South Jersey from the ocean to the Delaware River. It is as untarnished as it was when the first settlers came. Batsto Village in the Wharton Tract is probably the state's most impressive piece of reconstruction with a working sawmill, gristworks, baronial mansion, and resident artisans in the original workers' cottage. Clementon Amusement Park has a subdued rollercoaster and other rides for the small children. South Jersey's only ski area, Ski Mountain is located at Pinehill.

## COLUMBUS

This is a Federal style home, circa 1845, that has been featured in many country magazines. The country setting on which the home is featured covers 12 acres. The three guestrooms on the third floor are all air conditioned and furnished with period antiques and country decor. Bedroom three also contains a queen bed and working fireplace. The bath becomes private, as your hosts prefer to limit their accommodations to one family at a time or couples traveling together. All guests receive a full breakfast daily. Animal lovers will enjoy their pets — a dog, two cats, six Suffolk sheep, an Arabian horse, and a Welsh pony! Lots to enjoy nearby — from the racetracks to canoeing, antiquing, and nature walks.
**Rates:** S $60, D $66 DAILY.
**Reservations:** (201) 444-7409 MONDAY THROUGH FRIDAY 9 A.M. TO 4 P.M.

## EAST BRUNSWICK

Old-fashioned hospitality is in abundance at this lovely two-story colonial home. Your hosts are semiretired educators who love people. They also love crafts and evidence of their handiwork can be found throughout the house from the folk art paintings to the reupholstered ottoman. The guestroom, with shared (sometimes) bath, has a hand-stenciled border and features a queen-sized canopy bed. Guests are welcome to use the TV in the family room. An additional bedroom can be made available for children and a crib can be provided. Guests who are relocating are welcome for a longer stay. Your hosts are knowledgeable about the area and could provide much information. Children welcome.
**Rates:** S $40, D $58 DAILY.
**Reservations:** (201) 444-7409 MONDAY THROUGH FRIDAY 9 A.M. TO 4 P.M.

## EAST WINDSOR

Your hosts at this charming townhouse are famous dessert cookbook authors who might be persuaded to give the recipes for Bavarian Mint Chippers or Kuir Fruit Creme to an interested guest. Their home is filled with treasures they have collected over the years. One wall of the dining room is covered with autographs! The second floor air-conditioned guestroom has large sliding glass windows (overlooking the tennis courts) and shares a bath only during the summer. Guests can arrange to have access to the tennis courts and the swimming pool. A full breakfast with wonderful omelets, French toast, pancakes, and bacon can be served if desired.
**Rates:** S $47, D $53 DAILY.
**Reservations:** (201) 444-7409 MONDAY THROUGH FRIDAY 9 A.M. TO 4 P.M.

## NORTH WILDWOOD

Experience the American turn of the century — relax and enjoy a cool retreat in a gracious 80 year old Queen Anne guest house. Surround yourself in authentic antique furnishings that include an 1855 sofa, and an 1890 Eastlake piano. In the afternoon and evening you can sit and relax on the veranda that surrounds two sides of the house. There is always a calming cool breeze. Located within walking distance to three free beaches, the boardwalk, and shopping. Of the nine guestrooms, seven have a private bath. All the rooms are doubles except for one twin room. A great hearty breakfast is included with your rate. A three night minimum is necessary in July and August, but this wonderful accommodation is open year-round, with a glowing fireplace in winter. No Children. No Smoking.

**Rates:** A-G) $55-$75; AND H-I) $40-$60.
**Reservations:** (201) 444-7409 MONDAY THROUGH FRIDAY 9 A.M. TO 4 P.M.

## GATEWAY REGION

This is the vacation region where the Pallisades overlook the Hudson River. Gateway is a great place for watching things: sports of all sorts at the Meadowlands Sports Complex, the New York City skyline, and the Statue of Liberty. Visit the laboratory of Thomas Edison in Menlo Park or Grover Cleveland's home in Caldwell. The Turtleback Zoo in West Orange lets youngsters pet the animals and there is an ice skating rink behind the zoo for year-round skating. People enjoy the Aviation Hall of Fame and Museum at Teterboro Airport. This museum is dedicated to the story of flight and is crammed full of aviation artifacts, photographs, and magnificent vintage aircraft. Naval buffs might wish to board the U.S. Ling, a restored World War II submarine tied up at Court and River Streets in Hackensack. Enjoy green space at the Trainside Nature and Science Center on the Watchung Reservation, Palisades Interstate Park, or the Sacred Heart Cathedral/Branch Brook Park in Newark. The Gateway region offers easy access to New York City for business or sightseeing.

## ALLENDALE

A separate area of this expanded Cape Cod home has been set aside for guests. It offers a private entrance to the bright and cheerful twin room on the second floor. Private bath, air conditioning, TV, and separate heat control are included. Light kitchen privileges are available. The property borders on a wooded area and is away from the main traffic area by two blocks. Lots of fine restaurants and shopping nearby.

**Rates:** S $47, D $53 DAILY.
**Reservations:** (201) 444-7409 MONDAY THROUGH FRIDAY 9 A.M. TO 4 P.M.

## CHATHAM

A 4 year old Labrador retriever, Roaree, will be delighted to show you the walking paths surrounding this sprawling Colonial. Situated on 18 acres and tucked away at the end of a private road, the property boarders on a wildlife center. It is a beautiful setting, any time of the year! A twin room with private bath is ready for guests' use on the second floor, and a sitting room with TV is also available. Continental breakfast served. Easily accessible to major New Jersey routes with golf and many outdoor activities. Children welcome and a crib is available. Additional sleeping rooms for overflow.
**Rates:** S $35. D $47 DAILY.
**Reservations:** (201) 444-7409 MONDAY THROUGH FRIDAY 9 A.M. TO 4 P.M.

## CRESSKILL

A Georgian Colonial built in 1900 offers wonderful accommodations for the traveler or transferring executive. The large double guestroom on the second floor is beautifully decorated, it would fit into the most magnificent inn. The Red Room offers twin beds and a third room is available with a high-riser or can become an adjoining suite to the Red Room. All rooms share a bath. The hostess is in the theater and real estate and has many hobbies keeping her on the move. However, there is always time for her to prepare a continental breakfast of croissants, fresh fruit, and assorted cheeses, which is served in the cozy Butler's Pantry or on the porch in warmer weather. Excellent public transportation and many fine restaurants nearby. It is 15 minutes from the George Washington Bridge.
**Rates:** S $45, D $60 DAILY.
**Reservations:** (201) 444-7409 MONDAY THROUGH FRIDAY 9 A.M. TO 4 P.M.

## HAWORTH

If privacy is what you are after, then this Dutch Colonial will suit you perfectly. This attractive home has a separate driveway and entrance for guests and is located on a quiet street adjacent to a country club. The large bedroom features a private bath, color TV, phone, and separate heat control. An additional room is available to handle any overflow. Continental breakfast served daily. Public transfortation is available nearby from the center of the community. Children welcome.
**Rates:** S $35, D $45 DAILY.
**Reservations:** (201) 444-7409 MONDAY THROUGH FRIDAY 9 A.M. TO 4 P.M.

## JERSEY CITY

Easy access to New York City makes this new brick townhouse ideal for travelers. Journal Square and the PATH station are only a few blocks away! The guestroom features a double bed, private bath, and large closet. The apartment is filled with treasures from your hosts' many trips abroad working for the United Nations. Since they have traveled extensively, they are eager to help their fellow travelers in whatever way they can. The hosts are fluent in French, Dutch, and Tagalog. With luck, you might even be able to persuade them to share their special recipe for an exotic Middle East banana dish.

**Rates:** S $50, D $55 DAILY.
**Reservations:** (201) 444-7409 MONDAY THROUGH FRIDAY 9 A.M. TO 4 P.M.

## LYNDHURST

Nestled in the historic district of Lyndhurst, along a park, trails, and recreational facilities, lies a cozy B&B establishment. Private accommodations include a two-room suite with private bath and a continental breakfast. This historic landmark was completely restored in 1984. It was originally built in 1841 by a ship joiner who worked at the shipyards located on the Passaic River. The neighborhood is quiet and residential and offers jogging and bike paths, baseball fields, tennis courts, and so on. Excellent local restaurants are nearby, some within walking distance. A friendly welcome is extended to nonsmoking guests and a comfortable stay awaits you in this interesting cottage accommodation.

**Rates:** S $70, D $75 DAILY.
**Reservations:** (201) 444-7409 MONDAY THROUGH FRIDAY 9 A.M. TO 4 P.M.

## MONTCLAIR

A post-Victorian homestead in Upper Montclair offers three sleeping rooms for B&B guests. All rooms are on the second floor and share a bath. Accommodations include: A) queen-sized room with air conditioning; B) a twin room with color TV and air conditioning; and C) a single room. A wonderful English breakfast is served each morning by your hostesses, a mother and daughter, who have traveled extensively throughout the United Kingdom. Although this home is located in town, the neighborhood is very quiet. Close to shops and many restaurants. Arrangements can be made for pick-up at Newark Airport, just a half hour away. Nonsmokers and children over 8 welcome.

**Rates:** A & B) S $35, D $45; AND C) S $35 DAILY.
**Reservations:** (201) 444-7409 MONDAY THROUGH FRIDAY 9 A.M. TO 4 P.M.

This lovely white Colonial features all the homey touches for which B&B hospitality is known. Continental breakfast, sometimes with homemade apple butter or strawberry jam and English muffins, is served in the antique-filled dining room or the cheery kitchen. Guestrooms are on the second floor; one room has twin beds and the other a double bed. Shopping, restaurants, and theater are within walking distance, as well as the train station. Your hosts are well-traveled and will be happy to share tales of their adventures. Airport pick-up is also possible for an additional charge.
**Rates:** S $40, D $50 DAILY.
**Reservations:** (201) 444-7409 MONDAY THROUGH FRIDAY 9 A.M. TO 4 P.M.

## MORRISTOWN

A bit of New England is located just 4 miles from Madison or Morristown. This 200 year old grand home is recorded in the Historic American Buildings Survey and furnished with antiques and Oriental rugs. There are five fireplaces to warm the body and spirit on a cold day and a heated pool and parklike grounds to enjoy in warmer weather. The two guestrooms have private baths. A) The Brides Room has a queen-sized bed with handknotted canopy. The wicker settee overlooks the fountain and patio below. B) The second guestroom is decidedly a gentleman's room. The dark burgundy and regimental striped walls are a perfect background for the sturdy four poster bed, covered in Ralph Lauren paisleys. There is also a nursery with a crib and single bed that can be used by well-mannered children. Included in the rate is a continental breakfast featuring home baking and afternoon tea or evening wine and cheese. Nonsmokers welcome.
**Rates:** A & B) S $53, D $66, DELUXE PACKAGE $76 DAILY.
**Reservations:** (201) 444-7409 MONDAY THROUGH FRIDAY 9 A.M. TO 4 P.M.

## PALISADES PARK

Your hosts at this red brick home are a charming young couple who are fluent in French and Spanish. Their adorable and friendly dog also responds to French! The home has a European flavor to it, from the coziness of the single guestroom to the crystal lamp and grandfather's clock in the living room. The bath is shared with the hosts. Your hostess' mother is a New York City B&B hostess and has passed on the art of gracious hospitality to her daughter. You will be served a continental breakfast and also have refrigerator privileges. Public transportation is two blocks away and major highways only 3 minutes away, providing easy access to the Meadowlands Sports Complex and shopping outlets, as well as New York City. Nonsmokers welcome.
**Rates:** S $35 DAILY.

**Reservations:** (201) 444-7409 MONDAY THROUGH FRIDAY 9 A.M. TO 4 P.M.

## RIDGEWOOD

In a quiet neighborhood of this colonial village, an English tudor home is available for B&B guests. Although the community was recently voted one of the most desirable in the country in which to live, it is also a great place to visit! Many fine shops, recreational facilities, and restaurants are here. The hosts are former guest house owners and really enjoy meeting new friends. The bubbly hostess is a model and motivation speaker who sometimes does fashion commentary. The host has been consulting since his early retirement. Both love to travel. They share their home with a very friendly mini-retriever dog. A) The guestroom on the second floor has a double bed and guests share the bath with their hosts. B) The entire third floor is a complete studio apartment for guests. The huge bedroom is carpeted and contains a walk-in closet and double bed. The separate sitting room has a table and chairs. There is also a full private bath. This apartment is ideal for executives, since it is available for three months minimum rental. An extended continental breakfast is served in the breakfast room. Some Spanish spoken. Nonsmokers and children welcome.
**Rates:** A) S $46, D $53 DAILY. B) $600 MONTHLY.
**Reservations:** (201) 444-7409 MONDAY THROUGH FRIDAY 9 A.M. TO 4 P.M.

This traditional two-story home is located in a residential neighborhood yet is convenient to public transportation (bus and train) to New York City. Your hosts, a professional couple, have lived in Europe and various locations in the United States. They are accustomed to giving and receiving the hospitality that is the B&B hallmark. Cozy rooms on the second floor include a private bath, air conditioning, TV, and plenty of closet space. During the week, a continental breakfast is provided. On weekends a full breakfast is possible featuring the house specialty — puff pancakes — and you can dine in the cheerful screened porch overlooking the wooded garden.
**Rates:** S $40, D $50 DAILY.
**Reservations:** (201) 444-7409 MONDAY THROUGH FRIDAY 9 A.M. TO 4 P.M.

A continental breakfast with lots of home-baked goodies is featured in a large kitchen filled with hanging plants and copper pots. This professional couple share their home with a gentle collie and all really enjoy guests. Their four-bedroom Colonial offers two newly decorated rooms for guests. A single with pop-up bed converts to a double and the second room has a new queen convertible sofa, colored TV with remote control, and air

conditioning. Both sleeping rooms share the bath. Tennis and public transportation are within walking distance. Plenty of recreation, shopping, and fine restaurants within a few minutes drive. One hour from New York City.
**Rates:** WEEKLY ONLY S $430, D $435, ADDITIONAL PERSON $10 DAILY.
**Reservations:** (201) 444-7409 MONDAY THROUGH FRIDAY 9 A.M. TO 4 P.M.

## SUMMIT

Tucked away in a quiet neighborhood, this charming home can offer a hiatus from your hectic schedule. Your hosts are a well-traveled professional couple who lived in Europe for several years where they experienced the finest hospitality. Now they would like to share that experience with you. The guestroom on the third floor is bright and airy with lace curtains and a skylight. Antique furniture and a rocking chair contrast the platform double bed. The bath is reserved exclusively for guests' use. Your hosts love to cook and breakfast is bound to be delicious — especially when it is served in the screened sunroom! For further relaxation, try lounging around the pool in the lush backyard or take a stroll in the nearby park. Peace of mind comes easily in this tranquil setting.
**Rates:** S OR D $63 DAILY.
**Reservations:** (201) 444-7409 MONDAY THROUGH FRIDAY 9 A.M. TO 4 P.M.

## WASHINGTON TOWNSHIP

This stately two-story Colonial is located in a quiet residential area atop a hill overlooking the Pascack Valley. Your hosts, a Norwegian couple, take great pride in their home which they built themselves. Rough-hewn columns and paneling along with a collection of antique tools indicate that this is indeed a builder's home. Custom features are especially evident in the guest area. A private entrance leads into a huge living room with queen-sized sofabed, piano, and large antique pool table. The bedroom has two large closets (one becomes a desk area), a double bed, and a color TV with remote control. A kitchen and bath (with shower stall) complete the guest apartment. Your friendly hosts, who are active in their church, will gladly provide any information you may need about the area. Buses to New York City are only a short walk away and there is easy access to the Garden State Parkway and Routes 17 and 4.
**Rates:** S $75, D $90 DAILY.
**Reservations:** (201) 444-7409 MONDAY THROUGH FRIDAY 9 A.M. TO 4 P.M.

# WESTWOOD

This wonderful young host couple will make you feel very welcome to their country home in this suburban community. Both have used B&B accommodations throughout the world, through their travel in conjunction with his ministry and her employment with the airlines. The ranch home is situated in a secluded wooded area just off a main street. Pool and patio are available to guests. A twin-bedded room with TV and private bath on the main level has been decorated for guests. The finished basement is complete with bedroom, living room with color TV, eating area, and lavatory with shower. Study available for overflow. Blocks away from the bus/train commuter line to New York City. A continental breakfast is served daily.

**Rates:** S $35, D $45 DAILY.
**Reservations:** (201) 444-7409 MONDAY THROUGH FRIDAY 9 A.M. TO 4 P.M.

## MOUNT HOLLY
## COLUMBUS

An 1845 Federal farmhouse on 8 acres with a stable, carriage house, ducks, horses, and sheep. A lovely old home, filled with restored, antiques. Related guests only, no multiple guests. House written up and photographed in December 1985 *Country Living*. Host is in the military service; hostess is a family counselor. Near antique flea markets and mono bicycle museum. Accommodations include: A) double bed, shared bath with guests; and B) single bed, bath, working FIREPLACE, footed tub. Private guest sitting room with TV and air conditioning. Full breakfast. Must have a car. CAT in residence. Historic home.

**Rates:** A) S $55, D $65; AND B) S $55 DAILY.
**Reservations:** (215) 688-1633 MONDAY THROUGH FRIDAY 9:00 TO 5:00.

# NORTH SHORE

After you have stopped, sunned, and had enough swimming, the North Shore has more excitement and attractions. Get swept along the breathtaking amusement areas at Seaside Heights, Long Branch, and Point Pleasant. Travel a little inland and relive history while touring the restored village of Allaire. Spend an evening at the ballet or attend a concert at the Garden State Arts Center. Watch a race at Monmouth Park, trotters at Freehold, or stock cars at Wall Stadium. Then brave the 450 acres wild game safari and amusements at Great Adventure.

## BELMAR

The atmosphere at this seashore Dutch Colonial is friendly and informal. Built around the turn of the century, the home's furnishings are a mixed seashore special, consisting of some antiques, wicker, and the hosts' art collection. There are seven guestrooms, one with an oceanview, and all are equipped with fans. Most rooms have a private bath and some rooms can be combined to accommodate three or four guests. Guests are welcome to use the front porch, sitting room, and sun deck and off-street parking is provided. A full breakfast is served featuring spicy fruit compote, omletes, Jersey seafood quiche, cranberry orange bread, and much more. Enjoy dozens of local activities or take advantage of nearby features such as: Garden State Art Center, Monmouth Race Track, Great Adventure Amusement Park, or the Englishtown Flea Market.

**Rates:** S $45-$55; D $60-$70 DAILY.

**Reservations:** (201) 444-7409 MONDAY THROUGH FRIDAY 9 A.M. TO 4 P.M.

## LAKEWOOD

This home offers two inviting bedrooms, one twin bed with shared bath and a king-sized bed with private entrance and bath. A sitting room is available for reading, music, or TV. The professional couple who serve as hosts are eager to make a stay there pleasant, many little extra surprises are included. Golf and tennis are within walking distance. Enjoy a hansom cab ride around the town. It is 15 minutes from the shore and from Great Adventure/Safariland, but has many nearby attractions and restaurants. There is hourly bus service to Atlantic City. Choice of full or continental breakfast or use of the kitchen. Children welcome.

**Rates:** S $40, D $53 DAILY.

**Reservations:** (201) 444-7409 MONDAY THROUGH FRIDAY 9 A.M. TO 4 P.M.

## OCEAN GROVE

This Victorian village is a historic landmark and has been a popular seaside retreat since 1869. Stroll along tree-lined avenues and you will find this charming 100 year old inn, just four houses from the ocean! Step inside and conjure up memories of the by-gone era your hosts have recreated. Enjoy a cool breeze and a wonderful view of the ocean from the first and second story porches, or relax on a park bench in the rose garden. A continental breakfast features fresh-baked goods, fruit juices, and exotic coffees. All guestrooms are equipped with sinks and some have private baths. A two-bedroom suite is also available. Your hosts are healthcare professionals who are lifelong area residents. Their exuberance is infectious and you will become as captivated by Ocean Grove as they are.

**Rates:** S $38-$65, D $48-$75 DAILY.

**Reservations:** (201) 444-7409 MONDAY THROUGH FRIDAY 9 A.M. TO 4 P.M.

Known for its friendliness, hospitality, and quiet, this four story guest house was built over 100 years ago. With 20 rooms, 3 porches, and 2 full apartments, there is plenty of room for families. A simple continental buffet breakfast is available each morning and you are free to use the fully equipped communal kitchen during the day. There is also a lounge and music and TV are available for guests. Enjoy the true family atmosphere of Victorian Ocean Grove. where you can walk on the wooden boardwalk for miles seeing flowers and parks. There are no commercial buildings on the ocean. A nearby 8,000 seat auditorium offers cultural-musical events and shops and restaurants are just a short walk from your room. This inn is located just 1 1/2 hours from Manhattan, with buses every hour, and Atlantic City is an hour away.

**Rates:** A-P) S $20-$32, D $24-$55, FAMILY (4 PERSONS) $40-$64; G & H) (EFFICIENCIES) $40-$56; I & J) (APARTMENTS) $80-$94 DAILY. RATES DEPEND ON LENGTH OF STAY.

**Reservations:** (201) 444-7409 MONDAY THROUGH FRIDAY 9 A.M. TO 4 P.M.

## SOUTH BELMAR

Open year-round, there is much to enjoy in a rustic mountain lodge at the seashore. Built in 1908, it boasts of original wooden beams, great stone fireplace (one of four), and wood and brick floors. The six guestrooms have been completely redecorated, each with a private bath and a view of the lake and/or ocean. Some rooms also have a private porch or balcony. Across the street is Lake Como which is stocked with fish. It is also a migratory lake with a profusion of different birds each season. Bikes for loan. Beach badges available for Spring Lake and Belmar beaches located 5 minutes away. Buffet style continental breakfast with homemade goodies. Children over 12 welcome.

**Rates:** S $50-$80, D $50-$85 DEPENDING ON SEASON.

**Reservations:** (201) 444-7409 MONDAY THROUGH FRIDAY 9 A.M. TO 4 P.M.

## NORTH SHORE HEIGHTS
## ISLAND HEIGHTS

This unusual studio/home of a renowned artist was built in 1889 and has recently been completely restored. It retains a wonderful Victorian atmosphere with the artist's paintings, memorabilia, and antiques. The artist designed the studio first, with its large fireplace, and then built the rest of the house around it. In later years, a sun room and a large country kitchen were added. You will enjoy sitting on the old-fashioned porch and watching the boats sail by on Toms River or cycling through the town, which has recently been placed on the National Register of Historic Sites. Three beaches are within walking distance, along with lots of recreational facilities and fine restaurants. Three sleeping rooms are

available for guests, a twin, a double, and a double with a sitting area. All sleeping rooms share baths. A full gourmet breakfast is served in the sunny kitchen.
**Rates:** S $55-$72, D $65-$82 DAILY.
**Reservations:** (201) 444-7409 MONDAY THROUGH FRIDAY 9 A.M. TO 4 P.M.

## SKYLANDS REGION

This area includes all of northwestern New Jersey including the gulf of the Delaware Water Gap in the Gap National Recreation Area and New Jersey's largest lake, Lake Hopatcong. The mountain country of this area offers hiking ridge paths and superb birding at High Point State Park. The oldest road in the United States, the Old Mine Road, will take you from the Water Gap to the restored hamlet of Milbrook with a smithy and farms. Another reconstructed village, Stanhope's Waterloo dates back to the eighteenth century and plays hosts to old-time craftspeople at work and summer concerts. In season, ski at Vernon Valley/Great Gorge, home of the world's largest snowmaking apparatus, Craigmeur, and Hidden Valley. All have lots of summer activities, too. Excellent cross-country skiing is to be had on the region's mountian trails and pathways. The Great Swamp Nation Wildlife Refuge has 7,000 acres of living space for birds and a half mile walkway for birdwatchers. Open daily.

## CHESTER

Gracious country living is what you will find at this spacious, new Colonial home. It is located in an area renown for its antique and craft shops, yet convenient to the historic Morristown and Hackettstown communities. Your vivacious hostess has redecorated the king-sized room that is sure to please. It includes a private bath, TV, phone, and air conditioning. A double guestroom shares a bath with the hostess. Also a delight is a continental breakfast featuring fresh-baked coffee cake (an original recipe).
**Rates:** S $35, D $47 DAILY.
**Reservations:** (201) 444-7409 MONDAY THROUGH FRIDAY 9 A.M. TO 4 P.M.

## FLEMNGTON

To experience the pretty country town of Flemington, spend a night or two at this wonderful B&B. This turn-of-the-century Victorian has been totally renovated. Your hostess has a cheery, friendly personality and the house reflects her traits. Born and raised in the area, she is always ready to assist guests with dinner reservations, suggest shopping strategies, or even book a flight in a hot-air balloon! A continental breakfast of fresh fruit, breads, and pastries is served (make sure you try the pear bread).

When weather permits, guests can eat on the spacious screened porch. The five guestrooms are nicely decorated without appearing pretentious. Children over 12 and nonsmokers welcome.
**Rates:** $55-$70 DAILY.
**Reservations:** (201) 444-7409 MONDAY THROUGH FRIDAY 9 A.M. TO 4 P.M.

## HOPE

Originally the heart of the village economy, this impressive colonial grist mill complex is now a gracious country inn. It is situated on 23 acres along Beaver Brook and was built circa 1769 by Moravian pioneers. The individually decorated guestrooms, each with private bath, reflect the quiet elegance once found in fine homes of Colonial America. Distinctive antique furnishings, original wide board flooring, and handcrafted Oriental rugs heighten the feeling of colonial authenticity. Guests can take advantage of the almost unlimited number of area attractions including Waterloo Village with seasonal concerts, antique and craft shows, fishing or canoeing on the Delaware River, hiking in the Delaware Water Gap Recreation Area, and wine tasting at nearby vineyards.
**Rates:** S $49-$74, D $55-$80 DAILY.
**Reservations:** (201) 444-7409 MONDAY THROUGH FRIDAY 9 A.M. TO 4 P.M.

## MILLINGTON

Close your eyes and you might be able to picture a scene from colonial times when this home was a wing of a stagecoach inn. Originally built in 1764 and renovated in 1980, this historic home was recently featured on a house tour. The cozy atmosphere begins in the country kitchen where a fireplace will make your extended continental breakfast a real treat. The three guestrooms (one with private bath) all feature original hardwood floors with attractive area rugs. A Queen Anne desk, antique dressers, and rocking chairs add to the overall charm of the house. Your hostess, a personnel manager of an international corporation, invites you to experience her home's colonial heritage.
**Rates:** A) S $45, D $50; AND B & C) S $61, D $66 DAILY.
**Reservations:** (201) 444-7409 MONDAY THROUGH FRIDAY 9 A.M. TO 4 P.M.

## PHILLIPSBURG

Originally a miller's house, this gracious fieldstone manor is set in the midst of 16 acres of rolling hills and forests. The outdoor patio overlooks landscaped gardens with stone walkways, a huge free form pool, and numerous outbuildings that contribute to the pastoral setting. The interior of this historic estate includes a library with arched corner fireplace, a game room, a living room for casual conversation, and a workout room. There is even a trout stream on the property. The house has eight bedrooms, two with fireplaces and seven with baths. Each room has a queen-sized four-poster bed, its own TV, and private phone. A conference room is also available. Enjoy home baking for gourmet breakfasts and afternoon tea.

**Rates:** A-F) $75; AND G & H) $65 DAILY.
**Reservations:** (201) 444-7409 MONDAY THROUGH FRIDAY 9 A.M. TO 4 P.M.

## SOUTH SHORE

The wide beaches of the Wildwoods and Ocean City are perfect places to build sand castles and enjoy the exciting miles of boardwalks for rides and nighttime entertainment. Wander the tranquil ocean beaches of Stone Harbor and Avalon or the Delaware Bay. Find a nineteenth century retreat in Cape May where Victorian porch pillars, ornate railings and dormers, gables, chimneys, and cupolas seem to be everywhere. Explore one of the country's last free zoos and the state's largest historic district in Bridgeton. See glass being fired and shaped at an open furnace or create your own glass paperweight. Enjoy the annual "Night in Venice" boat parade and festival in Ocean City. Visit historic towns, museums, holly orchards, and award winning gardens of New Jersey's South Shore.

### BARNEGAT LIGHT
### LONG BEACH ISLAND

If a beach house with a spectacular view is what you are seeking, then look no further. This house is literally on the beach! Guest quarters are a complete apartment on the second floor of this contemporary home. They include a master (double) bedroom with access to the deck, two twin-bedded rooms, living room (with pull out sofa), kitchen (with dishwasher!), dining room, and full bath. Yet another terrific feature: a washer and dryer. One entire side of the apartment boasts floor to ceiling windows offering a truly magnificent view of the lagoon, channel, and lighthouse. Since the house is bounded by Barnegat Light State Park, recreational activities are right outside your door. A short walk will take you to the center for shopping, restaurants, and other activities. This is the perfect spot for anyone who is a beachcomber at heart. Available by the week only.

**Rates:** $425-$1,000 WEEKLY.
**Reservations:** (201) 444-7409 MONDAY THROUGH FRIDAY 9 A.M. TO 4 P.M.

## BEACH HAVEN

This charming Victorian cottage by the sea is located in Beach Haven's historical district, one block from the beautiful protected beach (complimentary beach badges). Six bright, airy guestrooms are equipped with ceiling fans to keep you comfortable on the hottest summer afternoons. Enjoy the sound of the surf and the cool ocean breezes from the spacious wraparound porch — you can even have your continental breakfast there! Six rooms include two with private bath. Most rooms can be converted from king to twin beds. Water sports are locally available, the National Wildlife Preserve is 2 miles away and it is only a 45 minute drive to the casinos of Atlantic City. Children over 7 and nonsmokers welcome.
**Rates:** $75 - $120 DAILY.
**Reservations:** (201) 444-7409 MONDAY THROUGH FRIDAY 9 A.M. TO 4 P.M.

## CAPE MAY

West Cape May now offers a small Victorian inn with lots of history. Just opened in the spring of 1987, it has been carefully restored with Oriental rugs and lace curtains throughout. The three guestrooms, containing an antique twin bed set, extra long twin beds, and a carved oak double bed, all share a bath. Only six short blocks to the beach; beach tags and bikes are available to guests. A great hunt breakfast is served in the dining room by the inn's chef who is a student at the Culinary Institute. Guests are also free to use the kitchen for later day snacks. With low rates and the many extras that are offered, this will surely become one of the most sought after accommodations in the area.
**Rates:** S $50, D $55 - $65 DAILY.
**Reservations:** (201) 444-7409 MONDAY THROUGH FRIDAY 9 A.M. TO 4 P.M.

## HISTORIC DISTRICT

This turn-of-the-century inn is situated in an excellent location, a half block from the beach, near the Victorian Mall in the Historic District. Restaurants, night spots, and most other attractions are no more than a short stroll away. Each of the nine bright, cheery guestrooms is furnished individually in Victorian decor; two rooms have private baths and seven share baths. A continental breakfast that includes fresh fruit, juices, cheese, and homemade breads and coffee cakes is served in either the peach and turquoise lobby or the dining room. Your congenial hosts took on the big but rewarding job of restoring the inn and they are very proud of the results. Children over 12 welcome.
**Rates:** A-G) $25-$65; H & I) $40-$75 DAILY DEPENDING ON SEASON. 10% DISCOUNT FOR WEEKLY STAYS.

**Reservations:** (201) 444-7409 MONDAY THROUGH FRIDAY 9 A.M. TO 4 P.M.

## ON THE OCEAN

Reserve your rocker overlooking the ocean in the heart of Cape May. There are 11 apartments with Victorian charm and modern conveniences that can be rented on a weekly basis or for the summer season. This is only one of a few accommodations in Cape May that welcome children. On site parking, cable TV, and laundry. Ask about off-season discounts. **Rates:** A & B) $450, C) $350, D & E) $400, F) $525, PENTHOUSE) $600, CROWS NEST) $350, SIDE) $325, CARRIAGE) 1 - $325, 2 - $575 WEEKLY. A WEEK RUNS SATURDAY TO SATURDAY. **Reservations:** (201) 444-7409 MONDAY THROUGH FRIDAY 9 A.M. TO 4 P.M.

At first glance, this three story turn-of-the-century mansion does not seem in keeping with the gingerbread architecture of Cape May. Built by a prominent Philadelphia physician, with fluted columns and colonial revival accents, it resembles an Italian palazzo townhouse. Once inside, however, a Victorian atmosphere is clearly in evidence. The 12 foot coffered ceilings and incredible hand-carved woodwork will delight you as much as the beautiful antiques of every kind. Of seven guestrooms, five have private baths and two share a bath. Full breakfast and afternoon sherry or tea are a treat. Bikes, beach passes, off street parking, and beach towels are available to guests. This peaceful inn is on the ocean, away from the bustle of town. It is a place to relax, savor the pleasures of a long-gone lifestyle, and, best of all, to sit on a rocker and watch the crystals of ocean spray dance over the seawall. **Rates:** A, B, H, & L) S $85, D $95; C, D, E, J, & K) S $79, D $87; G) S $89, D $99; AND I) S $95, D $105 DAILY. TAKE OFF 10% WEEKLY. OFF-SEASON RATES ON REQUEST. $20 FOR EACH ADDITIONAL PERSON IN ROOM. **Reservations:** (201) 444-7409 MONDAY THROUGH FRIDAY 9 A.M. TO 4 P.M.

## SECONDARY HISTORIC DISTRICT

Situated in a quiet section of Cape May, yet just three blocks from the beach, you will find this home, which offers two full apartments and a single room with trundle bed and private bath. The second floor apartment contains an eat-in kitchen with pantry, living room with sleeper sofa, cable TV and radio, a bedroom with queen bed, and a tile bath. It is well heated or air conditioned for year-round guests. The backyard is available for grilling and an outdoor shower has been installed for use after a day at the beach. The entire third floor is also heated and offers a living room with cable TV and sleeper sofa, foyer, a large air-conditioned bedroom,

and a private bath. A suite with double bed and private bath is also available. Beach badges are available. Children are always welcome.
**Rates:** A & B) $75-$125; C) $75 DAILY. A & B) $475-$550 WEEKLY.
**Reservations:** (201) 444-7409 MONDAY THROUGH FRIDAY 9 A.M. TO 4 P.M.

## OCEAN CITY

A private vacation complex on the beach provides a commanding view of the ocean. Six beachfront units include a refrigerator, bar sink, cable TV, phone, accommodations for two to four persons, contemporary furnishings, wall-to-wall carpeting, air conditioning, a beachfront deck, and access to a private courtyard, a large beach-level deck, a private party deck, laundry facilities, and food service. A beach front duplex has two floors, each with four bedrooms (two with walk-in closets and queen-sized beds); three bathrooms (one with jacuzzi); complete kitchen; ocean-view dining; and living room with cable TV and fireplace, central air conditioning, heat, and full carpeting; utility room with washer and dryer; and a private beach-front deck and access to courtyard and beach deck. Breakfast is available during the off-season and children welcome.
**Rates:** A) $95; B) $75; C) $485; AND D) $95 DAILY.
**Reservations:** (201) 444-7409 MONDAY THROUGH FRIDAY 9 A.M. TO 4 P.M.

This 15 room guesthouse usually rents five units for the entire summer season. Just 2 1/2 blocks to the beach, it is open Memorial Day through Labor Day and provides many types of accommodations, including three apartments which are available year-round. Each apartment can sleep four people comfortably and is equipped with cable TV, air conditioning, refrigerator, stove, and private bath. Single and double rooms share baths and two outside enclosed showers. Some parking on premises. Children are always welcome and will probably enjoy the bunk beds.
**Rates:** A-H) D $45-$75 (DEPENDING ON SEASON) S; 10% OFF DAILY. EFFICIENCIES SLEEP FOUR $450 PER WEEK.
**Reservations:** (201) 444-7409 MONDAY THROUGH FRIDAY 9 A.M. TO 4 P.M.

## BEACH BLOCK

Families love the comfortable, homey atmosphere of this six room guesthouse. Two rooms are large enough to accommodate two adults and one child and some rooms have TV and some have refrigerators. All rooms share a bath on each floor. The house is only 100 yards from the beach and boardwalk and is near the recreation center and tennis courts. A museum and many restaurants are only a few blocks away. Parking is not a problem — you will have a reserved spot in a lot on the same street. Your vivacious hostess takes pride in her bountiful buffet breakfast featuring specialty breads, jams, danish, juices, and casseroles. She will be glad to help you in whatever way possible to make your stay an enjoyable one.

**Rates:** A-F) D $45-$65, S LESS 10% DAILY. SEVENTH NIGHT FREE WEEKLY.

**Reservations:** (201) 444-7409 MONDAY THROUGH FRIDAY 9 A.M. TO 4 P.M.

# NEW YORK

## ADIRONDACKS

The Adirondacks are a mountain chain in the northeastern part of New York State. Lake George, Lake Placid, Whiteface Mountain (home of the Winter Olympics in 1980) are among the most famous places in the region. It is an area rich in history, the arts, and outdoor fun. Hiking, swimming, boating, skiing, and sightseeing make the Adirondacks an especially appealing vacation spot. The Adirondacks are an enjoyable all season playground easily reached from New York or Canada.

## CHESTERTOWN
### FRIENDS LAKE

FRIENDS LAKE ROAD — The inn, built in the 1860s, is furnished with antiques and boasts its original chestnut woodwork. Guests can relax in front of a crackling fire, or enjoy cocktails on the lakeview veranda. The inn has a full-service bar and is known for its original and imaginative cuisine served under the original tin ceiling. The 12 guestrooms are individually decorated with a warm country flair. A few have lakeviews. There are two cottages available that look over the lake. The inn is convenient to countless activities and attractions, yet it is in a private and quiet location. Guests can cross-country ski, hike, and swim on the premises. A very friendly DOG and CAT are in residence. PIANO. TV. White water rafting, bikes, rowboats, and a sunfish sailboat are available. Host is a commercial masonry contractor. Swedish is spoken here. Cots are available. Double accommodations are available in the guestrooms. Near Gore Mountain; 1 1/2 hours north of Albany. Children of all ages welcome.
**Rates:** D $85-$95 FOR BED & BREAKFAST. MODIFIED AMERICAN PLAN: D $118-$130, SPECIAL PACKAGE PRICES AVAILABLE UPON REQUEST.
**Reservations:** (914) 271-6228 MONDAY - FRIDAY 10 A.M. TO 4 P.M. APRIL - OCTOBER. 9 A.M. - 3 P.M. NOVEMBER - MARCH.

## COLD BROOK

A large 150 year old farmhouse on 165 acres with swimming POOL, TENNIS COURT, and working farm with animals. A 60 tree orchard, stocked fish pond with brook trout, horses, pigs and Moscovy ducks are on the farm. Guests can pick berries, walk the nature trails, watch the beaver frolic in the beaver pond, snow mobile, or cross-country ski on 180 acres. The home abuts the Adirondack park trails. Hostess is an educator. A CAT and two IRISH SETTERS live here. Accommodations include: A & B) double bed, shared bath; C) sofabed, shared bath; and D) double bed, private bath. Laundry facilities, pickup, TV available. Full breakfast served. Fireplace in house. No SMOKING in bedrooms.

CHILDREN over 12 are welcome.
**Rates:** A-D) S $30, D $35-$40 DAILY.
**Reservations:** (914) 271-6228 MONDAY - FRIDAY 10 A.M. TO 4 P.M.
APRIL - OCTOBER. 9 A.M. - 3 P.M. NOVEMBER - MARCH.

## ILION

MAIN STREET — An Italianate Second EMpire late Victorian home built in 1872. The home conveys a strong Victorian ambiance with some original furnishings, including a Steinway upright PIANO, several imported Italian marble fireplaces, and the first bathroom in the area, constructed completely of Venetian porcelain. Hosts are both retired. Home is located in small town nestled in rolling wooded hills and farm country. There is a FIREPLACE in the bedroom and home is accessible by public transportation. One CAT resides here. There are single and double bedrooms with either A) private bath or B) shared bath. Smokers are accepted.
**Rates:** A) S $35, D $40; AND B) S $25, D $30 DAILY.
**Reservations:** (315) 733-0040.

## KEESEVILLE

This 1797 Colonial farmhouse was once a tavern and stagecoach stop between Albany and Montreal. Major renovations have kept the authentic atmosphere of wide plank floors and beam ceilings. Hike or cross-country ski on 325 acres of beautiful Adirondack land; Lake Champlain is 10 minutes away; Lake Placid 45 minutes. Accommodations include: A) twin beds, share bath with family; B) double bed, share bath with family; C) sofabed, share bath with family; and D) queen-sized bed, FIREPLACE, private 1/2 bathroom. TV. Full breakfast served to guests. Children welcome.
**Rates:** A-C) S $30, D $40; D) D $50 DAILY.
**Reservations:** (914) 271-6228 MONDAY - FRIDAY 10 A.M. TO 4 P.M.
APRIL - OCTOBER. 9 A.M. - 3 P.M. NOVEMBER - MARCH.

## MALONE
### VILLAGE

MILWAUKEE STREET — The carriage house was built in 1820, owned by Senator Kilburn and his son Congressman Kilburn. House was on Daughters of American Revolution tour. Close to Titus Mountain ski center, 10 minutes to golf course. Swim in backyard POOL. Five minute walk to Main Street. Next door to Franklin County House of History. Hosts have three children living at home. NO SMOKING. All suites have sitting room and private bath. There are double beds in the three accommodations; also cots and cribs are available. Fireplace in home; TV and laundry facilities available. Continental breakfast is served to guests.

**Rates:** S $27.50, D $35 DAILY. S $150, D $210 WEEKLY.
**Reservations:** (914) 271-6228 MONDAY - FRIDAY 10 A.M. TO 4 P.M.
APRIL - OCTOBER. 9 A.M. - 3 P.M. NOVEMBER - MARCH.

## NICHOLVILLE

An 1810 Victorian with floating grand staircase, beautiful woodwork, and lots of antiques. Step back in time. Located in the North Country of New York State, 70 miles northwest of Lake Placid, 70 miles southwest of Montreal, and only 10 to 25 miles from 5 colleges including Potsdam and Canton. Hosts are retired, serve a full breakfast and aim to make your stay an enjoyable one. A Samoyed DOG also lives here. 150 miles to Syracuse. Accommodations include: A-D) double bed, shared bath. NONSMOKERS and CHILDREN over 12 welcome.
**Rates:** S $30, D $35 DAILY. S $175, D $210 WEEKLY.
**Reservations:** (914) 271-6228 MONDAY - FRIDAY 10 A.M. TO 4 P.M.
APRIL - OCTOBER. 9 A.M. - 3 P.M. NOVEMBER - MARCH.

## WARRENSBURG

MAIN STREET — An 1847 Victorian home in the heart of the queen village of the Adirondacks, an antiquer's paradise! The home is furnished with many Victorian antiques to send you back in time. Five minutes from Lake George Village, historical Fort William Henry plus Great Escape. In town, walk to restaurants, antique shops, and shopping areas. Enjoy the comfort of the air-conditioned television lounge for guests only. Wicker rockers and chairs are also available on the front porch. Accommodations include: all rooms with window fans, one room with two double beds, and four rooms with one double bed, sharing two large bathrooms. Bikes available. Gore Mountain nearby for downhill skiing. Pickup available. Host is a retired electrical inspector who enjoys antique cars, building old ships, and collecting antiques; hostess is a former supervisor of the Long Island Lighting Company who is also interested in antique cars (she has three), knitting, and refinishing antiques. Smokers welcome but not cigar SMOKERS. CHILDREN over 7 welcome.
**Rates:** $85-$110 S or D.
**Reservations:** (914) 271-6228 MONDAY - FRIDAY 10 A.M. TO 4 P.M.
APRIL — OCTOBER. 9 A.M. - 3 P.M. NOVEMBER - MARCH.

## CAPITAL REGION

This area is comprised of the six counties surrounding Albany, the capital city of New York State. As well as housing the state government, Albany is the home of the Empire State Plaza, which hosts many conventions and entertainment attractions. Universities abound including SUNY at Albany, Russell Sage, Siena, Rensselaer Polytechnic Institute, Union, and Skidmore. It is an area rich in history, culture, and outdoor activities in all seasons, convenient to both kinds of skiing in winter and swimming and hiking in summer.

## ALBANY
## COLONIE VILLAGE

LOCUST PARK — Host and hostess welcome you to their charming Cape Cod house located in the center of the tri-city area. The entire upstairs has been converted for guests with a separate entrance and stairway. There are two lovely rooms with one bathroom. One room features a cozy sitting room with wicker furniture, the second room features a small office area with desk and chair. There are many plants and a very attractive deck that guests are encouraged to use. Host is a production controller who enjoys golf; hostess is an executive secretary. Host has a very interesting bar in the family room, which he constructed, and hostess has a collection of cookbooks from around the world. Both host and hostess enjoy travel and love meeting people. They will pickup at airport, if convenient to their work schedule. Located in the heart of the capital district, they are convenient to all aspects of Albany-Schenectady-Troy areas and only 25 minutes to Saratoga Race Track and Performing Arts Center. They are surrounded by colleges, shopping centers, and social events. TENNIS courts are across the street, with basketball available, also. A truly pleasant place to stay. One CAT lives here. Double beds and a cot are available in the bedrooms. TV, VCR, and laundry facilities available. SMOKING downstairs only. CHILDREN over 5 years welcome.
**Rates:** S $35, D $40 DAILY. S $240, D $280 WEEKLY.
**Reservations:** (914) 271-6228 MONDAY - FRIDAY 10 A.M. TO 4 P.M. APRIL - OCTOBER. 9 A.M. - 3 P.M. NOVEMBER - MARCH.

## LOUDONVILLE

OFF ROUTE 9 — Situated in a lovely residential suburb of Albany, this charming Colonial home has an aura of country warmth. Many antiques and plants. Hearty breakfasts include homemade muffins and freshly ground and brewed coffee. During summer months, guests are served on the pleasant screened porch. Host is a sales manager; hostess is in advertising. Hosts are interested in fishing, travel, and theater. Accommodations in a separate guest wing of the second floor include: A) double bed, attractively decorated room, shared bath; and B) iron and brass double bed and antiques, sitting room (where guests find a decanter of sherry and fresh fruit), private guest bath. A folding bed can accommodate a CHILD over 10. This lovely home is conveniently located just minutes from Albany, SUNY at Albany, Siena College and only 20 miles from Saratoga, home of the Saratoga Performing Arts Center and Saratoga Race Track. Many fine museums, theaters, and restaurants are closeby. PIANO, fireplace, TV, and laundry facilities on premises.

SMOKING only on first floor.
**Rates:** A & B) S $40, D $50 DAILY. A & B) S $245, D $315 WEEKLY.
ADDITIONAL ADULTS $15 EACH DAILY.
**Reservations:** (914) 271-6228 MONDAY - FRIDAY 10 A.M. TO 4 P.M.
APRIL - OCTOBER. 9 A.M. - 3 P.M. NOVEMBER - MARCH.

## ALBANY

RAMSEY PLACE — A charming 1910 house that has been totally modernized and artistically renovated. It has parquet floors, beamed ceilings, and many beautiful antiques. There is a fireplace in the living room, a lovely breakfast nook and marvelous kitchen. A patio deck with many plants makes the small yard very inviting. Hostess is a legislative assistant in state government. She is interested in politics, classical music, and liberal causes. A CAT also lives here. Accommodations include: A) sofabed, porch; B) double bed, share family bath; and C) three-quarter bed, share family bath. Full breakfast served. Children welcome.
**Rates:** A-C) S $20, D $30 DAILY. S $105, D $175 WEEKLY.
**Reservations:** (914) 271-6228 MONDAY - FRIDAY 10 A.M. TO 4 P.M.
APRIL - OCTOBER. 9 A.M. - 3 P.M. NOVEMBER - MARCH.

TOWNWOOD DRIVE — Attractive townhouse development in a wooded, quiet area convenient to downtown Albany. Hostess works in vocational rehabilitation as a director of placement. She is active in business, professional, and community activities. She enjoys theater, dance, and cooking. Accommodations include: A) double flip couch, shared family bath; and B) double cabinet bed in living room, shared family bath. Children welcome. A full breakfast is served here. A fireplace is in the home and TV and laundry facilities are available.
**Rates:** A & B) S $20, D $30 DAILY.
**Reservations:** (914) 271-6228 MONDAY - FRIDAY 10 A.M. TO 4 P.M.
APRIL - OCTOBER. 9 A.M. - 3 P.M. NOVEMBER - MARCH.

## ALTAMONT

ROUTE 20 — A large white 75 year old renovated farmhouse on 14 acres of land with an apple orchard, inground 36 foot POOL, and an outdoor patio. Formal living room and dining room and a baby grand PIANO, large kitchen, den with television, and built-in stereo tape deck. Pool table and air hockey in the basement. Host is a retired research chemist who speaks German and enjoys photography as a hobby; hostess is a trainer/consultant; she enjoys travel and entertaining as hobbies, and understands and speaks some Spanish and French. Hostess' 89 year old mother lives here. Also in residence are a CAT and DOG. This residence is convenient to all historic, cultural, and outdoor activities available in this area. Accommodations include: A & B) two rooms each with a single bed. These rooms share a bath. C) Third floor suite including lovely

sitting area with double bed sofa, two rooms with double and single beds and private bath with shower. It is 15 minutes to Albany, 10 to Schenectady, 5 minutes to Altamont fairgrounds, 20 minutes off exit 24 of the New York Thruway and Interstate 87. Fireplace in home, laundry facilities and pickup available. SMOKERS NOT WELCOME.
**Rates:** A & B) S $30, D $40 DAILY. C) S $35, D $50, S $200, D $250 WEEKLY. ADDITIONAL CHILDREN $10 EACH DAILY.
**Reservations:** (914) 271-6228 MONDAY - FRIDAY 10 A.M. TO 4 P.M. APRIL - OCTOBER. 9 A.M. - 3 P.M. NOVEMBER - MARCH.

ROUTE 146 — This home is on the National Registry. It was built in 1765 as a tavern and is now run as a B&B. Downstairs is an antique shop specializing in bedroom furnishings and English Victorian linens. A full breakfast is served in a sun-filled solarium overlooking a flowing creek and swimming POOL or at your request have a white wicker tea cart wheeled to your bedside in order to enjoy an elaborate continental breakfast. Situated on six country acres complete with DOG, CATS (outside only), and horses but only minutes from Albany. Accommodations include: A) double bed with FIREPLACE and porch; B) queen bed with FIREPLACE and porch; C) twin beds; D) double bed plus a single bed. All rooms share two baths and are decorated with antiques throughout. VCR, TV, and bikes available, also laundry facilities. TENNIS COURT on property. Situated at the base of the Heldeberg Mountains, guestrooms have wide plank floors, antique beds and down comforters. Cross-country skiing and golf courses just minutes away. This inn is also available for weddings and business meetings. SMOKING OK, but not in bedrooms.
**Rates:** A & B) S or D $50; C) S or D) $45 DAILY. A & B) $280; C) S $200, D $250; AND D) S $200, D $280 WEEKLY. JANUARY THROUGH MARCH DINNER IN ROOM $75 WITH ROOM AND BREAKFAST DAILY.
**Reservations:** (914) 271-6228 MONDAY - FRIDAY 10 A.M. TO 4 P.M. APRIL - OCTOBER. 9 A.M. - 3 P.M. NOVEMBER - MARCH.

## BROADALBIN

Turn of the century home on 46 acre estate, once the summer home of a bishop. Hand cut stone fireplaces, hardwood peg floors, and Oriental and modern decor artistically blended in this one of a kind historic home. It is 10 minutes off exit 27 of the New York Thruway, 40 minutes to Albany, 25 minutes to Saratoga, 10 minutes to Lapland Lake for cross-country skiing, and 5 minutes to great Sagandaga Lake. Hosts are a writer and a psychiatrist. Accommodations include: A) king-sized bed, private bath, sitting room; B) double bed, private bath; C & D) queen-sized bed, shared bath; and E) double bed, shared bath. Cot available. Full breakfast served. TV. Children welcome. Two night minimum.
**Rates:** A) $70 B) $60 C & D) $55 E) $48 DAILY. EXTRA PERSON IN ROOM $15 DAILY.

**Reservations:** (914) 271-6228 MONDAY - FRIDAY 10 A.M. TO 4 P.M. APRIL - OCTOBER. 9 A.M. - 3 P.M. NOVEMBER - MARCH.

## CLARKSVILLE

A delightful restored Dutch farmhouse on 10 acres of wooded countryland with inground POOL, wide plank floors, beamed ceilings, and many antiques. Host is a retired business professor from SUNY at Albany; hostess is a retired first grade teacher. Host is on the board of the Albany League of Arts and Capital Repertory Company. Hostess sails and enjoys travel. A) B&B room has FIREPLACE, cathedral ceiling, canopy double bed, and private bath. B) Second room, only to members of the same family, has a double bed and shares the bathroom. Home is 20 minutes to Albany. One CAT lives here. Full breakfast is served. TENNIS COURTS. NO CHILDREN, however, young adults over 18 are welcome. Smoking restricted to downstairs.
**Rates:** A & B) S $35, D $45 DAILY. WHEN POOL IS OPEN S $45, D $55 DAILY.
**Reservations:** (914) 271-6228 MONDAY - FRIDAY 10 A.M. TO 4 P.M. APRIL - OCTOBER. 9 A.M. - 3 P.M. NOVEMBER - MARCH.

## NEWTONVILLE

NEWTON ROAD — This B&B is a 1953 yellow Cape Cod with several additions, redecorated on a quiet residential street. Convenient to everything in the capital district. Attractive patio, miniature playhouse for children, and a large double swing. Hostess is an outdoors type person who runs a summer camp for girls, officiates at sporting events, and is deacon for her church. The home is 5 minutes to Siena College, and 10 minutes to SUNY at Albany. Accommodations include: A) double bed, private bath, TV, and air conditioned; B) twin bed, shared bath; C) twin bed, shared bath; and D) single bed with comfortable living room/den, kitchen, private bath in basement apartment. Cot available. There is a COCKER SPANIEL here. Laundry facilities, fireplace in home. Full breakfast served to guests. HANDICAPPED ACCESSIBLE. Smoking permitted. Children welcome.
**Rates:** A-D) S $20-$30, D $40 DAILY. S $150, D $210 WEEKLY. ADDITIONAL CHILDREN $15 EACH DAILY.
**Reservations:** (914) 271-6228 MONDAY - FRIDAY 10 A.M. TO 4 P.M. APRIL - OCTOBER. 9 A.M. - 3 P.M. NOVEMBER - MARCH.

## RENSSELAER

OLD RED MILL ROAD — Beautifully restored Victorian home built in 1843 with emphasis on maintaining original details. The circular driveway and expansive lawn leads to the charming setting. There is a spectacular

view of the Albany skyline from this home, which is located on over 4 acres of land. It is a frame home with screened porch with its original "gingerbread" detail. Civil War antique safe, Pierre mirror, arched doorway, and original moldings in foyer. Living room has working marble fireplace, hardwood floors, and French doors leading to screened porch. Dining room has a leaded glass oak door. A very warm and inviting country kitchen completely remodeled in 1981 has large eating area plus brick fireplace, imported tile counter top and island. Host is a physician; hostess is a TV producer/writer. Accommodations include: A) master queen-bedded bedroom, marble FIREPLACE, large windows, double closet, shoe closet, adjoining full tile bath with tub and shower. Additional full bath is on the first floor. On the second floor is a full bath with square tub. B) Queen bed, FIREPLACE, crown molding, newly wallpapered, closet and dressing room with walk-in cedar closet. French door leading to balcony. Border designed hardwood floor. The den is a warm and inviting paneled room with built-in bookcases, FIREPLACE, recessed lighting. Wall-to-wall carpeting and French doors leading to balcony; C) cherry floor, newly papered, with crib and single bed. Two sons 15 and 13 live here. Three CATS reside here. PIANO. Bikes available. Smoking permitted.
**Rates:** A) S $55, D $60; B) S $50, D $55; AND C) S $40. ADDITIONAL CHILDREN $10 EACH DAILY.
**Reservations:** (914) 271-6228 MONDAY - FRIDAY 10 A.M. TO 4 P.M. APRIL - OCTOBER. 9 A.M. - 3 P.M. NOVEMBER - MARCH.

## SCHENECTADY

This is a 60 year old Colonial cottage on a quiet residential street. Living room with fireplace and cozy family room. Large tree-shaded deck. Host is psychotherapist in private practice; hostess is an administrator at a social service agency. Two adult 10 speed bikes and one child's bike available. Home is 10 minutes from Union College, 15 minutes to General Electric, and 30 minutes to Saratoga. Breakfasts on weekends are special and served at a time arranged with guests. Accommodations include: A) double bed, share bath with family, TV; B) sofabed suitable for child, share bath with family; and C) queen sofabed, share bath with family. Laundry facilities.
**Rates:** A-C) S $20, D $30 DAILY. S $105, D $175 WEEKLY. ADDITIONAL CHILDREN $10 EACH DAILY.
**Reservations:** (914) 271-6228 MONDAY - FRIDAY 10 A.M. TO 4 P.M. APRIL - OCTOBER. 9 A.M. - 3 P.M. NOVEMBER - MARCH.

## STOCKADE

Historic, circa 1790 Widow Kendall House, formerly run as a tavern, rebuilt 1830 and lovingly restored over the past years. Lots of charm plus Jacuzzi. Located in historic stockade district, a short walk to downtown

Schenectady, minutes to Union College or G.E. by car. Accommodations include: A) queen bed, B) double bed, FIREPLACE, and C) single bed. All share a guest bath. Your host, an attorney interested in skiing, swimming, antiquing, biking, and walking lives next door, but makes you a full breakfast.
**Rates:** A & B) D $60; C) S $35 DAILY.
**Reservations:** (914) 271-6228 MONDAY - FRIDAY 10 A.M. TO 4 P.M. APRIL - OCTOBER, 9 A.M. - 3 P.M. NOVEMBER - MARCH.

## SCOTIA

GLEN AVENUE — An unpretentious but cozy 40 year old center hall Colonial on a quiet residential street. A large country kitchen with woodstove and antique furniture overlooks a screened-in porch and backyard with a strawberry patch and vegetable garden, in season. Home is 1 mile from Erie Canal lock 8 and the Mohawk river, good for fishing. It is only 10 minutes from downtown Schenectady, Proctors Theater, Union College, and General Electric. In season, an invitation to board a pontoon boat at Arrowhead Marina 3 miles from home may be extended to guests. Albany is 20 minutes away and Saratoga 45 minutes. Host works in system procedures and enjoys coin collecting, history, boating, tennis, and travel; hostess is a speech/language therapist who recently became certified as an assistant chef and is noted for her gourmet cooking, flower arranging, kite flying, and decorating skills. Accommodations include: A) twin beds, shared family bath, and TV. B & C) Single bed shared family bath. Pickup available. A CAT is in residence.
**Rates:** A) S $20, D $30; AND B & C) S $20 DAILY. S $140, D $210 WEEKLY.
**Reservations:** (914) 271-6228 MONDAY - FRIDAY 10 A.M. TO 4 P.M. APRIL - OCTOBER. 9 A.M. - 3 P.M. NOVEMBER - MARCH.

## TROY
## HISTORIC DOWNTOWN

This is an 1890 townhouse in Troy's Victorian business district complete with stained glass, mosaic tiled hall, carved cherry staircase, and fireplaces in kitchen and dining room. There is also a private garden with deck. Breakfast with the family or use pantry kitchen and dining room. Host is a data base manager interested in history and Indian cooking; hostess is a legal secretary interested in swimming and family. It is a 10 minute walk to Rensselaer Polytechnic Institute and Russell Sage; 20 minutes to Albany; near Northway. Accommodations include: A) two large double-bedded rooms, carpeted, walk-in closets, 9 foot ceilings, original woodwork, new guests only bath, on third floor; B) small room with single bed on third floor; and C) single bedded room, quiet end of second floor, share bath with family. Some Italian and German spoken by host. TV and laundry facilities. NO SMOKING. Children of all ages welcome.

**Rates:** A-C) S $25, D $40 DAILY. S $175, D $280 WEEKLY.
**Reservations:** (914) 271-6228 MONDAY - FRIDAY 10 A.M. TO 4 P.M.
APRIL - OCTOBER. 9 A.M. - 3 P.M. NOVEMBER - MARCH.

2ND AVENUE — The wide plank floors and cooking fireplace in the kitchen from the farm days (built in 1810) combined with the mahogany paneling and abundant gingerbread from the Victorian era (remodeled in 1869) give this home a unique appeal. Host is a supervisor in a state department and enjoys windsurfing, carpentry, and historic homes; hostess is a leader in the Girl Scouts and is interested in crafts, chair caning, and fine cooking. They have a son (6), a daughter (12), and two CATS. Accommodations include: A) a double-bedded bedroom with Victorian furnishings and a private entrance. There is also a Victorian parlor for the guests' exclusive use and a B) queen-sized sofabed if needed. The private bath is off the kitchen. A gourmet breakfast includes a choice of waffled French toast, fresh fruit souffle, or quiche cups along with the usual fare. TV. NO SMOKING in the house.
**Rates:** A & B) S $35, D $40 DAILY. S $211, D $251 WEEKLY.
**Reservations:** (914) 271-6228 MONDAY - FRIDAY 10 A.M. TO 4 P.M.
APRIL - OCTOBER. 9 A.M. - 3 P.M. NOVEMBER - MARCH.

## NEAR RENSSELAER POLYTECHNIC INSTITUTE

GRAND VIEW AVENUE — A 50 year old Dutch Colonial on a deadend street overlooking the Hudson Valley. Host is a professor of economics; hostess is a psychiatric social worker. They have two sons, aged five and nine. Three CATS live here. Conveniently located off Route 7 within 5 minutes of Interstate 87 (the Northway). It is 20 minutes to Grafton State Park for swimming and hiking; and 35 minutes to downhill skiing at Willard, Jimney Peak, or Brody. Cross-country skiing at Frear Park is 2 minutes away. It is also 2 minutes to Rensselaer Polytechnic Institute, 5 minutes to Russell Sage College, 1 minute to Samaritan College, 5 minutes to historic downtown Troy, 15 minutes to Albany, 35 minutes to Saratoga, and 50 minutes to Tanglewood. Accommodations include a double-bedded room with shared family bath. A crib is available as are all baby items. Twin bunk beds are also available in an adjacent room for children over three. Laundry facilities and TV are also available.
**Rates:** S $20, D $30 DAILY. S $105, D $175 WEEKLY. ADDITIONAL CHILDREN 3-12 $10 EACH DAILY.
**Reservations:** (914) 271-6228 MONDAY - FRIDAY 10 A.M. TO 4 P.M.
APRIL - OCTOBER. 9 A.M. - 3 P.M. NOVEMBER - MARCH.

## SYCAWAY

OFF ROUTE 7 — A comfortable Cape Cod house overlooking the Hudson River Valley with a view of the Catskill and Adirondack Mountains and the skyline of the state capital, Albany, 10 miles away. The hostess' interests include working with flowers, gardening, and antiquing. Accommodations include: A) a twin-bedded double; and B) a single bed that could accommodate a teenager, both sharing the family bath. The home is located close to Rensselaer Polytechnic Institute and Russell Sage colleges and is convenient to Route 7 to Vermont and "The Northway," to Saratoga (30 to 40 minutes) and Lake George (1 hour). A CAT is in residence. Fireplace and TV on premises, and laundry facilities available. No SMOKING is permitted in the bedrooms but guests are encouraged to use the living room and the screened-in porch.
**Rates:** A & B) S $20, D $30 DAILY.
**Reservations:** (914) 271-6228 MONDAY - FRIDAY 10 A.M. TO 4 P.M. APRIL - OCTOBER. 9 A.M. - 3 P.M. NOVEMBER - MARCH.

15th STREET — A 70 year old home with oak parquet floors, beautiful fireplace in living room. This home is a block from Rensselaer Polytechnic Institute campus, 5 minutes to Russell Sage. Host is a professor of mechanical engineering; hostess is director of college personnel. Hosts enjoy reading, travel, theater, and sports. Accommodations include: A) twin beds, shared bath with family; and B) in living room a queen sofabed could be available. A three year old daughter and a CAT are also in residence. TV and laundry facilities.
**Rates:** A & B) S $20, D $30 DAILY. S $105, D $175 WEEKLY.
**Reservations:** (914) 271-6228 MONDAY - FRIDAY 10 A.M. TO 4 P.M. APRIL - OCTOBER. 9 A.M. - 3 P.M. NOVEMBER - MARCH.

## WATERVLIET
## HUDSON RIVER HIGHWAY 787

FIRST AVENUE — A white 1828 two story home with Shaker/Dutch design features on a residential street. Enclosed landscaped yard with deck. Host is an airline agent and artist with studio in house; hostess is a nurse interested in holistic health. Two children, girl 7 1/2 and boy 6. Accommodations include: second floor, private rear entrance, air conditioned, fully equipped kitchen, A) queen-sized bed, B) two single beds. Private bath. Can use artist studio bedroom on same floor. Nearby are parks, tennis, and skating rink (indoor seasonal). It is 15 minutes by car to Albany airport and the train station. Convenient access to Interstate 787 and 87, and Routes 9 and 7. In tri-city triangle of Albany, Troy and Schenectady. Major schools, Rensselaer Polytechnic Institute, Siena,

Union, SUNY at Albany, Russell Sage, Hudson Valley Community, and Saint Rose Colleges. TV and laundry facilities. NO SMOKING.
**Rates:** A & B) S $25, D $45 DAILY; S $125, D $225 WEEKLY. APARTMENT S $25, D $45 DAILY; S $200, D $400 WEEKLY. ADDITIONAL CHILDREN $10 EACH DAILY; ADDITIONAL ADULTS $20 EACH DAILY.
**Reservations:** (914) 271-6228 MONDAY - FRIDAY 10 A.M. TO 4 P.M. APRIL - OCTOBER. 9 A.M. - 3 P.M. NOVEMBER - MARCH.

## CATSKILLS

The Catskills are in Greene, Ulster, Sullivan, and Delaware counties of New York State. It is an area of mountains, swift running streams, and majestic beauty. Skiing, hiking, fishing, and good eating abound as well as plenty of antiquing. In Greene County, Hunter Mountain offers a range of skiing from novice to expert and in the summer, it is the site of many festivals. Cortina Valley is a good start for beginning downhill. Windham mountain offers a full range of difficulty. Hyer Meadow cross-country skiing is also nearby. The Catskill Game Farm is open year-round. Howe Caverns are nearby. Delaware County is very rural and unspoiled much as Vermont and New Hampshire used to be. It is famous for its fishing and hunting and has many good restaurants and lots of antiquing. Cross-country skiing can be done everywhere. There is little night life, save a weekly auction. The area is an outdoorsman's paradise and certainly a retreat from city life.

## ATHENS

A 300 year old farmhouse, expanded in Victorian times, furnished with beautiful Victorian furnishings. This fabulous home is on 8 1/2 acres with orchards. Nearby is cross country skiing, antiquing, auctions, hiking and the Bronk Museum. 20 min. to Catskill Game Farm, 40 min. to Hunter and Windham Mts. 18 miles to Albany. 1 hour to Saratoga or Tanglewood. 8.6 miles north of the Rip Van Winkle Bridge, Olana. Full breakfast and evening snack. Smoking only in the parlor. Accommodations include: 4 guest rooms all with double beds. The guest rooms share 2 full baths. Marinas for arriving by private boat. Host will make arrangements to meet you at the dock, or pick up at Hudson.
**Rates:** S $50, D $75, DAILY. S $280, D $350, WEEKLY

## CAIRO
## RURAL

MORRISON ROAD — Countryside area noted for serious HORSEBACK RIDING. The stable program includes riding instruction on well-trained horses geared to individual ability levels and interests. The farmhouse is

a mecca for visitors seeking country auctions, museums, famous Catskill Mountain attractions, and for the fine old-fashioned hospitality and excellent food offered at the charming nineteenth century Colonial farmhouse. Hiking, cross-country skiing, hunting, and fishing can be done on the farm. Nearby are Ski Windham, Hunter Mountain, Ski Bowl, Catskill Game Farm, Olana, Howe Caverns, the Durham Museum, the Hudson River, and many interesting antique shops and auction barns. In February and March there is maple syrup being produced at the sugarhouse. A harvest of wildflower honey takes place in the fall. Will meet Amtrak in Hudson, bus in Cairo or small planes in Freehold. Three guest bedrooms and shared bath. Double and twin beds available. Host is a teacher; hostess is a horse trainer. They enjoy photography and bridge. One DOG and four CATS reside here. Rowboat and horse stall available. A 160 acre horse ranch with fireplace and TV. Children welcome. For NONDRINKERS and NONSMOKERS only.
**Rates:** S $45, D $55 DAILY.
**Reservations:** (914) 271-6228 MONDAY - FRIDAY 10 A.M. TO 4 P.M. APRIL - OCTOBER. 9 A.M. - 3 P.M. NOVEMBER - MARCH.

## CHICHESTER

PARK ROAD OFF ROUTE 214 — A lovely Colonial home on a quiet country lane in the heart of the Catskill Mountains. This beautiful home is 12 miles to Hunter or Belleayre Mountains for cross-country and downhill skiing, and is nearby to fishing, tubing, hiking, and antiquing. It is 20 minutes from Woodstock. There is a fireplace in the living room, a fireplace and woodstove in the dining room, and both open and closed porches. The hosts have filled the spacious rooms with prized family heirlooms. The four bedrooms (A) king, B) queen, C) double with canopy, and D) twin) share two baths. Host is a sales representative for a major food company, interested in sports and politics; hostess is an accountant for Ulster County and enjoys crafts and gardening. Two CATS also reside here. Life long residents, the hosts are always ready to assist their guests with detailed maps of the area. Hosts are nonsmokers, but SMOKING is permitted downstairs. A full breakfast is served in their sunny dining room, or in season on their old-fashioned open porch overlooking their sparkling, inground POOL and picturesque gardens. PIANO. TV. A little French is spoken here. Laundry facilities and pickup service available.
**Rates:** A-D) S $40, D $55; ADDITIONAL ADULTS $15 EACH DAILY. S $200, D $280 WEEKLY.
**Reservations:** (914) 271-6228 MONDAY - FRIDAY 10 A.M. TO 4 P.M. APRIL - OCTOBER. 9 A.M. - 3 P.M. NOVEMBER - MARCH.

## FORESTBURGH

A full service inn that was formerly the summer home of Cardinals Hayes and Spellman. A large estate surrounded by thousands of acres, 250 acre LAKE, three TENNIS COURTS, and two guestrooms with FIREPLACES. Near Monticello. Full breakfast and gourmet dinner included. A carriage house with two queen-bedded rooms, sleeping loft, fireplace, sofabed in living room, great for family or group. King-sized beds as well as double beds are available in inn. Two night minimum. Full breakfasts and gourmet dinners included. TV and pickup available. Children welcome.
**Rates:** 9 ROOMS S $118, D $118-$178 DAILY. ADDITIONAL ADULTS $50 EACH DAILY.
**Reservations:** (914) 271-6228 MONDAY - FRIDAY 10 A.M. TO 4 P.M. APRIL - OCTOBER. 9 A.M. - 3 P.M. NOVEMBER - MARCH.

## HAINES FALLS
### NORTH LAKE STATE PARK

An 1867 country house on 6 1/2 acres, once a boarding house and working farm. Five minutes to Hunter Mountain Ski Area, convenient to Cortina Valley and Hyer Meadow Cross County Ski Area. Swimming at nearby North Lake State Park. Hosts are retired. They have beautifully redone three rooms: A) king bed, private bath; B & C) double bed, shared bath. Full breakfast. They have two French Poodles. CHILDREN over 12 are welcome. SMOKING outside, only.
**Rates:** A) S $60, D $65; AND B & C) S $45, D $50 DAILY.
**Reservations:** (914) 271-6228 MONDAY - FRIDAY 10 A.M. TO 4 P.M. APRIL - OCTOBER. 9 A.M. - 3 P.M. NOVEMBER - MARCH.

## HIGH FALLS
### VILLAGE

BRUCEVILLE ROAD — Beautifully restored 1830s Colonial, in lovely historic village with fine dining and antiquing. Close to Mohunk (3 miles) for all sports. Swimming in creek across the street. Host renovates houses; hostess is a social worker. Both are interested in music, flower gardening, antiques, and decorating, A teenage daughter and some PETS also live here. Accommodations include: A) two rooms with double beds, share a sitting room and each has direct access to bath; and B) separate cottage with double bed, kitchen, and heat. Fireplace and TV. Two night minimum. Children welcome.
**Rates:** A & B) S $45, D $55; AND C) S OR D $65 DAILY. A & B) S $315, D $385; AND C) S OR D $455 WEEKLY.
**Reservations:** (914) 271-6228 MONDAY - FRIDAY 10 A.M. TO 4 P.M. APRIL - OCTOBER. 9 A.M. - 3 P.M. NOVEMBER - MARCH.

## MT. TREMPER

WITTENBERG — A lovely Cape Cod style farmhouse with large cozy living room and woodburning stove, and old-fashioned three sided porch. Hostess is British born and raised with a West African and Jamaican background, all of which is reflected in her exotic cuisine. She is a textile designer. Walk to New York City bus, fine family restaurants, and Esopus Creek for swimming or fishing. Tubing, boating, swimming, and hiking nearby at state park. Skiing 10 minutes away. B&B guestrooms are available weekends only. Accommodations include: A) double bed, shared bath; and B) twin beds, shared bath. TV. Hearty breakfasts are served to guests. NO SMOKING. CHILDREN over 16 welcome.
**Rates:** A & B) S $35, D $45 DAILY.
**Reservations:** (914) 271-6228 MONDAY - FRIDAY 10 A.M. TO 4 P.M. APRIL - OCTOBER. 9 A.M. - 3 P.M. NOVEMBER - MARCH.

## NEW PALTZ
## HISTORIC

A historic, renovated barn restored by your hosts, two gentlemen who are both artists and interior designers. It is spacious, immaculately clean, and beautifully decorated with contemporary furnishings, lots of tile, wood, light, and a spectacular series of decks and inground POOL (open Memorial Day through Labor Day). A gourmet breakfast is served, walk into town, and walk to historic Huguenot stone houses. Very private. Accommodations include: A) two rooms with double bed, private bath; B) king-sized bed or twin beds, private bath; and C) on first floor (no steps) double bed, private bath. One DOG in residence. Fireplace in home. CHILDREN over 14 welcome. Arrive Thursday after 3:00 P.M., check out noon Sunday.
**Rates:** A-C) D $85 DAILY.
**Reservations:** (914) 271-6228 MONDAY - FRIDAY 10 A.M. TO 4 P.M. APRIL - OCTOBER. 9 A.M. - 3 P.M. NOVEMBER - MARCH.

A fabulous Victorian resort surrounding a glacier lake, atop a mountain. There are gazebos, an Alpine Climbing School, skiing, horseback riding, and special weekend events. Tower rooms are special. Many rooms have fireplaces. Two room suites are available. The entire inn and grounds are on the National Register of Historic Places. Rooms include three meals a day. There is no bar but drinks can be purchased with the evening meal.
**Rates:** START AT $139 DAILY.
**Reservations:** (914) 271-6228 MONDAY - FRIDAY 10 A.M. TO 4 P.M. APRIL - OCTOBER. 9 A.M. - 3 P.M. NOVEMBER - MARCH.

OLD FORD ROAD — A split level home on 20 acres near beautiful apple orchards. Hostess teaches costume design and pattern making. She is interested in exercise, singing, country dancing and offers to take guests along to country dancing evenings. She is a rock and shell collector and loves animals. She has four CATS, one DOG, a bird, and a bunny. Hunters are not welcome. Accommodations include: A) double bed, shared bath and B) double bed, private 1/2 bath. Crib available. Full breakfast served. Laundry facilities and TV.
**Rates:** A & B) S $35, D $45 DAILY. ADDITIONAL CHILDREN $10 EACH DAILY.
**Reservations:** (914) 271-6228 MONDAY - FRIDAY 10 A.M. TO 4 P.M. APRIL - OCTOBER. 9 A.M. - 3 P.M. NOVEMBER - MARCH.

### PALENVILLE

Built in the late 1800s, this mountain country home serves a full breakfast. The five double bedrooms share two baths. The living room has a fireplace, TV, VCR, and a large collection of old movies on tape. The front porch is done in white wicker. Convenient to lake and brook swimming, fishing, hiking, cross-country skiing, and 10 miles to Hunter and Hyer Meadow. An additional two twin-bedded rooms are also available. One DOG lives here, with your young energetic and friendly hosts. NO SMOKING.
**Rates:** S $35, D $40 DAILY. S $210, D $220 WEEKLY.
**Reservations:** (914) 271-6228 MONDAY - FRIDAY 10 A.M. TO 4 P.M. APRIL - OCTOBER. 9 A.M. - 3 P.M. NOVEMBER - MARCH.

### (NEAR HUNTER MOUNTAIN)

MILL ROAD — A charming 1927 Cape Cod with apple orchard, vineyard, and creek. The home is decorated with many pieces of original art work and includes a fireplace. Host is a paralegal, nature lover, and local historian. Hostess is an artist and vegetarian cook who caters to guest's particular dietary needs. One 2 1/2 year old who loves to greet guests. Accommodations include: A) queen-sized bed; and B) double bed futon. The two rooms share one bath. Host and hostess love to guide guests on interesting excursions to little known places in the Catskills. Pets not welcome. All baby equipment available. A shaggy MUTT lives outside. This home is convenient to the homes of artists Frederick Church and Thomas Cole, Opus 40, North Lake, Hunter Mountain, and Woodstock. It is accessible from New York City by bus (2 1/2 hours). Bus stop is two blocks from home. Children welcome. SMOKERS not welcome.
**Rates:** A & B) S $35, D $50 DAILY. S $200, D $250 WEEKLY. ADDITIONAL CHILDREN OVER 2 ARE $10 EACH DAILY.
**Reservations:** (914) 271-6228 MONDAY - FRIDAY 10 A.M. TO 4 P.M. APRIL - OCTOBER. 9 A.M. - 3 P.M. NOVEMBER - MARCH.

# SHANDAKEN

This house is 35 minutes west of Kingston in the heart of the Catskills. It is a spacious rustic nineteenth century lodging house that sits in a secluded setting, off the road, behind two little dashing brooks, and spanned by wooden bridges. Hiking and cross-country skiing trails are just behind the house. Swimming nearby. Hosts have rehabilitated this country home with lots of natural wood paneling, hardwood floors, and Early American style stencils. There are three spacious sitting rooms with a fireplace, a woodstove, and lots of views of woods and streams. An old stone fountain bubbles on the front lawn. Guests enjoy sitting on the sunny front porch to watch it. Breakfast specialties include a choice of crepes or omelets with specially prepared vegetable fillings (from the garden in season) and topped with special sauces (e.g., mushrooms sauteed with shallots and parsley with sorrel sauce). Host teaches fly fishing and cross-country skiing. Host and hostess are former New York City cliff dwellers who work in business consulting and management and enjoy fishing, hiking, gardening, cooking, cross-country skiing, history, and philosophy. Accommodations include: A) three rooms with double beds; and B) twin-bedded double. All share two baths. TWO DOGS and one CAT live here. Children welcome. Host smokes a pipe.
**Rates:** A & B) S $45, D $52 DAILY ON WEEKDAYS. S $51, D $58 DAILY ON WEEKENDS IN JULY, AUGUST, OCTOBER, AND HOLIDAYS.
**Reservations:** (914) 271-6228 MONDAY - FRIDAY 10 A.M. TO 4 P.M. APRIL - OCTOBER. 9 A.M. - 3 P.M. NOVEMBER - MARCH.

# STONE RIDGE

ATWOOD ROAD — A turn of the century farmhouse with country views and (20 x 40) inground POOL. Many Victorian antiques are to be found in this charming home. A STEINWAY GRAND PIANO graces one of the rooms. Host enjoys golf; hostess is an antiquer and has a shop on premises. Close to High Falls, New Paltz. This is a great area for cross-country skiing. Accommodations include: A) double brass bed, private bath; B) double bed, private bath; C) double rope bed, shared bath; D) king-sized bed or twins, shared bath; E) double pine bed, private bath; and F) double spindle bed, private bath. A fireplace is on the premises and TV is available. Full breakfasts are served to guests. CHILDREN over 12 welcome here.
**Rates:** A-F) S $40-$65, D $55-$65 DAILY. S $200-$250, D $280-$350 WEEKLY.
**Reservations:** (914) 271-6228 MONDAY - FRIDAY 10 A.M. TO 4 P.M. APRIL - OCTOBER. 9 A.M. - 3 P.M. NOVEMBER - MARCH.

## WEST SHOKAN

MOONHAW ROAD — This home is 12 miles from Woodstock, it is a 1840 farmhouse and working farm on 15 acres of woods and meadows that includes a cool running stream. A large living room with cozy fireplace, game table, cable TV, and VCR awaits guests. A full country breakfast with many homemade treats is served in an antique filled dining room or on a screened-in porch decorated with wicker furniture. Host is a teacher and farmer who enjoys cooking, hunting, fishing, and many sports; hostess is a bookkeeper with interests in cooking, canning, and local lore. They have two friendly CATS and a teenage son who can babysit. A relaxing atmosphere with the option to pursue local activities such as hiking, tubing, the Esopus, fishing, biking, skiing (cross country available on premises), or helping feed the numerous animals. Convenient to Hunter and Bellayre mountains (30 minutes), historic Kingston (New York's first capital), local winery tours, horseback riding, and antique shopping. It is 120 miles to New York City. Accommodations include: A) double bed with FIREPLACE; and B) large family room with four twin beds for family use. All have antiques and share a private guest bath. A cow named Ma also lives here. There are laundry facilities.
**Rates:** A) S $40, D $55; and B) S $40, D $45 DAILY. A & B) S $280, D $350 WEEKLY. ADDITIONAL ADULTS $15 DAILY; ADDITIONAL CHILDREN $10 EACH DAILY.
**Reservations:** (914) 271-6228 MONDAY - FRIDAY 10 A.M. TO 4 P.M. APRIL - OCTOBER. 9 A.M. - 3 P.M. NOVEMBER - MARCH.

## WOODBOURNE

BUDD ROAD — Large three story inn, completely refurnished with contemporary and deco decor. Immaculate, spacious, and comfortable throughout. In-ground swimming POOL, and all rooms have Casablanca fans. Host is a builder; hostess your innkeeper. Both enjoy skiing. Convenient to Big Vanilla and Holiday Mountains. In heart of Sullivan County, convenient to Monticello race track. Eight rooms available plus meeting space for conferences. Two CATS reside here, but never in guestrooms. Accommodations include: 8 rooms, double with private bath; queen-sized bed, private bath, and TV, Fireplace in inn. Two night minimum. Full breakfasts served. Dinner plan also available.
**Rates:** 8 ROOMS) S $45-$75, D $55-$75 DAILY. S $315-$385, D $385-$525 WEEKLY.
**Reservations:** (914) 271-6228 MONDAY - FRIDAY 10 A.M. TO 4 P.M. APRIL - OCTOBER. 9 A.M. - 3 P.M. NOVEMBER - MARCH.

# LEATHERSTOCKING
## ST. JOHNSVILLE
### RURAL

VEDDER ROAD — A contemporary Ranch, surrounded by trees and gardens. Self-sufficient lifestyle includes organic gardening, homemade jam and jelly, maple syrup, and so on, which are included in full breakfasts. Two DOGS live in the home; other animals on the property are sheep, chickens, ducks, and geese. An outstanding attraction in the area is collecting "Herkimer diamonds," unique quartz crystals, known worldwide. Host is retired, enjoys hunting, traveling, and woodworking; hostess is active in crafts, tourism, and ecology. Home is convenient to N.Y. Thruway, within 1 hour of the Albany area (east) and Utica (west). There are many historic sites, an art gallery, outlet stores, libraries (genealogy departments) within a few miles. Accommodations include: A) double bed with shared bath; and B) twin beds with shared bath. Cot available for child. SMOKING permitted but hosts prefer nonsmokers.
**Rates:** S $20, D $30, COT $10 DAILY.
**Reservations:** (315) 733-0040.

## UTICA
### RURAL-FRANKFORT HILL

BROCKWAY ROAD — This spacious home, circa 1828, done in Greek Revival style is accented by 100 year old maple trees, perennial gardens, and rose covered stone fences. The 60 acre homestead affords a spectacular view of the Mohawk Valley and foothills of the Adirondacks in every season. Trails winding through woodlands near ponds and streams. Relocators, business people, or visitors may reflect on nature's wonders. A cozy country kitchen, with exposed oak beams and a brick hearth fireplace, enhance the enjoyment of a full nutritious breakfast that may include French toast with New York maple syrup, homemade blueberry muffins, or tomato sausage and fresh fruit. Cheerful and airy guestrooms have paintings from local artists and are furnished with traditional and antique furnishings. Accommodations include: A) twin bed room; B) king-size room; and C) suite for families. Craft, specialty and antique shops, and outlets are an added plus. Historic forts, museums, and the brewery tour, or local fairs and seasonal recreation make vacations affordable and fun. This home is centrally located (4 miles south of Utica, 6 miles south of New Hartford, 5 miles west of Frankfort, and 40 minutes from Cooperstown). It is accessible to all colleges and hospitals. PIANO. DOGS and a CAT live here. Children welcome. No SMOKING in bedrooms.
**Rates:** A) $35; B) S $30; AND C) SUITE FOR FAMILY 2 ROOMS $60. CHILDREN/COT $10, CRIB $10 DAILY.
**Reservations:** (315) 733-0040.

## WATERVILLE
### HISTORIC TRIANGLE

WHITE STREET — The blend of charm and craftmanship creates an atmosphere of Americana personified within this lovely Victorian home situated in Waterville's historic triangle. Each room reflects the hostess' talents with quilts and needlework artistically displayed. Guestrooms include a spacious twin-bedded room with a private bath on the first floor. The other rooms are furnished with antiques and collectibles and are warm and cozy. Full breakfasts with delicious homemade breads and muffins, juices, and eggs satisfy the guests. The hosts have traveled extensively using B&Bs and extend gracious hospitality to their guests. Within minutes of Colgate University; Hamilton College; SUNY at Morrisville, Oneonta, and Cazenovia. It is 30 minutes south of Utica on Route 12, it is in the heart of New York's antique country. Children welcome.
**Rates:** A) S $25, D $40; AND B & C) S $20, D $35 DAILY.
**Reservations:** (315) 733-0040.

## CHAUTAUQUA COUNTY
### MAYVILLE

ERIE STREET — A large turn of the century Victorian home located in a small village adjoining Chautauqua Lake in western New York State. Many antiques and woodwork by European artisans will help make your stay pleasurable. Host is an insurance representative and two sons in their 20s live in the third floor apartment. Accommodations include: A) 1860 high poster double bed with depression vanity and dresser; B) cottage furniture with Oriental rug, double bed; and C) two single beds and eclectic furnishings. Breakfasts will be continental, featuring homemade waffles. Two bedrooms interconnect for family stays. Area interests are numerous. Chautauqua Lake is a short walk, Chautauqua Institution 3 miles, and Lake Erie 8 minutes. Ski resorts, wineries, vineyards, fruit farms, golf courses, and dozens of antique shops all within a 30 minute drive. All village streets except main highways are open for snow mobiling and a cross-country ski course is a few minutes away. Winter snow storms turn the village into a winter wonderland. Children welcome depending on other guests.
**Rates:** A-C) S $40, D $50 DAILY. S $240, D $300 WEEKLY.
**Reservations:** (914) 271-6228 MONDAY - FRIDAY 10 A.M. TO 4 P.M. APRIL - OCTOBER. 9 A.M. - 3 P.M. NOVEMBER - MARCH.

## COLUMBIA COUNTY

Columbia County is on the east side of the Hudson River and the east side of this area borders Connecticut and Massachusetts. It is convenient to the Berkshires. Claremont (the Livingston estate), Olana (Frederick

Church's estate), and the Mills House are located here. Tanglewood in the Berkshires is nearby.

## CHATHAM
### VILLAGE

Turn of the century farmhouse on 10 acres in village. Convenient to Tanglewood, Stockbridge, Pittsfield, and so on. Host is an architect; hostess a writer. They have two girls, aged 11 and 16. Home has pressed tin ceiling and GRAND PIANO. Near Berkshires for skiing, Tanglewood, antiquing, music festivals, and Shaker museums. A CAT, SHEEPDOG, and horse reside here. Accommodations include: king-sized bed, share bath with family. Full breakfasts served. Laundry facilities, TV. Children welcome. SMOKING outside only.
**Rates:** S $35, D $50 DAILY.
**Reservations:** (914) 271-6228 MONDAY - FRIDAY 10 A.M. TO 4 P.M. APRIL - OCTOBER. 9 A.M. - 3 P.M. NOVEMBER - MARCH.

### LEBANON SPRINGS
### BERKSHIRES

MAIN STREET NEAR ROUTE 22 — Elegant white Georgian Victorian mansion with wraparound porch on 60 acres, heated inground POOL, two TENNIS COURTS, and many fireplaces and antiques. It is 18 minutes to Tanglewood. A luxury accommodation. PIANO. Guests are welcome to use the parlor, wicker sitting room, or stroll on the manicured grounds. Hosts are two physicians who enjoy meeting guests. They have two young adolescent boys. Breakfast is a big delicious country fare. Spectacular view. Bikes, basketball, and ping pong available. Close to skiing and antiques. Accommodations include: two large bedrooms with private bath; two large bedrooms with shared bath; and one small bedroom with shared bath. King, queen, and bunk beds are available, as well as cots and cribs. TV. Two night minimum.
**Rates:** A-E) S $55-$70, D $70-$90 DAILY. ADDITIONAL CHILDREN $15 EACH DAILY. ADDITIONAL ADULTS $25 EACH DAILY. $10 LESS DAILY OFF-SEASON OCTOBER THROUGH MAY 30.
**Reservations:** (914) 271-6228 MONDAY - FRIDAY 10 A.M. TO 4 P.M. APRIL - OCTOBER. 9 A.M. - 3 P.M. NOVEMBER - MARCH.

## DELAWARE COUNTY
### WALTON

FEAK HOLLOW — A chalet type home on 200 beautiful acres with a large pond. A rowboat, pedal boat, and a canoe are available; also, fishing for rainbow trout, turkey hunting, and bow hunting. Host is retired but busy with gardening, toy making, and maple syrup production; hostess does tole painting, chair caning, and makes quilts. Hostess will gladly

babysit. This place is a nature lover's paradise. In December, guests can cut their own Christmas trees and in spring, help sugar the maples. When the snow is plentiful, guests can cross-country ski right on the property, then come inside to get warm in front of the huge fireplace. The wooded acres are a birdwatcher's paradise and the fall leaves are a sight to behold. Hostess is a wonderful cook (from scratch) and enjoys using her imagination. House is only 15 minutes from Delhi State College. Accommodations include: A) large room with double bed, three single beds, TV; and B) large room with double bed, two single beds, one cot, TV. Cribs available. Guests share a private guest bath. No pets. Prefer not to have unmarried couples. Fireplace and laundry facilities on premises. Two night minimum; one night for college only. SMOKING outside only. CHILDREN welcome if well supervised because of the pond.
**Rates:** S $30, D $40 DAILY. S $160, D $275 WEEKLY. EACH ADDITIONAL PERSON $10 DAILY.
**Reservations:** (914) 271-6228 MONDAY - FRIDAY 10 A.M. TO 4 P.M. APRIL - OCTOBER. 9 A.M. - 3 P.M. NOVEMBER - MARCH.

## DUCHESS COUNTY

A county on the east side of the Hudson River, just north of Westchester County. Known for unspoiled woodland, large estates, and historic sites including the Franklin D. Roosevelt home at Hyde Park and the Vanderbilt mansion. The Culinary Institute and Marist and Vassar Colleges are also well known. The Cascade Mountain vineyards won an award in 1986 for making the best wine east of the Rockies.

## CHELSEA

A 1932 Dutch Colonial currently being renovated. It is one block from the Hudson River. Hosts are an electrician and a mortgage banker who love to sail. The property is large and well landscaped. There is a lovely inground POOL and porch. It is 10 miles to Poughkeepsie, the Culinary Institute, FDR's Estate and many parks and historic sights. Vassar and Marist College are also close by. Just north of the Newburgh-Beacon Bridge. Accommodations include: A) queen bed, shared family bath, B) queen-sized bed, shared family bath. SMOKING restricted to downstairs. A continental plus breakfast is served.
**Rates:** S $45, D $50, EXTRA CHILD $10 DAILY. S $175, D $210 WEEKLY.
**Reservations:** (914) 271-6228 MONDAY - FRIDAY 10 A.M. TO 4 P.M. APRIL - OCTOBER. 9 A.M. - 3 P.M. NOVEMBER - MARCH.

# COLUMBIA COUNTY
## CRARYVILLE

ROUTE 23 — 1870 central hall Colonial 4 miles from Catamount ski area, 20 miles to Tanglewood, golf 9 miles, swimming 5 miles. Two women are hosts, a counsellor and a housing specialist. This home has three porches, antiques, and fine reproductions throughout. Accommodations include: A) king plus a single bed for a child, B) double bed, which adjoins, C) single bed shared bath, and D) double bed, private bath. Continental breakfast served. SMOKING limited to parlor only.
**Rates:** A & B) S $35, D $55, ADDITIONAL ADULT $15, CHILD $10; C) S $35; D) S $50, D $60 DAILY.
**Reservations:** (914) 271-6228 MONDAY - FRIDAY 10 A.M. TO 4 P.M. APRIL - OCTOBER. 9 A.M. - 3 P.M. NOVEMBER - MARCH.

## DOVER PLAINS

CRICKET HILL ROAD — An 1850 farmhouse on 30 acres with spectacular views of the Berkshires. Comfortable living close to main highways; 1 1/2 hours to New York; 1/2 hour to Poughkeepsie and Hyde Park; and 45 minutes to Catamount and Butternut ski areas. Cross-country skiing and hiking on premises. Many fine restaurants and antique shops nearby. Host is in construction; hostess cares for this lovely place. Accommodations include: A) double bed, shared bath; B) twin beds, shared bath; and C) double bed, shared bath. Full breakfast served. Fireplace in home, laundry facilities, and TV available for guests. Children welcome. NO SMOKING.
**Rates:** A-C) S $40, D $50 DAILY. S $280, D $350 WEEKLY.
**Reservations:** (914) 271-6228 MONDAY - FRIDAY 10 A.M. TO 4 P.M. APRIL - OCTOBER. 9 A.M. - 3 P.M. NOVEMBER - MARCH.

## RED HOOK
### VILLAGE

SOUTH BROADWAY — This is a 150 year old inn, conveniently located in the village of Red Hook, close to Rhinebeck. Short drive to Vanderbilt mansion, Franklin D. Roosevelt's estate, and the Culinary Institute. The inn has a taproom and full restaurant. Nightly entertainment on weekends. Book weekdays or full weeks only—not just weekends. SMALL PETS PERMITTED if well controlled. Accommodations include: A) queen-sized bed, private bath; B) suite, double bed, private bath; C) double bed private bath adjacent; D) twin beds, private bath; and E) queen-sized bed, private bath, FIREPLACE. Cots and cribs available. TV. Full breakfasts are served. Smoking permitted and children welcome.
**Rates:** A-E) S & D $55-$80 DAILY. $346.50-$504 WEEKLY.
**Reservations:** (914) 271-6228 MONDAY - FRIDAY 10 A.M. TO 4 P.M. APRIL - OCTOBER. 9 A.M. - 3 P.M. NOVEMBER - MARCH.

# RHINEBECK
## VILLAGE

MONTGOMERY ROAD — This is a turn of the century beige with blue trim Victorian with spacious wraparound porch in landscaped backyard in a quaint, historic village. The recipient of a visual environment award. It is 25 minutes to Vassar College or Hunter Mountain. Accommodations include: A) double bed, private bath; B & C) double bed, shared bath; and D & E) twin beds, shared bath. Fireplace in home and TV available. Full breakfasts are served to guests. Children welcome.
**Rates:** A-E) S OR D $65-$80 DAILY. A-E) $432.25-$532 WEEKLY. CORPORATE AND WINTER DISCOUNTS AVAILABLE.
**Reservations:** (914) 271-6228 MONDAY - FRIDAY 10 A.M. TO 4 P.M. APRIL - OCTOBER. 9 A.M. - 3 P.M. NOVEMBER - MARCH.

## WAPPINGERS FALLS

This historically significant brick Victorian mansion within walking distance of the Hudson River was once the home of a famous nineteenth century clergyman who designed the National Cathedral in Washington, D.C. Restored by the host, who is a data processing and financial consultant, it is furnished with period antiques, has working fireplaces, PIANO, and antique phonographs, large formal parlor and dining room, spacious porches with rocking chairs and porch swing, and central air conditioning. The private 7 acre hilltop estate has a 52 foot inground POOL, 200 year old trees in landscaped settings, picnic tables, and pond. Convenient to Vanderbilt mansion, Frankin D. Roosevelt's home, Vassar College, West Point, and other attractions. Many antique shops and wineries nearby, sometimes live theater shows. Continental breakfast features fine pastries, fruit, and exotic teas. Accommodations include: A) Double bed, twin bed, private bath TV B) Double bed, twin bed, private bath C) king bed, twin bed private bath. Suites have cable TV with HBO. No pets. Pickup available. Not advisable to bring CHILDREN unless extremely well behaved, due to the many fragile antiques.
**Rates:** A) S $70, D $80 DAILY; S $450, D $516 WEEKLY. B) S $55, D $65 DAILY; S $353, D $419 WEEKLY. C) S $30, D $40 DAILY; S $194, D $260 WEEKLY. ADDITIONAL ADULTS $25 EACH DAILY.
**Reservations:** (914) 271-6228 MONDAY - FRIDAY 10 A.M. TO 4 P.M. APRIL - OCTOBER. 9 A.M. - 3 P.M. NOVEMBER - MARCH.

# EASTERN LONG ISLAND

Eastern Long Island is best known for its beaches, terrific fishing, and boating. Both the north and the south fork are easily reachable by car. The south fork is reachable by the Long Island railroad and a jitney service operates to Montauk and the Hamptons in the summer. Shelter Island is nestled between the two forks and can be reached by ferry from

Greenport or Sag Harbor. The north fork connects to New London, Connecticut by ferry making it very easy to reach from New England. The ferry from Orient Point also goes to Block Island.

## E. QUOGUE
## SHORE

DUNE ROAD — A Contemporary OCEAN FRONT house on Dune Road in the Hamptons known as the "architect's playground"; 330 degree unobstructed views of ocean, bay, and wetlands (part of Atlantic flyway); swimming POOL in season; activities include birdwatching, swimming, surfcasting, star gazing, miles of sandy beaches to wander, and miles of wetlands to explore. Meade spotting scope available; host is a local attorney, reasonable ability in German; interests include sailing, swimming, and birdwatching. Accommodations include: A) large convertible queen-sized bed, private bath; B) double bed with ocean view, private bath; C) A and/or B with living room, FIREPLACE, sunspace; and D) large totally private bedroom, double bed, seating for two, panoramic ocean view; private bath with JACUZZI. Breakfast is gourmet continental and can be served on the deck if desired. CHILDREN 10 years and older welcome. Nonsmokers preferred; no SMOKING in bedrooms. TV. Available Labor Day to Memorial Day only.
**Rates:** A) S $85, D $95; B) S & D $110; C) S $60, D $75; AND D) S $95, D $110 DAILY. ADDITIONAL CHILDREN $10 EACH DAILY. SUITE WITH LIVING ROOM $145 DAILY. OFF-SEASON RATES AVAILABLE.
**Reservations:** (914) 271-6228 MONDAY - FRIDAY 10 A.M. TO 4 P.M. APRIL - OCTOBER. 9 A.M. - 3 P.M. NOVEMBER - MARCH.

## GREENPORT

NORTH ROAD — Built in 1940 by the co-owners of a prominent advertising agency for their personal use as well as to entertain some of their more distinguished clients, including Greta Garbo and Humphrey Bogart. This elegant Colonial is situated on Long Island's east end (North Fork). Swimming, sailing, fishing, wine tasting, golf, antiquing, riding, and fine restaurants minutes away. It has 2.8 acres of private BEACH. Host is in the computer business. The hosts have two children, ages 7 and 10. Corporate meetings welcome. Many porches. Accommodations include: A) queen-sized bed, private bath; B) queen-sized bed, private bath; and C) queen-sized bed, private bath, porch, and private entrance. Laundry facilities, pickup, and TV available. Fireplace in home. Two night minimum. Full breakfast served. NO SMOKING. Children welcome.
**Rates:** A-C) $95 DAILY. $500 WEEKLY.
**Reservations:** (914) 271-6228 MONDAY - FRIDAY 10 A.M. TO 4 P.M. APRIL - OCTOBER. 9 A.M. - 3 P.M. NOVEMBER - MARCH.

## HAMPTON BAYS
**WATERFRONT**

RAMPASTURE ROAD — Right on Shinnecock Bay, enjoy quiet WATERFRONT home with big garden, terrace, barbecue, TV, and kitchen privileges. A small motor boat, sailboat, windsurfer, and bikes are available. Hosts will gladly drive guests to ocean beach 2 miles away. Jitney from New York City or Long Island Railroad. Accommodations include: A) two rooms with twin beds, private bath; and B) twin beds, shared bath and available only in addition to two night minimum on long weekends. Laundry facilities. Full self-serve breakfast. Children welcome. **Rates:** A & B) S $50-$70, D $55-$75 DAILY. S $275-$395, D $305-$425 WEEKLY. ADDITIONAL ADULTS $15 EACH DAILY.
**Reservations:** (914) 271-6228 MONDAY - FRIDAY 10 A.M. TO 4 P.M. APRIL - OCTOBER. 9 A.M. - 3 P.M. NOVEMBER - MARCH.

## MATTITUCK

PIKE STREET — This home built in 1907 rests on a beautifully landscaped three-fourths of an acre parcel. Its wraparound porch and surrounding property offers a very peaceful and quiet environment conducive to relaxation. The interior was meticulously restored to its original grandeur reminiscent of the Victorian era. The detailed moldings throughout the entire structure beautify its interior. The home has been decorated throughout with fine antiques from the nineteenth century. Many of the rooms and hallways contain wallpaper and art work also reminiscent of the Victorian era. The main parlor has been decorated as a breakfast room with cafe tables and chairs, Oriental carpet, French doors, and antiques. The front parlor is a setting for the exclusive use of guests. This room contains comfortable seating, books, periodicals, TV with VCR, and fine period pieces. There is one private bath guestroom and 2 1/2 baths are shared with other guests. There are three queen-sized beds, two single beds, and one full bed in six rooms. Cots are available. Continental breakfast is served. Boats are available at the marina. Bikes can be rented nearby. Accessible by Long Island Railroad and Sunshine Bus Line. Smoking permitted. NO CHILDREN.
**Rates:** OFF-SEASON S OR D $40-$60 DAILY; IN-SEASON S OR D $50-$80 DAILY.
**Reservations:** (914) 271-6228 MONDAY - FRIDAY 10 A.M. TO 4 P.M. APRIL - OCTOBER. 9 A.M. - 3 P.M. NOVEMBER - MARCH.

A 1917 English country home on an acre of lush property, 1 1/2 miles to the Long Island Sound Beach and 1 3/4 miles to Gardiner's Bay Beach. Host and hostess have a 7 year old daughter. They enjoy having guests year-round and serve a full country breakfast. Accommodations include: A) small double-bedded room, B) large double-bedded room, shared bath, and C) two twin beds, stenciled room, shared bath. There is a fireplace

in the country living room. Two night minimum on weekends. Hosts have a DOG and CAT. No SMOKING. CHILDREN over 6 welcome.
**Rates:** A) S $60, D $75; and B & C) S $60, D $70.
**Reservations:** (914) 271-6228 MONDAY - FRIDAY 10 A.M. TO 4 P.M. APRIL - OCTOBER. 9 A.M. - 3 P.M. NOVEMBER - MARCH.

# MONTAUK
## VILLAGE

ESSEX STREET — Charming brick and stucco 1926 Tudor, situated on a picturesque 1 acre, surrounded by green hedges, located two blocks from magnificent public BEACH and one block from Montauk Village. Three excellent TENNIS courts are directly across the street. An indoor dining area, where breakfast is served, has a stone fireplace and small refrigerator for guests' use. A secluded solarium and a garden barbecue area are also available for breakfasting/relaxing. There are several excellent restaurants within walking distance; horseback riding, golf, surfing, and superb fishing are 10 minutes drive away. A well-known health spa is closeby and offers various therapeutic treatments. Hosts will meet guests at the Long Island Railroad Station or the Hampton or Montauk Jitney bus stop on request. Cannot accommodate CHILDREN under 7 years of age or pets of any kind. Hosts are management consultants. Host is interested in golf; hostess in gardening, quilting, and jewelry design. Two night minimum. Open March through November. Accommodations include: A) king-sized bed, large bedroom/sitting room suite, color TV, private bath; B) twin beds, color TV, private bath; and C) queen-sized bed, large bedroom/sitting room suite, color, TV, private bath.
**Rates:** FALL AND SPRING RATES D $60-$70 DAILY. JULY AND AUGUST RATES D $75-$90 DAILY. D $400-$500 DAILY.
**Reservations:** (914) 271-6228 MONDAY - FRIDAY 10 A.M. TO 4 P.M. APRIL - OCTOBER. 9 A.M. - 3 P.M. NOVEMBER - MARCH.

# PECONIC

PECONIC LANE — An 1875 Victorian with wraparound porch, white wicker furniture, and hammock in the shade of a towering beech tree. Extras include bikes, antiques, and VCR. It is 1 mile to Long Island Sound or Peconic Bay BEACHES; 1 hour to McArthur airport; and 15 minutes to ferry at Orient Point. Host is a cook on a tug boat who enjoys gardening, duck carving, and cooking; your hostess installs wallpaper and enjoys gardening, painting, and decorating. Accommodations include: A) double bed, shared bath; B) double bed, shared bath; and C) twin bed, shared bath. Hosts prefer not to have unmarried couples. A LABRADOR resides here. Full breakfasts are served. Fireplace in home and TV available. No SMOKING in bedrooms. CHILDREN over 7 are welcome.
**Rates:** A-C) S $40, D $65 DAILY. S $210, D $350 WEEKLY. ADDITIONAL CHILDREN $20 EACH DAILY.

Reservations: (914) 271-6228 MONDAY - FRIDAY 10 A.M. TO 4 P.M.
APRIL - OCTOBER. 9 A.M. - 3 P.M. NOVEMBER - MARCH.

## SHELTER ISLAND

NORTH FERRY ROAD — Large Dutch Colonial, close to village of
Shelter Island, two blocks to beautiful BEACH, walking distance to quaint
village shops, restaurants, and marinas. A mix of Early American and
deco. Hosts have a 7 year old little girl. Ferry from Sag Harbor or
Greenport, $4 each way for you and your car or $5 round trip.
Accommodations include: A) double bed, private bath; B) double bed,
single twin, private bath; C) two rooms with double bed, shared bath;
and D) sofabed, shared bath. Baths have tubs, no showers. Laundry
facilities, pickup available, and TV. Full breakfasts served. Two night
minimum. Smoking permitted. Children welcome.
Rates: A-D) S $50, D $65-$85 DAILY. S $300, D $450 WEEKLY.
ADDITIONAL PERSONS $15 EACH DAILY.
Reservations: (914) 271-6228 MONDAY - FRIDAY 10 A.M. TO 4 P.M.
APRIL - OCTOBER. 9 A.M. - 3 P.M. NOVEMBER - MARCH.

## SOUTHOLD
### BAY VIEW

WATERVIEW DRIVE — Large, comfortable creekside farmhouse on 7
acres. Quiet, secluded, and surrounded by woods. Civil War era house;
stone basement dates from 1780s. Cozy living room with fireplace.
PIANO. Hostess is a food teacher/writer, publishes Laura Ingalls Wilder
booklets, speaks some Spanish. Serves gourmet country breakfasts
(homemade jams, jellies, whole wheat pancakes, or apple rings, also
scrapple) in large eat-in kitchen with patio doors facing garden, and
backyard. Accommodations include: two double rooms and two singles,
shared bath. Golf, TENNIS, fishing, excellent BEACHES, antiquing, farm
stands, and vineyards within easy reach in this rural vacation area. Shelter
Island ferries nearby to south shore, Montauk and ferry to Block Island,
also ferry to New London, Connecticut. Laundry facilities and pickup
service available. NO SMOKING. Children of any age welcome.
Rates: A-C) S $40, D $60 DAILY. S $240, D $380 WEEKLY.
ADDITIONAL CHILDREN 1/2 PRICE.
Reservations: (914) 271-6228 MONDAY - FRIDAY 10 A.M. TO 4 P.M.
APRIL - OCTOBER. 9 A.M. - 3 P.M. NOVEMBER - MARCH.

INDIAN NECK LANE — A historic Victorian with five fireplaces, close
to Long Island and Peconic Bay BEACHES. Extras include bikes, VCR,
PIANO, and badminton. Host is in advertising sales and enjoys skeet
shooting, skiing, and fishing; hostess is in public relations and enjoys
sewing, music, and horseback riding. Visitors can charter fishing and
party boats, enjoy all outdoor activities or visit historic sites and the

Indian Museum library with friendly host. Open May 15 through October. Weekends preferred.

**Rates:** S $40, D $55 DAILY. ADDITIONAL CHILDREN $10 EACH DAILY.

**Reservations:** (914) 271-6278 MONDAY - FRIDAY 10 A.M. TO 4 P.M. APRIL - OCTOBER. 9 A.M. - 3 P.M. NOVEMBER - MARCH.

## FINGER LAKES

The Finger Lakes region encompasses a 14 county chain of 11 narrow glacial lakes spanning some 90 miles across west central New York State between Rochester and Syracuse. A thousand waterfalls splash down gorges into beautiful glens. Vineyards grace the lakes' gentle slopes and there are regularly scheduled tours and tastings at most of the vineyards. The Finger Lakes region is the home of Corning Glass, Buttermilk Falls, Letchworth State Park, numerous museums and historic homes, Greek Peak, automobile racing at Watkins Glen, Cornell University, Ithaca College, Alfred University, Eastman Kodak, many wineries, lots of antiques shops and auctions, and much more. All sports are popular here and cyclists are discovering the joy of exploring this natural paradise.

### AVON

BARBER ROAD — This 1852 Greek Revival home is on 1,200 acres, which include cross-country ski trails, a 20 by 40 foot inground POOL, and a CLAY TENNIS COURT. The home is on the Historic Register and has remained in the same family for generations. Convenient to Eastman House and Letchworth Park. It is still a working farm. Each of the two rooms share adjoining baths. The four guestrooms have three double beds and one twin bed. One CAT and one DOG live here. Full breakfast are served. Fireplace in home and TV. Children welcome.

**Rates:** S $40, D $45 DAILY. S $175, D $250 WEEKLY.

**Reservations:** (914) 271-6228 MONDAY - FRIDAY 10 A.M. TO 4 P.M. APRIL - OCTOBER. 9 A.M. - 3 P.M. NOVEMBER - MARCH.

### BATH
### NEAR TAYLOR WINERY

This home is a half hour to Corning and an easy drive to Watkins Glen. It is at the gateway to the Finger Lakes, Hammondsport with many wineries. Near Taylor winery. Circa 1865, stately Greek Revival home is just 4 1/2 miles from Interstate 390 and Route 17, nestled in the hamlet of Wheeler, on a 325 acre working farm. The atmosphere is one of calm serenity. The rooms decorated with crafts and quilts made by your hostess. Warm hospitality awaits you. Fireplace in home. TV. Accommodations include: A) large double bed, shared bath; B) double bed, shared bath; and C) double bed, single twin, private 1/2 bath. One

DOG lives here. CHILDREN over 12 permitted. SMOKING downstairs only.
**Rates:** A) S $50, D $55; B) S $30, D $40; AND C) S $50, D $55 DAILY. A) S $300, D $330; B) S $180, D $240; AND C) S $300, D $300 WEEKLY.
**Reservations:** (914) 271-6228 MONDAY - FRIDAY 10 A.M. TO 4 P.M. APRIL - OCTOBER. 9 A.M. - 3 P.M. NOVEMBER - MARCH.

## CANANDAIGUA

This 1857 Italianate B&B inn is beautifully restored with great attention to small details. This home was once part of the Sonnenberg estate. Located on a wooded site yet moments to the center of town. Near a large lake for swimming and boating. It is close to the Granger homestead and carriage museum, Roseland amusement park, and the Sonnenberg Gardens. Skiing at Bristol is 11 miles away. The Rochester Philharmonic summers here. Breakfast in bed is extra, free to newlyweds on first morning. Full breakfast is served on fine china and silver. Accommodations include: A) suite with private bath and double bed; and B) two rooms with double bed, shared bath. Fireplace in inn and TV available. Children welcome. NO SMOKING. Two night minimum.
**Rates:** A) S $60, D $65; AND B) S $40, D $45 DAILY. A) S $300, D $325; B) S $200, D $225 WEEKLY.
**Reservations:** (914) 271-6228 MONDAY - FRIDAY 10 A.M. TO 4 P.M. APRIL - OCTOBER. 9 A.M. - 3 P.M. NOVEMBER - MARCH.

## CANDOR
### NEAR CORNELL

MAIN STREET — This B&B is 9 miles to Ithaca. It is a 1908 Georgian home on one beautifully landscaped acre with arbor and many porches. Close to Cornell University and Ithaca College. Convenient to Watkins Glen, Corning, and Elmira's Mark Twain country. Also close to wineries and state parks. Host is an economics professor; hostess is a financial analyst. She enjoys cooking. sewing, quilting, and miniatures. There is a dollhouse here. Accommodations include: A) queen-sized bed, private bath, elevator; B) twin beds, shared bath; C) three rooms with double bed, shared bath; and D) double bed, private bath. Laundry facilities, fireplace, and TV. Full breakfast served. Children welcome. NO SMOKING.
**Rates:** A-D) D $30-$50 DAILY. $210-$350 WEEKLY.
**Reservations:** (914) 271-6228 MONDAY - FRIDAY 10 A.M. TO 4 P.M. APRIL - OCTOBER. 9 A.M. - 3 P.M. NOVEMBER - MARCH.

# HAMMONDSPORT

An Italianate Victorian home with widow's peak and small porch in front. Bedrooms upstairs. Home has sitting room and dining room. Accommodations include: A) king bed, double bed, air conditioning, B & C) double bed, AC, shared bath. Hosts are retired and have a DOG. Public beach is 4 houses away, costs $2.50, it has a launch for boats. Close to shopping, antiquing. Five minutes walk to Taylor, Gold Seal, and Bully Hill Wineries. SMOKING on porch only. Breakfast continental plus. **Rates:** S OR D A) $60, B) $55, C) $45. ADDITIONAL CHILDREN IN ROOM A $10 EACH. DAILY. **Reservations:** (914) 271-6228 MONDAY - FRIDAY 10 A.M. TO 4 P.M. APRIL - OCTOBER. 9 A.M. - 3 P.M. NOVEMBER - MARCH.

# ITHACA
## NEAR CORNELL UNIVERSITY

BOSTWICK ROAD — An 1865 farmhouse on 100 acres. It is 10 minutes to Cornell University and Ithaca College. Skate or ski on Cayuga Lake. Ski Greek Peak or Song Mountain 30 minutes away. Enjoy breakfast on screened-in porch in summer or before the fire in winter. Play the PIANO or PUMP ORGAN. Your hostess enjoys travel, cooking, reading, and welcoming guests. Accommodations include: A) double bed, private bath on first floor; B) two rooms with twin beds, shared bath; C) double bed, single twin bed and shared bath; and D) two rooms with double bed, shared bath. Crib available. Two CATS live here. Full breakfast served. Laundry facilities, TV. Fireplace in home. **Rates:** A-D) S $40, D $50-$60 DAILY. S $150, D $250 WEEKLY. **Reservations:** (914) 271-6228 MONDAY - FRIDAY 10 A.M. TO 4 P.M. APRIL - OCTOBER. 9 A.M. - 3 P.M. NOVEMBER - MARCH.

# OWEGO
## VILLAGE

FRONT STREET — Nestled along the bank of the Susquehanna River lives an 1866, two story brick Victorian with wraparound front porch, Mansard roof, leaded glass doors, decorated with antiques, wicker, and down comforters. An 18 by 35 foot heated, inground POOL, and deck make the garden a wonderful place to relax. This home is in Owego's Historic District next to a pretty park, just 5 minutes from IBM Federal Systems Division plant. Owego is 25 minutes from Binghamton and 35 minutes from Ithaca, at the gateway to the Finger Lakes. Your host is a utility company executive who enjoys fishing, sailing, and collecting antique lamps; your hostess enjoys music, antiquing, and making homemade soup. Two DOGS, two birds, and a CAT reside here. Accommodations include: A) three rooms with double bed; and B) single bed. All share two guest baths and a communal second floor kitchen is available for guest use. Full breakfast served. A fireplace is in home, pickup service and laundry facilities available. SMOKERS not permitted. Infants and CHILDREN over 10 welcome. **Rates:** A & B) S $35, D $45 DAILY. S $175, D $200 WEEKLY. **Reservations:** (914) 271-6228 MONDAY - FRIDAY 10 A.M. TO 4 P.M. APRIL - OCTOBER. 9 A.M. - 3 P.M. NOVEMBER - MARCH.

## PALMYRA

CANANDAIGUA STREET — A historic 1850s village home with numerous antiques and two working fireplaces. Walking distance to historic sights. It is 5 miles north of New York State Thruway exit 43. Your host is a business consultant conducting seminars and training programs; hobbies are winemaking and photography. Your hostess enjoys crafts, cooking, and antiquing. A 16 year old daughter can speak Spanish. Enjoy a farm fresh country breakfast. Accommodations include: A) double bed, single twin bed, and shared bath; and B) double bed, shared bath. Laundry facilities and TV. Children welcome. **Rates:** A & B) S $25, D $35 DAILY. ADDITIONAL CHILDREN $10 EACH DAILY. **Reservations:** (914) 271-6228 MONDAY - FRIDAY 10 A.M. TO 4 P.M. APRIL - OCTOBER. 9 A.M. - 3 P.M. NOVEMBER - MARCH.

## FULTON COUNTY
## JOHNSTOWN

EAST MADISON AVENUE — A tastefully decorated turn of the century U.S. home on a quiet street. Hostess is a part-time occupational therapist who enjoys weaving, gardening, the outdoors, and making distinctive jams and jellies which often appear at breakfast. Host is a retired printer who likes the outdoors, cross-country skiing, and handyman projects. This home has a PIANO in the large living room and a cozy den with a TV and a loom. There is a 24 foot above ground POOL. It is 20 minutes to several lakes and many hiking trails, 10 minutes to Gloversville, 45 minutes to Schenectady and Saratoga, and 1 hour to Utica or Albany. Cross-country skiing at several nearby areas. Downhill skiing at three areas within an hour's drive. TENNIS is half a block away. There are many historic sites only minutes away and several outlets for quality gloves and leather goods. Accommodations include: A) double bed with single trundle for child; and B) single bed. Both rooms share bath with family. Two canoes are available. Fireplace in home and laundry facilities available. SMOKING is permitted but not in the bedrooms. CHILDREN above 2 welcome. **Rates:** A) D $30 AND B) S $20 DAILY. S $105, D $175 WEEKLY. ADDITIONAL CHILDREN 2-12 ARE $5 EACH DAILY. **Reservations:** (914) 271-6228 MONDAY - FRIDAY 10 A.M. TO 4 P.M. APRIL - OCTOBER. 9 A.M. - 3 P.M. NOVEMBER - MARCH.

## GREAT LAKES
## SODUS POINT
### NEAR LAKE ONTARIO, ROCHESTER

BAY STREET — This 150 year old historic village home is 30 miles east of Rochester right on Lake Ontario. The village is known for its trout and salmon fishing. Your hostess is retired and enjoys playing the organ. Four rooms, each with two double beds share two baths. They are on the second floor. Nearby BEACH for swimming. TV. Continental breakfast served. SMOKERS ARE NOT WELCOME. Children welcome.
**Rates:** S $30, D $40 DAILY. ADDITIONAL PERSONS $10 EACH DAILY.
**Reservations:** (914) 271-6228 MONDAY - FRIDAY 10 A.M. TO 4 P.M. APRIL - OCTOBER. 9 A.M. - 3 P.M. NOVEMBER - MARCH.

## GREATER ROCHESTER
## ROCHESTER
### DOWNTOWN

Attractive city home located in Rochester, nearby to University of Rochester, downhill skiing at Bristol, parks, shopping outlets, historic homes, and museums. Xerox and Kodak are found in this city. Host is retired and is interested in computers; hostess is a social worker who enjoys travel. There are double accommodations available with either private attached bath or private bath in hall facilities. Children welcome.
**Rates:** S $45, D $50 DAILY.
**Reservations:** (716) 233-8877 MONDAY THROUGH FRIDAY 12 TO 5 P.M.

This home is like a tiny, antique farmhouse transplanted into the city! All of the houses on the street are small also—all have been restored in the last five years. The hostess is a teacher of home economics during the school year. She has chosen furnishings and plants that give a peaceful, comfortable feeling of "being home." One block from the Memorial Art Gallery, and you can walk to at least three other museums! City bus transportation available. Only open weekends during the school year, all summer and school vacations. One resident CAT. Accommodations include: two rooms with double bed, shared bath. NO SMOKERS. Children welcome.
**Rates:** S $40, D $45 DAILY.
**Reservations:** (716) 233-8877 MONDAY THROUGH FRIDAY 12 TO 5 P.M.

### PENFIELD

DUBLIN ROAD — Attractive Ranch style home surrounded by rolling countryside. Located 20 minutes east of Rochester. Nutrition conscious

hostess whips up apple raisin oatmeal or apple muffins for guests. Soft blue walls, traditional furnishings, and friendly hostess — the whole setting says "welcome" when you step onto the brick pathway under the old fruit tree. Hostess is a teacher in literacy training. Convenient to shopping and restaurants. Bikes available. PIANO. HANDICAPPED ACCESSIBLE. Accommodations include: room with twin beds, shared bath. Children welcome. NO SMOKING.
**Rates:** S $35, D $40 DAILY.
**Reservations:** (716) 233-8877 MONDAY THROUGH FRIDAY 12 TO 5 P.M.

## PERINTON

This home, built in 1975, is nestled in the woods where deer can often be seen, and it is furnished with antique country pine throughout. Host is a college professor (mechanical engineering): hostess creates stone mosaic pictures. Hiking and cross-country skiing on premises. Shopping and restaurants are near. Air conditioned. Breakfast on screened porch if weather permits. Located on southeast side of Rochester near exit 45 on New York State Thruway (Interstate 90), a 20 minute drive to downtown Rochester. Accommodations include: A) room with twin beds. and B) room with double bed. Extra cots and beds available. Private bath unless both rooms are taken. One resident CAT. PIANO, banjo, autoharp, guitars, and dulcimer. Children welcome. NONSMOKERS preferred.
**Rates:** A & B) S $40. D $45 DAILY. S $200, D $280 WEEKLY.
**Reservations:** (716) 233-8877 MONDAY THROUGH FRIDAY 12 TO 5 P.M.

## PITTSFORD

Beautiful new home tucked into a hollow between two hills. There is a small pond, trees, birds — and peace and quiet — but still only 20 minutes from downtown Rochester. Near exit 45 on New York State Thruway (Interstate 90) and Route 490. Host is a professor; hostess is lively and well-traveled and is writing a treatise on the carvers of early American gravestones in the New England area. Accommodations include: A) two rooms twin beds; and B) room with double bed. Bath is shared between the two rooms, will be private unless the other room is taken by extra persons in party. Air conditioned. Two resident Burmese CATS. NO SMOKERS. Older CHILDREN welcome.
**Rates:** S $40, D $45 DAILY.
**Reservations:** (716) 233-8877 MONDAY THROUGH FRIDAY 12 TO 5 P.M.

# HUDSON VALLEY
## KINGSTON
### RONDOUT

WEST CHESTER STREET — This 1905 house was built on a grand scale with three columned porches set on two restful acres of lawn and woods. Beveled glass windows refract sunlight in the living and dining rooms filled with paintings, prints, sculptures, and ceramics, reflecting hosts' eclectic taste. Comfortable paneled game room with gas fireplace. PIANO, TV, and fireplace in living room. Bed and breakfasters share bath in separate guest quarters with view of Catskill Mountains. Art, antiques, and books in every room. Welcoming refreshments. Hearty breakfast includes cinnamon waffles with homemade maple syrup, served with crystal and silver in large dining room or on airy porch. Host is an engineer; hostess is a teacher. Both enjoy flying, acting, travel, and Hudson Valley, where they have lived for 35 years. Personable 12 year old DOG and CAT live here. No pets. Close to Hudson River cruises, year-round recreation, five colleges, IBM, theatres, historic sites, antiquing, restaurants, and public transportation. Single and double accommodations available. Children welcome. SMOKING outside.
**Rates:** S $40. D $50 DAILY. $250 WEEKLY.
**Reservations:** (914) 271-6228 MONDAY - FRIDAY 10 A.M. TO 4 P.M. APRIL - OCTOBER. 9 A.M. - 3 P.M. NOVEMBER - MARCH.

# LAKE GEORGE AREA
## BOLTON LANDING
### NEAR LAKE GEORGE

LAKESHORE DRIVE ROUTE 9N — A spacious and recently renovated farmhouse once the caretaker "cottage" of an estate on "Millionaire's Row" of Lake George. Within a 10 minute walk are beaches, marinas, museums, restaurants, and shops. Lake cruises, historic forts, Winter Carnival, and several theme parks are nearby in Lake George Village. Concerts and racing at Saratoga, hot air balloon festival in Glens Falls, as well as downhill and cross-country skiing in nearby areas. The host is a retired guidance counselor; hostess is a former German teacher. Both enjoy gardening, concerts, cross-country skiing, traveling, and sharing renovation experiences. Three newly decorated guestrooms each with twin beds share one modern bath. A cozy guest cottage is available. Guests may use PIANO, picnic table, lawn games, porch and lawn chairs, and enjoy a woodstove in winter. Full breakfasts with daily specialties, some of German origin, are served with homemade jams and breads outdoors when possible. Hilltop is 9 miles from New York Northway, 45 minutes from Vermont, and 1 1/2 hours from Albany and Canada. Accomodations include: A & B) two twin beds; C) queen-sized bed. All share a guest bath. There is also a guest cottage with a private bath, refrigerator and queen-sized bed. House has fireplace and TV. One DOG and two CATS

live here. Pickup service is available. CHILDREN over 4 are welcome. No SMOKING in guestrooms.
**Rates:** S $25, D $35 DAILY. GUEST COTTAGE $45 FOR TWO. THIRD PERSON IN ROOM $10 DAILY. S $175, D $250 WEEKLY.
**Reservations:** (914) 271-6228 MONDAY - FRIDAY 10 A.M. TO 4 P.M. APRIL - OCTOBER. 9 A.M. - 3 P.M. NOVEMBER - MARCH.

## GLENS FALLS
## COUNTRYSIDE

RIDGE ROAD — Located in the Adirondack Mountain resort area, this restored two story Federal style home offers a relaxing atmosphere. The accommodations in this B&B are comfortable and spacious, featuring four poster beds. From the front porch guests may witness the panorama of mountains, shade trees, and old stone walls. Recreational possibilities exist at nearby Lake George and many cultural opportunities are present in Saratoga or across the border in Vermont. Host is a teacher; hostess is a former music teacher. One DOG and two CATS live here. PIANO. Accommodations include: double bedrooms with private baths. King, double, and twin beds are available. Fireplace in home and TV. No smoking.
**Rates:** WINTER S $35, D $45 DAILY. SUMMER S $45, D $55 DAILY. 7% TAX. ADDITIONAL CHILDREN $10 EACH DAILY. ADDITIONAL ADULTS $15 EACH DAILY.
**Reservations:** (914) 271-6228 MONDAY - FRIDAY 10 A.M. TO 4.P.M. APRIL - OCTOBER. 9 AM. - 3 P.M. NOVEMBER - MARCH.

## WHITEHALL

A quaint country inn on 134 acres of field and woodland. In the winter, sledding and cross-country skiing available to guests. In spring and summer the fields are covered with the wonders of nature. Fishing, swimming, and golf are nearby. Convenient to all kinds of seasonal adventures, Lake George, country fairs, Fort Ticondiroga, and so on. It is 30 minutes to Rutland and Killington in Vermont. PIANO, pond, bikes. Accommodations include: A) double bed, single twin, private bath; B) double bed, 3/4 bed, private bath; C) twin beds, semi-private bath; and D) double bed, private bath. Laundry facilities. Fireplace, TV. Full breakfast and dinner included in rates. Cots and cribs available.
**Rates:** A-D) D $90 DAILY. $630 WEEKLY. ADDITIONAL CHILDREN $22.50 EACH DAILY. BREAKFAST AND FOUR COURSE DINNER INCLUDED. 10% DISCOUNT TO SENIORS. 15% GRATUITY ADDED TO BILL.
**Reservations:** (914) 271-6228 MONDAY - FRIDAY 10 A.M. TO 4 P.M. APRIL - OCTOBER. 9 A.M. - 3 P.M. NOVEMBER - MARCH.

# LEATHERSTOCKING REGION

This is the area of central New York State including Utica, Cooperstown, and Syracuse. The famous Russian Orthodox Church at Jourdanville is here. It is an area of mountains and lakes convenient to the New State Thruway (Interstate 87) plus a number of other routes. A number of colleges are located here including: Hamilton, Colgate, Mohawk Valley Community College, and Syracuse University. Downhill and cross-country skiing as well as snow mobiling are all around. Bargain hunters enjoy the Charlestown Outlet Center, which is crammed full of retail outlets for famous maker items. The Munson Williams Art Center is another attraction. Hunting, fishing, and a full variety of outdoor sports abound. Cobleskill is the home of SUNY at Cobleskill and is 5 minutes from Howe Caverns.

## BAINBRIDGE
### RURAL

Hilltop 1820 farmhouse on 75 acres. Breathtaking views, peaceful, ideal for bird and wildlife watching, cross-country skiing, and swimming or ice skating in large pond. In Chenango County, 30 miles from Binghamton, 3 hours from New York City. Accommodations include: three rooms with double beds that share two baths. Entire house furnished with antiques and comfort amenities, like flannel sheets, down comforters, television, VCR, and stereo. Also a library. Nutritious breakfast included. Many restaurants nearby or share family meals on a coop basis, including outside barbecues. Free use of bikes, cross-country skis, snowshoes, and ice skates. Nearby TENNIS (free), golf, horseback riding, antiquing, and sightseeing (e.g., Cooperstown). Host is an antiques dealer and linguist (Spanish, French, Italian, German, Latin, etc.); hostess is a textile designer and dedicated renovator. No pets. CATS and a DOG live here. This is the place to get away from it all, to relax, to cleanse the heart and soul, to watch deer and hummingbirds, to read a whole book, to meditate, and to feel the earth under your feet. Fireplace in home and laundry facilities available. Children welcome. SMOKING OK outside and in living room.
**Rates:** S $35, D $45 DAILY. S $210, D $270 WEEKLY.
**Reservations:** (914) 271-6228 MONDAY - FRIDAY 10 A.M. TO 4 P.M. APRIL - OCTOBER. 9 A.M. - 3 P.M. NOVEMBER - MARCH.

## COBBLESKILL

WEST MAIN STREET — A turn-of-the-century brick home in the heart of Cobleskill. Convenient to Howe Caverns, SUNY at Cobleskill (5 minutes), Albany (45 minutes), Cooperstown (50 minutes), Saratoga (70 minutes), and New York City (4 hours away). Host is an economist with a managing consulting firm; hostess is an educator. Accommodations

include: A) three rooms with double bed, shared bath; B) twin beds, shared bath; and C) suite with double bed, twin beds, and private bath. The suite sleeps four at no extra charge. Continental breakfast is served to guests. This home is on a bus line and TV is available. Children welcome. Smoking permitted.
**Rates:** A-C) S $35-$60, D $40-$70 DAILY. S $210-$350, D $280-$385 WEEKLY.
**Reservations:** (914) 271-6228 MONDAY - FRIDAY 10 A.M. TO 4 P.M. APRIL - OCTOBER. 9 A.M. - 3 P.M. NOVEMBER - MARCH.

## COOPERSTOWN

An elegant 200 year old home offering beautiful furnishings and an elegant atmosphere for guests looking for something special. Acres of lawn, creek and dock for fishing and swimming. Host is a college administrator, state mediator, and arts consultant; hostess manages real estate holdings. Both are professional performers with the nationally famous Glimerglass Opera Theater. Enjoy breakfast on the wraparound deck. Accommodations include: A) queen-sized bed, queen sofabed, private bath; B) brass double bed, private bath; and C) double bed, private entrance, deck. Crib and cot available. Fireplace in home. Laundry facilities, TV on premises. Third floor suite is available. Well-behaved children welcome.
**Rates:** A-C) D $60-$70 DAILY. ADDITIONAL PERSONS OVER 12 ARE $10 EACH DAILY. ADDITIONAL CHILDREN 3-11 ARE $10 EACH DAILY.
**Reservations:** (914) 271-6228 MONDAY - FRIDAY 10 A.M. TO 4 P.M. APRIL - OCTOBER. 9 A.M. - 3 P.M. NOVEMBER - MARCH.

This 1903 Victorian cottage and reborn barn, furnished with period furniture, is located on 14 acres east of Cooperstown. Host is an educational consultant who enjoys gardening and sailing; hostess runs a gift shop in town and enjoys antiques and people. A little pond and barbecue grace the property. A wonderful breakfast is served here. Accommodations include: A) double bed, shared bath; and B) queen-sized bed, shared bath. There are three guestrooms in the barn as follows: C) twin beds, private bath; and D) two rooms with queen-sized bed, private bath. Fireplace in home and TV available. NO SMOKING in bedrooms. Children welcome.
**Rates:** A-D) D $54 DAILY. ADDITIONAL PERSONS $10 EACH DAILY.
**Reservations:** (914) 271-6228 MONDAY - FRIDAY 10 A.M. TO 4 P.M. APRIL - OCTOBER. 9 A.M. - 3 P.M. NOVEMBER - MARCH.

Second Empire home, circa 1868-1870. Located in the historic district, one mile to the village of Cooperstown. This home has a carved staircase, stained glass, 12 foot tin ceilings. Accommodations include: A) queen and double sofabed, private bath, and B) double bed, shared bath. Continental breakfast. SMOKING outside only. CHILDREN over 12 welcome. **Rates:** A) S OR D $75, EXTRA ADULTS OR CHILDREN $10 EACH; B) S OR D $65 DAILY. **Reservations:** (914) 271-6228 MONDAY - FRIDAY 10 A.M. TO 4 P.M. APRIL - OCTOBER. 9 A.M. - 3 P.M. NOVEMBER - MARCH.

## DOLGEVILLE

STEWART STREET — Modern Contemporary home with inground POOL, wildflower garden, and 9 acres of ground in foothills of Adirondacks. Hostess is a world traveler and elementary social studies teacher who delights in shopping and loves to listen. Accommodations include: A) large double-bedded room with private bath; B) large twin-bedded room, shared bath; C) large room with queen-sized brass bed, shared bath; and D) large single room (while son is in college). Ample parking, quiet street. Colleges, restaurants, shopping malls, and historic sites within minutes. Horse racing and performing arts in Saratoga, 1 hour's drive. Capital district only 1 1/2 hours away. It is 10 minutes from exit 29-A, New York State Thruway. Local sites: Daniel Green Slipper Outlet, International African Violet Nursery, Adirondack Bat factory, herb shops, gift shops, woodcrafts, and arts and crafts suppliers. Continental breakfasts served in lovely sunny dining room, and includes endless cups of coffee. Fireplace in living room. Italian is spoken here. One CAT resides here. TV and laundry facilities. CHILDREN over 12 welcome. **Rates:** A-D) S $30, D $35 DAILY. S $180, D $210 WEEKLY. **Reservations:** (914) 271-6228 MONDAY - FRIDAY 10 A.M. TO 4 P.M. APRIL - OCTOBER. 9 A.M. - 3 P.M. NOVEMBER - MARCH.

## FAYETTEVILLE
### HISTORIC DISTRICT

1850 Greek revival home offers: A) queen bedded room, and B) single room. Both share a guest bath. Your hostess is a freelance writer who volunteers for the National Park Service and enjoys botany, hiking, and antiquing. She has a DOG. This home is close to Syracuse (7 miles), Green Lakes State Park (2 miles), Erie Canal State Park (1 mile), and GE, Carrier, GM, and Bristol (5-10 miles). Extras include private terrace and overlooking gardens, cable TV, VCR, crib, and fireplace. Children welcome. No SMOKING. PETS OK with prior approval. **Rates:** S $30, D $40 DAILY. **Reservations:** (914) 271-6228 MONDAY - FRIDAY 10 A.M. TO 4 P.M. APRIL - OCTOBER. 9 A.M. - 3 P.M. NOVEMBER - MARCH.

## NELLISTON
## RURAL FARM AREA

ROUTE 5 — An 1842 limestone Victorian house with Greek Revival architecture. Stone porches on two sides of house. Completely restored for modern conveniences. Living room has handpainted ceiling with crystal chandelier and tiled fireplace. Guests are served in dining room atmosphere with large bay window. A 50 foot deck is attached to the back of the garage overlooking Mohawk River. Lounges, tables, umbrellas, and roof provide shade in summer. Quiet rural setting on main road with dairy farm opposite house. New to the area are Amish families, who may be seen riding by the house daily in their horse drawn carriages. It is 3 miles from exit 29 on the New York State Thruway. Two small POODLES are in residence. Double beds and twin beds as well as private bath and shared bath are available. CHILDREN over 5 welcome.
**Rates:** A) S $22; B) D $35; AND C) D $38 DAILY. A) $130; B) $220; AND C) $240 WEEKLY.
**Reservations:** (315) 733-0040.

## ONEIDA
## HISTORICAL

CORNER OF MAIN AND STONE — A beautiful Italian villa of the Victorian era in historic Oneida. This home is filled with arts, crafts, special collections, and antiques. There are fireplaces and chandeliers (one original gas). Guests are pampered with special breakfasts, down quilts and bed warmers in winter; flowers grace house and gardens in summer. There are two resident CATS. Hosts request NO ALCOHOL in their home. No pets. Hosts are world travelers. Host is a business consultant and media broker; hostess is an artist/crafstman who teaches spinning and other classes. Her studio is in the home. Located well in the upstate New York area, this home is within short drives to Syracuse, Adirondacks, Finger Lakes regions, sports areas, antique shops, and historical landmarks. Accommodations include: A) two rooms with queen-sized bed; B) two double beds: and C) two rooms with single twin bed. Large bath shared. DOGS and CATS live here. TV and laundry facilities available. Children that are quiet and well behaved will be accepted. NO SMOKING.
**Rates:** A-C) S $30-$35, D $55-$65 DAILY. S $200, D $280 WEEKLY.
**Reservations:** (914) 271-6228 MONDAY - FRIDAY 10 A.M. TO 4 P.M. APRIL - OCTOBER. 9 A.M. - 3 P.M. NOVEMBER - MARCH.

## PALATINE BRIDGE

WEST GRAND ROUTE 5 — This inn is a rambling stone mansion and has long been famous for its delicious menu. Beautiful, landscaped grounds with giant oaks and maple trees provide a relaxing setting. The

inn is beautifully decorated with Victorian tapestry and corniced windows and even a suit of armor; elaborate woodwork and chandeliers accent the decor. The guestrooms are furnished with antique and period pieces. Situated a short distance from Interstate 90, exit 29 at Canajoharie or a leisurely drive on Route 5 west of Ainsterdam, the inn is near SUNY at Fulton-Montgomery, Fort Klock, the Fonda Speedway, and Shrine of the North American Martyrs at Auriesville. Double bedrooms have shared baths. PIANO. Children welcome.
**Rates:** S $40, D $50 DAILY.
**Reservations:** (315) 733-0040.

## NEW SYRACUSE
## NEW WOODSTOCK

A 130 year old farmhouse with barns on 70 acres outside the village of Cazenovia. There are wide board floors, double staircase, parlor stove, and antiques throughout. It is 3 1/2 miles to Cazanovia and 20 minutes to Syracuse. LAKE privileges. Host is a hospital administrator interested in photography, outdoor sports, and gardening; hostess is a nutritionist interested in antiques and outdoor sports. There are two children ages 11 and 14. PIANO. Canoe, bikes, and exercycle available. Accommodations include: A) double bed, shared bath; and B) twin beds, shared bath. One DOG and two CATS reside here. There is a fireplace in the home, TV and laundry facilities are available. Full breakfasts are served to guests. Children of all ages welcome.
**Rates:** A & B) S $20, D $30 DAILY. S $105, D $175 WEEKLY. ADDITIONAL CHILDREN $10 EACH DAILY.
**Reservations:** (914) 271-6228 MONDAY - FRIDAY 10 A.M. TO 4 P.M. APRIL - OCTOBER. 9 A.M. - 3 P.M. NOVEMBER - MARCH.

## NEW YORK CITY

New York City is made up of five boroughs — Manhattan, Bronx, Queens, Staten Island, and Brooklyn. One of the most famous cities in the world it is known as a center of finance, trade, and business. It is easily reachable from LaGuardia, Kennedy, or Newark airports. This is a city in which a car is a handicap. Parking is rare and very expensive. The public transportation system combined with a healthy taxi force should fill your transportation needs.

## BROOKLYN

Brooklyn is basically a residential borough of New York City and is particularly well known for its ethnic neighborhoods and marvelous antique shops. It is the home of the famous Brooklyn Botanical Gardens as well as the Brooklyn Academy of Music. This borough is easily accessible to Manhattan via either subway or bus and accommodations can generally be found here at a more reasonable rate than in Manhattan.

## BRIGHTON BEACH

BRIGHTON 6TH STREET — This large, sunny apartment overlooks Brighton Beach. It contains original paintings by the host. The bedroom is very large with a king-sized bed. Located 1 1/2 blocks from the subway, half an hour to the city by car. From your window you can watch the sun rise and set on the OCEAN. There are Russian restaurants and nightclubs in the neighborhood, which is nicknamed "Little Odessa." TEENAGERS welcome. NO SMOKING.
**Rates:** SEPTEMBER THROUGH APRIL S $30, D $50. MAY THROUGH LABOR DAY S $50, D $80 DAILY. S $1,000, D $1,200 MONTHLY.
**Reservations:** (212) 645-8134 MONDAY THROUGH FRIDAY 8 A.M. TO 6 P.M.

## BROOKLYN HEIGHTS

Brooklyn Heights is a neighborhood in the borough of Brooklyn that has become very popular for many of New York's professional population because of its charming streets with brownstone residences and park areas. It is on the waterfront with spectacular views from a good part of the area. People flock to the famous promenade to enjoy the annual art shows.

An 1890 brownstone home with garden and large terrace on a lovely tree-lined street. Hostess is an artist who speaks Italian. There is no air conditioning, but fans. Accommodations are on the third floor with steep steps. They include: A) double bed, private bath; B) double bed, shared bath: and C) two rooms with sofabed, shared bath. Extras include PIANO, TV, and fireplace. It is a 5 minute subway ride to Wall Street. Short stays only; two weeks maximum. Laundry facilities. One CAT resides here. Gourmet continental breakfasts served here. Young adults over 21 welcome.
**Rates:** A-C) S $35. D $55-$60 DAILY. S $245-$420, D $385-$420 WEEKLY.
**Reservations:** (914) 271-6228 MONDAY - FRIDAY 10 A.M. TO 4 P.M. APRIL - OCTOBER. 9 A.M. - 3 P.M. NOVEMBER - MARCH.

## PARK SLOPE

PROSPECT PARK WEST — A magnificantly restored brownstone townhouse across the street from Prospect Park, beautifully decorated in the Victoriam manner. Available for guests are: A) queen bed, B) two twins, and C) twin sofa in sitting room. All share a guest bath, full kitchen, and sitting area. Breakfast is served upstairs in hostess's wonderful kitchen. Beautiful neighborhood, convenient to F train. CHILDREN over 7 welcome. Two night minimum stay on weekends.

**Rates:** S $60, D $75, ADDITIONAL ADULT IN SITTING ROOM $40, CHILDREN $10 DAILY. S $385, D $490 WEEKLY.
**Reservations:** (914) 271-6228 MONDAY - FRIDAY 10 A.M. TO 4 P.M. APRIL - OCTOBER. 9 A.M. - 3 P.M. NOVEMBER - MARCH.

## NEW YORK CITY
### MANHATTAN

Manhattan is the borough that most people think of when they think of New York. Close your eyes, think New York, and you will see the Manhattan skyline. It is a fast-paced city with lots to do both day and night. Once you are in town, ask your host to point you toward the half-priced ticket lines for theater or music. Do not miss the many fine museums throughout Manhattan. You will have your choice of some of the finest restaurants in the world. Shopping in this city is a pleasure that people travel far and wide to experience. It is said that if you can't find it in New York it isn't made.

### CHELSEA

WEST 24TH STREET — Twin-bedded room with shared bath in a two bedroom apartment. Elevator building. Host is a retired film editor who enjoys reading, tennis, classical music, food, and wine. TV available. Two night minimum. Full breakfast served. NO SMOKERS. NO CHILDREN under 12.
**Rates:** S $50, D $70 DAILY. S $350, D $490 WEEKLY.
**Reservations:** (914) 271-6228 MONDAY - FRIDAY 10 A.M. TO 4 P.M. APRIL - OCTOBER. 9 A.M. - 3 P.M. NOVEMBER - MARCH.

WEST 22ND ST. — An unhosted garden level studio apartment in a privately owned brownstone that your psychoanalyst hosts are restoring for their own use. This apartment has a double bed, full kitchen, and private bath. The neighborhood is a lovely tree-lined block between 7th and 8th Avenues in Chelsea. Two beds could be set up for teenagers in a back room on the same level if needed.
**Rates:** S $75, D $85, ADDITIONAL CHILDREN $10 DAILY. S $475, D $550 WEEKLY.
**Reservations:** (914) 271-6228 MONDAY - FRIDAY 10 A.M. TO 4 P.M. APRIL - OCTOBER. 9 A.M. - 3 P.M. NOVEMBER - MARCH.

### EAST VILLAGE

EAST 3RD STREET NEAR AVENUE A — Top floor apartment in an elevator building. Guests have their own sunny room with VCR, TV, use of kitchen, stereo, and telephone machine for messages. There is a laundry room in the basement. There is a queen-sized bed as well as a

sofabed available. PETS WELCOME. Hostess is an art dealer who speaks Italian. Children welcome. NO SMOKERS.
**Rates:** S $40, D $60 DAILY.
**Reservations:** (212) 645-8134 MONDAY THROUGH FRIDAY 8 A.M. TO 6 P.M.

## GRAMERCY PARK

19TH STREET NEAR 2ND AVENUE — Bright, sunny apartment in a doorman building on a quiet street. Residential area. Guests have choice of two single beds or one double bed. Available UNHOSTED up to a week or more. Breakfast food is there for guest. NO CHILDREN.
**Rates:** S $40, D $60 DAILY HOSTED. $80-$100 DAILY UNHOSTED WITH BREAKFAST FOOD.
**Reservations:** (212) 645-8134 MONDAY THROUGH FRIDAY 8 A.M. TO 6 P.M.

EAST 22 STREET NEAR 3RD AVENUE — An immaculately clean, large UNHOSTED apartment in a doorman building. Breakfast is left for guest. It has a queen-sized bed plus a single bed. Smokers welcome. NO CHILDREN.
**Rates:** $80-$100 DAILY. $400-$500 WEEKLY.
**Reservations:** (212) 645-8134 MONDAY THROUGH FRIDAY 8 A.M. TO 6 P.M.

## GREENWICH VILLAGE

Greenwich Village is a quaint and old-fashioned area in the city with very interesting architecture. It is the home of many artists who both work and live there. The off-off-Broadway theater is found in this neighborhood as well as many fine clubs with excellent comedians and musicians. Outdoor art shows abound, as do antique shops that feature many curios. It has a culture that young people generally find fascinating. Your hosts will be glad to guide you through the labyrinth of streets that help to make this part of the city unique.

WEST 9TH STREET — Located in a landmarked section of Greenwich Village, this five story brownstone was built in the early 1800s in the Greek Revival style. The guest apartment is a full floor in the building. Brick walls, original/restored hardwood floors, shutters, two working FIREPLACES (bedroom and living room) enhance this two bedroom apartment. Accommodations include: A) queen-sized bed, master bedroom; B) twin beds, second bedroom; and C) double-bedded sofabed, living room. Full kitchen, TV, air conditioning. Location is convenient to all New York City attractions, especially shopping and eating in Greenwich Village. No pets. NO SMOKING. UNHOSTED.
**Rates:** D $100 DAILY; ADDITIONAL ADULTS $20 EACH DAILY. D

$700 WEEKLY. $160 Q DAILY. $3,000 A MONTH FOR ANY NUMBER OF PEOPLE.
**Reservations:** (914) 271-6228 MONDAY - FRIDAY 10 A.M. TO 4 P.M. APRIL - OCTOBER. 9 A.M. - 3 P.M. NOVEMBER - MARCH.

EAST 8TH STREET NEAR 5TH AVENUE — Fourth floor walkup apartment in Greenwich Village brownstone. Ideal for single guest on a budget. Room with high-riser can sleep two. Share bath with hostess. Full breakfast served. Three CATS live here. TV. Smoking permitted although hostess does not smoke. Young adults over 18 are welcome.
**Rates:** S $45, D $55 DAILY. S $200, D $300 WEEKLY.
**Reservations:** (914) 271-6228 MONDAY - FRIDAY 10 A.M. TO 4 P.M. APRIL - OCTOBER. 9 A.M. - 3 P.M. NOVEMBER - MARCH.

EAST 11TH STREET — Fabulous decorator loft with high ceilings, bright colors, big windows, and designer bath. Hostess is a French artist who has her studio here. Accommodations include king bed and private bath with sunken tub. TV. Full breakfast served. CHILDREN over 12 welcome.
**Rates:** S $55, D $70 DAILY. S $350, D $475 WEEKLY. ADDITIONAL ADULTS $25 EACH DAILY.
**Reservations:** (914) 271-6228 MONDAY - FRIDAY 10 A.M. TO 4 P.M. APRIL - OCTOBER. 9 A.M. - 3 P.M. NOVEMBER - MARCH.

GROVE STREET NEAR BLEEKER — This is a very private apartment on a historic West Village block. The bedroom is huge with a double bed and a clean, modern private bathroom. It is available UNHOSTED, sleeping up to four with a king-sized convertible couch. Breakfast food is left for guests. Children welcome.
**Rates:** S $60, D $80 DAILY HOSTED. $100 DAILY UNHOSTED WITH BREAKFAST. $400-$500 WEEKLY.
**Reservations:** (212) 645-8134 MONDAY THROUGH FRIDAY 8 A.M. TO 6 P.M.

WAVERLY PLACE — A beautiful two bedroom UNHOSTED apartment on a high floor with magnificent view of Manhattan. Extras include TV and fireplace. Doorman and elevator building. Available mostly on weekends and when hosts are away. Accommodations include: A) queen-sized bed, private bath; and B) queen-sized bed, share bath. Laundry facilities available. Two night minimum. Breakfast is self-serve. Children welcome.
**Rates:** A & B) S OR D $100 DAILY. ADDITIONAL ADULTS $25 EACH DAILY. AVAILABLE MOSTLY WEEKENDS UNHOSTED.
**Reservations:** (914) 271-6228 MONDAY - FRIDAY 10 A.M. TO 4 P.M. APRIL - OCTOBER. 9 A.M. - 3 P.M. NOVEMBER - MARCH.

## JAVITS CENTER

10TH AVENUE, 50TH-51ST STREETS — A one bedroom apartment with additional Murphy bed in living room, available hosted (twin beds) or unhosted. One bathroom. Although not a luxury building, it is clean and comfortable with spectacular views of the Hudson River and the Statue of Liberty. Convenient to the new Jacob Javits Convention Center, Lincoln Center, the Intrepid Air and Space Museum, and all of midtown Manhattan. Laundry facilities and TV. Two night minimum. Full breakfast served. Children welcome.
**Rates:** A) S $60, D $70; AND B) APARTMENT $150 DAILY.
**Reservations:** (914) 271-6228 MONDAY - FRIDAY 10 A.M. TO 4 P.M. APRIL - OCTOBER. 9 A.M. - 3 P.M. NOVEMBER - MARCH.

## MIDTOWN

The midtown area of Manhattan houses headquarters for many of the country's leading industries and businesses. Rockefeller Center with its ice skating in season and Christmas tree in December is a popular tourist spot. The Broadway shows are famous and well attended. The Plaza Hotel in the grand old style can be found at the entrance to Central Park. Fifth Avenue and its world reknowned department stores as well as elegant specialty shops are here. Carnegie Hall is also to be found here.

51ST STREET NEAR 8TH AVENUE — Very sunny apartment in a renovated walkup building. Exposed brick walls, clean and nicely furnished. Centrally located near Broadway theaters, restaurants, museums, and one block from the subway. There is queen-sized bed and two pullout couches are available for unhosted situations. Food is left for breakfast. Hostess is a writer. Two Siamese CATS live here. Children welcome.
**Rates:** S $50, D $60 DAILY HOSTED. $80 DAILY UNHOSTED WITH BREAKFAST FOOD.
**Reservations:** (212) 645-8134 MONDAY THROUGH FRIDAY 8 A.M. TO 6 P.M.

TUDOR CITY PLACE — UNHOSTED studio apartment with queen Murphy bed and modular sofa that does not open but can comfortably sleep one or two children. This is a small apartment with a view of the Chrysler Building and one block to the United Nations. Color TV, VCR, cable, air conditioned, private bath, and kitchenette. PETS WELCOME.
**Rates:** UNHOSTED APARTMENT S OR D $90 DAILY.
**Reservations:** (914) 271-6228 MONDAY - FRIDAY 10 A.M. TO 4 P.M. APRIL - OCTOBER. 9 A.M. - 3 P.M. NOVEMBER - MARCH.

WEST 46TH STREET — Historic building restored to lovely apartments. B&B is on the second floor. Host is an arts professional and teacher. Convenient to midtown Manhattan and dayliner, and Broadway shows.

Accommodations include double bed and sleep chair for child, share bath. Do it yourself breakfast. TV, air conditioned. Elevator. Weekend guests only. Three CATS live here. Two night minimum. NO SMOKING.
**Rates:** S $50, D $60 DAILY. EXTRA PERSON $20.
**Reservations:** (914) 271-6228 MONDAY - FRIDAY 10 A.M. TO 4 P.M. APRIL - OCTOBER. 9 A.M. - 3 P.M. NOVEMBER - MARCH.

WEST 57TH STREET — UNHOSTED executive apartment in luxury, doorman, elevator building. Apartment has a lovely living room with antique pieces, air conditioned, color TV, sofa that opens to queen bed, single bed and full bath, tiny but fully equipped kitchen with microwave and dishwasher. Near Carnegie Hall. Self-serve breakfast. Laundry facilities available. Two night minimum. Children welcome.
**Rates:** S OR D $85 DAILY. $535.50 WEEKLY. ADDITIONAL ADULTS $25 EACH DAILY.
**Reservations:** (914) 271-6228 MONDAY - FRIDAY 10 A.M. TO 4 P.M. APRIL - OCTOBER. 9 A.M. - 3 P.M. NOVEMBER - MARCH.

## MURRAY HILL

MADISON AVENUE LOW 30s — Your hostess manages a few apartments. Each has a large living room, dining area, kitchen for guest use and a number of bedrooms. Occasional private bath. Never more than four people to a bath. Two rooms in each apartment can sleep four. A fabulous New York setting for business or pleasure. Close to the Empire State Building, the Javitz Center, and Midtown. The large rooms have a double bed and two twins, smaller rooms have two twins which can form a king.
**Rates:** S $75, D $85, $10 FOR EXTRA CHILD, $20 EACH EXTRA ADULT DAILY. $10 SURCHARGE FOR ONE NIGHT STAYS. A WHOLE APARTMENT MAY BE RENTED FOR UP TO 12 PERSONS AT $400 DAILY.
**Reservations:** (914) 271-6228 MONDAY - FRIDAY 10 A.M. TO 4 P.M. APRIL - OCTOBER. 9 A.M. - 3 P.M. NOVEMBER - MARCH.

## SOHO

CROSBY STREET NEAR HOUSTON STREET — A historic building now an artist's home and studio duplex. It features 12 foot ceilings, fireplaces, brick walls, rough hewn floors, and oversized windows. There is a cozy private master bedroom with an adjacent full bathroom. A queen-sized antique bed, down comforters, and a ceiling bed make your stay very comfortable. A 6 year old boy and an 8 year old girl live here. PETS WELCOME. Children welcome.
**Rates:** S $60, D $80 DAILY.
**Reservations:** (212) 645-8134 MONDAY THROUGH FRIDAY 8 A.M. TO 6 P.M.

GREAT JONES STREET NEAR LAFAYETTE STREET — The hostess of this Soho loft is a weaver and works in the back. The atmosphere is friendly and informal. She would be happy to include guests in her plans. Guestroom has a twin bed with separate mattress available. TV and VCR. There is also a washer/dryer on the premises. TEENAGERS welcome. NO SMOKERS.
**Rates:** S $40, D $60 DAILY.
**Reservations:** (212) 645-8134 MONDAY THROUGH FRIDAY 8 A.M. TO 6 P.M.

MERCER STREET NEAR SPRING & BROOME STREETS — A lovely duplex loft in Soho. Nicely furnished and spacious. Near art galleries, restaurants, and subways. Guestroom has a double bed. There is one resident CAT. VISITING CATS ARE WELCOME. Hostess is a designer. Children welcome.
**Rates:** S $60, D $80 DAILY.
**Reservations:** (212) 645-8134 MONDAY THROUGH FRIDAY 8 A.M. TO 6 P.M.

## TRIBECA

GREENWICH STREET NEAR CANAL STREET — This loft in Tribeca is owned by a film editor. A truly unique New York living space. Open and spacious. Guests have a double bed. Children welcome.
**Rates:** S $40, D $60 DAILY.
**Reservations:** (212) 645-8134 MONDAY THROUGH FRIDAY 8 A.M. TO 6 P.M.

## UPPER EAST SIDE

The upper east side of Manhattan is the very fashionable and high priced residential district. It is the place of both brownstones and skyscrapers with views, and excellent gourmet restaurants. Bloomingdales is located in the heart of this high society area. The Metropolitan Museum of Art, the Frick, and Guggenheim museums can be found here. Of course Central Park is easily accessible, too, where one can walk along the tree lined paths by day in the center of this most modern of cities or take a horse and carriage ride.

EAST 54TH STREET — A wonderful building containing 10 studio apartments and 6 one bedroom apartments set up for B&B guests. Each has a queen-sized bed, and queen sofa. Color TV, cable, air conditioned, and small kitchen with breakfast needs. Laundry facilities in the building. Elevator building. Phone in each apartment. Guests will be billed for phones. A stay of one or more months requires $599 phone deposit. Children welcome.
**Rates:** STUDIO APARTMENT S $95, D $95, ADDITIONAL ADULTS

$10 EACH, ADDITIONAL CHILDREN $10 DAILY. ONE BEDROOM APARTMENT $120 FOR 1 OR 2 PEOPLE, $20 FOR EACH ADDITIONAL ADULT, $10 FOR EACH ADDITIONAL CHILD. FOR DAILY MAID SERVICE ADD $25 WEEKLY.
**Reservations:** (914) 271-6228 MONDAY - FRIDAY 10 A.M. TO 4 P.M. APRIL - OCTOBER. 9 A.M. - 3 P.M. NOVEMBER - MARCH.

EAST 58TH STREET — Single accommodations with private bath in luxury, highrise building near Bloomingdales, the museums, and fine dining. Hostess deals in fine art and enjoys art, theater, and music. Amenities include air conditioning, TV, continental breakfast on weekdays, and full on weekends. Two night minimum. Laundry facilities. Accommodations include: A) a single room and B) a double-bedded guestroom are available with shared bath. Young adults over 18 welcome. SMOKING PERMITTED.
**Rates:** A) S $60; AND B) S $60, D $70 DAILY. S $350, D $400 WEEKLY.
**Reservations:** (914) 271-6228 MONDAY - FRIDAY 10 A.M. TO 4 P.M. APRIL - OCTOBER. 9 A.M. - 3 P.M. NOVEMBER - MARCH.

EAST 68TH STREET — A beautiful Upper East Side apartment with spectacular views of the Hudson and the East Rivers as well as the New York skyline. Convenient to all of midtown Mahanttan. Decorator designed furnishing. A luxury accommodation. Accommodations include: A & B) two rooms with double bed, private bath; and C) single twin bed, private bath. Laundry facilities and TV. Children welcome. NO SMOKING.
**Rates:** A-C) S $70, D $85.
**Reservations:** (914) 271-6228 MONDAY - FRIDAY 10 A.M. TO 4 P.M. APRIL - OCTOBER. 9 A.M. - 3 P.M. NOVEMBER - MARCH.

EAST 69TH STREET — Luxury hosted apartment in doorman, elevator building on New York's fashionable east side. Convenient to all museums, Radio City Music Hall, and Broadway shows. Full breakfast. Air conditioned. Double hung soundproof windows. Designer decor in mauve and gray. Fresh flowers are everywhere about the bright, sunny apartment with breathtaking views of the city. Hostess is in real estate. She speaks a little Swedish, French, and Spanish. Kitchen privileges. Guestroom has queen-sized bed, private bath, and TV. Laundry facilities. Full breakfast. NO SMOKING. CHILDREN over 12 are welcome.
**Rates:** S $75, D $100 DAILY. S $525, D $700 WEEKLY.
**Reservations:** (914) 271-6228 MONDAY - FRIDAY 10 A.M. TO 4 P.M. APRIL - OCTOBER. 9 A.M. - 3 P.M. NOVEMBER - MARCH.

EAST 75TH STREET NEAR 3RD AVENUE — A large room with queen-sized bed and a single bed and private bath in a lovely two bedroom apartment in a doorman, elevator bulding. Hostess is a free-

lance writer with a variety of interests. A CAT is also in residence. Prefer long stay. TV and garden view. Laundry facilities available. Single adults only.
**Rates:** S $60 DAILY. S $300 WEEKLY.
**Reservations:** (914) 271-6228 MONDAY - FRIDAY 10 A.M. TO 4 P.M. APRIL - OCTOBER. 9 A.M. - 3 P.M. NOVEMBER - MARCH.

EAST 76TH STREET NEAR YORK AVENUE — Beautiful, clean studio apartment with a garden in a luxury doorman building. Nicely furnished, quiet. Has a queen-sized bed plus a couch for third person. Host is in real estate. UNHOSTED. Children welcome.
**Rates:** UNHOSTED WITH BREAKFAST FOOD $100 DAILY. $600 WEEKLY.
**Reservations:** (212) 645-8134 MONDAY THROUGH FRIDAY 8 A.M. TO 6 P.M.

EAST 80TH STREET & FIRST AVENUE — This apartment is available hosted during the week, unhosted when host is away (usually on weekends). The apartment is in a contemporary east side building with elevator and doorman with 24 hour security and garage in building. Parking costs extra. Accommodations include: A) queen-sized bed, TV, and share bath with family with additional sofabed in living room. B) Unhosted the apartment has an additional sofabed in living room, private bath, and full kitchen. Air conditioned. Laundry facilities. Full self-serve breakfast. Children welcome.
**Rates:** A) S $55, D $75; AND B) S $55. D $95 DAILY. S $385, D $490 WEEKLY. ADDITIONAL PERSONS $10-$20 EACH DAILY.
**Reservations:** (914) 271-6228 MONDAY - FRIDAY 10 A.M. TO 4 P.M. APRIL - OCTOBER. 9 A.M. - 3 P.M. NOVEMBER - MARCH.

EAST 85TH STREET NEAR YORK AVENUE — UNHOSTED. Large studio in a doorman building with a beautiful flower garden. Very quiet. Apartment has a microwave oven, cable TV, queen-sized bed, and a sofabed for a third person. Breakfast food left for guests. Children welcome.
**Rates:** UNHOSTED S $100, D $110, T $120 DAILY WITH BREAKFAST FOOD. $600-$700 WEEKLY.
**Reservations:** (212) 645-8134 MONDAY THROUGH FRIDAY 8 A.M. TO 6 P.M.

EAST 85TH STREET NEAR 5TH AVENUE — An elevator building just off Fifth Avenue and a short walk from the Metropolitan Museum of Art. Your Israeli hostess speaks Hebrew, Spanish, and German. She is a former restauranteur, a smoker, and very outgoing. Her little YORKIE is gracious, too. Decor is ornate but old and apartment needs some renovation. AC. Accommodations include: twin beds, share bath with

family. Laundry facilities and TV. Two night minimum. Full breakfast served to guests. Children welcome.
**Rates:** S $55, D $65 DAILY.
**Reservations:** (914) 271-6228 MONDAY - FRIDAY 10 A.M. TO 4 P.M. APRIL - OCTOBER. 9 A.M. - 3 P.M. NOVEMBER - MARCH.

EAST 89TH STREET — Third floor of private limestone townhouse. Two bedrooms, each with private bath (A) one attached, B) one with bath in hall), share a sitting room with TV and kitchenette. This 1880s home is situated on a beautiful tree-lined street, a stone's throw from the Mayor's mansion. Your hostess is an artist. Her art work is displayed about the home. Breakfast is self-served, fixings provided. Double beds in guestrooms. Two night minimum. Children over 14 welcome.
**Rates:** A) S $70, D $80; B) S or D $80 DAILY. ADDITIONAL CHILDREN $25 EACH DAILY.
**Reservations:** (914) 271-6228 MONDAY - FRIDAY 10 A.M. TO 4 P.M. APRIL - OCTOBER. 9 A.M. - 3 P.M. NOVEMBER - MARCH.

89TH STREET — An 1845 brownstone townhouse with beautiful garden, PIANO, and a hostess who loves to pamper guests. Accommodations are romantically decorated, and include full private bath, double bed, view of gardens. Your host is English; your hostess from Jamaica. They especially enjoy people who love to travel. Two large and lovable DOGS and three children reside here, too. SMOKING outside only. No CHILDREN.
**Rates:** S $70. D $85 DAILY. S $490, D $595 WEEKLY.
**Reservations:** (914) 271-6228 MONDAY - FRIDAY 10 A.M. TO 4 P.M. APRIL - OCTOBER. 9 A.M. - 3 P.M. NOVEMBER - MARCH.

# NEW YORK CITY
## MANHATTAN
### UPPER WEST SIDE

The Upper West Side of Manhattan is the trendy, avant garde, and a popular residential area where real estate, while expensive, is not as high as the Upper East Side. In the heart of this area is found Lincoln Center which is world famous for its opera house, ballet theater, and concert hall. Day or night people are strolling along Columbus Avenue enjoying fine dining and unusual shops. The Museum of Natural History and the Hayden Planetarium are not to be missed.

### UPPER WEST SIDE

CENTRAL PARK WEST — Decorator designed apartment in elevator, doorman building. Host is a banker; hostess is a consultant to a publisher of college level texts. Host enjoys furniture restoration and chair caning; hostess needle work and fine cooking. A gourmet continental breakfast is served. Close to Central Park and the Museum of Natural History.

Convenient to Broadway, the trendy Upper West Side, and easy access cross town to the Metropolitan Museum of Art. Accommodations include: a twin-bedded room with connecting private bath, all cotton bed linens and towels, black and white TV, telephone; and B) queen bed and private bath, as well as full kitchen and dining room, is available. Pre-war apartment can be offered unhosted. When unhosted apt also includes two night minimum. Children over 10 welcome.
**Rates:** S $65, D $75 DAILY. S $455, D $525 WEEKLY. 4 PERSONS $175 DAILY ENTIRE APARTMENT UNHOSTED.
**Reservations:** (914) 271-6228 MONDAY - FRIDAY 10 A.M. TO 4 P.M. APRIL - OCTOBER. 9 A.M. - 3 P.M. NOVEMBER - MARCH.

CENTRAL PARK WEST & 103RD STREET — Top floor apartment in doorman building overlooking Central Park. One block from subway. Double bed and futon available for a third person in unhosted situations. Breakfast is available whether the apartment is unhosted or hosted. Hostess is a therapist. Children welcome. NO SMOKERS.
**Rates:** S $40, D $60, T $80 DAILY HOSTED. $80 DAILY UNHOSTED WITH BREAKFAST FOOD.
**Reservations:** (212) 645-8134 MONDAY THROUGH FRIDAY 8 A.M. TO 6 P.M.

WEST END AVENUE — An UNHOSTED one bedroom apartment on the fifth floor of an elevator building. Very convenient to all West Side activities including Lincoln Center, Broadway, and the Javits Convention Center. Accommodations include a double bed, single sofabed, TV, and air conditioning. Full self-serve breakfast. Laundry facilities. Smoking permitted and children welcome.
**Rates:** UNHOSTED APARTMENT S OR D $75 DAILY. $525 WEEKLY. ADDITIONAL ADULTS $25 EACH DAILY.
**Reservations:** (914) 271-6228 MONDAY - FRIDAY 10 A.M. TO 4 P.M. APRIL - OCTOBER. 9 A.M. - 3 P.M. NOVEMBER - MARCH.

WEST 66TH NEAR BROADWAY — A large, beautifully furnished apartment in a luxury doorman building near Lincoln Center. It includes Japanese sliding doors leading to a terrace. The subway is down the block. There are two lovely CATS that do not require much attention. Accommodations include a queen-sized bed plus a sleep sofa available. Hosted or UNHOSTED. Children welcome.
**Rates:** S $50, D $80 DAILY HOSTED. $120-$150 DAILY UNHOSTED WITH BREAKFAST FOOD.
**Reservations:** (212) 645-8134 MONDAY THROUGH FRIDAY 8 A.M. TO 6 P.M.

WEST 68TH STREET — UNHOSTED large studio apartment in a luxury doorman, elevator building complete with air conditioning, TV, and full

kitchen. The bedroom area is separated from the rest of this studio by a latticework partition. Host works nearby and is happy to provide help in getting oriented to the city. Accommodations include: double bed, private bath; and queen sofabed in living room. Self-serve breakfast. Laundry facilities. Children welcome. Smoking permitted.
**Rates:** S $75 OR D $85 DAILY. ADDITIONAL PERSONS $25 EACH DAILY. $490 WEEKLY. UNHOSTED APARTMENT.
**Reservations:** (914) 271-6228 MONDAY - FRIDAY 10 A.M. TO 4 P.M. APRIL - OCTOBER. 9 A.M. - 3 P.M. NOVEMBER - MARCH.

WEST 70TH STREET NEAR COLUMBUS AVENUE — This bright, spacious, and comfortably furnished two bedroom apartment in doorman attended elevator building has one twin-bedded room with adjacent private bath available when host is in residence. Host is a magazine editor who enjoys music, travel, and meeting people. Additional room with queen-sized bed and private bath en suite available when unhosted (possible only July and December). Close to Lincoln Center, Museum of Natural History, Central Park, and many boutiques and restaurants on Columbus Avenue and Broadway; convenient also to City Center, Rockefeller Center, Carnegie Hall, midtown theaters and department stores, and East Side museums. HANDICAPPED ACCESSIBLE. VCR and AC. Two night minimum. CHILDREN 12 years and over welcome. No SMOKERS.
**Rates:** S $65, D $70 DAILY. $135 DAILY. ENTIRE APARTMENT UNHOSTED. S $455, D $490 WEEKLY. $910 WEEKLY FOR ENTIRE APARTMENT UNHOSTED.
**Reservations:** (914) 271-6228 MONDAY - FRIDAY 10 A.M. TO 4 P.M. APRIL - OCTOBER. 9 A.M. - 3 P.M. NOVEMBER - MARCH.

WEST 71ST STREET & BROADWAY — A small airy studio near Lincoln Center Queen-sized black leather sofabed is firm and comfortable. UNHOSTED apartment includes TV, private bath, and tiny kitchen. Perfect for the business person, tight for a couple. Two night minimum. Young adults over 18 welcome.
**Rates:** S $60, D $70 DAILY UNHOSTED APARTMENT.
**Reservations:** (914) 271-6228 MONDAY - FRIDAY 10 A.M. TO 4 P.M. APRIL - OCTOBER. 9 A.M. - 3 P.M. NOVEMBER - MARCH.

WEST 71ST STREET — An owner occupied brownstone building has two unhosted apartments available for guests. Your host is an architect. Accommodations include: A) 2nd floor apartment completely renovated includes: AC, color TV with cable, stereo, king loft bed in living room, full kitchen, queen loft bed in bedroom, terrace. Beautifully decorated with African art; B) 4th floor apartment with a double loft and a single bed in the living room, full kitchen, and bath. No SMOKING. Children welcome.
**Rates:** A) S OR D $100, ADDITIONAL ADULT $25, CHILD $15; AND

B) S $50, D $60, ADDITIONAL PERSON $10 DAILY. A) $600; AND
B) S $300, D $350 WEEKLY.
**Reservations:** (914) 271-6228 MONDAY - FRIDAY 10 A.M. TO 4 P.M.
APRIL - OCTOBER. 9 A.M. - 3 P.M. NOVEMBER - MARCH.

WEST 72ND STREET — UNHOSTED fifth floor apartment in elevator
building. It has 20 foot ceilings and large windows. Accommodations
include queen-sized bed loft upstairs and double bed in the living room.
Includes well-equipped small kitchen with microwave and dishwasher,
private bath, eating area. Convenient to Lincoln Center, Central Park,
Museum of Natural History, fabulous eating, and shopping on Columbus
Avenue. Laundry facilities and TV available. Children welcome.
**Rates:** S OR D $90 DAILY. ADDITIONAL ADULTS $25 EACH DAILY.
UNHOSTED APARTMENT.
**Reservations:** (914) 271-6228 MONDAY - FRIDAY 10 A.M. TO 4 P.M.
APRIL - OCTOBER. 9 A.M. - 3 P.M. NOVEMBER - MARCH.

RIVERSIDE DRIVE, BETWEEN 75TH & 76TH STREETS — An
UNHOSTED, spacious studio apartment on the fourth floor of a landmark
brownstone townhouse. The apartment is romantically decorated with full
kitchen, private bath, dressing room, dining table, loveseat, and antique
double bed. Hosts live in the building and will gladly help with information.
Refrigerator is stocked for do-it-yourself breakfast.
**Rates:** S or D $100, ADDITIONAL CHILD $10 DAILY.
**Reservations:** (914) 271-6228 MONDAY - FRIDAY 10 A.M. TO 4 P.M.
APRIL - OCTOBER. 9 A.M. - 3 P.M. NOVEMBER - MARCH.

WEST 76TH STREET — An all apartment hotel on 76th Street near
Broadway. Convenient to Lincoln Center, Broadway, and all New York
has to offer. There is a 24 hour concierge. Tiny kitchen has sink,
refrigerator, and microwave. Food is not supplied. Each room has a
telephone, billed to you separately, TV, and air conditioning. Choose
between studios and suites. Suites have pullout queen sofas in living
room. King-sized beds are available in accommodations, as well as cots
and cribs. Smoking permitted. UNHOSTED.
**Rates:** S $80-$110. D $95-$115 DAILY STUDIOS. $120-$140 DAILY
SUITES. S $560-$770, D $665-$805 WEEKLY STUDIOS. $840-$980
WEEKLY SUITES. ADDITIONAL PERSONS $15-$21 EACH DAILY.
**Reservations:** (914) 271-6228 MONDAY - FRIDAY 10 A.M. TO 4 P.M.
APRIL - OCTOBER. 9 A.M. - 3 P.M. NOVEMBER - MARCH.

WEST 78TH STREET — An UNHOSTED duplex in a brownstone. This
apartment is four flights up, no elevator. Once there you will find a light
spacious apartment with full living room, kitchen, two baths, queen-
bedded bedroom, balcony overlooking the tree-lined street and spiral
staircase between the bedroom and living rooms. The living room also

has a queen-sized sleeper sofa so the apartment can easily sleep two couples or a family of four with considerable privacy. Do-it-yourself breakfast. CHILDREN over 7 welcome. Four night minimum stay. **Rates:** S OR D $100 DAILY. ADDITIONAL CHILD $10, ADULT $25 DAILY. $600 WEEKLY.
**Reservations:** (914) 271-6228 MONDAY - FRIDAY 10 A.M. TO 4 P.M. APRIL - OCTOBER. 9 A.M. - 3 P.M. NOVEMBER - MARCH.

WEST 81ST STREET — Two lovely UNHOSTED apartments in an owner occupied five story brownstone, lovely tree-lined street, convenient to cross town bus. Both apartments have built in queen-sized beds and sofas that open to sleep two, full kitchen, and private bath. A) Third floor studio has deck overlooking gardens; and B) fourth floor apartment has no deck. Walkup. Host is a carpenter; hostess is an estate salesperson. Hosts and their 12 year old daughter live on the first two floors. Do it yourself breakfast. Refrigerator is well stocked. TV. Two night minimum. Children welcome.
**Rates:** A) S OR D $110; AND B) S OR D $105 DAILY. ADDITIONAL ADULTS $15 EACH DAILY. ADDITIONAL CHILDREN $10 EACH DAILY. A) S OR D $725; AND B) S OR D $700 WEEKLY. TWO UNHOSTED APARTMENTS.
**Reservations:** (914) 271-6228 MONDAY - FRIDAY 10 A.M. TO 4 P.M. APRIL - OCTOBER. 9 A.M. - 3 P.M. NOVEMBER - MARCH.

WEST 95TH STREET — Just off Central Park West, wonderful restored townhouse with private garden. Hostess is in housing development. She has teenage children, often away at school or camp. Air conditioned and TV. A CAT lives here. Accommodations include: A) double bed, private bath; and B) sofabed, shared bath. Laundry facilities available and fireplace in home. On bus line. Two night minimum. Full breakfasts are served to guests. Children of all ages welcome. **Rates:** A & B) S $55, D $65 DAILY. A & B) S $385, D $455 WEEKLY. ADDITIONAL CHILDREN $10 EACH DAILY.
**Reservations:** (914) 271-6228 MONDAY - FRIDAY 10 A.M. TO 4 P.M. APRIL - OCTOBER. 9 A.M. - 3 P.M. NOVEMBER - MARCH.

WEST 96TH STREET — A twin-bedded room with private bath in a two bedroom hosted apartment. The building has an elevator, doorman, indoor swimming POOL, and racquetball courts for guests. Long-term guests staying a month or more can be trained on gym equipment, too. Host smokes a pipe. Laundry facilities available. TV. Children welcome.
**Rates:** S $45, D $60 DAILY. S $200. D $300 WEEKLY.
**Reservations:** (914) 271-6228 MONDAY - FRIDAY 10 A.M. TO 4 P.M. APRIL - OCTOBER. 9 A.M. - 3 P.M. NOVEMBER - MARCH.

# NEW YORK CITY
## QUEENS

Queens is basically a residential borough of New York City. It is the home of LaGuardia airport, the Forest Hills Tennis Club, and the U.S. Open Tennis Championships. It is also home base for the New York Mets. It is less expensive to stay in Queens than Manhattan and good public transportation makes access to Manhattan very simple.

## BRIARWOOD

Briarwood is a residential neighborhood in the borough of Queens that is equally distanced between LaGuardia and Kennedy airports and easily accessible to Manhattan via public transportation. Accommodations here will generally be less expensive than in Manhattan.

GRAND CENTRAL PARKWAY — A two story brick home, well kept, and equally close to Kennedy or LaGuardia airports. Host is a civil engineer who enjoys public speaking as a hobby and belongs to Toastmasters International; hostess does day care. This spot is ideal for a single parent since a child can be well cared for during the day by the hostess. The host speaks fluent German. Walking distance to subway. Thirty minutes to midtown Manhattan. Parking available. Accommodations include: A) twin-bedded double, air conditioning; and B) single bed (fan available). Both share family bath. Crib available. TV. Laundry facilities. SMOKING on porch only.
**Rates:** A & B) S $35, D $50 DAILY. S $200, D $250 WEEKLY.
**Reservations:** (914) 271-6228 MONDAY - FRIDAY 10 A.M. TO 4 P.M. APRIL - OCTOBER. 9 A.M. - 3 P.M. NOVEMBER - MARCH.

# ORANGE COUNTY

Orange County is just north of Rockland County, starting at Bear Mountain and including ski areas, vineyards, orchards, and waterfront. West Point is probably the most famous attraction. Storm King Mountain Art Center is nearby as well. Newburgh is interesting as it has a very active Historical Society that gives tours to the Crawford mansion, Knox's headquarters, and George Washington's encampment. A major restoration effort is under way in this community and many of the newly restored Victorian homes are sometimes open for viewing.

## GOSHEN
### NEAR COURT HOUSE

MAIN STREET — Once the Anthony Dobbins Stage Coach Inn, this home, built in 1749, offers four antique filled rooms. Guests especially enjoy the plant filled glass solarium looking out over the gardens. Goshen is the home of the Trotter's Hall of Fame and the Orange County

Courthouse. Close to Orange County Park for swimming, skating, skiing, and hiking. It is 30 miles to West Point. Hostess is director of a professional fashion modeling agency. Hostess has one CAT and one DOG. No pets. Accommodations include: A) double bed, private bath, FIREPLACE; B) two rooms with twin beds, shared bath; and C) double bed, private bath. On a bus line. TV. Two night minimum. Elevator. CHILDREN over 12 welcome. NO SMOKING.
**Rates:** A-C) S OR D $80 DAILY.
**Reservations:** (914) 271-6228 MONDAY - FRIDAY 10 A.M. TO 4 P.M. APRIL - OCTOBER. 9 A.M. - 3 P.M. NOVEMBER - MARCH.

## NEW WINDSOR

A split level home in a lovely community just south of Newburgh. Convenient to West Point and Storm King Mountain Art Center. It is 1 hour to Great Adventure Amusement Park. Skiing, swimming, hiking, and sightseeing nearby. Hostess is a public health aide who is active in church and enjoys meeting people. Her 12 year old daughter also lives here. A YORKSHIRE TERRIER lives here, too. Guest accommodations are on the ground floor. HANDICAPPED ACCESSIBLE. One guestroom with a double bed, single sofa, and single bed, also private bath. Laundry facilities and TV. Full breakfast served. Children welcome. NO SMOKING.
**Rates:** S $45, D $65 DAILY. $65 FOR UP TO FOUR PEOPLE. ADDITIONAL CHILDREN $10 EACH DAILY. S $105, D $175 WEEKLY.
**Reservations:** (914) 271-6228 MONDAY - FRIDAY 10 A.M. TO 4 P.M. APRIL - OCTOBER. 9 A.M. - 3 P.M. NOVEMBER - MARCH.

## NEWBURGH

OLD LITTLE BRITAIN ROAD — A pre-Revolutionary farmhouse restored to better than the original splendor, furnished tastefully with marvelous antiques. This farm and its surrounding land was used as a truck farm on which many lilacs were grown and people traveled from New Jersey to purchase them. There is also an outside root cellar for garden and orchard crops. This home is near almost anything you would like to do or just relax. Historic sites, wineries, antiques, all kinds of sports, for example horseback riding, are near. This home has a music room with a PIANO and ORGAN. Also a screened-in porch to enjoy in warm months. Host has his own insurance agency, loves golf, history, gardening and music; hostess enjoys birdwatching, which you can do on property, gardening, and music. She is active in the Historical Society. Accommodations include: A & B) two rooms with double beds; and C) twin beds. Shared bath. A cot is also available. There is a fireplace in the home and TV. Two CATS reside here but are not in house. Hosts prefer not to have unmarried couples. Children welcome. Pipe SMOKING only.

**Rates:** A-C) S $45, D $50 DAILY. ADDITIONAL CHILDREN OVER 2 ARE $10 EACH DAILY. S $200, D $250 WEEKLY.
**Reservations:** (914) 271-6228 MONDAY - FRIDAY 10 A.M. TO 4 P.M. APRIL - OCTOBER. 9 A.M. - 3 P.M. NOVEMBER - MARCH.

OLD SOUTH PLANK — A custom built brick home overlooking a 400 acre lake. The furnishings are early American. Hosts are retired and enjoy crafts, cooking, skiing, and sailing. Neither smoke. The accommodations are not fancy, but clean and very comfortable. Guests can enjoy the beach, sunning, swimming, sailing, or canoeing (if you bring your own boat). In winter, the skating is wonderful. It is 30 minutes to West Point. Accommodations include: A) double bed, single twin, shared bath; and B) sofabed, shared bath. Hosts do not wish to have unmarried couples as guests. Fireplace in home and TV available. Full breakfast served. NO SMOKERS. CHILDREN over 12 welcome.
**Rates:** WINTER RATES A & B) S $20, D $30 DAILY. S $140, D $210 WEEKLY. SUMMER RATES A & B) S $30, D $40 DAILY. S $210, D $280 WEEKLY.
**Reservations:** (914) 271-6228 MONDAY - FRIDAY 10 A.M. TO 4 P.M. APRIL - OCTOBER. 9 A.M. - 3 P.M. NOVEMBER - MARCH.

## PINE BUSH
## RURAL

FREY ROAD — A cedar shingled house set on 22 acres of wooded land on a quiet road in the foothills of the Shawangunk Mountains where Ulster, Orange, and Sullivan counties meet. It is easily accessible to all the Hudson Valley has to offer, including wineries (3 within 15 minutes), golf, skiing, horseback riding, and, of course, antiquing. The home features a large living/dining room with woodburning fireplace, separate TV/VCR room and rooms A and C have hand stenciled wall decorations. Your hostess is an artist who also makes and sells English plum puddings by mail order. She is originally from England and provides a British style breakfast. Accommodations include: A) single bed, first floor; and B & C) double beds. All rooms share a first floor bath. Six CATS, a DOG and a goat in residence. CHILDREN under 12 not welcome. SMOKING permitted, but not in bedrooms.
**Rates:** A-C) S $30, D $40 DAILY. S $210, D $280 WEEKLY.
**Reservations:** (914) 271-6228 MONDAY - FRIDAY 10 A.M. TO 4 P.M. APRIL - OCTOBER. 9 A.M. - 3 P.M. NOVEMBER - MARCH.

A custom designed cedar shingled energy efficient home with greenhouse on 30 acres. Your hosts raise Scottish Highland Longhaired cattle. They are English and have a beautiful English garden. A creek for canoeing, fishing, and wading is a short walk with a swimming hole not too far away. Horseback riding stables are a short drive. Guestroom is on its

own level. It has twin beds which can be pushed together and a high rise sofa for two additional children, private bath. No SMOKING. Children welcome.
**Rates:** S $30, D $45, ADDITIONAL ADULTS $15, CHILDREN $10 DAILY. S $175, D $210 WEEKLY.
**Reservations:** (914) 271-6228 MONDAY - FRIDAY 10 A.M. TO 4 P.M. APRIL - OCTOBER. 9 A.M. - 3 P.M. NOVEMBER - MARCH.

This house has been in existence since the late 1790s. Built in stages, it was completed in 1870. The house contains antiques and a collection of clocks. Host is supervisor of township; hostess teaches and paints watercolors. Both enjoy having B&B guests. Inground POOL on premises, as well as one CAT and one DOG. Accommodations include two 3/4 beds, share bath with family. A child can bunk in with hosts' child. Full breakfasts are served to guests. Fireplace in house; TV and laundry facilities are available. SMOKING outside only.
**Rates:** S $40, D $45 DAILY. S OR D $175 WEEKLY.
**Reservations:** (914) 271-6228 MONDAY - FRIDAY 10 A.M. TO 4 P.M. APRIL - OCTOBER. 9 A.M. - 3 P.M. NOVEMBER - MARCH.

## WALDEN
### RURAL

A restored 1740 stone farmhouse, predating a sister building that is now a county museum. On the Historic Register, this farm is on 12 acres with a pond. Host is an engineer and medical researcher; hostess, host's daughter, is a schoolteacher. This home is near horseback riding and Holiday Mountain for skiing. Cross-country skiing on the property. Ice caves are also nearby. PIANO. All guestrooms are on the third floor. Accommodations include three rooms with double bed, shared bath. There is a fireplace in the home; TV and laundry facilities are available. Full breakfasts are served to guests. NO SMOKING. Children of all ages welcome.
**Rates:** S $39, D $45 DAILY. ADDITIONAL CHILDREN $10 EACH DAILY. S $150, D $200 WEEKLY.
**Reservations:** (914) 271-6228 MONDAY - FRIDAY 10 A.M. TO 4 P.M. APRIL - OCTOBER. 9 A.M. - 3 P.M. NOVEMBER - MARCH.

## WEST POINT
### HIGHLAND FALLS
#### VILLAGE

HICKORY STREET — This 1924 village home is within walking distance to West Point. Accommodations include: A & B) two rooms with double bed, and C) twin beds. All rooms share bath with family. TV and laundry facilities available. Full breakfast served here. Two night minimum. Host is employed by the Palisades Interstate Park and enjoys travel and

athletics; hostess enjoys gardening, travel, and people. Children over 2 years old welcome. NO SMOKING.
**Rates:** S $30. D $40 DAILY. ADDITIONAL PERSONS $10 EACH DAILY. S $140, D $210 WEEKLY. NO WEEKLY RATES PLEBE OR GRADUATION WEEKS.
**Reservations:** (914) 271-6228 MONDAY - FRIDAY 10 A.M. TO 4 P.M. APRIL - OCTOBER. 9 A.M. - 3 P.M. NOVEMBER - MARCH.

ONDAORA — A small but comfortable Ranch house within walking distance to West Point. The living room has a fireplace and color TV. Hosts can speak German. They own and run an ice cream store. Hostess loves to do needle work, read, and is a good cook. Guests can arrive by Short Line Bus or Hudson River Dayliner. Accommodations include double bed, share bath with family. Laundry facilities. Full breakfasts are served to guests. One DOG and one CAT reside here. Children welcome. SMOKING permitted in living room only.
**Rates:** S $30, D $35 DAILY. S $150, D $210 WEEKLY.
**Reservations:** (914) 271-6228 MONDAY - FRIDAY 10 A.M. TO 4 P.M. APRIL - OCTOBER. 9 A.M. - 3 P.M. NOVEMBER - MARCH.

# PUTNAM COUNTY
## COLD SPRING
### NEAR BOSCOBEL

Once the home of the Marquis Agnes Rizzo Deiritii and built in the first half of the nineteenth century. This popular restaurant now offers three beautifully appointed rooms as well as fine dining in their romantic Victorian dining room. "The Marquis doesn't live here any more but a sense of style and a time gone by remain." Hosts are Swiss. One is the chef and the other the manager in the dining room. Their menu incorporates Swiss and seasonal specialties. Try the restaurant for a dinner you will never forget. Price fixed about $30 for dinner. Accommodations include three rooms with king-sized bed, private bath. Fireplace, TV. Continental breakfasts served. Smoking permitted. Children welcome.
**Rates:** S OR D $125-$150 DAILY.
**Reservations:** (914) 271-6228 MONDAY - FRIDAY 10 A.M. TO 4 P.M. APRIL - OCTOBER. 9 A.M. - 3 P.M. NOVEMBER - MARCH.

# ROCKLAND COUNTY

Rockland County is the part of New York State north of New Jersey along the west bank of the Hudson River. It is one third parkland and includes an antiquing center as well as the Antron and Elmwood theaters and lots of bargain hunters' outlets. Rockland is the home of Rockland Community College and St. Thomas Aquinas College. The Renaissance Fair takes place in Sterling Forest each summer. Because of its close proximity to New Jersey, it is easily accessible to the Meadowlands Race Track and many Bergen County businesses.

## BLAUVELT

GREEN HEDGES LANE — This is a 1968 Colonial home with rear deck facing woods on 3/4 acre. It is quiet, secluded, and a 5 minute drive to Nyack waterfront and antique shops. It is 30 minutes to Bear Mountain State Park and 40 minutes to West Point. Host is a school administrator; hostess is a social worker. Accommodations include: A) queen bed; B) twin-bedded room; and C) high-riser and crib. All share hall baths. Air conditioned, color TV, rollaway, crib available. Laundry facilities available. On bus line. Pickup available. Fireplace. Children welcome.
**Rates:** S $35, D $45 DAILY. ADDITIONAL ADULTS $15 EACH DAILY. ADDITIONAL CHILDREN $10 EACH DAILY. S $175, D $275 WEEKLY.
**Reservations:** (914) 271-6228 MONDAY - FRIDAY 10 A.M. TO 4 P.M. APRIL - OCTOBER. 9 A.M. - 3 P.M. NOVEMBER - MARCH.

## SARATOGA REGION

There are outdoor concerts and ballet at the Saratoga Center for the Performing Arts (SPAC) and of course the Saratoga Race Track. B&B homes are available in downtown Albany, its suburbs, nearby towns and cities, and in the country. Fulton County, northwest of Albany, attracts tourists to the Great Sacandaga Lake and leather goods outlets.

## BALLSTON SPA

WEST HIGH STREET — This is a 1856 Victorian home, restored but with attached but private guest quarters. Located in downtown Historic District, home is 3 to 5 miles from Saratoga. Host is coordinator of a hospital education program; hostess operates a charming gift shop from her home and coordinates business education courses. They have three sons aged 3, 6, and 21. Hosts enjoy decorating, gardening, and meeting people. A POODLE resides here. Accommodations include: A) three rooms with double bed, shared bath; and B) double sofabed in living room. Children welcome. Fireplace and TV. Full breakfast served. SMOKING restricted to downstairs.
**Rates:** A & B) S $45, D $55 DAILY. AUGUST ONLY S $60, D $75 DAILY.
**Reservations:** (914) 271-6228 MONDAY - FRIDAY 10 A.M. TO 4 P.M. APRIL - OCTOBER. 9 A.M. - 3 P.M. NOVEMBER - MARCH.

## GREENWICH

GRAY AVENUE — Lovely white house built in 1900 but restored and modernized since. This home is 20 to 25 minutes from Saratoga, the

track, SPAC, and Skidmore. Manchester, Vermont, is 50 minutes away. Lake George and Willard Mountain, which is a family type downhill ski area, are nearby. Guest accommodations are on second floor, hosts on main level. Accommodations include: A) queen-sized bed, private bath; B) sofabed; and C) sofabed. Full breakfasts are served to guests. TV and laundry facilities available. CHILDREN over 10 welcome. No SMOKING in bedrooms.
**Rates:** A-C) S $30, D $45 DAILY. S $210, D $280 WEEKLY.
**Reservations:** (914) 271-6228 MONDAY - FRIDAY 10 A.M. TO 4 P.M. APRIL - OCTOBER. 9 A.M. - 3 P.M. NOVEMBER - MARCH.

## SARATOGA

A completely restored Victorian farmhouse on 8 acres of cleared land with well cared-for barns and gardens. It is 2.3 miles to Saratoga Racetrack, SPAC, Skidmore, natural mineral baths, etc. Host is a Doctor of Education who works with the developmentally disabled. Hostess is interested in metaphysics and ancient philosophy. Both are gardeners and registered French Alpine goat breeders. A DOG also lives here. A tray with coffee and homemade bread comes to your room early in the morning. A full country breakfast is served between 8 and 10 A.M. which includes pancakes, waffles or local produce. Accommodations include: A) twin beds, shared bath; B) queen bed, shared bath; C) twin beds, private bath; and D) double bed, private bath. Two night minimum stay on weekends.
**Rates:** SEPTEMBER THROUGH JULY — ROOMS WITH SHARED BATH $65, PRIVATE BATH $85; AUGUST SHARED BATH $75, PRIVATE BATH $95 DAILY.
**Reservations:** (914) 271-6228 MONDAY - FRIDAY 10 A.M. TO 4 P.M. APRIL - OCTOBER. 9 A.M. - 3 P.M. NOVEMBER - MARCH.

## SARATOGA SPRINGS

Perhaps the oldest guest house in Saratoga, this inn has been welcoming visitors for almost 100 years. It is a Queen Anne style Victorian featuring two elaborate fireplaces. and distinctive wainscotting. All the charm and excitement of Saratoga are just a short walk. Park your car and walk to the Racetrack, the Springs, historic Congress Park, the Museums of Dance and Racing, shops, and fine restaurants. Accommodations include: A) single bed, shared bath; B) double bed, shared bath; C) double bed, shared bath, sink; and D) double bed, private bath. CHILDREN over 12 welcome. Two night minimum. Six night minimum in August (Tues.-Mon.). A DOG lives here, too.
**Rates:** A) S $35; B) S OR D $40; C) S OR D $50; D) S OR D $65 DAILY SEPTEMBER-JUNE. S $45, D $85 JULY; S $75, D $125 AUGUST DAILY.
**Reservations:** (914) 271-6228 MONDAY - FRIDAY 10 A.M. TO 4 P.M. APRIL - OCTOBER. 9 A.M. - 3 P.M. NOVEMBER - MARCH.

This brown shingle and brick 1886 Queen Anne Victorian house is complete with wraparound porch. It is on the National Register of Historic Homes. It has been restored with wonderful attention to detail accentuating the charm and elegance of a bygone era. It is located four blocks from the track, minutes to downtown Saratoga. Host is interested in restoration and involved in a doll company, he enjoys skiing, sailing, and racquetball; hostess has interests in antiques, theater, music, and designs Victorian bridal and children's wear. Son, age 8, and two daughters, 2 1/2 years and 3 months, are in residence. No unmarried couples. Accommodations include: A) Victorian cottage pine double bed; B) brass double bed; and C) guest sitting room with double bed daybed suitable for teenagers. All guestrooms are in a private guest area on the second floor and share a guest bath. TV and laundry facilities available. Two night minimum. Nonwalking infants or CHILDREN over 12 welcome. SMOKING limited to the porch.
**Rates:** JULY AND AUGUST S $65, D $75, CHILDREN $30 FOR 1, $50 FOR 2 DAILY. OFF-SEASON S $45, D $55, CHILDREN $25 FOR 1, $40 FOR 2 DAILY.
**Reservations:** (914) 271-6228 MONDAY - FRIDAY 10 A.M. TO 4 P.M. APRIL - OCTOBER. 9 A.M. - 3 P.M. NOVEMBER - MARCH.

QUEVIC DRIVE — Ten year old rustic Ranch on a quiet deadend street overlooking private backyard with above ground POOL. Host is an industrial specialist; hostess is a teacher's aide at Skidmore. It is 5 minutes to SPAC, 10 minutes to the track. Accommodations include suite with queen bed, and double sleeper in sitting room, HOT TUB, SAUNA, FIREPLACE, cable TV, VCR, and private bath. Guest suite is on its own level facing the private yard. One ferret lives here, as well as an 11 year old son. Laundry facilities available. Continental plus breakfast. Children welcome. NONSMOKERS only.
**Rates:** S $45, D $65 DAILY. JULY AND AUGUST S $65, D $75 DAILY. ADDITIONAL PERSONS $10 EACH DAILY.
**Reservations:** (914) 271-6228 MONDAY - FRIDAY 10 A.M. TO 4 P.M. APRIL - OCTOBER. 9 A.M. - 3 P.M. NOVEMBER - MARCH.

## WESTCHESTER COUNTY

Westchester County is the county north of New York City. It is an area of rolling hills, lush countryside, many historic sites, as well as parkland. The area closer to New York City is more suburban while the northern part of the country is more rural. Westchester is the home of Historic Hudson Valley (formerly Sleepy Hollow Restorations) (Van Cortlandt Manor, Philipsburg, and Sunnyside), Lyndhurst, and Caramoor. It is also home to a number of colleges and universities (Iona, Pace, Sarah Lawrence, Manhattanville, College of New Rochelle, Kings, Marymount, Mercy, SUNY at Purchase) as well as many businesses including General Foods, Nestle, Texaco, Hitachi, IBM, Avon, and many more. Westchester is bordered on the east by the Long Island Sound and on the west by the Hudson River making the shore and waterfront areas interesting attractions. Three train lines serve this region from Manhattan making a Westchester stay an easy way to see both city and country. Limousine service is available from LaGuardia and JFK airports. Westchester also has its own airport. A variety of sports activities are available in the county including excellent cross-country skiing (Pound Ridge and Pocantico Hills), horseback riding, hiking, skating, swimming, sailing, golf, and so forth. In the summer, Westchester is the home of the Croton Clearwater Revival, Summerfare at SUNY at Purchase, and concerts at both Lyndhurst and Caramoor. Summerstock theater is also abundant.

## ARDSLEY

A Cape Cod style home with guest quarters on a separate level. Accommodations include: A) twin beds, share bath and B) queen bed, share bath. Both rooms share a sitting room. Full breakfast. Basket available for baby. Nicely landscaped acre with patio. Two outdoor CATS live here. No SMOKING.
**Rates:** S $42, D $50 DAILY. S $252, D $250 WEEKLY.
**Reservations:** (914) 271-6228 MONDAY - FRIDAY 10 A.M. TO 4 P.M. APRIL - OCTOBER. 9 A.M. - 3 P.M. NOVEMBER - MARCH.

## BEDFORD

A custom designed classical home with a fabulous view, antiques throughout, on 6 landscaped acres with inground POOL. The guest wing has its own living room, kitchen, is on two levels and has two full bedrooms plus a den with a firm comfortable sofabed. Accommodations include: A) antique double, private bath, B) queen firm sofabed, and C) double sofa in den. B and C share a bath. Host is a retired but very active architect. This is a luxury accommodation throughout. CHILDREN over 12 welcome. Two night minimum stay.
**Rates:** S OR D $160, ADDITIONAL PERSONS $35 DAILY. S OR D $500 WEEKLY.
**Reservations:** (914) 271-6228 MONDAY - FRIDAY 10 A.M. TO 4 P.M. APRIL - OCTOBER. 9 A.M. - 3 P.M. NOVEMBER - MARCH.

## CROSS RIVER
### NEAR CARAMOOR

A Colonial farmhouse built in 1600, now adapted to contemporary lifestyle. Beautifully appointed and landscaped, the house sits above the reservoir. Convenient to Pound Ridge Reservation for cross-country skiing, Katonah, Mt. Kisco, John Jay homestead, Caramoor, and the Harvey School; Ridgefield, Connecticut is 8 miles away. Hostess is a home health aide whose family is now grown. Accommodations include: A) double bed,

private bath on second floor; B) two bunk beds; and C) two sleeping bags and crib. Full breakfasts are served. Laundry facilities and TV. **Rates:** A-C) S $35, D $50 DAILY. ADDITIONAL CHILDREN $10 EACH DAILY. S $200, D $280 WEEKLY. ADDITIONAL CHILDREN $50 WEEKLY.
**Reservations:** (914) 271-6228 MONDAY - FRIDAY 10 A.M. TO 4 P.M. APRIL - OCTOBER. 9 A.M. - 3 P.M. NOVEMBER - MARCH.

## CROTON-ON-HUDSON
### RURAL, NEAR TEATOWN

TEATWON ROAD — A pretty, white eight room house set back from the road, once the gatehouse to a large estate. This home is located on 4 acres of beautifully landscaped land including lots of woods. Furniture is a mixture of Oriental and American and the living room boasts a large stone fireplace. Host is a retired electronics engineer who was in broadcasting and is presently beginning a teaching career; hostess is a homemaker who operates a word processing business from the den. Host is interested in karate and gardening; hostess enjoys home baking and both enjoy traveling, reading, and music. They are interested in Japan and Orientalia, and a little Japanese and Spanish are spoken here. A friendly hound DOG named Dasher and lovable CAT, Isabel, live here. This home is in a rural area, yet 10 minutes by car to the village or train station to New York City, which is 50 minutes away. It is also convenient to Teatown Reservation, a 300 acre nature preserve with 12 miles of walking trails and cross-country skiing. Accommodations include a double bed, private bath, desk, chair, and TV. Light kitchen privileges in modern kitchen. Hearty country breakfasts served as well as complimentary glass of wine in early evening. Convenient to IBM and Hudson River Conference Center and White Plains corporations 30 minutes away.
**Rates:** S $35, D $50 DAILY. S $200, D $250 WEEKLY.
**Reservations:** (914) 271-6228 MONDAY - FRIDAY 10 A.M. TO 4 P.M. APRIL - OCTOBER. 9 A.M. - 3 P.M. NOVEMBER - MARCH.

## VILLAGE

VAN WYCK STREET — A large riverview Victorian home with a mini apple orchard and 35 foot inground POOL. The home is furnished with many Victorian antiques and includes two PIANOS and FIREPLACES. Host makes computer software; hostess is a psychologist. Hostess can speak a little French; host can understand Russian. A 8 year old daughter lives here, too, as does a sleepy FRENCH BULLDOG. Accommodations include: A) large double-bedded room with Victorian furnishings, day bed in sleeping alcove; B) two twin beds; and C & D) two rooms with double bed. The four rooms share two and a half baths. An apartment E) double bed, living room, full kitchen, and bath is also available with private entrance. F) A fireplaced sitting room, queen bedded 2-room suite with private bath. An unhosted one bedroom apartment is also sometimes available. Hostess enjoys serving elaborate breakfasts on the patio beside the POOL in summer or in a 35 foot sunroom. All baby equipment is available. Bikes available. This home is convenient to Van Cortlandt Manor, Teatown Reservation, West Point, and has easy train access to New York City (50 minutes). Ten minutes to IBM research center. On bus line and pickup can be arranged at station. TV available. Children of all ages welcome. SMOKERS not welcome.

**Rates:** A) S $40, D $55, T $75; B & D) S $35, D $50 DAILY; AND C) APT. $60 DAILY. ADDITIONAL CHILDREN $10 EACH DAILY. A-C) S $200, D $280; D) S $250, D $300; F) $125 S OR D WEEKLY.

**Reservations:** (914) 271-6228 MONDAY - FRIDAY 10 A.M. TO 4 P.M. APRIL - OCTOBER. 9 A.M. - 3 P.M. NOVEMBER - MARCH.

## HARTSDALE
## NEAR CENTRAL AVENUE

HILLCREST ROAD — An 1896 central hall Victorian home with wonderful antique Colonial decor. This home on a hillside acre with a country atmosphere is a 15 minute walk to the Hartsdale train station, a 5 minute drive to White Plains and easy access to New York City by bus or train. Your host and hostess are both retired and enjoy a variety of crafts and hobbies. Accommodations include: A) double bed, private bath with separate entrance; B) twin beds, private bath, large room; and C) double bed, shared family bath. Room C is not available unless other rooms are full. Fireplace in home, TV and laundry facilities available, on bus line, pickup available.

**Rates:** A) $50 S OR $55 D; B) S $35 D $50; AND C) S $30, D $40 DAILY. A & B) S $200, D $280; AND C) S $175, D $250 WEEKLY.

**Reservations:** (914) 271-6228 MONDAY - FRIDAY 10 A.M. TO 4 P.M. APRIL - OCTOBER. 9 A.M. - 3 P.M. NOVEMBER - MARCH.

## KATONAH

ROUTE 22 NEAR ROUTE 35 — A large, new stucco Mediterranean style home, beautifully furnished on 4 landscaped acres with a 20 by 50 HEATED POOL. An oasis of privacy with decks and terraces. House has air conditioning, two fireplaces, projection screen TV, and VCR. It is minutes from Saw Mill Parkway, Interstate 684, Pepsico, IBM, and Caramoor. Host is a veterinarian; hostess speaks Dutch and German, enjoys gardening, cooking, needlework, and music. Two CATS and two DOGS also live here. A large country breakfast is served and no effort is spared to make your stay a fond memory. Deluxe accommodations include: A) first floor suite, double bed, private bath, and family room with projection screen TV, VCR, FIREPLACE, and terrace; and B) upstairs queen-sized bed, private bath. Bidets in both baths. Laundry facilities available. CHILDREN over 4 years old welcome.

**Rates:** A) SUITE $85 AND B) S $60, D $65 DAILY. A) $500 AND B) S OR D $300 WEEKLY.
**Reservations:** (914) 271-6228 MONDAY - FRIDAY 10 A.M. TO 4 P.M. APRIL - OCTOBER. 9 A.M. - 3 P.M. NOVEMBER - MARCH.

## MT. KISCO

An inviting Colonial home on 2 wooded acres, very convenient to Interstate 684 to White Plains or Danbury and the Northern Westchester Hospital. This home is furnished with many Victorian antiques and has a lovely grand PIANO. Host is a minister interested in people and travel, and is a collector of political buttons; hostess is a historic preservation consultant interested in architecture and music. Two CATS also live here. Accommodations include: A) double bed, private bath; and B) a high-riser in the music room that can accommodate two people. Laundry facilities and TV. Full breakfast served. Children welcome. Smoking permitted, but not in the bedrooms.
**Rates:** A & B) S $40, D $50 DAILY. S $210, D $280 WEEKLY.
**Reservations:** (914) 271-6228 MONDAY - FRIDAY 10 A.M. TO 4 P.M. APRIL - OCTOBER. 9 A.M. - 3 P.M. NOVEMBER - MARCH.

## NEW ROCHELLE

Summer soldiers and sunshine patriots, Colonial on original Thomas Paine farmland. It is a 30 minute train ride to Manhattan; 15 minutes to Connecticut, Long Island, or White Plains corporate centers. Host is a college professor; hostess operates an insurance business. Both enjoy sports, music, and cooking. Two teenagers live here. Home is very large with grand, spacious, beautifully decorated rooms with lots of antiques. PIANO. Close to Iona College of New Rochelle and Sara Lawrence College. Two guestrooms are on the third floor. Accommodations include: A) double bed, private bath; and B) two rooms with double bed, shared bath. Playpen and carriage are available. Full breakfast served. Laundry facilities and TV available. Fireplace in home. Children welcome.
**Rates:** A & B) S $45 & D $60 DAILY. ADDITIONAL CHILDREN $10 EACH DAILY. $315 WEEKLY.
**Reservations:** (914) 271-6228 MONDAY - FRIDAY 10 A.M. TO 4 P.M. APRIL - OCTOBER. 9 A.M. - 3 P.M. NOVEMBER - MARCH.

## WYKAGYL

Large Norman Tudor home once featured in *Better Homes and Gardens*. Hostess is a real estate salesperson and master bridge player. Four Shitzu DOGS also live here as well as a teenage daughter. An elaborate breakfast is served on weekends, simpler ones during the week. Guests are welcome to barbecue on the patio. Convenient to New Haven train (20 minutes to New York City, 15 minutes to Greenwich), near Sara Lawrence and Iona

colleges and a golf club. Accommodations include: A) queen-sized bed, twin beds, and shared bath; and B) twin beds, shared bath. TV and laundry facilities available. Children welcome.
**Rates:** A & B) S $50, D $65 DAILY. ADDITIONAL PERSONS $10 EACH DAILY. S $283.50, D $378 WEEKLY.
**Reservations:** (914) 271-6228 MONDAY - FRIDAY 10 A.M. TO 4 P.M. APRIL - OCTOBER. 9 A.M. - 3 P.M. NOVEMBER - MARCH.

## NORTH SALEM
### RURAL, NEAR IBM & PEPSI

An 1848 Colonial with greenhouse on 4 landscaped acres of trees, meadow, and pond with raft. Antiques abound and a number of Franklin stoves keep the house warm and cozy. Host is a computer specialist; hostess is a teller. Both enjoy birdwatching, gourmet cooking, and horticulture. Horse boarding facilities 3 miles away. Convenient to Union Carbide, IBM, and Pepsi. Private sitting room and twin beds, private bath. A teenager can be accommodated on sofabed. One DOG resides here. Laundry facilities, TV. Full breakfast served. CHILDREN over 12 welcome. SMOKING OK, but no cigars.
**Rates:** $50 DAILY. $350 WEEKLY.
**Reservations:** (914) 271-6228 MONDAY - FRIDAY 10 A.M. TO 4 P.M. APRIL - OCTOBER. 9 A.M. - 3 P.M. NOVEMBER - MARCH.

## NORTH TARRYTOWN
### SLEEPY HOLLOW

A large, lovely central hall Colonial in the heart of Sleepy Hollow country. Host is an international banker; hostess is French. She gives classes in cooking and wine. Neither smoke. Accommodations include a twin-bedded double room with private bath. Ideal for relocating executives. Hostess works and an early breakfast is served, otherwise guests help themselves during the week. Breakfast is set up and ready. Arrivals after 5:00 P.M. only. Close to restorations and many big corporations, such as IBM, General Foods, and Ciba Geigi. Fireplace, TV, and laundry facilities premises. SMOKING not permitted. CHILDREN under 12 not accepted.
**Rates:** S $45, D $55 DAILY. S $250, D $300 WEEKLY.
**Reservations:** (914) 271-6228 MONDAY - FRIDAY 10 A.M. TO 4 P.M. APRIL - OCTOBER. 9 A.M. - 3 P.M. NOVEMBER - MARCH.

## OSSINING

A beautifully decorated and layed out 150 room inn and conference center. Full buffet breakfast served. Indoor POOL, TENNIS, and racquetball courts on premises. All food made here, pastry chef, too. Convenient to Historic Hudson Valley (formerly Sleepy Hollow Restorations), West Point, IBM, White Plains (20 minutes). Hudson Valley

Airporter to all metro airports. Full bar and room service. Accommodations include choice of one queen bed, or two double beds. All rooms have private bath.
**Rates:** S $95, D $110, EXTRA CHILD $10 DAILY.
**Reservations:** (914) 271-6228 MONDAY - FRIDAY 10 A.M. TO 4 P.M. APRIL - OCTOBER. 9 A.M. - 3 P.M. NOVEMBER - MARCH.

## SPARTA

An 1824 Colonial on the walking tour of historical Sparta. Hostess teaches home economics and enjoys gardening, cooking. and tennis. One French POODLE is in residence. One room is available: A) it is twin bedded, has its own bath, and a winter Hudson River view; and B) a single bed in the den may be used for a child at an additional cost. Breakfast can be served outdoors weather permitting. Easily reached by train (walking distance of 1/2 mile) and near movies, restaurants, and shops. Laundry facilities and TV available. SMOKERS not welcome, children welcome.
**Rates:** A) S $40, D $50 AND B) S $30 DAILY. ADDITIONAL CHILDREN $10 EACH DAILY. A) S $150, D $250 AND B) S $150 WEEKLY.
**Reservations:** (914) 271-6228 MONDAY - FRIDAY 10 A.M. TO 4 P.M. APRIL - OCTOBER. 9 A.M. - 3 P.M. NOVEMBER - MARCH.

A 1787 Georgian brick house with rounded front and marvelous antique furniture. Both bedrooms have canopied double beds with lace canopies, shared bath. One CAT resides here. Room has a FIREPLACE. Walk to public transportation and fine dining. Host teaches English and is active in the Historical Society. He goes to work early on weekdays. TV and laundry facilities. Full breakfast served. Children welcome.
**Rates:** A) S $35, D $50 AND B) S $40, D $60 DAILY. A) S $200, D $280 AND B) S $250, D $350 WEEKLY.
**Reservations:** (914) 271-6228 MONDAY - FRIDAY 10 A.M. TO 4 P.M. APRIL - OCTOBER. 9 A.M. - 3 P.M. NOVEMBER - MARCH.

## VILLAGE

ELLIS PLACE — An 1850 Greek Revival Victorian 20 room home now with many apartments. Accommodation include: A) an executive apartment with queen sofabed, private bath, equipped kitchen. B) A queen-bedded room with private bath is available in hostess' quarters. It will have a little kitchen. Hostess is music director and organist at St. Malachi's, the actors church in New York City. Full self-serve breakfast. Private entrance, fireplace, on bus line, and TV. One CAT resides here. CHILDREN over 18 welcome.
**Rates:** A & B) S $45, D $55 DAILY. S $270, D $330 WEEKLY.
**Reservations:** (914) 271-6228 MONDAY - FRIDAY 10 A.M. TO 4 P.M. APRIL - OCTOBER. 9 A.M. - 3 P.M. NOVEMBER - MARCH.

## PEEKSKILL

A historic 1770 Dutch Colonial farmhouse with four fireplaces. This house is on the original survey done for General Washington during the Revolutionary War. It has an above ground POOL. It is 20 minutes to West Point, and convenient to the Taconic Parkway. Accommodations include: A) doube bed, B) single bed which must be rented to the same party as they are adjoining and you must walk through B to A. Both share a family bath. Hosts have raised six children here, one of whom is a West Point graduate. An 11 year old still lives at home. No SMOKING or UNMARRIED COUPLES.
**Rates:** S $30, D $50, EXTRA CHILD $10 DAILY. S $200, D $280 WEEKLY.
**Reservations:** (914) 271-6228 MONDAY - FRIDAY 10 A.M. TO 4 P.M. APRIL - OCTOBER. 9 A.M. - 3 P.M. NOVEMBER - MARCH.

## RYE
## VILLAGE

CENTRAL AVENUE — An 1904 Edwardian home on lots of land, far from the road, backing on the Rye Nature Center. Host is self-employed; hostess is an administrative assistant. Both enjoy sailing and travel. One CAT also resides here. This home is filled with wonderful nooks and crannies all loaded with adorable collections of interesting things. A beautiful carved Victorian PIANO is a focal point. Convenient to Manhattanville College and SUNY at Purchase, as well as General Foods, Pepsi Cola, AT&T, and many other corporations, this home is within walking distance to Rye Village, fine dining, and terrific shopping. Accommodations include: A) double bed, private bath and B) suite with double bed, private bath, outdoor deck, upstairs living room with TV, VCR, and couches that do not open but could sleep two children comfortably. Fireplace in home. SMOKING in all rooms except bedrooms.
**Rates:** A & B) S $40, D $60; AND C) SUITE $85 DAILY. A & B) $200, D $300; C) SUITE $415 WEEKLY.
**Reservations:** (914) 271-6228 MONDAY - FRIDAY 10 A.M. TO 4 P.M. APRIL - OCTOBER. 9 A.M. - 3 P.M. NOVEMBER - MARCH.

A marvelous and large Georgian brick carriage house that has been converted with artful creativity. The home was just rebuilt with modern, all new utilities yet furnished with oak and marble floors and fine antiques. It has the quality of spacious luxury and includes an interesting library, a grand PIANO, sunfilled tea room, and a bubbling indoor hydraspa. Host is an investor, pilot, and architect; hostess is a teacher, pilot, and former model who enjoys serving elaborate breakfasts and morning trays of hot beverages and biscuits. Two sons in college are fairly fluent in Spanish and French. Two SAILBOATS are available with professional instruction. This home is only a half mile from the Long Island Sound; walk to town or to Playland for its amusement park and beach in summer or indoor ice skating yearround. Nearby are two free TENNIS courts, nature conservancy, churches, shops, bus, and railroad. Rye is the Amtrack stop for trains to major east coast cities and Canada and is a 45 minute ride to Manhattan. Convenient to all highways, clubs, and colleges. Accommodations include: A) large double bed with private bath, radio and TV and B) a large three room apartment. A DOG and CAT live here. A fireplace is in the home. Home is convenient to IBM, Pepsi, General Foods, and SUNY at Purchase.

**Rates:** A) S $60, D $75; AND B) S OR D $90 DAILY. ADDITIONAL ADULTS $15; ADDITIONAL CHILDREN $10 DAILY. A) S $300, D $375; AND B) $495 WEEKLY.
**Reservations:** (914) 271-6228 MONDAY - FRIDAY 10 A.M. TO 4 P.M. APRIL - OCTOBER. 9 A.M. - 3 P.M. NOVEMBER - MARCH.

## NEAR WESTCHESTER COUNTRY CLUB

A large and spacious but cozy Colonial on almost 2 acres with a lovely porch and lawn furniture. This home is beautifully decorated and has a comfortable den where the family sits around a blazing fireplace. Host is in advertising and enjoys racquetball, tennis, and skiing; hostess has a fashion background and enjoys many sports and cooking. She can speak a little Spanish. Convenient to the Hutchinson River Parkway, SUNY at Purchase, Interstate 287, New England Thruway, and Westchester Country Club. A RETRIEVER lives here. Accommodations include a double bed, private bath. Laundry facilities, TV. Two night minimum. Full breakfast served.
**Rates:** A S $50, D $55 DAILY.
**Reservations:** (914) 271-6228 MONDAY - FRIDAY 10 A.M. TO 4 P.M. APRIL - OCTOBER. 9 A.M. - 3 P.M. NOVEMBER - MARCH.

## HUDSON RIVER AREA

This 1870 Queen Anne Victorian has a panormaic view of Hudson River and Tappan Zee Bridge. Many Victorian antiques add to the flavor of a romantic past. Once part of the underground railroad, this home had secret rooms. Now one is a sunken tub. Hostess is a teacher and archeologist. There is a PIANO and CAT here. Convenient to Route 287, the Sleepy Hollow restorations, and Lyndhurst. Accommodations include: A) twin beds, private bath; B) double bed, private bath; C) two rooms with sofabed, shared bath; and D) twin beds, shared bath. Laundry facilities, fireplace, and TV. Full breakfast served. No CHILDREN under 6, however, infants okay, crib available. NO SMOKING.
**Rates:** A-D) S $50, D $70-$90 DAILY. S $295, D $425 WEEKLY.
**Reservations:** (914) 271-6228 MONDAY - FRIDAY 10 A.M. TO 4 P.M. APRIL - OCTOBER. 9 A.M. - 3 P.M. NOVEMBER - MARCH.

## WHITE PLAINS

A raised ranch style home which is a 5 minute drive to White Plains. Accommodations include twin beds, sitting room, private bath on guest level. Would prefer not to have unmarried couples as guests. TV and laundry facilities available. Full breakfast is served to guests. Located in the county center, this B&B is convenient to many corporations, fine stores, and restaurants and is 30 minutes by train to New York City. NO SMOKING.
**Rates:** S $40, D $50 DAILY. S $150, D $250 WEEKLY.
**Reservations:** (914) 271-6228 MONDAY - FRIDAY 10 A.M. TO 4 P.M. APRIL - OCTOBER. 9 A.M. - 3 P.M. NOVEMBER - MARCH.

## PACE UNIVERSITY

Turn of the century Victorian home with wraparound porch and swings. Beautifully furnished with many antiques and lovely fireplace in living room. Hostess speaks Italian, Polish, and Greek. She enjoys gardening and painting. Weekday guests preferred. Accommodations include: A) sofabed, private bath; B) queen-sized bed, private bath in apartment; and C) twin or king beds, private bath. TV. Full breakfast served. Children welcome. NO SMOKING.
**Rates:** A-C) S $60, D $60-$85 DAILY. S $350, D $420-$595 WEEKLY.
**Reservations:** (914) 271-6228 MONDAY - FRIDAY 10 A.M. TO 4 P.M. APRIL - OCTOBER. 9 A.M. - 3 P.M. NOVEMBER - MARCH.

## YONKERS

A 1910 Colonial with interesting artifacts exhibited throughout the house. Host is a design engineer who can speak some German; hostess tests recipes for Betty Crocker. Convenient to Seton Hall College, St. John's Hospital, the Hudson River Museum, and southern Westchester office park. Easy access to New York City by train or car. Accommodations include: A) queen-sized sofabed, TV, shared family bath; and B) highriser, TV, shared family bath. Full breakfast is served here. Refrigerator privileges and laundry facilities are optional extras. Pickup service is also available if needed. CHILDREN over 12 welcome. Smoking permitted.
**Rates:** A & B) S $45, D $55 DAILY. S $240, D $290 WEEKLY.
**Reservations:** (914) 271-6228 MONDAY - FRIDAY 10 A.M. TO 4 P.M. APRIL - OCTOBER. 9 A.M. - 3 P.M. NOVEMBER - MARCH.

# WESTERN NEW YORK
## BUFFALO

In the heart of Buffalo a 100 year old large historic Victorian style home, on tree-lined street, furnished most tastefully in antiques. Host is a banking executive; hostess is interested in crafts, tennis, and people. Very private setting for guests, a whole second floor, full bath and large sitting

room with television. Accommodations include: A) double bed; and B) two rooms with twin beds. Continental or full breakfast happily served. One DOG in residence. Easy walk to bus, subway, shopping, and galleries. Within 2 miles of Convention Center and sports arenas. Children over 10 welcome.
**Rates:** S $35, D $45 DAILY.
**Reservations:** (716) 283-4794 MONDAY THROUGH FRIDAY, 9:00 A.M. - 6:00 P.M.

## COLDEN
## SOUTH BUFFALO

Charming country mini estate, in the Boston Hills, 25 miles south of Buffalo and 50 miles from Niagara Falls. Winter offers Nordic and Alpine skiing (cross-country skiing free on hosts' trail) or snow mobiling 1 to 10 miles from the chalet. Spring, fall, and summer beautifully secluded countryside for hiking. Main attractions are the herb and flower gardens, ponds, herbtique gift shop, and greenhouse. Natural, country breakfast is served. Host is a medical doctor; hostess is an herbalist. Accommodations in a separate chalet include: A) three rooms, one bath, fully furnished kitchen, dining/living room, PIANO, pool table, and fireplace; and B) a rustic post and beam cabin in the woods that can accommodate two. Crib and high chair available. PETS WELCOME. Rowboat available. Children welcome. Smokers welcome.
**Rates:** A & B) S $35, D $45-$50 DAILY. $10 EXTRA FOR CHILDREN IN ROOM WITH PARENTS. CHALET MAY BE RENTED ON WEEKENDS WITHOUT BREAKFAST FOR $150.
**Reservations:** (716) 283-4794 MONDAY THROUGH FRIDAY, 9:00 A.M. - 6:00 P.M.

## LEWISTON
## NEAR NIAGARA FALLS

SOUTH FOURTH STREET — This gracious 150 year old Greek Revival home is beautifully furnished according to the period of the home. Large private guestrooms offer a veranda and FIREPLACE, lovely grounds and covered porches for relaxing before or after the theater. Artpark, New York State's performing arts complex, is just three blocks away. A short stroll to all of historic Lewiston, 15 minute drive to Niagara Falls. Host is an attorney; hostess is a homemaker with a home business. Breakfast might consist of hostess' homemade sausage among other family recipes and local specialties. Accommodations include: A) large master bedroom with queen-sized bed, FIREPLACE, private bath, and shower; and B) twin beds, private bath. Amenities include picnic table, antiques. bikes, and PIANO. Accessible by public transportation. Children welcome. No SMOKING in guestrooms.
**Rates:** S $25-$35, D $50-$55 DAILY.

**Reservations:** (716) 283-4794 MONDAY THROUGH FRIDAY, 9:00 A.M. -
6:00 P.M.

## NIAGARA FALLS

Enjoy a warm welcome in a comfortable, WATERFRONT family home
on a small residential island just 4 miles above Niagara Falls. Enjoy a
relaxing view of the river and conversation with knowledgeable hostess.
Hostess is a social worker who enjoys travel. Full breakfast served on
screened porch, weather permitting. Third floor rooms are private and
quiet, beautiful cool river breeze blows through on warm summer nights.
Accommodations include: A & B) two rooms with twin beds, shared bath
with guests. A crib and cot are available. Children welcome. SMOKING
permitted but not in the guestrooms.
**Rates:** A & B) S $30, D $40 DAILY.
**Reservations:** (716) 283-4794 MONDAY THROUGH FRIDAY, 9:00 A.M. -
6:00 P.M.

Walk to Niagara Falls, all its parks, attractions and two bridges to
Canada. Enjoy the beautiful stained and leaded glass windows in the large
recently renovated 1900s brick home. Host and hostess are long time
Niagara Falls residents and are anxious to help you enjoy your stay. Host
is an engineer; hostess is in real estate. Accommodations include: A) two
rooms with double bed, shared bath with guests; and B) twin beds, shared
bath with guests. Accessible by public transportation. NO CHILDREN.
SMOKING permitted but not in guestrooms.
**Rates:** A & B) S $30, D $40 DAILY.
**Reservations:** (716) 283-4794 MONDAY THROUGH FRIDAY, 9:00 A.M. -
6:00 P.M.

## YOUNGSTOWN

LOWER RIVER ROAD — This beautifully furnished 150 year old
WATERFRONT country home provides an almost idyllic getaway. It is
15 minutes north of Niagara Falls, 30 minutes to Buffalo, and features
huge verandas overlooking the lower Niagara River. Accommodations
include: A) double bed, private bath; and B) double bed, private bath and
one twin loft room. Hosts enjoy sailing and travel. A DOG and CAT are
also in residence. Amenities include a PIANO and cross-country skiing
nearby. CHILDREN over 10 welcome. NONSMOKERS preferred.
**Rates:** A) S $35, D $45-$50; AND B) S $45. D $50-$55 DAILY.
**Reservations:** (716) 283-4794 MONDAY THROUGH FRIDAY, 9:00 A.M. -
6:00 P.M.

# PENNSYLVANIA

## AMISH COUNTRY
### ATGLEN

At the end of a winding farmland, atop the knoll sits a green trimmed, white farmhouse. Your energetic hosts welcome you into a kitchen full of the smell of apple dumplings, shoefly pie, rising bread dough, and mincemeat bubbling on the stove. This Mennonite couple have been B&B hosts since 1950, when they offered accommodations through the Pennsylvania Farm Council. Your rooms have hand-hooked rugs and patchwork pillows and quilts, all made by your hostess. The produce of the farm, fresh eggs, chickens, fresh sausage, ham, and garden vegetables provide the makings of her bountiful family style breakfasts and dinners. This is a working farm with cattle, corn, and hay crops, where you may pick your own blackberries in season or swim in an old time swimming hole. Located on the Lancaster County Line, within easy reach of Lancaster and Pennsylvania German countryside. It is 30 minutes to Chadds Ford. Little Baker's Dinner Theatre is 15 minutes away. Amish buggy rides and sleigh rides nearby. Discount stores and antique shops abound. Accommodations include: A) twin beds, shared bath with guests, fan cooled; B) double bed, shared bath with guests, fan cooled; and C) bunk house, two doubles in one room and pullout sofa. No heat or cooling. Full breakfast and DINNER family style. German spoken. Off-street parking. Will pickup at station. Resident DOG and CATS. NO SMOKING OR DRINKING.
**Rates:** A & B) S $35, D $45 DAILY.
**Reservations:** (215) 688-1633 MONDAY THROUGH FRIDAY 9:00 TO 5:00.

### THORNDALE

This rural homestead of the 1800s sits quietly and majestically in the hills of Chester County. Post and Beams with elegant antiques are the theme of this lovely Colonial home. Your hosts are avid travelers, fresh water fishermen, sailors, and computer enthusiasts. Your guestrooms are roomy and pleasant, providing ample room to sit and relax before the fireplace. Easy access to the Pennsylvania Turnpike (5 miles), a 30 minute drive to Lancaster, Brandywine Valley, or Valley Forge, and 1/2 hour from Amish country. German and French are spoken here. Accommodations include: A) first floor, queen-sized, four poster bed, FIREPLACE, antiques, louvered French doors to patio; and B) first floor, queen sofabed, woodburning stove, desk, Iranian rugs. Powder room on first floor and share second floor bath with family. Greenhouse with HOT TUB attached to home. Need car. CAT and outside DOGS in residence. SMOKING NOT PERMITTED.
**Rates:** A & B) S $40, D $50 DAILY.

**Reservations:** (215) 688-1633 MONDAY THROUGH FRIDAY 9:00 TO 5:00.

## BARTRAM'S GARDENS
### DREXEL HILL

This big, rambling white house has nurtured a family of five sons and daughters and is now a favorite visiting spot for your hostess' grandchildren with its large fenced yard. You are sure to be comfortable here. It is located in an established suburban residential neighborhood, with good, inexpensive restaurants and a shopping area nearby. Your full breakfast will be served in the light and airy dining room. Your hostess is an elementary teacher, so on workdays, late sleepers may serve themselves breakfast. She also enjoys gardening, golf, and bridge and especially making guests feel at home. European travel has been a sabbatical pasttime. Located on southwest edge of the city, 5 minutes from junction to Routes 1 and 3. Trolley stop across the street. It is a 25 minute ride to Center City. 15 minutes to University of Pennsylvania campus, 20 minutes to Ridley Creek State Park with Colonial plantation, and 30 minutes to Chadds Ford and Valley Forge. Accommodations include: A) single bed, shared bath; and B & C) two rooms with double bed, shared bath. Crib available. Air conditioning and TV available. Off-street parking. Children welcome. NO SMOKING.
**Rates:** A-C) S $25, D $35 DAILY.
**Reservations:** (215) 688-1633 MONDAY THROUGH FRIDAY 9:00 TO 5:00.

## LANSDOWNE

A large shaded stone house on a quiet street in an established community. Cool porch invites you inside where comfortable rooms are furnished with extraordinary antiques, one of which is your canopied eighteenth century bed. Classical music is loved here and there is a grand PIANO in the living room where a collection of brasses is displayed on the large stone fireplace. Your host, who is an accountant and member of the Scottish Historical Society and Dickens' Fellowship, will guide visitors on weekends to outlying attractions of the city. He will also meet guests at the railroad station or airport if prearranged. German spoken here. Full breakfast, self-serve on workdays. Home is 1 1/2 miles west of city limits. "D" bus from Center City (35 minutes) within 1 mile. Other public transportation within 1 1/2 blocks. By car: accessible from Interstate 95, US 1, and US 13. Major colleges nearby: University of Pennsylvania, Swarthmore, Bryn Mawr, Rosemont, and Haverford. Accommodations include: A & B) two rooms on second floor, double bed; and C) third floor, twin beds. Private or semiprivate baths. Two rollaways available. Off-street parking. Children and PETS WELCOME. No SMOKING in bedrooms.
**Rates:** A-C) S $20, D $25 DAILY.

**Reservations:** (215) 688-1633 MONDAY THROUGH FRIDAY 9:00 TO 5:00.

# BIRCHRUNVILLE

Plush farmland and horse farms abound amid these historical acres. Proximity to Valley Forge National Park, Wyeth Museum, Winterthur, Longwood Gardens, and Lancaster Amish country. Country restaurants, local post office, and general store nearby. Cross-country skiing, horseback riding, and hiking possible, as well as antique shops tucked away at nearly every crossroads. Host is in the insurance business and enjoys cross-country skiing and riding. Accommodations include: private carriage house with Great Room, fireplace (nonworking); bedroom with twin beds and shower bath. Small refrigerator but no cooking facilities. POOL. Horse boarding for extra fee. Continental basket breakfast.
**Rates:** S $65, D $75 DAILY.
**Reservations:** (215) 688-1633 MONDAY THROUGH FRIDAY 9:00 TO 5:00.

# BLUE BELL

Stately brick posts guard the driveway entrance to this solid turn of the century home. Your hostess left during World War II to become a WAC, married an army officer, and returned to the homestead with her family. Here she became involved with her first love, art, at the local community art center. Now, with her two college age children, she welcomes you to share her home. Full breakfasts feature homemade jams and jellies. Your hostess is happy to offer tour suggestions. She will also pack picnic lunches and give guide service for a modest fee if prearranged. Located off Skippack Pike (Route 73); 10 minutes from exit 25, Pennsylvania Turnpike (Interstate 276); 10 minutes to Chestnut Hill commuter train to city. Good restaurants, shopping, and unique Colonial homes are nearby. Accommodations include: A) twin beds, private bath, TV, breeze-cooled; and B) single bed, shared guest bath. PETS WELCOME. Resident DOG and CAT. French spoken. Off-street parking. Swimming POOL. Children WELCOME.
**Rates:** A) S $25, D $35 AND B) S 25 DAILY.
**Reservations:** (215) 688-1633 MONDAY THROUGH FRIDAY 9:00 TO 5:00.

# BRANDYWINE VALLEY

A section of southeastern Pennsylvania and northern Delaware near Philadelphia and Wilmington that is visually characterized by its rolling green hills and valleys and rocky streams, with terrain good for pasturing dairy herds, sheep, and horses. The Brandywine River flows southwest from its beginnings near the Amish country down to the Delaware River at Wilmington. The area was the setting for Swedish settlements, then the William Penn land grants followed by the pre-Revolutionary Colonial settlements. It was the scene for numerous Revolutionary battles. The houses that were built are still standing and are lovingly cared for by the contemporary inhabitants of this historic land. The "Brandywine School" of art has become synonymous with American art. The Brandywine River Museum at Chadds Ford houses collections by the famous artists of this school. The region is equally famous for its bequeathed treasures from the Du Pont family, the renowned Longwood Gardens, Winterthur Museum, and numerous estate museums.

## BERWYN

An 1805 typical American home has been reconstructed internally to provide for the conveniences of modern living while retaining the warmth and charm of random width floors and oversized windows. The four new guestrooms and baths are light and airy and have queen-sized, twin and youth beds. A crib is also available. Inground POOL. PIANO. Pool table. NO SMOKING.
**Rates:** $65 DAILY.
**Reservations:** (215) 692-4575 NOON TO 4 P.M. MONDAY THROUGH FRIDAY.

## CHADDS FORD

UNHOSTED log cottage. A newly restored 1700 guesthouse on an important historic estate on the Brandywine River. The grounds include two large, stocked LAKES, paths, lawns, and ancient trees. The guesthouse has a queen bedroom and bath, living room, and fully stocked kitchen with dining area. Inground POOL, Air conditioned. NO CHILDREN. NO SMOKING.
**Rates:** $150 DAILY. MINIMUM TWO NIGHT STAY.
**Reservations:** (215) 692-4575 NOON TO 4 P.M. MONDAY THROUGH FRIDAY.

## GLEN MILLS

A historic Pennsylvania landmark private inn on 55 acres of lawns, old trees, and rolling fields of flowers and pastures. There are thoroughbreds, sheep, geese, ducks, and chickens contributing to the estate's gentle ambiance. There are nine guestrooms and suites, and four guesthouses for one or two couples. Cribs available. This exclusive, elegant accommodation has been featured recently in *Mid-Atlantic Country* magazine *Country* magazine, and *Colonial Homes*. Inground POOL. Air conditioned. FIREPLACE in bedroom. HORSE stall. PETS WELCOME BY PERMISSION ONLY. Children welcome. Smoking permitted.
**Rates:** A) $85; B) $100; C) $125; AND D) $150 AND D) $200 DAILY.

**Reservations:** (215) 692-4575 NOON TO 4 P.M. MONDAY THROUGH FRIDAY.

## LANDENBURG

A meticulously restored 1690 William Penn land grant estate, this private inn offers four rooms, also suites, with private baths in the manor house and three newly constructed guesthouses for one or two couples with complete kitchen and laundry facilities. Inground POOL. Air conditioned. HOT TUB. FIREPLACE in bedroom. French, German, and Spanish are spoken here. Children welcome. NO SMOKING.
**Rates:** A) $85; B) $95; C) $150; AND D) $200 DAILY.
**Reservations:** (215) 692-4575 NOON TO 4 P.M. MONDAY THROUGH FRIDAY.

## MARSHALLTON

This historic eighteenth century stone Pennsylvania farmhouse on the east branch of the Brandywine River, filled with charming Chester County antiques, offers private accommodations for guests up a private staircase to a charming double bedroom and bath with sitting room and FIREPLACE/antique stove. Hosts are both brokers. CHILDREN over 5 welcome. NO SMOKING.
**Rates:** $125 DAILY.
**Reservations:** (215) 692-4575 NOON TO 4 P.M. MONDAY THROUGH FRIDAY.

## MENDENHALL

This newly constructed house in the Williamsburg style accommodations include: A) queen-sized suite with FIREPLACE and private bath; and B) twin-bedded room with private bath. The hosts' breakfast recipes have been published recently. The host is a research engineer. German is spoken here. One toy POODLE resides here. A daughter and son, 11 and 8 respectively, live here. Inground POOL. AC. NO SMOKING.
**Rates:** A) $65 AND B) $75 DAILY.
**Reservations:** (215) 692-4575 NOON TO 4 P.M. MONDAY THROUGH FRIDAY.

## WAWA

An elegant Georgian mansion on the Pennsylvania Register of Historic Places, this 30 acre estate has been home to the host family since it was built at the beginning of the nineteenth century. The beautiful gardens are overseen by the host/chatelaine, a Philadelphia Flower Show blue ribbon winner. This exclusive accommodation offers commodious and comfortable rooms for guests. French is spoken here. Air conditioned. PIANO. Suites available. Also cribs and cots. NO SMOKING.

**Rates:** $85 DAILY.
**Reservations:** (215) 692-4575 NOON TO 4 P.M. MONDAY THROUGH FRIDAY.

## WEST CHESTER
## HISTORIC SECTION

On the National Register of Historic Places, this elegant three story brick "in towne" house offers four bedrooms (two to a floor with bath) and a guest common room furnished with family Chester County antiques. Cribs and cots available. Inground POOL. JACUZZI. VCR. NO SMOKING.
**Rates:** $75 DAILY.
**Reservations:** (215) 692-4575 NOON TO 4 P.M. MONDAY THROUGH FRIDAY.

The interior of this home is decorated with the hosts' collection of antiques and art work. The original house of 1825 reflects the spirit of the early nineteenth century. Located on Route 202 beside a 700 acre farm. Convenient to Brandywine, Winterthur, and Longwood Gardens. Each guestroom has a complimentary decanter of wine. Breakfast in the old dining room or on the screened porch with its view of rolling hills. You may join your hosts in the family room if you wish. Your hosts are interested in art. Host is a professional artist/painter and a retired art teacher; hostess has served as a docent at Winterthur and Rockwood Museums. They are also very interested in travel, having traveled throughout most of Western Europe. Some German is spoken. Accommodations include: A) double bed, pine floors, no closet, shared bath; B) double bed, antique quilt, shared bath; and C) double bed, desk, shared bath. Sitting room with period furniture, phone, and TV available to all guestrooms. A DOG and a CAT are in residence but do not go upstairs. No SMOKING in the bedrooms. May smoke on porch.
**Rates:** A-C) S $40, D $50 DAILY.
**Reservations:** (215) 688-1633 MONDAY THROUGH FRIDAY 9:00 TO 5:00.

Situated on a knoll curved round by a country road, this gracious "summer home," sheltered by ancient trees, stands serenely welcoming. High ceilings and tall windows bring cool breezes in summer while wintertime guests gather in the den with its crackling fire. Third floor bedrooms are spacious and airy, furnished with almost antique collectibles. Summertime relaxing is a joy around the beautifully landscaped POOL. Your host, a recently retired executive from a large corporation, is a cook of no mean talent and will make you feel at home immediately. It is 1 mile from town limits and West Chester University. Nearby is Brandywine Valley and Longwood gardens. Accommodations include: A & B) two rooms with double bed, share bath; and C) twin beds, shared

bath. Fan cooled. One family or compatible group only. Swimming POOL.
Full breakfast. Children welcome.
**Rates:** A-C) S $35, D $45 DAILY.
**Reservations:** (215) 688-1633 MONDAY THROUGH FRIDAY 9:00 TO
5:00.

Country roads take you to this serene setting. A winding lane is graced
with nursery stock as you approach this 1748 Pennsylvania farmhouse.
There are oak hand-hewn floors, walkin fireplaces, and the slate floors
are from an old railroad station. There is a pond and the guestrooms are
Colonial with a tiny working fireplace and antiques. Hospitality is a
trademark of your hosts and you may have a sing along in the parlor.
Breakfast may be a surprise of cinnamon buns or regional fare. A paradise
for nature lovers as you can swim, canoe, ice skate, cross-country ski,
or hike on this property. Host is a landscape artist; hostess is a teacher
whose hobbies are antiques and house history. Convenient to Winterthur,
Longwood, and Brandywine. Accommodations include: A) first floor,
private wing with twin beds, private bath, TV, air conditioning; B) second
floor, twin spool beds, marbletop dresser, share hall bath, FIREPLACE;
and C) second floor, double sleigh bed, FIREPLACE, TV, Persian rug.
Also auxiliary room for child with single bed, share hall bath. POND
swimming. CATS and DOGS in residence. SMOKING permitted in
common area.
**Rates:** A-C) S $50, D $60 DAILY.
**Reservations:** (215) 688-1633 MONDAY THROUGH FRIDAY 9:00 TO
5:00.

## UNIONVILLE

A country lane is edged by a Post and Rail fence. On the left a clipped
lawn is graced with 150 year old spruces, sycamores, oaks, and boxwoods.
On the right is an apple orchard, trellised grape arbor, barn, and rolling
pasture beyond. This white-washed stone farmhouse was built in 1700.
As the seventh family to live here, your hosts have lovingly restored the
lands and home, exposing hand pegged doors and original locks and
hardware. Antique touches are throughout the home. Your hosts'
avocations include raising and racing harness bred and dressage horses.
They will serve you a country style breakfast, possibly including home
fries, "real" French toast, local berries, and mushrooms. An avid
birdwatcher, the hostess is happy to take guests on a tour of their bird
trails. Located 5 minutes from West Chester, 2 1/2 miles from Unionville,
2 miles from Longwood Gardens, 2 miles off Routes 1 and 202 south.
Chadds Ford 4 miles, Brandywine River canoeing and tubing a quarter
mile. Excellent country road biking. Horseback riding and hot air balloon
rides arranged. Accommodations include: A) second floor, double bed,
private stall/shower bath, radio; and B) private back stairs, double canopy

bed, share tub/shower bath with host family, TV sitting room, air conditioned. Resident COLLIE, CATS, and HORSES. Double hide-a-bed in kitchen. Stalls for boarding horses. Off-street parking. CHILDREN welcome with sleeping bags. NO SMOKING in house.
**Rates:** S $50, D $60 DAILY.
**Reservations:** (215) 688-1633 MONDAY THROUGH FRIDAY 9:00 TO 5:00.

# BUCKS COUNTY
## CHURCHVILLE

This modern Colonial style home is situated in a picturesque rural area. From the porched entrance, you will enter a cheerful flagstone floored foyer. Your large, comfortable room is at the top of the stairs and has its own tiled bath. Your hostess is a gourmet cook and promises you a delicious breakfast. You are invited to relax in the family room, one entire wall of which is a stone fireplace graced by the family's heirloom spinning wheel. Tennis, golf, and a swim club are nearby. There is a park for hiking, biking, and canoeing. A racquetball club is also in the area. Access from US 1 and PA 232. It is 20 minutes to Peddler's Village; 15 minutes to New Hope; 20 minutes to northeast Philadelphia; and 45 minutes to Center City. Near Philmont Dinner Theater. Accommodations include: A) double bed, shared bath with guests, air conditioning, TV; and B) double bed, shared bath with guests. Rollaway available. Easy street parking. No SMOKING in house.
**Rates:** A & B) S $35, D $45 DAILY.
**Reservations:** (215) 688-1633 MONDAY THROUGH FRIDAY 9:00 TO 5:00.

## LANGHORNE

At the end of a long drive bordered by century old trees stands a 1682 field stone farmhouse, built by Nicolas Wain, who accompanied William Penn in his fleet of 23 ships to our shores. This house was the site of the first Friends Meeting in Bucks County and Penn was known to have attended. Your guestrooms are decorated with warm Colonial prints and furniture handcrafted by your talented hosts. The "window in the wall" from the original construction shows the various stages of restoration. Handmade Pennsylvania Dutch quilts, random width pine floors, and beamed ceilings abound in this home. Your hosts may serve you breakfast in front of a 250 year old walkin fireplace. Breakfast will, in season, include fresh raspberries, blueberries, or strawberries from their large fruit and vegetable garden. Host is a food consultant. It is 3 miles to Sesame Street Park, 15 miles to New Hope, 10 miles to Washington's Crossing and Peddler's Village, and 6 miles to Tyler State Park. Accommodations include: A) double canopy bed, crafted by host, shared full bath; and B)

double bed, shared full bath. Outdoor CATS, resident DOG. German spoken. Off-street parking.
**Rates:** A & B) S $50, D $60 DAILY.
**Reservations:** (215) 688-1633 MONDAY THROUGH FRIDAY 9:00 TO 5:00.

## NEW HOPE
## DOYLESTOWN

As you approach this white stone farmhouse, your eyes rise to the date stone, "1819." You enter the room of today's home, but the feeling is of the warmth and busyness of the Colonial farmhouse kitchen. The room is dominated by the warm wood tones of a long trestle table echoed in the hand finished barnwood paneling of the fireplace wall. Old wooden and tin farm implements and artifacts are suspended from the exposed beams of the ceiling. Your host is an experienced teacher of industrial arts, but his heart is in antiques, particularly pie safes, which, with his wife and teenaged son, he buys and refinishes for sale. As natives of this Colonially farmed picturesque area, your hosts are happy to share their knowledge and expertise. It is 5 miles north of Doylestown, off PA 611; 8 miles to Peddler's Village; 12 miles to Peace Valley Pond; and 7 miles to Mercer Museum. Accommodations include: A) second floor, double bed, shared bath with guests, TV, fan cooled; B) second floor, den type room, antique double bed, woodburning stove, cot available, fan cooled, shared bath with guests; and C) first floor, double room, bath, and kitchenette. PETS WELCOME. Resident CAT. Off-street parking. Full breakfast. Coffee pot always on. CHILDREN WELCOME.
**Rates:** A-C) S $40, D $52 DAILY.
**Reservations:** (215) 688-1633 MONDAY THROUGH FRIDAY 9:00 TO 5:00.

## YARDLEY
## SESAME PLACE

French country ambience and casual living lie within this clapboard and brick Colonial community home. Young hosts, with two small boys, welcome you to their creative living place. Host is an insurance manager and also an accomplished sailing buff; hostess is a gourmet cook, with visually apparent interior design talents. Breakfast may be served in a glassed-in breezeway filled with plants, with views of the POOL, screened porch, and handsome hand crafted pottery filled kitchen. It is 20 minutes to New Hope, Peddler's Village, and Princeton; and 45 minutes to center of Philadelphia. Golfing and tennis facilities nearby. Your charmingly authentic country French and antique pine room beckons you and overlooks the backyard. Accommodations include: A) double bed, shared bath; and B) twin beds, shared bath. Crib available. TV and air conditioning. Children welcome. NO SMOKING.

**Rates:** A & B) S $35, D $45 DAILY.
**Reservations:** (215) 688-1633 MONDAY THROUGH FRIDAY 9:00 TO 5:00.

## GREAT LAKES
## NORTH EAST

This inn is an outstanding example of Colonial Revival architecture. It was built in 1929 with great attention to detail in the leaded windows, transoms, fireplace, and woodwork. The rooms have been decorated with antiques and collectibles, carefully selected from the hosts' European travels and years of patient collecting. Beautiful gardens and a lakeside park surround the inn. It is 2 miles from North East with its small shops and village green. World famous Chatauqua Institution is just a short drive away. The local wineries and fruit stands are always a good attraction. The inn is on Route 89 North just off Routes 5 and 20 and Interstate 90. Accommodations include: A) king/twin with private bath; B) double bed, private bath; and C) two rooms with double beds, shared bath. Full breakfast included. The host is the headmaster of a day school; your hostess is the innkeeper. Dutch is spoken here. A CAT is in residence here. SMOKING permitted in the solarium. Guests are discouraged from including young CHILDREN and pets.
**Rates:** A & B) S $35, D $45; AND C) S $25, D $35 DAILY.
**Reservations:** (412) 367-8080 MONDAY THROUGH FRIDAY 9:00 A.M. TO 5:00 P.M.

## GREATER PHILADELPHIA
## CHESTNUT HILL

A historically certified home, one of the "Spite Houses," built, according to legend, with their backs to their neighbors, this five story home and its owner are a joy for the history buff! The home is comfortably furnished with warmth and antiques. There is a flagstone patio and fireplace, as well as a grand PIANO and the dining room has an original soap stone sink in the Butler's Pantry. Your hostess is an energetic and informed lady, a former museum council president and retired from the Historical Society. Located in the Mt. Airy area, 1 block to West Chestnut Hill train line, 23 minutes to Suburban Station, 1 block to Spring Garden College, and the Lutheran Seminary. Accommodations include: A) third level master bedroom with Lincoln period high double bed, Morris chair, shared bath (no shower); B) fourth level pineapple cherry poster beds, shared bath (no shower); and C) twin brass beds with sink in room, shared bath (no shower). Street parking, hostess smokes.
**Rates:** A-C) S $40, D $50 DAILY.
**Reservations:** (215) 688-1633 MONDAY THROUGH FRIDAY 9:00 TO 5:00.

## JENKINTOWN

Stone Victorian just off main thoroughfare. Walk through traditional double glass doors into a high ceilinged, oak paneled vestibule. The hosts have glass collections and the furniture is accented with old time linens, lace and crochet, handmade by your hostess. Outside your second floor room hangs an enormous quilt—each square hand done by friends and family as an anniversary gift. Brilliant colors, Victorian print wallpaper, and restored 20s furniture. A full breakfast (in summer) will include fresh picked berries and vegetables from your host's large productive garden and flowers will be on the table. Your host is a chrysanthemum specialist. It is a 5 minute walk to train station, 15 minutes to Chestnut Hill, 25 minutes to Center City, and 35 minutes to New Hope. Close to Beaver College, Temple University, Penn State, and Ogontz campus. Accommodations include: A) second floor, double bed with sitting room, double hide-a-bed, private bath, TV, air conditioning (shared bath with family if more than four nights); and B) two rooms on third floor, single bed, shared bath. Third floor is warm in summer. SMOKING NOT PERMITTED.
**Rates:** A) S $30, D $40; AND B) S $30 DAILY.
**Reservations:** (215) 688-1633 MONDAY THROUGH FRIDAY 9:00 TO 5:00.

## MAIN LINE

Stately elegance describes this large pre-Revolutionary home which is centrally located to Villanova University and Valley Forge Park. Oversized rooms and high ceilings easily accommodate the magnificent antique furnishings. A large, bright, and sunny third floor guestroom beckons you to make yourself at home. Accommodations include: A) comfortable chairs to relax in front of the TV, and two double beds and a hide-a-bed make it as perfect for the whole family as for the individual traveler desiring extra space. The private adjoining bath is complete with a small refrigerator. B) Two additional rooms, one on the second floor and the other on the third, are comfortably arranged for the single traveler. Features include an antique sleigh bed, desks, built-in bookshelves. TVs, and private baths. Your host and hostess have lived in France and speak "rusty French." If your schedule permits, they will enjoy preparing for you a full gourmet breakfast to be served in their elegant dining room or on the porch. The backyard POOL is also available for a quick dip during the summer months. Resident DOG and CATS. Host is a financial advisor; hostess is a lawyer. A 17 year old son lives at home. Children welcome.
**Rates:** A) S $50, D $60; AND B) S $45 DAILY.
**Reservations:** (215) 687-3565 9 A.M. TO 6 P.M. MONDAY THROUGH SATURDAY. NOON TO 6 P.M. ON SUNDAY.

## PHILADELPHIA

Open an "iron grid" gate and step down through a terraced yard filled with roses, flowering shrubs, banana plants, and apple and cherry trees. A heavy door leads you into the paneled and stained glass windowed vestibule of this turn-of-the-century home. This is the manor built by a Philadelphia wood entrepreneur in 1860. Your hosts have restored this home to its former elegance of polished oak carvings, marble fireplace, gaslight, and period furniture. Your quarters are separated from the rest of the house by arched glass double doors. It is a master suite of rooms with complete privacy. On weekends your hosts will add "light as air" biscuits to their adequate Creole breakfast menu. Located 1 block from train station. It is 20 minutes to Center City, and 15 minutes to Chestnut Hill. Near Einstein Medical Center. Accommodations include private wing on second floor: A) double bed; B) sofabed; and C) alcove room with double bed. Shared full bath. Air conditioning. Two resident CATS and three resident DOGS. Louisiana breakfast. Children welcome.
**Rates:** A-C) S $35, D $45 DAILY.
**Reservations:** (215) 688-1633 MONDAY THROUGH FRIDAY 9:00 TO 5:00.

## ALIAN MARKET

Charming tiny row house with great knowledgeable hosts. Host was born in Japan; hostess goes to Italy every summer for the opera season and hosts Philadelphia Opera Company guests. Italian and Spanish are spoken here. Pennsylvania Hospital 4 blocks away, also Italian Street Market. Accommodations include: A) third floor, twin beds, shared bath; and B) single with trundle bed, shared bath. Air conditioning, TV. Free parking 3 blocks away. Full breakfast served. Children welcome. NO SMOKING.
**Rates:** A) S $35, D $40; AND B) S $35 DAILY.
**Reservations:** (215) 688-1633 MONDAY THROUGH FRIDAY 9:00 TO 5:00.

## ANTIQUE ROW

Complete third floor privacy awaits the guest in this townhouse located along Antique Row and also within walking distance of the Historic District. Simply, yet tastefully furnished, the guestroom is bright and inviting with double bed accommodations, TV, and telephone. Sliding glass doors lead to a deck where you can relax and enjoy the city skyline and the beauty of the patio gardens below. With private adjoining bath and full breakfast, this accommodation could not be more perfect for the business traveler or the long-term guest. Hostess is a school psychologist. PETS WELCOME. Two CATS reside here. Children welcome.
**Rates:** S $45, D $55 DAILY.

**Reservations:** (215) 687-3565 9 A.M. TO 6 P.M. MONDAY THROUGH
SATURDAY. NOON TO 6 P.M. ON SUNDAY.

## BALA CYNWYD

The location of this comfortable, suburban home provides easy access to
both Center City attractions and to Main Line universities. Two second
floor guest accommodations offer a private suite arrangement for the
family traveling together or may be reserved separately. Accommodations
include: A) one bright and sunny double that features an antique brass
bed, TV and vanity; and B) smaller double available across the private
hallway. Shared bath. Port-a-crib available for the family traveling with
infant. Your host, an artist, displays many of his originals throughout the
home. If you recognize your hostess, it may be from the many magazine
and TV ads for which she has modeled. Be sure to see her scrapbook.
Continental plus breakfast. Resident DOG. VCR. Children welcome.
**Rates:** A) S $50, D $55; AND B) S $40, D $50 DAILY.
**Reservations:** (215) 687-3565 9 A.M. TO 6 P.M. MONDAY THROUGH
SATURDAY. NOON TO 6 P.M. ON SUNDAY.

## CENTER CITY

The proper Colonial facade of this home is incongruous to the
Contemporary design within. Purchased as a shell by its present owner
whose clever architect has retained the 170 year old brick walls, the
fireplaces, staircases and a few sound original beams, and has added a
"greenhouse"—a large window in the back. Your hostess, a psychotherapist
who works in a children's hospital, is an established resident of the
neighborhood and will be happy to advise you with tour plans or choices
among the many excellent restaurants in the area. Located near Society
Hill and Historic District. Accommodations include on the third floor,
double bed, private bath, air conditioning, TV. Full breakfast. Arrivals:
weekdays after 6:30 P.M. NO SMOKING.
**Rates:** S $60, D $65 DAILY.
**Reservations:** (215) 688-1633 MONDAY THROUGH FRIDAY 9:00 TO
5:00.

Gracing one of Philadelphia's most prestigious streets, this is a many
leveled 1860 historically certified townhouse. Classical music pervades.
Original paintings and graphics, plus an extensive arts library are shared
with guests by your hosts, whose vocations and home reflect their artistic
involvement. Polished pine floors, country prints, and furnishings in your
accommodations are warmly touched with antique linens and basketry
from your hostess' fine collections. The surprise of a chilled carafe of
fresh chilled juice, spiced tea or sherry, a filled ice bucket, a delectable
sweet on the pillow of a turned down bed, or breakfast in a flower filled

city garden return guests to the elegance of eighteenth century Philadelphia. Near museums, bus to Independence Hall. Centrally located within minutes of all Philadelphia's cultural and historic attractions. It is 35 minutes to Valley Forge. Bus stop half block away. Airport 15 minutes. Accommodations include: A) second floor, double bed (oversize antique— 1820 sleigh bed), private attached bath, air conditioning; B) third floor, twin beds, share bath with one room; and C) double bed, share bath, breeze/fan cooled. Street parking or lot nearby (3 blocks). CAT in residence. CHILDREN over 12 welcome. NO SMOKING.
**Rates:** A & B) S OR D $70 DAILY.
**Reservations:** (215) 688-1633 MONDAY THROUGH FRIDAY 9:00 TO 5:00.

This 100 year old home is furnished attractively but unpretentiously; the living room walls and shelves are showcases of the artistic products of the hands of talented children and friends. Beveled glass French doors and PIANO overlook the outdoors. Your hostess is a teacher of elementary aged children with special problems and is an inveterate traveler. She has been a city resident for 20 years. It is a 15 minute bus ride from Center City. Walk to Presbyterian and University Hospitals, Armory, Civic Center, Drexel, and University of Pennsylvania. It is 15 minutes driving to Art Museum, Liberty Bell, rowing regattas, historic park houses. Accommodations include: A) second floor suite: large room, double bed, double hide-a-bed, private bath with shower, air conditioning, TV; B) one room, double bed, television, radio, semiprivate bath; and C) one small room with single bed, semiprivate bath. Street parking. Resident shaggy DOG. Full breakfast, self-serve weekdays. Infants and children welcome.
**Rates:** A & B) S $20, D $40; AND C) S $20 DAILY.
**Reservations:** (215) 688-1633 MONDAY THROUGH FRIDAY 9:00 TO 5:00.

## GERMANTOWN INSTITUTE

This magnificent stone manor home is at the top of Germantown hill. It is a 140 year old Victorian home. Step into a 14 foot ceilinged foyer through draped, double leaded glass doors, into European elegance, furnished with antiques and accented with memories of your hostess' world travels and with her commemoration of growing up on the continent. She is a former gymnast, ballerina, and teacher, and will offer her typical Hungarian breakfast in the cheery country kitchen, or out on the flower filled backyard patio. Germantown Hospital is 5 minutes away. Three historic Germantown houses are nearby. Chestnut Hill east train station is 5 minutes away, 20 minutes to Center City, Philadelphia. Short distance to Better Baby Institute (Institute for Human Potential). Accommodations include: A) second floor, double bed, private tub bathroom, sitting room, FIREPLACE, TV, air conditioning; and B) third floor, efficiency apartment

with C) one room twin beds, D) one room double bed, E) one room single bed. Efficiency kitchenette, dining area, and bath. TV and air conditioning. Sheltered parking. Resident DOG and finch. Hungarian and German spoken. Walk to train. For extra fee, hostess drives to Institute of Human Potential. CHILDREN over 12 on third floor only. NO SMOKING.
**Rates:** A-D) S $35, D $45; AND E) S $35 DAILY.
**Reservations:** (215) 688-1633 MONDAY THROUGH FRIDAY 9:00 TO 5:00.

## MT. AIRY

Located within minutes of Chestnut Hill and its charming shopping district, this magnificent 1901 English Tudor mansion has been featured in area newspapers and selected as a Chestnut Hill Art and Design Showhouse home. Four poster beds and winged back chairs suggest the sophisticated elegance that awaits you. The third floor "Dutch Room" recalls the cool and serene lifestyle of Holland with its Delft blue wall stencils, double four poster bed and additional Dutch bed cozily built into one wall and covered with white lace. A second third floor room is also tastefully appointed with a double four poster bed. A hall bath is shared by both rooms. Two elegant rooms are available on the second floor, one with queen bed accommodations and the other a double bed. A connecting bath with antique tub and shower serves these rooms. You are invited to relax in front of a fire in the library or engage in a lively game of billiards. A full gourmet breakfast is served in the dining room and be sure to ask your hosts about the interesting history of this home. A year old son lives here. Host is a hotel consultant. Children welcome.
**Rates:** S $50-$60, D $55-$65 DAILY.
**Reservations:** (215) 687-3565 9 A.M. TO 6 P.M. MONDAY THROUGH SATURDAY. NOON TO 6 P.M. ON SUNDAY.

## MAIN LINE
### ARDMORE

You will be greeted by your charming host at the solid front door of this 50 year old home. As the door closes, peek at the massive wrought iron lock and key. Your bedroom is furnished in California pine pieces. You are invited to watch TV or relax in the adjoining sitting room, where your hostess' green thumb is evident in the healthy plants grouped among the white wicker chairs and table. Two finches in a bamboo cage lend a busy, if exotic, touch. Breakfast on weekdays is self-serve. Blueberry pancakes are a specialty. An old hand at B&B travel through Europe, your host will be happy to help you with local attraction information or better still, trade travel yarns. Location is a western suburb of Philadelphia. By train, city is 20 minutes. Access from US 1, PA 3. Near St. Joseph's, Haverford, Bryn Mawr Hospital, and Merion Golf Club. Plush residential

area. Accommodations include a second floor suite, one room with queen-sized bed, attached parlor, and private bath. Two sleeping bags, cot available. Fan cooled. Off-street parking. Public tennis nearby. Children welcome.
**Rates:** S $40, D $50 DAILY.
**Reservations:** (215) 688-1633 MONDAY THROUGH FRIDAY 9:00 TO 5:00.

A modern townhouse with traditional French Provincial furnishings. Guest bath with French porcelain pedestal basin and mirrored full bath. Hostess excels in baking and is a grandmother with many interests. Backyard accessible from family room. Guests are welcome to lounge in family room or have use of the patio on nice days. Convenient location to all Main Line colleges and Center City. Breakfast strictly Kosher. Other special dietary meals may be arranged. Accommodations include: twin beds, private hall bath, crib. Need car. Street parking. A CAT is in residence. Children welcome. NO SMOKING.
**Rates:** S $40, D $50 DAILY.
**Reservations:** (215) 688-1633 MONDAY THROUGH FRIDAY 9:00 TO 5:00.

## BERWYN

This rambling 1770 field stone home, nestled in rolling pastureland, is one of the period houses in which farmers who tilled fields for Colonial landowners lived. The original house, "the keeping room," takes guests back three centuries, with exposed beam ceilings, walkin fireplace and tightwinder stairway to guest accommodations. Your talented hostess has deftly stenciled the walls of your rooms and retained the warmth of wide pine floors, rag rugs, and country primitive furnishings. Breakfast is served in the brick floored, multiglass windowed "garden" room. Your hostess is an equestrian and tennis player, extremely knowledgeable in the history of the area and the important events of the present as well. It is 3 minutes to historic Waynesborough; 15 minutes to Valley Forge National Park, Pennsylvania Turnpike exit 24; 5 minutes to train station; and 25 minutes to Center City and Brandywine Valley via Route 202. Accommodations include: A) queen-sized bed, shared hall bath; B) queen-sized bed, shared hall bath, FIREPLACE; C) suite: large room, king-sized bed, FIREPLACE with woodburning stove; and D) small room, 3/4 antique bed, connecting semiprivate bath. Trundle bed available. Fan cooled. Resident DOG. Use of "keeping room," with television, wet bar. Good turnout and pasture for one HORSE. NO SMOKING. Children welcome.
**Rates:** A-D) S $45, D $55-$65 DAILY.
**Reservations:** (215) 688-1633 MONDAY THROUGH FRIDAY 9:00 TO 5:00.

Over the kitchen table of this lovely suburban home is a stylized fabric picture of busy barnyard birds done in glowing colors, which was designed and embroidered by your hostess. It seems to symbolize the warmth, talent, and energy of this host family. The hosts' sons have gone to college, so there is ample room for guests, who have always been welcome. Host is a management consultant; hostess is a guidance counselor; both enjoy sports, especially golf. In summer, living is out of doors on the tree-shaded brick terrace, the screened porch, or by the landscaped POOL. You will be close to Valley Forge National Park, Devon Horse Show, Wharton Esherick Museum, and so on. It is 4 minutes from exit 24, PA Turnpike (Interstates 76 and 276) via US 202, Devon exit. Accommodations include twin beds, private bath, additional single bed also. Swimming POOL. Full breakfast, self-serve on workdays. Off-street parking. NO SMOKING.
**Rates:** S $35, D $45 DAILY.
**Reservations:** (215) 688-1633 MONDAY THROUGH FRIDAY 9:00 TO 5:00.

## CHESTERBROOK

A historic Pennsylvania 1700 stone farmhouse on the edge of Valley Forge Park. Private guest floor has convenience hall with refrigerator and oven. There are two large guestrooms: one with queen-sized bed and private hall bath; the other with a double and single bed, attached private bath. A crib is also available. Inground POOL. Children welcome. NO SMOKING.
**Rates:** $65 DAILY.
**Reservations:** (215) 692-4575 NOON TO 4 P.M. MONDAY THROUGH FRIDAY.

## GLADWYN

This Ranch style home is located halfway between two very visited areas, Valley Forge and Philadelphia. Lovers of Victorian furniture will be especially happy here. The guestroom boasts an ornate mahogany dresser, a marbletopped washstand complete with pitcher and bowl, and a working victrola in beautiful condition. It is easy to imagine yourself back at the turn of the century. Your hosts have welcomed many guests from overseas, usually through the church, but also from a two year stay in Germany. Your host is a doctor; your hostess a former nurse. Growing plants is a special interest as seen by the healthy collection on the patio and well-kept lawns. Your hostess will send you a fat packet of local and outlet store information and is happy to help with your daily touring plans. Located 5 minutes from Schuylkill Expressway (Interstate 76). It is a 15 minute drive to Center City or Valley Forge. Bus to Center City at corner. Near Barnes Foundation and Buten Museum, Bryn Mawr Haverford Harcum and Rosemont Colleges. Accommodations include:

first floor, double bed, private bath, air conditioning. Full breakfast. Special diets available. Resident DOG and CAT. Off-street parking. SMOKING in den or on sunporch only.
**Rates:** S $45, D $50 DAILY.
**Reservations:** (215) 688-1633 MONDAY THROUGH FRIDAY 9:00 TO 5:00.

This suburban single stone home sits on an acre, giving it privacy and peace. There is a first floor suite that can be available for HANDICAPPED use. The second floor guestrooms are very private, even the resident DOG does not go up there. Breakfast may be served on the enclosed patio overlooking the fountain or in the bright, skylit nook. Your hostess has many interests, including collections of dolls, frogs, and children's toys. She is also a talented cheese sculptress! You will feel most welcome and at home here in a setting that is convenient to all that the Main Line has to offer, including access to Philadelphia! Near railroad and bus, and cabs available. Accommodatioms include: A) first floor handicapped, single pullout, study with TV, air conditioning, private bath; B) first floor, twin beds, private bath; C) second floor, queen-sized bed, very masculine room, shared bath; and D) second floor, twin beds, rag rugs and patch quilts, shared bath. SMOKING NOT PERMITTED.
**Rates:** A-D) S $40, D $50 DAILY.
**Reservations:** (215) 688-1633 MONDAY THROUGH FRIDAY 9:00 TO 5:00.

## MALVERN

Ground floor apartment in National Register bank home, part of eighteenth century milling village, all on the National Register. Host prepares gourmet breakfast. He is an attorney who enjoys cooking. Located in the Great Valley's high tech corridor. There is a CAT in residence. Accommodations include: ground floor apartment, private entrance, bedroom/sitting room with double bed, sofa, woodburning stove, full kitchen, wet bar, full bath, additional room with single bed, TV. VCR, pond view. Auxiliary room for emergencies: Lincoln room with 1840 Lincoln double bed on second floor, host quarters.
**Rates:** S OR D $70 DAILY.
**Reservations:** (215) 688-1633 MONDAY THROUGH FRIDAY 9:00 TO 5:00.

The last addition to this beautiful big old stone house was built 300 years ago. A walk up the flagstone path between tall hedges of boxwood, holly and yews leads you to an unusual experience. Your enthusiastic hosts who recently bought this treasure are working hard to restore it to its original appearance. Walk the original random width plank floors, fastened with hand-forged nails, admire the thick stone walls and the beautiful

condition of the ground floor room with its walkin fireplace, pot crane, and rare stone "sink" built into the outside wall. Upstairs is a charming Victorian bath. In summer you may share the POOL or fish in the meandering stream that flows through the 4 acres of ground. A full country breakfast will be served before a warming fire in the 1690 kitchen in winter, or on the terrace under ancient trees in summer. Host is a marketing manager. Hosts have a 3 1/2 year old daughter. French and some Spanish and German are spoken here. Just off US 202 via PA 252. It is 10 minutes from exit 24 Pennsylvania Turnpike, 5 minutes drive to Valley Forge Park and Music Theater, and 30 minutes to Philadelphia. Accommodations include: A) private third floor, queen-sized canopy bed, private bath; and B) double brass and iron bed with private bath en suite, small sitting room between with small refrigerator. Resident DOG and CAT. Off-street parking. Arrivals after noon.
**Rates:** A & B) S $55, D $65 DAILY.
**Reservations:** (215) 688-1633 MONDAY THROUGH FRIDAY 9:00 TO 5:00.

## MUSEUM AREA

An 1850 turn-of-the-century row house on a street that is fully restored. Flowering cherry and apple trees are fragrant in the spring. You will appreciate the beautiful beams and floors in this townhouse. A middle parlor has a fireplace. Guestroom decor is in Queen Anne mode. Breakfast may be served in the sunny kitchen greenhouse or in the city garden. Within walking distance of the Museum of Art, Boat House Row, Logan Center, Franklin Plaza, and Franklin Institute. The city bus is a 2 block walk. Your host is in the video documentation field; your hostess is in the entertainment business and can arrange special tours for an additional fee. Many restaurants nearby. Accommodations include: A) third floor, private guest wing, twin beds, refrigerator, full bath, air conditioning; and B) auxiliary room with twin beds and private shower bath. Full English breakfast. Street parking or lot 3 blocks (approximately $4.00/day). Some French and German are spoken here. NO SMOKING.
**Rates:** A & B) S $40, D $50 DAILY.
**Reservations:** (215) 688-1633 MONDAY THROUGH FRIDAY 9:00 TO 5:00.

## NEWTOWN SQUARE

This lovely, suburban home, centrally located to historic Philadelphia, the Brandywine Valley, and Valley Forge Park, was designed to recall the elegance of an earlier era. Although just minutes from the hubbub of the Main Line, you will be able to leave the cares and bustle of the city behind as you wind up the long drive to this stately cobblestone Colonial overlooking 5 acres of rolling hunt country. Three second floor guestrooms have been tastefully appointed and offer complete privacy. Two rooms

are available separately or as a suite. One provides twin or king bed comfort and the other a charming 3/4-sized bed with canopy. There is a private bath to serve both rooms. The third room may be conveniently reached via the backstairs, which also provides a CHAIR LIFT for those who may require it. It offers double bed accommodations and a private bath. You are invited to enjoy the spacious family room with TV. Your hostess, who is a history buff, also loves to cook and will prepare a delicious full breakfast which you may choose to have served in the garden room or on the terrace overlooking the beautiful Pennsylvania countryside. Resident DOG.
**Rates:** S $55, D $65 DAILY.
**Reservations:** (215) 687-3565 9 A.M. TO 6 P.M. MONDAY THROUGH SATURDAY. NOON TO 6 P.M. ON SUNDAY.

## PHOENIXVILLE

This modern two story Colonial style house is nestled on a hillside bordered by flowering shrubs and trees. Attractively furnished, this home reflects order and serenity. Your hostess is a caterer by profession with grown children. She is a green thumb gardener and gourmet cook. She has been a college instructor and is knowledgeable about many cultural and human service organizations. Your feather light, homemade croissants may be served at breakfast time in the large kitchen/activity room that overlooks the back garden terraced down to a lily pond. Having traveled in Sweden, Norway. Switzerland, and the Netherlands, your hostess wishes to make your stay in Valley Forge equally pleasant. She speaks French. Located northwest of Philadelphia, 3 miles from the Pennsylvania Turnpike (Interstates 76 and 276) exit 24 via PA 363 and PA 23. It is 5 minutes from Valley Forge Park, King of Prussia; and 20 minutes to Pottstown. Accommodations include: A) twin beds, private bath, air conditioning; and B & C) two rooms with single bed, shared bath, fan cooled. Rollaway. Full breakfast. Off-street parking. Resident GOLDEN RETRIEVER. CHILDREN over 8 welcome. NO SMOKING.
**Rates:** A) S $25, D $40; AND B & C) S $20 DAILY.
**Reservations:** (215) 688-1633 MONDAY THROUGH FRIDAY 9:00 TO 5:00.

## RITTENHOUSE SQUARE

This charming townhouse is located just off Rittenhouse Square on a lovely city street. The focal point of its magnificently appointed guestroom is the massive walnut antique double bed beautifully adorned with a Marseilles spread. Floral drapes reach floor to ceiling and bookcases line the wall. Select a book, make a hot cup of tea from the electric kettle, and curl up on the hide-a-bed sofa to rest from the day's activities. TV is also available should you prefer, or catch up on your correspondence at the desk. All the comforts of home are yours, including a small

refrigerator tucked behind the closet doors. Private adjoining bath. Private entrance. Gourmet continental breakfast served in your room. Hostess is an art student interested in ceramics. Resident CATS. Air conditioned. Children welcome. NO SMOKING.
**Rates:** S $60, D $65 DAILY.
**Reservations:** (215) 687-3565 9 A.M. TO 6 P.M. MONDAY THROUGH SATURDAY. NOON TO 6 P.M. ON SUNDAY.

## SOCIETY HILL

A wrought iron fence surrounds the cluster of unique brick townhouses designed by architect I. M. Pei. After passing through the gate, you will enter a charming home located just 1 block from Independence Park. A spiral staircase leads to the elegant second floor sitting room with grand PIANO where you are invited to relax. Continuing on up the stairs, you will come to the third floor guestroom comfortably appointed with two twin beds and a TV. Your private bath is just across the hall. On returning downstairs in the morning, you will find that the massive antique dining room table makes an impressive setting for your continental breakfast. Or if you like, adjourn to the back patio where your hostess, a high school English teacher, will join you for a cup of coffee. Resident DOG. PIANO. Children welcome. NO SMOKING.
**Rates:** S $50, D $55 DAILY.
**Reservations:** (215) 687-3565 9 A.M. TO 6 P.M. MONDAY THROUGH SATURDAY. NOON TO 6 P.M. ON SUNDAY.

## STRAFFORD

The quietness of this high side, split level home nestled in the trees, belies the energy of your hostess, whose interests are centered in the arts. Her avocation as a singer with choral arts societies, local theater group, and her church choir are part of her musical bent. Her love of the arts is reflected in soap stone sculptures, paintings, prints, and a collection of Swiss music boxes. Breakfast specialties include blueberry crepes, eggs, and quiche. It is 5 minutes to train, Valley Forge National Park, Main Line colleges, or King of Prussia; 25 minutes to center of Philadelphia via train or Interstate 76. Accommodations include: A) second floor, den room, twin beds, radio, air conditioning, shared bath; B) second floor, bunk beds, shared bath. Resident DOG and CAT. Off-street parking. Living room for television viewing. Complimentary afternoon libation. Full breakfast. CHILDREN over 5 welcome. NO SMOKING.
**Rates:** A & B) S $30, D $40 DAILY.
**Reservations:** (215) 688-1633 MONDAY THROUGH FRIDAY 9:00 TO 5:00.

## UNIVERSITY CITY

This historically registered row home provides generous third floor guest quarters and is conveniently located to the University of Pennsylvania, Drexel University, and Children's Hospital. At one end of the third floor you will find the bedroom that can accommodate a family with its two twin beds and a double bed. Private bath. The sitting room is located at the opposite end of the hall and is a perfect place to relax in front of the TV or curl up with a book. Your hostess, a retired businesswoman, provides a continental plus breakfast. Laundry facilities and refrigerator space are also available. Children welcome.
**Rates:** S $40, D $50 DAILY.
**Reservations:** (215) 687-3565 9 A.M. TO 6 P.M. MONDAY THROUGH SATURDAY. NOON TO 6 P.M. ON SUNDAY.

## VALLEY FORGE

Just minutes from Valley Forge Park, this comfortable old stone home reflects the care and innovation of its carpenter host. Once a duplex, it now boasts double the space, extra wide hallways and creative additions to its guestrooms. Three very inviting second floor rooms are available. A) one a twin and B & C) two rooms offer double bed accommodations. Shared or private bath. Your hostess, a grandmother of 15, welcomes you to relax in the living room in front of the fireplace after a day of sightseeing. A continental breakfast is provided. NO CHILDREN. NO SMOKING.
**Rates:** A) S $30; AND B & C) S $35, D $40 DAILY.
**Reservations:** (215) 687-3565 9 A.M. TO 6 P.M. MONDAY THROUGH SATURDAY. NOON TO 6 P.M. ON SUNDAY.

## WAYNE

This 1760s house was formerly an inn. Now it is owned by history buffs who have filled it with charming antiques and a wonderful library. Host is an investment consultant and is interested in computers; Hostess is interested in gardening. Your breakfast might be served in your light, cheery bedroom or in the plant-filled formal dining room, or, in sunny weather, by the POOL. Some French is spoken here. Located near (176). Accommodations include: A) third floor, king-sized bed, private bath, sitting room, black and white TV, air conditioning, and double pullout sofabed; B) third floor, single bed, private bath in hall, black and white TV, air conditioning, and C) second floor, single bed, private bath in hall, air conditioning. black and white TV.
**Rates:** A & B) S $50, D $55; AND C) S $45 DAILY.
**Reservations:** (215) 688-1633 MONDAY THROUGH FRIDAY 9:00 TO 5:00.

# LANSDALE
## NORTH WALES

This charming rancher is graced by an abundance of flora and fauna of herbs, perennials, and exotic plantings. Your hostess prepares an extra special breakfast enhanced by these home grown fresh herbs. The hosts are two very active senior citizens who enjoy company. Breakfast is often served in front of a toasty fire in the country kitchen or on the garden patio. You can walk to town. Near Ursinus College, North Wales, Skippack Village, and Collegeville. It is 10 minutes to Valley Forge; 20 minutes to King of Prussia; 35 minutes to New Hope. Accommodations include on the first floor, double bed, share hall bath with hosts.
**Rates:** S $25, D $35 DAILY.
**Reservations:** (215) 688-1633 MONDAY THROUGH FRIDAY 9:00 TO 5:00.

# LAUREL HIGHLANDS
## DONEGAL

An 1865 Pennsylvania farmhouse situated on 6 acres in the Laurel highlands. Hosts are antique dealers and have their shop in a chestnut bank barn on the premises. This country home offers magnificent views of the Laurel Mountains from every room and has two porches for relaxation. There are three quaint guestrooms with double beds furnished with period antiques. Guests share bath with other guests. PETS WELCOME. A Steinway Grand PIANO is available. Skiing nearby at Seven Springs and Hidden Valley. One hour drive to Pittsburgh. A DOG and two CATS are in residence here. CHILDREN WELCOME. NO SMOKING.
**Rates:** S $35, D $40 DAILY.
**Reservations:** (412) 367-8080 MONDAY THROUGH FRIDAY 9:00 A.M. TO 5:00 P.M.

# SCOTTDALE
## MT. NEBO

A charming country home furnished with antiques and collectibles, surrounded by 4 acres of woods, wildflowers, herb and flower gardens, and a small creek. Located 10 miles from the New Stanton exit of the Pennsylvania Turnpike and Interstate 70; 45 miles from downtown Pittsburgh; and 3 miles from the borough of Scottdale. Host is an editor of a religious weekly and a Mennonite minister; hostess is a self-employed floral designer, gourmet cook, and involved in various phases of the fiber arts. Both enjoy the outdoors, gardening, and conversation with guests. Accommodations include three rooms on the second floor: A) double bed, shared bath; B) double bed and twin beds, shared bath; and C) double

bed and bunk beds, shared bath. A crib is available. A CAT is in residence. PETS ARE WELCOME. Children welcome.
**Rates:** A & B) S $34, D $38; AND C) S $36, D $40 DAILY.
**Reservations:** (412) 367-8080 MONDAY THROUGH FRIDAY 9:00 A.M. TO 5:00 P.M.

## LEHIGH VALLEY
## ALLENTOWN-BETHLEHEM
### SALSBURY TOWNSHIP

EAST EMMAUH AVENUE — Built in 1810 this historic 17 room stone Plantation house is surrounded by acres of lawn, flowers, venerable hardwood trees, fruit trees, boxwood gardens, and has an Egyptian water lily pond. Spring fed creek and nature trails cut through a hardwood forest that is a few feet from your room. To enter the Plantation house is like stepping into the past. The roomy interior is crowded with furnishings representing much of American history. Guests sleep in antique beds, hang their towels on Victorian hatracks and lounge on early twentieth century chairs. The ground floor is a rambling maze of living rooms, formal dining room, full size library, enclosed all-season sunporch, attached greenhouse, and unexpected hideaways. Antiques, fine old objects d'art, and colorful pieces of whimsey brighten every corner cupboard and recessed window sill. Over 100 original paintings by early twentieth century artists cover the walls. The building's second level consists of five antique filled bedrooms, baths, and a living room. Five Rooms with double beds and shared baths available. The hosts live on the third floor. Host is a retired engineer; hostess a retired technical writer. The hosts offer a style of lodging in the very finest B&B style tradition. Full breakfasts are served on fine old china. One DOG and three CATS live here. Fireplace in home and TV available. SMOKING in common rooms. CHILDREN NOT WELCOME.
**Rates:** ROOMS A-E) S OR D $85 DAILY.
**Reservations:** (914) 271-6228 MONDAY - FRIDAY 10 A.M. TO 4 P.M. APRIL - OCTOBER. 9 A.M. - 3 P.M. NOVEMBER - MARCH.

## BETHLEHEM

This is a tree-shaded house set back from the road. Your hosts are retired and keep active with tennis and swimming. They also love to play bridge. Your host speaks fluent Spanish and your hostess feels she "gets by in it." They have an above ground POOL in an immaculate garden and guests may take a quick dip in the pool. CHILDREN under 14 must be accompanied by a parent. On the second floor, they offer a double room with an adjoining private bath. Full breakfast will be served between 7 and 9 A.M. This home is within 2 miles of historic Bethelem. No pets. PIANO. CHILDREN over the age of 5 welcome. SMOKING permitted only on first floor.

**Rates:** S $35, D $45; FAMILY 3 $65; FAMILY 4 $70; CHILD WITH OWN SLEEPING BAG $3 DAILY.
**Reservations:** (215) 845-3526 MONDAY THROUGH FRIDAY 8 A.M. TO 8 P.M. ANSWERING MACHINE AT OTHER TIMES.

## LONGWOOD
### GLEN MILLS

This is a 1690 stone cottage—a drive through miles of rural acreage attests to the fact that this is the real "Penn's Woods." Cherry trees flank the farm lane and angora goats graze in the field. Afar lie the outbuildings of a former farm estate—a barn, stone cottage, tenant quarters, spring house, and slaughter shed. A warm welcome by an active family, who enjoy travel, fellowship, and an array of sport, awaits you. The stone cottage is charming with its rustic beams, family heirlooms, hooked rugs, and potbelly stove. Breakfast is served in the main house dining room or on the screened summer porch. Car convenient, however, suburban train to Center City. Long-term guests may have cooking privileges in the main house. Accommodations include: A) first floor, double bed, share bath; B) second floor, loft with twin beds and cot, share bath.
**Rates:** A & B) S OR D $60 DAILY.
**Reservations:** (215) 688-1633 MONDAY THROUGH FRIDAY 9:00 TO 5:00.

## MERCERSBURG
### THE CORNER

PUNCH BOWL ROAD — A brick home on a 200 acre farm surrounded by mountains, fields of corn, and wildlife. Guests have use of TENNIS COURTS, POOL, PRIVATE FISH POND. Stocked trout stream 1 mile away. Horseback riding and trail riding available. FIREPLACE in master bedroom and living room. Enjoy evenings on the sunporch and watch the deer come out of the mountains and graze in the fields. Open year-round. Available for an overnight, weekend, or week. Accommodations include: A) master bedroom with FIREPLACE and queen-sized bed, shared bath; B) first floor bedroom with king-sized bed, shared bath; C) West Room with queen-sized bed, shared bath; D) North Room with double bed, shared bath; and E) East Room with double bed, shared bath. VCR.
**Rates:** A & B) D $55; C-E) D $45 DAILY.
**Reservations:** (703) 955-1246 MONDAY THROUGH SATURDAY 9 A.M. TO 1 P.M. ANSWERING MACHINE AT OTHER TIMES.

## PITTSBURGH
### BUFFALO MILLS

This lodge is a log home in a rural, peaceful valley with a stocked BASS POND, hiking trails, and cross-country skiing available. A modern lodge is maintained by a retired couple. Host enjoys woodworking and gardening; hostess enjoys crafts, sewing, and quilting. Two DOGS and one CAT reside here. Rooms have double accommodations and a crib and cot are available. Located nearby to Pennsylvania State game lands. Children welcome. SMOKING NOT PERMITTED.
**Rates:** D $35 DAILY. D $230 WEEKLY.
**Reservations:** (412) 367-8080 MONDAY THROUGH FRIDAY 9:00 A.M. TO 5:00 P.M.

### MERCER
### NEAR COURTHOUSE

ROUTE 58, EAST MARKET STREET — This 150 year old Colonial Empire style red brick home offers you a peaceful night's rest amid antiques native to the region. Working fireplaces and ceiling paddle fans add to your comfort. The host family has been part of Mercer's history since the 1820s. Your host is the fourth of his family line to practice law in Mercer. He golfs and does civic work; hostess enjoys antiquing, reading, and needlepoint. They have two children. Just a few steps from County Courthouse, site of old-fashioned summer band concerts, and Historical Society. Close to Amish country, forges, grist mills, antique and specialty shops, Thiel, Westminster, Grove City colleges and Slippery Rock University. Children welcome. NO SMOKING. Convenient to Interstates 79 and 80. Accommodations include: A) double bed with Victorian furnishings and private bath; and B) two double beds, antique furniture, FIREPLACE, shared bath. Brochure available. A crib and a cot are available, as are bikes.
**Rates:** A & B) S $45 DAILY, D $50 DAILY. S $250, D $280 WEEKLY.
**Reservations:** (412) 367-8080 MONDAY THROUGH FRIDAY 9:00 A.M. TO 5:00 P.M.

## MONTGOMERY COUNTY
### HUNTINGTON VALLEY

Tucked away in a corner of the large forest rimmed back lawn of a comfortable home is a small cottage with an attached greenhouse. This was the potting shed. Your hosts have installed a Franklin stove and sink. The bathroom is a special delight: a greenhouse walled and curtained for privacy, but open to the sun above. A shower in the quaint four-footed tub could be an unforgettable experience. There are 7 acres of woods with deer; also a large POOL at the far edge of the sloping lawn. A jogging trail is nearby. A breakfast basket will be left at your doorstep.

The tiny kitchen is stocked with all supplies for your convenience. Located in a northwest suburb, accessible from Interstate 96 and Pennsylvania Turnpike (Interstate 276). It is a 30 minute drive to New Hope and historic Philadelphian Colonial towns. River floats and horseback riding nearby. Accommodations include: private guesthouse with queen-sized bed, TV, skylights, ceiling fan, woodburning stove.
**Rates:** S OR D $80 DAILY.
**Reservations:** (215) 688-1633 MONDAY THROUGH FRIDAY 9:00 TO 5:00.

## SOUTHEAST PENNSYLVANIA
## BERNVILLE-NEAR READING

This farm was built in 1830, 100 yards from the Tulpehoken Creek, a RIVER stocked by the state. Your host and hostess are semiretired and she has a service for restoring old quilts. They are antique buffs who try to attend all local auctions and guests may join them. Accommodations include: A) queen-sized bed, powder room en suite on the second floor, shared bath; and B) double room, shared bath. A full breakfast will be served. There is a friendly DOG, however, no pets allowed. CHILDREN over 10 welcome with their own sleeping bags. SMOKING allowed but not in bedrooms.
**Rates:** A) S $35, D $45; AND B) S $32, D $40. FAMILY 4 $70. CHILD WITH SLEEPING BAG $3.00 DAILY.
**Reservations:** (215) 845-3526 MONDAY THROUGH FRIDAY 8 A.M. TO 8 P.M. ANSWERING MACHINE AT OTHER TIMES.

## EAST GREENVILLE

This mill is a lovely Victorian home furnished with antiques. It is on a famous trout STREAM and fishing is allowed with the proper license. Your host and hostess are retired but busier than ever with the Chamber of Commerce and mental health organizations. On the second floor are two double rooms each with a private bath. There is also a single room on the same floor for a school age child or single parent but who would share the parent's bath. On the third floor are three rooms with two single beds each, suitable for a family—summers only—a bath would be shared with the second floor. A full breakfast is served on the screened porch in summer and the bay window of the kitchen at other times. One LABRADOR and two CATS live here. Bikes available. Children welcome. NO SMOKING.
**Rates:** S $35, D $45; FAMILY 3 $60 DAILY. PRIVATE BATH $50 DAILY.
**Reservations:** (215) 845-3526 MONDAY THROUGH FRIDAY 8 A.M. TO 8 P.M. ANSWERING MACHINE AT OTHER TIMES.

## EPHRATA-ADAMSTOWN

Straddling the county line of Berks and Lancaster is a Civil war frame farmhouse that has been added to and tastefully restored. Your hostesses, a mother and daughter, are keen gardeners and proud of the work they have done on the property. They offer a double bed with private bath on the second floor and a second double bed, also on the second floor, which has a bathroom with shower en suite. There is also a larger room with a queen-sized bed and two chair beds suitable for children, which makes an ideal family room. It may share a bath with a room on the third floor that has a 3/4 bed but normally the family room has the private bath and is priced accordingly. A sitting room with TV is available for the use of guests. The house is tree shaded and well equipped with fans, but there is a window air conditioner that can be put in if necessary for an extra charge. There is a resident DOG and two CATS. There is an INGROUND POOL that guests may use, but children must be supervised. Bikes may be borrowed and 5 minutes away is a golf course open to the public. CHILDREN 4 years and up may bring their own sleeping bags. Children under that age should have their own port-a-crib or whatever. On the 11 acres are interesting walks with springs and grottoes. Convenient to Amish country and antique emporiums. Full breakfast of your choice will be served up to 10:00 A.M. Pennsylvania Dutch and a little German are spoken here. Children welcome. SMOKING in the sitting room only. **Rates:** S OR D $55; FAMILY 3 $70; FAMILY 4 $85. CHILD WITH OWN SLEEPING BAG $5. UNDER 4 YEARS NO CHARGE DAILY. **Reservations:** (215) 845-3526 MONDAY THROUGH FRIDAY 8 A.M. TO 8 P.M. ANSWERING MACHINE AT OTHER TIMES.

## FOGELSVILLE

Within 2 miles of the intersection of Interstate 78 (Route 22) and Route 100 is a CONVERTED BARN set amid hills and orchards. Accommodations include: A) 12 rooms, each with queen-sized beds and private bath, TV, telephone, and individual climate control; and B) there is also a conference room for 10 available for guests. On the property there is also the old farmhouse now converted into three private self-contained suites, each consisting of a living/dining room and kitchen area. Upstairs is a bedroom with queen-sized bed and bathroom. Four guestrooms with FIREPLACE. Long-term stays by arrangement. A full breakfast is served in the converted hayloft, now the living/dining area with a large open fireplace. Ideal for business travelers and getaway weekends. Host enjoys windsurfing, skiing, and biking; hostess enjoys reading cooking and decorating. One DOG resides here. AC. HOT TUB. Canoe and sailboat available. Bikes available. **Rates:** A) S $60 D $80; AND B) S $70, D $90. DAILY. ROOMS WITH FIREPLACE D $125 WEEKENDS.

**Reservations:** (215) 845-3526 MONDAY THROUGH FRIDAY 8 A.M. TO 8 P.M. ANSWERING MACHINE AT OTHER TIMES.

## LANDIS STORE

This COTTAGE makes you think you are in the English Cotswolds with acres of woodland. It has been skillfully decorated by the hostess using antiques, handmade furniture, and quilts. The living room with a woodburning stove has a bay window. Hand-hewn stairs lead to a bedroom with a double bed and a Laura Ashley bathroom with a 4 foot Victorian tub. The bedroom is air conditioned. The hostess offers a full breakfast that will be served in the cottage. No pets as the hosts have two CATS. Handmade country furniture and quilts are for sale. Ideal for a hideaway vacation. Walk on the country roads and watch deer in the fields. Good restaurants and antique shops in the area. AC. NO CHILDREN. SMOKING in the living room only.
**Rates:** COTTAGE S $40, D $50 DAILY.
**Reservations:** (215) 845-3526 MONDAY THROUGH FRIDAY 8 A.M. TO 8 P.M. ANSWERING MACHINE AT OTHER TIMES.

## OLEY

This house is in the heart of the Oley Valley, a National Historic site. Host is a retail automotive parts salesman and a fire chief who enjoys auto racing; hostess has a small shop on the first floor that sells local hand crafted items. She offers on the second floor one room with a double bed. A bathroom shared by all bedrooms is reached through the guest sitting room which has TV. There is a full kitchen for the use of guests and where a continental breakfast will be served by the hostess. Guests may prepare their own cooked breakfast. Off the kitchen is a balcony with chairs and an umbrella table. The house is well ventilated with ducts and a fan. On the third floor there are two rooms, each with a double bed and one has a daybed for a third person. There is a crib and rollaway available. No pets. One of the guestrooms has a private balcony. CHILDREN sometimes accepted. SMOKING is permitted, but not in the bedrooms.
**Rates:** S $35, D $50; FAMILY 3 $60; FAMILY 4 $70; CRIB $5 DAILY. ENQUIRE ABOUT WEEKLY RATES.
**Reservations:** (215) 845-3526 MONDAY THROUGH FRIDAY 8 A.M. TO 8 P.M. ANSWERING MACHINE AT OTHER TIMES.

## PLUMBSTEADVILLE

On 5 acres in the middle of Bucks County is a restored farmhouse, circa 1819. The second floor offers a room with a double brass bed and another room that is really a bed-sitting room because it has an antique double bed, a sofa, and a working FIREPLACE. If both rooms have guests they share the bath, otherwise it is a private bath. Children welcome. Children may bring their own sleeping bags. The hosts can put up a cot if necessary. A full breakfast will be served. New Hope and Peddlers Village are only 15 minutes away. Both host and hostess are teachers. There are animals in the house and GUESTS MAY BRING SMALL PETS (well behaved of course). The hosts do not smoke but smoking is allowed.

**Rates:** S $40-$45, D $52-$57, COT $15. CHILD WITH OWN SLEEPING BAG $7.50 DAILY. $5 SURCHARGE FOR A ONE NIGHT STAY.

**Reservations:** (215) 845-3526 MONDAY THROUGH FRIDAY 8 A.M. TO 8 P.M. ANSWERING MACHINE AT OTHER TIMES.

## POTTSTOWN

The original owner of this house obtained the land grant from William Penn and the first house was built in 1750 with two additions in 1800 and 1840. The host's interests include photography, restoring antiques, and golf; hostess likes to arrange dried flowers. They offer on the second floor, up very steep stairs, a double-bedded room with a private bath. There is a resident DOG. A continental breakfast will be served. Children welcome. SMOKING outside the house only.

**Rates:** S $35, D $45. ROLLAWAY $5. CHILD WITH OWN SLEEPING BAG $3. DAILY.

**Reservations:** (215) 845-3526 MONDAY THROUGH FRIDAY 8 A.M. TO 8 P.M. ANSWERING MACHINE AT OTHER TIMES.

## READING

A 180 year old stone farmhouse with a wide porch in sight of the RIVER. Your hostess, who was raised on a farm, prepares her own bread, relishes, and jellies. She offers on the second floor a Victorian suite of a double bedroom, sitting room with TV, and a private bath. A full breakfast will be served on the porch in summer and in the dining room at other times. A boat is available for fishing and bikes may be borrowed. With advance notice the hostess will serve a farm supper (cost to be arranged). CHILDREN welcome with their own sleeping bags. No pets since there is an outside DOG. SMOKING permitted in the sitting room but not in the bedroom.

**Rates:** S $40, D $50; CHILD WITH OWN SLEEPING BAG $5 DAILY.

**Reservations:** (215) 845-3526 MONDAY THROUGH FRIDAY 8 A.M. TO 8 P.M. ANSWERING MACHINE AT OTHER TIMES.

## RIVERTON

This house is on the west side of the Delaware River and reached by a bridge. It has lawns running down to the water and the owners have carefully restored this Victorian gem. They have filled the three guestrooms

with furnishings from antique shops and their own collection. All rooms
are on the second floor and all have a washbasin in them. One has twin
beds and the other two double beds. They share a full bath on the same
floor. Children with their own sleeping bags are accepted and a rollaway
is available. No pets because there is a resident COLLIE. A continental
breakfast will be served outside on the deck facing the RIVER in fine
weather, otherwise in the formal dining room. There is a guest sitting
room and game room that has a billiard table and TV. Three teenagers
live here. Host is a wholesale car dealer and land developer who enjoys
skiing, racquetball, and boating; hostess enjoys decorating, skiing, and
water sports. PIANO. Canoe available. NO SMOKING permitted in the
house.
**Rates:** S $35, D $55; CHILD WITH OWN SLEEPING BAG $5 DAILY.
**Reservations:** (215) 845-3526 MONDAY THROUGH FRIDAY 8 A.M.
TO 8 P.M. ANSWERING MACHINE AT OTHER TIMES.

## ROBESONIA

You will be welcomed by the bell that called children in 1875 to the old
schoolhouse. With a first floor addition it has been converted into a
lovely home by a talented couple. Your hosts are birdwatchers and flower
growers. They invite guests to take a quick dip in the INGROUND
POOL. This home is equipped with RAMPS and can handle a wheelchair.
Surrounded by cornfields teaming with wildlife. There are hiking trails
and cross-country skiing. It is within easy reach of Blue Marsh Dam for
boating, fishing, and swimming. They offer a double room with a private
bath. Full breakfast will be served in the living/dining area with a fireplace
for the use of guests. NO CHILDREN.
**Rates:** S $36, D $48. MAY 15 THROUGH OCTOBER 15, S $48, D $60.
DAILY.
**Reservations:** (215) 845-3526 MONDAY THROUGH FRIDAY 8 A.M.
TO 8 P.M. ANSWERING MACHINE AT OTHER TIMES.

## SUMNEYTOWN

Imagine yourself in a country hotel at the turn of the century with no TV
or telephone. The innkeeper has four double rooms on the third floor and
two shared baths. Each room has its own personality and the three largest
face the front of the building. "The Elevator Room" has a four poster
bed and it is named for the machinery still to be seen in the corner of
the ceiling when the building was a cigar factory. "The Brass and Wicker
Room" explains itself. "The East Room" has a tall Victorian bed and
matching turn-of-the-century furniture in the sitting area. The fourth room
is smaller, faces the back of the house, and has a four poster canopy
bed. Two of the rooms have working gas FIREPLACES and there is
central heat and air conditioning. A full country breakfast is served
downstairs in the "Hunt Room," one of four dining rooms. There is also

a country bar. Last minute guests can be accommodated. NO CHILDREN. **Rates:** S $70, D $80 DAILY. CORPORATE RATES MONDAYS THROUGH THURSDAYS. RATES INCLUDE TAX. **Reservations:** (215) 845-3526 MONDAY THROUGH FRIDAY 8 A.M. TO 8 P.M. ANSWERING MACHINE AT OTHER TIMES.

## WOMELSDORF

Log house and although this is a new one the charm and convenience are evident. Your hostess is a keen gardener and does substitute teaching in a one room Amish school. She offers a double room and private bath, use of the living room and large front porch, all on the first floor. A rollaway is available. Children may sleep on the living room floor or on the screened porch. Full or continental breakfast is offered. Ideal family base as it is only 16 miles from Reading outlets, 20 miles from Hershey, and 30 miles from Lancaster. German is spoken here. Bikes are available and there is a picnic area. CHILDREN over age of 4 welcome with their sleeping bags. SMOKING outside only. **Rates:** S $35, D $40. ROLLAWAY $7.50. CHILD WITH OWN SLEEPING BAG $2.50 DAILY. **Reservations:** (215) 845-3526 MONDAY THROUGH FRIDAY 8 A.M. TO 8 P.M. ANSWERING MACHINE AT OTHER TIMES.

# SOUTHERN ALLEGHENIES
## EVERETT

LUTZVILLE ROAD NEAR ROUTE 30 — A restored farmhouse, listed on the National Register of Historic Places, begun in 1805. Each generation expanded the physical dimensions of the house into the current blend of stone, brick, and log. Host likes to scuba; hostess likes Wall Street. It is country on the RIVER. A house can not be seen in any direction, but it is on a macadam road maintained by the state. It is close to both the Bedford and Breezewood exits of the Pennsylvania Turnpike. It is near Fort Bedford, Old Bedford Village, and the Bedford Historic District with over 200 well-preserved buildings. Fishing and canoeing from the premises. Bedrooms have private baths and individual FIREPLACES. The rooms are furnished in antiques, reproductions, and family heirlooms. Double accommodations are available. Occupancy is limited to two persons per room. No pets. Color TV, VCR, and Steinway PIANO in the library. Full continental breakfast. CHILDREN over 12 welcome. SMOKING permitted on the first floor only. **Rates:** A) (LARGER ROOM) SUNDAY THROUGH THURSDAY S $30, D $42, FRIDAY & SATURDAY S $35, D $48; B) SUNDAY THROUGH THURSDAY S $28, D $36, FRIDAY & SATURDAY S $33, D $40 DAILY. **Reservations:** (412) 367-8080 MONDAY THROUGH FRIDAY 9:00 A.M. TO 5:00 P.M.

## SCHELLSBURG

ROUTE 30 — This inn is a gracefully built Georgian style stone house. The large pillared side porch invites guests to sit and fantasize. The beautifully landscaped grounds are enclosed by a white picket fence. The living room, which is decorated with antiques, displays a delightful player PIANO and the fireplace features an ornate mantel built by Robert Wellford in the late 1800s. A similar mantel is located in the White House. The four guests' bedrooms are adorned with homemade quilts and embroidered linens. Accommodations include double accommodations in: A) the Schell room; B) Bankers Room and Vault (for additional person); C) the Erin room; D) Pennsylvania Room. Homemade breads, muffins, and pastries are a favorite of the guests. Host enjoys collecting coins and listening to Blue Grass music; hostess likes cooking, gardening, and crafts. The inn is located in historic Bedford County. History comes alive when one visits Old Bedford Village, Fort Bedford, the covered bridges, and other landmarks. Children welcome. SMOKING permitted in the living room and the porch only.

**Rates:** A) D $36; B) D $48; AND C & D) D $55 DAILY.
**Reservations:** (412) 367-8080 MONDAY THROUGH FRIDAY 9:00 A.M. TO 5:00 P.M.

## WASHINGTON COUNTY
## WASHINGTON
### VILLAGE OF HICKORY

CALDWELL ROAD — Restored early 1800 Colonial mansion home on 140 acre working farm in rolling hill country of southwestern Pennsylvania. Guest suite with FIREPLACE and private bath accommodates family with children. Home is furnished with antiques, PIANO, and ORGAN. Fireplaces in most rooms. Swimming and fishing POND at farm and excellent fishing and boating at beautiful Cross Creek Park 3 miles away. Baby equipment is available. Guests may take nature walks on farm and view wildlife, horses, cattle, geese, crop planting and harvesting, and other farming activities. Close to Washington and Jefferson College, the Meadows Racetrack, and antique and craft shops at Meadowcroft Village, West Alexander Village, and Scenery Hill. Host is a retired electrical engineer; hostess is a registered nurse. It is 35 minutes to downtown Pittsburgh and Three Rivers Stadium. Located on Caldwell Road just off Pennsylvania Route 18, 8 miles north of Interstates 70 and 79 intersection in Washington, Pennsylvania (Interstate 70 exit 6). Gourmet continental breakfast. A DOG and a CAT are in residence. Pool table.

**Rates:** S $36, D $42 DAILY.
**Reservations:** (412) 367-8080 MONDAY THROUGH FRIDAY 9:00 A.M. TO 5:00 P.M.

# 3

# South Atlantic

- [ ] **District of Columbia**
- [ ] **Florida**
- [ ] **Georgia**
- [ ] **Maryland**
- [ ] **North Carolina**
- [ ] **South Carolina**
- [ ] **Virginia**
- [ ] **West Virginia**

# DISTRICT OF COLMBIA

## DISTRICT OF COLUMBIA
## WASHINGTON, D.C.
### ADAMS-MORGAN (NORTHWEST)

LANIER PLACE NEAR CONNECTICUT AVENUE — A large 1910 townhouse on a quiet street in historic Adams-Morgan, close to Metro and bus, National Zoo, Rock Creek Park, shops, and restaurants of all kinds. Furnished with antiques. Oriental rugs, art, and PIANO. Guests have use of library and kitchen. Host works in international development; hostess is an energy analyst. Elaborate continental breakfast with fresh juice and homebaked goodies served. Accommodations include: A) large dormer room with two twin beds; B) queen-sized bed; and C) queen-sized waterbed. All have own color TVs and share baths. French and some Spanish are spoken here. Air conditioning. Victorian style home. Children welcome. NO SMOKERS.
**Rates:** A-C) S $40, D $50 DAILY.
**Reservations:** (202) 363-7767 MONDAY - THURSDAY 9:00 - 5:00; FRIDAY 9:00 - 1:00.

Renovated 1890s Victorian row house on a quiet street in the Capitol Hill Historic District. Convenient to public transportation, Amtrak, and restaurants. It is a 15 minute walk to the Capitol, Supreme Court, Library of Congress, and congressional office buildings. Home is air conditioned, with three fireplaces on the first floor, and a friendly DOG. Hostess likes her home clean and casual. She is interested in antiques, history, and whatever is going on in Washington, D.C. Accommodations include: A) a large room with bay window, double bed, and private bath; and B) double bed. share bath with hostess. NO SMOKERS.
**Rates:** A) S $45, D $58; AND B) S $35, D $45 DAILY.
**Reservations:** (202) 363-7767 MONDAY - THURSDAY 9:00 - 5:00; FRIDAY 9:00 - 1:00.

### CAPITOL HILL

E STREET NEAR UNION STATION — A typical Capitol Hill townhouse of the Victorian era, modernized but retaining touches of the old days. Hostess is a single lady (five grown children and one grandchild) now in a second career as a real estate agent. She is a pianist, enjoys knitting and lively conversations with her always interesting guests. Good walkers can visit many tourist attractions on foot, as well as good restaurants and sidewalk cafes. AMTRAK/Metro are 6 blocks away; street parking available. Accommodations include: A) large pleasant room with private bath, queen and single bed; B) middle size room with queen bed; and C) single room with balcony. All rooms have color TV. Children of all ages welcome. SMOKERS permitted but not encouraged.

**Rates:** A) S $35, D $40; B) S $40, D $50, T $60; AND C) S $25 DAILY.
**Reservations:** (202) 363-7767 MONDAY - THURSDAY 9:00 - 5:00;
FRIDAY 9:00 - 1:00.

**FIFTH STREET, S.E.** — Townhouse built in 1919 for former House of
Representatives' Speaker, Champ Clark of Missouri. Three blocks from
subway, and 1 block from historic Eastern Market. Within walking
distance of Capitol. One bedroom apartment in basement with all amenities
including washer/dryer. Sleeps four using queen-sized sofabed. UNHOSTED
but continental breakfast provided. Air conditioned. Host is a political
consultant; hostess is a lobbyist. Hostess speaks some French and a little
Greek. NO SMOKERS.
**Rates:** S $50, D $60, T $80 DAILY.
**Reservations:** (202) 363-7767 MONDAY - THURSDAY 9:00 - 5:00;
FRIDAY 9:00 - 1:00.

**SOUTH CAROLINA AVENUE, S.E.** — A 1915 three story townhouse
ideally situated on a wide street in a quiet residential section yet only 6
blocks from the Capitol, and 1 block from Metro and bus routes. National
Airport can be reached by Metro and Union Station is a 10 minute car
ride away. Walk to the Congress, the Library of Congress, Supreme
Court, and museums. Accommodations include: A) English room with
one double and one single bed; B) Irish room with one double bed; C)
Scottish room with two single beds; and D) Welsh room with one single
bed. Bathrooms are shared with other guests. Bountiful, complimentary
English breakfast or continental breakfast. Hostess' interests include
gourmet cooking, music, camping and the outdoors, ballroom dancing,
and world traveling. In lounge, guests may enjoy a complimentary glass
of wine in the evenings, or chat with your hosts on the front porch.
Guests may use the hibachi in the garden to cook dinner. Friendly DOG
in residence. Street parking available with free temporary residential
sticker obtained by hostess. Please advise if you will be driving and give
registration number and state of registration. Interstates 95, 395, and 295
are 1 mile from the house. The Pennsylvania Dutch country, Gettysburg,
Harper's Ferry, and the Shenandoah Valley and Blue Ridge Mountains
are all convenient day trips. Air conditioned. CHILDREN over 12
welcome. SMOKING permitted in the lounge.
**Rates:** A) S $30; B) S $35, D $45; C) S $40, D $50; AND D) S $45, D
$55, T $65 DAILY.
**Reservations:** (202) 363-7767 MONDAY - THURSDAY 9:00 - 5:00;
FRIDAY 9:00 - 1:00.

**SOUTH CAROLINA AVENUE, S.E.** — A townhouse built in 1908.
Three UNHOSTED apartments are available. Each beautifully decorated
apartment sleeps 4 to 5 persons, has a fully equipped kitchen, bathroom,

bedroom with queen-sized bed, living room with color TV and pullout couch, and dining area. Kitchens are stocked with coffee beans, bacon and eggs, bread and pastries, milk and juice, cereals, wines, spices, and all the basics. Host provides a car tour of Washington, D.C., bikes can be borrowed, and hosts can be a French or Spanish translator/tour guide. Dozens of restaurants and shops are within a few blocks; the immediate neighborhood is residential, safe, and pleasant. The U.S. Capitol, Supreme Court, Library of Congress, and other governmental buildings are an easy 10 minute walk; the Smithsonian Museums and downtown Washington are 15 minutes away. The bus stop and subway are only 2 blocks away. VCR. Air conditioning. PETS WELCOME. Victorian style home. Children welcome.
**Rates:** S $50, D $60-65. T $75-$80, Q $85-100 DAILY.
**Reservations:** (202) 363-7767 MONDAY - THURSDAY 9:00 - 5:00; FRIDAY 9:00 - 1:00.

## CLEVELAND PARK

NEAR CONNECTICUT AVENUE — Attractive and quiet three story brick townhouse in country setting. Located in historic Cleveland Park. Five minute walk to Metro. Short ride to downtown Washington. Neighborhood features include the National Cathedral, Zoo, Rock Creek Park, post office, library, banks, stores, and a variety of restaurants. Hosts, a foreign language educator and an interior designer, speak French and German. Accommodations include: A) double bed and B) single bed. Two second story comfortable rooms. A CAT resides here. Baths are shared with other guests. A PIANO is here and bikes are available. Children welcome. NO SMOKERS.
**Rates:** S $30-$40, D $50 DAILY.
**Reservations:** (202) 363-7767 MONDAY - THURSDAY 9:00 - 5:00; FRIDAY 9:00 - 1:00.

## DU PONT CIRCLE

17TH STREET, N.W. — A turn-of-the-century brick Victorian home containing original architectural features, such as oak woodwork, pocket shutters and doors, gas fireplaces with ornate mantels, and a walkin silver safe. The five bedrooms are furnished with antiques, period reproduction wallpapers, antique chandeliers, and lace curtains. Accommodations include: A) double bed, single bed; B) double bed; C) double bed; and D) two double beds. The house is minutes from downtown, the White House, and the Capitol Mall, and within walking distance of shops, galleries, restaurants, and the subway. SMOKERS are not welcome, but CHILDREN over 10 are. Merlin is the resident cockatiel. The hosts are government lawyers; he enjoys woodworking; she loves choral singing; they both enjoy antiquing and baking, especially for breakfast. Air conditioning.

**Rates:** A & D) S $55, D $65, T $75; B & E) S $50, D $60; C) S $45, D $55 DAILY.
**Reservations:** (202) 363-7767 MONDAY - THURSDAY 9:00 - 5:00; FRIDAY 9:00 - 1:00.

18TH STREET, N.W. — Two bedroom apartment in small, turn-of-the-century, fully renovated apartment building in the Du Pont Circle section of Washington, D.C. Convenient walking distance to shops, restaurants, movie theaters, and convention sites. It is a 5 minute walk to Metro and 10 minute Metro ride to Capitol Hill, government buildings, mall, and monuments. Accommodations include a single bedroom with one full and one half bath shared with the hostess. Hostess is an attorney in private practice in the District of Columbia.
**Rates:** S $40 DAILY.
**Reservations:** (202) 363-7767 MONDAY - THURSDAY 9:00 - 5:00; FRIDAY 9:00 - 1:00.

## GEORGETOWN

39TH STREET, N.W. — A 1920s English cottage type row house with front and back gardens on one of Washington's most charming and tranquil streets. Street deadends into a park on a hilltop, across the street is woodland and house is backed by woodland also. Back porch is delightful in warm weather, and for viewing Washington Monument and Capitol in leafless winter. Pretty house is furnished with antiques and family possessions. Air conditioning and VCR. Hostess is an economist, can speak a little French and Spanish, and loves to cook. Bus transport to downtown and the subway is at the bottom of the hill, as is Georgetown University and Hospital. Accommodations include: twin beds, shared bath with hostess. A cot is available. Children welcome.
**Rates:** S $40, D $50 DAILY.
**Reservations:** (202) 363-7767 MONDAY - THURSDAY 9:00 - 5:00; FRIDAY 9:00 - 1:00.

## NORTHWEST

NEAR CONNECTICUT AVENUE — A Tudor style townhouse located in an excellent residential area near the heart of the city. The home is furnished with antiques inherited from the hostess' family, including antique Oriental rugs. The hostess manages her own business in an office well separated from the guestrooms. The subway is an 8 minute walk from the house and several bus lines are a 3 to 5 minute walk. The Washington Cathedral and American University are a 20 minute walk, a private school running track and tennis courts are a 5 minute walk. Downtown Washington, the Mall, the White House, and U.S. Capitol are 5 to 10 minutes away by subway. Guests are welcome to use the porch and garden in good weather and there is off-street parking available. One

elderly, friendly DOG is in residence. Accommodations include: A) two
four poster twin beds and attached private bath; B) a four poster double
bed and private bath; and C) a double bed and shared bath. Air
conditioning. CHILDREN over 12 welcome.
**Rates:** A) S $48, D $60; B) S $40-$45, D $50-$58; AND C) S $30-$35
DAILY.
**Reservations:** (202) 363-7767 MONDAY - THURSDAY 9:00 - 5:00;
FRIDAY 9:00 - 1:00.

UNICORN LANE — Four story townhouse in northwest Washington
near the zoo. The home is beautifully and ornately furnished. Both
double-bedded rooms share a guest bath. Arrivals after 6:00 P.M. only.
Delicious full breakfast is served here. House is on a bus line and there
is a fireplace and TV. Children welcome.
**Rates:** S $50, D $55 DAILY.
**Reservations:** (914) 271-6228 MONDAY - FRIDAY 10 A.M. TO 4 P.M.
APRIL - OCTOBER. 9 A.M. - 3 P.M. NOVEMBER - MARCH.

## SOUTHWEST

M STREET — A lovely apartment in a luxury highrise offers a beautiful
view of the Washington skyline and the Capitol. Your suite includes a
separate sitting room with TV, radio, cable, VCR, and private bath.
POOL privileges in summer. Easy access to parking. One block from the
riverfront and waterfront restaurants. Public transportation outside the
front door. Two blocks to subway. It is 15 minutes by cab from National
Airport and 10 minutes from Union Station. Walking distance to
Smithsonian and many major Washington sites. Your hostess, who works
for a large D.C. law firm, smokes. "Happy hour" on the patio during
warm months. PETS WELCOME. Air conditioning. Children welcome.
**Rates:** S $40, D $50 DAILY.
**Reservations:** (202) 363-7767 MONDAY - THURSDAY 9:00 - 5:00;
FRIDAY 9:00 - 1:00.

## WESTOVER AREA OF NORTH ARLINGTON

WASHINGTON BOULEVARD — A beautifully and lovingly restored
1899 Victorian home rich in local history. On several area house tours.
Featured in a Christmas issue of *Washington Home*. Marvelous surprises
of color, ornamentation, and design await the visitor inside and out. Wall
stenciling, many period antiques, and prize winning needlepoint as well
as much that has been transformed from "trash to treasure." Extremely
convenient to historic sites of Arlingon and the nation's capital. On bus
line, 1 block from subway station and 3 blocks from Interstate 66. Family
enjoys many hobbies including interior design, restoration work, handcrafts,
and gardening. Accommodations include: A) double bed, private bath;
and B) single bed. Teenager or adult could be accommodated occasionally

on family level. Bikes available. Air conditioning. ORGAN. No young CHILDREN. NO SMOKING.

**Rates:** A) S $47, D $53; AND B) S $35 DAILY.

**Reservations:** (202) 363-7767 MONDAY - THURSDAY 9:00 - 5:00; FRIDAY 9:00 - 1:00.

## WOODLEY PARK

Overlooking the grounds of the Swiss Embassy, this house offers two comfortable double bedrooms, sitting room, and bath on the third floor. Only minutes away from the Washington Sheraton and Shoreham Hotels, and a short walk to the Woodley Park Zoo Metro. Hostess is active in literary and artistic organizations and the townhouse reflects these interests. There is off-street parking. Resident CAT and DOG. French and German are spoken here.

**Rates:** S $40-$50, D $50-$65 DAILY.

**Reservations:** (202) 363-7767 MONDAY - THURSDAY 9:00 - 5:00; FRIDAY 9:00 - 1:00.

# FLORIDA

## GULF COAST
### PENSACOLA
### NORTH HILL DISTRICT

This town, settled by the Spanish before 1700, was ceded to the United States in 1821. It has been the home of the Pensacola Naval Air Station since 1914; has interesting historic area and delightful beaches and seafood restaurants. Restored Victorian house in Historic District. Accommodations include: A) six rooms with private bath and B) two rooms, shared bath. Two wraparound porches; a complete breakfast. All this besides being in the midst of antique shops and only 10 minutes from the beach.

**Rates:** A-C) S $65, D $70; D) S $75, D $80; E & F) S $55, D $60 DAILY. $5 OFF EACH NIGHT ON STAYS OF TWO OR MORE NIGHTS. CHILDREN UNDER 6 $5, OVER 6 $10. OFF-SEASON SUBTRACT 10%.

**Reservations:** (504) 346-1928 SEVEN DAYS 8 A.M. TO 8 P.M.

## SOUTHERN FLORIDA
### FORT LAUDERDALE BEACH
### BEACH

ALHAMBRA STREET — This historic two story home has been lovingly restored to its original 1930s Florida Mediterranean architecture with all its charm and beauty. Nestled right on Fort Lauderdale's BEACH, it overlooks the beautiful warm Atlantic Ocean. All rooms are air conditioned and designed to make your stay more comfortable. A decked garden area and SPA are available for your use. Continental breakfast is served daily. After a day in the sun guests gather in the lovely Coconut Palm sitting room and enjoy complimentary cocktails and hors d'oeuvres. King-, queen-, and double-bedded rooms are available. PIANO, VCR. Two night minimum; three on holiday weekends. The feel of Casablanca—lots of rattan furnishings, potted palms, relaxation, and romance. Breakfast 8:30 to 10:30 A.M. CHILDREN over 10 welcome.

**Rates:** OFF-SEASON RATES S OR D $50-$75 DAILY. $315-$472.50 WEEKLY. IN SEASON RATES S OR D $80-$125 DAILY. $504-$787.50 WEEKLY. ADDITIONAL ADULTS $10 EACH DAILY.

**Reservations:** (914) 271-6228 MONDAY - FRIDAY 10 A.M. TO 4 P.M. APRIL - OCTOBER. 9 A.M. - 3 P.M. NOVEMBER - MARCH.

# GEORGIA

## NORTHWEST GEORGIA MOUNTAINS
### KENSINGTON
### CHATTANOOGA VALLEY

A large country Victorian home, built in 1878, its porch on three sides overlooks the 25 mile length of the Chattanooga Valley and Lookout Mountain's eastern slope. The house, at the center of a 130 acre horse farm, stands on a ridgetop at the entrance of McLemore's Cove, made by the junction of the Pigeon Mountains to the east. It is 15 miles south of Chattanooga. The host is the fifth generation on the land and a former professor of communication. The home has an extensive library; excellent hiking, biking and riding areas, with trout fishing in nearby mountain streams. There are four rooms and two full baths for guests. A large kitchen/Great Room with fireplace makes it possible for guests and host to enjoy the scenic, uncommercial location in this undeveloped valley. Accommodations include: A & B) two rooms with double bed, private bath; and C & D) two rooms with twin-bedded double, shared bath.
**Rates:** S $35, D $50 DAILY.
**Reservations:** (615) 331-5244 MONDAY THROUGH FRIDAY 9 TO 5 (ANSWERING MACHINE OTHER TIMES).

# MARYLAND

## CHESAPEAKE BAY
### ANNAPOLIS
### HISTORIC DISTRICT

KING GEORGE STREET — Three story brick residence in center of Historic District. Located outside Naval Academy within easy walking distance of all the historic homes, the historic State Capitol building, many antique and craft shops and the famous Annapolis restaurants. Intimate back garden area. Waterfront is 3 blocks away. Host is an Academy graduate and retired naval officer with recent employment in Washington, D.C. in the legislative scene; hostess has health care background but now focuses on old home rehabilitation and restoration. During your stay you will be a part of the family, but you can enjoy privacy as you wish. Accommodations include: A) double bed and two trundle beds and B) double bed. One guestroom has a private bath and the other is shared with other guests. Home is Colonial style. Children welcome.
**Rates:** S $50, D $60. $5-$15 EACH ADDITIONAL PERSON DAILY.
**Reservations:** (202) 363-7767 MONDAY - THURSDAY 9:00 - 5:00; FRIDAY 9:00 - 1:00.

## CHESTERTOWN

On the beautiful Chesapeake Bay, 30 new air-conditioned YACHTS are available on three options of lengths of stay. Everything is provided except boating shoes. These options are: A) overnight at dock, breakfast at yacht club; B) overnight at dock, breakfast at yacht club, afternoon sail; C) overnight at dock, breakfast at yacht club, afternoon sail, overnight anchorage, dinner, morning sail, and continental breakfast. NO CHILDREN. NO SMOKERS.
**Rates:** A) OVER NIGHT AT THE DOCK, BREAKFAST AT THE YACHT CLUB: $100 DAILY; B) (A) PLUS AFTERNOON SAIL: $325 DAILY; C) (B) PLUS DINNER, ANCHORAGE, MORNING SAIL, AND CONTINENTAL BREAKFAST ABOARD YACHT: $450 DAILY.
**Reservations:** (215) 692-4575 NOON TO 4 P.M. MONDAY THROUGH FRIDAY.

## GREATER WASHINGTON
### CHEVY CHASE

CONNECTICUT AVENUE — Charming beamed ceiling country type house and garden in historic Chevy Chase. Furnished from around the world combining American country charm with old world foreign cultures. Hosts have lived and traveled in Latin America, Europe, the Middle East, and Turkey and warmly welcome opportunities to greet guests from across

the United States and other countries and help them experience the greatest enjoyment in their visit to the capital. French, German, and Turkish are spoken here. Amenities include a PIANO, VCR, air conditioning, antiques, picnic area. Bikes are available. Accommodations include: A) double bed, private bath and B) single bed, private bath. Children welcome.
**Rates:** S $45, D $60 DAILY.
**Reservations:** (202) 363-7767 MONDAY - THURSDAY 9:00 - 5:00; FRIDAY 9:00 - 1:00.

## ROCKVILLE
### THE WEST END

ABERDEEN ROAD — A 1902 Victorian farmhouse in a historic area of Rockville located on a wooded, very private lot, yet only 2 blocks from Interstate 270. Two charming brick patios are used for weekend breakfasts, weather permitting. Landscaping includes English boxwood and dozens of azaleas and dogwoods, that are spectacular in spring. Host is an engineer; hostess is a management analyst. Host and hostess enjoy sailing, traveling, and cooking. Both are experienced users of B&Bs in Britain. There is a resident CAT. Home is ideally located for business travelers to Montgomery County. The Rockville Metro station is 1 mile away and the bus stop 1 block away. A variety of good restaurants and shopping centers are nearby as well as many places of historic interest. Accommodations include: A) queen-sized bed with desk and private full bath; B) twin beds or king-sized bed with desk and private full bath. B can be combined with A, when available, to provide a private sitting room for A. Air conditioning. NO CHILDREN. NO SMOKERS.
**Rates:** A & B) S $45, D $58 DAILY. S $300-$345, D $360-$425 WEEKLY.
**Reservations:** (202) 363-7767 MONDAY - THURSDAY 9:00 - 5:00; FRIDAY 9:00 - 1:00.

## WESTERN MARYLAND
### HAGERSTOWN
#### KEEDYSVILLE

POFFENBERGER ROAD — A working farm. There are beef cattle, horses, sometimes pigs and chickens. There is a gorgeous pair of peacocks and trio of pheasants in the aviary. And one can see deer and wild turkey on occasion. There is a spring fed pond within sight of the house. The house itself is a pre-Civil War stone home with an added 40 foot sunroom. The guestrooms, as well as the living areas are furnished with antiques. Guestrooms are on the very private third floor. Accommodations include: A) one huge room with four or five double beds and B) double bed, shared bath. The hosts are life long farmers and are presently involved in adult foster care as well. There are two live-in grandfathers. You will be offered a farm breakfast of fresh foods prepared and processed by your hosts. Homemade breads and jellies. Fresh or home preserved fruits and vegetables and meats. Eggs fresh from the hen house! Other meals available. You can visit and have a traditional farm Thanksgiving feast. Hosts attend a Mennonite church and will welcome you to go with them. Three DOGS.

**Rates:** A) S OR D $30 AND B) S OR D $30 DAILY. CAN SLEEP FAMILY OF 7.

**Reservations:** (703) 955-1246 MONDAY THROUGH SATURDAY 9 A.M. TO 1 P.M. (ANSWERING MACHINE AT OTHER TIMES.)

# NORTH CAROLINA

## COASTAL REGION
### BEAUFORT

A Victorian summer home by the SEA with heart pine floors, friendly hosts, and a large parlor welcome you to historic Beaufort. Three guestrooms, one with two double beds and a FIREPLACE, all have private baths. Large rocking chair porch; continental breakfast and a "salute to the sunset."
**Rates:** $65-$95 DAILY.
**Reservations:** (919) 787-2109 MONDAY THROUGH FRIDAY 9 A.M. TO 8 P.M.

### NEW BERN

Open the Victorian frosted glass doors and enter this warm, charming home built in 1870. Oriental rugs, antique and reproduction furniture, and a player PIANO add to the inn's charming elegance. A complete country breakfast is included. Within walking distance to Tryon Place and other New Bern attractions. Five rooms with private baths.
**Rates:** $50-$75 DAILY.
**Reservations:** (919) 787-2109 MONDAY THROUGH FRIDAY 9 A.M. TO 8 P.M.

### OCRACOKE

Beautifully restored estate on the harbor of an Outer Banks fishing village on Ocracoke Island. There are 11 individually decorated guestrooms, 10 with private baths. Accommodations for small conferences, meetings, and receptions. Shops and restaurants nearby.
**Rates:** $55-$75 DAILY.
**Reservations:** (919) 787-2109 MONDAY THROUGH FRIDAY 9 A.M. TO 8 P.M.

### WILMINGTON

Charm and privacy are provided in this quaint inn in historic downtown Wilmington. The two rooms, each individually decorated with antiques, have a FIREPLACE, ceiling fan, private bath, and entrance. The full breakfast is served on the piazza or the gaslit dining room.
**Rates:** $50-$65 DAILY.
**Reservations:** (919) 787-2109 MONDAY THROUGH FRIDAY 9 A.M. TO 8 P.M.

Located in historic Wilmington, this inn is a turn-of-the-century residence lovingly renovated. Four spacious guestrooms are furnished with antiques

and ceiling fans, suite available. Private baths with claw-footed tubs. Enjoy a continental plus breakfast in the beautiful dining room.
**Rates:** $40-$85 DAILY.
**Reservations:** (919) 787-2109 MONDAY THROUGH FRIDAY 9 A.M. TO 8 P.M.

Housed in a mansion in the Historic District of Wilmington, this inn has 14,000 square feet that include a music room and parlor. Six guestrooms are decorated with luxurious appointments; four have private baths. Continental breakfast served in your room; sherry and fruit in the evening. Free airport pickup.
**Rates:** $70-$95 DAILY.
**Reservations:** (919) 787-2109 MONDAY THROUGH FRIDAY 9 A.M. TO 8 P.M.

# MOUNTAIN REGION
## ASHVILLE

Charming Dutch Tudor inn filled with antiques of Southern heritage and collected from a decade of traveling and living in Europe. Within walking distance of streams and walkways of botanical gardens. The hosts will help you plan your sightseeing. Three rooms with semiprivate baths. Continental breakfast served on the covered side porch, in the formal dining room, or in the rock walled garden amid the wildflowers.
**Rates:** $35-$50 DAILY.
**Reservations:** (919) 787-2109 MONDAY THROUGH FRIDAY 9 A.M. TO 8 P.M.

Lovely, comfortable home built in the early 1900s sitting on an acre of parklike grounds. Six guestrooms, some with private baths and FIREPLACES, decorated in antique and traditional furnishings. Cottage with kitchen also sleeps six. "All you can eat" continental breakfast; coffee service in rooms.
**Rates:** $30-$75 DAILY.
**Reservations:** (919) 787-2109 MONDAY THROUGH FRIDAY 9 A.M. TO 8 P.M.

Visit this turn-of-the-century inn within easy walking distance of Asheville's business district. Four upper floor guestrooms, two with private baths, restored to remind you of "grandmother's house." Complete Southern breakfast served; rocking chair porch; hosts also provide a touring service.
**Rates:** $45-$55 DAILY.
**Reservations:** (919) 787-2109 MONDAY THROUGH FRIDAY 9 A.M. TO 8 P.M.

## GLENDALE SPRINGS

Not a true B&B, but a lodge and cabins on 5 acres of land in the Blue Ridge Mountains. Quiet surroundings, hidden from the road, and at the top of a mountain. Cabins available for families. Rustic wood structures, cabins have kitchenettes; four rooms in lodge have a full breakfast included. Popular area for craft shops and beautiful scenery. Ski package.
**Rates:** $35-$55 DAILY. WEEKLY RATES ON REQUEST.
**Reservations:** (919) 787-2109 MONDAY THROUGH FRIDAY 9 A.M. TO 8 P.M.

## MARS HILL

A charming, inviting inn located in the Appalachian Mountains, 18 miles north of Asheville. Wide rocking chair porches and gardens surround the home. Five guestrooms, some with working FIREPLACES and two with private baths. Suite available. Breakfast included.
**Rates:** $36-$55 DAILY.
**Reservations:** (919) 787-2109 MONDAY THROUGH FRIDAY 9 A.M. TO 8 P.M.

## TRYON

Located on 3 acres near the charming town of Tryon, this inn is a 1939 stone home. The eight bedrooms are furnished in modern traditional decor, each with a private bath. Buffet breakfast served; guests are encouraged to use the inn as their home, including the TV and video file.
**Rates:** $40-$90 DAILY.
**Reservations:** (919) 787-2109 MONDAY THROUGH FRIDAY 9 A.M. TO 8 P.M.

## PIEDMONT AREA
### CHAPEL HILL

Beautiful home combining Greek Revival and Federal styles. Guests are welcome to enjoy the eighteenth century living room and formal dining room or roam the surrounding 10 acres of woodland. Six rooms, each with private baths. Full English breakfast. Also available for receptions and business meetings. It is 11 miles west of Chapel Hill.
**Rates:** $75-$85 DAILY.
**Reservations:** (919) 787-2109 MONDAY THROUGH FRIDAY 9 A.M. TO 8 P.M.

## CLINTON

Take a step back in time in this Greek Revival home featuring leaded glass, double parlors filled with antiques, dining room, wraparound porch,

and deck in back. Five rooms, each with private bath and TV, period furniture. Continental or full breakfast provided.
**Rates:** $40-$65 DAILY.
**Reservations:** (919) 787-2109 MONDAY THROUGH FRIDAY 9 A.M. TO 8 P.M.

## DURHAM

Step back into the eighteenth century, but be near the technology of the Triangle area. Select one of the six guestrooms, individually decorated in Colonial or Victorian themes; two with private baths. Complimentary tea or sherry as well as continental or full breakfast. Visit historical areas or stroll the 3 1/2 acres.
**Rates:** $55-$75 DAILY.
**Reservations:** (919) 787-2109 MONDAY THROUGH FRIDAY 9 A.M. TO 8 P.M.

## GREENSBORO

Chalet style home lovingly renovated; living area, two fireplaces, TV room, dining area, and kitchen. POOL. Hearty continental breakfast served. Five rooms, one with waterbed, another with fireplace; three private baths, two shared. Park nearby for jogging, picnics, or other recreation.
**Rates:** $35-$50 DAILY. (SURCHARGE DURING FURNITURE MARKET.)
**Reservations:** (919) 787-2109 MONDAY THROUGH FRIDAY 9 A.M. TO 8 P.M.

## HERTFORD

Beautifully restored home with wraparound porch, located on the historical tour of Hertford. Three spacious rooms, carpeted, with private or semiprivate baths. Full country breakfast and the bakery is right next door.
**Rates:** $30-$40 DAILY.
**Reservations:** (919) 787-2109 MONDAY THROUGH FRIDAY 9 A.M. TO 8 P.M.

## PIEDMONT AND OTHERS
### MILTON

A Greek Revival plantation manor house overlooking the hills of Northern Piedmont, North Carolina near the Dan River valley; historic Caswell County landmark. Federal and American Empire antique furnishings, canopied beds and other elegant touches. Four rooms, each with half or full bath. Full Southern breakfast. Dinner and Sunday brunch also available.

**Rates:** $47-$52 DAILY.
**Reservations:** (919) 787-2109 MONDAY THROUGH FRIDAY 9 A.M.
TO 8 P.M.

## PINEHURST

Charming five story country inn just minutes from golf, tennis, quaint shops, and riding trails. Modern hotel amenities; 81 rooms, including 33 suites, all with private baths. Victorian dining room serves three meals; breakfast included with room. Entertainment in the lounge; conversation in the parlor. Packages available. Meeting facilities.
**Rates:** $55-$180.
**Reservations:** (919) 787-2109 MONDAY THROUGH FRIDAY 9 A.M.
TO 8 P.M.

## RALEIGH

Beautifully restored Victorian inn built in 1871 and on the National Register of Historic Places. Furnished with period antiques throughout. Located in downtown historic area. Full breakfast, walking tour guide and newspaper. Six rooms, some with shared bath.
**Rates:** $60-$75 DAILY.
**Reservations:** (919) 787-2109 MONDAY THROUGH FRIDAY 9 A.M.
TO 8 P.M.

# SOUTH CAROLINA

## COASTAL AREA
### CHARLESTON

If history and beauty appeals to you, you will be surrounded by it in Charleston, South Carolina. The gentle tolling of church bells, magnificent eighteenth century homes, gardens, plantations, and public buildings that have remained in daily use for centuries and a people noted for their warmth and hospitality are all found in this unique city. The area's beaches are superb and accessible (10 miles) by car or bus. Harbor tours take visitors to Fort Sumter, where the Civil War began. Horse and buggy tours give visitors a real feel for the past while giving them an excellent history lesson as they ride over brick and cobblestone streets. Come and discover America's best kept secret!

### HARLESTON VILLAGE

BEAUFAIN STREET — Unique circa 1837 gracious dwelling overlooking Colonial Lake. Accommodations include king-sized bed in master suite with twin bed in adjoining room. Full private bath. Piazza with hammock. Lighted public tennis courts in view. Antiques throughout home. Your very own refrigerator, toaster oven, and kettle. Gourmet continental breakfast. Complimentary wine and goodies. Host is a realtor; hostess is a preservation activist. Both enjoy gardening and are do it yourselfers. Affectionate DACHSHUND in residence. Convenient to house museums, historic churches, theater, museums, galleries, antiquing, and outstanding restaurants. It is 12 to 14 miles to plantations and gardens. Parks, beaches, recreation abound for sports and nature lovers. Come for a memorable visit. CHILDREN over 16 welcome. NO SMOKERS.
**Rates:** S OR D $90 DAILY MARCH THROUGH JUNE. JULY THROUGH FEBRUARY S OR D $80 DAILY. (T $115 DAILY.)
**Reservations:** (803) 722-6606 MONDAY THROUGH FRIDAY 9:30 A.M. - 5:30 P.M.

RUTLEDGE AVENUE — Four room brick carriage house overlooking fish pond. Tile bath and furnished kitchen. Furnished with antiques. Built in 1840 as a kitchen building, still has old fireplace (nonworking). Host is an attorney; hostess is a journalist. Two daughters ages 12 and 9, a son age 6, live here. Can accommodate one child of any age. Convenient to all of Charleston's historic areas and antiques shops. It is a 30 minute drive to historic gardens or to beaches. Continental breakfast. Air conditioning. Accommodations include: bedroom with double bed and private bath; sleeper sofa in the living room. NO SMOKERS.
**Rates:** $75 OFF-SEASON; $85 SPRING SEASON DAILY. OFF-SEASON ONLY: $350 WITHOUT BREAKFAST WEEKLY.

**Reservations:** (803) 722-6606 MONDAY THROUGH FRIDAY 9:30 A.M. - 5:30 P.M.

RUTLEDGE AVENUE AT QUEEN — Hospitable accommodations in a gracious mansion overlooking beautiful Colonial Lake here in Charleston's Historic District. Outside, visitors may sit on the two story porches and view the sunset over the water. Inside, guests are greeted by beveled glass doors, inlay floors, crystal chandeliers and family antiques. Spacious guestrooms feature old FIREPLACE mantels, private baths, ceiling fans, individually controlled heating and air conditioning, all with individual character. Accommodations include: A) queen-sized bed and B) two rooms with double bed. A continental breakfast is served daily in the dining room and sherry is available in the evenings. The guests also enjoy the use of a refrigerator, bikes, brochure and menu collection, music room with PIANO, and library. Staying here is like a visit with old friends. Host is an architect who enjoys windsurfing, show dogs, and antiques. One PET is in residence. CHILDREN over 10 years old welcome.
**Rates:** $85 DAILY.
**Reservations:** (803) 722-6606 MONDAY THROUGH FRIDAY 9:30 A.M. - 5:30 P.M.

SMITH STREET — An 1870 Charleston single house with a small garden located in Harleston Village in historic Charleston. The house is furnished with antiques, wicker, and reproductions. The hostess is a retired medical technologist and enjoys serving a full breakfast to her guests. There are two connecting bedrooms. One room has a 3/4 bed, and the other room has a single bed. There is a connecting bath with tub and European shower. The bedroom with the 3/4 bed also has a lavatory in the bedroom. It is ideal for two ladies or two gentlemen. Hostess has had many couples, however, who have enjoyed her accommodations. Besides being in the Historic District of Charleston, it is within 2 blocks of the College of Charleston and 3 blocks from the Medical University of South Carolina. The hostess has no pets. CHILDREN over 10 years are welcome. The hostess does not smoke and prefers that guests not SMOKE in the bedrooms.
**Rates:** S $45; D $60 DAILY.
**Reservations:** (803) 722-6606 MONDAY THROUGH FRIDAY 9:30 A.M. - 5:30 P.M.

WENTWORTH STREET — A very grand 1838 Greek Revival pillared mansion rated in the very highest category in the architectural survey of Charleston buildings. The house is magnificently restored and furnished with museum quality antiques of the eighteenth century, including Charleston and Philadelphia furniture. The host is a William and Mary

College alumnus and a retired interior designer who is well versed in the arts, architecture history, and genealogy of the area. All rooms are well appointed and a full breakfast is served in a beautiful, bright solarium. Your host will direct you to points of interest, historic places, restaurants, and the like. The mansion is located in the heart of the historic area, close to the College of Charleston and the Medical University of South Carolina, and 4 blocks from the Charleston Convention Center. The terraces and garden with fountain are large and formal and guests are welcome to enjoy them. Accommodations include: A) king canopy bed, private bath; and B) two bedroom suite with a queen canopy bed and a double bed. There is a full bath between and suite is let to one party only; C) Gazebo Garden Suite, king-sized bed and a double canopy bed, two bedroom suite with a private bath. CHILDREN over 12 welcome. SMOKERS NOT WELCOME.

**Rates:** A) D $75-$85; B) TWO ROOMS WITH ONE BATH $110; AND C) GAZEBO GARDEN HOUSE $85 DAILY.

**Reservations:** (803) 722-6606 MONDAY THROUGH FRIDAY 9:30 A.M. - 5:30 P.M.

## HISTORIC DISTRICT

ANSON STREET NEAR MARKET STREET — Historic District near market area. Everything is a short walk from this centrally located colonaded 1820s house. The garden is shaded by a huge pecan tree. The two apartments have private entrances on the garden level. Brick walls, beamed ceilings, and working FIREPLACES. Apartment accommodations include: A) one bedroom with two double beds, private bath and B) queen-sized bed in bedroom, sleeper sofa in living room, private bath. Host is a textile merchant; hostess is an artist. French and fluent Spanish are spoken here. A GOLDEN LABRADOR is in residence here. HANDICAPPED ACCESSIBLE. Breakfast is usually served in the garden.

**Rates:** A) $85 AND B) $65 DAILY.

**Reservations:** (803) 722-6606 MONDAY THROUGH FRIDAY 9:30 A.M. - 5:30 P.M.

The oldest frame house in Charleston, built sometime before 1715. Much of the early Georgian woodwork remains and there is a beautiful keystone arch in the hall. There are five working fireplaces and a small garden. Accommodations include: A) twin beds, shared bath; B) single bed, FIREPLACE, shared bath; and C) sitting room where breakfast is served that has one bed. The accommodations are on the third floor. There is no off-street parking. The county parking garage is 1 block away. There is an elevator to the second floor. One DOG is in residence. A little French is spoken here. PIANO. NO SMOKING.

**Rates:** D $60,T $90, Q $110 DAILY.

**Reservations:** (803) 722-6606 MONDAY THROUGH FRIDAY 9:30 A.M. - 5:30 P.M.

BROAD STREET — House circa 1880 situated on south side of Broad Street in Historic District. Everything within walking distance. It is 1 block to King Street antique shops and America's top designer shops. Walking in another direction you pass many of Charleston's most beautiful houses and historic landmarks on your way to the Battery. All rooms have 10 foot ceilings, original wide board floors, FIREPLACES, and antiques. Elevator! Accommodations include: A) large double room and bath, four poster bed, French doors to piazza with wicker furniture. Adjoining is large sitting room and B) off piazza with double pullout couch, and C) master bedroom with king-sized bed, bath with bidet. Balcony. Continental breakfast served to guests in C. A and B have refrigerator and continental setup. Crib and cot available. Entire floor ideal for large party or family. D) is charming two room, queen bed, carriage house in pretty walled garden. TV, air conditioning, bikes available. Hostess loves people, her house, and garden. Children welcome. Smokers welcome.

**Rates:** A) $75; A & B AS SUITE) D $90 PLUS $15 EACH ADDITIONAL PERSON; C) $90; AND D) $85 DAILY.

**Reservations:** (803) 722-6606 MONDAY THROUGH FRIDAY 9:30 A.M. - 5:30 P.M.

BROAD & KING STREETS — Carriage house of a large pre-Revolutionary War home set in middle of downtown area with separate carriage house for B&B. Carriage house has a separate entrance, is furnished with antiques, includes two FIREPLACES and a charming courtyard. Host is an attorney; hostess is a housewife and they have four children (3 teenagers). Accommodations include: A) two single beds, private bath; B) Charleston queen-sized rice bed, FIREPLACE, and private bath; C) two single beds, FIREPLACE, and private bath; and D) double bed. private bath. Breakfast is delivered to the rooms each morning. A kitchen is available for guests' use including a washer and dryer. Bikes and a crib are available, as well as air conditioning. A friendly GOLDEN RETRIEVER is in residence. This home is in the middle of the Historic District. Historic sites, shops, and restaurants are within easy walking distance. A picnic area is also available. Children are welcome. Smokers welcome.

**Rates:** A & D) S OR D $75 AND B & C) S OR D $85 DAILY. S OR D $450 WEEKLY.

**Reservations:** (803) 722-6606 MONDAY THROUGH FRIDAY 9:30 A.M. - 5:30 P.M.

BROAD STREET AT MEETING — Charming carriage house converted into a two bedroom unit for B&B rental. Perfect for one or two couples traveling together. The carriage house is beautifully furnished with antiques. It includes a full kitchen, living room, and A) queen-sized bedroom with private bath and B) bedroom with double bed, private bath. Off-street parking. Excellent location in the heart of Charleston's Historic District is within walking distance of most of Charleston's historic attractions. Host is a real estate broker; hostess is a housewife who is interested in tennis, sailing. and bridge. Air conditioning. Fireplace. **Rates:** S $85, D $140 DAILY. **Reservations:** (803) 722-6606 MONDAY THROUGH FRIDAY 9:30 A.M. - 5:30 P.M.

BROAD STREET AT SAVAGE — Classic Charleston single house with double side verandas, built in 1868. Heart of Charleston district. B&B is the original detached kitchen house, now attached to the main house. Recently renovated, country antiques, and JACUZZI blend old with new. Host is a pathologist; hostess is an exercise instructor. Parents of three children: 2 girls, 5 and 7 years; and a boy 1 1/2 years. Queen-sized bed, separate vanity area with double sinks and makeup lights, and eat-in area with table and chairs. Continental breakfast placed outside door in hallway. Stays hot or cold for late sleepers. Bikes available. College of Charleston, the Citadel, and the Medical University of South Carolina are all within 5 to 10 minute drive. Within walking distance to town for sightseeing, antiques, and tennis courts. Beaches are 20 minutes away. One DOG is in residence. NO SMOKERS. **Rates:** ON SEASON $90; OFF-SEASON $80 DAILY. **Reservations:** (803) 722-6606 MONDAY THROUGH FRIDAY 9:30 A.M. - 5:30 P.M.

BULL STREET — This 1811 single house with separate entrance, formal rose garden; off-street parking; bikes; near antique mart and in historic Harleston Village; walk to famous King Street shops. Accommodations include: two bedrooms A) queen-sized bed; B) queen-sized bed and C) living room with sleeper sofa; private bath; full kitchen. Sleep like a lamb after famous low country seafood dinner in one of the nearby four star restaurants; wake to two "pet" cardinals at feeder in garden; private brick patio. Host is minister of nearby historic downtown First (Scots) Presbytrian Church; hostess is newspaper columnist. A "retired" LHASA APSA will greet you with a smile, two teenage daughters help with breakfast. Air conditioning. HANDICAPPED ACCESSIBLE. Children welcome. **Rates:** S OR D $85, OR $120 DAILY. **Reservations:** (803) 722-6606 MONDAY THROUGH FRIDAY 9:30 A.M. - 5:30 P.M.

CHURCH STREET — According to *Charleston Interiors* published by the Preservation Society of Charleston, this house circa 1745 is one of

the most impressive double houses in the city. It retains its original Georgian paneling along with Adam mantels that were added shortly after the Revolution. Like the main house, a charming outbuilding at the rear is built of low country brick. This former kitchen and servant facility has windows with pointed arches, an architectural departure from the normal style of houses of the period. It was lately the studio of nationally known artist, Alice Ravenel Huger Smith. Accommodations include: A) double bed, private bath; B) double canopy bed, private bath; and C) twin beds, private bath.
**Rates:** $70-$80 DAILY.
**Reservations:** (803) 722-6606 MONDAY THROUGH FRIDAY 9:30 A.M. - - 5:30 P.M.

CHURCH STREET — This is a 1,800 square foot, former servants' quarters and cook kitchen buildings. Property is a National Historic Landmark. All landmark properties are automatically on the National Register. Kitchen with washer/dryer, dishwasher, and the like. Located within the heart of the Historic District of Charleston. Living room, dining room, kitchen downstairs. Accommodations include: A) queen-sized canopy bed in master bedroom and B) twin beds in guestroom. Both share bathroom. Central heat and air conditioning. Private, walled garden in rear with fountain, table and chairs for guests. Continental breakfast in house, prepare yourself. Private entrance, separate telephone. Appropriately furnished in period reproductions. Host is a medical doctor and speaks a little German. One DOG is in residence here. CHILDREN over 12 welcome.
**Rates:** S OR D $100, $150, Q $175 DAILY. $1,800-$5,000 MONTHLY. RATE DEPENDS ON WHICH MONTH.
**Reservations:** (803) 722-6606 MONDAY THROUGH FRIDAY 9:30 A.M. - 5:30 P.M.

LEGARE STREET — In the walled garden of this 1759 Charleston home, guests find the two bedroom, two bath carriage house. The living room and eat-in kitchen open onto the patio and garden with fountain. Full breakfast fixings and complimentary wine await the visitor. Host is a family physician; hostess is the owner of Historic Charleston Bed & Breakfast Reservation Service. Within walking distance to many excellent restaurants, museums, historic places of interest, and unique shops. Tennis courts nearby. Beaches 20 minutes away. Accommodations include: A) double bed, private bath; and B) two twin beds, private bath. Limited French is spoken. One DOG and one CAT are in residence here. Air conditioning. CHILDREN over 6 years old welcome.
**Rates:** S $90, D $90, T $135, Q $150 DAILY. $355 WEEKLY.
**Reservations:** (803) 722-6606 MONDAY THROUGH FRIDAY 9:30 A.M. - 5:30 P.M.

MEETING STREET — Enjoy eighteenth century history and twentieth century hospitality in this 1740 Charleston single house. Three bedroom-parlor suites are authentically restored for your comfort with every modern convenience. Each suite has canopy double beds, private baths, heart pine floors, and FIREPLACE. A crib and single daybeds are available. Breakfast food in the kitchenette includes a different homebaked bread or muffin each day in addition to coffee, tea, juice, milk, cereal, English muffin, butter, and jelly. Fresh fruit, flowers, and a morning newspaper are provided. Located in residential, historic Charleston within walking distance of restaurants, theater, and shops. Host will play harpsichord on request; hostess will give information about sightseeing and restaurants. One black LABRADOR is in residence. Children of all ages welcome.
**Rates:** $75-$100 DAILY.
**Reservations:** (803) 722-6606 MONDAY THROUGH FRIDAY 9:30 A.M. - 5:30 P.M.

ORANGE STREET — The kitchen dependency of a 1770s Charleston style single house accommodates visitors who want to enjoy the elegance and charm of one of America's most historic cities. Within a short walking distance of the residential area home are White Point Gardens, the "Four Corners of Law," the city market, museum houses, historic churches, and the antique shops and boutiques of King Street. Furnished with Southern antiques, the attached two story apartment with private entrance from the rear garden of the house has a sitting room and kitchen unit on the first floor, a bedroom (with a double antique sleigh bed and an iron and brass single bed) and modern bath with shower on the second floor. Breakfast is provided, and varied offerings include fresh fruit and pastries and breads baked by the hostess. The host is in public relations. German and French are spoken here. Air conditioning. Children welcome. NO SMOKERS.
**Rates:** S $90, D $90, T $110 DAILY.
**Reservations:** (803) 722-6606 MONDAY THROUGH FRIDAY 9:30 A.M. - 5:30 P.M.

ORANGE STREET — Located in the former slave quarters of a Charleston single house built in 1770 in an area of historic Charleston formerly known as the "Orange Garden." One bedroom only with canopy double bed, private shower bath, and private entrance. Offers off-street parking and a walled garden for your pleasure. Breakfast prepared by hostess and served in dining room or garden. Host is a physician who enjoys sailing and running; hostess enjoys gardening and antiquing. A little French and Spanish are spoken here. Air conditioning, bikes, and PIANO are available. Public transportation is nearby. CHILDREN cannot be accommodated. NO SMOKING.

**Rates:** S OR D $75 DAILY.
**Reservations:** (803) 722-6606 MONDAY THROUGH FRIDAY 9:30 A.M. - 5:30 P.M.

RUTLEDGE AVENUE NEAR CANAL — Antebellum kitchen building servants' quarters in rear garden of circa 1830 Charleston single house. On corner of picturesque Colonial Lake, home is within walking distance from historic sites, antique shopping district, and deep sea flshing at marina. Golf and beaches within 15 minutes. Host is a retired naval officer and navy mementos fill the rooms; hostess is an attorney. Accommodations include: A) double bed, shared bath; B) twin beds, shared bath; and C) living room/double sleep sofa, shared bath. Playpen and bassinette available. Perfect for families or couples traveling together. Help yourself to full breakfast in well-stocked kitchen. After sightseeing, relax in a rope hammock or on porch swing. Light a fire and sip a glass of wine in the living room before retiring. Your private entrance is through semitropical garden scented with wisteria and honeysuckle. Accessible to public transportation.
**Rates:** S OR D $85, T/Q $120, 5 OR 6 PERSONS $145 DAILY (ALL BOOKED AS ONE UNIT). $325 WEEKLY WITHOUT BREAKFAST.
**Reservations:** (803) 722-6606 MONDAY THROUGH FRIDAY 9:30 A.M. 5:30 P.M.

TRADD STREET — Circa 1732, "the Kitchen House," which has been completely restored, is situated in the heart of the Historic District. The patio overlooks a Colonial herb garden. Entire house at your disposal including living room, dining area, and full kitchen on first floor. Accommodations include: A) queen-sized bed, a FIREPLACE, share bath; B) two twin beds, share bath on the second floor. The refrigerator and pantry are stocked for a hearty breakfast; sherry and fruit as well. Host is an executive; hostess is a gourmet cook. C) A twin-bedded room and bath in the main house can be used as overflow accommodations. Within walking distance to most Charleston attractions. Airport is 25 minutes away. Featured in November-December 1986 *Colonial Homes* magazine. A POODLE is in residence. Well-behaved children welcome. SMOKERS tolerated.
**Rates:** A) ONE BEDROOM D $115. A & B) TWO BEDROOMS $160.
**Reservations:** (803) 722-6606 MONDAY THROUGH FRIDAY 9:30 A.M. - 5:30 P.M.

TRADD STREET AT CHURCH — Main house is pre-Revolutionary, located in the center of the old Historic District. Guest facilities are in separate outbuilding with private entrance from street. Ground level room has entrance from courtyard, private bath, twin brass beds, air conditioning, black and white TV. Second floor room upstairs from

breakfast room, has private bath, twin beds, air conditioning, black and white TV. Cot is available. Continental breakfast (homebaked breads, host's blended coffee, juice). Served either in breakfast room or in courtyard. Host is an apparel manufacturer; hostess is an apparel designer. They are very knowledgeable on restaurants, what to see, menu file, books on antiques, and Charleston. Host speaks good French. There is one DOG in residence. CHILDREN cannot be accommodated.
**Rates:** S OR D $55 DAILY EXCEPT HIGH SEASON MARCH 15 THROUGH JUNE 15 WHEN S OR D IS $65 DAILY. WEEKLY AND MONTHLY RATES ARE NEGOTIABLE.
**Reservations:** (803) 722-6606 MONDAY THROUGH FRIDAY 9:30 A.M. - 5:30 P.M.

WENTWORTH NEAR EAST BAY — An 1840 carriage house in an urban residential setting, within walking distance of market area, historical sites, and antique row. Fort Sumter tours and marina are nearby. The carriage house is one complete unit with living room, dining room, and kitchen downstairs. Two bedrooms (one with twin beds, one with double bed) upstairs. Small private yard. Off-street parking. Supplies for full breakfast included. Ideal location to see historic Charleston by foot, horse carriage, or tour bus. Your host is a physician. Two DOGS are in residence here. Air conditioned.
**Rates:** S OR D $85, T $145, Q $145 DAILY.
**Reservations:** (803) 722-6606 MONDAY THROUGH FRIDAY 9:30 A.M. - 5:30 P.M.

## SUMMERVILLE
### HISTORIC DISTRICT

SOUTH HAMPTON STREET — In this small town of charming historic homes, the lovely double wraparound porches of this National Register circa 1865 house draw many camera bugs. In the comfortable main house family antiques join the eclectic collection of 30 years of navy travel. A FIREPLACE warms the A) canopy double bedroom that opens to the upstairs porch for breakfast or enjoying complimentary wine and fruit. NONSMOKERS here. Hostess' country kitchen is the starting point for local walking tours and cooking classes as well as family and guest meals. The dependency B) cottage, beamed ceiling, fireplace, and country furniture offers charm, privacy, and a view of garden and swimming POOL. Cottage guests may prepare breakfast or join house guests by the pool or in the flower filled greenhouse. Walk or bike to tennis, shops, restaurants, or follow the Preservation Society Tour. Tired of eating out, use the cottage kitchen along with grill, relax by the pool, or picnic in park gardens. Colleges, shopping, and historic spots are within easy range. Cozy for two to escape the winter. Air conditioned. PIANO. Bikes available. NO CHILDREN. Smoking permitted in cottage only.

**Rates:** A) D $50, T $75 DAILY AND B) D $45, T $65, Q $75 DAILY.
$210 WEEKLY. $500 MONTHLY.
**Reservations:** (803) 722-6606 MONDAY THROUGH FRIDAY 9:30 A.M. -
5:30 P.M.

# VIRGINIA

## ALLEGHENIES
## WARM SPRINGS
### OLD GERMANTOWN

This is an eighteenth century log tavern, the second house was joined in the early nineteenth century. Within the walking distance of the Warm Springs pools. Good restaurants nearby. A rambling old house with porches. A place for sitting, reading, walking, and generally quiet times. Active recreation such as golf is available 5 miles away. Hostess may leave all in readiness, may be there to make breakfast. Accommodations include six rooms: A) king-sized bed, FIREPLACE, private bath; B) two rooms with twin-bedded double, private bath; C) queen-sized bed, private bath; D) double bed and single bed, shared bath; and E) double bed. Hostess is a real estate broker who speaks a little French. SMALL, WELL-BEHAVED PETS WELCOME. PIANO.
**Rates:** A-E) S $40, D $50 DAILY.
**Reservations:** (703) 955-1246 MONDAY THROUGH SATURDAY 9 A.M. TO 1 P.M. (ANSWERING MACHINE AT OTHER TIMES.)

## BLUE RIDGE MOUNTAINS

The Blue Ridge Mountains are the heart of the historical hunt country in Virginia. Found here are the rolling hills of Virginia. You are close to historical houses, Oatlands, Morgan's Mill, Carter Hall, and many famous horse farms. There are the Clarke and Loudoun Hunts as well as Point-to-Point hunt races. You are close to historical battlefields and world reknowned restaurants, including the oldest tavern in the United States. Many antique shops and estate auctions abound.

## AMISSVILLE
### VIRGINIA HUNT COUNTRY

A gracious 1923 farmhouse surrounded by lawns and tree-filled park. Still in original family. Filled with memorabilia of five generations. Present owner is an art historian. Furnishings are both antique and modern, but all are family pieces and many reveal long associations with fox hunting and racing. Shingle house combines wide center hall and high ceilinged rooms of traditional Virginia architecture with subtle flavor of Irish heritage of owners. Two NORWICH TERRIER DOGS in residence. Accommodations include: A) twin beds, private bath, and working FIREPLACE; B) double bed, private bath, and working FIREPLACE; and C) two rooms with twin beds, shared bath. Enjoy hearty breakfast in formal dining room with cheery fire in winter or on open porch amid birdsong in warm weather. In foothills of Blue Ridge Mountains, Bunree is convenient for hiking, antiquing, historic sites, local vineyards, and fine restaurants. CHILDREN over 10 welcome.

**Rates:** A & B) S $45, D $55; AND C) S $35, D $45 DAILY.
**Reservations:** (703) 955-1246 MONDAY THROUGH SATURDAY 9 A.M.
TO 1 P.M. (ANSWERING MACHINE AT OTHER TIMES.)

## BLUEMONT

BLUE RIDGE MOUNTAIN HIGHWAY — A cozy 50 year old field
stone house, barn and springhouse on 7 acres atop the Blue Ridge
Mountains (1,700 feet). Overlooking scenic and historic Shenandoah
Valley. Rocky Top is just 3 miles from the Shenandoah River for fishing
and canoeing, and 20 miles from Middleburg, the heart of Virginia's hunt
country. Access to the Appalachian Trail for hiking is a mile away. One
can enjoy Harper's Ferry, West Virginia and the Skyline Drive in 30
minutes and the nation's capital in an hour. The entire area has an
abundance of Civil War sites and quaint specialty and antique shops. The
home is furnished with country antiques including the 1830s rope bed you
will sleep on. Eat a gourmet breakfast including homemade jam and
waffles cooked on the Franklin stove. One can relax at this romantic
secluded mountain retreat watching birds, counting deer in the pasture,
and sunbathing on the deck. A 50 year old blue spruce shares the evening
sky with the setting sun. Host is a data processing consultant who enjoys
spelunking, boomerangs, and books; hostess is a dietitian who takes pride
in her violets, postcard collecting, and home decoration. PETS must be
able to spend the night in the barn. Sixty minutes from Dulles International
Airport and minutes from Interstates 66 and 95. Accommodations include
a double bed (rope), private bath. PIANO. Children welcome. SMOKERS
NOT WELCOME.
**Rates:** S OR D $45 DAILY.
**Reservations:** (703) 955-1246 MONDAY THROUGH SATURDAY 9 A.M.
TO 1 P.M. (ANSWERING MACHINE AT OTHER TIMES.)

## FLINT HILL
### SCENIC FARMLAND

With Virginia's Blue Ridge Mountains in the background, this farm offers
its guests a beautiful setting year-round. Scenic pasture lands are
surrounded by stone fences. The Federal style house and companion
summer kitchen were completed in 1812. The two have remained intact
— mantels, paneled window, and wide pine floors are original—restoration
was completed in 1965. It was granted one of Virginia's first scenic
easements in 1973. Three porches offer a variety of views during the
warmer months. A working cattle farm, adjacent to the Shenandoah
National Park. Many activities are nearby: Skyline Drive, caves, riding,
hiking, canoeing, tennis, golf, winery, antiquing, historic sites, and superb
dining. A NONSMOKING HOME. CHILDREN UNDER 12 AND PETS
ONLY BY SPECIAL ARRANGEMENT. Evening social hour and full
breakfast menu. There is a 2 1/2 room summer kitchen. International

broadcaster Phil Irwin is host. Accommodations include: A) double bed, FIREPLACE, shared bath; B) double bed, single bed, FIREPLACE, shared bath; and C) queen-sized bed, FIREPLACE, private bath. Air conditioned, VCR, and canoe.
**Rates:** MAIN HOUSE $70 DAILY; SUMMER KITCHEN $100 DAILY. WORKING FIREPLACES SURCHARGED.
**Reservations:** (703) 955-1246 MONDAY THROUGH SATURDAY 9 A.M. TO 1 P.M. (ANSWERING MACHINE AT OTHER TIMES.)

## WASHINGTON
### HISTORIC DISTRICT

MAIN STREET — Circa 1900, the inn is located in the heart of historic Washington, Virginia—"the first Washington of them all." The house is now a showcase for the host, who is a renovation specialist and decorative painter. The upstairs guestrooms have been tastefully decorated in country Victorian style and are air conditioned. Many furnishings are antiques. Guests enjoy relaxing on the front porch or soaking in views of the surrounding mountains and country estates from the guest suite. Favorite pastimes of guests include hiking, fishing, antique shopping, dining at the renowned "Inn at Little Washington," taking a walking tour of the town, and exploring "the First Washington Museum." Accommodations include: A) private suite with kitchen, bath, bedroom, and sitting room; B) double room with private bath; and C) two double rooms with shared bath. Cot can be supplied for a third person. PIANO. Air conditioned and VCR. Small bikes available.
**Rates:** A) S $65, D $75; AND B & C) S $45, D $55 DAILY. DISCOUNTS APPLY AFTER FIRST TWO DAYS.
**Reservations:** (703) 955-1246 MONDAY THROUGH SATURDAY 9 A.M. TO 1 P.M. (ANSWERING MACHINE AT OTHER TIMES.)

## CENTRAL PIEDMONT
### SCOTTSVILLE
### CHARLOTTESVILLE AREA

CONSTITUTION BYWAY ROUTE 20 — The perfect place for people who love to travel but hate to leave home. A Virginia Historic Landmark on 22 acres with dwellings built in 1832 and 1882 joined by a longitudinal grand hall. On the National Register of Historic Homes. Four guestrooms, each with a private bath, are part of 17 available rooms furnished with individually collected period perfect antiques. Nine fireplaces, antique rose and flower gardens, acres of Pinot Noir grapevines, two ponds and streams, gazebo, and four porches. Bikes available. It is 15 minutes to Charlottesville, Jefferson's Monticello, Monroe's Ash Lawn, University of Virginia, 5 minutes to James River for fishing, tubing, and canoeing, and 2 hours from D.C. area. Wine touring and tasting at numerous local wineries. Shenandoah and Blue Ridge mountains provide fall foliage or

skiing. Picnicking, hiking, croquet, badminton, horseshoes, birdwatching on premises. Host is a retired naval submarine officer; hostess is a financial analyst. Their 14 year old son plays classical guitar. The 6 year old DACHSHUND frolics. Pets welcome. Accommodations include: four double bedrooms with attached private baths. Cot available. JACUZZI. FIREPLACE in bedroom. Children welcome.
**Rates:** S $49, D $59 DAILY.
**Reservations:** (202) 363-7767 MONDAY - THURSDAY 9:00 - 5:00; FRIDAY 9:00 - 1:00.

# CENTRAL VIRGINIA
## BOWLING GREEN

This home is the oldest in Caroline County and one of the best preserved Georgian houses in Virginia. It was designated a historic site by the Virginia Historic Landmarks Commission in 1967. Guests entertained here are thought to include George Washington on his way to Yorktown and Lafayette during his triumphal tour. The house features a center hall plan, gambrel roof, and wide plank pine floors. The upstairs offers three bedrooms, A & B) double beds and C) queen-sized bed with tall posts. Two bedrooms have FIREPLACES and guests are encouraged to use them. There is a full bath with tub upstairs and full bath with shower downstairs. Located on 125 acres, the house is surrounded by boxwoods and ancient holly trees and cedars. It is just over an hour to Williamsburg, 20 miles from Fredericksburg and 32 miles from Richmond. Host and hostess are interested in antique restoration and are wildflower enthusiasts. Children of any age welcome. NO SMOKING.
**Rates:** A-C S $46, D $55; WITH PRIVATE BATH ADD $10. CHILDREN OVER THREE $10 PER DAY.
**Reservations:** (804) 648-7560 11 A.M. TO 6 P.M. MONDAY THROUGH FRIDAY.

## GWYNN'S ISLAND

Located 45 minutes from Williamsburg and a little over an hour from Richmond, in the Middle Peninsula off the Chesapeake Bay, Gwynn's Island is a paradise for boaters and water skiers as well as a haven for seafood lovers. The surrounding area offers golf, tennis, boating. swimming, and antiquing. Further inland, country roads replete with fruit stands, country markets, and local crafts lead to other attractions such as the Ingleside Winery at Oak Grove; a working eighteenth century farm; Stratford Hall, where Confederate general Robert E. Lee was born, completed in 1732 and considered one of the finest unaltered examples of Colonial church architecture in the nation. With a wealth of sun and surf, historic attractions, and sporting opportunities, the Middle Peninsula of Virginia promises a perfect adventure.

Located just 45 minutes from Williamsburg and a little over an hour from Richmond is a wonderful B&B originally built by a sea captain in the 1730s. The house overlooks the Chesapeake Bay, which is a paradise for those loving WATER-related activities and those who enjoy good seafood restaurants. There is boating, fishing, crabbing, swimming, and skiing nearby as well as antiquing. During the summer months regularly scheduled all day cruises leave from a nearby dock. Built of clapboard in the true Williamsburg style, many of the original windows, fireplace mantels, floors, and doors remain in the house. The house offers five bedrooms, each with FIREPLACE, and two are very large rooms with private bath. There is a private half bath off the third bedroom, which shares a bath for showering with the others. Double accommodations available in the guestrooms (A-E). Your host and hostess enjoy fishing, collecting antiques, history, and writing. There are two resident DOGS. No SMOKING in the upstairs guestrooms due to the age of the house. Well-behaved children of any age welcome.

**Rates:** A & B) S $66, D $75; C) S $48, D $60; AND D & E) S $40-$45, D $44-$50 DAILY.

**Reservations:** (804) 648-7560 11 A.M. TO 6 P.M. MONDAY THROUGH FRIDAY.

## PETERSBURG

HIGH STREET — Located 25 minutes south of Richmond and built in the 1890s, this 14 room yellow brick Queen Anne style inn offers its guests the opportunity to experience the elegance and splendor of the Victorian period. House has a corner turret, Tuscan columns, and a color patterned slate roof. Many of the original lighting fixtures and fireplace mantels remain. Furnished in period antiques, the inn offers five guestrooms, including a honeymoon suite, with furnishings reflecting different periods ranging from Empire (1840s) to Eastlake (1880s). Double accommodations are available in the guestrooms. The inn is within walking distance of the Trapezium House, built in the 1800s without right angles or parallel sides; the Siege Museum, which documents the daily life of the townspeople during the Civil War; and the Old Blanford Church which was dedicated in 1901 as a shrine to the Confederate troops and which contains 15 original Tiffany windows. The inn is in close proximity to the Petersburg National Battle Field and U.S. Army Quartermaster Museum. Hosts are interested in historic preservation and travel. Air conditioned. NO SMOKING.

**Rates:** A) S $65, D $70; B & C) S $55, D $60; AND D & E) S $45, D $50 DAILY.

**Reservations:** (804) 648-7560 11 A.M. TO 6 P.M. MONDAY THROUGH FRIDAY.

This lovely three story home was built in 1915. It features fine architectural details throughout the first floor and includes a walnut paneled library, large renovated kitchen, and private, walled garden in the rear of the house. The home is beautifully furnished with antiques and Oriental rugs and offers its guests a twin-bedded room with private bath. The host is an attorney, who joins his wife in enthusiastic support of civic and cultural activities in Richmond. Their interests include sailing, classical music, entertaining, and travel. Resident DOG. Air conditioned. NONSMOKING guests only.

**Rates:** S $72, D $84 DAILY.

**Reservations:** (804) 648-7560 11 A.M. TO 6 P.M. MONDAY THROUGH FRIDAY.

## RICHMOND

Located just over an hour from Charlottesville, 50 minutes from Williamsburg, and 2 hours from Washington, D.C. Richmond is centrally located for day trips to various parts of Virginia. The city has a history dating back to 1607. There are great plantations along the James River. Richmond is rich in Revolutionary War sites where Patrick Henry, Lafayette, Washington, Jefferson, and others played out their roles. In the early 1800s Aaron Burr was tried for treason at the State Capitol in Richmond before Chief Justice John Marshall. Great architecture is everywhere, including Jefferson's magnificent Capitol, and work by Latrobe, Mills, Pope, Bottomley, and others. Today you can still stand where Robert E. Lee took command of his army, visit the White House of the Confederacy, tour famous battlefields, and see the pew where in 1865 Jefferson Davis received word of Petersburg's fall which would result in the Confederacy's ultimate demise. Museum lovers are delighted to find a wide array of choices in Richmond. There is the Poe Museum in Church Hill, the Valentine Museum (which depicts the history of life in Richmond), the Virginia Museum (one of the finest art museums of its size in the South), the Science Museum, Children's Museum, and the Museum of the Confederacy.

### FAN DISTRICT

This is a portion of central Richmond 8 to 10 minutes from downtown. It is known for urban townhouses, lovely gardens, beautiful architecture, small neighborhood restaurants, and shops. On the north, it is bound by Monument Avenue, one of the few historic avenues in the nation. Its monuments are dedicated to the heroes of the South, including several Confederate generals.

This charming 1912 row house has been completely remodeled by your host. Walls in the kitchen and living room have been removed to give the entire downstairs an open, airy feeling. The double-bedded room upstairs is large and spacious and the big bright yellow and white private bath is a delight. The front of the house and backyard are filled, in season, with blooming flowers reflecting one of the host's many leisure time pursuits. This home is within walking distance of neighborhood restaurants and close to the Virginia Museum and other local sites and attractions. Air conditioned. CHILDREN over 8 welcome. NO SMOKING. **Rates:** S $46, D $55 DAILY. **Reservations:** (804) 648-7560 11 A.M. TO 6 P.M. MONDAY THROUGH FRIDAY.

This lovely 1916 brick home is a Monument Avenue adaptation of the London townhouse. The large double parlor in the front of the home is open and airy, and leads back to the rear garden that in season is full of azaleas, camellias, and roses, which surround a Victorian gazebo. The home, which offers one double- and one queen-bedded guestroom, each with private bath is furnished with antiques, reproductions, and family pieces. The hosts, an engineer and personnel administrator, jointly love gardening, tennis, travel, football, and are involved in historic preservation. They are enthusiastically joined in welcoming guests to Richmond by two COCKER SPANIELS, Lady Virginia and Captain Rhett Butler. This home is within minutes of the Virginia Museum and other local sites and attractions. NONSMOKING guests only. **Rates:** S $48, D $60 DAILY. **Reservations:** (804) 648-7560 11 A.M. TO 6 P.M. MONDAY THROUGH FRIDAY.

This stunning, three story brick Georgian home was designed by Bottomley, who is well known for his fine architectural detailing. The rooms within the home are nicely proportioned and beautifully appointed. It is furnished with a combination of English and American antiques, fine antique Orientals, rich fabrics, and both traditional oil painting and contemporary art. The moldings and pediments over the doorways are of special interest as are the sconces in the living room, which were commissioned by Bottomley and made in Paris. The library is richly decorated with exotic raised paneling made of red gum. Accommodations include: A) a second floor queen-bedded room with sitting area, FIREPLACE, private bath, and optional adjoining sitting room and B) third floor double-bedded room with adjoining bath. The host is self-employed with interests in travel, cooking, music, and reading. Air conditioned. NO SMOKING. **Rates:** A) S $94, D $100, WITH ADJOINING SUITE S $100, D $125 AND B) S $88, D $94 DAILY. **Reservations:** (804) 648-7560 11 A.M. TO 6 P.M. MONDAY THROUGH FRIDAY.

MONUMENT NEAR ALLISON — This large home has been recently renovated. It was designed in the Italian Renaissance style, with a slightly French accent. The use of natural wood raised paneling to the wainscotting,

leaded glass windows, and coffered ceilings with dropped beams add a slightly medieval flavor. There are four second floor bedrooms, each with private bath. A) The front bedroom is large and sunny and features a queen-sized bed, FIREPLACE, separate sitting area by the bay window, and large oversized bath with JACUZZI. B) The second bedroom has a twin bed, private bath, and delightful FIREPLACE. C) The third and D) fourth bedrooms each have a queen-sized bed with private bath. Crib available. The hosts are B&B reservations service owners. Resident CAT. Located minutes from the Virginia Museum and from most local sites and attractions. Within a block of a bus line. Ideal for honeymooners. Well-behaved children are welcome. No SMOKING in the upstairs bedrooms.
**Rates:** A) S $66, D $75; B-D) S $56, D $65 DAILY. MONTHLY S $750, D $900.
**Reservations:** (804) 648-7560 11 A.M. TO 6 P.M. MONDAY THROUGH FRIDAY.

MONUMENT NEAR ROBINSON — The interior of this large, gracious house sparkles with the new life recently given it by your creative hosts. Heavily damaged while in other hands some years ago, the millwork has been faithfully reproduced and now showcases the brightly colored walls, fireplaces, and detailed windows throughout. This home, which was featured on the 1986 Fan Christmas Tour, offers: A) a second floor queen-bedded room and private bath with optional adjoining suite with FIREPLACE; and B & C) adjoining third floor twin bed and queen bed guestrooms with private bath between them, wet bar, and beautiful view of the city. The owners are both working professionals who love collecting antiques, art, and new friends. Resident DOG. This home is within 10 minutes of local sites and attractions and one block from public bus lines. Air conditioned. NO SMOKING in upstairs guestrooms.
**Rates:** A) S $72, D $84; WITH OPTIONAL SUITE S $90, D $105; AND B & C) S $65, D $72 DAILY.
**Reservations:** (804) 648-7560 11 A.M. TO 6 P.M. MONDAY THROUGH FRIDAY.

Some of the furnishings in this 1924 cottage style home, whose style is derived from the houses of the Cottswold District in England, were acquired at the 1922 Davanzanti Palace sale in Florence, Italy. Among the heirlooms are genuine Renaissance pieces including tapestries and rugs. The main rooms have art deco cornices with a running design of vines or flowers, and each opens through French doors onto the marble paved loggia (now enclosed) or the garden. The bedroom features a queen bed with private bath (shower only). Your hostess has been instrumental in starting the preservation movement in Richmond and is a sixth generation Richmonder. This house is minutes away from the Virginia Museum, Science Museum, and other local sites and attractions. Resident DOG and CAT. CHILDREN over 10 welcome.

**Rates:** S $46, D $55 DAILY.
**Reservations:** (804) 648-7560 11 A.M. TO 6 P.M. MONDAY THROUGH FRIDAY.

MONUMENT NEAR STRAWBERRY — This very large Gothic home was built in 1910 and is thought to be designed by Baskerville, one of Richmond's most prominent architects. The interior of the home is very grand, with mahogany paneling throughout the downstairs entry, living room, study, and dining room. There is a spacious feeling to the home, which is decorated in an eclectic blend of antiques and traditional furnishings. The home offers three guestrooms. Accommodations include: A) on the second floor a large, queen-bedded room with bay window and private bath with JACUZZI as well as a large double-bedded room with FIREPLACE, window seats, and private bath across the hall and B) on the third floor there is a twin-bedded room with private bath. The hosts, both self-employed professionals with grown children, enjoy various activities including jazz, photography, entertaining, and travel. Resident DOG. There is public transportation within a block. The home is within minutes of the Virginia Museum and other local sites and attractions. AC.
**Rates:** A) S $56, D $65 AND B) S $72, D $84 DAILY.
**Reservations:** (804) 648-7560 11 A.M. TO 6 P.M. MONDAY THROUGH FRIDAY.

This lovely three story home was built in 1915. It features fine architectural details throughout the first floor and includes a walnut paneled library, large renovated kitchen, and private walled garden in the rear of the house. The home is beautifully furnished with antiques and Oriental rugs and offers its guests a twin-bedded room with private bath. The host is an attorney, who joins his wife in enthusiastic support of civic and cultural activities in Richmond. Their interests include sailing, classical music, entertaining, and travel. Resident DOG. Air conditioned. NONSMOKING guests only.
**Rates:** S $72, D $84 DAILY.
**Reservations:** BEN00232

MONUMENT NEAR THOMPSON — This 1927 Tudor home has been lovingly restored. The gleaming wood floors showcase the hosts' interest in and collection of Oriental rugs. The house is nicely furnished with a blend of antiques and contemporary furnishings. The house offers a double bedroom with private bath. Host is a sales representative with his own business; hostess teaches emotionally disturbed children. Both enjoy the theater, symphony, and outdoor activities. This home is within minutes of the Virginia Museum and other local sites and attractions. Air conditioned. NONSMOKING guests only.
**Rates:** S $48, D $60 DAILY.

**Reservations:** (804) 648-7560 11 A.M. TO 6 P.M. MONDAY THROUGH
FRIDAY.

## HISTORIC CHURCH HILL

This 1870s Victorian structure features four working fireplaces, exposed
wood and brick walls, and several skylights. Filled with plants, the house
contains baskets and other craft pieces from all over the world, especially
from Brazil, where the hosts vacationed frequently. This home offers an
antique quilt covered double bed, with private half bath and private
courtyard off the guestroom. The upstairs bath must be shared for
showering. Your hostess, a snorkler and shell collector, draws finely
detailed studies of pine cone shells and other natural phenomena. This
home has been featured on the Church Hill tour. It is within walking
distance of historic St. John's Church and within 10 to 15 minutes of
most local sites and attractions. Resident CAT. Air conditioned.
**Rates:** S $46, D $55 DAILY.
**Reservations:** (804) 648-7560 11 A.M. TO 6 P.M. MONDAY THROUGH
FRIDAY.

## MECHANICSVILLE

The property on which this 1750 home stands was the site of the Battle
of Mechanicsville in 1862 and the house was used as a Civil War hospital
at that time. Nicely restored, it has lovely wide pine floors and is
furnished with a blend of antique and traditional pieces. The family room
offers a wonderful place to visit. The hostess is involved in the travel
industry. It is located on 5 1/2 acres that give it a country atmosphere. It
is 20 minutes from the center of Richmond. This home offers a canopied
queen-bedded room with private bath. Air conditioned. Children of any
age welcome.
**Rates:** S $48, D $60 DAILY.
**Reservations:** (804) 648-7560 11 A.M. TO 6 P.M. MONDAY THROUGH
FRIDAY.

## NORTH RICHMOND

Located just a short distance off Interstate 95, this brick, four bedroom
home is located in a quiet, peaceful neighborhood 15 minutes from
downtown Richmond. Guests have a twin-bedded room with private bath
and can use the large den with TV or, if they prefer, relax on the rear
deck in good weather. Hostess is a recently retired, but very active,
energetic, and delightful. She enjoys travel, cooking, biking, and refinishing
antique furniture. Air conditioned. PIANO. NONSMOKING guests only.
**Rates:** S $38, D $48 DAILY.
**Reservations:** (804) 648-7560 11 A.M. TO 6 P.M. MONDAY THROUGH
FRIDAY.

## UNIVERSITY OF RICHMOND AREA

This lovely old frame home is located in a wooded and nicely landscaped area within minutes of the University of Richmond. The home is comfortably furnished with antiques and Orientals and offers a twin-bedded room with private bath. The hostess is an active, energetic woman who loves to travel and is involved in many activities in the Richmond area. Air conditioned. CHILDREN over 12 welcome.
**Rates:** S $46, D $55 DAILY. CHILDREN $10 EACH PER NIGHT.
**Reservations:** (804) 648-7560 11 A.M. TO 6 P.M. MONDAY THROUGH FRIDAY.

This cozy, wonderful Williamsburg style townhouse is within minutes of the University of Richmond. Furnished with nineteenth century American antiques and porcelains, this inviting home offers its guests a room with antique twin sleigh beds, small adjoining sitting room, and private bath. There is an enclosed porch, with a terraced garden behind it, off the living room where guests can relax and enjoy the out of doors in good weather. Hostess loves travel, gardening, knitting, bridge, and entertaining parents visiting their children at the University! Air conditioned. CHILDREN over 6 welcome.
**Rates:** S $6, D $55 DAILY.
**Reservations:** (804) 648-7560 11 A.M. TO 6 P.M. MONDAY THROUGH FRIDAY.

## WILLIAMSBURG
### HISTORIC DISTRICT

This charming rust and cream colored 1 1/2 story Williamsburg clapboard cottage offers its guests complete privacy. UNHOSTED. Located behind the main house on a quiet, wooded lot with a small private garden in front, the cottage is within a mile of Colonial Williamsburg. The interior of the cottage is furnished with quaint and comfortable Colonial style furnishings. The downstairs offers a living room, with color TV, queen-sized sofabed, small pullman kitchen, and half bath. The upstairs offers a double brass bed and full bath. A continental breakfast is placed in the kitchen so that guests may enjoy breakfast at their convenience. Host is a physician. Air conditioned. Well-behaved children of any age welcome.
**Rates:** S $72, D $85 DAILY.
**Reservations:** (804) 648-7560 11 A.M. TO 6 P.M. MONDAY THROUGH FRIDAY.

### NEAR HISTORIC DISTRICT

This beautifully proportioned home is a copy of the eighteenth century Sheldon's Tavern in Litchfield, Connecticut. Built in 1983, it is located 1 mile from Colonial Williamsburg and the College of William and Mary, in

a quiet, wooded area. One of the homes participating in the 1986 Garden Week Tour, it features a large Palladian style window on the second floor, handpainted tiles of flowers and birds from the Caribbean in the living room fireplace, antique heart pine wide plank floors from Philadelphia, and beautiful oak paneling in the family room from an old church in Indiana. The hosts have younger children. The third floor guestroom with queen-sized bed, FIREPLACE, and private bath offers complete privacy and overlooks a boxwood garden below. A port-a-crib and queen-sized sleep sofa are available for children. Breakfast consists of special homemade ham rolls, apple cake, fresh fruit, and beverages. Bikes are available. Families welcome. Swimming POOL privileges are available nearby. Resident DOG and CAT. Air conditioned. NO SMOKING.
**Rates:** S $56, D $65, CHILDREN OVER THREE $10 EACH PER NIGHT.
**Reservations:** (804) 648-7560 11 A.M. TO 6 P.M. MONDAY THROUGH FRIDAY.

# EASTERN PANHANDLE
## SHEPHERDSTOWN
### TERAPIN NECK

TERAPIN NECK ROAD — A restful wildlife preserve and farm nestled between the banks of the Potomac River with a pleasant atmosphere in the Shenandoah Valley. The river is there for fishing, tubing, or simply to be enjoyed for its own grandeur. There is an inground SWIMMING POOL; trails for hiking, jogging, or cross-country skiing. Host enjoys managing this inn, cooking, woodworking, and watching nature, hostess is a teacher who enjoys birdwatching, nature, and art. Accommodations include: A) four rustic duplex cabins with private kitchen and bathroom; B) main lodge with two large bedrooms and private bathrooms. Four queen-sized beds are available, as well as crib and cot. The meals are prepared country style and served in the main lodge. There is a recreation room, dining room with library, and fireplace in the lodge. Located near Harper's Ferry, West Virginia (15 miles), Antietam, Maryland (9 miles), and only 1 1/2 hours from Washington, D.C. and Baltimore, Maryland. Convenient to both Interstate 81 (14 miles) and Interstate 70 (20 miles); historic Shepherdstown, West Virginia (5 miles), and outlet shopping in Martinsburg. West Virginia (14 miles). Farm DOG, 10 CATS. Children of all ages welcome.
**Rates:** A) D $50, EACH ADDITIONAL PERSON $5; AND B) D $40, EACH ADDITIONAL PERSON $10 DAILY. A) D $310 AND B) $240 WEEKLY.
**Reservations:** (703) 955-1246 MONDAY THROUGH SATURDAY 9 A.M. TO 1 P.M. (ANSWERING MACHINE AT OTHER TIMES.)

## SUMMIT POINT

A charming country lodging in the quaint village of Summit Point, located in the beautiful Shenandoah Valley of West Virginia's Eastern Panhandle. Near historic Harper's Ferry, the area provides splendid hiking, cycling, antiquing, and sightseeing opportunities. Old-fashioned hospitality welcomes the crowd weary traveler with a cheerful room, bath, and breakfast amidst rural peace and quiet. Accommodations include: A) double bed, shared bath and B) double bed, shared bath. One DOG resides here. Host is a public relations officer; hostess enjoys reading and antiquing.
**Rates:** S OR D A) $40 DAILY AND B) $50 DAILY.
**Reservations:** (703) 955-1246 MONDAY THROUGH SATURDAY 9 A.M. TO 1 P.M. (ANSWERING MACHINE AT OTHER TIMES.)

## FREDERICK COUNTY

APPLE PIE RIDGE — Farmhouse built in 1792 on Apple Pie Ridge in Frederick County, Virginia. Many historical features such as door locks, windows, floors, and so on. Two story with two basements and attic. Presently operates as a small beef cattle farm. Visitors welcome. Accommodations include a double bed, shared bath. Cot available. Four DOGS. Host is retired school principal who enjoys farming and sports; hostess is a guide for the Historical Society. CHILDREN over eight welcome. No smoking.
**Rates:** S OR D $45 DAILY.
**Reservations:** (703) 955-1246 MONDAY THROUGH SATURDAY 9 A.M. TO 1 P.M. (ANSWERING MACHINE AT OTHER TIMES.)

## GREATER WASHINGTON
## ALEXANDRIA
## MOUNT VERNON

A large Colonial home in wooded suburban area nestled between Old Town Alexandria and Mount Vernon, minutes from the Potomac River. Lovely landscaped garden with sweeping decks and inground POOL. Host is assigned with the air force at the Pentagon; hostess is in direct sales. Accommodations include: A) large double bed and B) twin beds. Both rooms have Victorian furnishings. Hostess serves breakfast with homemade breads on the patio by the pool or in the solarium. Hosts do not smoke. Nearby bike trail. It is 15 minutes from Old Town and George Washington's Home, Mount Vernon. Lots of lovely old homes in area. Minutes from Washington D.C. Accessible from National Airport, Washington, D.C. Approximately 20 minutes by cab. Buses run by door. Close to Metro subway. Two CATS reside here. Air conditioning. Children welcome.
**Rates:** A & B) S $48, D $58 DAILY. A & B) S $280, D $350 WEEKLY.

**Reservations:** (202) 363-7767 MONDAY - THURSDAY 9:00 - 5:00; FRIDAY 9:00 - 1:00.

## HISTORIC TRIANGLE
## FREDERICKSBURG
## MASSAPONAX

STATE ROUTE 607 — Large 1838 classical Revival manor house on 10 rural acres with stocked pond in Historic Triangle of Virginia. House occupied by both armies in Civil War. Six fireplaces, antiques, and original contemporary art. Second story portico with fluted columns offers guests lovely view of farm fields and woods from wicker chairs. Host is a sculptor who works at Hirshhorn Museum in Washington, D.C.; hostess is a former teacher. Both enjoy nature study and historic preservation. Children include son 7 and daughter 5. Accommodations in sunny English basement. Four room suite with kitchen, private bath and entrance, two FIREPLACES. Full breakfast, country eggs. Two bikes and fishing tackle available. One DOG in residence. Near Kenmore, four Civil War battlefields, Rising Sun Tavern, Mary Washington House, Melcher's Gallery, King's Dominion, Interstate 95. It is 1 hour to Monticello, Washington's and Lee's birthplaces, Mt. Vernon, Skyline Drive, Richmond, Washington, D.C., and Alexandria. HANDICAPPED ACCESSIBLE. Air conditioning. Children welcome.
**Rates:** S $45, D $65, $10 EACH ADDITIONAL PERSON DAILY.
**Reservations:** (202) 363-7767 MONDAY - THURSDAY 9:00 - 5:00; FRIDAY 9:00 - 1:00.

## LOUDOUN COUNTY
## HAMILTON

BUSINESS ROUTE 7 — Located near the Blue Ridge Mountains, this inn offers a romantic setting for guest accommodations. The four delightfully decorated guestrooms (two with FIREPLACES) are appointed to provide visual pleasure and physical comfort. All rooms are equipped for double occupancy and are accessible to two full baths. A full breakfast is included in the price of the room. The inn also provides an elegant, yet casual restaurant. Dinner is served Monday through Saturday, 6 to 9:30 P.M., Sunday brunch 11 A.M. to 2:30 P.M. The restaurant is closed for dinner Sunday and Tuesday nights. In the fall and winter, the three fireplaces give the restaurant a special glow. In the spring and summer, the beautiful English gardens are a perfect backdrop for enjoying a drink or dinner on the porches. CHILDREN over 6 welcome. One CAT. HANDICAPPED ACCESSIBLE. Air conditioned. Host enjoys tennis and bike riding; hostess enjoys bike riding.
**Rates:** A) & D) D $75; B) D $45; AND C) $55 DAILY.
**Reservations:** (703) 955-1246 MONDAY THROUGH SATURDAY 9 A.M. TO 1 P.M. (ANSWERING MACHINE AT OTHER TIMES.)

# NORTHERN VIRGINIA
## ARLINGTON
### CRYSTAL CITY

Large apartment in a modern highrise just 15 minutes by car or Metro from downtown Washington, Alexandria's Old Town, Pentagon, Smithsonian, Capitol, National Airport, and Arlington Cemetery. Apartment furnished with antiques and the debris of 27 years collecting while in the Foreign Service. Hostess loves gardening, is a genealogy nut and manages a George Washington University center for graduate studies. Amenities include cable TV, climate control, outdoor POOL, garage parking, laundry facilities, exercise room, and secretarial service. Accommodations include: A) queen-sized bed and single bed, private bath and B) twin beds, shared hall bath. The location is convenient for both vacationers and business persons. Major firms are located here as well as Navy Intelligence Headquarters and the U.S. Patent Office. Shopping, restaurants, and the necessities of life are all built into the lifestyle here. Continental breakfast. French is spoken here. HANDICAPPED ACCESSIBLE. CHILDREN over 12 welcome.
**Rates:** S $40-$45, D $50-$58 DAILY. $500-$600 MONTHLY.
**Reservations:** (202) 363-7767 MONDAY - THURSDAY 9:00 - 5:00; FRIDAY 9:00 - 1:00.

## SHENANDOAH VALLEY

Home of the famous Shenandoah River and most of the major battlefields of the Civil War. Located close to mountain climbing, fishing, hunting, canoeing, as well as both skiing and cross-country skiing. Lots of wonderful country restaurants with outstanding cuisines. Famous auctions, antique shops, and estate sales. Winchester, "Apple Capital of the World," hosts Apple Blossom Parade, one of America's longest parades. Bryce Mountain Ski Resort is here, as well as Skyline Drive, Shenandoah Caverns, Luray Caverns, New Market Battle Field, Belle Grove Plantation, George Washington's Headquarters, Stonewall Jackson's Headquarters, and the Appalachian Trail. Located between Shenandoah National Forest in the Blue Ridge Mountains and George Washington National Forest in the Allegheny Mountains. You will find Shenandoah College and Conservatory of Music, James Madison University, Lord Fairfax Community College, Massanutten Military Academy, and Randolph Macon Military Academy here. Breathtaking views of the mountains.

## BENTONVILLE
### INDIAN HOLLOW

ROUTE 613 — Vacation in a beautiful, rustic but modern, air conditioned, secluded but not isolated, year-round home on 5 acres of pine trees, with views of horses, cows, and animals from neighboring farms, as well as view of mountains and the river. The home includes a woodburning stove in the parlor, a large deck overlooking the POOL with diving board, use of a canoe with life preservers (as available), and a bountiful and varied deluxe continental breakfast, use of the grill to picnic on the grounds. The South Fork of the Shenandoah River is a quarter mile and has excellent fishing and canoeing. Horseshoes, badminton, ping pong, bocci cards, chess, and a hammock in the pines are available. It is 10 miles from the Skyline Drive, the Thunderbird Archeological Museum, Skyline, and Luray Caverns. Luray Pottery, the Oasis Vineyard, and golf clubs are a few minutes drive. Bryce and Massanutten ski resorts are about 50 miles on excellent roads. At times the home may be UNHOSTED, but guests will always be advised when the reservation is made and breakfast will be available in the refrigerator. Accommodations include: A) queen-sized bed, shared bath; B) king-sized bed, shared bath; and C) twin-bedded room, shared bath. Bikes available. Air conditioned. Host is a physician; hostess is a nurse. CHILDREN over 10 welcome.

**Rates:** S OR D A) $55 OR B) $60, AND C) $50. LOWER RATES OFF-SEASON. COT IN ROOM $10 DAILY. WEEKLY HOUSE RENTAL AVAILABLE.

**Reservations:** (703) 955-1246 MONDAY THROUGH SATURDAY 9 A.M. TO 1 P.M. (ANSWERING MACHINE AT OTHER TIMES.)

## BERRYVILLE
## AURBON FARMS

A large Colonial Williamsburg reproduction in the middle of 11 acres of Christmas trees. Furnished with lovely antiques and includes large stone fireplace. Accommodations include: A) two large cheerful antique filled rooms that share a bath; one has a brass bed and the other a high four poster bed and B) two rooms with private bath; one filled with antiques and sledge bed, and the other white wicker, and private patio. Full country breakfasts served on deck overlooking foothills of the Blue Ridge Mountains, in formal dining room, or in antique kitchen by woodstove. Walking distance of Shenandoah River; within 30 minutes Harper's Ferry, Appalachian Trail, Skyline Drive, outstanding cuisines, many antique shops, skiing, swimming, and golfing. Host invites guests to hunt and fish. Convenient to Interstate 81. CHILDREN, WELCOME.

**Rates:** A) D $60 AND B) D $50 DAILY.

**Reservations:** (703) 955-1246 MONDAY THROUGH SATURDAY 9 A.M. TO 1 P.M. (ANSWERING MACHINE AT OTHER TIMES.)

## BOYCE
## HUNT COUNTRY OF VIRGINIA

Two story farmhouse with second floor for guests. Accommodations include: A) large room with antique double bed, TV, and comfortable chairs overlooking beautiful mountain view and B) smaller room with

sofabed that can accommodate two children or one adult. Bath between the two rooms. Host is a retired dentist who is training his pair of horses to drive the carriages he built; hostess has retired from teaching learning disabled children. An old, spoiled WHIPPET and a BARN CAT live here. Breakfast is served on a screened porch. This home is an ideal place for a quiet vacation. Only 6 miles from Winchester, a charming town with shops, and Shenandoah College.
**Rates:** A & B) S $40, D $50 DAILY.
**Reservations:** (703) 955-1246 MONDAY THROUGH SATURDAY 9 A.M. TO 1 P.M. (ANSWERING MACHINE AT OTHER TIMES.)

## CLARKE COUNTY
### SHENANDOAH RIVER BANKS

ROUTE 50 — Located less than 60 miles from Washington, D.C., on 15 heavily wooded, secluded, peaceful, and rural acres. The field stone house was built in 1780 on a hill bordering the Shenandoah River. Easy access to Route 50 ensures proximity to activities appealing to every age and taste, from antiques to vineyards, and from sports to historical and scenic areas. The superb neighboring restaurants are unique and well thought of and reviewed. Attractively but eclectically furnished for comfort, four of the five guest bed/sitting rooms boast fireplaces with unlimited wood and books on almost every subject. Host is a semiretired independent school head with multiple interests, whose main hobby is reading; hostess is a former stage actress/director, who has also taught in her husband's schools. Their extensive theater collection is the result of both their involvement. Hostess speaks fluent French, minimal Spanish, but owns dictionaries in both languages. Equipment for the comfort and safety of both the HANDICAPPED AND CHILDREN is available, as is babysitting (with adequate notice). Layout of rooms adapts easily to either privacy or families and small groups. Choice of self-served, or host-served breakfast (the latter for $10 per couple surcharge). Accommodations include: A) large double bed, sofabed, private bath, FIREPLACE; B) double bed, sofabed, private bath, FIREPLACE; C) double bed, private bath, FIREPLACE; D) twin beds, share bath, FIREPLACE; and E) double bed.
**Rates:** A) S $55, D $65 1 NIGHT, S $45, D $55 2 NIGHTS DAILY; S $340, D $350 WEEKLY; B) S $40, D $50 1 NIGHT, S $30, D $40 2 NIGHTS DAILY; S $235, D $245 WEEKLY; C) S $50, D $60 1 NIGHT, S $40, D $50 2 NIGHTS DAILY; S $305, D $315 WEEKLY; D & E) S $35, D $45/$40 DAILY.
**Reservations:** (703) 955-1246 MONDAY THROUGH SATURDAY 9 A.M. TO 1 P.M. (ANSWERING MACHINE AT OTHER TIMES.)

## GORE
### TIMBER RIDGE

ROUTE 259 — Relax and enjoy your stay at this comfortable country home that is located on Timber Ridge in the beautiful Appalachian Mountains in Gore, Virginia. Near old town Winchester, with its quaint shops, the area provides many historic attractions, antiquing, heritage days, fairs, old churches, hiking trails, with fishing and hunting (in season). Your sightseeing opportunities are endless, including the nearby Skyline Drive and the many famous caverns. Every season has much to offer you. As the sun breaks over the mountains, you can enjoy your continental breakfast, while deer, fox, or any of the many species of colorful birds that frequent the pond nestled among the pines, greet the new day. Come rest and enjoy old-fashioned hospitality amidst rural quiet in apple country. Host is in sales and enjoys fishing, whittling, and working with computer; hostess is a homemaker and is involved with quilting, various crafts, and birdwatching. They have a 20 year old son. House CAT in residence. Accommodations include a double bed with shared bath. Air conditioned. CHILDREN over 12 welcome. SMOKING NOT PERMITTED.
**Rates:** S $30, D $35 DAILY.
**Reservations:** (703) 955-1246 MONDAY THROUGH SATURDAY 9 A.M. TO 1 P.M. (ANSWERING MACHINE AT OTHER TIMES.)

## HINTON
### RAWLEY SPRINGS

A riverside home built in stone, surrounded by shrubbery in a 7 acre parklike setting. The Rawley Springs area provides paths for strolling or serious hiking and a river with genuine swimming holes. Terraces, a wide front porch, and a gazebo offer outside sitting places in the summer. The high ceilinged, pine paneled living room (50' x 30') has a large stone fireplace at one end to provide a winter evening's warmth. Bedrooms are large. Accommodations include: A) double bed, single bed, and pullout bed, shared bath; B) double bed, private bath; C) double bed, shared bath; and D) queen-sized bed, private bath. The hostess writes, teaches, and collects American art. One DOG lives here. VCR and picnic area. Children welcome. SMOKING OUTSIDE ONLY.
**Rates:** A-D) S $35, D $45 DAILY.
**Reservations:** (703) 955-1246 MONDAY THROUGH SATURDAY 9 A.M. TO 1 P.M. (ANSWERING MACHINE AT OTHER TIMES.)

## LURAY

PRIVATE ROAD — A small but unique mountaintop house. Great room with fireplace and unmatched views. On top of Massanutten Mountain at approximately 2,100 feet above Shenandoah Valley and River. Views of

50 square miles looking at Blue Ridge Mountains and Shenandoah National Park. Bordered by George Washington National Forest. Six miles from Luray Caverns. Two bedrooms. All amenities. Accommodations include: A) queen-sized bed, shared bath and B) twin-bedded room, shared bath. Well-behaved PET DOGS WELCOME. Host is in public relations and enjoys classical music and history; hostess is a counselor and enjoys photography, decorating, and wildflowers.
**Rates:** A) D $45 AND B) D $35 DAILY.
**Reservations:** (703) 955-1246 MONDAY THROUGH SATURDAY 9 A.M. TO 1 P.M. (ANSWERING MACHINE AT OTHER TIMES.)

## "SMALL SLEEPY TOWN"

MAIN STREET — A late eighteenth century log house with four bedrooms, recently restored by owner/host who is presently restoring an early nineteenth century house in Woodstock. Located in Middletown, Virginia (settled 1755), which is in the heart of the northern Shenandoah Valley, an area rich in history and folklore. Nearby are: Winchester (15 minutes) and Front Royal (10 minutes). Just south of town is Belle Grove Plantation (constructed in 1794 with the guidance and advice of Thomas Jefferson), a property of the National Trust, and now a working farm and center for regional crafts. It was General Sheridan's headquarters during the decisive Battle of Cedar Creek in 1864. Accommodations include: A) large cathedral ceilinged room with king-size and single beds and private bath; B & C) two rooms with double bed, shared bath; all on second floor and D) first floor beamed ceilinged room, queen-sized bed with private bath. Entire house furnished with antiques and original works of art. Inn also contains antique shop where afternoon refreshments are served. A FRIENDLY YELLOW LABRADOR (fishes, swims, and hunts tennis balls) is also in residence. Several good restaurants nearby or host can serve dinner with good local wines at additional cost of $30 per couple. VCR and Air conditioning. CHILDREN over 12 welcome.
**Rates:** A) S & D $65; B) S & D $50, SUITE $105; C) S & D $60 DAILY.
**Reservations:** (703) 955-1246 MONDAY THROUGH SATURDAY 9 A.M. TO 1 P.M. (ANSWERING MACHINE AT OTHER TIMES.)

## MOUNT JACKSON

An 1830 Colonial homestead on 7 acres in the Shenandoah. You would know this "visiting grandmother" home anywhere; friendly rooms filled with antiques, family photographs, bric-a-brac, lace curtains, and Boston fern. SIX BEDROOMS HAVE WORKING FIREPLACES; three have private baths. Handcrafted quilts grace four poster Lincoln and spindle beds. Memories are everywhere you look. Every article in here is for sale. Life is offered at a gentler pace. After a full country breakfast, lie by the 32 foot POOL, enjoy a book picked from an extensive collection with complimentary sherry, or daydream on the "Lillian Gish" side porch. For a faster pace, attend area auctions, hike, canoe, ski, golf, or explore caverns—all nearby. Bikes are provided for a jaunt through a nearby apple orchard, and a picnic lunch is available to take with you. This inn is an intimate retreat, reflecting a 1910 to 1920 era, for anyone wanting to escape their daily routine. Double accommodations. VCR. **Rates:** S $45, D $50-$60 DAILY. SEPARATE COTTAGE $65. **Reservations:** (703) 955-1246 MONDAY THROUGH SATURDAY 9 A.M. TO 1 P.M. (ANSWERING MACHINE AT OTHER TIMES.)

## WHITE POST

NEAR ROUTES 50 AND 340 — Pre-Civil War Federal brick home on 17 private acres perfect for picnics and walks in Shenandoah Valley. Mountain views, Opequon Creek borders property. Large bed-sitting rooms, sunny with attention to comfort and beauty. Antiques and books throughout, every effort made to refresh the soul and refuel the body. Graciously appointed public rooms with fireplaces, porches with breathtaking westward views, perfect for sunset celebrations. Retired couple and daughter (public relations executive) share hosting. Hostess offers wine and cheese, afternoon tea, and full country breakfast on porch or fireside. Specialties are pound cake and French toast. In season, fruit, vegetables, and flowers from host's garden. Near Skyline Drive, Harper's Ferry, Winchester, and Virginia Hunt Country. Nearby boating on Shenandoah River, hiking, antiquing, historic sites, and fine dining. Third floor exclusively for guests: A) double bed, private bath (JACUZZI for 2); B) queen-sized bed with shared bath; and C) double bed with shared bath. Friendly COLLIE in residence. No pets, kennel nearby. It is 90 minutes from Washington, D.C.; 60 minutes from Interstate 495 (Fairfax); 10 minutes from Interstate 81 (Winchester); and 45 minutes from Dulles Airport. Air conditioned. NO CHILDREN. Teenagers 16 and older traveling with parents welcome. **Rates:** A) D $95 AND B & C) D $75 DAILY. $15 DISCOUNT MONDAY THROUGH WEDNESDAY. **Reservations:** (703) 955-1246 MONDAY THROUGH SATURDAY 9 A.M. TO 1 P.M. (ANSWERING MACHINE AT OTHER TIMES.)

## WINCHESTER

Home is in a quiet tree-shaded neighborhood. All on one floor, this Contemporary Ranch is furnished with Early American antiques from New England. In the back of the house are flower gardens off the patio, on the lower level a 30 foot inground POOL beckons you to dive off the board! The woods behind ensure privacy as you swim. Two friendly CATS lazily wander in and out. Accommodations include two rooms with single bed, shared bath. HANDICAPPED ACCESSIBLE. VCR. Host is an administration manager; hostess enjoys bridge, calligraphy, and swimming.

**Rates:** S $25 DAILY.

**Reservations:** (703) 955-1246 MONDAY THROUGH SATURDAY 9 A.M. TO 1 P.M. (ANSWERING MACHINE AT OTHER TIMES.)

## BRADDOCK HILLS ESTATES

ROUTE 856, OFF ROUTE 522 NORTH — Ranch home on 1 1/2 acres lovely wooded area located only minutes from heart of Winchester, North/ South Skirmish, Berkley Springs, and Summit Point Raceway. Fishing, swimming, golf, racquetball, hiking, antiquing, and fruit picking all close. Wild game often seen from dining room window. Apple Blossom Festival in spring and fall harvest and craft shows nearby. Host and hostess are retired and enjoy cooking, traveling, birdwatching, gardening, music, needlepoint, and photography. Cookbook and dwarf fruit tree collections. Many wild and domestic flowers. Accommodations include a double bed, private bath. NONSMOKERS ONLY. Full country breakfast in garden, weather permitting. Will accommodate special diets. Hostess invites you to bring your tennis racket. Host and hostess speak a smattering of French, Spanish, and Yiddish. One DOG. PIANO.

**Rates:** D $40 DAILY.

**Reservations:** (703) 955-1246 MONDAY THROUGH SATURDAY 9 A.M. TO 1 P.M. (ANSWERING MACHINE AT OTHER TIMES.)

## HISTORIC DISTRICT

A large historic home built shortly after the Civil War, filled with antiques. The home has been lovingly restored by owners, who spent countless weekends painting, scraping, plastering, and haunting flea markets and auctions. You will find many touches that reflect their sense of whimsy. A typical Victorian era home with three fireplaces and large rooms. Hosts are in the public relations/marketing business with wide-ranging interests. Well-trained PETS welcome. The hosts are very active; they enjoy all kinds of sports, travel, arts, and adventures. They will happily give you advice on what is available in the area. They maintain a large library of information on local historic sites, events, and eateries. Nearby are many historic sites and lovely homes. There is a nearby track and health club. Breakfast is an event for these two hosts, who love serving elaborate meals in the formal dining room. The hosts will attempt to accommodate any dietary restrictions. Each bedroom has its own special character. The hosts prefer to entertain one couple or family at a time. Accommodations include: A) bedroom with private bath and B) two bedrooms with shared baths. Double accommodations. Air conditioned, VCR, canoe, and bikes available. No children. SMOKING IS STRICTLY FORBIDDEN.

**Rates:** A OR B) S 35, D $45, W/ SHARED BATH, A & B) D $45 DAILY.

Reservations: (703) 955-1246 MONDAY THROUGH SATURDAY 9 A.M.
TO 1 P.M. (ANSWERING MACHINE AT OTHER TIMES.)

## WOODSTOCK

NORTH CHURCH STREET — This turn-of-the-century Victorian inn is located on a quiet street facing the mountains. Settle in for a peaceful stay in rooms decorated with cozy quilts, ruffled curtains, and antiques. The window seat in the sitting room is the perfect spot to enjoy a cup of tea and a good book. Wake to the sound of church bells and the aroma of homebaked breads and flavorful coffee served in your room, the cozy country kitchen or on the bright sunporch. One of the hostesses is an administrative assistant for a national honor society. The other is a lease administrator and makes crafts for their shop in her spare time. Accommodations include: A) double bed, private bath; B) twin-bedded room, private bath; and C) four rooms with double bed, share two baths; Air conditioned. Bikes available. Children over 12 welcome.
Rates: A & B) S OR D $50 AND C) S $40, D $45 DAILY. SPECIAL WEEKDAY AND GROUP RATES.
Reservations: (703) 955-1246 MONDAY THROUGH SATURDAY 9 A.M. TO 1 P.M. (ANSWERING MACHINE AT OTHER TIMES.)

NORTH MAIN STREET — Historic home built in the 1800s. Hostess enjoys crafts, stenciling, sewing, and furniture refinishing. Double accommodations include: A) room with fireplace private bath and B) two double rooms with bath shared with other guests. A suite can be made available. Air conditioned. SMOKING in designated areas only.
Rates: A) S OR D $50 AND B) S $35, D $40 DAILY.
Reservations: (703) 955-1246 MONDAY THROUGH SATURDAY 9 A.M. TO 1 P.M. (ANSWERING MACHINE AT OTHER TIMES.)

## MIDDLETOWN

FIRST STREET — A Victorian home that has been in this family since 1910. All antique furnishing. Breakfast served. There are two guestrooms that share a bath. Guests have access to the whole house. There are double accommodations in the bedrooms. Small well-behaved PETS welcome.
Rates: $60 DAILY.
Reservations: (703) 955-1246 MONDAY THROUGH SATURDAY 9 A.M. TO 1 P.M. (ANSWERING MACHINE AT OTHER TIMES.)

# WEST VIRGINIA

## CUMBERLAND AND POTOMAC RIVER
### BERKELEY SPRINGS
### SECLUDED DOWNTOWN

INDEPENDENCE STREET — A three story brick Colonial. The first floor had been an auto mechanic's garage for over 30 years. This floor now has a 48 seating capacity American-Italian restaurant with a lovely outdoor garden and grotto. The first house has four rooms with shared baths, color TV, air conditioning, and antiques. In the house adjacent to the outdoor garden, four additional rooms are offered, two of which offer four poster beds, Casablanca fans, private showers, and porch. The perfect gateway. Children welcome.

**Rates:** PRIVATE BATHROOMS S $40-$45, D $50-$55; SHARED BATHROOMS S $30-$35, D $40-$45 DAILY.

**Reservations:** (703) 955-1246 MONDAY THROUGH SATURDAY 9 A.M. TO 1 P.M. (ANSWERING MACHINE AT OTHER TIMES.)

## EASTERN PANHANDLE
### CHARLES TOWN

SUMMIT POINT ROAD — This romantic and dramatically beautiful English half timbered manor house set on 17 acres of rolling lawns and unspoiled woodlands is open year-round to a limited number of discerning guests. Only the birds in the trees, the ducks on the pond, and the ripple of Bullskin Run interrupt the quiet. Your privacy is assured. Candles and firelight, the rich patina of old wood, the glow of polished brass, and the deep jewel tones of Oriental carpets combine to create a seductively relaxing and intimate atmosphere. Featherbeds and goosedown comforters dispel the winter cold; open fires cheer the spirit. In summer the hammock under the willows by the pond provides perfect relaxation. Accommodations include A-C) three rooms with double bed, private bath, and FIREPLACE. One CAT. French is spoken here.

**Rates:** S $100-$120, D $100-$130 DAILY.

**Reservations:** (703) 955-1246 MONDAY THROUGH SATURDAY 9 A.M. TO 1 P.M. (ANSWERING MACHINE AT OTHER TIMES.)

## HARPER'S FERRY
### MIDDLEWAY

Circa 1760, a romantic stone house of early Georgian design, listed on the National Register of Historic Places. Set in the eighteenth century village of Middleway, house is fronted by the oldest flagstone sidewalk in the state. Interesting graffiti inside includes drawing of President Polk. Eighteenth century log house rebuilt in backyard; environs include old churches, creeks, footbridges, and gazebo. Walking tour offered. Antiques and Oriental rugs add to the elegance of the large rooms; FIREPLACE IN EVERY ROOM EXCEPT THIRD FLOOR. Listen to the rain on the tin roof upstairs. House has no ghosts, but ask about the Legend of Wizard Clip. Host practices various engineering disciplines, loves to cook, and talk history. Speaks Spanish and German. Hostess is a chartered financial analyst, retired president of investment company, dabbles in art, and is a community leader. Located in heart of historic region. Convenient to Interstate 81 (exit 5 for 5 miles), 5 miles to Charles Town and thoroughbred racing, near Summit Point sports car raceway, Antietam Battlefield, Shepherd College, 11 miles from Harper's Ferry. Also near Winchester, Virginia and 60 miles from Washington, D.C. beltway. No pets. Full, leisurely breakfast, refreshments. Accommodations include: A) FIREPLACE, double bed, private bath; B) FIREPLACE, double bed, private bath; and C) double bed, private bath. PIANO and air conditioning. NO CHILDREN.

**Rates:** $85 DAILY. SUITE $125 DAILY.

**Reservations:** (703) 955-1246 MONDAY THROUGH SATURDAY 9 A.M. TO 1 P.M. (ANSWERING MACHINE AT OTHER TIMES.)

# 4

# North Central (East)

- [ ] Indiana
- [ ] Michigan
- [ ] Ohio
- [ ] Wisconsin

# INDIANA

## WHITEWATER VALLEY
## METAMORA

DUCK CREEK CROSSING — A circa 1850 home that has the serenity of quiet country living. Located in a historic 1838 canal town, 8 miles west of Brookville, Indiana on US 52, and 12 miles north of Interstate 74 from Batesville. This home contains four rooms, one of which is a two room family suite. Although this home is unhosted, the annex to this is hosted and is 2 blocks away. The annex contains two additional rooms. Host is a semiretired architect; hostess is a shopkeeper in town. There are two toy POODLES in residence. SMALL PETS WELCOME. Gift, craft, and specialty shops are all within a short walk. Brookville Lake reservoir is 9 miles away. and is 16,000 acres. It has excellent fishing, boating, and swimming. Flowing adjacent to Metamora is the Whitewater River, which offers canoe trips and fishing. Canoe rentals are available for any distance excursion. Metamora also has a water canal and grist mill and the only operating wood aqueduct in the United States. Inn operates on a seasonal basis, mid-April through Christmas. All rooms have twin beds. Twin size rollaways and air beds are available. Children of all ages welcome.

**Rates:** A) D $30; B) D $35; AND C) D $45 DAILY.

**Reservations:** (606) 356-7865 8 A.M. TO 9 P.M. MONDAY THROUGH SATURDAY. SUNDAY, CALLS ANSWERED DEPENDING ON AVAILABILITY.

# MICHIGAN

## GREAT LAKES
## ANN ARBOR
### NEIGHBORHOOD HOME

OFF US 23, EXIT 37B — A very special neighborhood home away from home. Located just off US 23 (exit 37B) near the Holiday Inn East, there is easy access to Eastern Michigan University and the University of Michigan, cultural and sports events, and shopping, hospitals, parks and the beautiful Huron River and its recreational activities. Willow Run and Metropolitan airports are minutes away. Complimentary evening snacks, coffee, and tea are available on request. Breakfast is continental plus, with more elaborate breakfasting on weekends. Complimentary early morning Yogasana lessons are available if desired. The two available bedrooms have comfortable beds. One room has an antique double bed, while the other has two sleek singles. Bathrooms shared. Enjoy the living room in front of the woodburning stove reading, listening to music, or talking. TV is available in a separate room. Hostess speaks some French. Inground POOL. NONSMOKERS ONLY.

**Rates:** S OR D $45 DAILY.

**Reservations:** (313) 561-6041 MONDAY THROUGH FRIDAY, 6 P.M. TO 11 P.M. SATURDAY AND SUNDAY 9 A.M. TO 9 P.M.

## IRISH HILLS
## BROOKLYN

CHICAGO STREET — Nestled in the foothills of the Irish Hills, this 1886 Queen Anne style Victorian home sits on an acre of land within walking distance of quaint shops, antique mall, restaurants, and more. If you are a car racing buff, you will happily find yourself 2 miles from Michigan International Speedway. The inside of this home has the original woodwork in oak and cherry, family antiques, stained glass windows, cherry fireplace, wraparound porch, and original paintings. This house lends itself to romance and a sense of a time gone by. Accommodations include four A-D) double-bedded, antique filled rooms with private baths. One hour from Detroit, Lansing, or Toledo. Host is in real estate and enjoys tennis and golf; hostess enjoys reading and decorating. Both have a love for antiques. Hosts make special occasions SPECIAL! SMOKING allowed downstairs only.

**Rates:** A-C) S $50, D $55 AND D) S $40, D $45 DAILY. S $300. D $330 WEEKLY.

**Reservations:** (313) 561-6041 MONDAY THROUGH FRIDAY, 6 P.M. TO 11 P.M. SATURDAY AND SUNDAY 9 A.M. TO 9 P.M.

# METRO DETROIT
## BIRMINGHAM

NEAR SOUTHFIELD ROAD — Large, beautifully furnished guestroom with double bed. Spacious private bath. Ranch home in suburban neighborhood near freeway. Twenty minutes to downtown Detroit. Close to elegant shopping and good restaurants. Your hosts are an active retired couple. They play golf. She teaches crafts. This home is close to business offices in Troy and Birmingham, Michigan. Pool table. Small well-behaved DOGS WELCOME. CHILDREN over 12 welcome.
**Rates:** D $45 DAILY.
**Reservations:** (313) 561-6041 MONDAY THROUGH FRIDAY, 6 P.M. TO 11 P.M. SATURDAY AND SUNDAY 9 A.M. TO 9 P.M.

## DEARBORN
## WEST DEARBORN

Brick bungalow furnished in traditional style with a combination of antiques and reproductions. Upstairs private for guests. Two adjoining rooms with double bed in one room, single bed in the other. Rollaway available. Bath shared with family. Host makes custom made golf clubs; hostess has a large collection of teddy bears. One small DOG resides here, too. Discount tickets to Henry Ford Museum-Greenfield Village available. TV and air conditioning in bedrooms. Breakfast is an event here, not just a snack. Guests can enjoy early morning coffee on the patio in the flower filled backyard or in the dining room. It is 20 minutes to downtown or to Metro Airport via Ford Freeway (Interstate 94). NONSMOKERS ONLY.
**Rates:** S $30, D $40; $10 EACH ADDITIONAL PERSON DAILY.
**Reservations:** (313) 561-6041 MONDAY THROUGH FRIDAY, 6 P.M. TO 11 P.M. SATURDAY AND SUNDAY 9 A.M. TO 9 P.M.

## DETROIT

Just 5 minutes from downtown Detroit, Tiger Stadium, Cobo hall, and Ambassador Bridge to Windsor, Canada. This home is in a restored historic area. Host and hostess have been active in the civil rights' movement and NAACP. Hostess has written two books about her role in the civil rights' movement. Accommodations include: A) two twin beds, private 1/2 bath; B) double bed; and C) and king bed. B and C share a bath. Southern style breakfast served. Two CATS and a DOG live here. Children welcome.
**Rates:** S $25, D $35 DAILY.
**Reservations:** (313) 561-6041 MONDAY THROUGH FRIDAY, 6 P.M. TO 11 P.M. SATURDAY AND SUNDAY 9 A.M. TO 9 P.M.

# NORTHERN MICHIGAN
## HARBOR SPRINGS

NORTH STATE STREET AND LAKE ROAD — Do not miss Harbor Springs on Little Traverse Bay and its outstanding beautiful Shore Drive. There is a private outside entrance to this guestroom and a private bath; TV and radio furnished. The hostess is a native to the area and will help you enjoy this northern Michigan resort community like a native. A short walk down the hill will take you to many interesting shops and delightful restaurants on the waterfront. General information: Boyne Highlands and Nub's Nob are two popular ski resorts just minutes away. Outstandingly beautiful area for fall color season. Lovely beaches in summer. You will enjoy the waterfront with its protective harbor for the many yachts and sailboats. Three challenging golf courses are also minutes away. Young American Dinner Theater performs weekly through the summer months at Boyne Highlands. Accommodations include a double bed with private bath and private entrance. NO CHILDREN. No SMOKING in bedroom.
**Rates:** S $35, D $45 DAILY.
**Reservations:** (313) 561-6041 MONDAY THROUGH FRIDAY, 6 P.M. TO 11 P.M. SATURDAY AND SUNDAY 9 A.M. TO 9 P.M.

## OMENA
## NEAR NORTHPORT

OMENA POINT ROAD — You are invited to a contemporary designer chaletlike home nestled in the woods on the bay with private BEACH. Walk the beach or stroll in the woods, or take the two bikes and experience God's country. Eat breakfast in the dining room or on the deck. Enjoy a continental breakfast with homemade bakery and fresh fruits. Close to fine restaurants and antique shows, marinas, airport, and golf courses. Accommodations include: A) room with double bed; and B) room with twin beds. They share a bathroom and powder room. One DOG lives here. PIANO. CHILDREN age 12 or more welcome. NO SMOKING.
**Rates:** S $45, D $50 DAILY. $300 WEEKLY. PLUS TAX.
**Reservations:** (313) 561-6041 MONDAY THROUGH FRIDAY, 6 P.M. TO 11 P.M. SATURDAY AND SUNDAY 9 A.M. TO 9 P.M.

## TRAVERSE CITY

Victorian farmhouse built in 1898 has the original wood floors and oak trim. Comfortable rooms overlook Lake Leelanau. Accomodations include: A) a bay room with double bed and twin; and B) large room with double bed and queen-sized hide-a-bed sofa. There is a shared bath and a sitting room with TV. The rooms are upstairs and could be rented as a suite. Breakfast is served in the dining room. Host is recently retired from

military service; hostess works at a nearby ski resort in the winter. They are located 15 miles northwest of Traverse City and are convenient to Sleeping Bear Dunes National Lakeshore, golf courses, skiing, wineries, fine restaurants, Interlocken Music Academy, and all of the beautiful Leelanau Peninsula. Guests are welcome to explore the grounds and the barns and to climb the hill for a magnificient view of the lake. Boat launching and swimming are available at the nearby township park, where swans and Canadian geese are often seen. Open all year. CHILDREN over 5 welcome.
**Rates:** D $45; $10 EXTRA PERSON SHARING ROOM DAILY.
**Reservations:** (313) 561-6041 MONDAY THROUGH FRIDAY, 6 P.M. TO 11 P.M. SATURDAY AND SUNDAY 9 A.M. TO 9 P.M.

## SOUTHEASTERN MICHIGAN
## ANN ARBOR

Historic 1859 home just out of Ann Arbor. Close to antique shows, all affairs of the University of Michigan. The city is one of the 10 best cities in the country in which to retire or begin a new business. House is filled with antiques. Hostess is a principal of an elementary school who enjoys collecting, theater, reading, and traveling. One Dalmation DOG lives here. Accommodations include: A) downstairs room, double bed with sitting room and private bath; B) double bed; C) double bed and sofabed; and D) twin-bedded double. VCR and bikes available.
**Rates:** D $45, S $35 DAILY.
**Reservations:** (313) 561-6041 MONDAY THROUGH FRIDAY, 6 P.M. TO 11 P.M. SATURDAY AND SUNDAY 9 A.M. TO 9 P.M.

A 1950s Ranch home located on a quiet, tree-lined street, 10 minutes from downtown Ann Arbor and the University of Michigan campus. The home is filled with antiques from the early 1900s, particularly birds' eye maple furniture. Adjacent to the property is the County Farm Park, 113 acres of meadowland with walking and jogging trails and cross-country skiing. Host is a forensic security officer; hostess is a social worker. Both enjoy jazz, old movies, and cooking, especially canning and preserving. Three friendly CATS are in residence. No pets. Lodging includes one room with double bed and shared bath. Bikes available, also VCR. No CHILDREN.
**Rates:** S OR D $40 DAILY.
**Reservations:** (313) 561-6041 MONDAY THROUGH FRIDAY, 6 P.M. TO 11 P.M. SATURDAY AND SUNDAY 9 A.M. TO 9 P.M.

# SOUTHWESTERN MICHIGAN
## FENNVILLE
## SAUGATUCK/DOUGLAS

2125 LAKESHORE DRIVE — A restored 1800s logging beach house in a 2 acre wooded setting across from a 2,000 foot BEACH on Lake Michigan. It is 4 minutes from the artist and boating colony of Saugatuck, Michigan; 2 1/2 hours from Chicago, Detroit, and most of Indiana. Accommodations include: private cottage with double bed and private bath. Cottage: A) two double beds, private bath, private entrance; Mainhouse: B & C) two rooms with queen beds; D) double bed; and E) large queen bed. Gourmet continental breakfasts are served on a huge atrium topped screened porch in season (Easter through Halloween). The owners are professionals at a major Chicago bank who cook and serve on weekends. A resident manager provides during the week. Two wineries are 15 minutes away and a thousand other activities within minutes. American authors and quotes are featured for a Walden Pond reflective hiatus. Guestrooms B, C, D, and E are on the second floor; each room has its own sink and guests share two bathrooms. One small DOG resides here. Windsurfer available, JACUZZI, pool table. CHILDREN over 10 welcome.
**Rates:** A-C) S $43, D $49; D) $55; AND E) $49 DAILY. S $250, D $280 WEEKLY.
**Reservations:** (313) 561-6041 MONDAY THROUGH FRIDAY, 6 P.M. TO 11 P.M. SATURDAY AND SUNDAY 9 A.M. TO 9 P.M.

# WESTERN
## ROMULUS

SIBLEY ROAD, EXIT 13 — Friendly family on farm welcomes guests to their 20 acre farm where guests may pick their own berries and fruit in season. Two large guestrooms: A) with double and twin beds and B) with double bed and cot or crib if needed. Country fresh breakfast. Many ANIMALS are present. Kennel and HORSE facilities available. Close to Interstates 275 and 75, Detroit Metropolitan Airport, Huron Metroparks, bike trails, golf courses, and walleye fishing with host on Lake Erie. Twenty minutes to Detroit, Windsor, and Greenfield Village. Children welcome.
**Rates:** $35-$40 DAILY.
**Reservations:** (313) 561-6041 MONDAY THROUGH FRIDAY, 6 P.M. TO 11 P.M. SATURDAY AND SUNDAY 9 A.M. TO 9 P.M.

# OHIO

## EAST FORK
### NEW RICHMOND

NORTH ALTMAN — Charming country house on 10 acres. Pond, fishing, birdwatching, small sheep farm. Award winning design, public golf course 5 miles. Cincinnati 45 minutes. Hostess enjoys cooking country style. It is 25 miles to symphony, opera, ballet, sports, and downtown attractions; 30 minutes to King's Island; and 20 minutes to East Fork State Park. Dinner by private reservation in nearby historical establishment. Boating facilities 15 minutes away. Village of New Richmond on the Ohio River. Hostess regards her guests as "company" and hospitality reflects same. Accommodations include: A) double bed, private bath; and B) double bed, shared bath. One DOG in residence here. HANDICAPPED ACCESSIBLE. Air conditioned. CHILDREN over 6 are welcome.
**Rates:** A) $45 AND B) S $30 D $35 DAILY.
**Reservations:** (606) 356-7865 8 A.M. TO 9 P.M. MONDAY THROUGH SATURDAY. SUNDAY, CALLS ANSWERED DEPENDING ON AVAILABILITY.

## NORTH CENTRAL
### DANVILLE

ROUTE 715 EAST OF ROUTES 62 AND 36 — A large country home nestled in the hills of the Walhonding Valley. Surrounded by woods and rolling countryside. The Kokosing River winds its way less than half a mile from the inn providing prime fishing area, canoeing, and peaceful respites. The inn is filled with comfortable antiques, handmade quilts on each bed, a large country porch with swings for restful afternoons, and a common room for relaxing with a cool drink in the summer or being warmed by the fireplace in the winter. Hosts have extensive corporate management backgrounds. Two Labrador Retriever DOGS reside here, too. The inn is 14 miles from Mount Vernon, 11 miles east of Kenyon College, and 50 miles northeast of Columbus. Accommodations include: A) one double bed, private bath with shower, B) one double bed, one twin bed, private bath with shower, C & D) two rooms with one double bed with private shower each, and E & F) two rooms with one double bed in each room, shared bath with tub and shower. Older children welcome. NONSMOKERS only.
**Rates:** S OR D A-D) $60 AND E & F) $50 DAILY.
**Reservations:** (504) 346-1928 SEVEN DAYS 8 A.M. TO 8 P.M.

## OHIO VALLEY

The Ohio Valley is one of the most unique regions of our country with the Ohio River winding its way from Pittsburgh, Pennsylvania to the

Mississippi. The Ohio Valley includes the tri-state area of southwestern Ohio, northern Kentucky, and southeastern Indiana—a hub of activity. Antiquing in nearby Maysville, Kentucky; Metamora, Indiana; and Lebanon, Ohio is awaiting the traveler within an hour in all directions from the city. A visit to the old German Mainstrasse Village in Covington, Kentucky is a must. The University of Cincinnati, Xavier University, and Northern Kentucky University offer lecture series and theater. The banks of the Ohio River provide breathtaking scenic views. The Miami Whitewater area provides thrills of whitewater rafting for the adventurous. Visit Metamora, Indiana, with its working Grist Mill built in 1900 and the only functioning wood aqueduct in the United States. Enjoy a horsedrawn canal boat ride, turn-of-the-century homes and buildings, and over 100 specialty shops. Kentucky's extraordinary state park system is within a day's drive. Come for the Kentucky Derby, to the Horse Park in Lexington, Kentucky, or the many Blue Grass horse farms.

## BETHEL

SOUTH CHARITY STREET — Turn-of-the-century farmhouse on wooded 12 acres. Creek to sit by. Large eat-in kitchen. Vine covered back porch. Peaceful surroundings. Host sells antiques and collectibles and is president of the Historic Society. Accommodations include three rooms with double bed, shared bath. A cot is available. One CAT and two outside DOGS are in residence here. PIANO. Children are welcome. SMOKING NOT PERMITTED.
**Rates:** S $30 DAILY; D $40 FIRST NIGHT, $35 SECOND NIGHT.
**Reservations:** (606) 356-7865 8 A.M. TO 9 P.M. MONDAY THROUGH SATURDAY. SUNDAY, CALLS ANSWERED DEPENDING ON AVAILABILITY.

## CINCINNATI

Cincinnati, Ohio, is fast becoming a major tourist attraction and convention city. Riverfront Stadium, Cincinnati's crown jewel, boasts the Cincinnati Reds baseball and the Bengals football teams. Cincinnati most recently was chosen to host the World Figure Skating Championships. The Cincinnati Zoo is world famous as is its symphony, opera, playhouse, ballet, chili parlors, and German cuisine. Carriage rides and one day steamboat cruises on the Ohio River are available. Nearby King's Island Amusement Park beckons travelers from all over the world. The Jack Nicklaus Sports Center hosts the LPGA.

## DELHI

Enjoy a quiet corner of middle America. Home is newly decorated, immaculate, and comfortable. Sit on the front porch to watch the beautiful Cincinnati sunsets. Only 10 minutes to downtown. Near shopping centers

and fine restaurants. Two guestrooms available: A) double bed and B) twin beds. Bath shared among guests. CHILDREN over 12 welcome. NO SMOKING.
**Rates:** S $35, D $40 DAILY.
**Reservations:** (606) 356-7865 8 A.M. TO 9 P.M. MONDAY THROUGH SATURDAY. SUNDAY, CALLS ANSWERED DEPENDING ON AVAILABILITY.

## EAST WALNUT HILLS

Newly furnished apartment in a one floor California style home with private entrance. Living/bedroom with queen-sized sofabed; kitchen bar, completely equipped; private bath, and patio with parking area. Beautifully tree lined and shrubbed. Daily newspaper and maid service available. Many amenities. Professional host offers an insider's view of Cincinnati. Six minutes from downtown.
**Rates:** S or D $35 DAILY.
**Reservations:** (606) 356-7865 8 A.M. TO 9 P.M. MONDAY THROUGH SATURDAY. SUNDAY, CALLS ANSWERED DEPENDING ON AVAILABILITY.

## EAST WALNUT HILLS, HYDE PARK

DEXTER PLACE — A large stone Victorian, circa 1901, completely restored, with natural oak floors and woodwork throughout, fireplaces, some stained glass, and chef's gourmet kitchen. At the end of a private lane with large yard, deck, and original pond fountain restored as a swimming POOL. Host is in sales; hostess owns her own clothing boutique. Both enjoy collecting 1930s, 1940s, and 1950s things, and have a very friendly Old English SHEEPDOG. Accommodations include: A) double bed, shared bath, gas FIREPLACE; and B) larger room with double bed, private bath, gas FIREPLACE. Both guestrooms are filled with deco and Victorian antiques. Convenient location near Interstate 71, within 3 miles of downtown, University of Cincinnati, Xavier University, zoo, hospital complexes, just off city bus route. Hosts will make airport pickup for small fee. A little Spanish is spoken here. Air conditioned. NO CHILDREN. SMOKERS NOT WELCOME.
**Rates:** A & B) S $40, D $50 DAILY. S $225, D $250 WEEKLY.
**Reservations:** (606) 356-7865 8 A.M. TO 9 P.M. MONDAY THROUGH SATURDAY. SUNDAY, CALLS ANSWERED DEPENDING ON AVAILABILITY.

## PLEASANT RIDGE

BRIARCLIFFE — Located in the geographic center of Cincinnati, 15 minutes by car to most major destinations in the city. The hostess is well informed about the area and how to get around as she is also employed at the information desk in a large hotel. This is a Tudor home on a gaslit street surrounded by large shade trees. Tennis and golf nearby. Near Cincinnati Gardens. Accommodations include: A) king-sized waterbed, shared bath; and B) queen-sized waterbed, shared bath. Some Spanish is spoken here. Pool table. Above ground POOL. Children under 2 or over 12 welcome.

**Rates:** D $35 DAILY. LONGER STAYS, REDUCED RATES.

**Reservations:** (606) 356-7865 8 A.M. TO 9 P.M. MONDAY THROUGH SATURDAY. SUNDAY, CALLS ANSWERED DEPENDING ON AVAILABILITY.

# WISCONSIN

## MILWAUKEE

The nation's 24th largest city, Milwaukee is known for its cleanliness and friendliness. It is a city of many ethnic festivals and cultural celebrations. World class museums, universities, restaurants, and shopping malls are abundant. The extensive park system contains golf courses, cross-country ski trails, bike paths, botanical gardens, and miles of Lake Michigan shoreline. Home to all of the performing arts and major league sports. Milwaukee truly lives up to its slogan, "A Great Place on a Great Lake."

## EAST SIDE

A lovely Tudor home feauturing leaded glass windows and natural woodwork. The British hosts offer their special touch of traditional B&B in America. The second floor guestroom has twin beds and a full private bath. A CAT resides here. HANDICAPPED ACCESSIBLE. NON-SMOKERS, only.
**Rates:** S $35, D $40 DAILY.
**Reservations:** (414) 271-2337 MONDAY THROUGH FRIDAY 9 A.M. TO 6 P.M. CENTRAL TIME.

This lovely home is on the Historic Register. Accommodations include: A) master bedroom with adjacent sitting room, queen four poster bed; and B) tower room has a beautiful view, queen bed and private bath. Breakfast is served on heirloom china in the sunroom overlooking the garden. Sitting room has a fireplace. Smoking allowed.
**Rates:** A) S OR D $65 AND B) $55 DAILY.
**Reservations:** (414) 271-2337 MONDAY THROUGH FRIDAY 9 A.M. TO 6 P.M. CENTRAL TIME.

## LAKE MICHIGAN

An UNHOSTED, luxurious downtown penthouse in a historic district. Spectacular views of the skyline and Lake Michigan. Separate apartment contains a bedroom with choice of king or extra large twin beds, living room (queen sleeper sofa), full kitchen, full bath with whirlpool, central air conditioning, elevator, heated, secured parking. NO SMOKING, pets, or INFANTS.
**Rates:** S $70, D $75 (HONEYMOON SPECIAL—A DOZEN ROSES AND CHAMPAGNE—$90) DAILY.
**Reservations:** (414) 271-2337 MONDAY THROUGH FRIDAY 9 A.M. TO 6 P.M. CENTRAL TIME.

## SOUTHWEST

A rustic suburban home overlooking a beautiful wooded lot with a bubbling stream and hiking paths. The hostess is an artist and her talents are evident throughout her home. Accommodations include: A) double bed, private bath; and B) double bed, shared bath. A DOG and two CATS live here. Continental breakfast served. Children welcome. NONSMOKERS, only.

**Rates:** S $35, D $40 DAILY.

**Reservations:** (414) 271-2337 MONDAY THROUGH FRIDAY 9 A.M. TO 6 P.M. CENTRAL TIME.

## WAUKESHA

Built in 1915, this home has old world charm. It is situated on spacious grounds in Waukesha, 20 miles west of Milwaukee. The second floor bedroom contains a queen-sized brass bed, antique furniture, and floral wallpaper. Great for cross-country skiing and convenient access to Brewer Stadium and the Milwaukee Zoo. Children and NONSMOKERS welcome.

**Rates:** S $30, D $35 DAILY.

**Reservations:** (414) 271-2337 MONDAY THROUGH FRIDAY 9 A.M. TO 6 P.M. CENTRAL TIME.

# 5

## North Central (West)

☐ **Missouri**

# MISSOURI

## GREATER KANSAS CITY
### INDEPENDENCE
### TRUMAN HISTORIC DISTRICT

DELAWARE STREET — Four doors from the Truman Home, in walking distance of other Truman sites and tour houses. Step back in time to the turn of the century. This 1850s house will overwhelm you with its feeling of generations past. Hundreds of details have been added to a basic setting of antique walnut furniture, period rugs, and lighting to recreate the Victorian era. Sleep in an 1880s bed and use your private 1900s bathroom yet experience the comforts of the present! Accommodations are a double bed, private bath, second floor bedroom, air conditioned. Nearby porch available for guest use in nice weather. Full breakfast is served in dining room. Information on sightseeing, antiquing, and restaurants in Independence and nearby Kansas City (20 minutes) provided. Other small towns in area make interesting side trips for antique and history buffs. Stay in the neighborhood the Trumans loved! One CAT. NONSMOKERS ONLY.
**Rates:** S $42.50, D $45.00 DAILY.
**Reservations:** (913) 268-4214 8 A.M. TO 9 P.M. (USUALLY) MONDAY THROUGH FRIDAY, ANSWERING MACHINE OTHERWISE.

### KANSAS CITY
### COUNTRY CLUB PLAZA

WEST 50TH STREET — A fine Tudor residence, situated in a wooded residential area on the Civil War battlefield of the Battle of Westport, near Nelson Art Gallery, the University of Missouri at Kansas City, Missouri Repertory Theater, Rockhurst College, the Country Club Plaza Shopping District, several four star restaurants, public transportation, public tennis courts, and a park. Accommodations include a twin-bedded room, air conditioning, TV, and private bath. A cot is also available. Full or continental breakfast on request. No pets. Host is a retired college professor; hostess works for an airline. Both are avid tennis players. NO SMOKERS.
**Rates:** S $52, D $58 DAILY.
**Reservations:** (913) 268-4214 8 A.M. TO 9 P.M. (USUALLY) MONDAY THROUGH FRIDAY, ANSWERING MACHINE OTHERWISE.

### OLD NORTHEAST

VANBRUNT NEAR HIGHWAY 24 — Retired hosts treat visitors to genuine midwest hospitality in this 1910 family home located in a quiet residential neighborhood on a tree-lined boulevard. Off-street parking for car. Near major highways Interstates 29, 35, and 70; and US 40 and US

24. Hosts furnish brochures and maps to amusement parks, stadiums, zoo, Truman home, hallmarks, country club plaza, and convention centers—all under 30 minutes by car. It is 1 1/2 blocks to city bus. Accommodations include: A) third floor has two single beds, sofa, space for sleeping bags or cot; and B) second floor has two double bedrooms, reading room, and guests' bath. Highchair. Crib. Host completely redecorated after children married and moved away. Each room is carpeted and features hand-embroidered linens, crocheted spreads, and other decorative touches hostess added for guests to enjoy. She serves full breakfast with freshly made jams and marmalades from fruit in season. (Also evening meal with sufficient notice.) Children welcome. SMOKING permitted in limited areas.
**Rates:** S $35, D $45 DAILY. CHILDREN UNDER 12 $5 EACH. AIRPORT PICKUP PREARRANGED $12-$15. 7TH DAY FREE.
**Reservations:** (913) 268-4214 8 A.M. TO 9 P.M. (USUALLY) MONDAY THROUGH FRIDAY, ANSWERING MACHINE OTHERWISE.

## WEATHERBY LAKE

75TH TERRACE — Large Contemporary home situated on a private LAKE. The home has a view of the lake from each window. Deck and patio available for guests use along with TV and fireplace. Host and hostess are self-employed. Accommodations include one wing separate from the rest of the house: A) king-sized waterbed; and B) two rooms with double bed. The three rooms share two baths. The hostess enjoys serving full breakfasts in the kitchen or dining room overlooking the lake and in summer on the deck. This home is convenient to Worlds of Fun, Kansas City International Airport, Old Historic Weston with McCormick Distillery, Historic Old Westport, the Plaza, downtown Kansas City, and Historic Liberty, Missouri. Air conditioned. Picnic area. One DOG. CHILDREN over 6 welcome.
**Rates:** S $40, D $45 DAILY. S $200, D $250 WEEKLY.
**Reservations:** (913) 268-4214 8 A.M. TO 9 P.M. (USUALLY) MONDAY THROUGH FRIDAY, ANSWERING MACHINE OTHERWISE.

## PARKVILLE (KANSAS CITY SUBURB)

NORTH CROOKED ROAD — Unusual earth integrated home features private entrance to four bedrooms, each with private bath. Accommodations include: three rooms with double beds, one room with twin beds. Each have a private bath. A crib and rollaway are also available. INDOOR SWIMMING POOL, EXERCISE ROOM, and jogging path. Breakfast is special order—from country to continental. A quiet country setting conveniently located near Parkville between Kansas City International Airport and downtown Kansas City. Host is a farmer and livestock salesman; hostess is a former college music teacher, now full time in

B&B. One DOG, two horses, cows, and many Canadian geese call this home their home. PIANO.
**Rates:** S $55, D $65 DAILY.
**Reservations:** (913) 268-4214 8 A.M. TO 9 P.M. (USUALLY) MONDAY THROUGH FRIDAY, ANSWERING MACHINE OTHERWISE.

## OZARK FRINGE
### WARRENSBURG
### RURAL

MONKEY MOUNTAIN — A Contemporary home located on 20 acres of quiet woodland atop a hill overlooking rich farmland and the Blackwater River. Furnished with a mixture of antiques, contemporary furniture, and Oriental rugs. An easy 1 hour drive to Truman Sports Complex, 75 minutes from Kansas City Plaza's fine shops and food of downtown convention area, 45 minutes to Truman Lake and excellent boating, fishing, and waterfowl hunting. The host is a professor of English at Central Missouri State University; the hostess is a public school counselor and special education teacher. Both enjoy conversation, good books, and listening to classical music. Grounds afford ample opportunity for hiking, bird and wildlife observation, photography, while escaping from civilization. Wraparound deck provides same without exercise plus glorious star watching. Accommodations include: A) room with twin beds, shared hall bath B) double-bedded room, shared hall bath; and C) a recreation room downstairs has a bath and queen hide-a-bed sofa or double waterbed. All have TV and radio. TRAINED PETS WELCOME inside, large kennel available. Located 5 miles northeast of Warrensburg, 13 miles south of Interstate 70 via US 13; 2 miles north of US 50. Children welcome.
**Rates:** S $25, D $30 DAILY. S OR D $175 WEEKLY.
**Reservations:** (913) 268-4214 8 A.M. TO 9 P.M. (USUALLY) MONDAY THROUGH FRIDAY, ANSWERING MACHINE OTHERWISE.

## PONY EXPRESS REGION
### ST. JOSEPH
### HARRIS ADDITION

NORTH 20TH AT JULE STREET — A gracious turn-of-the-century home with beveled glass, beautiful oak woodwork, and many antiques. Tea or sherry is served by the fire in cool weather or on the porch during warm months. A full breakfast is offered with homemade pastries. Centrally located, you can easily visit Patee House, Jessee James Home, Pony Express Stables, St. Joseph Museum, Albrecht Art Gallery, and the Doll Museum. Many antique shops and other places of interest are in the area. Located 45 minutes north of Kansas City International Airport. Accommodations include: A) elegant window treatment, Eastlake furniture, double bed. FIREPLACE; B) Victorian furniture, double bed, shares 1/2 bath with A; and C) antique iron double bed and baby bed, bath with claw-foot tub, separate shower room. Crib available. Air conditioned. Host is an insurance agent who enjoys refinishing antiques, golf, and hunting; hostess is a retired teacher and businesswoman. Her hobbies are cooking, reading, and collecting antiques. Both enjoy music and people. One CAT. Children welcome. NO SMOKING indoors.

**Rates:** A & B) S $35, D $45; AND C) S $30, D $40 DAILY. 7TH NIGHT FREE. CHILDREN OVER 3 $10.

**Reservations:** (913) 268-4214 8 A.M. TO 9 P.M. (USUALLY) MONDAY THROUGH FRIDAY, ANSWERING MACHINE OTHERWISE.

# 6

**South Central (East)**

☐     **Kentucky**

☐     **Mississippi**

☐     **Tennessee**

# KENTUCKY

## BLUE GRASS AREA

Center of the thoroughbred horse industry of Kentucky, the Blue Grass region draws visitors from all over the world, with its miles of fences, some dry-laid stone over 100 years old and its gently rolling fields. Keeneland Race Track, between Versailles and Lexington, across from Blue Grass Airport, was patterned after the track at Saratoga, New York and is said to be one of the most beautiful in the United States. The Red Mile Trotting Track shows off the saddlebred horse. But the Blue Grass has a guilty secret: It only shows blue when it is allowed to grow tall enough to bloom. At that time, there is a definite blue cast to the tiny flowers.

## CYNTHIANA
## US 62—RURAL

ROUTE 6 — Located on an 80 acre farm, this circa 1830 restored servants' quarters consists of a large brick-floored room with DOUBLE FIREPLACES and twin beds, a bedroom with an antique brass double bed, a kitchenette with breakfast foods provided (continental to full), plus a bath and a half. This antique filled cabin is part of a National Register complex made up of a Federal style main house, separate kitchen, smokehouse, and a wayfarer's station (now Broadwell Antiques). Guests are welcome to see and enjoy these buildings and the farm. Host is a school administrator; hostess buys and sells antiques. Convenient to both I-64 and I-75, this B&B is in the heart of Kentucky's horse farms and antiquing sites. CHILDREN over 12 welcome.
**Rates:** D $80, T $90, Q $100 DAILY.
**Reservations:** (502) 635-7341 8-11 A.M., 4-7 P.M. WEEKDAYS. MACHINE ALL OTHER TIMES.

## FRANKFORT
## HISTORIC SOUTH FRANKFORT

SHELBY NEAR 2ND STREET — Kentucky state capital strategically situated between Louisville and Lexington; 80 miles from Cincinnati. Large, late Victorian frame home located 100 yards from the scenic Kentucky River and on a beautiful tree-lined street. Six blocks from historic district and State Capitol. Home is furnished with several antiques and has two fireplaces on each floor. Host works for Kentucky General Assembly, speaks Spanish fluently and some French, and is a private pilot; hostess is a schoolteacher, speaks some Spanish, jogs, and canoes. Both do not smoke but SMOKERS (except cigar) are welcome. One CAT in residence. Large, elaborate breakfasts are offered. Accommodations include a queen-sized bed and private bath. CHILDREN over 8 welcome. Air conditioned.

**Rates:** S $39, D $44 (EXCEPT DERBY WEEK) DAILY.
**Reservations:** (502) 635-7341 8-11 A.M., 4-7 P.M. WEEKDAYS.
MACHINE ALL OTHER TIMES.

## INDEPENDENCE

TAYLOR MILL ROAD — This is an 18 acre mini farm in rural setting.
Fishing and swimming lakes, gardening, small animal reserve, ice skating
in winter. A perfect retreat from the hustle and bustle of the city yet just
20 minutes from downtown Cincinnati. Host is a manufacturer's rep and
social service administrator. His hobbies include fishing, snorkeling,
theater, travel, crafts, and boating. Hostess enjoys cooking. Full country
breakfast offered outside when weather permits. Two story family home
offering comfort and hospitality to the traveler—a home away from home.
Accommodations include: A) double bed, shared bath; and B) single bed,
shared bath. Both guestrooms are upstairs. Air conditioned. Pool table.
Bikes and rowboat available. Also speed boat for water skiing. NO
SMOKING.
**Rates:** A) S $25, D $40; B) S $25 DAILY. S $140, D $200 WEEKLY.
**Reservations:** (606) 356-7865 8 A.M. TO 9 P.M. MONDAY THROUGH
SATURDAY. SUNDAY, CALLS ANSWERED DEPENDING ON
AVAILABILITY.

## LOUISVILLE
### CHEROKEE TRIANGLE

EDGELAND AND WILLOW — Gracious southern living in historic
Cherokee-Triangle neighborhood on edge of beautiful Cherokee Park,
designed by the famous Frederic Law Olmstead. Within walking distance
of antique center and restaurant row on Bardstown Road. Old line duplex
home is professionally decorated with Oriental antiques and art. High
ceilinged rooms are sunlit and spacious. Accommodations on first floor
include: A) double bed, private bath and B) double bed, shared family
bath. NO SMOKING. AC.
**Rates:** A) S $45, D $50 AND B) S $40, D $45 DAILY (EXCEPT DERBY
WEEK).
**Reservations:** (502) 635-7341 8-11 A.M., 4-7 P.M. WEEKDAYS.
MACHINE ALL OTHER TIMES.

WILLOW NEAR CHEROKEE PARK — An airy and large apartment
now privately owned, awaits your arrival through the spacious Art Decco
lobby of this 1929 highrise apartment building. Located at the entrance of
Cherokee Park (designed by Olmstead in the nineteenth century) where
you can jog, play golf, tennis, or simply enjoy the beauty of the wooded
setting. Some of Louisville's best restaurants are within walking distance
and the location is convenient to downtown, hospitals, General Electric,
and Kentucky Fried Chicken headquarters, Churchill Downs and the

airport can be reached by either car or bus. Interstate 64 is within a mile and connects with Interstates 65 and 71. Accommodations include twin beds and private bath. The room is predepression size. Air conditioned.
**Rates:** S $45, D $50 DAILY (EXCEPT DERBY WEEK).
**Reservations:** (502) 635-7341 8-11 A.M., 4-7 P.M. WEEKDAYS. MACHINE ALL OTHER TIMES.

## DUNDEE-HAYFIELD

GARDINER LANE — Middle school teacher/counselor shares her spacious Contemporary home with large backyard enclosed by a creek and trees. Conveniently located near expressways and airport. Two blocks from Interstate 264, 3 miles east of airport, Interstate 65, and State Fair/ Expo Center. Guests are welcome to relax in large family room. Breakfasts of fresh fruits—Kentucky ham—hostess prides herself on good cooking and hospitality. Accommodations include: A) large double-bedded room, private bath directly across hall and B) small single room, shares guest bath. PIANO. NONSMOKERS ONLY.
**Rates:** A) S $37, D $42 AND B) S $37 DAILY (EXCEPT DERBY WEEK).
**Reservations:** (502) 635-7341 8-11 A.M., 4-7 P.M. WEEKDAYS. MACHINE ALL OTHER TIMES.

## GLEN HILL

OFF LIME KILN LANE — Large Colonial style home set on 1 1/2 landscaped acres in exclusive suburb of Louisville. Only half block from public transportation, 20 minutes from airport. Hosts will pickup at airport on request. Host is a professional musician, reads, fishes; hostess enjoys sewing, cooking, and traveling. PETS and Children WELCOME. Location, 1 mile from Interstate 264 and historic Locust Grove, the last home of General George Rogers Clark, only 5 minutes to center of city, shopping centers minutes away, and 30 minutes to Churchill Downs for the races. Hostess goes all out with full Kentucky breakfasts. Accommodations on second floor include three double bedrooms. Two baths.
**Rates:** S $40, D $45 DAILY. 7TH DAY FREE (EXCEPT DERBY WEEK).
**Reservations:** (502) 635-7341 8-11 A.M., 4-7 P.M. WEEKDAYS. MACHINE ALL OTHER TIMES.

## OLD BROWNSBORO ROAD

LEXINGTON LANE — A spacious hideaway amid a 3 acre park atmosphere with woods and brook, 15 minutes from downtown. Books, music, nature, and relaxation abound. Host is a product manager; hostess is a marketing director. Both enjoy nature, the arts, people, travel, and gourmet cooking. Accommodations include: private guest suite, overlooking

wooded area, encompasses entire lower level. Master bedroom features floor to ceiling FIREPLACE, bookcase wall, stereo. Sitting room contains sofabed. Room-sized dressing suite with walk-in closet and bath. Housekeep or snack in full kitchen with microwave; washer and dryer available. Direct access to picnic area and hammock in woods. Guests invited to use BABY GRAND PIANO and half bath upstairs, large lighted front deck. Full deck, weather permitting. Bear, the lovable LABRADOR, will accompany guests on walks or jogging. NO SMOKERS. CHILDREN over 10 welcome.
**Rates:** D $60, $40 2nd COUPLE DAILY. D $250, $300 2nd COUPLE WEEKLY. (EXCEPT KENTUCKY DERBY WEEK.)
**Reservations:** (502) 635-7341 8-11 A.M., 4-7 P.M. WEEKDAYS. MACHINE ALL OTHER TIMES.

## OLD LOUISVILLE

The National Register District kmown as Old Louisville was built on the grounds of the site of the Great Southern Exposition of 1883. Immediately to the south of the downtown resurgence of the arts and business, and only 2 miles from Churchill Downs of Kentucky Derby fame. The area is one of the most interesting architectural mixes in the city. Of significance is the variety of styles, ranging from the formal designs of Renaissance Revival to the romance of Queen Anne and Chateauesque, best viewed from the street by a walking tour. Three story homes in this neighborhood are the largest and most elaborate of Louisville's oldest housing stock. Owing to their size, most have been made into apartments, though some remain single family dwellings. Because of its proximity to downtown, it is very popular with visitors to the races, Actor's Theater, and Center for the Performing Arts.
**Rates:** CONTACT RESERVATION SERVICE FOR CURRENT RATES.
**Reservations:** (502) 635-7341 8-11 A.M., 4-7 P.M. WEEKDAYS. MACHINE ALL OTHER TIMES.

BELGRIVIA COURT AND SAINT JAMES — Iron gate opens onto brick walk to entrance on side and a small city garden. The 1890 restored duplex has three floors and is located in an area on the National Historic Register. The guest suite occupies all three rooms on the second floor. Accommodations include: A) double-bedded room with antique brass bed, other antique furniture and a FIREPLACE; B) a smaller, single-bedded room, with a refrigerator in its closet. The closet can be used as a dressing room if unoccupied. Both share a sitting room which also has a FIREPLACE, PIANO, television, and bath. Host spoils his guests almost as he does Nellie, his GERMAN SHEPHERD. Restaurants, the University of Louisville, and Churchill Downs are within walking distance. Breakfasts are ample Kentucky fare.
**Rates:** A) D $55; A & B) S $50, T $80 DAILY (EXCEPT KENTUCKY DERBY WEEK).

**Reservations:** (502) 635-7341 8-11 A.M., 4-7 P.M. WEEKDAYS. MACHINE ALL OTHER TIMES.

NEAR CENTRAL PARK/MAGNOLIA — An 1887 large Victorian home near Central Park with a private English garden. High ceilings and details such as stained glass windows, antique woodwork, and many fireplaces make this home especially interesting to guests. Host is with a major airline; hostess is an interior decorator. Both are active in community volunteer work. Home is furnished with antiques and owners' collection of primitive art. Within walking distance to downtown Galleria shopping to the north, and the University of Louisville to the south. Churchill Downs 2 miles. The Art Center, restaurants, and museums nearby. Public transportation at door. Off-street parking in garage. Full breakfast served; refrigerator available other times for guests to help themselves. CAT and DOG in residence. Accommodations include: A) double-bedded room with bath in suite and B) twin-bedded room with private bath down one fiight of stairs. NONSMOKERS ONLY.
**Rates:** A & B) S $55, D $60 (EXCEPT DERBY WEEK).
**Reservations:** (502) 635-7341 8-11 A.M., 4-7 P.M. WEEKDAYS. MACHINE ALL OTHER TIMES.

ST. JAMES COURT — A large three story stately Victorian home in yellow brick, built in the 1890s. Was occupied in the early years by members of the du Pont family. The property still has a carriage house converted to living quarters. The home is decorated with Victorian antiques. Among the amenities are nine fireplaces; rare and exotic imported wood trim, paneling, and staircase; imported marble fireplaces; an updated marble Victorian bathroom; a PIANO; and a sitting room. The host is a former Naval officer, deep sea diver, business manager, business owner, entrepreneur, high school and college teacher and counselor; hostess is a dealer in antiques with an avid interest in gardening. She has served as chairperson of "The Annual Garden Tour of Historic Farmington," annual fundraiser for the Historic Homes Foundation, and of other community projects. Both are world travelers and enjoy sharing experiences with guests. Host and hostess are nonsmokers but welcome smokers. Home is within walking distance of downtown. Excellent restaurants within 3 or 4 blocks, and the University of Louisville, home of the NCAA basketball championship team of 1986, is 6 blocks away. Accommodations include two rooms with double beds, private bath. Both rooms are available as a suite with a spacious sitting room. One DOG. CHILDREN over 10 welcome.
**Rates:** A & B) S $55, D $60 DAILY (EXCEPT KENTUCKY DERBY WEEK).
**Reservations:** (502) 635-7341 8-11 A.M., 4-7 P.M. WEEKDAYS. MACHINE ALL OTHER TIMES.

UNHOSTED efficiency apartment on third floor of 1890s house in picturesque Old Louisville. It is 10 minutes from downtown, University of Louisville, and Churchill Downs; 15 minutes from airport and fairgrounds. Six blocks from Highway 165. Private bath, living room with full size Simmons hide-a-bed, equipped kitchen with bar. Rollaway cot available. Central heat and air conditioning with controls. Breakfast makings are supplied. Hosts live in apartment next door. Minimum stay three nights. One DOG. Children welcome (subject to limitations of facility).
**Rates:** S OR D $38, T $46 DAILY. S OR D $200, T $240 WEEKLY. (NO WEEKLY RATES DURING DERBY WEEK).
**Reservations:** (502) 635-7341 8-11 A.M., 4-7 P.M. WEEKDAYS. MACHINE ALL OTHER TIMES.

2ND STREET BETWEEN OAK 7 ORMSBY — A Queen Anne house built in 1895, restored and furnished with antiques in keeping with that period, offers warm, informal hospitality for a nostalgic sojourn into the past. Relax around the fireplace and watch TV in your own sitting room before retiring to the elaborately ornate queen-sized antique bed. Awaken to breakfast including fruits in season and homemade muffins. From this Historic Preservation District you are minutes away from downtown Louisville, the University of Louisville, Spalding College, Churchill Downs, major hospitals, antique shops, and other attractions. All interstate highways through this area conveniently converge less than 2 miles north of this neighborhood. One and one-half baths shared with family. Host is a chemical operator; hostess is a floral designer. One 14 year old daughter lives here. Air conditioned. NO CHILDREN.
**Rates:** S $39, D $44 DAILY. 7TH NIGHT FREE WEEKLY (EXCEPT KENTUCKY DERBY WEEK).
**Reservations:** (502) 635-7341 8-11 A.M., 4-7 P.M. WEEKDAYS. MACHINE ALL OTHER TIMES.

OFF LEXINGTON ROAD — The Louis Seelbach House, built in 1912 for Louisville's most famous hotelier, is a gem of the Georgian architecture of the period. The portico and the balustrades relate the building to the elegant, formalized Beaux Arts style. Present owners bought the home when the estate was sold off, retaining a broad scenic easement at the front with sweeping view of Cherokee Park. In 1982, the home was the Bellarmine Designers' Showcase house. Hostess has reinforced the themes laid down by the Showcase design team. Host is a professional lobbyist who plays golf and enjoys traveling with hostess; hostess, a postal manager, collects antique dolls. Both are fond of arts and crafts shows. Only 10 minutes from city's center. This luxurious home offers double and twin bedrooms, each with bath en suite. One can be used via connecting bath along with a king-sized waterbed room. Guests welcome to use the billiard room. Full Kentucky breakfast served in formal dining

room or in one of the spacious glassed-in porches that grace the ends of the house. Tastefully done efficiency with separate entry available in the summer. PIANO.
**Rates:** S $70, D $75 DAILY (EXCEPT DERBY WEEK).
**Reservations:** (502) 635-7341 8-11 A.M., 4-7 P.M. WEEKDAYS. MACHINE ALL OTHER TIMES.

# BLUE GRASS AREA
## NICHOLASVILLE

RICHMOND AVENUE—HIGHWAY 169 — This 1805 house has had several changes in architecture. It has been designated a Kentucky landmark worthy of preservation by the Kentucky Heritage Commission. Located in the Blue Grass section there are many historical places that are a must. Located within 10 miles of the University of Kentucky Medical Center and the University of Kentucky, home of the Wildcats. Food is served in a traditional manner of excellence and courtesy at Pleasant Hill, home of the Shakers; Boone Tavern in Berea; and Beaumont Inn in Harrodsburg; all within a distance of 30 miles. Antiques are predominant in this area and this home contains many, mostly Victorian. Hostess has traveled extensively. When not traveling she spends most of her time as a community volunteer. Accommodations include three rooms with double beds. Two of the bedrooms adjoin the bath and also a sitting room.
**Rates:** S $39, D $44, 3RD PERSON IN SLEIGH BEDROOM $22 DAILY.
**Reservations:** (502) 635-7341 8-11 A.M., 4-7 P.M. WEEKDAYS. MACHINE ALL OTHER TIMES.

# RICHMOND
## FOUNTAIN PARK

RIVA RIDGE — University professor and his Brazilian wife welcome visitors to their Contemporary Ranch home just 1 mile from Interstate 75, 30 minutes from Lexington. One story at front, two stories at rear. Decor an interesting mix of antiques and South American arts and crafts. Host likes working with wood; hostess' hobby is cooking. She serves homemade sugar free cakes, breads, and cookies. And she will gladly babysit while visitors tour nearby Bybee pottery, the oldest pottery west of the Alleghenies, or Berea, famed for its unique college, Churchill Weavers and Boone Tavern with its fine regional food. Portuguese and Spanish spoken here. Guest suite below stairs opens onto a patio. Accommodations include: double bedroom with bath, sitting room adjoining. There is a sofabed for children or extra couple. Wicker furniture is in the suite. Park at private entrance. Air conditioning and VCR. WHEELCHAIR ACCESSIBLE.

**Rates:** S $35, D $42 DAILY.
**Reservations:** (502) 635-7341 8-11 A.M., 4-7 P.M. WEEKDAYS.
MACHINE ALL OTHER TIMES.

BARNES MILL ROAD—STAR ROUTE 876 — Located on 100 acres of rolling Blue Grass farmland at the foot of the Appalachian Mountains. Enjoy Southern hospitality in the comfort and privacy of this home. A full breakfast will be served in the large dining room furnished with antiques. Guests may explore the farm and talk to the animals, or play TENNIS on a private clay court. Host is a physician, who enjoys tennis and horseback riding; hostess, a homemaker, likes reading, cooking, and swimming. They have a 15 year old son. Just 2 miles from Interstate 75; 5 minutes from Eastern Kentucky University; and 20 to 50 minutes from Berea College, Ft. Boonesborough, Shakertown, University of Kentucky, and Kentucky Horse Park. An upstairs den/library has a fireplace, TV, and refrigerator. Accommodations include: A) double bed; B) twin beds; and C) queen-sized hide-a-bed. The three rooms share a split bath. SMOKERS/RESTRICTED. Children welcome.
**Rates:** A-C) S $41, D $46 DAILY.
**Reservations:** (502) 635-7341 8-11 A.M., 4-7 P.M. WEEKDAYS.
MACHINE ALL OTHER TIMES.

## SHELBYVILLE
### BAGDAD

NEAR US 421 BETWEEN INTERSTATES 71 AND 64 — Deep in the country, halfway between Interstates 71 and 64, is a 200 acre tobacco/dairy farm ideal for families with children who wish to leave the city behind. Home built in 1800s but has been completely modernized. Fish the ponds and hike the farm bordered at rear by old hand laid stone fence. About 25 minutes from Frankfort and Louisville. It is 10 miles from historic Shelbyville for antiquing at Wakefield-Scearce Galleries and the fine regional food at Science Hill Inn. Host farms full time except when hunting and fishing; he likes to sing, too; hostess is a homemaker with two part-time jobs with antiques shops in Shelbyville. Accommodations include three rooms with double beds. There is a guest bath and a crib available. Four DOGS live here.
**Rates:** S $37, D $42 DAILY. S $200, D $250 WEEKLY.
**Reservations:** (502) 635-7341 8-11 A.M., 4-7 P.M. WEEKDAYS.
MACHINE ALL OTHER TIMES.

## WILLIAMSTOWN

FALMOUTH STREET — Ranch home in quiet setting on 24 acres with view of surrounding woodlands and wildlife. Large apartment consisting of double bedrooms, bath, living room, dining room, and kitchen furnished

with early American antiques and collectibles. Rent all or part. Two miles from Williamstown Lake; 3 miles off Interstate 75. It is 50 minutes to downtown Lexington or Cincinnati. Retired hosts enjoy travel and refinishing antique furniture. Two DOGS are in residence here. Air conditioned. HANDICAPPED ACCESSIBLE.
**Rates:** FULL APARTMENT: S $40, D $45, T OR Q $85, 5 OR 6 PERSONS $120 DAILY. S $215, D $250 WEEKLY.
**Reservations:** (606) 356-7865 8 A.M. TO 9 P.M. MONDAY THROUGH SATURDAY. SUNDAY, CALLS ANSWERED DEPENDING ON AVAILABILITY.

## CENTRAL KENTUCKY
### SONORA

HIGHWAY 357 — Modern farmhouse situated on a 100 acre working farm where alfalfa hay and Polled Hereford cattle are the main enterprises. Farm is located in gently rolling central Kentucky approximately 10 miles south of Abraham Lincoln's birthplace and 45 miles north of Mammoth Cave National Park. Nearest restaurants are located about 8 miles from the home; access to major interstates is available within 10 miles. A privately owned lake with swimming, paddleboats, volleyball, and putt golf is located within a quarter mile. Host is a full-time farmer; hostess works full-time as a computer operator/bookkeeper. Their 12 year old son is a 7th grader with a keen interest in basketball. Accommodations include a double bed and private bath on second floor. One DOG. NONSMOKERS ONLY. HANDICAPPED ACCESSIBLE.
**Rates:** S $39, D $45 DAILY.
**Reservations:** (502) 635-7341 8-11 A.M., 4-7 P.M. WEEKDAYS. MACHINE ALL OTHER TIMES.

## CUMBERLAND LAKE
### SOMERSET

PUMPHOUSE ROAD — A Contemporary farmhouse on 4 landscaped acres. The home is cozy with wood floors, exposed oak post and beam framework, woodstove, and fireplace. Host is an attorney; hostess is a potter. They have a 3 year old boy and a 1 year old girl. They enjoy backpacking, eating from their garden, and gourmet cooking. South central Kentucky provides plenty of outdoor recreation with Lake Cumberland, the Big South Fork Recreation Area, Cumberland Falls, whitewater rafting, and lots of hiking trails within 40 minutes. Convenient to Interstate 75. Accommodations include: A) double-bedded room with private bath and B) sitting room with pullout bed. Separate entry. One DOG and a CAT. VCR. Children welcome. No SMOKERS.
**Rates:** S $39, D $44 DAILY.
**Reservations:** (502) 635-7341 8-11 A.M., 4-7 P.M. WEEKDAYS. MACHINE ALL OTHER TIMES.

# KENTUCKY LAKE
## PADUCAH
### SUBURBAN

Large new two story red brick Federal style home in exclusive neighborhood. Period antiques include some American Country pieces. Host is a semiretired electrical contractor; hostess gardens and works with antiques. Large white PERSIAN CAT lives in the utility room, but occasionally joins host couple for television. Home easily accessible from Interstate 24 and is much used by those coming to or from St. Louis. This tip of the state is at the heart of the Kentucky Lake Area, just minutes from the Lakes and the Land Between. Accommodations include three large double bedrooms. They share a guest bath. CHILDREN over 12 welcome.
**Rates:** S $39, D $44 DAILY.
**Reservations:** (502) 635-7341 8-11 A.M., 4-7 P.M. WEEKDAYS. MACHINE ALL OTHER TIMES.

# MAMMOTH CAVE REGION
## BOWLING GREEN

A Ranch style home with an all year panoramic view. Located on 1 1/2 landscaped acres with wooded area, in rolling farmland, minutes from old-fashioned general store and post office. A major shopping mall and numerous restaurants are only 10 minutes away. The home is furnished with a number of antiques as well as some Pennsylvania Dutch. It is minutes from Western Kentucky University, antique and craft shops, and numerous historic sites including Shakers at South Union. Old Union Church can be seen from the lawn. Located 7 miles from Interstate 65 and 8 miles from Bowling Green. A scenic 45 minute drive to Mammoth Cave and hostess will guide guests to nineteenth-century style Mennonite Community, 15 minutes away. Host is with G.M. Corvette and invites guests to a tour of the plant; he enjoys woodworking; hostess enjoys collecting antiques and gardening. Accommodations are limited for children. They include double-bedded room with private bath. Air conditioning and VCR. Children of all ages welcome.
**Rates:** S $37, D $42 DAILY.
**Reservations:** (502) 635-7341 8-11 A.M., 4-7 P.M. WEEKDAYS. MACHINE ALL OTHER TIMES.

# OHIO VALLEY
## MAYSVILLE

WEST 2ND STREET — This home is 60 miles east of Cincinnati in historic river town. Scenic drive from Cincinnati; ferry ride, if desired, in Augusta, Kentucky to near Ripley, Ohio. Apartment occupies top floor in small apartment building overlooking Ohio River with balcony for

breakfast, boat watching, or peaceful contemplation. Private entrance, bath, and sitting room complete this antique filled apartment. There is an elevator in the apartment. VCR. Hosts are local travel agent and farmer/businessman. Hobbies are travel and community theater. Air conditioned. HANDICAPPED ACCESSIBLE.
**Rates:** S OR D $40 DAILY.
**Reservations:** (606) 356-7865 8 A.M. TO 9 P.M. MONDAY THROUGH SATURDAY. SUNDAY, CALLS ANSWERED DEPENDING ON AVAILABILITY.

## PROSPECT-GOSHEN

This area, a few miles east of Louisville, is the Arabian horse capital of Kentucky. Set in gently rolling terrain, a little more chilly than the Blue Grass area, it is as lush, and contains some of the most famous horse farms in the state: Paramont, Hermitage, and Lasma East. The saddlebred horse is represented, too, in this neighborhood, around Covered Bridge Road and Wolf Pen Mill Road. Lasma East offers tours of their incredibly posh facilities just off US 42, the old road to Cincinnati.
**Rates:** CONTACT RESERVATION SERVICE FOR CURRENT RATES.
**Reservations:** (502) 635-7341 8-11 A.M., 4-7 P.M. WEEKDAYS. MACHINE ALL OTHER TIMES.

### GOSHEN NEAR LOUISVILLE

OFF US 42 — Your "Old Kentucky Home" in Goshen, Kentucky. An 80 year old rustic restored tenants' house located on a scenic 1,700 acre working farm with crops, cattle, and horses. The cottage has two bedrooms, living room with Ben Franklin fireplace, full size kitchen, bathroom, and cozy front porch with rockers. Plenty of hiking in woodlands, fishing on ponds, wild deer roaming nearby. City of Louisville only 25 minutes away; Standiford Field Airport 35 minutes; and Interstates 71 and 64 are 15 to 20 minutes away. A generous breakfast is provided in refrigerator for guests to prepare. Accommodations include: A) double bed on first floor and B) double bed on second floor. Bath on main floor. Children welcomed. Open April through October. UNHOSTED.
**Rates:** S OR D $55, T OR Q $75 DAILY (EXCEPT KENTUCKY DERBY WEEK).
**Reservations:** (502) 635-7341 8-11 A.M., 4-7 P.M. WEEKDAYS. MACHINE ALL OTHER TIMES.

### LOUISVILLE
### PROSPECT

HUNTNG CREEK — Deluxe condominium in prestigious country club setting. Backs up to wooded area that disguises path to stables. Home is 30 minutes from city center, short drive to the heart of Arabian Horse

farm country on US 42. Within 5 minutes of club house, golf, tennis, swimming pool. Walking, biking. Hostess, telecommunications director for major newspaper, offers gracious interior with antiques and traditional furnishings. Enjoys sharing interest in travel in relaxed, informal surroundings. Hostess will meet guests at Standiford Field and provide escort to residence. Accommodations include: A) queen-sized bed, private bath and B) queen sofabed, bath shared by other guests only. PIANO, Air conditioned, HANDICAPPED ACCESSIBLE. NONSMOKERS. Children and small well-behaved PETS WELCOME.
**Rates:** A) S $45, D $50 AND B) S $40, D $45 DAILY.
**Reservations:** (502) 635-7341 8-11 A.M., 4-7 P.M. WEEKDAYS. MACHINE ALL OTHER TIMES.

## PROSPECT

UPPER RIVER ROAD — A cozy Colonial style home in a quiet residential neighborhood out the River Road. Screened porch and patio. A beautiful drive to Prospect anytime, but especially in the early spring and fall. Hostess is retired, but has a part-time position with New Neighbor, a welcoming service for new people who move into the area. It is 7 miles from Interstates 64, 65, and 71. Home is convenient to beautiful Churchill Downs, famous for Kentucky Derby, and Keeneland Race Track is only 77 miles away. A few minutes' drive on US 42 is the area famed for its Arabian horse farms. This residence is located about 15 minutes from Louisville, Kentucky along the beautiful Ohio River. A hearty breakfast will be served. Accommodations include: A) twin beds; and B) king-sized bed, private bath. CHILDREN over 12 welcome.
**Rates:** A & B) S $33, D $38 DAILY (EXCEPT KENTUCKY DERBY WEEK).
**Reservations:** (502) 635-7341 8-11 A.M., 4-7 P.M. WEEKDAYS. MACHINE ALL OTHER TIMES.

## FOX HARBOR

Spacious Ranch style home backs up to a mini-horse farm. It is surrounded by acres of rolling hills and such famous horse farms as Hermitage, Longfield, Paramont, and Lasma East, center of the Arabian horse industry in Kentucky. Enjoy game room with pool table, and, in season, a HEATED POOL in backyard. It is 20 minutes from Standiford Field, 15 minutes from Bowman Field if you are flying your light plane, and 10 minutes to exclusive shopping. Running and bike routes in the neighborhood; the Ohio River close at hand for more outdoor sport. Host and hostess are avid runners and bikers. Accommodations include: A) king-sized bed, private bath and B) trundle bed that can sleep two. Both bedrooms are located on the first floor. One DOG, Air conditioning.
**Rates:** A) S $45, D $50; B) S $35, D $40 DAILY (EXCEPT KENTUCKY DERBY WEEK).

**Reservations:** (502) 635-7341 8-11 A.M., 4-7 P.M. WEEKDAYS.
MACHINE ALL OTHER TIMES.

# SOUTH CENTRAL KENTUCKY
## HODGENVILLE

HIGHWAY 21 EAST OF HOGENVILLE — In the heart of Lincoln
Country, this B&B provides a pastoral setting on a working farm in the
south central area of Kentucky. The two story pillared Colonial home is
framed with a white board fence and the approaching driveway is lined
with pine and oaks. Antiques are predominant in the decor in a home
that has seen four children grow up. The view from all directions is that
of beautiful rolling countryside and a large lake in the rear. All of this is
enhanced with the beauty of the changing seasons. On the farm one can
enjoy sheep and baby lambs, cattle, hogs, tobacco production, the growing
of a large vegetable garden, corn, soy beans, and hay making. In this
setting the visitor has the best of the two worlds—rural and urban. One
hour by Interstate 65 from Louisville, Kentucky's largest city; 5 minutes
from Abraham Lincoln National Historic Birthplace; 45 minutes from
Mammoth Cave National Park; and 30 minutes from My Old Kentucky
Home State Park. With advance arrangements, evening supper is available.
Expect a bountiful Kentucky country breakfast. Accommodations include:
A) mother-in-law wing on main level, double bed, private bath, all
antiques; and B) on second floor, two rooms with double bed, shared
bath. One DOG and a CAT.
**Rates:** A) S $40, D $45 AND B) S $35, D $40.
**Reservations:** (502) 635-7341 8-11 A.M., 4-7 P.M. WEEKDAYS.
MACHINE ALL OTHER TIMES.

## RUSSELLVILLE

FRANKLIN ROAD — The log house is a unique home built from hand-
hewn logs recovered from old cabins and barns. Set in 15 wooded acres
and decorated in the American Country style, the house is filled with
antiques and auction finds that are for sale. Host is a production manager
and enjoys flying; hostess is a textile designer and has her fiber studio
and shop on the premises where guests may take classes in the fiber arts
during their stay. The CAT, Lucy, can be found in the greenhouse in the
cooler weather where guests may use the HOT TUB. The DOGS, Sophie
and Emma, enjoy company on their romps through the woods. Shakertown
at South Union, Bowling Green, Mammoth Cave, and Lake Malone State
Park, Opryland and Nashville, Tennessee are all within easy driving
distance. Russellville's antique and craft shops offer delightful shopping.
Memorable gourmet food. Accommodations include: A) double bed, single
bed, and private bath; B & C) two rooms with double bed, private bath;
and D) twin-bedded double, private bath. All bedrooms are on second

floor. TWO OF THE BEDROOMS HAVE WORKING FIREPLACES. CHILDREN over 6 welcome.

**Rates:** S $50, D $55 DAILY. 7TH NIGHT FREE WEEKLY.

**Reservations:** (502) 635-7341 8-11 A.M., 4-7 P.M. WEEKDAYS. MACHINE ALL OTHER TIMES.

## WESTERN KENTUCKY
## OWENSBORO
### FARM

OLD HENDERSON ROAD — Rustic two bedroom restored tenants' house on 100 acre farm and tennis ranch. Host is a farmer interested in philosophy, hunting and fishing; hostess is a noted tennis professional who speaks Spanish and a little French. An INDOOR TENNIS CLUB with three tennis and three racquetball courts located on the property. Other facilities include three outdoor tennis courts, a large swimming and small wading POOLS, fishing ponds with small boats, HORSES FOR RIDING, and bikes. Large playground and picnic area near the creek running through the farm also fruit trees and berries on farm. Guests met at airport at no charge. Hosts own a 500 acre farm 20 miles away, with deer, quail, dove, for HUNTING, two FISHING ponds. Professional tennis instruction available; hosts arrange matches. Accommodations include a COTTAGE that includes living room with queen sofabed, Franklin stove, carpet, and antique furnishings; kitchenette and bath. UNHOSTED. PIANO and air conditioned. Children of all ages welcome.

**Rates:** D $60, $25 ADDITIONAL ADULT, $10 PER CHILD UNDER 16 DAILY. 7TH NIGHT FREE WEEKLY.

**Reservations:** (502) 635-7341 8-11 A.M., 4-7 P.M. WEEKDAYS. MACHINE ALL OTHER TIMES.

## THE DELTA
### INDIANOLA

Enjoy a full breakfast of country ham and homemade biscuits at this extremely attractive two story home in the heart of the Mississippi Delta. The hosts, known for their hospitality, will take guests on a tour of the area, pointing out crops in season and directing them to restaurants. Accommodations include: double bed, private bath. Extras include: PIANO and antiques. CHILDREN over 6 welcome.

**Rates:** S OR D $45 DAILY.
**Reservations:** (601) 482-5483.

## GULF COAST
### BILOXI

Restored turn-of-the-century hotel overlooking the Mississippi Gulf. Continental breakfast. Swimming POOL and other modern ammenities. All guestrooms have private baths. Cribs and cots available.

**Rates:** $55-$65 DAILY.
**Reservations:** (601) 482-5483.

### LONG BEACH

A Contemporary home with swimming POOL on property, convenient to the BEACH. Hostess is well traveled, originally from Germany, and delights in preparing German breads for breakfast and sharing her knowledge about wonderful seafood and French restaurants along the coast. Accommodations include: A) double bed, private bath; and B) double bed, shared bath. The second room is only available to people traveling with those in A. Cribs and cots available. Bikes also available. PIANO. Pool table.

**Rates:** S OR D $45 SHARE BATH, $55 PRIVATE BATH DAILY.
**Reservations:** (601) 482-5483.

### PASS CHRISTIAN

A 2,100 square foot log Cajun cottage situated on 45 acres of rolling land with orchard, live Christmas trees, picnic, and hiking area plus inground POOL (15 × 36 feet). Two and a half miles north of Interstate 10, 8 miles to beach, convenient to Andrew Jackson's "Beauvoir," Marine Life, NASA Space Center, and Keesler Air Force Base. Boat to Ship Island, part of national seashore within 30 minutes and New Orleans only 62 miles west. Accomodations include: A) downstairs double-bedded room, private bath, exit to large screened porch facing the pool; and B) a loft that can sleep two adults or school age children, share bath with A. Host is in sales and speaks French; hostess is a registered nurse and

can speak a little Spanish. Hosts invite guests to share hamburgers by the pool during the summer months and a relaxing drink by the fireplace in winter. Dinners of regional favorites can be arranged. CHILDREN over 6 welcome.
**Rates:** S OR D $55 DAILY. $280 WEEKLY.
**Reservations:** (601) 482-5483.

## THE HEARTLANDS

The bluffs that overlook the vast Mississippi River are rich with images of a past grandeur and grace. The Civil War battlefields are a historic reminder of the end of an era. Mississippi's Heartlands offer a playground in which to see history come to life. Natchez and Vicksburg present the antebellum life complete with hoop skirts and mint juleps. In contrast, the capital city of Jackson abounds with cultural events. Events include: Natchez—spring and fall pilgrimage (March, April, and October); Medicine Show (fall), Christmas Pilgrimage (December). Vicksburg—spring Pilgrimage (March). Jackson—Mississippi State Fair (October). Port Gibson—spring Pilgrimage (March).
**Rates:** CONTACT RESERVATION SERVICE FOR CURRENT RATES.
**Reservations:** (601) 482-5483.

## BROOKHAVEN
### HISTORIC

A beautiful nineteenth century completely restored and furnished in Victorian style with antiques of the period. Four large bedrooms, all with private baths. One downstairs bedroom with antique canopied bed. Perfect for honeymooning couple or for a special occasion. The three upstairs bedrooms are also furnished in antiques and beautifully decorated. Bedrooms have double accommodations. Suites available. The host is a well-known Mississippi decorator and architectural designer. Gourmet dinner is available by special and prior arrangement. A full breakfast is served in the formal dining room. Air conditioned. HANDICAPPED ACCESSIBLE.
**Rates:** S $75, D $95-$125 DAILY.
**Reservations:** (601) 482-5483.

## JACKSON
### BELHAVEN

Located in Belhaven, an older area with many restored homes; near downtown and historic buildings, Art Museum, Agriculture and Forestry Museum, Millsaps College, Belhaven College. and four major medical complexes. This home is the arch typical Southern mansion. It is on the National Register of Historical Places and has often been compared to Mount Vernon. The grounds are spacious and provided with dramatic

landscape lighting. Furnishings have been provided with an eye to comfort as well as style. It is the scene of many wedding receptions and enjoys a reputation for elegant hospitality. Guests are made welcome to enjoy the Southern graces within the ambience of a private mansion. Full Southern breakfast. Suite includes hosts' personal library and adjoining bedroom with king-sized bed. Furnished beautifully with family antiques. Private bath, color TV on second floor. The second accomodation is a lovely large room with sitting area and two double beds. Furnished with antiques and reproductions, private bath, and color TV. Host and hostess are well traveled, interesting, and will direct guests to all area and Jackson attractions. French is spoken here. Welcoming beverage and tour of home included. Air conditioned. PIANO. NO CHILDREN.
**Rates:** S OR D $75 DAILY.
**Reservations:** (601) 482-5483.

## LORMAN

This 100 acre working plantation with 125 year old Classic Greek Revival mansion. On National Register, a truly elegant home with most gracious hosts. Relax and enjoy antiques, spacious grounds, plantation tour, fish in their well-stocked pond, read first owner's journal, perhaps meet the friendly ghost. Plantation breakfast, a welcoming julep and fresh fruit in your room. Accommodations include: A) two rooms with double bed, private bath, B) double bed, share bath; and C) three twins, share bath. Competent baby sitter can be secured. Pets include: three DOGS, one CAT, peacocks, chickens, and ducks. Host is a Christmas tree grower. He is interested in model railroads and Civil War history; hostess is an antique buff. Children welcome.
**Rates:** S $85, D $95 DAILY. CHILDREN $25 EACH NIGHT. TAKE $5 OFF EACH NIGHT ON STAYS OF TWO OR MORE NIGHTS.
**Reservations:** (504) 346-1928 SEVEN DAYS 8 A.M. TO 8 P.M.

## NATCHEZ

An 1818 Federal style home on 18 landscaped acres. Where Jefferson Davis married Varina Howell in 1845. It is furnished with period antiques, Oriental rugs, and Audubon prints. Fee includes a guided tour, cocktails in Riverview Lounge, and full Southern breakfast. A gourmet dining pavilion is on the premises. On the National Register. Accommodations include: A) first floor, 1790 poster bed, FIREPLACE, TV, private bath; B) adjoining the parlor, 1830 pine and maple double bed, sitting area. Sarouk carpet, private bath; C) second floor, eighteenth century English four poster bed, hooked rugs, TV, private bath; D) very large rooms with pineapple twin beds and maple daybed (for extra person), sitting area with sofa and wing chair, TV, private bath; and E) an elegant room with view of the Mississippi River, antiques, Acanthus four poster double bed, TV, private bath. Extras include: inground POOL, HOT TUB.

HANDICAPPED ACCESSIBLE. SMOKING allowed in restricted areas. CHILDREN over 12 welcome.
**Rates:** S OR D $90 DAILY.
**Reservations:** (601) 482-5483.

Circa 1818, completely restored in 1978. All 14 guestrooms feature private baths, period antiques, including four poster canopy beds, phones, and TVs. Located on 26 acres of beautifully landscaped gardens. Full Southern breakfast included.
**Rates:** A, C, & D) (IN SLAVE QUARTERS) S $70, D $75; E) (IN SLAVE QUARTERS) S $80, D $85; F, G, L, & M) (IN MAIN HOUSE) S $95, D $100; Q) SUITE D $135, $20 EACH EXTRA PERSON, GARDEN COTTAGES H, I, J, & K) S $80, D $85.
**Reservations:** (504) 346-1928 SEVEN DAYS 8 A.M. TO 8 P.M.

A one room cottage with a fireplace, cathedral ceiling with skylight, wood floors, kitchenette, central heating, air conditioning, and private bath designed by your architect hosts. Cable TV, no phone unless requested. Your cottage opens onto a flagstone patio with fish pond shaded by oak trees. Guests make their own continental breakfast. Baby equipment is available as are books about local sights and history, including a tourbook for walkers. A GOLDEN RETRIEVER and two CATS live on the property as do your hosts who have traveled widely and speak fluent French, Japanese, and German. Children welcome.
**Rates:** S OR D $45 DAILY.
**Reservations:** (601) 482-5483.

The hostess of this historic home is a professional interior decorator. Her lovely home reflects her talent, both in the decor and in the fine collection of outstanding Federal furniture. The master bedroom contains a Sheraton canopied bed and other family antiques. The other bedrooms are all furnished with plantation made furniture. Six bedrooms available. all with private baths. One twin bedroom available. The others have double beds. Plantation breakfast is served and a tour of the home included. Hostess will direct you to all there is to see and do in the historic city of Natchez. Air conditioned. CHILDREN over 12 welcome. SMOKING in restricted areas.
**Rates:** S OR D $70-$75, $90 DAILY.
**Reservations:** (601) 482-5483.

Building of this gracious National Register home spans years from 1791 to 1950s. Descendants of family that purchased it in 1849 still live in it. Note its magnificent collection of period furniture and Audubon prints. There are seven bedrooms with private baths. Full Southern breakfast (served on the veranda when weather is good) is provided. Accommodations include: first floor—A) double bed, tub, nonworking fireplace, private

entrance; B) king bed, tub/shower, nonworking fireplace, private entrance; and C) double bed, one 3/4 bed, tub/shower, private entrance, 3 people share room. Second floor—D) two double beds, tub; E) queen and twin beds. tub/shower; F) west wing, two twin beds, shower, entrance from upper gallery; and G) same as F only double bed.
**Rates:** S $65, D $75, T $95 DAILY.
**Reservations:** (504) 346-1928 SEVEN DAYS 8 A.M. TO 8 P.M.

## DOWNTOWN

CORNER PEARL AND ORLEANS — A 3 story, 18 room Greek Revival style townhouse (circa 1835) on the National Register because of its magnificent staircase, interior millwork, and historically prominent past residents. Accommodations include a first floor master suite. Five lovely bedrooms are all furnished with period antiques and reproductions. All guestrooms are double occupancy, with the exception of the master bedroom, which is on the second floor. Other bedrooms are on the first floor. One twin-bedded room; all others are four poster canopied beds. All have private baths. Adjoining sitting room with TV and telephone for guests' use. A full plantation breakfast is served, and a tour of the house is included in the price of lodging, along with a welcoming beverage. One DOG lives here.
**Rates:** D $75 DAILY.
**Reservations:** (601) 482-5483.

## HISTORIC

CORNER OF HOMOCHITTO STREET — Each guestroom is unique and furnished with antiques. One of the bedrooms has twin beds, joins the bedroom with canopied bed and is perfect for a couple with older children or four people traveling together. FIREPLACE in bedroom. Hostess and daughter will make you feel very much at home by offering suggestions, giving directions and of course typical Mississippi hospitality and graciousness. AC. CHILDREN over 7 welcome.
**Rates:** S OR D $80 DAILY. EACH ADDITIONAL PERSON $20 DAILY.
**Reservations:** (601) 482-5483.

NORTH UNION STREET — An elegant inn built circa 1832. A historical home of pure Greek architecture. The three story mansion is especially noted for its semispiral stairway, unique gardens, and exquisite collection of priceless antiques. An original dependency is still on the grounds. The front portico is supported by large, dark columns, and the paneled doorway is framed in sidelights of early glass. During the Civil War this home was used as headquarters by the Federal troops and later became a hospital for Union soldiers. All of the bedrooms include authentic antiques and four poster tester beds, private baths, air conditioning, and TV. There are 4 acres of terraced gardens and an outdoor swimming

POOL available. Home is within walking distance of the downtown area and the Mississippi River. Rates include a seated plantation breakfast each morning, a tour of the antebellum mansion, and a complimentary wine at check in. The home has been the private residence of three mayors of Natchez, including the present mayor. Children of any age welcome.
**Rates:** S OR D $75 DAILY. EACH ADDITIONAL PERSON $20 DAILY. TAX EXTRA.
**Reservations:** (601) 482-5483.

CEMETERY ROAD — Circa 1855, an outstanding example of Greek Revival style overlooking the Mississippi River. Furnished in fine antiques of the period, four double rooms have private entrances and private baths. A fifth room is available with private hall bath. Elegant dining in the original dining room includes a full plantation breakfast and beverage or cocktail in the evening overlooking the river. Many historic homes are available for viewing close by. A true glimpse of the pre-Civil War past. PIANO. SMOKING on the veranda, only.
**Rates:** S OR D $65-$75 DAILY.
**Reservations:** (601) 482-5483.

CORNER QUITMAN PARKWAY — Circa 1818, completely restored in 1978. All 14 guestrooms feature private baths, period antiques, including four poster canopy beds, also telephones and TVs. Located on 26 beautifully landscaped acres of gardens. A full Southern breakfast is served. Extras include: PIANO, air conditioning, and antiques. CHILDREN over 14 welcome and limited SMOKING permitted.
**Rates:** A-D) S $70, D $85; E-H) S $80, D $85; I-M) S $95, D $100; AND N) S $125, D $135 DAILY.
**Reservations:** (601) 482-5483.

## PORT GIBSON

Hosts whose families have been in Mississippi for 200 years love to show this elegant National Trust antebellum home with private baths, antiques, and TV artfully combining old and new for your pleasure. Full breakfast and tour of the house. Hostess will prepare picnic lunches (for extra charge) and direct guests to many historic sites in the area. Six double guestrooms, air conditioning, PIANO, and chairlift for the handicapped are available. Your hosts are a retired merchant and Civil War historian and an area historian who is serving as Governer. General of the Order of First Families of Mississippi. Host organized the Grand Gulf Military Monument, a 400 acre park. SMOKING in designated areas only, not in bedrooms.
**Rates:** 2ND FLOOR IN GUESTHOUSE A) $80; B) $80; C) $85; D & E) $70 DAILY. ROLLAWAY $15 ADDITIONAL NIGHTLY. $5 OFF

ROOM RATE EACH NIGHT ON STAYS OF TWO OR MORE DAYS. 2ND FLOOR OF MAIN HOUSE HAS TWO BEDROOM SUITE G & H) $155 DAILY.
**Reservations:** (504) 346-1928 SEVEN DAYS 8 A.M. TO 8 P.M.

## HISTORIC

A palatial 30 room mansion on the National Register of Historic Places. Port Gibson is the town General Grant said was "too beautiful to burn." The mansion and adjoining guesthouse are furnished with antiques and family heirlooms. The bedrooms are beautifully decorated. The grounds include a beautiful courtyard with both fountain and gazebo. Host is a Civil War historian and has a rare collection of Civil War memorabilia; hostess is an area historian and is active in the Daughters of the American Revolution. A full breakfast is served in the family's formal dining room. A tour of the house is included. Telephone and sitting room with TV available. Off-street parking. Six bedrooms available, all with private baths and air conditioning. Also rollaway beds available. There is a queen-sized eighteenth century canopied bed as well as double beds. Refrigerator in one guestroom. CHILDREN over 12 welcome. SMOKING permitted in restricted areas.
**Rates:** D $75 AND UP DAILY. ADDITIONAL PERSON $15 EACH DAILY.
**Reservations:** (601) 482-5483.

## VICKSBURG

Situated on 6 landscaped acres, this outstanding home designed in the Federal style hosts exquisite milled woodwork, sterling silver doorknobs, French bronze chandeliers, and a lonely ghost—all echoes of the past. Three lovely guestrooms all furnished in antiques: a Mallard bed, a Heppelwhite tester, or a plantation style room are yours to enjoy. A tour of the home, plantation breakfast, and mint juleps included. Host is a physician; hostess enjoys gardening, antiques, and art. One teenager lives here. SMOKING in restricted areas. Air conditioned.
**Rates:** S OR D $75 DAILY.
**Reservations:** (601) 482-5483.

An 1830 Greek Revival townhouse located on the brick paved streets of Vicksburg. The home is furnished with period antiques and artifacts, complete with gas burning chandeliers. All guestrooms are furnished with antiques and all have private baths. A full Southern breakfast is served in the main house after which guests receive a tour of the home. A large inground POOL and JACUZZI HOT TUB are a few of the modern amenities for guests to enjoy. PETS WELCOME. Enjoy sightseeing in the many museums and tour homes along with the National Military Park.

There are nine double guestrooms with private baths. Suites are also available. FIREPLACES in some bedrooms, also antique queen-sized tester bed. PIANO. HANDICAPPED ACCESSIBLE. Children of all ages welcome.
**Rates:** MARCH THROUGH NOVEMBER S $70-$100, D $75-$105 DAILY. DECEMBER THROUGH FEBRUARY S $60-$80, D $65-$85 DAILY.
**Reservations:** (601) 482-5483.

## HISTORIC

Enjoy your own charming cottage in Vicksburg. Hosts are involved in promoting Vicksburg and are certain to direct you to many historical sites as well as outstanding restaurants. Southern breakfast in the family dining room and a tour of the home is included. Double bedroom has private attached bath; suite available with a sofabed. HANDICAPPED ACCESSIBLE. CHILDREN over 10 welcome.
**Rates:** S OR D $65 DAILY. EACH ADDITIONAL PERSON $10 DAILY.
**Reservations:** (601) 482-5483.

Elegant 150 year old town house and slave quarters. Nine delightful rooms all have private baths and are furnished in antiques. Enjoy the splendor of yesterday with modern conveniences (TV, JACUZZI, HOT TUB, and POOL). Gracious hostess greets you with a mint julep or glass of wine. Small pets allowed. Full breakfast and tour of the house included in all rates. Children welcome.
**Rates:** MARCH THROUGH NOVEMBER ON GROUND LEVEL A) S $90, D $95; B) S $80, D $85; F) S $80, D $85; G & H) S $80, D $85; I) S $70, D $75. ON SECOND FLOOR C) S $80, D $85; D) S $90, D $95; E) IN MAIN HOUSE S $100, D $105. ROLLAWAY AVAILABLE FOR ANY ROOM EXCEPT I AT $15 ADDITIONAL. DECEMBER THROUGH FEBRUARY $10 LESS EXCEPT I $5.
**Reservations:** (504) 346-1928 SEVEN DAYS 8 A.M. TO 8 P.M.

## THE HILLS
## HOLLY SPRINGS

MASON AVENUE — Built in 1838 by William F. Mason, Treasurer of the Illinois Central Railroad, this home is listed on the National Register of Historic Places. It is filled with eighteenth and nineteenth century antiques. Accommodations include three double rooms with private baths. Guests may choose the formal dining room, the veranda, or the gazebo as the location for their breakfast. It includes juice, coffee, fresh fruit, sausage and egg casserole, angel biscuits, and strawberry butter. In the afternoon, guests may enjoy a complimentary drink by the POOL. There is also a year-round HOT TUB. Bikes are available. The carriage house

is now an antique shop. Nearby are over 100 antebellum homes and the 1837 Hillcrest Cemetery. HANDICAPPED ACCESSIBLE. Air conditioned. Children welcome.
**Rates:** S $55, D $65 DAILY.
**Reservations:** (601) 482-5483.

## OXFORD

A turn-of-the-century historic home with hostess who is there during the day, but not at night. Accommodations include six bedrooms with private baths. Extras include: air conditioning, antiques, and access by public transportation. Convenient to the Faulkner home, University of Mississsippi, and more. CHILDREN over 6 welcome.
**Rates:** S $42, D 45 DAILY.
**Reservations:** (601) 482-5483.

Built in 1838, this lovely antebellum home is made entirely of native timber and is on the National Register. The hostess is a world traveler and retired university professor. Treasures abound here. There are 150 years of fashion displayed on mannequins in the attic. With their breakfast guests can enjoy cakes that are still warm on the balcony on warm spring mornings. Conveniently located near the William Faulkner home. Accommodations include: A) downstairs suite with double bed, private bath; and B & C) second floor—two double rooms, share bath. CHILDREN over 12 welcome.
**Rates:** A) $65 SUITE; B OR C) $55 PRIVATE BATH; AND B & C) $80 TWO ROOMS WITH SHARED BATH DAILY.
**Reservations:** (601) 482-5483.

## THE PLAINS

Known for the mysterious stillness of its Indian Mounds, stimulation of its festivals, excitement of harness racing and taste of country cooking, the Mississippi Plains offer a wealth of choices. Events: Meridian—Lively Arts Festival (April). The Jimmie Rodgers Memorial Festival (May). Symphony Orchestra, Little Theater, and Art Museum (year-round). Columbus—spring Pilgrimage, tour of antebellum homes and gardens, (April). Philadelphia—Neshoba County Fair, crafts, harness racing, and political speaking (August).
**Reservations:** (601) 482-5483.

## COLUMBUS
## HISTORIC

This house is a Federal style house and the oldest brick house in Columbus. It was built in 1828, the year Andrew Jackson was elected president. The house has been completely restored and is furnished with

antiques of the period. Three bedrooms with double accommodations, each with private bath. CHILDREN over 12 welcome. SMOKING in restricted areas.
**Rates:** A) D $65; B) D $75; AND C) D $65 DAILY. PRICED BY SIZE.
**Reservations:** (601) 482-5483.

This home is in the heart of historic downtown Columbus. This two story Italianate style house is furnished with period antiques that recount the splendor of the historical South. It has been fully restored. Convenient to all attractions and Mississippi State University for Women. Air conditioned. CHILDREN over 12 welcome.
**Rates:** $45 DAILY.
**Reservations:** (601) 482-5483.

# MERIDIAN

This is an eighteenth century Williamsburg reproduction home. Upstairs suite with bedroom and sitting room, private bath. Triple accommodations available in suite. Hosts are well traveled and have collections from various parts of the world. One DOG resides here. PIANO. Air conditioned. CHILDREN over 12 welcome.
**Rates:** S OR D $50, T $70 DAILY.
**Reservations:** (601) 482-5483.

This lovely traditional home is furnished with both reproductions and antiques of the period. House is high on a hill overlooking beautiful pastureland. A lovely swimming POOL on premises is available for guests' use. Convenient to highway. Hosts have a fine collection of art done by Mississippi artists. Host is a banker who is interested in photography, travel, and art; hostess enjoys bridge, antiques, and travel. Full breakfast included. HANDICAPPED ACCESSIBLE. Children of all ages welcome. NO SMOKING.
**Rates:** S OR D $65 DAILY.
**Reservations:** (601) 482-5483.

Restored Victorian home filled with antiques and located on 10 wooded acres within the city limits of Meridian. Host is a TV executive; hostess is a noted gourmet cook and collects antiques. Both are very interesting and have collected antiques for their home from their many trips both in this country and abroad. Hostess will prepare a special gourmet dinner for guests by special arrangement made at the time of reservation for an additional charge. Both hosts will direct you to area attractions and make you feel very much at home. One bedroom available with antique poster canopied bed, beautifully decorated and private bath. Tour of the home and welcoming beverage included. Spanish is spoken here. One resident small DOG. Air conditioned. PIANO. Children welcome.

**Rates:** S OR D $65 DAILY. EACH ADDITIONAL PERSON $10 DAILY. CRIB $5 DAILY.
**Reservations:** (601) 482-5483.

## RESIDENTIAL

In one of Meridian's loveliest neighborhoods, this home is set among flowering shrubs and dogwood trees. The hosts have always been active in civic, as well as cultural activities, both locally and within the state. Host is a retired pharmacist; hostess is a historian. Attractively furnished, two bedrooms with shared bath (for family or four people traveling together, only) or a double bedroom with private bath. Full Mississippi breakfast. Host and hostess will direct you to all area restaurants and attractions. Very special Mississippi hospitality here! Air conditioned. CHILDREN over 10 welcome.
**Rates:** S OR D $45, T OR Q $70 DAILY.
**Reservations:** (601) 482-5483.

This Contemporary home is hosted by hosts who are active in both local and state affairs. Host is an attorney; hostess is a well-known Mississippi artist. Their home is filled with art and collections from their travels. One guestroom with double accommodations, private bath. Suite also available. Air conditioned. NO CHILDREN.
**Rates:** S OR D $45 DAILY.
**Reservations:** (601) 482-5483.

# TENNESSEE

## CUMBERLAND PLATEAU
## CROSSVILLE
## PLEASANT HILL COMMUNITY

CLAYSVILLE ROAD — Large home of Country French architectural design, native field stone exterior, and known by many locals as "The Castle." It is nestled on 6.33 manicured and very secluded acres, just 10 miles from Crossville, Tennessee, on the great Cumberland Plateau. The 2,000 feet elevation makes for an ideal four seasons' climate. The home features five double bedrooms, four full baths, plus two powder rooms. There is 4,600 square feet of living area, central heat and air conditioning, plus two fireplaces. The large rear patio affords a breathtaking view of the mountains and frequently deer can be seen grazing nearby. The property is located just off I 40 approximately 100 miles from Nashville, and 65 miles from Knoxville. It is less than an hour's drive to three different state parks. Fishing, tennis, golfing, and swimming are available nearby. An ideal spot to escape to and enjoy the peace and quiet—and forget the hustle bustle of city life. Accommodations include three double rooms. Full breakfast.

**Rates:** A & B) S $45 AND C) D $60 DAILY.
**Reservations:** (615) 331-5244 MONDAY THROUGH FRIDAY 9 TO 5 (ANSWERING MACHINE OTHER TIMES).

## MONTEREY

HIGHWAY 70 — A restored turn-of-the-century home decorated with many period pieces. The home's primary function is as a restaurant, opened by the owners and dedicated to Southern cooking and Southern hospitality. Located in a small town on the edge of the historic Cumberland Plateau, major tourist attractions are available, and easily accessible. Gatlinburg, Knoxville, and the Gran Ole' Opry are easily reached by Interstate 40. Accommodations include: A) room on the main floor and B) two rooms upstairs. Two centrally located baths on the main floor. Single and double accommodations are available in the rooms. Guests will be served a Tennessee country ham breakfast either in their room or in a private dining room. One DOG lives here. Air conditioned.

**Rates:** A & B) S $30, D $40 DAILY.
**Reservations:** (615) 331-5244 MONDAY THROUGH FRIDAY 9 TO 5 (ANSWERING MACHINE OTHER TIMES).

# KENTUCKY LAKE REGION
## BUCHANAN
### RURAL

CYPRESS CREEK ROAD — Log home on 7 acre woodland setting in northwest Tennessee near Kentucky Lake. The home is filled with country charm and includes a large stone fireplace in the "Great Room" which provides a comfortable and cozy retreat. Great Room and other amenities added in 1977. Hosts are both retired and enjoy oil painting, sculpturing, arts and crafts, and country cooking. Original log home was a schoolhouse built in mid 1800s. Kentucky Lake, land between the lakes, and Paris Landing State Park just minutes away where fishing, swimming, boating, hunting, golf, hiking, tennis, archery, birdwatching, and full scale marina are available. Playfull CAIRN TERRIER is in residence and confined when in house. Reachable by auto only. Accommodations include: A) queen-sized bed; B) single bed; and C) loft double bed. Guests share two baths. Dinner provided on special request. CHILDREN over 5 years welcome.
**Rates:** A & B) S $40, D $65; AND C) D LOFT S $35. CHILDREN $10 DAILY.
**Reservations:** (615) 331-5244 MONDAY THROUGH FRIDAY 9 TO 5 (ANSWERING MACHINE OTHER TIMES).

## MEMPHIS

On the mighty Mississippi River, Memphis is home to colleges, universities, medical centers, fine restaurants, art galleries, regional theater, and opera. Famous for Mud Island, street fairs and flea markets, cotton and magnolias, and old-fashioned Southern hospitality.
**Rates:** CONTACT RESERVATION SERVICE FOR CURRENT RATES.
**Reservations:** (901) 726-5920 8 A.M. TO 6 P.M. MONDAY THROUGH FRIDAY. SATURDAY AND SUNDAY 1 P.M. TO 4 P.M.

## CORDOVA

A large UNHOSTED mother-in-law wing separated from the main house by a breezeway. Spacious upstairs has a twin-sized bedroom, living room with queen-sized sofabed downstairs along with a dining area, fully equipped kitchen, and bath. A private line telephone, shared laundry facilities and housekeeper once a week are included. Host is a manufacturer's representative; hostess is an energetic family woman and Spanish teacher. This is a favorite of families with children. Conveniently located just minutes to the expressway and midtown or downtown.
**Rates:** S OR D $45, AND $60 FOR FAMILY DAILY. $270 WEEKLY. $762 MONTHLY.
**Reservations:** (901) 726-5920 8 A.M. TO 6 P.M. MONDAY THROUGH FRIDAY. SATURDAY AND SUNDAY 1 P.M. TO 4 P.M.

Situated on 11 acres, with fishing pond and swimming POOL just outside your door, this UNHOSTED accommodation has an elegant living room, fireplace, kitchen, sleeping alcove with double featherbed, and shower bath as well as patio. Minutes to Germantown and east Memphis business hub.
**Rates:** S OR D $80 DAILY. $480 WEEKLY. $762 MONTHLY. 3 NIGHT MINIMUM.
**Reservations:** (901) 726-5920 8 A.M. TO 6 P.M. MONDAY THROUGH FRIDAY. SATURDAY AND SUNDAY 1 P.M. TO 4 P.M.

## GERMANTOWN

An elegant country home with formal gardens, gazebo on lake with resident ducks, geese, grey fox, and scampering rabbits. Accommodations include: A) double-bedded room with pond view and full bath, use of microwave and refrigerator; and B) suite with antique double bed, private bath, and sitting room. Guests can enjoy the swimming POOL. Host is an interior designer.
**Rates:** S OR D $65 DAILY. $391 WEEKLY. $700 MONTHLY.
**Reservations:** (901) 726-5920 8 A.M. TO 6 P.M. MONDAY THROUGH FRIDAY. SATURDAY AND SUNDAY 1 P.M. TO 4 P.M.

## DOWNTOWN

UNHOSTED luxury highrise on the river with balcony. Large living room, dining room, generous closet space, utility room with washer/dryer, and the latest in fabulous kitchens. Sleek contemporary furnishings. Accommodations include: A) king bed and B) double bed. Both with private baths (one with whirlpool). Walk to fine restaurants, shopping, famous Beale Street, Mud Island, and the majestic Orpheum Theater. Indoor swimming POOL. TENNIS COURTS, racquetball, exercise room. Indoor assigned parking.
**Rates:** S OR D $80 DAILY. $480 WEEKLY. $1,450 MONTHLY.
**Reservations:** (901) 726-5920 8 A.M. TO 6 P.M. MONDAY THROUGH FRIDAY. SATURDAY AND SUNDAY 1 P.M. TO 4 P.M.

Downtown luxury highrise on the river. Accommodations include a room with whirlpool bath, double accommodations, handsome country English furnishings. Large living room, dining room, generous closet space, utility room with washer/dryer, and the latest in modern kitchens. Walk to fine restaurants, shopping, famous Beale Street, Mud Island, and the majestic Orpheum Theater. Indoor swimming POOL, TENNIS COURTS, racquetball, exercise room. Indoor assigned parking. UNHOSTED. SMOKING outside only.
**Rates:** S OR D $80 DAILY. $479.99 WEEKLY. $338.81 MONTHLY. ALL RATES INCLUDE TAX.

**Reservations:** (901) 726-5920 8 A.M. TO 6 P.M. MONDAY THROUGH FRIDAY. SATURDAY AND SUNDAY 1 P.M. TO 4 P.M.

High on the bluff overlooking the mighty Mississippi River, near Interstates 55, 40, and 240. This luxury condo includes a plant filled patio for quiet evenings enjoying spectacular sunsets or crisp mornings with your coffee and paper. It is furnished in antique and reproductions, parquet floors, light and airy in a distinctive urban setting. Accommodations include a queen-sized bed with private bath. Extras include private parking, washer/dryer, security, and more.
**Rates:** S OR D $55 DAILY. $330 WEEKLY. $1,550 MONTHLY.
**Reservations:** (901) 726-5920 8 A.M. TO 6 P.M. MONDAY THROUGH FRIDAY. SATURDAY AND SUNDAY 1 P.M. TO 4 P.M.

## LAURELWOOD

A pretty one bedroom mother-in-law wing with private entrance. Living room has a bay window overlooking gardens in one of Memphis' most beautiful areas. Accommodations include a queen bed, private bath, full kitchen, shared laundry room. Housekeeper comes in once a week. Extras include: cable TV. Your host is a prominent attorney. Conveniently located to Dixon Gallery and Gardens, the Agricenter, Licterman Nature Center, fine restaurants, and excellent shopping.
**Rates:** S OR D $45 DAILY. $270 WEEKLY. $735 MONTHLY.
**Reservations:** (901) 726-5920 8 A.M. TO 6 P.M. MONDAY THROUGH FRIDAY. SATURDAY AND SUNDAY 1 P.M. TO 4 P.M.

## MIDTOWN

UNHOSTED charming stucco guesthouse with twin bedroom, generous closet space, living room, galley kitchen, shower bath, and plenty of off-street parking on elegant grounds. Close to Chickasaw Gardens on one of Memphis' most beautiful streets. Host is a physician and he and his wife have decorated this guesthouse in excellent taste.
**Rates:** S OR D $45 DAILY. $270 WEEKLY. $705 MONTHLY.
**Reservations:** (901) 726-5920 8 A.M. TO 6 P.M. MONDAY THROUGH FRIDAY. SATURDAY AND SUNDAY 1 P.M. TO 4 P.M.

## MIDDLE TENNESSEE
## BRENTWOOD

MURRAY LANE — A beautiful country setting on 12 acres in the hills of Tennessee but within the city limit of Brentwood. Home is brick Georgian style with many antiques, central heat, and air conditioning. There is a large garden and barn. Many fruit trees are behind the house. Family pets live outside. Host is a veterinarian; hostess is a homemaker and does occasional part-time work. Two sons in high school. Guest bedroom has a private entrance and private bathroom. Full breakfast with homemade biscuits is served. Home is convenient to the interstate that can easily take you to places such as Opryland, Hermitage, Grand Ole' Opry, Music Row in Nashville, Parthenon, Wave Pool, Franklin, Vanderbilt University, Belmont College, four hospitals, and many businesses. PIANO. NONSMOKERS only.

**Rates:** S $30, D $40 DAILY.

**Reservations:** (615) 331-5244 MONDAY THROUGH FRIDAY 9 TO 5 (ANSWERING MACHINE OTHER TIMES).

OLD HICKORY — Contemporary two story home just 12 miles from historic Franklin and 8 miles from Nashville; 2 miles off Interstate 65 South. Accommodations include a private suite, with queen bedroom, well appointed, with private bath and private entrance. Just off the suite is a beautiful deck and SWIMMING POOL. The sitting area is a hide-a-bed. Neighborhood is very quiet and there is a lovely view of the surrounding area. Host is an independent broker; hostess is homemaker. Hosts are Christians and enjoy opening their home to guests. FIREPLACE in den guestroom. Air conditioned. Children of all ages welcome.

**Rates:** S OR D $65 DAILY.

**Reservations:** (615) 331-5244 MONDAY THROUGH FRIDAY 9 TO 5 (ANSWERING MACHINE OTHER TIMES).

## NEAR NASHVILLE

Lovely two story home located in prestigious Brentwood, on the southern outskirts of Nashville, home of country music and many well-known universities. Hosts always welcome guests with open arms and do everything possible to make them enjoy their stay in Music City. Located within 15 minutes of three large universities, Opryland, Grand Ole' Opry, and many homes of well-known music stars. This home will make you feel right at home. History and Civil War buffs will enjoy visiting Franklin, Stones River, and Nashville battlefields as well as the home of President Amdrew Jackson (the Hermitage) and Cheekwood (mansion built by Maxwell House Coffee and given to Nashville to be used as a museum and art gallery). Accommodations include: A) queen room with a single bed and couch, private bath and B) double room furnished in antiques, a private bath. Host is a retired space scientist interested in photography, travel, and genealogy; hostess is a retired teacher and speaks French. There are two DOGS residing here. PIANO. NONSMOKERS only.

**Rates:** A) S $30, D $40 AND B) S $30, D $38 DAILY.

**Reservations:** (615) 331-5244 MONDAY THROUGH FRIDAY 9 TO 5 (ANSWERING MACHINE OTHER TIMES).

Large Colonial style home in quiet neighborhood on two landscaped acres, including four types of fruit trees, HEATED INGROUND POOL

(20 × 40 feet), surrounded by flowers and decorative picket fence around 1 acre. Elegantly furnished 1,350 square feet guest suite has private entrance, private bath, FIREPLACE, billiard table, color TV, central heat, and air conditioning. Bedroom is furnished in Queen Anne style with queen-sized bed. Fully carpeted suite opens to patio and pool area and fish lily pond. Breakfast will be served on patio beside pool or in suite. Host is employed by glass manufacturer; hostess is in sales. Two DOGS are in residence, but do not come in contact with guest area. Bikes are available. Home is convenient to Opryland, Belle Meade Mansion, the Hermitage, the Parthenon, State Museum, Tennessee Performing Arts Center, and Nashville Symphony Orchestra. Within 30 minutes are seven major shopping centers. No CIGAR SMOKERS.
**Rates:** S $50, D $80 DAILY. 7TH NIGHT FREE WEEKLY.
**Reservations:** (615) 331-5244 MONDAY THROUGH FRIDAY 9 TO 5 (ANSWERING MACHINE OTHER TIMES).

## COLUMBIA
### NORTHERN MAURY COUNTY

DOUBLE BRANCH ROAD — Home is on a small sheep farm in the peaceful Tennessee countryside, with ducks and geese and 15 acres of woods, yet 15 minutes from Columbia, with President James K. Polk's home, walking horse show, 10 minutes from GM's new Saturn plant, and 50 minutes from Nashville. Enjoy hummingbirds and chickadees while you eat your breakfast of biscuits and homemade blackberry jam. Host is employed by the Social Security Administration; hostess by a local bank. Both are kmowledgeable about local history, historic homes, and other attractions. Both enjoy wildflowers, photography, hiking, and the outdoors. Children welcome. Accommodations include: A) private suite with large double bed, sitting room with Franklin stove FIREPLACE, private bath and B) extra people accommodated on cots or in nearby twin-bedded double with 1/2 bath.
**Rates:** A) S $28, D $38 DAILY. $10 EACH NIGHT EACH ADDITIONAL PERSON. S $175, D $235 WEEKLY.
**Reservations:** (615) 331-5244 MONDAY THROUGH FRIDAY 9 TO 5 (ANSWERING MACHINE OTHER TIMES).

## FRANKLIN
### RURAL

SWEENEY HOLLOW ROAD — If you enjoy seeing stars at night instead of smog, smelling wild honeysuckle instead of gas fumes, come to this lovely farm with its large "U" shaped modern home of earth color brick that marries itself to the hillside. Many windows with beautiful views from each makes one feel part of the lovely rural setting. A few pheasants and fancy chickens are nearby and ducks stroll from the pond to eat from your hand. Graceful Arabian HORSES romp in the fields and

Angus cattle graze peacefully beside the creek. Accommodations include: A) double bed with antique iron bed and B) double bed in a Japanese style room sleeping on a futon, a Japanese garden just outside glass doors. Rooms share bath. Accommodations for a child in a nearby room. Nashville with its many attractions is only 30 minutes away and charming historic Franklin is 10 miles. Hostess is a full-time farmer and part-time actress. She enjoys people from all over the world. Air conditioned, Horse stalls, HANDICAPPED ACCESSIBLE. NONSMOKERS preferred.
**Rates:** A & B) S $32, D $40 DAILY. 7TH NIGHT FREE WEEKLY.
**Reservations:** (615) 331-5244 MONDAY THROUGH FRIDAY 9 TO 5 (ANSWERING MACHINE OTHER TIMES).

## GALLATIN
## DOWNTOWN

This 1840 carriage factory has been remodeled and furnished in antiques and reproductions. The rooms have high ceilings and hardwood floors. There is a spacious, cherry sunroom and a full kitchen. Six can sleep here in A) a double room and B) a twin room and a hide-a-bed. There is a private entrance and the unit is very private. This tastefully decorated suite is only 30 minutes to Opryland and Nashville. Nearby there is a lake and boating can be arranged. Your hostess is a realtor and stockbroker who is interested in decorating, antiques, and travel. UNHOSTED. Air conditioned. NO SMOKING.
**Rates:** A & B) S $40, D $50 DAILY.
**Reservations:** (615) 331-5244 MONDAY THROUGH FRIDAY 9 TO 5 (ANSWERING MACHINE OTHER TIMES).

## GOODLETTSVILLE
## PAGE HEIGHTS

This three year old brick and clapboard Ranch on 2 1/2 acres sits atop the highest hill in town offering an unparalleled 360 degree view that includes Old Hickory Lake. Guests can enjoy the plant filled Florida room or the 32 foot back deck, where their tasty breakfast is served in fine weather. One BASENJI (barkless African dog) and one LABRADOR RETRIEVER charm the guests as they romp in the large fenced yard. The hosts keep maps and brochures on hand so they can direct guests to all the nearby attractions, which include the Hermitage, Opryland, Music Village, and Parthenon. One of the loveliest parks in the area is within walking distance. This is near Mansker's Fort and the Bowen Campbell house, the oldest brick home in middle Tennessee. The area abounds with country music, both easily recognizable stars and locals who perform in barns and inns and your hosts know them all. Accommodations include A & B) two double rooms and C) a trailer.
**Rates:** A & B) S $30, D $40 AND C) TRAILER $50 DAILY.
**Reservations:** (615) 331-5244 MONDAY THROUGH FRIDAY 9 TO 5 (ANSWERING MACHINE OTHER TIMES).

## NEAR RIVERGATE

Located in oldest community in majestic middle Tennessee is this large suburban Colonial home. Private lower level, twin beds, private bath. Large sitting room with two sofas that sleep one, TV, pool table, patio with swings, and front porch with rocking chairs. It is 20 minutes from colleges, airport, historical points of interest, Parthenon, museums, Country Music Hall of Fame, Music Row, and Hermitage; 10 minutes from downtown Nashville, Opryland, Music City, USA; 5 minutes to parks, tennis courts, jogging trails, historical fort, and the largest shopping area in state. Near Interstates 65, 40, and 24. Host is director of federal property utilization; hostess is a homemaker. Both love sports, music, children, art, and travel. PIANO. SMOKING AND SOCIAL DRINKING NOT WELCOME.
**Rates:** S $30, D $40, EXTRA PERSON $10 DAILY.
**Reservations:** (615) 331-5244 MONDAY THROUGH FRIDAY 9 TO 5 (ANSWERING MACHINE OTHER TIMES).

## HENDERSONVILLE

SHACKLE ISLAND — This three and a half story Greek Revival home is located atop one of the highest hills in middle Tennessee, with a spectacular panoramic view. Host is a residential building contractor; hostess is a realtor and decorator who likes to collect crystal and fine dishes. Both love antiques, which are in abundance in the home. A large DOG is also in residence. Accommodations include a private suite, with bedroom of Victorian antiques, sitting area, kitchen with stocked refrigerator, full bath, and pool table. There is also a POOL (20 × 20 feet) that the guests may use. The home is near Opryland, Music City, USA, and homes of many country music stars. Continental breakfast is provided as are snacks and softdrinks. NO CHILDREN. NO SMOKERS.
**Rates:** S OR D $80 DAILY.
**Reservations:** (615) 331-5244 MONDAY THROUGH FRIDAY 9 TO 5 (ANSWERING MACHINE OTHER TIMES).

## LYNCHBURG
## COUNTY LINE COMMUNITY

DOG TAIL ROAD — Rustic cottage with catherdral ceiling on 70 acre farm. It is 5 miles out of town, total country environment. Cottage in wooded area consists of large main room with woodburning stove, sleeping loft, and kitchen facilities. Modern bath and screened-in back porch. Large front porch with pastoral view. It is 30 minutes from Trims Ford, the newest of the TVA lakes has a state park providing swimming, boating, and fishing facilities; 1 hour ride to the University of the South at Sewanee provides facilities for golf, tennis, and cultural events; 20 minutes to Tullahoma's Arnold Air Force Testing Center, shopping, dining, and theaters; and 25 minutes to Shelbyville, the Walking Horse Capitol of the World. Couples with one or two children could comfortably be accommodated for a short stay using a pullout couch or space for sleeping bags. Lynchburg is the home of Jack Daniels distillery, the oldest one in the country. Tours available every hour.

**Rates:** S $26, D $32 DAILY. $100 WEEKLY. $300 MONTHLY.
**Reservations:** (615) 331-5244 MONDAY THROUGH FRIDAY 9 TO 5 (ANSWERING MACHINE OTHER TIMES).

## NASHVILLE

This city, the home of the Grand Ole' Opry, abounds with country music, yet the capitol of Tennessee boasts of being called "The Athens of the South." The Parthenon in Centennial Park, the many universities and colleges around the area have certainly given this title to Nashville, and justifiably so. Among them are Vanderbilt University, David Lipscomb, Trevecca College, Free Will Baptist College, and Vanderbilt School of Medicine. There are many historic sites to enjoy, such as the Hermitage, the home of President Andrew Jackson, the Opera and Broadway presentations at the Tennessee Performing Arts Center, and many museums including the Tennessee State Museum. All enhance "Music City, USA."

**Rates:** CONTACT RESERVATION SERVICE FOR CURRENT RATES.
**Reservations:** (615) 331-5244 MONDAY THROUGH FRIDAY 9 TO 5 (ANSWERING MACHINE OTHER TIMES).

A brick Contemporary house on 1 acre, with trees, flowers, covered carport, brick patio, and picnic tables. Accommodations include: A) twin antique beds, private bath and B) antique four poster bed with private bath in adjoining hall. Both rooms have Oriental rugs. Paneled den has fireplace and TV. This home is near Vanderbilt University, the Grecian Parthenon, Belle Meade Mansion, and Opry Land (Opry Land by way of Interstate 24, 15 minute drive). This house is hosted and a continental breakfast is served each morning. Host is retired from the office of the state attorney general; hostess is interested in refinishing antique furniture and sewing. Air conditioned. CHILDREN over 5 welcome. NO SMOKING.

**Rates:** A & B) S $30, D $40 DAILY.
**Reservations:** (615) 331-5244 MONDAY THROUGH FRIDAY 9 TO 5 (ANSWERING MACHINE OTHER TIMES).

## CARONDELET

Cape Cod four bedroom house, furnished in antique reproductions, is located 10 to 15 minutes from Nashville. Tennis and swimming are available nearby. Host is marketing director for Baptist bookstore who enjoys travel and meeting people; hostess is a French teacher. Accommodations include: A) king bedroom, private bath; and B) double

bedroom with private bath in the hall. TV is available. Family likes to visit with guest. A continental breakfast is provided. One CAT and one DOG live here. A very small house trained DOG WOULD BE WELCOME. Air conditioned. Children past infancy welcome.
**Rates:** A) S $30, D $40 AND B) S $30, D $40 DAILY.
**Reservations:** (615) 331-5244 MONDAY THROUGH FRIDAY 9 TO 5 (ANSWERING MACHINE OTHER TIMES).

## DONELSON-MAPLECREST

WEONA DRIVE — This Contemporary home is located in a quiet neighborhood with a nice yard, patio, and grill that guests may use. The home, with central air conditioning and heat, has a large living room with console ORGAN that guests are welcome to use. PETS welcome. Accommodations include: A) king bedroom, remote TV, small refrigerator and B) double room, TV, radio. Both rooms open into hall with guest bath. Off-street parking is available. Opryland is 5 minutes away and the Hermitage and other historical sights are nearby; Downtown Nashville is but 10 minutes away; the airport is very near. CHILDREN welcome.
**Rates:** A) S OR D $40 AND B) S OR D $38 DAILY. 7TH NIGHT FREE WEEKLY.
**Reservations:** (615) 331-5244 MONDAY THROUGH FRIDAY 9 TO 5 (ANSWERING MACHINE OTHER TIMES).

## DOWNTOWN

This is an older three story row house that was built in 1859, Nashville's oldest existing townhouse. Built by Nashville's first eye surgeon, Dr. Savage, as his residence and office. The rooms have 12 foot ceilings with a FIREPLACE in each bedroom. The first floor of the house is a restaurant serving breakfast and lunch. The old ballroom of the house is a mini mall with various shops. The house is located in the downtown business district of Nashville, 1 1/2 blocks from the convention center. There are many sightseeing tours available from the area to the homes of the Opry stars, the Hermitage (home of Andrew Jackson), the state capital, and many other places of historic value. Opryland and the Grand Ole' Opry are 15 minutes away. Rooms furnished in antiques. Double accommodations available in bedrooms. PIANO. Air conditioned. Bikes available.
**Rates:** S $45, D $65 DAILY.
**Reservations:** (615) 331-5244 MONDAY THROUGH FRIDAY 9 TO 5 (ANSWERING MACHINE OTHER TIMES).

## MOUNT JULIET AREA

CENTRAL PIKE — A California Country Comtemporary home and guesthouse on 8 wooded acres surrounding tranquil 7 acre FISHING

LAKE with ducks, geese, and two Australian swans. Guesthouse has Great Room (30 × 52 feet) with fireplace, pool table, game table, wet bar, GRAND PIANO, and audio-video center. A & B) Two large bedrooms with private bathrooms. EXERCISE ROOM with SAUNA and HOT TUB. Inground unheated POOL (60 × 20 feet) with dressing rooms and kitchen. Host is in music business and enjoys fishing and hunting; hostess is former background singer now in real estate, who loves competitive ballroom dancing, writes short stories, and enjoys meeting people. Host speaks a little Spanish. Convenient to Interstate 40, airport, Opryland, the Hermitage, colleges, Music Row, AVCO, and Nissan. Main house has C & D) two bedrooms with private baths. Continental breakfast either house. Jody the POODLE and Boots the CAT in residence. Bear is friendly outside DOG. HANDICAPPED ACCESSIBLE. Double accommodations available. Air conditioned. Three horse stalls. CHILDREN over 12 welcome. NO SMOKING IN HOUSE.

**Rates:** A & B) S $100, D $120 AND C & D) S $60, D $75 DAILY. 10% DISCOUNT WEEKLY.

**Reservations:** (615) 331-5244 MONDAY THROUGH FRIDAY 9 TO 5 (ANSWERING MACHINE OTHER TIMES).

## OAK HILL

GRASSLAND LANE — Ranch style home on 2 acres, quiet, secluded yet only 3 minutes from Interstate 65, 8 minutes from downtown Nashville, 15 minutes from the airport, and 20 minutes from most tourist attractions, including Opryland. Host is a retired airline pilot; hostess is a homemaker. Accommodations include: A) large double room with TV and B) twin double room with TV, one private bath. Crib and rollaway cot are also available. Full continental breakfast included, with coffee and tea available anytime. Air conditioned. Children welcome.

**Rates:** A & B) S $30, D $40 DAILY.

**Reservations:** (615) 331-5244 MONDAY THROUGH FRIDAY 9 TO 5 (ANSWERING MACHINE OTHER TIMES).

## PERCY PRIEST LAKE

Large, cheerful townhouse on beautiful Percy Priest Lake. Lovely patio, barbecue. Home has SWIMMING POOL, TENNIS, EXERCISE ROOMS, and SAUNA. Marinas nearby, good fishing and lake swimming as well. Good running track. Home is furnished with many beautiful antiques. Many antique shops in area. Within 6 miles is the lovely Opryland Hotel and Gran Ole' Opry. President Andrew Jackson's home is nearby. Many fine shopping malls are in the area. Downtown Nashville is only a 12 mile drive; Airport 7 miles. Vanderbilt University, Cheekwood Fine Arts Center and Botanical Gardens, Tennessee Performing Arts Center are all within an easy drive. Host is international sales manager for a large German firm, hostess is retired nursery woman. Both speak a little

German. Accommodations include: A) twin beds, private bath and B) double bed, private bath. Both rooms have antiques as does the whole house. Air conditioned and HANDICAPPED ACCESSIBLE.
**Rates:** A & B) S $30, D $40 DAILY.
**Reservations:** (615) 331-5244 MONDAY THROUGH FRIDAY 9 TO 5 (ANSWERING MACHINE OTHER TIMES).

## SOUTH

A comfortable, attractive two story home. Central air conditioning keeps this house cool and pleasant during the hot, humid summer. Host is insurance broker who works out of his home; hostess is a registered nurse. Both enjoy birdwatching. Convenient to Interstates 65 and 24. This home is ideal for the busy visitor. Music City within a few minutes of Opryland, music row, Metro Airport, Vanderbilt University, downtown Nashville, and many other attractions. Accommodations include: A) double bed with color TV and B) twin bed. The rooms share a bath. Host will supply maps and information if desired. He will host a short (approximately 1 hour) tour for guests staying two or more nights. One DOG resides here. CHILDREN 12 and over welcome. NO SMOKERS.
**Rates:** A & B) S $30, D $40 DAILY.
**Reservations:** (615) 331-5244 MONDAY THROUGH FRIDAY 9 TO 5 (ANSWERING MACHINE OTHER TIMES).

## WEST MEADE

WINDROWE DRIVE — One mile to Interstate 40 across Tennessee east and west. Convenient to grocery and shopping mall. Residential with churches nearby. Close to 3 universities and restaurants, and 10 miles to downtown Nashville, Music City, USA, and colleges in between. Neat twin bedroom with full closet and private bath in hall. A crib is available. TV in den with family. Quiet neighborhood. Host is a business consultant interested in golf, bridge, and dancing; hostess is in sales and enjoys golf and dancing. PIANO. CHILDREN over 3 welcome.
**Rates:** S $30, D $40 DAILY.
**Reservations:** (615) 331-5244 MONDAY THROUGH FRIDAY 9 TO 5 (ANSWERING MACHINE OTHER TIMES).

## WHITEHOUSE PORTLAND AREA

Located 22 miles from Opryland and 28 miles from Nashville is this country home styled much like the Hermitage and built by the hostess and her architect husband by his design. The setting is a large grove of tall oaks which inspired the name, the place where Joshua of Old commanded the sun and the moon to stand still. There are five bedrooms and four baths on the two main floors and one bedroom and bath in the basement. Furniture and trimmings are "All American" in no particular

style, but only a conglomeration of comfort and coziness that has been collected over a period of years. Crib available. Hostess, who is a writer and poet, loves to cook Southern breakfast for her guests. Air conditioned. HANDICAPPED ACCESSIBLE. ORGAN. Bedrooms have double accommodations. Children of all ages welcome. NONSMOKERS are preferred but smokers are not forbidden.
**Rates:** S $35, D $50 DAILY.
**Reservations:** (615) 331-5244 MONDAY THROUGH FRIDAY 9 TO 5 (ANSWERING MACHINE OTHER TIMES).

FRANKLIN ROAD — Contemporary Ranch home on 1 acre of wooded lot on quiet deadend street. Host does offset printing for a blueprint supply company, speaks Spanish, and is a veteran ham radio operator; hostess is an elementary schoolteacher who enjoys decorative sewing, music, reading, and travel. A PERSIAN CAT is lord of the manor. Some antiques make the home interesting and antique malls are nearby. The college community is 15 minutes away, as are fine shopping areas and many ethnic restaurants. Homes of two U.S. presidents are within 30 miles, as are other historic homes and buildings. Also close are many homes of country music stars and other country music attractions are easily accessible. Nissan and Saturn automotive plants are within 50 miles. There is easy access to Interstates 65, 40, and 24. Accommodations include: A) private room with double bed and B) private room with sofa double bed for teens. Both rooms share off-hall bath. CHILDREN over 12 welcome. SMOKERS not welcome.
**Rates:** A & B) S $30, D $35 DAILY.
**Reservations:** (615) 331-5244 MONDAY THROUGH FRIDAY 9 TO 5 (ANSWERING MACHINE OTHER TIMES).

# NORTH CENTRAL
## CLARKSVILLE

MADISON STREET — One hour from Nashville is one of the most famous facilities of its kind in the South. Your hostess is renowned as TV personality and author of numerous cookbooks, including *The United Nations' Cookbook, Kountry Kooking, Old Timey Recipies,* and *The Tennessee Homecoming '86 Cookbook.* Overlooking a wildflower garden and a bird sanctuary are cozy rooms in a historic 1790 house attractively decorated in authentic primitives. Guest cottages are available in Clarkesville's oldest log houses. Accommodations include: A) can sleep 4; B) can sleep 10; and C) can sleep 7. Cottages are fully equipped and are furnished with beautiful antiques. HANDICAPPED ACCESSIBLE. FIREPLACE in bedroom. Air conditioned. Children welcome.
**Rates:** $55 DAILY. $250 WEEKLY.
**Reservations:** (615) 331-5244 MONDAY THROUGH FRIDAY 9 TO 5 (ANSWERING MACHINE OTHER TIMES).

# SMOKY MOUNTAINS
## CHATTANOOGA
### HIXSON

Contemporary house with view of Chickamauga Lake (Tennessee River). Near public access to lake, public swimming, and picnic areas. Guest accommodations are separate from hostess and include bedroom with twin beds and private bath, living and dining rooms, kitchen, and patio. Guests prepare their own breakfast (hostess provides food). Hostess is sometimes free to act as tour guide to the many historical places, amusement areas, shopping areas, and campuses. There are many fine restaurants in the area as well as the usual fast food restaurants, and tourist attractions such as Lookout Mountain and Chattanooga Choo Choo. Convenient to Interstates 24 and 75 and Tennessee 153. All of these are within 30 minutes of the house. The Great Smoky Mountains or Florida are within a day's drive from this area. Atlanta is about 3 hours away. Birdwatchers will find some waterfowl of interest as well as many inland birds. Guests can have as much as quiet and privacy as they want.
**Rates:** S $40, D $50 DAILY. $300 WEEKLY.
**Reservations:** (615) 331-5244 MONDAY THROUGH FRIDAY 9 TO 5 (ANSWERING MACHINE OTHER TIMES).

### KNOXVILLE
### DOWNTOWN NEAR UNIVERSITY OF TENNESSEE

NEAR HENTEY STREET — This small (15 rooms) luxury hotel is furnished primarily in eighteenth century antiques and reproductions. A penthouse with an oversized JACUZZI and skylight are featured in the bath. There is a living room/bedroom with remote controlled TV and a sundeck with a riverview. Several accommodations have jacuzzis while others have sunken marble soaking tubs, Roman tubs, or regular-sized ones. All have private baths and a sitting area. A continental breakfast featuring homemade blueberry muffins is served with various pastries, teas, and coffees. A private honor bar is open 24 hours for guests and their guests. Room service is available through one of the city's best restaurants. Located downtown near the edge of the University of Tennessee campus in a small historic district and convenient to all courts of law and the business, arts, and entertainment centers, transportation is never a problem. Complimentary parking is on premises. There is easy access to Interstates 40 and 75. It is 20 minutes to the major airport, 5 minutes to the city private aircraft airport, 45 minutes to Gatlingburg, Dollywood, and the Great Smoky Mountains National Park.
**Rates:** S $55-$85, D $55-$125, PENTHOUSE $125 DAILY. S OR D $200, PENTHOUSE $375 WEEKLY.
**Reservations:** (615) 331-5244 MONDAY THROUGH FRIDAY 9 TO 5 (ANSWERING MACHINE OTHER TIMES).

# UPPER EAST TENNESSEE
## GREENEVILLE

NORTH MAIN STREET — A charming three story turn-of-the-century home located in a storybook town nestled in the hills of upper east Tennessee. Perfect for antique lovers, history buffs, and romantics. Many lovely antiques, fireplace, PIANO, library, guest parlor, spacious porches, and huge tree-filled yard. Hearty breakfast (complimentary) and elegant dinners ($12) are served in either the country oak kitchen or the formal dining room. Hostess A is an airline pilot who also raises Arabian horses. Hostess B is a former schoolteacher who loves antiques, quilting, and innkeeping. Silky (short for French) is the residence TOY POODLE. Accommodations include: A) two double beds with single bed; B) double bed with single bed; C) king-sized bed with private bath; D) two double beds with private bath; and E) two twin beds with half private bath. Inn is within walking distance of downtown Greeneville, and close to Smokies, Gatlinburg, Appalachian Trail, Biltmore mansion, and many lakes and rivers. Airport pickup available from Knoxville or Tri-City. Children over 12 welcome.
**Rates:** S or D A & B) $50; C & D) $70; AND E) $60 DAILY.
**Reservations:** (615) 331-5244 MONDAY THROUGH FRIDAY 9 TO 5 (ANSWERING MACHINE OTHER TIMES).

## LIMESTONE

DAVY CROCKETT ROAD — This is an 1815 Federal brick home. Largely original, set in farm country with view of mountains and creek within walking distance of Davy Crockett Birthplace State Park with swimming pool, golf, and fishing closeby. It is a 15 minute drive to historic Jonesborough or Andrew Johnson home in Greeneville. Host has recently retired from the Boeing Company, Seattle, Washington to enjoy the country life and bluegrass music of upper east Tennessee. Home is furnished with antiques, including a Victorian reed ORGAN, drapes made in the old style by hostess, and pool table. Blue room is furnished in Victorian oak, rose room in Eastlake walnut. There is a rollaway bed for one extra person (adult or child). Shared bath, lovely wide staircase which guests must tread, full back porch where the large family DOG or three CATS may be found. They are not allowed in the house. Neither host or hostess smoke and prefer that guests SMOKE outside.
**Rates:** S $35, D $40 DAILY.
**Reservations:** (615) 331-5244 MONDAY THROUGH FRIDAY 9 TO 5 (ANSWERING MACHINE OTHER TIMES).

# WEST TENNESSEE
## GERMANTOWN

A Southern Colonial home with antiques. Hostess is a graduate student at Memphis State. There is a 16 year old son at home. Home is 5 minutes to the PGA Players Tournament, tennis, trail, horse shows, parks, antique shops, and restaurants on Interstate 240; 30 minutes to Memphis, where one will find St. Judes Hospital, Graceland, University of Tennessee Medical School, Billards School, Rhodes College, Memphis State University, Liberty Bowl, Libertyland Theme Park, Mud Island, and enjoy Beale Street and greyhound racing. Accommodations include: A) double bed, private bath; and B) double bed, share bath with A if both rooms are used. One LABRADOR lives here. Air conditioned. Bikes available. HANDICAPPED ACCESSIBLE. Children welcome.
**Rates:** A & B) S $26, D $40 DAILY.
**Reservations:** (615) 331-5244 MONDAY THROUGH FRIDAY 9 TO 5 (ANSWERING MACHINE OTHER TIMES).

## MEMPHIS
### EAST MEMPHIS

Guesthouse has living room with hide-a-bed, kitchenette, bath, bedroom with twin beds, and screened porch. Provisions for continental breakfast provided or guest may choose to have continental breakfast with hosts. This guesthouse is near a major shopping center where restaurants abound. All the Memphis sights are easily accessible. Host is in sales of industrial supplies and interested in golf and football; hostess is a guide with the Memphis Tourist Bureau. A POODLE and SCOTTIE live here. Air conditioned. NONSMOKERS only.
**Rates:** S OR D $45. EXTRA PERSON $10 DAILY.
**Reservations:** (615) 331-5244 MONDAY THROUGH FRIDAY 9 TO 5 (ANSWERING MACHINE OTHER TIMES).

### VICTORIAN VILLAGE (NEAR)

POPLAR AND INTERSTATE 240 — This long house is a magnificently restored Victorian mansion located near several points of interest in Memphis. It is a 15 minute walk to downtown, Beale Street, near Mud Island; 10 minute drive to Overton Park, Fair Grounds Stadium, Christian Brothers College, Rhodes College, and 15 minute drive to Memphis State University, Graceland, and other points of interest. This house resembles a small castle with four floors and a full basement. All rooms are spacious and furnished with replica period furniture and ceiling fans and central air conditioning. All baths are large with tile or marble. The main floor is open for viewing, and visitors are welcome to sit on the side and front porches. Accommodations include four rooms with double bed, private bath. Three gentle DOBERMANS live here. FIREPLACE in bedroom. VCR. HANDICAPPED ACCESSIBLE. Children welcome.
**Rates:** S OR D $50. $10 EXTRA FOR ROLLAWAY. $15 FOR YOUTHS IN HOSTEL ROOMS DAILY.
**Reservations:** (615) 331-5244 MONDAY THROUGH FRIDAY 9 TO 5 (ANSWERING MACHINE OTHER TIMES).

# 7

# South Central (West)

☐ **Arkansas**
☐ **Louisiana**
☐ **Texas**

# ARKANSAS

## OZARK MOUNTAINS

Craggy limestone bluffs and clear streams of the steep, forested Ozark foothills of north Arkansas dominate this part of the Natural State. At Calico Rock, towering multicolored bluffs overlook the White River; known nationally for swimming, fishing, canoeing, and float trips. The Ozark Folk Center shares the pioneer skills, music, and lore. Nearby Blanchard Springs Caverns rivals Mammoth and Carlsbad Caves and is rated as one of the most beautiful in North America. Dogwood, redbud, and wildflowers in the spring, and the fall colors of the changing foliage make a year-round photographer's haven. Inside this 30 mile radius abounds all the live entertainment, natures pleasures, warm and friendly people (most of them wave as you pass), and no need for a traffic signal. Come home to the Ozarks.

## CALICO ROCK

Modest residence attractively furnished by retired schoolteacher. Shared bath only. Five blocks from the White River where there is a boat landing and several boat docks and a canoe rental. The Norfork Dam and the National Fish Hatchery are just 15 miles to the north. There is excellent river and lake fishing with all day guide service available as well as float trips or party barges. One CAT resides here. Air conditioned. NO SMOKING.
**Rates:** S OR D $30 DAILY.
**Reservations:** (501) 297-8764 8:00 A.M. TO 12:00 P.M. MONDAY THROUGH FRIDAY.

## "ON THE HILL"

The hostess is a stained glass artisan and owns a shop downtown. She invites you to stay in her Victorian style cottage furnished with antiques. Enjoy full gourmet breakfast served tastefully. The quaint town of Calico Rock is located on high bluffs overlooking the White River and beautiful rolling hill scenery. A shared bath or complete upstairs apartment is available. A small house DOG also lives here. WELCOME PETS and children. Smoking is allowed. There is lots to see and do here. Come share the Ozark experience.
**Rates:** A) S $30, D $35 AND B) D 45; $5 OFF SECOND NIGHT DAILY. B) D $240 WEEKLY.
**Reservations:** (501) 297-8764 8:00 A.M. TO 12:00 P.M. MONDAY THROUGH FRIDAY.

## RURAL

There are two log cabins with more planned located on this acreage surrounded by the Ozark National Forest. Decorated with the past in mind but offering modern comforts. A sleeping loft in each cabin sleeps two. Downstairs one cabin A) hide-a-bed and B) a double bed. Both have kitchens available. and bath (showers only) as well as fireplace or woodstove. The cabins are UNHOSTED but provided with coffee, milk, cereal, and homemade fruit bread. Relax on the front porch and enjoy a panoramic view of river, forest, and ever present wildlife. This is a place to really get away and relax, yet only minutes from town, the Ozark Folk Center, Blanchard Springs Caverns, antique shops, and live music shows. Air conditioned. Children welcome.
**Rates:** A) S $40, D $47, $10 EACH ADDITIONAL PERSON AND B) S $40, D $47 DAILY. $10 EACH ADDITIONAL PERSON, $5 DISCOUNT EACH NIGHT AFTER FIRST.
**Reservations:** (501) 297-8764 8:00 A.M. TO 12:00 P.M. MONDAY THROUGH FRIDAY.

HIGHWAY 5 SOUTH — Modern home perched on 300 foot bluff overlooking the beautiful, clear White River. A large country breakfast is served on a deck outside your room. Wake up to a view of the mountains and sometimes mist filled river valley below. At night see lights of town 6 miles up the river. Business administrator host and agency coordinator hostess can arrange trout fishing, river float trips, or direct you to nearby Blanchard Springs Caverns and the Ozark Folk Center. A ramp makes easy access to the front entry, and hiking trails in the surrounding woods are inviting to explore. There are folk music hootenannies, craft and antique shops as well as flea markets only minutes away. One outside DOG lives here. ORGAN. Children of any age welcome.
**Rates:** A) S $35, D $40 AND B) S $30, D $35 DAILY. $5 DISCOUNT EACH NIGHT AFTER FIRST.
**Reservations:** (501) 297-8764 8:00 A.M. TO 12:00 P.M. MONDAY THROUGH FRIDAY.

HIGHWAY 56 EAST — This new Contemporary home located in a secluded woodland setting offers amenities that are bound to please even the most demanding. The gracious hostess provides a full, delicious breakfast in a private sunroom adjoining your spacious quarters, or if you wish enjoy the meal with the family in their dining room. Also offered for your pleasure is a large family room, satellite TV, a HOT TUB in the sunroom, a pool table, and other enjoyable pastimes such as a library. The surrounding scenery includes pasture, woodland, and only a short walk or ride away is a year-round spring fed stream. During some periods of the year this is a good tubing creek. Beautiful stained glass creations by the hostess as well as collectibles from around the world make this a delightful setting. Garage parking is an additional benefit. Double accommodations in one guestroom with private bath and another with a shared bath. A crib and cot are available. Two DOGS reside here. A 9 year old daughter and a 14 year old son also live here. PETS ARE WELCOME IF A CAGE IS PROVIDED. Air conditioned. **Rates:** S $30, D $40 DAILY. $5 DISCOUNT FOR SECOND AND SUBSEQUENT DAYS. **Reservations:** (501) 297-8764 8:00 A.M. TO 12:00 P.M. MONDAY THROUGH FRIDAY.

## DES ARC

Eclectic collection of antiques and collectibles decorate this Colonial Revival home recorded on the National Register of Historical Places. Located 14 miles north of Interstate 40 halfway between Memphis and Little Rock, this home is indeed a treasure. Wildlife management areas, lake bayous, and Stuttgard's famous duck hunting are all nearby. This beautiful home offers private suite, private and shared bath, and an unhosted garage apartment with stocked breakfast makings. Host is a retired petroleum engineer; hostess is a retired science teacher who serves full and healthful breakfasts and will accommodate special dietary needs if advised. Large wraparound porch shaded by pecan trees invites you to relax on the porch swing. One DOG lives here. Air conditioned. VCR. Double accommodations available in guestrooms and cots and crib if needed. Children welcome, but they must be supervised. NO SMOKING. **Rates:** A) S $45, D $50; B) S $37, D $42; C) S $37, D $42 FIRST NIGHT, S $32, D $37 SECOND NIGHT; AND D) S $42, D $47.50 FIRST NIGHT, S $37, D $42.50 SECOND NIGHT. $5 EACH ADDITIONAL PERSON. **Reservations:** (501) 297-8764 8:00 A.M. TO 12:00 P.M. MONDAY THROUGH FRIDAY.

## EUREKA SPRINGS
### HISTORIC DISTRICT

Restored Victorian style house decorated with antiques, folk art, and curious and unexpected treasures. Handmade quilts, brass and iron bedsteads, and fresh flowers add to the old-fashioned feeling. The balcony is for breakfast and watching the animals in the unique garden below. The interior decorator and art educator hostess speaks some Spanish. Location within walking distance of the historic town's quaint shops and cafes makes this an ideal place to stay. Enjoy local crafts' festivals and the internationally known and acclaimed Passion Playland, or have dinner on a real train while visiting this old spa town. CHILDREN over 12 welcome. SMOKERS are restricted to smoking areas.

**Rates:** S OR D $60-$70 DAILY. $5 DISCOUNT EACH NIGHT AFTER FIRST.
**Reservations:** (501) 297-8764 8:00 A.M. TO 12:00 P.M. MONDAY THROUGH FRIDAY.

## MOUNTAIN VIEW

Isolated country home located on a tree farm surrounded by the Ozark National Forest. Host is a retired USMC Officer who will advise you about the best hunting and fishing or canoeing spot around; hostess is a crafts instructor and artisan who has made stained glass for this contemporary home. There is a large three keyboard ORGAN in the spacious living room that guests are welcome to play as well as satellite TV and video games for your enjoyment. Large breakfasts always include homemade breads, cinnamon rolls, or biscuits rounded out with a hearty main dish. Enjoy country music, go crafts shopping, roam the many shops, or see Blanchard Springs Caverns and the Ozark Folk Center only 18 miles away. Accommodations include A) large double room and B) small double room. Shared baths. Children welcome.
**Rates:** A) S $35, D $40 AND B) S $30, D $35 DAILY. $5 DISCOUNT AFTER FIRST NIGHT.
**Reservations:** (501) 297-8764 8:00 A.M. TO 12:00 P.M. MONDAY THROUGH FRIDAY.

## COURT HOUSE SQUARE

WASHINGTON — This inn has been a traditional stopping over place for people coming home to the mountains since 1886. Faded entries in the old guest book show people coming back again and again. They did so not only because the inn was friendly and plesant, but because it was also close to the court house, the land office, general stores, churches, and just about anything a traveler needed in those days, and it still is! The weathered old stone buildings of the historic Court House Square, where the Folklore Society holds its open air music shows, is only a block away. Restaurants, drugstores. real estate offices, craft and antique shops, and churches are within a short walk. If you have the time it can be a pleasant half hour walk on marked nature trails along a white water creek. You can also go by car to the Ozark Folk Center in less than 5 minutes. Host is a superintendent for natural gas transmissions. Air conditioned. PIANO. Canoes and rafts available. Double accommodations in nine guestrooms with private baths are available. CHILDREN over 16 welcome. NO SMOKING.
**Rates:** S $35, D $41, $8 EACH ADDITIONAL PERSON DAILY. $5 DISCOUNT FOR SECOND AND SUBSEQUENT DAYS.
**Reservations:** (501) 297-8764 8:00 A.M. TO 12:00 P.M. MONDAY THROUGH FRIDAY.

## NORFORK
## OLD JOE

ARKANSAS HIGHWAY 5 SOUTH — A mountain retreat with a country club setting, the lodge sits on the banks of the White River and overlooks the beauty, serenity, and lush growth of the Ozark National Forest. In the large, antique furnished dining room, family style home cooked meals including hand selected meats, fresh vegetables, fresh baked bread, and European desserts are served. The bedrooms, also done in antiques, have their own entrances into a private, open air courtyard. A complete breakfast is included. Fly fishing schools and complete RIVER and lake guide services are offered throughout the year. The White River provides some of the best year-round trout fishing in the country and has produced many trophy browns and rainbows. Dutch is spoken here. An infant daughter as well as two DOGS, one CAT, and a parrot also reside here. Ten guestrooms with private baths are available, most with double accommodations. Air conditioned. PIANO. VCR. CHILDREN over 16 welcome.
**Rates:** S $55, D $67.50. ADDITIONAL PERSON $25 DAILY.
**Reservations:** (501) 297-8764 8:00 A.M. TO 12:00 P.M. MONDAY THROUGH FRIDAY.

## YELLVILLE AND HARRISON

You have got to see this to believe it. It is a large native stone house originally built as a general store in a bygone mining community. It is located on a creek with a private beach and swimming area. There are cows, goats, chickens, two friendly DOGS, as well as two lively young boys on this small farm. Roam this 18 acre farm, 4 miles off the paved highway, and enjoy country living. Large country style breakfasts are served in the dining room or outside on the patio. Packed picnic lunches and dinners are available on request. Host is a schoolteacher in a nearby Mountain Home; hostess is Australian born and speaks French. The large living room has books, games, and music available. Accommodations include: the entire second floor; A) large double and B & C) smaller double bedrooms shared bath is reserved for guests. Double accommodations in each guestroom as well as crib available.
**Rates:** A) D $40, $5 EACH ADDITIONAL PERSON AND B & C) S $30, D $35 DAILY. B & C) $5 DISCOUNT EACH NIGHT AFTER FIRST.
**Reservations:** (501) 297-8764 8:00 A.M. TO 12:00 P.M. MONDAY THROUGH FRIDAY.

# LOUISIANA

## ACADIANA
## VACHERIE

GREAT RIVER ROAD — Three cottages located in the residential quarters of the plantation, not far from the Big House, provide five independent sleeping units with private baths. Constructed circa 1880, each cottage has been renovated recently to include central heat and air conditioning, wall to wall carpeting, ceiling fans, and a fresh country decor. Two of the cottages have been divided in half, representative of the popular style of Louisiana architecture known as the Shotgun Double. The third cottage is a free-standing building with three bedrooms, combination living-dining room, fully equipped kitchen, and one bath. A nonsmoking environment is offered in some of the units. The absence of either a TV or phone (AM/FM radio available) will result in guests settling into the peaceful country atmosphere of plantation life. Rates include continental breakfast. Overnight guests are welcome to enjoy the grounds and gardens. Tours of the antebellum mansion are conducted daily by the Oak Alley Foundation.
**Rates:** A-E) S $60, D $70 DAILY. $10 EACH FOR EXTRA PERSONS DAILY.
**Reservations:** (504) 346-1928 SEVEN DAYS 8 A.M. TO 8 P.M.

## CAJUN COUNTRY

Cajun Country includes the University of Southern Louisiana, Acadian Country, and Avery Island Bird Refuge. Hear Cajun music and eat delicious French food. Enjoy a variety of different lifestlyes and people in antebellum homes, on sugar plantations, and shrimp boats on the bayou. There are also authentic swamp tours, year-round fresh or salt water fishing, and hunting. Enjoy Cajun Country, the Capitol of French Louisiana.

## FRANKLIN

IRISH BEND ROAD — Restored 1880s raised cottage and antebellum cabin are lavishly furnished with a variety of antiques in large rooms. On the bank of Bayou Teche, it is hosted by a French speaking descendant of Acadian settlers. Getaway to the bayou country, relax in this peaceful setting, enjoy the region's fishing, view historic homes, play golf or tennis, tour sugar mills, take a swamp tour, enjoy the profusion of winter blooming camellias, and sample superb food. Accommodations include: A & B) double and single beds; and C) double bed only.
**Rates:** S OR D A) $125; B) $100; AND C) $75 DAILY.
**Reservations:** (504) 346-1928 SEVEN DAYS 8 A.M. TO 8 P.M.

281

## JEANERETTE

Under the great oaks and cypress tree shading the edge of the Bayou is this separate and private guesthouse (600 sq. ft.) with furnished kitchenette, three twin beds, bath, TV, and refrigerator containing food for breakfast. Evening meal sometimes available for additional fee. Hosts are hospitable natives of area and sugar cane growers, speak some French. HANDICAPPED ACCESSIBLE. Air conditioned. Children welcome.
**Rates:** S $40, D $45 DAILY. TWO OR MORE DAYS, TAKE $5 OFF FOR EACH DAY.
**Reservations:** (504) 346-1928 SEVEN DAYS 8 A.M. TO 8 P.M.

## LAFAYETTE

Cajun Victorian, circa 1880. Two guestrooms with private baths; one has working fireplace and JACUZZI, one double bed in each bedroom. You will be greeted with a complimentary drink and served a full Cajun country breakfast in the morning.
**Rates:** S $55, D $65 DAILY. TWO OR MORE DAYS, TAKE $5 OFF FOR EACH DAY.
**Reservations:** (504) 346-1928 SEVEN DAYS 8 A.M. TO 8 P.M.

## NAPOLEONVILLE
## BAYOU LAFOURCHE

Napoleonville on Bayou Lafourche-National Historic Landmark (1846). An exquisite Greek Revival style plantation home with wide galleries, furnished with antiques, surrounded by moss draped Live Oak trees, and located in Cajun sugar cane country. Host is a business executive who enjoys architecture and gardening; hostess is a journalist whose hobbies are traveling and reading. Both enjoy music. No pets. Accommodations in main house include: dinner and breakfast. Accommodations include: A) two rooms with double bed; B) two double beds, C) three suites in outer buildings that include: D) cabin with fireplace, sitting room, double bed, twin bed and sofa bed. Suites: E) has sitting room. B and one of the rooms under A are rented as unit to one family or friends, with shared bath. On arrival, all guests are served wine and cheese. This gracious home is convenient to bayou browsing, charterfishing, and other plantations. French and Spanish are spoken. Children welcome. SMOKING outdoors only.
**Rates:** S OR D A & B) $150 AND C-E) $85 DAILY.
**Reservations:** (504) 346-1928 SEVEN DAYS 8 A.M. TO 8 P.M.

## NEW IBERIA

Comfortable modern home. Accommodations include: A) room on first floor with separate entrance, twin beds, private bath with shower; and B) room on second floor with double bed, private bath with tub. Baby bed

and rollaway available at additional charge. Host is retired engineer; hostess a tour guide and teacher and knows area thoroughly.
**Rates:** A) S $35, D $45; AND B) S $30 D $40 DAILY. TAKE $5 OFF PER DAY FOR STAYS OF TWO DAYS OR MORE.
**Reservations:** (504) 346-1928 SEVEN DAYS 8 A.M. TO 8 P.M.

Victorian cottage offers two bedrooms each with double bed and private bath. Furnished with antiques and interesting art objects collected by hosts as they have lived all over the world. Complimentary continental breakfast. Delightful hosts knowledgeable about the area.
**Rates:** S $45, D $50 DAILY. TAKE $5 OFF EACH NIGHT ON STAYS OF TWO NIGHTS OR MORE.
**Reservations:** (504) 346-1928 SEVEN DAYS 8 A.M. TO 8 P.M.

## CENTRAL CROSSROADS
### ALEXANDRIA
### RURAL LAKESIDE

Delightful contemporary lakeside home overlooking beautiful Lake Kincaid in the Kisatchi National Forest. Hosts are retired from big city corporation life and love sharing their gorgeous home with guests. Sailboat and canoe available, fishing pier for your use. Accommodations include: A) double bed, private entrance, full bath; and B) twin beds, direct entrance, shared bath. Can be used by party of four or one room only with private use of the bath.
**Rates:** A & B) S $35, D $40 DAILY. $5 OFF EACH DAY ON STAYS OF TWO OR MORE DAYS. CHILDREN HALF PRICE.
**Reservations:** (504) 346-1928 SEVEN DAYS 8 A.M. TO 8 P.M.

## FRENCH ACADIAN
### NEW ROADS
### BUSINESS DISTRICT

Accommodations include: Dogtrot House—Second Floor—A) two double beds, bath; B) double bed, twin bed, bath; first floor, suites—C) one room with double bed, one room with three twin beds, shared bath; and D) same as A. Turn-of-the-century house—first floor, two twin beds in living room, one twin bed in dining room, one double bed in bedroom, bath, kitchen. Two story turn-of-the-century house—first floor—living/diningroom/kitchen A) bedroom with two double beds, bath. Second floor—B) double bed, bath; and C) double bed, twin bed, bath. Continental breakfast.
**Rates:** S $45, D $50 DAILY. ADDITIONAL PERSONS $5 EACH. $5 OFF ON STAYS OF TWO OR MORE DAYS.
**Reservations:** (504) 346-1928 SEVEN DAYS 8 A.M. TO 8 P.M.

## NORTH
## RUSTON

NORTH VIENNA — Victorian B&B inn. Rock your cares away on the shady porch. Five rooms with private baths. Twin-, double-, or king-sized beds available. TV provided. No pets. Continental breakfast. Older children welcome. SMOKING areas provided.
**Rates:** A-C) S $45, D $50; D & E) S $50, D $55; AND D) SUITE $80 DAILY. $5 OFF EACH DAY FOR STAYS OF TWO OR MORE DAYS.
**Reservations:** (504) 346-1928 SEVEN DAYS 8 A.M. TO 8 P.M.

## NORTHWEST
## SHREVEPORT

This inn dates back to 1890 and is convenient to Centenary and Louisiana State University. Near Louisiana Downs for racing. Walk to village and restaurants. It has six bedrooms and all have private baths. Extras include: air conditioning, PIANO, antiques.
**Rates:** A-C) S $70, D $79; AND D-F) S $60, D $69 DAILY. $5 OFF EACH NIGHT FOR TWO OR MORE NIGHTS.
**Reservations:** (504) 346-1928 SEVEN DAYS 8 A.M. TO 8 P.M.

## PLANTATION COUNTRY

Plantation Country includes Baton Rouge, the Capitol city, over which seven flags have flown, 75 miles from New Orleans, fifth largest U.S. port, industrial center, home of Louisiana State University, Catfish Town (a river front historic district restoration), and central to many plantation homes. Located on the Mississippi River, Interstates 10 and 12, and US 61 and 190. St. Francisville is a 200 year old town, most of which is on the National Historic Register, first settled in the late eighteenth century. The area offers interesting walking and auto tours of historic homes in Audubon's "Happy Land" where he painted many pictures for his "Birds of America." Jackson, named after Andrew Jackson after his 1815 victory at New Orleans, has a large collection of Greek Revival buildings. Plantation Country has many historic sites, festivals, numerous antique shops, excellent restaurants, and peach orchards.

## BATON ROUGE

Lovely modern two story home in beautiful subdivision convenient to LSU, governmental complex, business and banking, Catfish Town complex, and shopping areas. Large upstairs bedroom with 8 foot desk with track lighting, ideal for someone on business. Large private bath. Double bed, kitchen privileges, full or continental breakfast. Delightful neighborhood to walk or to ride bikes. Hosts enjoy sharing their home and knowledge of the area.

**Rates:** S $45, D $50 DAILY. TAKE $5 OFF EACH NIGHT FOR STAYS OF TWO NIGHTS OR MORE.
**Reservations:** (504) 346-1928 SEVEN DAYS 8 A.M. TO 8 P.M.

If you like tennis or fishing this city home is your place. Two second floor rooms, double beds, sitting area, large bath, lovely antiques, refrigerator and microwave, HBO, and VCR. Kitchenette available. Host knows fishing spots and can arrange fishing trips, also tennis lessons or matches for amateurs or experienced (extra fee) players. Hostess puts fruit juice and fresh fruit in the rooms and serves a gourmet breakfast.
**Rates:** S $42.50, D $50 DAILY. TAKE $5 OFF FOR STAY OF TWO OR MORE DAYS.
**Reservations:** (504) 346-1928 SEVEN DAYS 8 A.M. TO 8 P.M.

## OUTSIDE BATON ROUGE
## PORT VINCENT

This river camp is built on stilts 11 feet in the air, which puts it in the tree tops. Contemporary design with lots of glass. Accommodations include: A) master bedroom, queen-sized waterbed, double size JACUZZI bathtub is part of the bedroom. There is a separate door to the deck and HOT TUB; and B) smaller bedroom has a double bed and private hall bath. The cabin has a woodburning fireplace, full kitchen, satellite dish, and TV. Grounds have ponds with bridges, ducks, geese, and boat slip for launching your own boat.
**Rates:** A) D $100; AND B) D $50 DAILY. A) $100 TWO NIGHTS B) $100; WHOLE CABIN $250 WEEKENDS, $600 WEEKLY.
**Reservations:** (504) 346-1928 SEVEN DAYS 8 A.M. TO 8 P.M.

## JACKSON

HIGHWAY 68 — Country inn is in Audubon's Happy Land, the Felicianas with woods and rolling hills. Rooms are in small cottages nestled among the trees, each room with private bath, some with fireplaces and sleeper sofas to accommodate extra people. Twin-, queen-, and king-sized beds are available. There is a 10% Senior Citizen discount. Excellent weekly rates on request. Lunch and dinner are available in excellent restaurant in historic building on the grounds. Sip your afternoon cocktail or tea on the verandah, cool off in the swimming POOL, or enjoy a walk in the woods. Excellent facilities are here for family vacations, group meetings, and soon, with quick access to and from Baton Rouge airport.
**Rates:** A, B, C, D, L, & M) S $50, D $55; E, F, G, H, P, & Q) S $70, D $75; J, K, N, & O) S $60, D $65; AND SUITE I) D $95, Q $130 DAILY. TAKE $5 OFF EACH NIGHT FOR STAYS OF TWO OR MORE.
**Reservations:** (504) 346-1928 SEVEN DAYS 8 A.M. TO 8 P.M.

This plantation home is considered the finest example of Victorian Gothic Architecture in the state (on National Register of Historic Places). Four rooms in house, two in each of four Victorian cottages with lake view total 12 rooms, all with private baths and double bed. Enjoy the swimming POOL, TENNIS COURT, and fishing ponds (bring equipment but no live bait) in the quiet of this 1,000 acre working plantation. Full breakfast.
**Rates:** A & B) D $70; C & D) $85; AND COTTAGES $60.
**Reservations:** (504) 346-1928 SEVEN DAYS 8 A.M. TO 8 P.M.

## HISTORIC DISTRICT

Built in 1825-1836, this National Register property has been a home, a bank, occupied by Union troops, and is now restored to its former elegance and furnished with period antiques. Accommodations include: A) room with double bed, private bath on first floor; B) two rooms with double bed and bath suites on second floor; C) three rooms with double bed; and D) two twins. Children welcome. All rates include full southern style breakfast. There is a 10% Senior Citizen discount. TV and bar available if desired, also champagne for special occasions. Sample the house special—frozen peach daiquiris made with Louisiana peaches. Picnic lunches and private sightseeing tours may be arranged. Weddings, banquets, and receptions are specialties of these hosts.
**Rates:** A & B) D $75 AND C & D) D $65 DAILY. $450 WEEKLY.
**Reservations:** (504) 346-1928 SEVEN DAYS 8 A.M. TO 8 P.M.

## ST. FRANCISVILLE

Enjoy the seclusion of this picture book spot just minutes from town and many other places of historic and scenic interest. This antebellum home belongs to one of Louisiana's famous sons who has retired, with his wife, to his childhood home. They have a guest apartment above a modern carriage house that sleeps four with use of sofabed in living room, queen bed in bedroom which has compartmented full bath. Use of the guesthouse kitchen available for extended stays. This overlooks a view beyond description—watch Canada Geese that live on the pond and the deer occasionally drinking there, or stroll the beautifully landscaped grounds. Host, an authority on area history, looks forward to sharing his knowledge with history buffs. Two weeks notice for reservations necessary.
**Rates:** S OR D $85, T $90 AND Q $100 DAILY. S OR D $80 FOR TWO OR MORE NIGHTS.
**Reservations:** (504) 346-1928 SEVEN DAYS 8 A.M. TO 8 P.M.

## HISTORIC DISTRICT

This home dates back to 1809. All rooms have iron-work balconies, lovingly restored wood floors, and are furnished with antiques. Accommodations include: A) first floor bedroom with private bath; and B

& C) two second floor rooms that share a bath all with double beds. First floor suite in secluded corner of house has bedroom, sitting room, bath and for special anniversary or honeymoon package a gourmet dinner by candlelight, champagne, and breakfast served in bed is very special. Continental breakfast included. Gourmet breakfast is $50. Hostess' hobby is cooking!

**Rates:** A & B) $60; AND C) $50 DAILY. $5 OFF EACH NIGHT FOR STAY OF TWO OR MORE NIGHTS.

**Reservations:** (504) 346-1928 SEVEN DAYS 8 A.M. TO 8 P.M.

## SOUTHEAST
## NATCHITOCHES
### HISTORIC DISRICT

Guest may expect a warm welcome, a room tastefully decorated with king-sized beds, private baths, makeup vanities for m'lady, a sitting area, as well as the many amenities one expects in a friend's home. Downstairs, the living room offers TV and comfortable furnishing where guests may chat with hosts and other guests. Each morning, with a breakfast call, a 12 foot long table is set for a plantation breakfast.

**Rates:** S $50, D $60 DAILY. $5 OFF EACH NIGHT FOR STAYS OF TWO OR MORE NIGHTS.

**Reservations:** (504) 346-1928 SEVEN DAYS 8 A.M. TO 8 P.M.

## SOUTHERN LOUISIANA
### MADISONVILLE

Downstairs and upstairs porches, high ceilings, wide hallways, and bright airy rooms welcome you to the casual atmosphere of this 100 year old house furnished with antiques. Just steps to the river where you can fish, canoe, or ski. Bikes, canoe, windsurfer available for a fee. Three guestrooms with double bed, shared bath. Full breakfast may include crab omelet, pancakes, or popovers.

**Rates:** S $40, D $45 DAILY. $5 OFF EACH NIGHT FOR STAYS OF TWO NIGHTS OR MORE. S $150, D $200 WEEKLY.

**Reservations:** (504) 346-1928 SEVEN DAYS 8 A.M. TO 8 P.M.

### NEW ORLEANS

This is the city most famous for its Mardi Gras, jazz clubs, and French cuisine with Cajun flair.

### CARROLTON

Cottage near universities, parks, museums, easy access to all highways, and French Quarter, downtown. Hostess speaks fiuent Spanish. Small pets allowed. Shared bath, continental breakfast, two twin beds. Resident CAT. No CHILDREN.

**Rates:** S $32, D $37 DAILY. $5 OFF EACH NIGHT FOR STAY OF TWO NIGHTS OR MORE. SIX NIGHTS FOR THE PRICE OF FIVE WEEKLY.
**Reservations:** (504) 346-1928 SEVEN DAYS 8 A.M. TO 8 P.M.

## CHATEAU ESTATES, KENNER, LOS ANGELES

BRITTANY DRIVE — Away from the busy downtown area, home is located on a quiet suburban street in New Orleans, most prestigious neighborhood—Chateau Estates. This 10 year old English Tudor home is uniquely furnished with antiques and collectibles. A short 10 minute ride from the New Orleans International Airport, 2 minutes from the area's newest shopping Center—The Esplanade. 2 minutes from Lake Pontchartrain, which offers a linear park/path for jogging or bike riding on the tandem bike. Jefferson Downs Race Track is within walking distance for those who enjoy horse racing. French Quarter and Convention Centers are an easy 20 minute drive. Host works for the Department of Defense and enjoys racquetball, jogging, and golf; hostess is an information specialist who enjoys antiques, ventriloquism, history, and square dancing. An 18 year old daughter lives at home as well as a DALMATIAN who stays in the yard. Accommodations include: A) double bed, private bath; and B) double bed, private hall bath. Air conditioning. NO SMOKING.
**Rates:** A & B) S $30, D $40 DAILY. WEEKLY AND LONG-TERM RATES QUOTED.
**Reservations:** (504) 525-4640 FOR BOOKINGS (800) 288-9711 - DIAL TONE - 184; HOURS MONDAY THROUGH FRIDAY 8:00 - 5:00.

## FRENCH QUARTER

The French Quarter is the "original city" of New Orleans. Often called a European city in the United States, world famous restaurants and jazz clubs are within short walking distance. Excitement is everywhere. Mississippi paddlewheelers ride visitors up the river to plantation homes of the nineteenth century. Convention senters are near. Antiquing and window shopping are favorites of strollers as the sweet sounds of music seems to always be floating in the air. Away from the bustle is a quiet residential neighborhood where many New Orleanians live in century old homes. There is ample public parking for those with cars.

A 1940s Contemporary ranch house located in a quiet, secluded neighborhood, 10 minutes to downtown. Host and hostess enjoy evening meetings with guests over glass of wine. Their interests are art, academia, classical music, theology, travel (have lived abroad) but are open to all. Two CATS and two DOGS also reside here. Accommodations include a double bed full bath, shower, cable TV, refrigerator, coffee maker. Sliding glass doors open onto beautifully landscaped POOL and patio. Separate

entrance through garden gate. Self-serve continental breakfast. Air conditioned. CHILDREN welcome if they can swim.
**Rates:** A S $30, D $40 DAILY.
**Reservations:** (504) 525-4640 FOR BOOKINGS (800) 288-9711 - DIAL TONE - 184; HOURS MONDAY THROUGH FRIDAY 8:00 - 5:00.

BARRACKS AT ROYAL — A newly renovated Victorian building located in the quiet residential section of the historic French Quarter. Within a few blocks of 24 hour restaurants, bars, and delicatessens. And, because this area was designed for walkers, you are minutes by foot from any place in the Quarter. Neighborhood banks, hair salons, and grocers are readily available. Leave your car at home—you will not need it here. Hosts take care of the housekeeping but beyond that, your room is strictly and privately yours. You have access to the street through a security gate for which you have your own key. No doorkeeper, no lobby, no hassle. Hosts are always available if needed, but most guests seem to find their way around amazingly fast. The rooms open onto a secluded patio that is maintained just for the guests' pleasure. The patio, with its wet bar, refrigerator, and ice maker, is a popular place to relax. The patio is where you are served a complimentary continental breakfast each morning. The three guestrooms have air conditioning and heating, and ceiling fans, too, for your comfort. Big double beds are standard, as are individual baths with newly tiled showers. TV sets, roomy storage closets, and ice buckets are a few of the additional amenities. Each room is individually decorated with furniture and art befitting a gracious New Orleans home. NO CHILDREN.
**Rates:** S $55, D $60 DAILY. WEEKLY AND LONG-TERM RATES POSSIBLE.
**Reservations:** (504) 525-4640 FOR BOOKINGS (800) 288-9711 - DIAL TONE - 184; HOURS MONDAY THROUGH FRIDAY 8:00 - 5:00.

BURGUNDY — An 1820s two story cottage with balcony off bedroom with double bed on secluded patio. It also has a living area with a double-bedded sofa, kitchen, and bath. The furnishings are contemporary. Host is a business manager; hostess is self-employed in a multiple service company. This cottage is convenient to the business district, shopping, entertainment, fine restaurants, convention and sports centers, and historic points of interest. Hostess is eager to share knowledge of New Orleans with guests so they leave loving New Orleans and are already planning a return trip. Children welcome.
**Rates:** S $65, D $75, T $85 DAILY. S $100, D $125, T 150 DAILY DURING MARDI GRAS, JAZZ FESTIVAL, OR SPORTS SPECIALS. WEEKLY AND LONG-TERM RATES QUOTED.
**Reservations:** (504) 525-4640 FOR BOOKINGS (800) 288-9711 - DIAL TONE - 184; HOURS MONDAY THROUGH FRIDAY 8:00 - 5:00.

**CHARTRES** — This garconniere, located on one of the French Quarter's choicest residential streets is an unhosted guesthouse at the rear of the enclosed courtyard and a real New Orleans hideaway. Queen-sized sofabed in ground floor living room sleeps two, spiral stairway takes you upstairs to a large bath with shower and a large airy bedroom with twin beds and balcony overlooking courtyard. Pullman kitchenette in living area, fireplace with gas burner, phone, TV, covered and locked parking across the street add to your enjoyment. Two weeks notice required for reservations.
**Rates:** $80 DAILY. $5 OFF EACH NIGHT FOR STAYS OF TWO OR MORE NIGHTS. $450 WEEKLY.
**Reservations:** (504) 346-1928 SEVEN DAYS 8 A.M. TO 8 P.M.

**ESPLANADE AVENUE** — Be a part of the French Quarter in a home from the 1800s. Your hostess has recently retired from 35 years of owning an internationally known French Quarter guesthouse. Her knowledge of the area is expansive. She now enjoys a handful of guests who stay in separate apartments in her home. Built as a grand home of its time, Gothic details decorate the facade. Convenient to mini bus and streetcar, guests can easily attend conventions and sightsee. Each guest apartment has its own private entrance. Apartments include: A) two bedrooms with king and double beds, 1 1/2 baths. kitchen (self-serve continental breakfast) and living room on front balcony; B) four poster queen bed, sitting area (sofabed), bath and kitchen (self-serve continental breakfast); and C) twin beds, bath, kitchen (self-serve continental breakfast). Children welcome. AC.
**Rates:** A-C) S $55-$70, D $65-$85, T $100-$105, Q $125 DAILY. WEEKLY AND SPECIAL RATES QUOTED.
**Reservations:** (504) 525-4640 FOR BOOKINGS (800) 288-9711 - DIAL TONE - 184; HOURS MONDAY THROUGH FRIDAY 8:00 - 5:00.

## ST. CHARLES AVENUE LINE

The streetcar begins at the French Quarter and downtown Convention Center area, then meanders along an oak-lined boulevard through the Nineteenth Century Garden District to the turn-of-the-century uptown area. It runs 24 hours a day. Visitors can spend a day getting off and on to dine at local restaurants. See historic sites, go antiquing, visit coffee houses, and tour the Louisiana Swamp Exhibit, a walk through attraction of the Audubon Zoological Gardens. Visitors will also encounter many New Orleanians who use the streetcar daily.

## LOWER GARDEN DISTRICT

Late nineteenth century Italianate mansion in Lower Garden District has central courtyard with balconies. Six bedrooms: all have private baths, some with both tub and shower, four with nonworking fireplaces, all with

TV, all furnished with unusual antiques. Hosts' hobbies are gourmet cooking and antique collecting and they delight in seeing that their guests get to see and do all the things that are special and unique in New Orleans. French and Spanish spoken.
**Rates:** A & B) $95; C) $80; D) $65; E) $65; AND F-T) $80 DAILY. $5 OFF EACH NIGHT FOR STAYS OF TWO OR MORE NIGHTS.
**Reservations:** (504) 346-1928 SEVEN DAYS 8 A.M. TO 8 P.M.

COLISEUM SQUARE — Antebellum townhouse faithfully restored and elegantly furnished with antiques. Balconies and courtyard add charm. Excellent facilities for meetings, private parties, and weddings. Ten rooms in mansion and carriage house with private baths. Complimentary breakfast and afternoon cocktail. Public transportation at door, easy access to any part of the city.
**Rates:** S OR D A & B) $75; C) $85; D-H) $65; AND I) $60 DAILY.
**Reservations:** (504) 346-1928 SEVEN DAYS 8 A.M. TO 8 P.M.

This turn-of-the-century home on historic St. Charles Avenue is furnished in lovely antiques. Accommodations include A & B) two rooms each with twin beds. They both share a hall bath, plus the use of another bath and a half. A delicious continental breakfast, complete with Southern biscuits and homemade preserves, is served on fine china in the formal dining room. The home is convenient to Interstate 10, within walking distance to the universities and Audubon Park with its magnificent zoo. It is minutes away from jazz clubs, Cajun music, and New Orleans' special coffee houses. The French Quarter, steeped in history and loads of fun, is a 20 minute drive or a 35 minute delightful streetcar ride down the oak-shaded "Avenue." Within walking distance there are also several excellent restaurants for weary visitors. The host and hostess are knowledgeable walking chambers of commerce, with a Southern accent. One small DOG also resides here. Air conditioned.
**Rates:** S $50, D $50 DAILY. LONG-TERM AND SPECIAL EVENTS RATES QUOTED.
**Reservations:** (504) 525-4640 FOR BOOKINGS (800) 288-9711 - DIAL TONE - 184; HOURS MONDAY THROUGH FRIDAY 8:00 - 5:00.

NAPOLEON & ST. CHARLES — Restored nineteenth century home: antiques and artifacts abound this elegant home. The hosts have lovingly restored their Greek Revival style house. They have traveled to auctions and shows to select their treasures. Host is an architect; hostess is a furniture designer. Host has done much of the actual craftsmanship himself, from hand painted ceilings to lush draperies. Hosts willingly assist guests in choosing things to do, places to tour, music to hear, and anything else. They give a complimentary tour of their own home. Home is conveniently located a short drive or romantic streetcar ride to the French Quarter and Convention Center. Several fine, intimate restaurants are closeby. Continental breakfast in country kitchen usually becomes the scene of exciting plan making for the day. Extras include: air conditioning, PIANO, VCR, many antiques, and a horse stall. Accommodations include: A) double bed, private bath; B) queen-sized bed, private bath; and C) king-sized bed, private bath; and D) twin beds, hall bathroom. One indoor CAT.

**Rates:** A) S $60, D $70; B & C) S $50, D $60; AND D) S $40, D $50 DAILY. WEEKLY OR LONG-TERM RATES QUOTED. SPECIAL EVENTS RATES QUOTED.

**Reservations:** (504) 525-4640 FOR BOOKINGS (800) 288-9711 - DIAL TONE - 184; HOURS MONDAY THROUGH FRIDAY 8:00 - 5:00.

PINE STREET CORNER GREEN STREET — A New Orleans Style Raised Cottage on a quiet uptown street near Tulane University. The atmosphere is casual. Host is a professor of engineering at Tulane University doing research in climatlogy; hostess enjoys all types of handwork and ultrasuede sewing. Both enjoy traveling, playing tennis, and raising Louisiana's Catahoula dogs. One block from public transportation on the Streetcar. Ten minutes from Garden District and 40 minutes to the French Quarter. Walking distance to Tulane Campus, Audubon Park, and many uptown restaurants. Accommodations include a double bed, private plus den with double sofabed. AIR CONDITIONED AND PIANO. CHILDREN AND PETS WELCOME. PREFER NONSMOKERS.

**Rates:** S $30, D $40, T $50, Q $60 DAILY.

**Reservations:** (504) 525-4640 FOR BOOKINGS (800) 288-9711 - DIAL TONE - 184; HOURS MONDAY THROUGH FRIDAY 8:00 - 5:00.

ST. CHARLES & NAPOLEON — The two private guest cottages sit behind an 1876 uptown Victorian home. Stained and leaded glass windows, French doors, cypress staircases, and a brick courtyard enhance the romantic atmosphere of the cottages. Three blocks from St. Charles Avenue and minutes away from major New Orleans attractions including the French Quarter, Audubon Zoo, Convention Center, Tulane and Loyola Universities, the Mississippi River, the Superdome; and seasonal events including Mardi Gras and Jazz Festival. The historic St. Charles Streetcar Line makes the food, music, and ambiance of New Orleans accessible without a car. Each cottage has a telephone, refrigerator, tea and coffee pot, TV, stereo, queen bed (cottage B has twin beds and queen bed in different rooms), laundry room, fruit basket, flowers, maps and restaurant recommendations. Guests have a choice of a full sit down breakfast in the main house, a private breakfast served in their cottage, a gourmet buffet in the kitchen, or continental breakfast in a basket served at the yard swing or in the courtyard. PETS WELCOME. Children welcome.

**Rates:** A & B) S $50, D $60, T $70, Q $80 DAILY.

**Reservations:** (504) 525-4640 FOR BOOKINGS (800) 288-9711 - DIAL TONE - 184; HOURS MONDAY THROUGH FRIDAY 8:00 - 5:00.

6TH STREET NEAR ST. CHARLES — Big family atmosphere and beloved family pets create an informal, friendly feeling to this Creole style cottage in the garden district. Only 1 1/2 blocks from St. Charles Avenue, this is a perfect location for viewing Mardi Gras parades and riding the historic St. Charles Streetcar. It is a short 20 minute ride by streetcar to downtown and the French Quarter. It is near Audubon Park and Tulane and Loyola Universities. Most major churches are within walking distance. Accommodations include two rooms with twin beds that share a hall bath. Kitchen privileges. Breakfast supplied. PETS POSSIBLE. Both host and hostess enjoy helping visitors find the best places to eat, enjoy jazz, and their historic city. Two DOGS and two CATS. VCR. Children welcome.
**Rates:** S $35, D $40 DAILY.
**Reservations:** (504) 525-4640 FOR BOOKINGS (800) 288-9711 - DIAL TONE - 184; HOURS MONDAY THROUGH FRIDAY 8:00 - 5:00.

7 ST AND ST. CHARLES — This residence is a large five bedroom Queen Anne Victorian home built in 1887. It has a large wraparound porch on the first floor and two smaller balconies on the second floor. The home furnishings are eclectic and include many antiques, and a large number of original paintings and drawings. Also a STEINWAY GRAND PIANO. The home is conveniently located half a block from historic St. Charles Avenue and in the beautiful Garden District. New Orleans' famous Streetcar runs on St. Charles Avenue and is used for transportation to the French Quarter, parks, and universities. A 6 block walk to Magazine Street will find you many antique shops and art galleries. Accommodations include: A) king-sized bed; B) double bed plus twin bed. and C) two rooms each with king-sized bed plus twin bed. The four rooms share three baths. Bikes available. Hosts do not smoke, but allow guests to do so. It is 10 minutes by streetcar and 5 minutes by car to the French Quarter and Convention Center. Air conditioned. Children of all ages welcome.
**Rates:** A & B) S $40, D $50 AND C) S $40, D $50, T $60 DAILY. SPECIAL EVENTS QUOTED. WEEKLY OR LONG-TERM RATES QUOTED.
**Reservations:** (504) 525-4640 FOR BOOKINGS (800) 288-9711 - DIAL TONE - 184; HOURS MONDAY THROUGH FRIDAY 8:00 - 5:00.

# PONCHATOULA
## TANGIPAHOA PARISH

HIGHWAY 22 WEST — Delightful country home with attached Bavarian Bakery operated as an Austrian style guesthouse in the heart of South

Louisiana. Host is baker and operates Bakery Tea Room; hostess owns gift shop in Baton Rouge and works both places. Home is built of all old wood materials and furnished in antiques. Each room has a double bed and large compartmented private baths. European full breakfast is served in the Bakery Tea Room.

**Rates:** S $40, D $50 DAILY. $5 OFF EACH NIGHT FOR STAY OF TWO OR MORE NIGHTS.

**Reservations:** (504) 346-1928 SEVEN DAYS 8 A.M. TO 8 P.M.

# TEXAS

## BLACKLAND PRAIRIE
### TEMPLE
### NORTHSIDE

NORTH 13TH OFF ZENITH — Large POOL, new SPA, and gazebo all may be used by guests to this lovely home in tree-lined neighborhood away from noise of freeway. Hosts are eager to have travelers come and share ideas. Host is a research scientist. Continental breakfast. Accommodations include: A) king bed, private bath and B) double bed, private bath. Located halfway between Dallas and San Antonio. Near two area lakes with fishing and boating; 35 miles from Baylor University. HANDICAPPED ACCESSIBLE. Well-behaved children welcome. NO SMOKING.
**Rates:** A) S OR D $40 AND B) S OR D $30 DAILY.
**Reservations:** (214) 298-8586.

## BRAZOS VALLEY
### BRYAN

BRISTOL — A spacious, traditional home on tree-shaded lot with heated inground POOL. Casual, comfortable atmosphere. An entertainment center has 13 foot antique marble bar; four living areas. It is 10 minutes from Texas A&M University. Hostess in on marketing/advertising staff of regional home life magazine. A CAT is on premises. Centrally located on Brazos Valley Historical Trail. Winery just outside city limits. Close to shopping and restaurants. Accommodations include: A) queen bed, private bath and B) double bed, private bath. CHILDREN over 6 welcome.
**Rates:** S $35, D $40 DAILY.
**Reservations:** (214) 298-8586.

## CENTRAL TEXAS
### AUSTIN

33RD STREET OFF GUADALUPE — Located in the heart of Austin, this B&B is convenient to town, the Capitol Complex, and the University of Texas. Travelers receive warm hospitality in true British style with all the ambiance of a country inn. Five rooms are tastefully decorated and furnished with antiques and reproductions. Guests gather in the dining room for breakfast around an original Stickley Brothers oak table that extends to accommodate a full house. Your hosts are happy to bring a tray to your room should you prefer the special treat of "breakfast in bed." The hearty continental breakfast consists of pecan or blueberry muffins, sausage rolls, or English beer biscuits as well as a delightful selection of fresh fruits in season or a broiled grapefruit dripping with honey, nutmeg, and cinnamon. No guests leave this table hungry. There is also your choice of a special blend of coffee, teas, and juices. Accommodations include: A) twin beds; B) double bed; C) queen-sized bed, private bath; D) guest cottage; and E) retreat D&E sleep four. There are two DOGS here. Air conditioned. Host is an engineer; hostess is an interior designer. Both enjoy tennis.

**Rates:** A & B) $49; C) $65; D) $75; AND E) $65 DAILY.
**Reservations:** (713) 868-4654 MONDAY THROUGH FRIDAY, 7:30 A.M. TO 9:00 P.M., SATURDAY AND SUNDAY 8:00 A.M. TO 5:00 P.M.

## CLIFTON

FARM TO MARKET HIGHWAY — On beautiful, uncluttered, rolling prairie and farmland sits this simple, farm style home. Pleasant views, fresh, clean, gentle, summer breezes and quiet starlight nights are standard equipment at this second generation home. Toast your toes on a chilly night by the woodburning stove and snuggle to sleep under a colorful, handmade quilt. Owner is a self-employed architectural designer and shares the farm with two large, friendly DOGS. Accommodations include: A) a double room, private bath inspired by a former Swedish exchange student. Romantic fabric wallcovering with matching drapes and comforter trimmed in blue and an antique double iron bedstead; B) room with double bed, shared bath. Breakfast is a glass of fresh squeezed juice, fruit compote, homemade pork sausage, country fresh eggs, and hot from the oven biscuits. It is 10 minutes to Texas Safari, world's largest exotic animal drive through wildlife park; 15 minutes to Lake Whitney for excellent fishing and boating; and 45 minutes to Waco and Baylor Bear territory. Blacked out Dallas Cowboy games are available on color TV. Good restaurants within 10 minutes. Horse stall. HANDICAPPED ACCESSIBLE. Children of all ages welcome. SMOKING on patio.

**Rates:** A) S $25, D $30 AND B) D $40 DAILY.
**Reservations:** (214) 298-8586.

## FREDRICKSBURG
### HILL COUNTY

This is a 1912 Victorian frame, blue with white trim. Early Texas home furnished with family heirlooms, stained glass windows, large yard, garden, kitchen facilities. Accommodations include: A) twin bedroom; B) king bedroom; C) double bedroom; and D) king pullout sofa bed as well. Guestrooms share two baths. Rooms have ceiling fans and air conditioning. This is a favorite spot for families and honeymooners who always want to return again. Set in the supreme beauty of Texas hill country. Offering the antique shopping of Fredricksburg. Off-street parking, half block to bus line. Host is a teacher interested in photography and sports; hostess enjoys genealogy and calligraphy. Both are active in church and scouting. Two outside COLLIES. German is spoken here. HANDICAPPED ACCESSIBLE.

**Rates:** S $44, D $49.50, CHILDREN $11, UNDER 5 YEARS FREE, DAILY.
**Reservations:** (214) 298-8586.

## LAMPASAS

KEY AVENUE AND 6TH STREET — A large Victorian home built at the turn of the century, furnished with numerous antiques. The house has three fireplaces, one of which is in the downstairs suite. The hostess is a former home economics teacher and speaks some Spanish. Accommodations include: A) downstairs suite with double bed, FIREPLACE, sitting room, private bath; B) upstairs two rooms each with double bed, shared bath; and C) suite, three double beds, sitting room, private bath. Hostess serves full breakfast in dining room or breakfast can be served in bed. The home is accessible to downtown areas, 9 hole golf courses, and summer swimming. CHILDREN over 10 welcome. SMOKERS may use outside porches.
**Rates:** A & C) SUITE $75 AND B) S $40, D $55 DAILY.
**Reservations:** (214) 298-8586.

## STEPHENVILLE

NORTH GRAHAM — One time family ownership and was a restoration project of Bill and Paula Oxford. The home was built around 1898 by Judge W.J. Oxford, Sr. The Victorian home is furnished throughout with antiques, including a PIANO and family pump organ along with many framed family photographs. Host is a practicing attorney carrying on the tradition of law in Oxford; hostess is a housewife and enjoys watercolor painting. They have four children. (Family does not reside here; caretaker/ manager living in house.) Hostess enjoys serving continental breakfast with a formal setting in the family dining room with silver and china or in a country atmosphere on the patio. Each bedroom has its own decorated style along with a private bath. Accommodations include: A) queen bed; B & C) two rooms each with double bed; and D) 3/4 bed. House is within walking distance to downtown shopping and eating. Museum grounds are 8 blocks away. CHILDREN over 10 welcome. SMOKING only in parlor and outside porch.
**Rates:** D $65 DAILY.
**Reservations:** (214) 298-8586.

## WACO
## COUNTRY SETTING

TEXAS HIGHWAY 6 — UNHOSTED guest cottage in country setting on 7 acres. Next to the host house, large trees, and pond. It includes a full kitchen with microwave oven and refrigerator stocked with breakfast fixings. Accommodations include two rooms each with double beds. One

bathroom. Divan also makes a double bed. Color TV, outside barbecue and picnic area. Host speaks and understands some Spanish and German. Host is a dentist; hostess is a computer programmer. It is 10 minutes from Lake Waco with swimming, boating, and fishing; 15 minutes from golf and restaurants; and 20 minutes from shopping Baylor, University, Browning Library, Ft. Fisher, Texas Ranger Texas Safari, Meridan State Park, and Lake Whitney. Two DOGS and four CATS live here. Air conditioned. Children welcome.
**Rates:** S $35, D $50 DAILY. S $200, D $300 WEEKLY.
**Reservations:** (214) 298-8586.

## DALLAS/FORT WORTH
## DALLAS

Spacious home near Olla Podrida and Richardson. It has three available bedrooms. They include: A) double bed, pullout sofa, a sitting room, private bath and B) two rooms each with double beds, share a bath. The rooms are good for families or groups traveling together. TV and VCR. Hosts are very outgoing and make it easy for guests to enjoy themselves. Breakfast will be full or continental, your choice. Two CATS are on the premises.
**Rates:** S $30, D $35-$40 DAILY.
**Reservations:** (214) 298-8586.

Stunning two story home across from the country club in Lakewood, two bedrooms upstairs. Hosts are sailing enthusiasts. Host will prepare his biscuits and gravy for guests' enjoyment. Accommodations include: A) double bed with charming canopy, lovely antique pieces, private bath and B) twin bedroom overlooks the POOL and backyard. Public bus runs in front of home, 20 minutes to downtown. Scottie DOG named Valentine will snuggle you. One outside CAT. PIANO. VCR.
**Rates:** S $40, D $45 DAILY.
**Reservations:** (214) 298-8586.

## ARLINGTON
## DALWORTHINGTON GARDENS

NEAR INTERSTATE 20 AND BOWEN — Enjoy the flavor of the southwest in this 5,500 sqare foot home with its Mexican Colonial architecture and decor. There is an outdoor POOL, small private LAKE, and a HOT TUB in the Garden Room. Fishing and canoeing are available and there are even FACILITIES FOR YOUR HORSES. There are four bedrooms available, one with a king-sized round bed. Small crib, playpen available. Located 2 blocks north of Interstate 20, you are equidistant to either Dallas or Fort Worth. Attractions in Arlington include Six Flags Over Texas, the Ranger Stadium, wax museums, Wet and Wild, many

fine restaurants, and good shopping. Coverage of the Dallas Cowboys may be enjoyed in winter in the spacious living room, in front of the fireplace. Host is a family physician; hostess is with a mission agency. PIANO. HANDICAPPED ACCESSIBLE. SMOKING and ALCOHOL are not welcome. Children welcome.
**Rates:** D $60 DAILY.
**Reservations:** (214) 298-8586.

## BRYAN PLACE

Comfortable Contemporary style home located centrally for downtown, Dallas market center and the best eateries and entertainment in town. The hostess lived abroad for three years and entertains you with stories of her adventures in Europe. All you need do is ask her about them. The downstairs bedroom and adjoining private bath can accommodate either single or double occupancy (queen-sized bed). The home owners have built an outdoor POOL that is available for your use as a house guest. You can also accompany the hostess to her health club. Hostess is a food product developer who is interested in art history. Air conditioned. NO CHILDREN or pets. NO SMOKING in house, however, smoking on the patio allowed.
**Rates:** S $35, D $40 DAILY. S $165, D $185 WEEKLY.
**Reservations:** (214) 298-8586.

## COLLEYVILLE

FRONTIER — Two story Spanish style home on Big Bear Creek and a secluded 5 acres. This is a no industry, rural, bedroom community. It is 15 minutes west of Dallas/Fort Worth Airport and convenient to all metroplex activities. Accommodations include on second floor, two bedroom suite, attached bath, small private sitting room, and outside second floor sitting balcony. Host is retired from computer industry and does woodcarving in the ozark/western style; hostess does artificial flowers and trees, paints husband's woodcarvings and is a bridge enthusiast. Both are interested in friends, community affairs, and your comfort. PETS WELCOME. Three horses here. Videocassette recorder. Children of all ages welcome.
**Rates:** S $40, D $50; TWO BEDROOM SUITE $60 DAILY.
**Reservations:** (214) 298-8586.

## DALLAS
## LAKEWOOD-OLD EAST DALLAS

REIGER AT ABRAMS ROAD — Newly built cottage in restored area that was Dallas' original residential area (circa 1910-1925). Bedroom with double bed, private bath. Home features wooden deck in center of house with French doors leading outside on three sides. Breakfast served there,

weather permitting. Continental breakfast served during the week, more elaborate on weekends. POOL in service from April through November in rear yard. Host is computer consultant, world traveler, avid supporter of the arts and professional sports. Fair Park (Cotton Bowl, Science Place, Natural History Museum, Music Hall, Garden Center); White Rock Lake: Lakewood shopping area; six inexpensive restaurants within 5 minutes walking distance. PIANO. NO CHILDREN.
**Rates:** S $30, D $40 DAILY. $5 SURCHARGE FOR 1 NIGHT STAY. S $210, D $245 WEEKLY.
**Reservations:** (214) 298-8586.

## LOVE FIELD WEST

BROOKFIELD AND MOHAWK — Convenient to Love Field, Market Center, Convention Center, and Bachman Lake, these budget accommodations include a small kitchenette, private bath, and queen-sized bed. Also a small sitting area off the kitchen, private entrances and off-street parking. Hostess is a designer of children's wear and speaks French. Gourmet cooking can be included (dinner). Bikes available. PETS WELCOME. CHILDREN may bring their own sleeping bags.
**Rates:** S $30, D $35 DAILY.
**Reservations:** (214) 298-8586.

## PRESTONWOOD

GOLDEN CREEK ROAD — North Dallas Contemporary home with a lovely side patio off of the living room and den. A mixture of country and Early American furniture with a few antiques. Accommodations include a queen bed and private bath. Share den and living room with family. Breakfast served in country kitchen. Host is a property tax consultant; hostess does all kinds of crafts and volunteers at Dallas Museum of Art and church. Close to Valley View, Prestonwood, and Galleria shopping malls. Two blocks from Dart bus service and 5 minutes from Dallas Tollway. Air conditioned. NO CHILDREN or SMOKERS.
**Rates:** S $40, D $45 DAILY. S $240, D $270 WEEKLY.
**Reservations:** (214) 298-8586.

NEDRA/NEAR HILLCREST — Antique fan displayed in lovely twin bedroom with a private bath adds charm to this restful place. Home is near prestigious malls for shopping delights: Sakowitz, Prestonwood, and Galleria. Southfork from "Dallas" TV show is 15 minute drive away. Hosts traveled B&B in England and Scotland and decided to share their space with travelers. Full breakfast including Jalepeno muffin for first time Texas visitors. Downtown Dallas and Convention Center just 20 minutes away by car. PIANO. VCR. Children of all ages welcome.
**Rates:** S $ 40, D $45 DAILY.
**Reservations:** (214) 298-8586.

REGALHILL CIRCLE — A Mediterranean style home. Some antiques. Hostess enjoys aerobics, art, history, and antiquing. There is one DOG and two CATS, however, the pets are not allowed in the guest area. Hostess does not smoke but will permit smokers. Nice shopping center within walking distance. Very convenient to major north Dallas shopping: Prestonwood Town Center, Valley View Mall, and the Galleria. Has a homeowners' association with POOL, TENNIS COURT, and jogging areas. Accommodations include a queen-sized bed, private bath. CHILDREN over 5 welcome.
**Rates:** S $35, D $40 DAILY.
**Reservations:** (214) 298-8586.

## SWISS AVENUE HISTORICAL DISTRICT

SWISS AVENUE — A 1910 Prairie style mansion on three-quarters of an acre. There are many large trees and the area is nicely landscaped. The street is landscaped parkway. The house contains pink marble fireplace, antiques, music room, and three sunporches. Large swimming POOL and carriage house apartment. The area lends itself to jogging, walking, and sightseeing. Downtown is 10 minutes away; public transportation near. Convenient to Interstates 130 and 135 and central expressway. Accommodations include: A) king-sized bed with private sunporch; and B) double bed in room. Both rooms have an attached bath. Host is an electrical engineer; hostess enjoys gardening, arts, and cooking. A 20 year old son lives at home. One CAT also resides here, but outside. PIANO. CHILDREN over 12 welcome. NO SMOKING.
**Rates:** S $50, D $60 DAILY.
**Reservations:** (214) 298-8586.

## WHITE ROCK LAKE AREA

PROVINCE OFF PEAVY ROAD — Hosts are a retired couple. They enjoy traveling and have had guests from France, Scotland, and England as well as many from all over the United States and Canada. They have a three bedroom, two bath house with living/dining room, large eat-in kitchen, and a breakfast room in a glassed-in porch. Off-street parking is available. Accommodations include: A) single bed, shared bath and B) double bed, private bath. Air conditioned. PIANO and ORGAN. TV and VCR. NO CHILDREN OR SMOKING.
**Rates:** S $30, D $40 DAILY. WEEKLY RATES AVAILABLE.
**Reservations:** (214) 298-8586.

LOVERS LANE — Small brick cottage home near Southern Methodist University campus. Lovely homes in quiet neighborhood. Home is furnished with interesting mix of furniture and collectibles. There is a PIANO and fireplace in the home. Hostess is a flight attendant for a major airline who speaks some Spanish and a bit of Hebrew. A son, nine

years old, loves having B&B company. One double bed is available in the suite. There is a small music room, library, and private bath. Guests are welcome to use kitchen, living/dining rooms and laundry facilities. Ten minute drive to town, Convention Center, Market Center. Hostess will drive guest around for a small fee if time permits. One outside DOG. Air conditioned. Children welcome. NO SMOKING.
**Rates:** S $35, D $40, CHILDREN $5 EXTRA DAILY.
**Reservations:** (214) 298-8586.

NEAR MARSH LANE — Pleasant family neighborhood, home of professional woman, active in Business and Professional Women's Club, Inc. Huge garden with flowers, vegetables, herbs, fruits, and berries. Hostess is interested in cooking, traveling, reading, volunteer activities, and people. This home is convenient to two airports and three colleges, as well as market centers. Private room with bath. Adjacent to large dining room and kitchen, separating room from hostess' quarters. May use refrigerator. At times hostess can accommodate another person in another bedroom in home. Accommodations include: A) queen bed and B) suite with sofabed. NO SMOKERS.
**Rates:** S $35, D $45 DAILY.
**Reservations:** (214) 298-8586.

# GARLAND
## RICHLAND MEADOWS

RICHLAND — This 12 year old yellow brick home with three bedrooms. three baths, skylighted patio, oversized dining room, woodburning fireplace, study, breakfast nook and super relaxed atmosphere gives one the feeling, "I can be me here." One can have as much privacy or socializing as the mood strikes. Since there is a fenced backyard, small, well-behaved PETS ARE WELCOME in the yard or on the patio. Hostess is a retired home economics teacher with a special yen for people who express individuality. She prizes all guests for just being themselves. She enjoys setting a pretty table and making a full breakfast according to wishes of guests. She thoroughly enjoys serving food in a leisurely manner. Hostess will help transport guests short distance, but private car is to be desired for extensive sightseeing. Accommodations include: A) double bed, private bath and B) sofabed, private bath. This can be a suite. Children of all ages welcome.
**Rates:** $30-35 DAILY.
**Reservations:** (214) 298-8586.

# GRANBURY
## MITCHELL BEND

MITCHELL BEND — On the bend of the Brazos River is a host home with one bedroom, a double-sized bed and private bath for guests. The

iron double bed in the guestroom has a handmade spread appliqued with oak leaf clusters. Above a marbletopped washstand is a wreath made from grapevines growing in hosts' own backyard. Host is a civil engineer and enjoys old cars; hostess is a homemaker and enjoys doing volunteer work. Both are eager to receive visitors and share a secluded bit of the river environment. They enjoy making guests feel like part of the family. The house itself is modest, but it offers a quiet haven from hectic city life. CATS on premises. Nice breads for continental breakfast. Children welcome. NO SMOKERS.
**Rates:** S $35, D $40 DAILY.
**Reservations:** (214) 298-8586.

## PECAN PLANTATION

BRIERFIELD — This large, fine home in the controlled community of Pecan Plantation has golf course, tennis, swimming, and country club dining available. Guests are welcome to use all of the services as friends of the host and hostess. Host is a retired physician from Wisconsin. They have come to Texas to escape harsh winters. The bedroom has twin beds, private bath. New upbeat decor, many fine amenities in the home. There is a HOT TUB on the enclosed porch that guests may use. Breakfast will be full western style of omeletes or scrambled eggs. There is a CAT, which is outside most of the time. CATS AND OUTDOOR DOGS WELCOME. Nearby Granbury has great plays at the Opera House on the Square, art, antique, and dress shops as well as wonderful restaurants. Bass fishing boats available.
**Rates:** $50 DAILY.
**Reservations:** (214) 298-8586.

## PLANO
## LOS RIOS

BOSQUE DRIVE — A traditional home in a country club setting. TENNIS COURTS, golf, beautiful park all within complex. Large sports center nearby. Three miles from Interstate 75. Near Southfork Ranch of "Dallas" fame. Ten miles to downtown Dallas. Close proximity to Texas Instruments, EDS, and many other high-tech industries. Host is a chemical engineer (retired); hostess enjoys horticulture, sewing, and crafts; both enjoy entertaining. Accommodations include: A) double bed and B) twin beds. The two rooms share a bath. Children of all ages welcome. NO SMOKING.
**Rates:** S $35, D $40 DAILY.
**Reservations:** (214) 298-8586.

## WAXAHACHIE
## 28 MILES SOUTH OF DALLAS

HOWARD ROAD — Victorian farm cottage with five rooms, one bath. Completely restored. Host is a physician and this is his weekend retreat. Furnished throughout with family antiques. Central heat and air conditioning. Landscaped, fenced yard. It is 28 miles south of Dallas; 2 1/4 miles from town on paved road; and 1/4 mile from large LAKE. Boating, swimming, and fishing available. Two bikes furnished. UNHOSTED, breakfast supplied for guests to prepare. Accommodations include: double bed, private bath. TRAINED PETS WELCOME. **Rates:** D $75 DAILY. **Reservations:** (214) 298-8586.

## DEEP EAST TEXAS
## BROADDUS
### SAM RAYBURN LAKE

Located in the Angelina National Forest among tall hardwoods and long needle pine trees, this is a delightful getaway. Very private, no traffic, situated on the shore of Sam Rayburn Lake. WATERFRONT. A cozy five room cottage, with large glassed-in porch, overlooking the lake. Cottage sleeps seven adults easily. Two bedrooms, each with king-sized and twin bed, shared bath. All electric kitchen with everything furnished, except the food. Air conditioned and heat. Furnished with antiques and many primitive pieces are scattered throughout the house. The host will take you on a tour of the area of the lake on his party barge for a small fee. UNHOSTED. **Rates:** S $37.50, D $55 DAILY. S $245, D $350 WEEKLY. **Reservations:** (214) 298-8586.

## EAST TEXAS
## BIG SANDY

Originally built in 1901, a restored Victorian inn situated among the stately pines of northeast Texas. The house is surrounded by a white picket fence and features decorative porches and balconies. Each guestroom is furnished with antiques, decorative rugs, and handmade quilts. A gourmet breakfast is served across the street in Annie's Tea Room, also housed in a restored home. Annie's Pantry is in a small blue house in back of the Tea Room and features freshly baked pies, pastries, and gourmet coffees. Annie's Gift Shop, located in a third restored home across the street, offers for sale old-fashioned gifts, handmade items, fine linens, and antiques. This is a 13 room inn with all beds available. Five rooms have private baths; others share baths in hall. VCR. Bikes available. HANDICAPPED ACCESSIBLE. Children of all ages welcome. NO SMOKING.

**Rates:** $38, $48, $68 AND $88 DAILY.
**Reservations:** (214) 298-8586.

## JACKSONVILLE

A guesthouse on a small, beautiful LAKE in the rolling hills of east Texas. Separate from the main house and facing the lake, complete privacy is assured. A specialty of the house is the full country breakfast. Enjoy water skiing, swimming, bass and crappie fishing, or a ride on the hostess' pontoon boat to see a beautiful sunset. Good hiking trails and bikes are available. Take a ride on the Texas State Railroad from Rusk to Palestine to enjoy the foliage in the fall or dogwoods in the spring. Fishing, ceramics, oil painting, and woodcrafts keep the two hostesses busy. Pets include a Schnauzer, a Benji-type DOG, and a CAT. Hostesses do not smoke, but smokers are welcome. Jacksonville is 4 miles from Lake Jacksonville, 28 miles from Tyler, home of the beautiful Tyler Rose Gardens, and Palestine and the dogwood trails in the spring. UNHOSTED guesthouse. Accommodations include a king bed, private bath. Spanish is spoken here. Air conditioned. HANDICAPPED ACCESSIBLE.
**Rates:** $50 DAILY.
**Reservations:** (214) 298-8586.

HIGHWAY 69 NORTH — Two story Colonial home, beautifully decorated and situated on 27 1/2 heavily wooded acres. Home has fireplace and PIANO. Each room has a view of the woods. Guest bedroom opens onto covered deck with many hanging plants and small table and chairs for breakfast outdoors, if desired. Hiking trails lead to two old wagon trails used by early settlers. Spring fed creek runs through property with several small waterfalls and heavily laced with fern, moss, and other vegetation. It is 25 minutes to Tyler, home of the Rose Garden and Rose Parade. Host enjoys golf and reading; hostess enjoys cooking, crafts, and writing, and speaks Spanish. He also enjoys conducting tour of property with guests. NO SMOKERS. Accommodations include a double bed, private bath. Baby crib and cot available. PIANO.
**Rates:** S $40, D $45 DAILY.
**Reservations:** (214) 298-8586.

## JEFFERSON

LINE — This B&B inn is another example of the Victorian charm of historic Jefferson in beautiful east Texas. Overnight accommodations are available to individuals and small groups in a gracious, homelike atmosphere. Charming guestrooms, some with private baths, are furnished in turn-of-the-century antiques of oak and pine. The spacious parlor and sunporch provide additional comfort for the guests, who can enjoy the morning paper while savoring the aroma of the "best breakfast south of the Mason Dixon Line." This inn overlooks City Park and historic

churches. Easy walking distance to fine museums and most other attractions (Jefferson is the fifth oldest city in Texas). Host is in gaphic arts; hostess is a paralegal. Accommodations include: two rooms with private bath (one queen, one double); and four rooms that share two other baths (one queen, three doubles). Two CATS reside here. Air conditioned. Bikes available. Children of all ages welcome. SMOKING is not encouraged.
**Rates:** D $60 AND $70 DAILY. WEEKDAY DISCOUNTS SUNDAY THROUGH THURSDAY.
**Reservations:** (214) 298-8586.

## PALESTINE
### BOIS D'ARC COMMUNITY

Nestled in the heart of east Texas is this B&B house. Here easy country living is invited, either relaxing on the front porch while watching the deer graze in the field or the hummingbirds darting about. Or perhaps taking a stroll or paddle boat ride around the pond or a walk among the Christmas trees. Hearty breakasts are served with homemade breads and jellies, fresh farm eggs, and perhaps quail and gravy. For sleeping accommodations, there is a guesthouse with twin beds and bath. Convenient for antique shopping, historical sites, and steam engine rides. The spring dogwood trails are well known for their beauty and the fall foliage is spectacular. Convenient for Canton's First Monday Sales and Athens Blackeye Pea Festival. UNHOSTED guesthouse. Host is a CPA; hostess enjoys cooking, crafts, and calligraphy. Children welcome.
**Rates:** S $35, D $45 DAILY.
**Reservations:** (214) 298-8586.

## EAST TEXAS/PINEY WOODS
### WOODVILLE

FM ROAD 256 — This country home is spacious and inviting. Accommodations include: A) king-sized bed and B) queen-sized bed. Both with private bath. Also on the ranch property is a cabin that is available for use by guests. It is unhosted and without breakfast, and has two double beds. Extras include a TENNIS COURT on the property and a small SAUNA inside the main house. The FISHING LAKE a few yards from the house is well stocked. Nearby are Texas' only Indian reservation and the Big Thicket. Golf is only 5 minutes away. A PIANO is in the home. Air conditioned. Pool table. CHILDREN over 5 years old welcome.
**Rates:** A & B) $50 DAILY. $300 WEEKLY. COTTAGE $40 DAILY. $200 WEEKLY.
**Reservations:** (713) 868-4654 MONDAY THROUGH FRIDAY, 7:30 A.M. TO 9:00 P.M., SATURDAY AND SUNDAY 8:00 A.M. TO 5:00 P.M.

# GOLDEN SPREAD/PANHANDLE
## AMARILLO

HIGHLAND STREET — Contemporary home with flower garden. Host is retired from the automobile business; hostess is a registered nurse. Family oriented people who raised nine children and enjoy traveling the United States and visiting their children and grandchildren. Located close to airport, Amarillo Junior College, West Texas State University, Palo Duro Canyon State Park, and Boys Ranch. Large medical center and athletic facilities nearby. Have two double rooms and two single rooms available. One room with private bath and others have shared bath. Children welcome.
**Rates:** S $35, D $40 DAILY. S $150, D $200 WEEKLY.
**Reservations:** (214) 298-8586.

# GULF COAST
## ALVIN

COUNTY ROAD 146 — A large Contemporary home located in the midst of 9 1/2 acres south of Houston. Relax in a country atmosphere by the 50 foot POOL, gazing at the moon and stars as your ceiling. Spend the cooler nights relaxing in a completely enclosed HOT TUB. For businesspeople, an IBM computer is available for your use. Two VRCs are available for tape copying or entertainment. For sports or TV fans, a satellite dish and large screen TV provide a wide range of entertainment. Loft contains a pool table. Host is a mechanical engineer; hostess is a nurse anesthetist. They enjoy bowling. bridge, chess, and raise ST. BERNARDS for show. Close to five theaters. Car is needed. Centrally located to Astrodome, NASA, and GALVESTON. Accommodations include: A) two king beds, remote control TV, private bath; B) king bed, private bath; and C) trundle bed and queen-sized hide-a-bed available for larger groups.
**Rates:** A-C) S $25, D $35 DAILY.
**Reservations:** (713) 868-4654 MONDAY THROUGH FRIDAY, 7:30 A.M. TO 9:00 P.M., SATURDAY AND SUNDAY 8:00 A.M. TO 5:00 P.M.

## BACLIFF
## CLEAR LAKE AND NASA

BAYSHORE DRIVE SOUTH OF GRAND — A quaint FISHING VILLAGE located on Galveston Bay; exit front door of Contemporary one story home, pass swimming POOL and walk out on dock to witness glorious sunrises and sunsets. The fishing in the area is superb and restaurants abound. Hosts know all the good spots for recreation, touring, and eating. Johnson Space Center is 20 minutes north, Houston 35 minutes north, and Galveston 35 minutes south. House is barrier free. Hostess warns all to be careful of her friendly ST. BERNARD and

COLLIE who sleep in doorways to watch what is going on. Accommodations include a king bed and bath with own entrance A cot is also available. Join the family for meals or have the caterer hostess prepare a picnic lunch and rent a sailboat, go to the beach, or lounge around the clover shaped pool. Host is a chemical engineer; hostess is a psychologist and teacher. Children welcome.
**Rates:** S $45, D $50 DAILY.
**Reservations:** (713) 868-4654 MONDAY THROUGH FRIDAY, 7:30 A.M.. TO 9:00 P.M., SATURDAY AND SUNDAY 8:00 A.M. TO 5:00 P.M.

## BELLAIRE/GREATER HOUSTON

A modest urban home that provides comfortable, homey accommodations. The bedrooms feature family quilts and crocheted spreads. Although located in a quiet suburb, it is convenient to all Houston has to offer. Enjoy a breakfast of beignets and seasonal fruits. Unwind after a busy day with tea and hors d'oeuvres made with home grown herbs. Arrangements can be made for hostess to meet you at the airport or bus and for various tours around the area. Air conditioned. Bikes available. Accommodations include: A) double bed and B) single bed available for an extra guest. CHILDREN over 5 welcome. Light SMOKING is permitted.
**Rates:** A & B) S $25, D $35 DAILY.
**Reservations:** (713) 868-4654 MONDAY THROUGH FRIDAY, 7:30 A.M. TO 9:00 P.M., SATURDAY AND SUNDAY 8:00 A.M. TO 5:00 P.M.

## GALVESTON

Included in the many attractions of the Galveston area are the 1877 tall ship Elissa, Ashton Villa, Bishop's Palace, an 1894 Grand Opera House, Seawolf Park, and Sea-Arama Marine World. The restored Galveston Strand features fine restaurants and shopping and the famous Railroad Museum. The University of Texas boasts the state's first medical school in its Galveston location. Of interest to visitors are the Gulf of Mexico and Galveston Bay fishing and many water activities available year-round. Galveston has two major festivals, Dickens on the Strand (December) and Mardi Gras (February or March).

## SILK STOCKING HISTORIC DISTRICT

AVENUE K AT 24TH STREET — Built in 1907, this 7,500 square foot home is the only B&B in Galveston's Silk Stocking Historic District. The architecture is neo-Mediterranean, with arches over nine porches. The exterior is stucco, and the interior has been restored and furnished with antiques, many of which are family heirlooms. This home offers a step back in history when gracious living resulted from warm Southern hospitality. Restoration includes complete central air conditioning. The inn and gardens are surrounded by live oaks and palms, which provide shade and a place for croquet and badminton. The gardens also afford a seasonal birdwatching. Rates include a cheese tray in the afternoon and an abundant continental breakfast served in the dining room, your private balcony porch, or in your room. When you arrive, you will be 7 blocks from Galveston's historic downtown featuring the Strand shopping and sightseeing, and an equal distance from the seawall and beaches of the Gulf of Mexico. Exercise equipment is provided in the basement and bikes are provided. A sailboat is also used for excursions for guests. Accommodations are five bedrooms, one with private bath, and the other four sharing two baths. Bedrooms include: A) king-sized bed: B & C) two rooms each with double beds; D) king-sized bed; and E) 3/4 size bed. One DOG resides here. PIANO and VCR. CHILDREN over 12 welcome.

**Rates:** A) $125; B & C) $85; D) $95; AND E) S $60, D $75 DAILY.
**Reservations:** (713) 868-4654 MONDAY THROUGH FRIDAY, 7:30 A.M. TO 9:00 P.M., SATURDAY AND SUNDAY 8:00 A.M. TO 5:00 P.M.

## HOUSTON

Houston offers visitors the variety of attractions expected of one of the largest cities in the United States. Some of the most famous points of interest are the Johnson Space Center, NASA, the San Jacinto Battleground and Monument, the battleship Texas, the Houston Ship Channel, the Houston Zoo, and the Astrodome. Museums include Bayou Bend, Museum of Fine Arts, and the Natural Science Museum. The Houston Grand Opera, Ballet, and Symphony are among the finest in the nation, and from April through October Miller Outdoor Theater offers nightly productions free of charge. Houston has 18 art galleries and one or two festivals monthly throughout the year. Houston's world famous rodeo takes place in February. Shopping in Houston offers a full range from Oriental specialities in Chinatown to Mexican imports in El Mercado del Sol. Of course, Houston's Galleria has representation by every major retailer along with a huge ice skating rink and running track. Universities in Houston include the University of Houston, St. Thomas University, Rice University, and Houston Baptist. The Medical Center of Houston is without equal anywhere.

This comfortable, multilevel townhouse is situated on a secluded cul-de-sac in the Galleria area of Houston. It is within 2 miles of many of Houston's finest restaurants, shopping facilities, and churches; Memorial Park, offering an 18 hole golf course, lighted tennis courts, 3 mile jogging track, picnic grounds, swimming pool, nature trails; airport, bus terminal to both airports is nearby as is easy access to Loop 612 and Houston Metro bus lines. Your hostess is a secretary interested in travel, gardening, and walking. Accommodations include: A) twin beds, adjoining bath and

B) queen bed, private hall bath. Both baths have shower and tub. An upstairs sitting room is available for reading, visiting, or watching TV. NO CHILDREN or pets. SMOKING is permitted in the sitting room only.
**Rates:** S $35, D $45 DAILY.
**Reservations:** (713) 868-4654 MONDAY THROUGH FRIDAY, 7:30 A.M. TO 9:00 P.M., SATURDAY AND SUNDAY 8:00 A.M. TO 5:00 P.M.

## BRAESWOOD PLACE 610S LOOP

DURNESS BY BEECHNUT — A modern Ranch style brick house inside Loop 610. Older neighborhood with large trees. Host is a realtor. Hosts both enjoy having company, including children, and bowling. Very convenient to Medical Center, the Astrodome, 20 minutes to downtown Houston, 30 minutes to NASA. Accommodations include: A) double bed and B) twin beds. Both share a private guest bath. One CAT and a DOG reside here.
**Rates:** A & B) S $30, D $40 DAILY.
**Reservations:** (713) 868-4654 MONDAY THROUGH FRIDAY, 7:30 A.M. TO 9:00 P.M., SATURDAY AND SUNDAY 8:00 A.M. TO 5:00 P.M.

## GALLERIA

POST OAK AT 610 LOOP — This is a fully furnished two bedroom, with queen-sized beds, two bath condo unit which is the owner's home away from home. A cot is also available. Breakfast foods are provided for the guests to make breakfast. There is cable TV, telephone, POOL, and coin operated washer and dryer. Within walking distance there is the finest shopping and dining in Houston's Galleria area. UNHOSTED. A PIANO is on the premises. HANDICAPPED ACCESSIBLE.
**Rates:** D $60; WHOLE CONDO $75 DAILY.
**Reservations:** (713) 868-4654 MONDAY THROUGH FRIDAY, 7:30 A.M. TO 9:00 P.M., SATURDAY AND SUNDAY 8:00 A.M. TO 5:00 P.M.

RICHMOND AT SAGE — Originally an apartment community, this all suite hotel is truly unique. Service is the key motto for all personnel with the staff and regular corporate guests throwing weekend barbecues, attending ball games, and other social city functions. The small staff enjoys bowling, racquetball, tennis, basketball, swimming, dancing, and jogging. A complimentary continental breakfast is served daily and for those who prefer to have their first cup in the suite, a coffee pot is also provided with coffee supplied daily. Complimentary cocktails are served Monday through Thursday, guests and their guests are welcome. All 650 square feet, two room suites have private bedrooms, large living rooms with queen-sized sofa sleepers, dinette, and fully equipped kitchens. For at home entertainment, 30 channel cable TVs, two swimming POOLS, and access to a health spa are also available. Tennis, golf, racquetball,

jogging trail, airport bus terminal, and the famous Galleria mall are less than 5 minutes away. Air conditioned.
**Rates:** $45 DAILY.
**Reservations:** (713) 868-4654 MONDAY THROUGH FRIDAY, 7:30 A.M. TO 9:00 P.M., SATURDAY AND SUNDAY 8:00 A.M. TO 5:00 P.M.

WELLESLEY — Large, spacious home has three walls of glass looking out onto enclosed courtyard and large swimming POOL. Guests are invited to use pool, cabana room, TENNIS COURTS, kitchen, and other living areas. Bedroom is large with queen-sized bed, white bear rug, telephone, couch, and desk. Bed is brass, covered with quilt, decorated in comforting pastels. Private bath has shower and large tub. TV and air conditioning. Style of decor is southwestern with southwest and Indian art. Host is corporate president; hostess is homemaker/fitness advoacate. Hobby is travel. No pets. Resident pets: one fish, two white YORKSHIRE TERRIERS, trained and caged. Home is Contemporary with 5,000 sqare feet in very exclusive area. Walk to restaurants and shopping. Near Galleria Mall, Arboretum, Memorial Park, Astrodome, Astro World, Galveston Beach, NASA, museums, Goodyear Blimp Headquarters. NO SMOKERS.
**Rates:** S $50, D $60, ADDITIONAL ADULTS $10 DAILY.
**Reservations:** (214) 298-8586.

## GLENBROOK NEAR HOBBY AIRPORT

GLENLOCH AT BELLPORT — A large Colonial home in a quiet neighborhood with lovely landscaping and 25 foot inground POOL. The backyard is wooded with a deck overlooking a small spring fed creek. Small GREENHOUSE. This home is furnished with antiques including a grand PIANO in a 30 foot sunroom. Small den has fireplace, TV, and VCR. Inside deck overlooks pool and wooded area. Can be used as reading area or quiet room. Some exercise equipment is available. Host and hostess are retired florists who enjoy horticulture, antiques, traveling, and church activities. Accommodations include: A) double bed, private bath on main level; B) upstairs twin bed, shared bath; C) double bed, shared bath with B or host family bath. B & C are suitable for a family with children. A playpen is available. Easy access to freeways and inner loop around Houston. Ten minutes to downtown, 20 minutes to Medical Center and Astrodome, 30 minutes to NASA, 45 minutes to Galveston, 5 minutes to Hobby airport, and 10 minutes to Intercontinental airport. A full breakfast in dining room, sunroom, or by the pool. Air conditioned. PETS welcome. Children of all ages welcome.
**Rates:** A-C) S $30, D $35 DAILY.
**Reservations:** (713) 868-4654 MONDAY THROUGH FRIDAY, 7:30 A.M. TO 9:00 P.M., SATURDAY AND SUNDAY 8:00 A.M. TO 5:00 P.M.

## HOUSTON HEIGHTS

HEIGHTS BOULEVARD OFF INTERSTATE 10 — A beautiful home on a boulevard in Houston's oldest residential section. Decor in 1890s Victorian and older, completed by lace curtains, crocheted bedspreads, and claw-foot bathtubs. Other vintage attractions are a tandem bike for guest use, a player PIANO, and a front porch with swing and wicker furniture. A full breakfast is served daily with homebaked muffins. Host speaks German and understands some Spanish. Accommodations include: A) double bed and B) twin-sized bed. One DOG is in residence here. Host is in marketing; hostess is an antique dealer. NO SMOKERS. CHILDREN over 12 accepted.
**Rates:** A) S $35, D $45 AND B) S $35 DAILY.
**Reservations:** (713) 868-4654 MONDAY THROUGH FRIDAY, 7:30 A.M. TO 9:00 P.M., SATURDAY AND SUNDAY 8:00 A.M. TO 5:00 P.M.

## MEMORIAL

MEMORIAL DRIVE/WEST BELT — This home is located in the suburbs to the west of central Houston. The grounds are beautifully landscaped and there are flowers year-round. The accommodations include twin beds with crocheted spreads, private hall bath. It offers quiet comfort with a lovely view. Your hosts are a retired couple who are active in church activities and traveling. The home has a PIANO and many antique Oriental rugs. Guests may use the community swimming POOL on the next block. Well-behaved PETS welcome.
**Rates:** S $30, D $35 DAILY.
**Reservations:** (713) 868-4654 MONDAY THROUGH FRIDAY, 7:30 A.M. TO 9:00 P.M., SATURDAY AND SUNDAY 8:00 A.M. TO 5:00 P.M.

## MEYERLAND/BRAESMONT, BY LOOP 610

GRAPE STREET OFF BEECHNUT — A traditional, French Provincial style home. Your hostess is retired, loves people, and likes to welcome you to her abode. It is comfortably furnished with soft colors, sofas, lounge chairs, a baby grand PIANO, fireplace in den, plate collection. and ceramics. Convenient to the Galleria, Astrodome, Medical Center. Westbury Square, and the Summit. Easy access to NASA and Galveston. Very convenient to LOOP 610 and Interstate 59. Accommodations include two rooms each with double bed. Both share a private guest bath. CHILDREN over 10 welcome.
**Rates:** S $30, D $35 DAILY.
**Reservations:** (713) 868-4654 MONDAY THROUGH FRIDAY, 7:30 A.M. TO 9:00 P.M., SATURDAY AND SUNDAY 8:00 A.M. TO 5:00 P.M.

## MONTROSE

RIDGEWOOD AT VERMONT — A cute cottage beside the main house in a quiet older neighborhood. The furnishings are English Country and reflect the owner's New Zealand heritage. The apartment comes equipped with shower and tub, twin beds, and private patio for breakfast or sunbathing. The owner is a world traveler who loves art, antiques, cooking, and gardening. She owns three placid CATS and has a 16 year old daughter living at home. Air conditioned. HOT TUB. HANDICAPPED ACCESSIBLE. A gourmet continental or vegetarian breakfast is available. Kitchen privileges are also available. Children welcome. SMOKING outdoors on patios only.
**Rates:** S $30, D $40 DAILY.
**Reservations:** (713) 868-4654 MONDAY THROUGH FRIDAY, 7:30 A.M. TO 9:00 P.M.. SATURDAY AND SUNDAY 8:00 A.M. TO 5:00 P.M.

WOODROW — A 1920s bungalow, updated in colors of the French Impressionist painters and furnished with pieces from New Orleans and Kentucky. Its inner city location is minutes to downtown Houston, the Museum Corner, the Astrodome, Medical Center, Herman Park, and several universities. Walk to turn-of-the-century mansions, highrise condos, miniature parks, sidewalk cafes, glimpses of the downtown skyline, wide spreading live oaks, elegant restaurants, jazz spots, and jogging paths. Transportation choices include: Metro bus line and the freeway system. Your hostess, a social worker, serves continental breakfast in the mauve dining room and enthusiastically directs guests to favorite spots in the city. A yellow tabby CAT also greets guests. Accommodations include twin beds with private attached bath. CHILDREN over 12 welcome.
**Rates:** S $30, D $35 DAILY.
**Reservations:** (713) 868-4654 MONDAY THROUGH FRIDAY, 7:30 A.M. TO 9:00 P.M., SATURDAY AND SUNDAY 8:00 A.M. TO 5:00 P.M.

## MONTROSE-AVONDALE

STRATFORD AT HELENA — A gracious Victorian three story mansion in a historic neighborhood adjoining downtown Houston. It is within walking distance of restaurants, museums, art galleries, and antique shops. Morning coffee or afternoon tea is served on the front porch, which wraps around the house and is conspicuous for its wicker swing and rocker. Full breakfast is served in the first floor garden room. Accommodations include two full apartments: A second floor, large double bed and private sitting room with daybed and trundle, private bath and kitchen; B) third floor, two double beds and bath, kitchen and a breathtaking view of downtown Houston. Hostess is an interior designer who does research for the Historical Society. CHILDREN over 12 welcome.

**Rates:** A & B) S $30, D $40 DAILY.
**Reservations:** (713) 868-4654 MONDAY THROUGH FRIDAY, 7:30 A.M. TO 9:00 P.M., SATURDAY AND SUNDAY 8:00 A.M. TO 5:00 P.M.

## NORTH CHANNEL AREA

WHITE CEDAR — A special guest getaway room, both enchanting and private, was built as a B&B area over the garage of this Contemporary home east of Houston. A full bath with antique claw-footed tub is part of this guestroom. Inside the main house there are two more rooms for guests. Accommodations include: A) queen-sized bed; B) double bed; and C) twin beds. An unusually large living area with a center fireplace and a shaded patio provide many locations for dining and relaxing. This stunning home is near the world famous Gilley's and the Houston Ship Channel. PIANO available, as are bikes. NO CHILDREN.
**Rates:** $30-$35 DAILY.
**Reservations:** (713) 868-4654 MONDAY THROUGH FRIDAY, 7:30 A.M. TO 9:00 P.M., SATURDAY AND SUNDAY 8:00 A.M. TO 5:00 P.M.

## SHARPSTOWN

A one story home with 32 foot inground POOL, 25 minutes to Rice and the University of Houston, 20 minutes to downtown and Medical Center, and 10 minutes to the Galleria. Convenient to bus. A public golf course is only 5 minutes away. Walk to New Chinatown. Accommodations include a queen-sized bed with private bath. Your hostess has a small DOG. A large homemade breakfast is served. Hostess is an office manager who enjoys cooking and travel. No SMOKERS.
**Rates:** S $30, D $35 DAILY.
**Reservations:** (713) 868-4654 MONDAY THROUGH FRIDAY, 7:30 A.M. TO 9:00 P.M., SATURDAY AND SUNDAY 8:00 A.M. TO 5:00 P.M.

## SOUTHWEST MEMORIAL/GALLERIA

OFF VOSS — A large, luxurious old English townhome furnished with antiques, convenient to excellent shopping, (Neiman Marcus, Macy's, and Saks Fifth Avenue) and many fine restaurants. A private Pool for B&B guests' use is only half a block away. Breakfast is served on a banquet-sized table in the formal dining room that looks into the indoor garden and fountain area. Host is a builder designer; hostess is a local and national tour guide. When at home, she is available for guided tours of the city and surrounding area including San Jacinto Museum and Monument, Galveston, NASA, and other closeby historical sites. Both hosts enjoy bridge, sports, and sailing. Oilers tickets are available. For the music lover, the formal living room is furnished with a baby grand PIANO. During the holiday season, the home is decorated with nine different Christmas trees, one per room. This townhome was featured in

a local newspaper last year as "The Christmas House." Accommodations include: A) master suite with king bed, fireplace, and small kitchen and bath, B) twin beds, and C) antique double bed. Guests share a connecting bath. A crib and cot are available. Air conditioned.
Rates: S $40, D $50-$60 DAILY.
Reservations: (713) 868-4654 MONDAY THROUGH FRIDAY, 7:30 A.M. TO 9:00 P.M., SATURDAY AND SUNDAY 8:00 A.M. TO 5:00 P.M.

## SPRING BRANCH

NEAR GESSNER, NORTH OF INTERSTATE 10 — Contemporary French style home furnished with country accents. Hostess has many interests, including crafts, antiques, and seashells. They all add to the warmth of the home. Host is a U.S. postal inspector and enjoys sports, especially baseball and football. Accommodations include a four poster double bed with a large private hall bath. The home is located near two large shopping malls and many good restaurants. Public transportation is within 1 block and tennis courts are in walking distance. A large public park, swimming pool, library, running track, and athletic fields are within 2 miles. PIANO. Host smokes and smokers are welcome. No pets or young CHILDREN.
Rates: S $25, D $35 DAILY.
Reservations: (713) 868-4654 MONDAY THROUGH FRIDAY, 7:30 A.M. TO 9:00 P.M., SATURDAY AND SUNDAY 8:00 A.M. TO 5:00 P.M.

## WOODLAKE

GESSNER AT WESTHEIMER — A charming townhouse in a community featuring a beautifully landscaped all adult swimming POOL, complete HOT TUB, JACUZZI, as well as two family swimming pools. There are lovely wooded hiking trails, four lighted TENNIS COURTS, four racquetball courts, and convenient parking next to the house. It is convenient to the Galleria, Memorial City, and town and country shopping centers as well as to the heart of the southwest Houston business center. Bus transportation to all parts of the city. Your hostess is an executive secretary with a seismic exploration company. Her 14 year old daughter is in high school and enjoys horseback riding and participates in hunter/jumper competitions. This home is a quiet and cozy retreat in a bustling city. A racing bike is available for hire. Breakfast features homemade English scones with jam and cream as a specialty, and a full English breakfast on weekends that includes grilled mushrooms and tomatoes, and even kipper herrings for the adventurous! Accommodations include: A) double bed, private bath and B) double bed, shared family bath. Children welcome.
Rates: A) S $30, D $35 AND B) S $25, D $30 DAILY.
Reservations: (713) 868-4654 MONDAY THROUGH FRIDAY, 7:30 A.M. TO 9:00 P.M., SATURDAY AND SUNDAY 8:00 A.M. TO 5:00 P.M.

## INDUSTRY
### BLUEBONNET TRAIL

MAIN STREET — Circa 1900 restored farmhouse is located in the "Bluebonnet Trail" area on 1 acre with fruit and pecan trees. The home is furnished with antiques and includes a library. It is within walking distance from an antique store, a country store, and a small park with historical site. Located just 10 minutes from two very large lakes. Also located very close to many other historical towns and sites. Great area for biking. Hostess loves cooking and music (bring your instruments). Relaxed and comfortable atmosphere. Your choice of hearty continental or country style breakfast. Accommodations include: A) double bed; and B & C) suite with two double-bedded rooms. A little Spanish is spoken here. Hostess is a bank officer. One DOG, two CATS, and four birds live here. WELL-BEHAVED PETS ARE WELCOME. CHILDREN over 2 years old welcome.
**Rates:** A & B) D $50 AND C) D $65 DAILY.
**Reservations:** (713) 868-4654 MONDAY THROUGH FRIDAY, 7:30 A.M. TO 9:00 P.M., SATURDAY AND SUNDAY 8:00 A.M. TO 5:00 P.M.

## MAGNOLIA
### RURAL, NORTHWEST HOUSTON

Ten year old New England Colonial farmhouse on 50 acres furnished with antiques. Half heavily wooded, other half cattle and horse pasture, with 5 acre lake and swimming POOL. Host has own chemical brokerage. Daughters aged 13 and 10 are both Suzuki musicians. Violin and flute. Accommodations include: A) queen-sized bed, attached bath, attached sitting room with color TV, FIREPLACE and B) twin beds, bath next to but not connected, living room with fireplace. Kitchen facilities (not family kitchen) also available. Tennis nearby. Hostess invites guests to play at club, time permitting. Automobile essential but Metro to downtown Houston comes twice daily. It is 20 minutes to every kind of shopping. Annual Texas Renaissance Festival (October). Spanish is spoken here. Three DOGS reside here. HANDICAPPED ACCESSIBLE.
**Rates:** S OR D $60 DAILY.
**Reservations:** (713) 868-4654 MONDAY THROUGH FRIDAY, 7:30 A.M. TO 9:00 P.M., SATURDAY AND SUNDAY 8:00 A.M. TO 5:00 P.M.

## PASADENA
### HOUSTON SUBURB

CORNER FLORENCE: FLYNN — A warm, informal, two story house that welcomes travelers and makes them friends. The bedrooms are upstairs, private and very large, complete with comfortable couches and chairs, TV, and books. The bath is shared with the other bedroom. There is a large fenced backyard. PETS ARE WELCOME if they are like other

pets who think they are people. There is always a new crop of kittens
out in the backyard. Privacy, accessibility to downtown Houston,
Galveston and the Bay, the chemical companies, and the ship channel
area; near NASA, Hobby Airport, University of Houston, and the
Astrodome, as well as the Medical Center and Galveston Hospital. Be a
part of the family (scrabble tournaments are a specialty) or enjoy the
privacy of your own comfortable room with queen-sized bed. Hostess is
an office manager who enjoys needlework and walking. Two DOGS reside
here, too. Air conditioned. Children welcome.
**Rates:** S $35, D $40 DAILY. SPECIAL DISCOUNTS FOR FAMILIES
OF PEOPLE BEING TREATED AT MEDICAL CENTER.
**Reservations:** (214) 298-8586.

## SEABROOK
### THE WATERFRONT

11TH STREET — A Small WATERFRONT cottage facing Galveston Bay
and Clear Creek. Offers an ongoing view of ships in the distance and
colorful shrimp boats unloading their catch across the way. The house is
furnished Cape Cod style with antiques and a large kitchen with large
fireplace where breakfast is served family style. Host is a building
designer; hostess is a local and national tour guide. When at home she is
available for guided tours of the local area including San Jacinto Museum
and Monument, Galveston, NASA, and the Houston area. Both hosts
enjoy bridge and sailing. Activities, such as swimming and tennis, are
available for guests at nearby yacht club. Bay fishing charters are only a
half mile away and several seafood restaurants are within walking distance.
Hosts invite guests to join them for a day of sailing should schedule and
weather permit. During fall and spring breakfast is usually served on the
large veranda that surrounds two sides of this quaint 50 year old bayside
cottage. Accommodations include: A) two rooms each with double bed
and B) upstairs loft with two double beds and one twin-sized bed.
CHILDREN over 6 years old welcome.
**Rates:** S OR D $40 WINTER; $50 SUMMER DAILY.
**Reservations:** (713) 868-4654 MONDAY THROUGH FRIDAY, 7:30 A.M.
TO 9:00 P.M., SATURDAY AND SUNDAY 8:00 A.M. TO 5:00 P.M.

## HILL COUNTRY
### AUSTIN
### BARTON CREEK

STEARNS — Charming, efficiency apartment adjacent to host home
offers complete privacy. Breakfast is stocked in refrigerator; there is also
hot plate, coffee maker, toaster, and electric skillet in kitchenette. Linens
in soft burgundy and rose for double sofa-bed. An additional single foldout
chair bed in apartment. Crib available. Shower only, private bath.

Telephone, off-street parking, and laundry facilities available. Air conditioned. Alcohol in moderation okay. Apartment 400 square feet. Home is 18 year old Ranch style. Quiet 2 acre refuge just inside Austin city limits. Enjoy the deck patio overlooking the yard with hiking trails to Barton Creek and an original Austin homestead now reduced to stone walls. Listen to owls, mourning doves, and watch racoons and possums come to be fed by two sons. HANDICAPPED ACCESSIBLE. Host is an attorney; hostess is a social worker. Spanish and Japanese are spoken here. UNHOSTED. NO CHILDREN, except babies. SMOKING outside. **Rates:** S $40, D $45, $10 ADDITIONAL ADULT, $5 ADDITIONAL CHILD DAILY. $150 WEEKLY.
**Reservations:** (214) 298-8586.

## ONION CREW

Located 12 miles south of downtown Austin and 45 minute drive to LBJ Ranch. Near Canyon Lake for tubing and canoeing. Accommodations include private bath, twin beds, use of living room, dining room, and kitchen. Full breakfast on weekends. Continental breakfast on weekdays. Fresh fruit and homemade breads served. Swimming POOL on property. Bikes available. Wonderful park, pond with ducks and swans, golf, and tennis nearby. Craft shows and flea markets scheduled throughout the year. Airport pickup.
**Rates:** S $35, D $40 DAILY. SPECIAL WEEKLY RATES ON REQUEST.
**Reservations:** (214) 298-8586.

## UNIVERSITY AREA

WOODRAW NEAR 38TH STREET — A charming older home surrounded by large trees, grass, gardens; a half acre of green in the heart of the city. Two room suite on the second floor overlooks backyard, creek and pecan trees; main room has queen bed, sleeping porch has queen hide-a-bed. Guests are invited to enjoy the fireplace in the living room; a PIANO is available in the library; ceiling fans throughout the house add comfort and charm. Enjoy breakfast out on the gazebo hung with plants and birdfeeders: bring your birdbook and binoculars or borrow from hosts. The whole family shares a special interest in visitors from other countries. Sons are aged 8 and 15, daughter 13. Within walking distance to University of Texas; minutes from downtown business and historic sites; on the edge of the hill country and highland lakes. Just off Interstate 35, 8 minutes from airport, 3 blocks from city bus. Children of all ages welcome. SMOKING is not permitted in the guestrooms.
**Rates:** S $40, D $45; 2 ROOM SUITE $60 DAILY.
**Reservations:** (214) 298-8586.

# BUCHANAN DAM
## LAKE BUCHANAN

Large, LAKEFRONT home on 2 acres with SWIMMING POOL, private fishing pier, and boat ramp. This spacious house, located on Lake Buchanan in Highland Lakes Hill country, was built around the concept of entertaining in style and comfort. It features: three bedrooms with king-sized beds, ceiling fans, and private bathrooms; use of expansive living and dining areas with panoramic view of lake; and modern kitchen with all amenities. Golf courses, fishing, state park, caves, Falls Creek Winery, and Vanishing Texas River Cruise located nearby. The American bald eagle nests in the area from November through March and package deals are available for Vanishing Texas River Cruise Eagle Expeditions. Breakfast is served on poolside deck when weather permits. Air conditioned. Host is in investments, enjoys water skiing, and scuba diving; hostess also enjoys scuba diving.
**Rates:** S OR D $80 DAILY.
**Reservations:** (713) 868-4654 MONDAY THROUGH FRIDAY, 7:30 A.M. TO 9:00 P.M., SATURDAY AND SUNDAY 8:00 A.M. TO 5:00 P.M.

# UTOPIA
## RURAL

HIGHWAY FM 1050 — A private cabin on a creek in a secluded corner of this 260 acre ranch home is now available for guests. In the complete kitchen breakfast will be left in the refrigerator. Cabin will accommodate six people; host home will also sleep four adults. Host is retired from the Air Force; hostess is a story teller of local historical legends. They build and put out bluebird boxes to attract birds to their ranch. Hummingbirds by the dozen flock to the feeders. Near Gardner State Park and the Frio River, 1 hour to San Antonio. Perfect for those who wish complete privacy and rest for recuperation. Two night minimum. Accommodations include: A) queen bed, Queen Anne furnishings, love seat, wicker chair and B) queen sofabed in library. Will only let second room when four people are traveling together. Guestrooms have beautiful views and the two rooms share a bath. Cabin is UNHOSTED. SMOKERS outside.
**Rates:** A) S OR D $65 AND B) S OR D $50 DAILY.
**Reservations:** (214) 298-8586.

HIGHWAY FM 1050 — Early Texas homestead cabin, with tin roof, circa 1840, romantic, hideaway that provides privacy, peace, and tranquility. Open beams, bare floors, skin rugs. Claw-foot red bathtub (shower). Antiques, complete kitchen, beaded ceiling in kitchen and bath. No telephone, no TV. Separate from main ranch house, 250 acres, excellent viewing for birds, deer, wild hogs, armadillos, and fall foliage. Hiking and mountain climbing on property. Swimming and tubing in Frio and Sabinal Rivers. Garner State Park 4 minutes, Lost Maple Nature

Area, tennis, horse riding, antiquing, fruit picking within 30 minutes, village, where there are restaurants, is 15 minutes away. Host is a rancher and potter; hostess is a writer/storyteller. She enjoys baking bread and pastries and breakfast is prepared for you. Both enjoy square dancing, horticulture, and gourmet cooking. Accommodations include: A) loft with king-sized bed, view up the creek; B) 3/4 width antique Betsy Ross bed in main room circa 1840; and C) log room, extra long twin bed, antique daybed converts to sleep two, wing back rocker, FIREPLACE, game table, antique decor. The cabin itself is rented to 1 party of up to 8 people.

**Rates:** CABIN S OR D $65, EACH ADDITIONAL PERSON ADD $5 UP TO EIGHT PEOPLE. $364 WEEKLY FOR TWO PLUS $5 EACH EXTRA PERSON PER DAY.

**Reservations:** (713) 868-4654 MONDAY THROUGH FRIDAY, 7:30 A.M. TO 9:00 P.M., SATURDAY AND SUNDAY 8:00 A.M. TO 5:00 P.M.

## WIMBERLEY
### HILL COUNTRY-RANCHES

ROUTE 183 — Great getaway ranch 30 miles southwest of Austin and San Marcos. A queen-sized sofa bed and a double waterbed, with a private bath. POOL is available for warm weather visitors; fishing in the private LAKE. Gourmet breakfast of eggs and cheese casserole, fruit cup, sausage, coffee, tea, or milk. DOGS and farm animals live here. Air conditioned. CHILDREN over 6 welcome.

**Rates:** D $50 DAILY.

**Reservations:** (214) 298-8586.

# HISTORIC WASHINGTON COUNTRY
## BURTON
### RANCH AND HORSE COUNTRY

HIGHWAY FM 390 — Texas hospitality in a luxury home copied inside and out from Old World chalets. Outside the balcony, fretwork, and window boxes with geraniums are a picture of Europe. Inside the stair and loft railings copied from a centuries old house in Norway, the German crystal chandelier in the dining room, the paintings, and the paneled and boxed ceiling in the family room continue the continental theme. Central air conditioning and heat, ceiling fans, a fireplace, and a hearthstone woodburning heater are here, as are family heirlooms, European antiques, and mementos from 27 years of military service. Bouquets in all rooms from flower gardens with more than 70 rose bushes. This 175 acre cattle ranch overlooks Lake Somerville. A big Texas ranchhands breakfast is served in a formal setting of china, crystal, and silver. Gourmet lunches and dinners are available by prior arrangement. Host is an attorney, a retired U.S. Army Colonel, a rancher, and a free-lance writer; hostess

has been a teacher. Both converse in German. The area is rich in history. Accommodations include: A) twin beds, private bath; B) double bed, private bath; and C) sitting rooms adjoining-bedrooms have hide-a-beds for family members or groups who can share baths. Family room with hide-a-bed shares bath with hosts. PIANO. SMOKING is not permitted in bedrooms.
**Rates:** A & B) D $60 AND C) D $45 DAILY.
**Reservations:** (713) 868-4654 MONDAY THROUGH FRIDAY, 7:30 A.M. TO 9:00 P.M., SATURDAY AND SUNDAY 8:00 A.M. TO 5:00 P.M.

## LACOSTE

Historical hotel reopens and looks similiar to when it was originally built in 1890. Just 18 miles from San Antonio, this small town is a weekend getaway at its best. Antiques have been used throughout the restoration. Three bedrooms offer king-sized, queen, and double beds. Each has a private bath and a sitting area on the upstairs veranda. Breakfast is included in the price, lunches and dinners are extra. Enjoy high tea or hear the hostess play classical guitar for dinner guests in the evening. Hosts lived in Europe for seven years and are thrilled to welcome all to their lovely new inn. NO CHILDREN. SMOKING limited.
**Rates:** S $40, D $45 DAILY.
**Reservations:** (214) 298-8586.

## LAKE RAY HUBBARD
## ROCKWALL
## HEATH

DARR ESTATES OFF FM ROAD — Near Lake Hubbard, this is a two story salt box country cottage built on a landscaped acre. Large native trees shade yard's picnic area. Two upstairs bedrooms, one with king-sized bed, the other with two twins. Both have private access to full bath in hall. A downstairs half bath is exclusively for guests' use as well. Though most prefer breakfast in den viewing woods behind, coffee, juice, and homemade blueberry muffins may be enjoyed on a bedroom tray. Bright chintz prints dominate the decor. Single, employed hostess has sewn most drapes and bedspreads and gardening is her hobby. It is 26 miles on scenic country roads to TV's "Dallas" Southfork Ranch, with tours from $2 to $8 365 days a year. The Texas Queen, a touring paddle wheeler, Captain's Cove Fishing Barge, and the Shores Golf Course are located on the lake. Friendly female Lhasa Apso DOG will greet you. Home is accessible on Interstates 20 and 30 east of Dallas (30 miles). Children of all ages welcome, there is no specific baby equipment available.
**Rates:** S $35, D $40 DAILY.
**Reservations:** (214) 298-8586.

# LAKE TEXOMA
## DENISON
### GRANDPAPPY POINT MARINA

HIGHWAY 84/BOATHOUSE 30 — A sparkling 51 foot blue water motor YACHT, for a unique, romantic B&B with Texas brunch and morning cruise on beautiful Lake Texoma which borders Texas/Oklahoma, 60 miles north of Dallas. It has two staterooms complete with bath facilities. Your hosts each operate their own business during the week and invite you to enjoy a portion of your weekend with them. An optional, but very popular, gourmet dinner cruise is offered. One and a half hours north from Dallas and northwest of Denison, Texas, Highway 84 West leads you 8 miles to Pappy's Store, left past the Point Restaurant to the first boat house parking lot, over breakwater via wooden walkway to end of boat house, third yacht on right after reaching blue carpet. Operated all year. Air conditioned. CHILDREN and pets are not permitted in this romantic environment. SMOKING is permitted topside.
**Rates:** GOURMET DINNER CRUISE $250/COUPLE PER NIGHT INCLUDING B&B.
**Reservations:** (214) 298-8586.

# MID CITIES
## HURST

PLEASANTVIEW DRIVE — This home with backyard SPA is conventional and situated in a residential neighborhood. There are two guest bedrooms with bathroom/shower in the hall. One large bedroom with twin beds and ceiling fan; the other a double bed with canopy and French Provincial furniture. If both rooms are in use the bath is shared by guests. A large den is available with fireplace. TV, VCR, and comfortable couches to relax on. Coffee, cold drinks, dessert always available. Hosts' motto is "make yourself at home." The hosts are avid world travelers and especially welcome visitors from abroad. Geographically situated between Dallas and Fort Worth with easy access to a main freeway to either city or airport. Six Flags Over Texas approximately 20 minutes away. Hosts will collect and deliver guests to the airport for a reasonable fee. Children of all ages welcome. NO SMOKING.
**Rates:** S $35, D $40 DAILY.
**Reservations:** (214) 298-8586.

# MISSOURI CITY
## QUAIL VALLEY

LA COSTA, AT PEBBLE BEACH — A one story Colonial home in southwest Houston. The property is well shaded and the backyard is lovely for sitting on the patio and relaxing. There is a small electric ORGAN and a VCR available for guest use. The hostess is an insurance

coordinator for 10 doctors. She reads Tarot cards and collects unicorns. Her breakfast specialty is blueberry muffins. HANDICAPPED ACCESSIBLE. Air conditioned. Accommodations include queen bed with private hall bath. NONSMOKERS ONLY.
**Rates:** S $25, D $35 DAILY.
**Reservations:** (713) 868-4654 MONDAY THROUGH FRIDAY, 7:30 A.M. TO 9:00 P.M., SATURDAY AND SUNDAY 8:00 A.M. TO 5:00 P.M.

# NORTH CENTRAL TEXAS
## WICHITA FALLS
### COUNTRY CLUB

MIRAMAR — The guesthouse is nestled under massive pecan trees behind a Southern Colonial home built when the town was only 40 years old. It is decorated in authentic antiques, oil paintings, and Oriental rugs. The host is an oil producer/attorney; the hostess collects antiques. The guest suite includes bedroom with twin beds, sitting room, breakfast room, and bath. The hostess enjoys serving gourmet continental breakfasts of homemade breads, jellies, and fresh orange juice. The home is convenient to public tennis and golf, state university, several shopping malls, and is near several recreational and fishing lakes. Accessible by commercial airline, bus, and several highways. One CAT and one DOG live here, both outside. Teenage children live at home. Air conditioned. TV. NO SMOKING. CHILDREN are not encouraged but can bring their own bedrolls for floor.
**Rates:** S $35, D $55 DAILY.
**Reservations:** (214) 298-8586.

# NORTHEAST TEXAS
## ROYSE CITY

SOUTH HOUSTON STREET — A two story white Victorian house with white picket fence, wraparound porch on rear of house, and upstairs balcony. The home is furnished with antiques and contemporary furniture. Family history to the early days of Dallas gives a personal sparkle to the meaning of "Native Texan." Host is a teacher and mayor of Royse City; hostess is also a teacher and free-lance artist. Both love to travel. Guests will stay in upstairs bedroom furnished with two twin four poster, antique beds, adjoining sitting room, balcony, and bath. Small rural community within minutes of two large lakes, Caddo Mills and Soaring, and within 25 minutes of Dallas Metroplex. No indoor pets. Air conditioned. VCR. Children welcome. NO SMOKING.
**Rates:** S $38, D $45 DAILY.
**Reservations:** (214) 298-8586.

# PARKER COUNTY
## ALEDO

Brick and shingle home with lovely view on 28 acres in the rolling Texas ranch land, 20 minutes west of Fort Worth. Wooded hiking trail on property and you may see deer and wild turkey. General Dynamics, Carswell Air Force Base, and Opera House, and west Fort Worth with restaurants within easy 20 minute drive; and historic Granbury museums, theaters, gardens, and historic old Fort Worth 30 minute drive. Accommodations include: A) large country room, queen bed, private entrance, private bath and shower, decorated with antique furniture and B) smaller room with private hall bath for teenager or adult. Crib, highchair and play equipment provided. Country breakfast provided; dinner available with advance arrangements. No pets. Washer and dryer available. Host is a retired teacher (history and social science). Air conditioned. Nonsmokers preferred. Children of all ages welcome.
**Rates:** A) S $35, D $45 AND B) S $20 DAILY.
**Reservations:** (214) 298-8586.

# SOUTH CENTRAL TEXAS
## NEW BRAUNFELS
### COUNTRYSIDE

INTERSTATE H35 EXIT: LAKE McQUEENEY — Snuggle into this cozy double bed bedroom with brand new mattress, but lovely restored antiques otherwise. Private bath. Home is new, hosts are owners of an antique shop in town and will offer 10% on anything they sell to their B&B guest. Hostess serves a choice of breakfast, either wurst and eggs (German) or taquitas (omelettes wrapped up in a flour burrito (Mexican)). They will help with tips on canoeing or rafting in the Guadalupe or Comal Rivers. CHILDREN over the age of 12 welcome. SMOKERS will be asked to use the porch. No cigars.
**Rates:** S $50, D $60 DAILY.
**Reservations:** (214) 298-8586.

# SOUTH TEXAS
## SAN ANTONIO
### 4 MINUTES FROM DOWNTOWN

HAGGIN AT PALMETTO — Just a unique "Hacienda from the 1920s," with antique and contemporary furnishings, inground swimming POOL (20 × 30 feet). Hosts initiated the horsedrawn carriage trade in San Antonio, offering sightseeing tours to historic downtown and Mission Trail. Riding and driving training is available in the nearby stable. Bikes, morning gymnastics fitness, or fencing only on schedule. Breakfast is poolside, front porch, dining room, or in your room. Relax in the multicultural library with books and records, chess, or cards. Host speaks Swedish,

Norwegian, Danish; hostess speaks Hungarian, German, Russian, and a little French. Accommodations include: A) king-sized bed; B) twin beds in the Blue Room; and C) double bed. **Rates:** S $40, D $55 DAILY. S, D, OR T $280 WEEKLY. **Reservations:** (214) 298-8586.

## FORT SAM HOUSTON HISTORICAL DISTRICT

PIERCE AT GRAYSON STREET — This inn, a registered Texas Historic Landmark, is in a large white mansion built in 1909 for famed cavalryman General John L. Bullis. The large columned home was designed in the Neoclassical style, and has geometrically patterned floors of fine woods, chandeliers, marble fireplaces, and decorative 14 foot ceilings within. A spacious veranda surrounds much of the home. Host is a former engineer; hostess is an artist. Both enjoy travel, canoeing, hiking, and camping. There are a total of eight guestrooms, several with FIREPLACES, and some with private baths. Several rooms are equipped for families. Enjoy special continental breakfast in your room, the parlor, or veranda. No pets. This inn is next door to historic Fort Sam Houston and army museums. The Alamo, Riverwalk, and downtown are a short 2 miles away (10 minutes by city bus). Closeby are golf, tennis courts, art and natural history museums, and the zoo. Convenient to both Interstate 35 and US 281. Bikes available. Air conditioning. Spanish is spoken here. Children welcome. **Rates:** A & B) S $39, D $45; C & E) S $33, D $39; G) S $26, D $32; AND D & H) S $22, D $28 DAILY. A & B) S $201, D $252; C & E) S $161, D $217; G) S $136, D $172; AND D & H) S $116, D $157 WEEKLY (WITH BREAKFAST). A & B) S $180, D $210; C & E) S $140, D $175; G) S $115, D $130; D & H) S $95, D $115 WEEKLY (NO BREAKFAST). **Reservations:** (713) 868-4654 MONDAY THROUGH FRIDAY, 7:30 A.M. TO 9:00 P.M., SATURDAY AND SUNDAY 8:00 A.M. TO 5:00 P.M.

## GLEN OAKS

MERKENS AT WURZBACH — Spanish style residence. Home has lovely bric-a-brac, some antiques. PIANO and color TV in living room for guests. Hostess is former legal secretary now working part time for three accountants. Accommodations include: A) queen bedroom; B) double bedroom; and C) twin bedroom. All share bath, or have private bath if no other guests. Full breakfast. Fenced-in backyard. Friendly DOBERMAN is in residence but out of sight unless requested. Home is 5 minutes from Medical Center with six major hospitals and many doctors' offices; Downtown is 20 minutes by auto and 35 minutes by bus, which stops across the street. Hostess plays tennis nearly every morning and guests may join. Children welcome. NO SMOKING.

**Rates:** A & B) S $35, D $40 AND C) S $40, D $45 DAILY. S $175, D $200 WEEKLY.
**Reservations:** (214) 298-8586.

# TEXAS PANHANDLE
## AMARILLO

WASHINGTON & 16TH STREET — A large, totally modernized commercial space designed after New York artist loft living style. It has 16 skylights, 6 ceiling fans, and 14 foot ceiling. Air conditioned. The home abounds with contemporary art. Accommodation is one bedroom with double bed, private entrance, and bath. Cots provided. Off-street parking. Host is an art center (museum) director and award winning film maker; hostess is a sculptor and teacher. Bikes available. Jogging, tennis, and basketball courts can be found in nearby park. Transportation includes three airlines and two bus lines. Home is 2 1/2 blocks from Interstate 40. Visit includes free guided tour of the art center and the campus of Amarillo College. It is 20 minutes to Panhandle Plains Historical Museum (oldest and largest in Texas) and spectacular Palo Duro Canyon. Gourmet dinners possible. Welcoming drink provided. Children over 10 only. NO SMOKING in the home.
**Rates:** S $32, D $38 DAILY. S $196, D $238 WEEKLY. CHILDREN $10 EACH DAILY.
**Reservations:** (214) 298-8586.

# WASHINGTON COUNTY
## CHAPPEL HILL

CHESTNUT — On the National Register of Historic Homes this recently restored house was built in 1855. The two large downstairs guest bedrooms each have twin beds, exquisite antique linens, armoires, and adjoining private baths. One of these also has its own large FIREPLACE. Upstairs the guest bedroom has a queen-sized bed, chaise lounge, and large private bath. Host is a wood sculptor; hostess, who is retired, is a charity worker for many causes. There is also a two bedroom, 1 1/2 bath apartment for guest use over the barn. One DOG. CHILDREN over 12 welcome. NO SMOKING.
**Rates:** S $65, D $75-$85 DAILY.
**Reservations:** (713) 868-4654 MONDAY THROUGH FRIDAY, 7:30 A.M. TO 9:00 P.M., SATURDAY AND SUNDAY 8:00 A.M. TO 5:00 P.M.

An 1857 Colonial mansion on a 220 acre working plantation. The home is set in landscaped 11 acres complete with POOL, log cabin, antique shop, orchard, and beautiful flowers. The rolling countryside, horse farms, antique shops, and historic site is located 1 hour from Houston. The area is famous for wildflowers in April and the house is beautifully decorated

in December. Furnished with antiques throughout. Large verandas overlook countryside. A seated gourmet breakfast is served around a large Victorian antique table. Accommodations are: three double rooms and one room for four in the manor house and two double rooms with private baths in the "Station House." A perfect place for a restful weekend in the country. PIANO available for guests use. Host is a hunting enthusiastic; hostess enjoys bridge. CHILDREN over 12 welcome. SMOKING permitted on verandas.
**Rates:** S OR D $110.
**Reservations:** (713) 868-4654 MONDAY THROUGH FRIDAY, 7:30 A.M. TO 9:00 P.M., SATURDAY AND SUNDAY 8:00 A.M. TO 5:00 P.M.

# WEST TEXAS
## FORT STOCKTON (21 MILES)

Modern day "bunk houses" are more like well-appointed guesthouses at this ranch just 27 miles east of Fort Stockton. Three miles from the newest Texas winery with 250 acres of vineyards. Hosts will give you a first hand look at the vineyards and serve a complimentary glass of St. Genevieve's wine. King-sized beds and baths in two guesthouses, each with air conditioning, carpeting, antique dressers, and so on. Breakfast is served in the main home and will be hearty with egg and cheese casserole, fresh fruit, and coffee or tea. Town of Bakersfield was named after the owner of this large spread. See deer and other wildlife wander through the dry creek bed just below the home. VCR and pool table. CHILDREN over 6 welcome.
**Rates:** S $37.50, D $47.50 DAILY.
**Reservations:** (214) 298-8586.

## MIDLAND

Quiet, Contemporary ranch house in horse country, boarding available for three HORSES. Accommodation is a large secluded bedroom with a queen-sized bed and adjoining private bathroom with shower. Inground POOL and WHIRLPOOL SPA (spa available year-round). Complete Texas breakfast is served. Two friendly DOGS in residence. Well-behaved PETS WELCOME. Ten minutes to downtown, close to restaurants and Midland College. Host is a financial analyst; hostess is a clinical scientist. VCR. Air conditioned. HANDICAPPED ACCESSIBLE. NONSMOKERS.
**Rates:** S $30, D $40 DAILY.
**Reservations:** (214) 298-8586.

## RURAL

Typical Texas style home that was built in 1898 is a superb example of Prairie craftsmanship with ornate tin ceilings and hardwood floors. Hosts do weddings and parties for large groups, but now wish to have B&B

guests. Breakfast will be continental and dinners may be available for an extra fee with advance reservation. Hosts have lived in Washington, D.C. and the Virginia hunt country, so guests will be treated to special eastern hospitality. Catch the evening breeze on the large wraparound porches as you contemplate the prairie dog town across the road. PETS welcome. Two bedrooms available: A) four poster bed and B) a double trundle bed. PIANO. VCR. Air conditioned. Children welcome.

**Rates:** A) S OR D $50 AND B) S OR D $40 DAILY.

**Reservations:** (214) 298-8586.

# 8

# Mountain

- [ ] **Arizona**
- [ ] **Colorado**
- [ ] **Montana**
- [ ] **New Mexico**
- [ ] **Utah**
- [ ] **Wyoming**

# ARIZONA

## CENTRAL ARIZONA
### PRESCOTT

Two story home surrounded by pines and feels secluded, though it is near downtown Prescott. Living room on first floor with large fireplace and TV. Guestrooms are on the second floor near a patio. Hostess enjoys catering parties and is an excellent cook. She is also an executive secretary, and enjoys gardening with a variety of flowers and bushes and grandmothering. Accommodations include: A) double bed and B) king-sized bed. Share one full bathroom in home. Dinners served to guests for reasonable fee. No pets in home. NO CHILDREN. NONSMOKERS preferred.
**Rates:** A) S OR D $45 AND B) S OR D $55 DAILY.
**Reservations:** (602) 990-0682 8 A.M. TO 8 P.M. DAILY, MOUNTAIN TIME.

## EASTERN ARIZONA
### SHOW LOW

Small farmhouse near lake with hostess a retired surgical nurse from Chicago who speaks German, Rumanian born, is hospitable in a joyous, European manner. She enjoys handicrafts, gardening, and traveling. Guestroom has a king-sized bed with private bathroom in the hall. Convenient to excellent fishing, boating, Fort Apache, prehistoric Kinishba Ruins, and snow skiing. Hostess smokes. One friendly, large DOG in residence.
**Rates:** S $35, D $40 DAILY. S $210, D $240 WEEKLY.
**Reservations:** (602) 990-0682 8 A.M. TO 8 P.M. DAILY, MOUNTAIN TIME.

## FLAGSTAFF AREA

Canyons, pine covered mountains, forests and lakes, prehistoric and pioneer scenes, and quirks of nature abound in this area. Within easy driving distance are the Grand Canyon; 186 mile long Lake Powell; the Painted Desert; Sunset Crater; Meteor Crater; museums; Oak Creek Canyon and Sedona set amid the famous red rocks; Jerome, one of the United States' most fantastic "ghost" mining town; Prescott and the Sharlot Hall and Smoki Museums; ancient cliff dwellings at Walnut Canyon and Montezuma Castle National Monuments; Navajo lands with the world famous Monument Valley and the Hopi Indian Reservation and the Second Mesa unexcelled for coiled basketry.

## CLARKDALE

Ranch style home on 60 acre ranch in one of most beautiful, lush green areas in Arizona. Ranch surrounded on three sides by Verde River. For those who enjoy a peaceful, rural setting with many cottonwood trees, wild birds, animals, walking by the river, and fishing. Hostess in this new home is a realtor who enjoys Indian history and antiques. Accommodations include: A) double bed and B) twin bed. Rooms share bath in hall. Resident outside CATS. Children welcome. NONSMOKERS preferred.
**Rates:** S $30, D $40 DAILY.
**Reservations:** (602) 990-0682 8 A.M. TO 8 P.M. DAILY, MOUNTAIN TIME.

## COTTONWOOD

RANCHO MANANA CIRCLE — A new Ranch home in the Mingus Mountain foothills. The guestroom has a private bath, radio, and built-in double bed with matching dresser. Being retired, hosts have time to visit with guests and share their knowledge of local attractions. They offer a choice of foods for breakfast and serve outdoors in good weather. The views from the deck are panoramic; Sedona red rocks and Mingus Mountains. The area is 4 miles outside of Cottonwood, 15 miles to Jerome, 20 miles to Sedona, and 40 miles to Flagstaff for skiing. NO SMOKING.
**Rates:** S $30, D $45 DAILY.
**Reservations:** (602) 990-0682 8 A.M. TO 8 P.M. DAILY, MOUNTAIN TIME.

## FLAGSTAFF

Handsome new Tudor mansion in tall pines and lawn setting, 2 1/2 miles from Interstate. Hostess is warmly hospitable, and enjoys travel, people, and her family. She is very knowledgeable about Arizona. Accommodations include on second floor: A) two queen beds; B) queen bed; and C) twin beds. A-C share bath. On first floor, D) queen bed, private bath. The home is within an easy drive to many tourist attractions in northern Arizona. No pets in the home. Children of all ages welcome. Prefer NONSMOKERS.
**Rates:** A) $60; B) $50; AND C) S OR D $50 DAILY.
**Reservations:** (602) 990-0682 8 A.M. TO 8 P.M. DAILY, MOUNTAIN TIME.

Two story Ranch style home in one of nicest areas among tall pines, in quiet neighborhood in north Flagstaff, near scenic route to Grand Canyon and San Francisco Peaks. Guest area and family room with TV, VCR, and fireplace on first floor. Host is a businessman; hostess is a teacher. They enjoy meeting new people and outdoor activities such as golf,

hiking, camping, skiing, and traveling. A little German and Spanish spoken. King bed and king waterbed in two guestrooms, and a sofabed are available. One full hall bath. Convenient to Northern University, museums, art galleries, historic observatory, ice caves, Sunset Crater, Walnut Canyon, Meteor Crater, Montezuma Castle, Sedona, Oak Creek, and Grand Canyon. Resident elderly DOG. Children welcome.
**Rates:** S $35, D $40 DAILY. S $210, D $240 WEEKLY. CHILD UNDER 5 IS $5; CHILD UNDER 10 IS $10 DAILY.
**Reservations:** (602) 990-0682 8 A.M. TO 8 P.M. DAILY, MOUNTAIN TIME.

## PAYSON
## OX BOW ESTATES

OX BOW ESTATES & US 87 — A large, three story modified "A" Frame mountain type of home, 4 miles south of Payson, bordering a national forest with pinon trees, good for hiking. Host is a retired industrial arts teacher, now in building; hostess is retired from teaching home economics and has furnished this home with a decorator's flair. They enjoy gardening, landscaping, camping, and birdwatching. A continental breakfast is served. Resident CAT. Accommodations include: A) queen-bedded room with large inside balcony overlooking living room, exterior deck with view, full bath, up one flight of stairs; B) one bedroom studio, queen bed, private bath, own patio, carport; C) two bedroom apartment with queen beds, private bath, private parking and ground level entry; and D) one bedroom studio. CHILDREN over 12 welcome. NO SMOKERS.
**Rates:** A) S $25, D $35 DAILY. S $180, D $210 WEEKLY. B) B-D AVAIL MONTHLY ONLY, $290; C) $390; AND D) $290 MONTHLY.
**Reservations:** (602) 990-0682 8 A.M. TO 8 P.M. DAILY, MOUNTAIN TIME.

## SEDONA

One of the most spectacular areas in Arizona with panoramic views of red rock formations from Contemporary home with many windows. Host couple are from Germany. Full breakfasts are served, but no meat, as hosts are vegetarians. Breakfast is served in formal dining room, in the living room by the fireplace, or outside. Breakfasts include homemade whole grain breads and muffins. Home is light, airy, and tranquil. Accommodations include: A) king bedroom, adjacent bath, double whirlpool, and atrium, full views of red rocks, free standing FIREPLACE; B) queen bedroom, sofa bed, private bath in hall, view, and deck; and C) bedroom is large with adjacent bath. Inground POOL. No pets. NO CHILDREN. NO SMOKING.
**Rates:** A) S $75, D $80 AND B) S $60, D$65; AND C) S $50, D $55 DAILY. WEEKLY RATES QUOTED.

**Reservations:** (6021 990-0682 8 A.M. TO 8 P.M. DAILY, MOUNTAIN TIME.

# HUACHUCA MOUNTAINS (BASE OF)
## HEREFORD
### RAMSEY CANYON

RAMSEY CANYON ROAD — A rambling home on a small ranch (where chickens and turkeys are raised) nestled in the beautiful Huachuca Mountains with magnificent views from the 5,050 foot elevation. A heated POOL and indoor SPA are available for your pleasure. You may picnic or barbecue on the patio. A full breakfast is included with fresh eggs. Host is a computer systems analyst; hostess a retired nurse. There are one DOG and two CATS in residence. The home is just 2 miles from the internationally famous Mile High Nature Conservancy (14 varieties of hummingbirds in season). Wildlife include deer, javeline, mountain lions, and more abundant wildlife in the canyon. The home is near Fort Huachuca and its excellent historical museum. Tombstone, "the town too tough to die," and Bisbess, a colorful old mining town with tours of the famous Lavender Pit (once a mountain) and Copper Queen mines are close by, too. Old Mexico is just south of the Huachuca's. For a glimpse of another culture and great shopping, both Nogales and Agua Prieta are pleasant and easy drives. Accommodations include: A) queen bed, private bath with shower and B) twin-bedded double with private hall bath with both shower and tub. CHILDREN over 6 welcome.
**Rates:** A & B) S $35, D $45 DAILY.
**Reservations:** (602) 990-0682 8 A.M. TO 8 P.M. DAILY, MOUNTAIN TIME.

# MINGUS MOUNTAINS
## JEROME

Originally a Mexican miner's home, now remodeled and restored and the home of an artist. It is on a quiet road with fantastic views, yet only steps from Jerome's enchanting main street and overlooking the red rocks of Sedona and the Verde Valley. Accommodations are completely private with own entrance, double bed, full bath, and dressing room. Additional space for children or traveling companions (hide-a-bed in entry room, share bath). Guests have full use of patio, perfect for outdoor meals, birdwatching, and star gazing. Full gourmet breakfast features fresh fruit egg entree, ham or bacon, homemade hashbrowns, fresh baked bread or rolls, homemade preserves and jellies, and tea or coffee, and a choice of juice. For the more adventurous, choices can include a variety of ethnic breakfasts (with advance notice) ranging from Korean "bim bim bop," a rice, vegetable and meat dish served with poached egg and hot sauce to a French country breakfast. From Jerome it is an easy drive to many scenic points of interest: 25 miles to Sedona and the shops and galleries

of Tlaquepaque, Oak Creek Canyon, and Slide Rock just beyond Sedona; 30 miles of breathtaking beauty takes you to Prescott and its historic homes, Sharlott Hall Museum, and many antique shops. Not to be missed are Prescott's quaint town square and the once notorious "Whiskey Row." Also nearby are: the Indian ruins of Tuzigoot and Montezuma's Castle, Sycamore Canyon for hiking, and the many artists and craftsmen of Jerome.
**Rates:** S $40, D $45 DAILY. S $200, D $250 WEEKLY.
**Reservations:** (602) 990-0682 8 A.M. TO 8 P.M. DAILY, MOUNTAIN TIME.

## MOHAVE DESERT
### BULLHEAD CITY
#### PUNTA DE VISTA

Rambling home in natural desert setting with acres of desert vegetation available for hiking. Star studded skies and fresh desert air help you to relax on the deck overlooking the Colorado River. Host enjoys spectacular sports; hostess enjoys sewing and cooking. Hosts are retired and they enjoy the desert plants. Accommodations include: A) queen bed, private adjacent baths; B) two queen beds, private hall bath; and C) double bed, private adjacent bath. One outside BRITTANY SPANIEL resident. Six miles from Laughlin, Nevada, famous for gambling casinos. Near Davis Dam and Lake Mohave. Historic areas include Oatman, a gold mining town, and the Indian petroglyphs. Children welcome.
**Rates:** A & C) S $35 D $40 AND B) S $30 D $40 DAILY.
**Reservations:** (602) 990-0682 8 A.M. TO 8 P.M. DAILY, MOUNTAIN TIME.

## NORTHWEST ARIZONA
### LAKE HAVASU CITY

Retired hostess welcomes guests to Lake Havasu City, home of the London Bridge. She enjoys square dancing, travel, and antiques, and offers extra large breakfast. Minutes to Lake Havasu where there is good boating and fishing. No pets. There is one double bed and private full bath. No CHILDREN. NONSMOKERS preferred.
**Rates:** S $30 D $40 DAILY.
**Reservations:** (602) 990-0682 8 A.M. TO 8 P.M. DAILY, MOUNTAIN TIME.

## SOUTHERN ARIZONA
### AMADO

This ranch and vineyard is located on 80 acres (4,000 foot elevation) just southwest of Green Valley, Arizona. They have lush green pastures for the cattle and horses, mesquite forests with an abundance of native birds,

ponds with geese and wild heron. The 1,600 square foot guesthouse is a double wide mobile home. It is surrounded by its own orchards and offers tranquility and beauty. It is newly furnished with king, queen, and double beds; library; and washer and dryer. The kitchen is stocked with fresh eggs, bacon, muffins, and everything you will need. A lovely POOL by the main house is also for guest use. The back gate opens onto 10,000 acres of the Coronado National Forest (spectacular!). Located near two old missions, an artist colony (Tubac), fishing lakes, numerous golf courses and of course Old Mexico. Tucson International Airport is 60 minutes away. Accommodations include: A) king bed, private bath, dressing room; B) queen bed, private bath; and C) double bed, shared bath. DOG and other barnyard animals. SMALL DOGS OR CATS ON LEASH WELCOME. Two teenage children live here. Host is a mortgage broker; hostess is a real estate developer. Horse stall and picnic area. Children of all ages welcome. SMOKING, outside only.
**Rates:** A) $50; B) QUEEN $40; AND C) $50. WHOLE UNIT (BOTH ROOMS TOGETHER) $150 DAILY.
**Reservations:** (602) 990-0682 8 A.M. TO 8 P.M. DAILY, MOUNTAIN TIME.

## SOUTHWEST ARIZONA
### YUMA

Large, beautiful adobe home on quiet, pretty residential area. Sociable hostess is bridal consultant. Accommodations include: A) double bed, adjacent full bath; furnished with exceptional Victorian antiques; B) king bed, mirrored wall, door leading to POOL area; and C) twin bed with antique furniture, many books. B and C share hall bath. HANDICAPPED ACCESSIBLE.
**Rates:** A) D $50; B) D $35; AND C) S $25 DAILY.
**Reservations:** (602) 990-0682 8 A.M. TO 8 P.M. DAILY, MOUNTAIN TIME.

## GREATER TUCSON

Points of interest include Ajo and its tremendous copper pit; Tombstone, Bisbee with underground mine tours; and Nogales is nifty for Mexican shopping bargains, and on the way, it is interesting to visit the Tubac Presidio State Historic Park, first Spanish settlement. The University of Arizona campus, Arizona State Museum, Flandrau Planetarium, and the Arizona Historical Society collections are worth seeing as is Kitt Peak National Observatory where huge telescopes can be seen near an explanatory museum.

## TUCSON

Desert flora and colorful mountains dominate southern Arizona, Numerous destinations show the diversity. The Arizona-Sonora Desert Museum featuring live displays, the movie set of Old Tucson, petroglyphs, the Saguaro and the Organ Pipe National Monuments, Colossal Cave and the gleaming Spanish Mission, San Xavier del Bac restored to its 1700 splendor. Birdwatchers enjoy Madera Canyon and Ramsey Canyon Road leading to the world's hummingbird capital, and Sierra Vista with the Fort Huachuca Museum which gives a glimpse of the area's military past.

Friendly hosts welcome guests to central Tucson. Host is an administrator at the University of Arizona; hostess is a realtor associate. They enjoy sports, gardening, camping, sailing, music, and photography. Three well-behaved small DOGS. Large breakfasts if desired. SPA, light kitchen, and laundry privileges. In private wing of home are two guestrooms and den, and one bathroom. Accommodations include: A) king or twin beds; B) one twin bed; and C) sofa-bed. Ranch style home.
**Rates:** S $28, D $35 DAILY. S $168, D $210 WEEKLY. S $675, D $840 MONTHLY.
**Reservations:** (602) 990-0682 8 A.M. TO 8 P.M. DAILY, MOUNTAIN TIME.

## CATALINA FOOTHILLS

Rambling Ranch home with separate guesthouse. Host is a lawyer; hostess is a housewife. They enjoy reading, art, travel, Indian rugs, grandparenting, pet GOLDEN RETRIEVER, and cockatoo. A warm, friendly atmosphere in Catalina foothills in a unique garden setting near 127 acres for walking. Mountain and city views; and quail, other wild birds, rabbits, and squirrels are numerous. Convenient to shopping, theater, churches, restaurants, golf courses, University of Arizona, and the University Hospital. Accommodations include: A) in main house, guestroom with comfortable queen sleeper, private hall bath and B) in large guesthouse, host serves hearty breakfast first morning, make your own at leisure thereafter in fully equipped kitchen from stocked refrigerator. Comfortably furnished with honey maple, braided rugs. Has living room, dining room, bedroom with twin beds, bath, private parking and entrance. Living room opens on POOL and patio and private covered porch. HANDICAPPED ACCESSIBLE. Children welcome.
**Rates:** A) S $30, D $35 AND B) $60 DAILY. B) $390 WEEKLY. THREE DAY MINIMUM STAY.
**Reservations:** (602) 990-0682 8 A.M. TO 8 P.M. DAILY, MOUNTAIN TIME.

## EL PRESIDIO

ST. MARY'S ROAD AND MAIN — The historic "Julius Kruttschnitt" house is a charming 1886 American Territorial adobe mansion, located in the El Presidio Historic District, amidst other historic mansions. It has been restored by the owners and is a delightful oasis complete with private courtyards with fountains and lush gardens. Host is an airline pilot; hostess is active as a cateress and interior decorator. They enjoy antiques, architecture, horticulture, travel, and painting. Guest accommodations include a carriage house (1,850 sq. ft.) apartment with living room, kitchen, bedroom with double bed and adjacent bath fully equipped and furnished with period antiques. There is an additional sofa bed in the living room. Enjoy unique shopping, museums, and restaurants ranging from authentic Mexican to nouvelle French. Within easy driving distance are Tubac and San Xavier del Bac as well as cultural and sports events and the University of Arizona. A little Spanish is spoken here. One CAT is in residence. CHILDREN over 10 welcome. NONSMOKERS ONLY.
**Rates:** S $65, D $75 DAILY. S $390, D $450 WEEKLY. THREE NIGHT MINIMUM. EXTRA PERSONS ADDITIONAL.
**Reservations:** (602) 990-0682 8 A.M. TO 8 P.M. DAILY, MOUNTAIN TIME.

## FOOTHILLS

BIG ROCK ROAD NEAR SKYLINE — Located in a natural desert setting in the foothills of the Santa Catalina Mountains, this home offers the privacy of the desert yet is only minutes from shopping centers, a variety of restaurants, and the University of Arizona. Accommodations include: A) a large bedroom with dressing area, private bath, cable TV, and your own entrance to the POOL and patio and B) twin-bedded double, close to the bath. A CAT is in residence. CHILDREN over 12 welcome.
**Rates:** A) S $32, D $40 AND B) S $32.50, D $35 DAILY.
**Reservations:** (602) 990-0682 8 A.M. TO 8 P.M. DAILY, MOUNTAIN TIME.

## RANDOLPH PARK

BROADWAY AND ALVERNON — A private, newly remodeled guesthouse including a sitting/bedroom with queen-sized bed and 19 inch color TV. Full kitchen includes dishes, pots, and pans. There is a full bath with ample towels. In town, but quiet, located on back of property. Minutes to University of Phoenix, golf, tennis, park, and zoo. Shopping center 3 blocks away; half a block from public transit. Breakfast food is provided for the first morning. Hosts also provide homemade muffins. Host enjoys golf and all sports, military history, and politics; hostess

enjoys cooking, gardening, people, and is a dental hygenist. He is an editor of a large daily newspaper.
**Rates:** S $40, D $ 50 DAILY. S $280, D $350 WEEKLY. S $900, D $1,000 MONTHLY.
**Reservations:** (602) 990-0682 8 A.M. TO 8 P.M. DAILY, MOUNTAIN TIME.

## ROLLING HILLS

CAMINO SECO AND 22ND STREET — Townhouse with host who is a retired fighter pilot and hostess who is German and presently an insurance secretary. Hostess speaks German. Host enjoys golf, cooking, and fixing things up, walking; hostess enjoys painting, cooking, golfing, and walking. They enjoy making jams, jellies, marmalades, and homemade breads. The home is furnished in contemporary style. There are many trees and grassy areas, with a HEATED SWIMMING POOL available. Accommodations include: A) queen bed, private bath across the hall and B) suite with adjacent bath on the second floor. Easy driving to Old Tucson, Sonora Desert Museum, San Xavier del Bac, Kitt Peak, Sabino Canyon Park, Colosssal Cave, and University of Arizona. Near city bus. Resident CAT. Pickup at the airport is available for a small fee. Dinners are also available for a reasonable rate. Bikes available. TEENAGERS welcome.
**Rates:** A) S $35, D $45 AND B) D $56 DAILY.
**Reservations:** (602) 990-0682 8 A.M. TO 8 P.M. DAILY, MOUNTAIN TIME.

## VALLEY OF THE SUN

The area of the Valley of the Sun includes Phoenix, Mesa, Scottsdale, and Tempe. Within easy driving distance is the Boyce Thompson Southwestern Arboretum State Park, Gila River Indian Arts and Crafts Center, the Casa Grande National Monument, and the Fort Verde State Historic Park. There are many fine arts and sporting events programs during the year as well as ethnic festivals and restaurants.

## MESA

A large Contemporary Spanish style home set on 1 1/4 acres in a quiet neighborhood of a rapidly growing city. Mesa is winter home to thousands who come to enjoy the mild winters. Host enjoys gardening and woodworking; hostess enjoys cooking, sewing, and crafts. Large breakfasts are served including fresh bread, butter, homemade jams, and fresh eggs raised on premises. Host is a teacher; hostess is a former teacher. They have three daughters aged 8, 9, and 13. The home is 1 mile from a freeway and close to shopping, golf, spring baseball training, and Arizona State University. A MINIATURE SCHNAUZER and two CATS are present. Accommodations include a double bed, private hall bath. Inground POOL. PIANO.

**Rates:** S $30, D $35 DAILY. S $180, D $210 WEEKLY.
**Reservations:** (602) 990-0682 8 A.M. TO 8 P.M. DAILY, MOUNTAIN TIME.

## EAST VALLEY

McKELLIPS AND VAL VISTA — Enjoy country living in your own guesthouse nestled in an orange orchard 10 minutes from Mesa's center. Guesthouse has living room, bedroom with twin beds, large closet, dressing room, full bath, and fully equipped kitchen. Linens are furnished, as is a color TV. All oranges you can eat in season! Breakfast not included in rates. SMALL DOGS WELCOME. Has attached, enclosed garage. Easy driving distance to Saguaro Lake (fishing and boating), Superstition Mountains, prehistoric Indian dwellings and museums, horses, golf, tennis, art galleries of Scottsdale, and adult center. Hostess enjoys quilting, golfing, fishing, and grandmothering. UNHOSTED. HANDICAPPED ACCESSIBLE. CHILDREN WELCOME. NONSMOKERS ONLY.

**Rates:** S OR D $42 DAILY. $260 WEEKLY. $850 MONTHLY.
**Reservations:** (602) 990-0682 8 A.M. TO 8 P.M. DAILY, MOUNTAIN TIME.

## NORTHEAST MESA

NEAR MCKELLIPS & LINDSAY — Large Spanish style, red tiled roofed home (new in 1985). Inground POOL, covered ramada poolside. Home is furnished with touches of antiques. Cozy fireplace in family room—breakfast nook—kitchen combo. Guests can eat poolside, on patio, covered ramada, or breakfast nook. Hostess is a caterer so great breakfasts are guaranteed. Hosts enjoy traveling, golf, flea markets, and entertaining. Located by orange groves, excellent area for walking. Children of all ages welcome. GUEST PETS WELCOME. Laundry and kitchen privileges. Baby equipment available. Bikes are too. A BOSTON TERRIER pup is in residence. Home is convenient to all retirement areas of Mesa and Apache Junction, Superstition Mountains, and restaurants. Accommodations include: A & B) double rooms with shared bath, and C) double with private bath. Double accommodations as well as master suite available. TVs in all bedrooms. HOT TUB and JACUZZI. Air conditioning. NONSMOKERS preferred.

**Rates:** A & B) S $30, D $40; C) (MASTER SUITE); AND D $50 DAILY.
**Reservations:** (602) 990-0682 8 A.M. TO 8 P.M. DAILY, MOUNTAIN TIME.

## PHOENIX

Irrigated by water from nearby recreational lakes; palm, olive, and eucalyptus trees grace homes and streets. Rugged mountains jut sharply above citrus groves and farms of cotton and vegetables. Outdoor living (golf, swimming, boating, and some 40 other sports) bring year-round pleasure in this land of abundant sunshine. There are 500 annual special events in Arizona from art shows to rodeos. A few of the more popular places to visit include the Heard Museum with Indian exhibits, the Desert Botanical Garden, Phoenix Zoo, South Mountain (world's largest city park), Frank Lloyd Wright's Taliesen West, Scottsdale with the third largest number of art galleries in the United States, the Phoenix Art Museum, Arizona State University, and the Hohokam ruins at Pueblo Grande.

CACTUS AND 58TH STREET — A large Ranch style home with landscaped desert front yard, green backyard with POOL, on a quiet cul-de-sac near a major street. Convenient to Paradise Valley Mall. The home is furnished with contemporary comfortable furniture and includes a PIANO, large fireplace, and welcoming patio. Hostess was formerly in insurance, is from Korea, and can also speak Japanese. Accommodations include: A) double bed and B) single bed. Both have private baths. Continental breakfast and kitchen privileges. CHILDREN above 6 welcome.
**Rates:** S $30, D $35 DAILY. S $180, D $210 WEEKLY.
**Reservations:** (602) 990-0682 8 A.M. TO 8 P.M. DAILY, MOUNTAIN TIME.

NORTH 53RD DRIVE — A couple, of Swedish descent, welcomes you to a modest home with large breakfast. Kitchen privileges as long as your cooking fits into hostess' schedule. Gas barbecue, picnic table, glider in yard. A small DOG WELCOME. Backyard enclosed; screened-in patio. PIANO and ORGAN for music lovers. City park with large pool (for summer swimmers) and tennis courts within walking distance. It is 2 miles to golf course; 1 mile to shopping centers; near city bus stop. Hosts enjoy bowling and going to Las Vegas. Cable TV. Accommodations include: A) two rooms each with double bed, share full private bath in hall; and B) den with queen sofabed for overflow, also shares bath. HANDICAPPED ACCESSIBLE. Children welcome. SMOKING on patio only.
**Rates:** S $20, D $30 DAILY. S $120, D $180 WEEKLY.
**Reservations:** (602) 990-0682 8 A.M. TO 8 P.M. DAILY, MOUNTAIN TIME.

## AHWATUKEE

TONALEA DRIVE (2 MILES TO INTERSTATE 10) — Spanish style tri-level custom home located in a quiet residential area in one of Phoenix's finest locations. This is a planned community 4 miles south of Tempe, east of the Phoenix South Mountain Park Preserve. The home has a comfortable, friendly atmosphere. For golf lovers, choose from either of two year-round 18 hole golf courses. Hosts works with two Arizona utility companies. They enjoy traveling, entertaining, cooking, golf, and the hostess likes needlework. POOL. Host couple speak English, Burmese, Shan, and Cantonese. Near shopping and restaurants. Easy access to Interstate 10, Sky Harbor Airport, Arizona State University. Laundry and kitchen privileges. Accommodations include: A) separate wing with double bed, shower and private entrance, own thermostat; B) queen water bed with full bath in hall (shared with C); and C) queen with extra firm mattress. Available by week or month. NO CHILDREN. NONSMOKERS preferred.
**Rates:** S $175, D $210 WEEKLY. S $550, D $650 MONTHLY.
**Reservations:** (602) 990-0682 8 A.M. TO 8 P.M. DAILY, MOUNTAIN TIME.

## BILTMORE AREA

Prime location in fashionable Biltmore Park area in east central Phoenix, near best shopping and restaurants. An extra large rambling, handsome home with private guest wing with parking, private entrance, and inground POOL. Friendly hostess is retired business lady, enjoys collecting art, fine antiques, travel, and horses. Easy driving from Convention Center, Heard Museum, Phoenix Art Museum, theaters, Arizona State University, Phoenix College, and Sky Harbor Airport. One friendly DOG, POOL, TV. Near bus stop, golf, parks. Accommodations include: A) extra large room with king-sized bed, sitting area, shares hall bath and B) smaller room with double bed, shares hall bath with other guestroom. Children over 6 welcome.
**Rates:** A) S $55, D $65 AND B) $40 DAILY.
**Reservations:** (602) 990-0682 8 A.M. TO 8 P.M. DAILY, MOUNTAIN TIME.

## ENCANTO PARK

Charming home in pleasant, quiet central Phoenix neighborhood, Encanto Park area. Host is spokesman for Phoenix Fire Department; hostess is self-employed. They enjoy traveling, sailing, dancing, handcrafts, cooking, collecting antiques, and entertaining. The red tiled, white stucco home is surrounded by trees, manicured grass and bushes, and retains all its original 1937 charm, with beamed living room, sculpted fireplace, arched

doors. Accommodations include: A) airy room with two walls of windows with double bed; B) twin bed; and C) queen bed. There are two hall baths for the guests. There is a large, friendly outside host DOG. Hostess enjoys serving homemade cookies on arrival and special place settings at breakfast with a variety of food. Children welcome.
**Rates:** A) S $40, D $45; B) S $35; AND C) S $40, D $45 DAILY. CHILD $10 DAILY.
**Reservations:** (602) 990-0682 8 A.M. TO 8 P.M. DAILY, MOUNTAIN TIME.

### METRO CENTER

28TH DRIVE — New townhouse located within walking distance to large Phoenix mall, Metrocenter; also near lake and bus stop. Host is from Germany, speaks German, is retired, and enjoys gardening and travel. He has an extra large guestroom with a balcony, queen bed, and an adjacent bath. Easy access to freeway, downtown Phoenix, International School of Management, and the thoroughbred race track. No pets in home. Full breakfasts with German specialties. Inground POOL. NO CHILDREN. NONSMOKERS preferred.
**Rates:** S $35, D $40 DAILY. S $210, D $240 WEEKLY.
**Reservations:** (602) 990-0682 8 A.M. TO 8 P.M. DAILY, MOUNTAIN TIME.

### MUMMY MOUNTAIN

SHEA & 23RD STREET — A Spanish style home with arches and desert landscaped front yard with tall eucalyptus and ironwood trees. Small backyard with resident, friendly large DOG. Views, near Mummy Mountain. It is 20 minutes from Sky Harbor Airport and 25 minutes from central Scottsdale. Hostess is educational consultant who enjoys travel, reading, and Indian history. Home is furnished with white carpeting, Indian and Oriental art, and light fabrics on furniture. It has a tranquil feeling. Accommodations include: A) large guestroom with private entrance, with extra long twin beds, dressing room, full bath; B) guestroom with one twin bed, shares hall bath; and C) guestroom has round king bed, shares hall bath. NO CHILDREN. NONSMOKERS preferred.
**Rates:** S OR D A) $50; B) $40; AND C) $50 DAILY. S $210, D $240 WEEKLY.
**Reservations:** (602) 990-0682 8 A.M. TO 8 P.M. DAILY, MOUNTAIN TIME.

### PARADISE VALLEY

Luxurious and spacious style of a Seville, Spain home, The attractively decorated home features both desert and tropical gardens with a beautiful

POOL, patio, lacy white gazebo and croquet lawn. Family room has a large fireplace where sherry and cheese are offered in the late afternoon in the winter months. Located in the Camelback Golf and Country Club Estates. Hostess enjoys traveling, art, music, architecture, and anthropology. She speaks Italian, Spanish, and French. Guests can enjoy a large twin bedroom with a French daybed and arcadia doors opening to the very large patio with a panoramic mountain view. Gourmet breakfasts served. Light kitchen privileges; arrangements can be made for private entertaining. One shy CAT in residence. HANDICAPPED ACCESSIBLE. VCR.
**Rates:** D $60 DAILY OCTOBER THROUGH APRIL; D $50 DAILY JUNE THROUGH AUGUST.
**Reservations:** (602) 990-0682 8 A.M. TO 8 P.M. DAILY, MOUNTAIN TIME.

## NORTHERN SCOTTSDALE

A private guesthouse on 5 acres, a ranch in rural Paradise Valley, 5 miles north of central Scottsdale. The guesthouse is 600 square feet with a combined living room/bedroom with twin beds. The bathroom has a shower. The fully equipped kitchen has a large refrigerator, electric stove, oven, and so on. All new carpeting and drapes, cable TV, private phone. Host is mortgage banker; hostess is Welsh and speaks Spanish. They enjoy trail riding, own four HORSES, and hunt their own pack of BEAGLES twice a week during the hunt season. Breakfast for the first morning included in rates (fresh farm eggs, homemade marmalade). Available October 15 through May 15. HANDICAPPED ACCESSIBLE. Inground POOL. NONSMOKERS only.
**Rates:** D $50 DAILY.
**Reservations:** (602) 990-0682 8 A.M. TO 8 P.M. DAILY, MOUNTAIN TIME.

## SCOTTSDALE

EAST CORONADO ROAD — Friendly, Canadian lady who is a realtor with a good sense of humor lives in a Ranch style home in Scottsdale near the Botanical Gardens and the Phoenix Zoo. Quiet, safe neighborhood within walking distance of canal with jogging path, has quick access to Phoenix, Tempe, or central Scottsdale. Hostess enjoys travel, needlepoint, and antiques. No pets in home. Washer available. Guests have use of den with TV, telephone. Accommodations include a double bed, private bath with shower down hall. Extra large breakfast offered. PIANO. No CHILDREN. NONSMOKERS preferred.
**Rates:** S OR D $35 DAILY.
**Reservations:** (602) 990-0682 8 A.M. TO 8 P.M. DAILY, MOUNTAIN TIME.

MILLER AND MONTECITO — Pretty townhouse in nice, quiet neighborhood, but within easy driving distance of stores, restaurants, Civic Center, and churches. Hostess, who is Irish, has a quick wit and is thoughtful of her guests' comfort. She enjoys her family, travel, cards, collecting Irish porcelain, horse prints, and people. There are three bedrooms on the second floor. Accommodations include: A) double bed and B) room for children only, two twin beds. Both rooms share a private bath in the hall. Large breakfasts are served on the patio or in the dining area. POOL and club house available. Hostess smokes, but would be glad to smoke outside for nonsmoking guests. A small DOG could be kept in the fenced backyard and patio area. Children of all ages welcome. **Rates:** S $35 D $40 DAILY. CHILDREN (2 MAX) $10 EACH DAILY. **Reservations:** (602) 990-0682 8 A.M. TO 8 P.M. DAILY, MOUNTAIN TIME.

VALLEY VIEW ROAD — Lovely tri-level home, POOL and heated SPA in center of Scottsdale's resort area. Outgoing hostess who is in sales, loves travel and arts and crafts. Five minutes from downtown and resort areas. Walking distance to bus transportation. A small TERRIER and a canary live here. Hostess will pick guests up at the airport for a reasonable charge. Near golf, tennis, and riding stables. Accommodations include: A) lower level, double bed, TV, phone, and private full bath; B) overflow room on third level for extra adult traveling with those in A. Both share bath. No pets. A continental breakfast is served. NO CHILDREN. NONSMOKERS preferred. **Rates:** S $25, D $35 DAILY. S $150, D $210 WEEKLY. **Reservations:** (602) 990-0682 8 A.M. TO 8 P.M. DAILY, MOUNTAIN TIME.

## CENTRAL GREEN BELT AREA

THOMAS AND HAYDEN ROADS — Beautiful two story townhouse on 18 hole executive golf course with view of Camelback Mountain. There is a patio, and the living/dining room area has a TV and fireplace. Adjoining Green Belt area has miles of paved walkways, well lighted. This area contains several small stocked lakes, with ducks, swans, and pedal boats; tennis courts, baseball diamonds (where San Francisco Giants train); picnic areas, two golf courses, and a Visitors' Center. Three shopping centers are a short walk away. Visit nearby Scottsdale Mall with its Center for the Arts; visit Old Town with its many charming boutiques. Host is retired from advertising and a little German and Spanish are spoken here; hostess enjoys dancing and sightseeing. The king-sized bed with posturepedic mattress is bound to please you. The room also looks out on the golf course; it has a walk-in closet, phone, TV, and private bath. Relax in a JACUZZI after a brisk swim in a heated POOL. Laundry privileges. Full breakfast. SMOKING on patio only.

**Rates:** IN SEASON, DECEMBER 1 THROUGH APRIL 1 D $60 DAILY.
**Reservations:** (602) 990-0682 8 A.M. TO 8 P.M. DAILY, MOUNTAIN TIME.

## MCCORMICK RANCH

Architect's spacious, modern home with golf course frontage, near small lake, views of surrounding mountains. Host is an urban architect and enjoys golf and snow skiing; hostess is a registered nurse and enjoys bridge. POOL, SPA. Five semipublic golf courses within 1 mile. Pool table. Continental breakfast. Accommodations include: A) queen bed, tub and B) double bed. Both share adjacent roman bath. Easy drive to mid-Scottsdale, fine restaurants, and Arizona State University. PIANO. No pets in home. CHILDREN over 10 welcome. SMOKING outside.
**Rates:** JANUARY THROUGH APRIL S OR D $60; MAY THROUGH DECEMBER $50. CHILDREN OVER 10 $45 DAILY.
**Reservations:** (602) 990-0682 8 A.M. TO 8 P.M. DAILY, MOUNTAIN TIME.

## MIDTOWN

MINNEZONA AVENUE NEAR 76TH — A large guestroom/sitting room is available in a tri-level townhouse in midtown Scottsdale. It is situated in a parklike setting with many orange trees and desert plants on the condominium property. An inground free form POOL is heated except in December and January. Shuffleboard is found here. The townhouse is 4 blocks from a large public park with many amenities, 1 mile from Scottsdale Civic Center, and 7 miles from Arizona State University. The guestroom with private entrance is on a separate level from other living quarters and has an adjacent covered carport. Hostess enjoys cooking, sewing, and bridge and is active in the local Presbyterian Church. There are many fine restaurants and resorts within a 2 to 3 mile radius. SMALL DOGS WELCOME here.
**Rates:** D $50 DAILY. $1,200 MONTHLY.
**Reservations:** (602) 990-0682 8 A.M. TO 8 P.M. DAILY, MOUNTAIN TIME.

## TEMPE

HUNTINGTON DRIVE EAST OF PRICE — Convenient attractive home minutes from Arizona State University and Mesa Community College. Two large shopping malls; central Mesa, Tempe, Scottsdale area; trolley access at end of street. Five minutes from Superstition Freeway; close to numerous restaurants, churches, recreation centers, and points of interest. Home has a tranquil, pleasant atmosphere with POOL and fireplace. Light cooking privileges. No pets. Host is a lawyer and college instructor; hostess enjoys cooking and making superior bagels and muffins.

Accommodations include: A) king bed with adjacent 3/4 bath, private entrance to outside pool through Arcadia doors; B) twin beds; and C) double bed. B & C share a full bath in hall. CHILDREN over 10 welcome. NONSMOKERS preferred.
**Rates:** S OR D A) $50 AND B & C) $40 DAILY. A) $300 AND B & C) $240 WEEKLY. MONTHLY RATES NEGOTIABLE.
**Reservations:** (602) 990-0682 8 A.M. TO 8 P.M. DAILY, MOUNTAIN TIME.

McCLINTOCK AND BROADWAY — Efficiency apartment in nice, quiet neighborhood. Enthusiastic hostess lives in main house. She has been a teacher and a travel agent, and enjoys travel, tourism events, and adult education. The apartment has a compact living room with two chairs that can be made into twin beds, a small kitchen, a bedroom with queen waterbed (semiwaveless), and bath. No pets. POOL, patio, citrus in season. UNHOSTED. HANDICAPPED ACCESSIBLE.
**Rates:** $40 DAILY, THREE NIGHT MINIMUM; $500 MONTHLY.
**Reservations:** (602) 990-0682 8 A.M. TO 8 P.M. DAILY, MOUNTAIN TIME.

**THE LAKES**

BASELINE — Ranch style home in the most beautiful area in Tempe, The Lakes. Host is an executive engineer involved in Western States' Water Projects, he enjoys swimming, travel, movies; hostess enjoys antiques, art, interior design. Accommodations include: A) twin beds and B) twin bed. Both rooms share a large hall bath. Convenient to Arizona State University, Motorola, Hughes, Garrett, and Sky Harbor Airport. Host couple smokes. No pets. Swimming in HEATED POOL. TENNIS, EXERCISE ROOM, and JACUZZI available to guests. Breakfast served on bougainvilla covered patio or by the fireplace. VCR. NO CHILDREN.
**Rates:** A) S $35, D $40, T $65 AND B) S $35 DAILY.
**Reservations:** (602) 990-0682 8 A.M. TO 8 P.M. DAILY, MOUNTAIN TIME.

# WESTERN ARIZONA
# PEORIA

New, large Spanish style home. Large guestroom near front door. Guests have full use of adjacent living room with TV. Host is a metal worker from Scotland; hostess was born in Berlin and speaks German, she is a homemaker who enjoys homemaking and cooking, crafts (knitting and crocheting) "but most of all people." Accommodations include twin beds, private hall bath. Host couple are nonsmokers. Extra large breakfasts, laundry privileges. Home is near Sun City, Pioneer Village, Luke Air Force Base, International School of Management, thoroughbred race

track, Interstate 10, and Lake Pleasant. One DOG is in residence.
HANDICAPPED ACCESSIBLE.
**Rates:** S $25, D $35 DAILY. S $150, D $210 WEEKLY.
**Reservations:** (602) 990-0682 8 A.M. TO 8 P.M. DAILY, MOUNTAIN
TIME.

# COLORADO

## COLORADO SPRINGS

Imagine the pioneers crossing Kansas suddenly face to face with a 14,000 foot snow covered peak—Pike's Peak! Blessed with bountiful natural beauty and an exciting array of attractions, Colorado Springs lies at the foot of Pike's Peak and is considered one of the world's great resort areas. "Pike's Peak or Bust" was the rallying cry of the gold seekers who rushed to the Rockies in 1859. The view from the summit of Pike's Peak is awesome, stretching 165 miles eastward to the Kansas border. The Garden of the Gods is 700 acres studded with huge masses of red sandstone rocks. Some of the great attractions in the area are: the U.S. Air Force Academy, Pike's Peak Cog Railroad to the top, Seven Falls, Cave of the Winds, Will Rogers Shrine, and the Royal Gorge with rafting within an hours drive, to name but a few. Truly a city for all seasons there is exceptional dining from French gourmet to the famous "chuck wagon supper." The scenery is beautiful whether in summer for hiking, fishing, photography, or birdwatching; in fall with the golden aspens changing; or in winter during the height of the ski season.

Ranch style home near city center in very quiet neighborhood, three bedrooms. Budget A) twin bedroom with B) double bedroom share bath down the hall (bring your robe and slippers). C) Modest queen with private attached bathroom (shower only) and separate dressing area. It is located 1 1/2 miles from downtown, near shopping center. Amenities include a nearby municipal golf and tennis courts. Host is officer of a national trade association, a car buff, and is very active in the Boy Scouts, he was born in Aspen, Colorado and knows interesting history of the entire Rocky Mountain area. Hostess enjoys travel, reading, needlecraft, and bridge after a busy career. Home is on bus line, pickup at airport can be arranged. Full breakfast.
**Rates:** A) $30; B) $25; AND C) $45 DAILY.
**Reservations:** (303) 630-3433 MONDAY THROUGH FRIDAY, 9:00 - 6:00 SUMMER; MONDAY THROUGH FRIDAY, 1:00 - 6:00 NONSUMMER.

Comfortable double bed, room decorated with a touch of nostalgia, private bath (five steps down hallway), great view of Pike's Peak. It is located near northeast Colorado Springs, 2 miles to U.S. Air Force Academy south entrance, 15 minutes to downtown. Amenities include: TV and laundry facilities. The living room is available for guests. There is a resident well-behaved son. Small PET ALLOWED. Hosts are professional educators who enjoy an excellent rapport with friends and neighbors. Cooking is a hobby, so you may have a variety of delicious choices for a full breakfast. Formal Sunday breakfast. PIANO. Bikes available. Children of all ages welcome.

**Rates:** S $27, D $42 DAILY. SINGLE BED AVAILABLE IN SON'S ROOM FOR CHILD $5 ADDITIONAL DAILY. 7TH NIGHT FREE. **Reservations:** (303) 630-3433 MONDAY THROUGH FRIDAY, 9:00 - 6:00 SUMMER; MONDAY THROUGH FRIDAY, 1:00 - 6:00 NONSUMMER.

Two interesting mountain CABINS next to a small, private mountain estate 15 minutes west of Colorado Springs nestled on a hill overlooking Ute Pass. It is also close to famous tourist attractions. Accommodations include: A) large cabin with antique double bed, living room with queen sofa sleeper, home center/cable TV, stereo/cassette library, small separate kitchen, claw-foot tub/shower. Cabins have private patios with cookout privileges. Fully equipped kitchens in each cabin. Amenities include: picturesque communities nearby with fishing, riding, and restaurants. Communicate any special dietary requirements to the host at least three days in advance. Hosts are interested in antiques, fishing, reading, and traveling. A DOG and CAT are in residence. CHILDREN over 12 welcome.
**Rates:** A) S OR D $55, T OR Q $70; DAILY. 3 NIGHT MINIMUM.
**Reservations:** (303) 630-3433 MONDAY THROUGH FRIDAY, 9:00 - 6:00 SUMMER; MONDAY THROUGH FRIDAY, 1:00 - 6:00 NONSUMMER.

Located out of town in the Black Forest. Two twin beds in nicely decorated, spotlessly clean, cheery room. Private bath across hallway. Second bedroom has double sleeper sofa—excellent for third person or two children. Firm mattresses. Resident outside DOG. It is located northeast of the city, 25 minutes from downtown, lovely forested area, east of the Air Force Academy. Allow a good half hour to locate this quiet home, or more if you initially arrive at night. Amenities include: country living, natural wood floors in bedrooms. Nearby horses to rent, tennis court, excellent walking and jogging, fresh air, peaceful. Full breakfast includes homemade breads. Hostess is retired Licensed Practical Nurse, gracious lovely person, excellent conversationalist. Has traveled in Europe (cousins run a B&B in Ireland). Enjoys Nordic skiing, sailing, hiking, and travel. PIANO. Picnic area and bikes available. Children of all ages welcome. SMOKING in dining room permitted.
**Rates:** S $22, D $34 DAILY. IN SECOND OR THIRD ROOM ADDITIONAL ADULTS $12 EACH; CHILDREN $7 EACH DAILY.
**Reservations:** (303) 630-3433 MONDAY THROUGH FRIDAY, 9:00 - 6:00 SUMMER; MONDAY THROUGH FRIDAY, 1:00 - 6:00 NONSUMMER.

Private entrance, private bath, one queen bedroom (large room) in modest one story home of older neighborhood near jogging park. Surrounded by huge old homes (this is not one of them), price is modest. Resident TOY

POODLE. One mile from downtown. Amenities include: large yard, laundry facilities, public transportation, bumper pool in family room, TV in room, shower only. Continental breakfast plus. Host is retired bank president; hostess is retired, enjoys needlecraft. No pets. NO CHILDREN. **Rates:** S $30, D $40 DAILY. 7TH DAY FREE. 10% SENIOR CITIZEN'S DISCOUNT.
**Reservations:** (303) 630-3433 MONDAY THROUGH FRIDAY, 9:00 - 6:00 SUMMER; MONDAY THROUGH FRIDAY, 1:00 - 6:00 NONSUMMER.

A three story Queen Anne shingle Victorian, one of the original seven hotels of this area. Excellent for wedding receptions. Has served as boarding house, lodge, apartment building, and private residence. Recently restored to a B&B inn. Some antiques, some are from host's native Hawaii. Redecorated in casual and fun fashion by family. It is located in Old Historic Manitou Springs. Amenities include: Special honeymooners' treat (anniversaries, too). Within walking distance of restaurants and shops. Large "common area" with games, puzzles, PIANO, and VCR. Full breakfast. No pets. Host is a real estate broker interested in hiking, painting, and fishing: hostess acts as innkeeper. Two DOGS reside here. No CHILDREN under 10.
**Rates:** S OR D $40-$60 DAILY. WINTER (DECEMBER THROUGH FEBRUARY) S OR D $36-$54 DAILY.
**Reservations:** (303) 630-3433 MONDAY THROUGH FRIDAY, 9:00 - 6:00 SUMMER; MONDAY THROUGH FRIDAY, 1:00 - 6:00 NONSUMMER.

Two bedroom suite, king bed in one, queen bed in second. Private bath and living room with pullout bed and TV. It is Located 15 minutes from U.S. Air Force Academy, 12 minutes from airport, near shopping centers and restaurants. Amenities include: private daylight lower level, laundry facilities. Full breakfast. Host enjoys electronics and computers; hostess enjoys needlework. Both are active and enjoy traveling in their own motor home as well as church work and do it yourself projects. No pets. Ranch style home. Children of all ages welcome. NO SMOKING.
**Rates:** S $30, D $38 DAILY, ADDITIONAL ADULTS $12 EACH; CHILDREN $8 EACH DAILY. 7TH NIGHT FREE.
**Reservations:** (303) 630-3433 MONDAY THROUGH FRIDAY, 9:00 - 6:00 SUMMER; MONDAY THROUGH FRIDAY, 1:00 - 6:00 NONSUMMER.

Comfortable modern home with spectacular view of Pike's Peak. Privacy afforded with large sitting area, fireplace, and adjoining game room. Bedroom with double bed, writing desk, includes adjacent private bath, folding double sleeper sofa. Crib and layaway cot available. Host has two children, 11 and 12, and two miniature SCHNAUZERS, and a PERSIAN

KITTEN. Amenities include: FIREPLACE in your own sittingroom, extra privacy. Home is located approximately 3 miles from U.S. Air Force Academy. Full breakfast. Host is a professional engineer whose hobbies are golf, bridge, woodworking, and skiing; hostess is a homemaker (former RN) who enjoys golfing, hiking, skiing, and gourmet cooking. No pets. PIANO. Bikes available. Children of all ages welcome.
**Rates:** S $45, D $45 DAILY. EACH ADDITIONAL PERSON $15 DAILY.
**Reservations:** (303) 630-3433 MONDAY THROUGH FRIDAY, 9:00 - 6:00 SUMMER; MONDAY THROUGH FRIDAY, 1:00 - 6:00 NONSUMMER.

Charming 1902 Victorian, recently restored with antique furnishings, family heirlooms, quilts, comforters, and claw-foot tub. Three unique and cozy rooms. The queen room and double room upstairs have private baths, another double room downstairs has private bath across the hall. Rollaway bed available. Resident CAT "Mingtoy." It is located near historic Old Colorado City, Manitou Springs, and major attractions. Amenities include: story book Victorian. Parlor and living room have TV, VCR, stereo, antique fireplace, and PIANO. Telephone available. Turn down service with mints on the pillows. Breakfast is served on veranda, weather permitting. Freshly ground coffee, homemade baked goods. Sunday champagne brunch. Host is a research scientist; hostess enjoys tennis, hiking, crafts, and cooking. CHILDREN over 12 welcome. NO SMOKING.
**Rates:** S OR D $40-$46 DAILY.
**Reservations:** (303) 630-3433 MONDAY THROUGH FRIDAY, 9:00 - 6:00 SUMMER; MONDAY THROUGH FRIDAY, 1:00 - 6:00 NONSUMMER.

This is a fourth generation ivy covered, gorgeous English Tudor home that offers a unique blend of privacy and quiet. It is an ideal retreat for businesspeople featuring a private office with desk and telephone. Three rooms with double, queen, or twin beds, each with adjoining, shared, or private baths and showers. TV available. Amenities include: sunporch with view of Cheyenne Mountain, covered outdoor patio with table, and grill for evening meals. Located 1 mile from city center, 2 blocks from Colorado College. Breakfast includes fresh baked specialty breads and fresh squeezed orange juice. Host enjoys fishing, gardening, and gourmet cooking, hostess is a docent of Fine Arts Center and Pioneer Museum. Two night minimum. No CHILDREN under 10. NONSMOKERS preferred.
**Rates:** S $40 D $55 DAILY. FAMILY OF 4 $70 DAILY.
**Reservations:** (303) 630-3433 MONDAY THROUGH FRIDAY, 9:00 - 6:00 SUMMER; MONDAY THROUGH FRIDAY, 1:00 - 6:00 NONSUMMER.

Downstairs suite with queen bed and private shower. Includes private living area and sleeper sofa for two additional people. Views of Pike's Peak, Cheyenne Mountain, and Garden of the Gods. Located 5 miles from Manitou, west of city center, 5 minutes from downtown. TV. Near churches and Garden of God. Full breakfast may include homemade delicacies. Hosts are gracious, enthusiastic, retired (teaching and military), and would love to help you plan your visit (have lived here 30 years). NONSMOKERS preferred.

**Rates:** S $30, D $40; ADDITIONAL ADULT $10 EACH; ADDITIONAL CHILDREN ON SLEEPER SOFA $6 EACH DAILY (LESS FOR LONG-TERM VISITS). 7TH NIGHT FREE. SENIOR CITIZENS 10% DISCOUNT.

**Reservations:** (303) 630-3433 MONDAY THROUGH FRIDAY, 9:00 - 6:00 SUMMER; MONDAY THROUGH FRIDAY, 1:00 - 6:00 NONSUMMER.

## MANITOU SPRINGS
### SMALL HISTORIC CITY

Private guest cottage ("on street" entrance). Centrally located in Manitou Springs. Queen bed, queen sofa sleeper in living room. Nicely furnished with hardwood floors, built in 1909, newly restored. Fully equipped kitchen and sunshine breakfast area. One resident CAT who believes this is her cottage. Located 4 miles from Colorado Springs, 3 blocks to bus. Perfect long-term visit spot with kitchen. Amenities include: catered dinner by appointment, living room with woodstove, flagstone patio, crib available, kitchen for exclusive use of guests. Full breakfast. Host couple lives next door, originally from New York. Host is an architect; hostess owns an import/export business. Both enjoy travel, skiing, tennis, golf, biking, jogging, and historic preservation. Two night minimum. PETS WELCOME. A DOG resides here. Children of all ages welcome.
**Rates:** D $75 DAILY. ADDITIONAL PERSON $5 DAILY. WINTER RATES NEGOTIABLE.
**Reservations:** (303) 630-3433 MONDAY THROUGH FRIDAY, 9:00 - 6:00 SUMMER; MONDAY THROUGH FRIDAY, 1:00 - 6:00 NONSUMMER.

## DENVER AREA

Denver is known as the "mile high city" at 5,280 feet above sea level. It is often golf weather when snow is flying in the mountains (a dramatic backdrop for the city). Attractions include the Denver Botanic Gardens, the Denver Art Museum, one of the finest Natural History Museums in the world, and the multimillion dollar Colorado Heritage Center. Two extraordinary theaters in the Denver area are the natural outdoors Red Rock Amphitheater with its amazing natural acoustics and splendid view of city below, and the unique Boettcher Concert Hall. The U.S. Mint and the State Capitol are also points of interest. There are two very large amusement parks, Lakeside, and Elitch Gardens. Denver is one of the gateways to the famous old mining towns of the central Rockies and several ski areas.

## BOULDER

Lovely old gray stone home with European flavor, beautifully decorated. Accommodations include: A) Large room decorated in pinks and ruffles, second floor, bright, cheerful, chaise lounge, rocking chair and B) twin bedded room decorated in antique pine furniture. Both with firm mattresses and electric blankets. Shared compartmented bath. It is for those who value fresh flowers, fine furniture, peacefulness, and simple elegance. Located next to university campus in Boulder. It is within walking distance to downtown (no cab fares). Pickup from airport limo services in Boulder. TV available. Full breakfast including fresh ground coffee, homemade breads. Host is an economist interested in tournament tennis; hostess is vivacious, interesting, energetic, one of those "ageless" people that you can not imagine really raised three children. She is interested and accomplished in fashion design, sewing, ski touring, hiking, and jogging. A wonderful conversationalist. One CAT in residence. NO SMOKING.
**Rates:** A) D $30 AND B) D $20 DAILY.
**Reservations:** (303) 630-3433 MONDAY THROUGH FRIDAY, 9:00 - 6:00 SUMMER; MONDAY THROUGH FRIDAY, 1:00 - 6:00 NONSUMMER.

## EVERGREEN

It is 30 miles west of Denver (45 minutes from downtown). Secluded home on three quiet timbered acres. Bedroom with double bed and adjoining shower/bath is private, includes TV. Large bedroom areas. It is located 1 hour from Stapleton Airport. Amenities include: nearby village that provides choice of dining, varied cuisine in settings casual or splendid, night club entertainment, and shops. Swimming, tennis, boating, fishing, and golfing nearby (country club nearby may honor your private club membership). Full breakfast either indoors or on deck. Host is retired nationwide investigator, amiable, traveled United States, home based in Evergreen 35 years. Varied hobbies. NO CHILDREN. NO SMOKING indoors.
**Rates:** S $40, D $50 DAILY.
**Reservations:** (303) 630-3433 MONDAY THROUGH FRIDAY, 9:00 - 6:00 SUMMER; MONDAY THROUGH FRIDAY, 1:00 - 6:00 NONSUMMER.

## GOLDEN

Restored Victorian inn less than 30 minutes from Denver's Stapleton airport. Shuttle service for nominal charge available through Golden West. Four guestrooms with double accommodations include: A) separate entrance, private bath; B) private half bath; and C & D) two with shared bath. It is located in the foothills areas—Golden (Near Coors Brewery and Colorado School of Mines). Amenities include: TV in rooms, tray service in rooms for breakfast available, baby crib available. Full breakfast. Host is a pilot; hostess is a former decorator. They can give you many ideas on attractions in the Denver area. No unmarried couples. SMOKING and PETS OK in B only.
**Rates:** S $29-$44, D $39-$49; ADDITIONAL PERSON $5 EACH DAILY. 10% DISCOUNT WEEKLY.
**Reservations:** (303) 630-3433 MONDAY THROUGH FRIDAY, 9:00 - 6:00 SUMMER; MONDAY THROUGH FRIDAY, 1:00 - 6:00 NONSUMMER.

This home has two king bedrooms, private baths. Charming, above lake overlooking snow capped mountains. On frosty winter mornings geese on the lake could awaken you from your snuggly bed, otherwise expect peace and quiet in this country home. Near Coors Brewery, Railroad Museum, Buffalo Bill's Museum, Heritage Square, Melodrama, Colorado School of Mines, and antique shops. It is located at the foothill areas of west Denver. It is 25 minutes to downtown and Stapleton International Airport. Amenities include: paddle boat on lake, air conditioning, crib, TV. HANDICAPPED OK—only one stair up. Enjoy morning coffee on the deck as you watch sailboats in the summer. Full breakfast. Hostess is a travel agent who likes cooking and gardening. Modern Ranch style home.
**Rates:** S $45, D $50, T OR Q $80 DAILY. ONE NIGHT ONLY ADD $5 EXTRA.
**Reservations:** (303) 630-3433 MONDAY THROUGH FRIDAY, 9:00 - 6:00 SUMMER; MONDAY THROUGH FRIDAY, 1:00 - 6:00 NONSUMMER.

## LAKEWOOD (DENVER SUBURB)

Two rooms available in modest home. Double bed and queen sofa sleeper downstairs includes "family room suite" with FIREPLACE (nice privacy and space), private shower (no bath). TV and phone in room. Additional single room upstairs with bath. Located in west Lakewood. It is 6 scenic miles from Interstate 70 near Coors Brewery, Heritage Square, and Red Rocks Theater, 25 to 30 minutes from downtown. Full breakfast (on patio in summer). Amenities include: hiking trails nearby, quiet, nice view. No unmarried couples. Must have own transportation. Host is retired from the airlines; both host and hostess enjoy travel. Contemporary style home. NO CHILDREN under 8. NO SMOKERS. **Rates:** S $27, D $35, T $43, Q $51 DAILY. **Reservations:** (303) 630-3433 MONDAY THROUGH FRIDAY, 9:00 - 6:00 SUMMER; MONDAY THROUGH FRIDAY, 1:00 - 6:00 NONSUMMER.

## LITTLETON

Lovely, newly built home bordering gorgeous hiking acreage and foothill! Two bedrooms, one with queen bed, one with double. Private bath. Listen to beautiful sounds of meadowlarks in backyard as you sip a cool summer soda (or ask your host what a "fuzzy navel" is!) It is 35 minutes from downtown. Perfect for hikers or businesspeople. Close to J-M, Martin-Marietta, and Denver Tech Center. Amenities include: rolling hills, black and white TV in queen room. Family room available (to share) with fireplace for crisp fall and winter evenings. Full and hearty breakfasts. Host enjoys making lead soldiers, history, and coin collecting; hostess is very English and enjoys medieval brass rubbing, gardening, and interior decorating. Fitness center downstairs with bikes, rowing machine, and "fit for life" exerciser. VCR. CHILDREN over 10 only. No SMOKING. **Rates:** S $29, D $39; EACH ADDITIONAL PERSON IN SECOND ROOM $15 DAILY. **Reservations:** (303) 630-3433 MONDAY THROUGH FRIDAY, 9:00 - 6:00 SUMMER; MONDAY THROUGH FRIDAY, 1:00 - 6:00 NONSUMMER.

## WINTER PARK

Quiet, scenic, peaceful, no TVs, surrounded by pine forest and wildflower meadows. Either B&B accommodations or Modified American Plan available in winter. Seven nicely appointed rooms with private baths, maximum 20 guests. Games, cards, fireplace as a central focus for skiing guests in main lodge. It is 8 miles from Winter Park/Mary Jane and Silver Creek ski areas. Snacks and hot beverage apres ski. Hydro SPA in sunroom with flowers growing year-round. Full and filling breakfasts featuring homebaked goodies. Host is professional ski instructor; hostess enjoys being creative in cooking and watercolor painting. One DOG, two CATS reside here. Children of all ages welcome. Smoking is permitted but not at dining tables. **Rates:** SUMMER AND FALL S $47, D $47-$57, T $57 AND WINTER S $47, D $65-$75, T $85 DAILY. MODIFIED AMERICAN PLAN AVAILABLE IN WINTER FOR S $62, D $104 PER PERSON INCLUDES DINNER NIGHTLY. **Reservations:** (303) 630-3433 MONDAY THROUGH FRIDAY, 9:00 - 6:00 SUMMER; MONDAY THROUGH FRIDAY, 1:00 - 6:00 NONSUMMER.

# ROCKY MOUNTAINS
## ASPEN

Three story Contemporary home at base of Smuggler Mountain, great view of ski town and slopes. Your private suite has private entrance, two bedrooms (one queen, one double), double sleeper sofa, full bath, half kitchen with hot plate and refrigerator and small dining area. Located on free shuttle to the Mall and ski areas. Amenities include woodburning stove and TV in your living room, pool table, baby grand PIANO. Babysitting on request. Continental or full breakfast depending on hostess' work schedule. Hosts built home, cabinets, and some furniture. Family love woodworking and all sports. Two resident, attractive, well-behaved children live upstairs with parents. No unmarried couples. One outside DOG resides here. NO SMOKING.
**Rates:** S OR D $75, TWO COUPLES $55 PER COUPLE, CHILDREN ADD $10 PER DAILY.
**Reservations:** (303) 630-3433 MONDAY THROUGH FRIDAY, 9:00 - 6:00 SUMMER; MONDAY THROUGH FRIDAY, 1:00 - 6:00 NONSUMMER.

Nice little inn or converted lodge, 20 rooms, within walking distance to the center of Aspen and the ski slopes. Mostly queen-sized beds, includes TVs and phones in the rooms. May include extra trundle bed and/or kitchenette. Located in the heart of Aspen. Amenities include brass beds and puffy comforters, mint on your pillows. Full view of Aspen Mountain, an intimate apres ski with hot hors d'oeuvres, cider, and friends. Continental breakfast in summer; full breakfast in winter. HOT TUB. Children of all ages welcome.
**Rates:** S $50-$125, D $50-$155; EACH ADDITIONAL PERSON $10 AND STUDIO $200-$350 FOR UP TO EIGHT DAILY. CHRISTMAS SEASON RATES ARE THE HIGHEST. CHILDREN UNDER 12 FREE.
**Reservations:** (303) 630-3433 MONDAY THROUGH FRIDAY, 9:00 - 6:00 SUMMER; MONDAY THROUGH FRIDAY, 1:00 - 6:00 NONSUMMER.

## BUENA VISTA

Small inn located in scenic mountain area. Quiet. Caters to cross-country skiers in winter. Beautifully decorated (with antiques), terraces, grounds, and garden room. Shared bath (or private) depending on availability. Amenities include: country inn elegance, stroll by river bordering property, library, fireplace, charming and gracious hosts. Full breakfast or homemade pastries. Hosts are vivacious, retired couple. Host can teach cross-country skiing to you; hostess will be glad to fix you a picnic lunch. SMOKING permitted on the terrace.

**Rates:** S $45-$49, D $49-$62.50; EACH ADDITIONAL PERSON $12.50; AND ADDITIONAL CHILD $10 DAILY.
**Reservations:** (303) 630-3433 MONDAY THROUGH FRIDAY, 9:00 - 6:00 SUMMER; MONDAY THROUGH FRIDAY, 1:00 - 6:00 NONSUMMER.

## EAST VAIL

ON GORGE CREEK — Gorge Creek sings you to sleep in large, comfortable home, fishing at door. Fantastic mountain views from every room. Guestrooms and entrance on ground floor, spacious, cozy, wood paneled living areas upstairs with views from all directions including up from glass roofed breakfast room—furnished in antiques, leathers and tweed, player grand PIANO and collections of western art, fireplace/stove. Host is ranch real estate broker and cowboy for buyers of livestock and recreation ranches in 11 western states; hostess skis, rides, and plays tennis. Your host knows back roads and local history, his specialty. Horse boarding available. Huge cowboy gourmet breakfast cooked and served from antique wood burning cook stove—wake up juice, coffee in room. Ski, ride, golf, fish, hike, raft, private tennis, and health club. Accommodation include: A) two twin beds, private bath and B) double bed, private bath in hall, antiques. Located 10 minute east of Vail Village on free bus route. Access by public transportation. Children welcome. NONSMOKERS only.
**Rates:** WINTER S $65, D $55; SUMMER S $35, D $45 DAILY.
**Reservations:** (303) 949-1212 WINTER DAILY 9 A.M. TO 6 P.M. SUMMER MONDAY THROUGH FRIDAY 12 - 5 P.M.

## ESTES PARK

Soak in HOT TUB overlooking majestic Long's Peak. Start your day with breakfast on the deck. Tastefully redecorated, older home, on terraced hillside with outstanding views. Accommodations include two rooms, both with queen-sized beds. Share one adjacent full bath. Located a stone's throw from Rocky Mountain National Park, within 2 miles of the town of Estes Park. Amenities include hiking, golfing, fishing, and horseback riding nearby. Continental breakfast served. Host enjoys traveling, gardening, and people, he is a retired banker; hostess enjoys genealogy, crafts, and hiking, she is very knowledgeable about the area, a wonderful resource person to advise on elevation and difficulty of trails, nature walks, and park information. Hostess smokes. CHILDREN over 15 years old only.
**Rates:** S $33, D $44 DAILY. 7TH DAY FREE.
**Reservations:** (303) 630-3433 MONDAY THROUGH FRIDAY, 9:00 - 6:00 SUMMER; MONDAY THROUGH FRIDAY, 1:00 - 6:00 NONSUMMER.

## FORT COLLINS

Newly restored small red brick inn built in 1905. Turn-of-the-century atmosphere. Within walking distance to Colorado State University and downtown Fort Collins. The charming single or double accommodations are all uniquely decorated. Spotlessly clean, all share bath down the hall (have sinks in the rooms). Amenities include coffee or tea, games available. Dining area can be used as conference area; private little sitting room with desk and phone. Full breakfast. Host is a consulting engineer and gifted handyperson, he is responsible for a great deal of restoration, as is your inventive hostess; hostess enjoys porcelain doll making. SMOKING in living room area only. One DOG lives here.
**Rates:** S $28, D $38; ADDITIONAL PERSONS $6 EACH DAILY. WHOLE HOUSE $125 DAILY.
**Reservations:** (303) 630-3433 MONDAY THROUGH FRIDAY, 9:00 - 6:00 SUMMER; MONDAY THROUGH FRIDAY, 1:00 - 6:00 NONSUMMER.

## GLENWOOD SPRINGS

Restored Victorian with charming wallpapers and antiques. Elegant without being formal, a true country inn atmosphere in a best yet location, the four upstairs bedrooms include two with doubles, one with twins, and one single. All share the three bathrooms in the inn. Crib available. Two resident BOXERS are well behaved and friendly. Host smokes occasionally. Located on quiet street within walking distance of downtown, hot pools, Amtrack. Amenities include: down stuffed king pillows, fluffy towels, and complimentary seasonable beverage after your day of driving, hiking, or skiing. Free pickup from AMTRAK or nearby airport. Full breakfast. Hosts are vivacious, energetic skiers. Hostess fills her inn with enthusiasm. Really enjoys people of same and different interests. SMOKING on main floor only.
**Rates:** S $27, D $42 AND CARRIAGE HOUSE D $55, $10 ADDITIONAL ADULT, $5 ADDITIONAL CHILD DAILY.
**Reservations:** (303) 630-3433 MONDAY THROUGH FRIDAY, 9:00 - 6:00 SUMMER; MONDAY THROUGH FRIDAY, 1:00 - 6:00 NONSUMMER.

## LEADVILLE

This 1880s Victorian, original hotel recently renovated includes private baths or showers (cleverly built into old closet areas). Four suites offer connecting rooms. Located on the main street in the heart of the town. Home of gold busts, mining claims, ghost towns, and prospector trails. TV in rooms. Paperback library, excellent views. Discounts to Ski Cooper. Snowmobiling available. Health club facilities nearby for your use,

compliments of inn. Continental breakfast served in restaurant/lounge on second floor. Host is an innkeeper interested in guests' comfort. Spanish and Hebrew are spoken here. PIANO. Bikes available. Children of all ages welcome. SMOKING in designated rooms, only. Advise if you require a "smoking room."
**Rates:** S $35, D $40-$45 AND SUITES $55-$65 DAILY. 15% DISCOUNT ON SIX DAYS OR MORE.
**Reservations:** (303) 630-3433 MONDAY THROUGH FRIDAY, 9:00 - 6:00 SUMMER; MONDAY THROUGH FRIDAY, 1:00 - 6:00 NONSUMMER.

## MINTURN

New Mexico charm in the Colorado Rockies. Newly remodeled inn sits along side the Eagle River, 7 miles north of Vail. Twelve rooms (six with king beds, six with two twins); each have private baths. They are decorated in southwestern decor with brightly colored rugs, Indian art, rustic furniture, and a cozy beehive fireplace in the lounge. Gourmet continental breakfast. Wine and cheese in the afternoon. No PETS. Prefer CHILDREN over 12. NONSMOKERS only.
**Rates:** DECEMBER THROUGH APRIL $85; JUNE THROUGH NOVEMBER $60-$65 DAILY. CLOSED IN MAY.
**Reservations:** (303) 949-1212 WINTER DAILY 9 A.M. TO 6 P.M. SUMMER MONDAY THROUGH FRIDAY 12 - 5 P.M.

## OURAY

Lovely renovated historic old hotel built in 1898, now a quaint B&B inn. Includes Victorian furniture. Semiprivate baths available (two rooms share one). Lovely lobby and sitting room. Located in the southwest corner of the state. Amenities include: excellent restaurant serves dinner nightly. Continental breakfast, fresh fruits, homemade breads, and muffins. No pets. Furnished with antiques, stained glass, polished wood and brass trim throughout. Nearby is the national historic district with its quaint shops and Victorian homes. Once bustling with gold and silver seekers, today Ouray is a picturesque hamlet, nestled in the majestic San Juan mountains of Colorado. Host is a former banker; hostess a former legal secretary. One DOG and one CAT reside here. Double accommodations and suites available as well as cribs and cots. PIANO, SAUNA.
**Rates:** S OR D $38-$62 DAILY.
**Reservations:** (303) 630-3433 MONDAY THROUGH FRIDAY, 9:00 - 6:00 SUMMER; MONDAY THROUGH FRIDAY, 1:00 - 6:00 NONSUMMER.

## SNOWMASS VILLAGE

Beautifully decorated host home (condo) within 1 block of free shuttle (every 20 minutes) to slopes and Aspen (runs till 1:00 A.M. ski seasons). Shuttle to pool, sauna, laundry facilities, and aiport pickup. King bed, private bath, shower, private entrance. Home has fireplace and TV. Within walking to Snowmass village and shops. Full breakfast. Host is self-employed painting/wallpapering; hostess has catered; great cook, very aware of any special diets required by guests. Both enjoy hiking, backpacking, skiing, travel, and art. CHILDREN over 7 welcome. SMOKING is restricted to bedroom.
**Rates:** S $47, D $60 DAILY. 7TH NIGHT FREE FOR RETURNING GUESTS ONLY.
**Reservations:** (303) 630-3433 MONDAY THROUGH FRIDAY, 9:00 - 6:00 SUMMER; MONDAY THROUGH FRIDAY, 1:00 - 6:00 NONSUMMER.

## VAIL

WESTMEADOW DRIVE — Centrally located, on the free bus route, in the heart of Vail. You are within walking distance to the village, slopes, Vail's nightlife, Vista Bahn, and Lions Head Gondola. The general living area, TV, fireplace, and kitchen are shared in common with vivacious hostess. This townhouse, filled with hostess's art work, is a favorite! Full breakfast or continental. Accommodations include: A) two twin beds and B) double bed. Both share a bath. Children welcome.
**Rates:** SUMMER S $40, D $45 AND WINTER S $50, D $60 DAILY.
**Reservations:** (303) 949-1212 WINTER DAILY 9 A.M. TO 6 P.M. SUMMER MONDAY THROUGH FRIDAY 12 - 5 P.M.

## EAGLE VAIL

Located west of Vail, close and easy access to both Vail and Beaver Creek Ski Areas, this duplex offers the guest a large room with a queen bed and private bath with a warm JACUZZI tub. A haven for recreational activities, summer and winter, especially for cross-country skiers, golfers, and bikers. Continental breakfast. Car necessary. Amenities: electric blanket, plenty of parking and ski storage, use of kitchen facilities, and TV and fireplace in living area. Hostess is a ski school supervisor. Children welcome.
**Rates:** S $40, D $55 DAILY.
**Reservations:** (303) 949-1212 WINTER DAILY 9 A.M. TO 6 P.M. SUMMER MONDAY THROUGH FRIDAY 12 - 5 P.M.

## MATTERHORN

GENEVA DRIVE — A comfortable mountain home situated on a hill, with a view of the Gore Valley from the breakfast table. Host manages commercial condominiums; hostess is employed in a gift shop. A 16 year old daughter and two CATS complete the family. All speak German and the daughter speaks some Spanish. Guest accommodations are on the lower level, consisting of two bedrooms: A) two twin beds and B) a single bed with a trundle bed. Both bedrooms share a large shower in the same hallway. TVs are in both bedrooms. Guestrooms are wheelchair accessible. Home located on the town bus route, and situated within walking to restaurants and movie theater. Continental or full breakfast served.

**Rates:** S $35, D $55 DAILY.
**Reservations:** (303) 949-1212 WINTER DAILY 9 A.M. TO 6 P.M. SUMMER MONDAY THROUGH FRIDAY 12 - 5 P.M.

## WEST VAIL

CIRCLE DRIVE — Host are warm, earthy, well traveled, and very interesting. House has a lot of warm charm and character. This cozy mountain chalet is nestled against a hillside with a creek running nearby. Hosts tailor breakfast to guests' request. Home is half a block from frequent bus to Vail and short walk to restaurants and shopping. There is a frequent bus to Vail and short walk to restaurants and shopping. Full use of the home is extended to guests, and guests are treated to snacks, occasional wine and cheese parties, or a day of skiing with hosts. This comfortable home has a unique atmosphere and is especially good for the single traveler. One never leaves this home without many warm smiles and great memories. Weather permitting breakfast is served on large deck overlooking the scenic Gore Valley. Accommodations include a double bed, shared family bath. Small DOGS permitted. Amenities include: PIANO, antiques, picnic area, access by public transportation, and bikes. CHILDREN over 5 welcome. NONSMOKERS only.

**Rates:** S $45, D $55 DAILY.
**Reservations:** (303) 949-1212 WINTER DAILY 9 A.M. TO 6 P.M. SUMMER MONDAY THROUGH FRIDAY 12 - 5 P.M.

CORTINA LANE — A mountain home with a view of Gore Range. Family is a skiing one with 25 years in Vail Valley. Fireplace, great breakfast, skiing hints available. One bedroom with two twin beds. Share bath with family. It is 10 minutes from Vail. On bus route and host will drive skiers in. Children welcome.

**Rates:** S $45, D $60 DAILY.
**Reservations:** (303) 949-1212 WINTER DAILY 9 A.M. TO 6 P.M. SUMMER MONDAY THROUGH FRIDAY 12 - 5 P.M.

## WINTER PARK

Comfortable, "cozy, homey" feeling. All rooms have two beds (two doubles or double and twin) and private bath. Crib and cots available.

Modified American Plan during ski season (breakfast and dinner included in rate). Book early here! INDOOR POOL and SAUNA! Free transportation to and from Winter Park slopes in winter. Spa, restaurant, lounge area, TV in common area, patio in summer. Hosts are conscientious couple who have their guests' comfort in mind at every turn. Pool table.
**Rates:** NONSKI SEASON S $39, D $45 DAILY. MODIFIED AMERICAN PLAN DURING SKI SEASON. SKIER'S SPECIAL PACKAGE FROM TWO TO SEVEN DAYS.
**Reservations:** (303) 630-3433 MONDAY THROUGH FRIDAY, 9:00 - 6:00 SUMMER; MONDAY THROUGH FRIDAY, 1:00 - 6:00 NONSUMMER.

## TABERNASH

Passive solar home nestled in wooded area outside small town near Winter Park. Host is stone mason and has created fabulous fireplace and archway in home, he coaches skiing after a successful career of racing; also enjoys fishing; hostess enjoys biking, tennis, and cooking. Both hike, read, and enjoy travel. Two second floor rooms each with balcony opening into solar GREENHOUSE and HOT TUB below. Both rooms have queen beds, private bath (will host two to four people). Resident CATS and DOG. Located approximately 15 minutes from Winter Park and Mary Jane ski areas. Hosts invite you to join them for TV or to share fireplace. Near golf, wonderful hiking. Hostess enjoys creating dinners for nominal fee for her guests (given 24 hour notice). Gourmet breakfast. Need four wheel drive or front wheel drive with chains in ski season. CHILDREN over 10 welcome.
**Rates:** S $40, D $50; ADDITIONAL ADULTS $15 EACH; AND ADDITIONAL CHILDREN $10 EACH DAILY.
**Reservations:** (303) 630-3433 MONDAY THROUGH FRIDAY, 9:00 - 6:00 SUMMER; MONDAY THROUGH FRIDAY, 1:00 - 6:00 NONSUMMER.

## SOUTHWEST COLORADO
### DURANGO

Newly built home not far from downtown. Two very comfortable bedrooms and full bath in daylight basement suite. One room with double bed, cozy, pretty antiques. Second room has twin beds, sleeper sofa in family room could accommodate one more. Located less than 10 minutes to downtown, quiet location. Amenities include: private entrance, two outside decks. Full breakfast. Hosts are gracious, conscientious, retired couple who have traveled B&B in Europe. They built their own lovely home. Host does terrific woodworking; hostess enjoys needlepoint, cross stitching, and is active in Gideon and Christian Women's Club. No pets. It is 25 minutes to airport, 20 minutes to Ft. Lewis College, 10 minutes to Durango-Silverton Narrow Gauge Rail Road and river rafting, and 30 minutes to Mesa Verde. All sports activities nearby. Contemporary home. CHILDREN over 15 welcome. NO SMOKING. **Rates:** MAY THROUGH NOVEMBER S $30, D $35-$40. EXTRA PERSON $12.50 EACH DAILY. **Reservations:** (303) 630-3433 MONDAY THROUGH FRIDAY, 9:00 - 6:00 SUMMER; MONDAY THROUGH FRIDAY, 1:00 - 6:00 NONSUMMER.

## TELLURIDE

Small three story inn, carefully restored, family owned and operated. Suites and double accommodations are available. Handmade quilts on each bed are color coordinated, each room different, shared bathroom "down the hall" (bring your robe). Located near excellent ski area, half block fron new Oak Street lift. Free shuttle bus to slopes just minutes away. Advance ski tickets sales available. Continental breakfast include homemade muffins and coffee. Host is in real estate and enjoys golf and fishing; hostess enjoys skiing and hiking. One LABRADOR RETRIEVER lives here. Children welcome. **Rates:** SUMMER D $22-$46; WINTER D $45-$60 DAILY. HOLIDAYS AND FESTIVALS MORE. **Reservations:** (303) 630-3433 MONDAY THROUGH FRIDAY, 9:00 - 6:00 SUMMER; MONDAY THROUGH FRIDAY, 1:00 - 6:00 NONSUMMER.

Restored Victorian boarding house. Eight rooms, one has private bath, others share. Twin and double beds. Some rooms accommodate three to four people. Located in southwest corner of Colorado in San Juan mountains, 1 block from new Oak Street lift! Amenities include: cable TV, HBO/movie theaters, books and games, apres ski refreshments, advance lift ticket sales. Within walking distance to restaurants. Continental plus breakfast. Hosts know area well. Host is a real estate salesman; hostess enjoys skiing and hiking with her husband. One LABRADOR RETRIEVER lives here. Many antiques. Children of all ages welcome. **Rates:** SUMMER $30-$40; WINTER $45-$50 DAILY. ADDITIONAL PERSONS $8 EACH DAILY. **Reservations:** (303) 630-3433 MONDAY THROUGH FRIDAY, 9:00 - 6:00 SUMMER; MONDAY THROUGH FRIDAY, 1:00 - 6:00 NONSUMMER.

## SUMMIT COUNTY

This home is 1 1/2 hours west of Denver via well-maintained Interstate 70. It is in a lovely valley surrounded by the four international resorts of Breckenridge, Keystone, Copper Mountain, and A-Basin. (Vail is only another 30 minutes away.) A free shuttle connects the four in winter. Ski all conveniently by purchasing a "ski on the summit" pass. Excellent shopping and dining in the quaint Victorian kingdom of Breckenridge, ranging from elegant dining and lodging to budget dorms. Olympic champions Phil and Steve Mahre Training Centers at Keystone; and with the largest snowmaking equipment in the west, the Summit County area is the place to go for "earlybird skiing" (October 15 approximate opening). Sleigh rides, hot air ballons, indoor tennis, and jacuzzis. Add this to Dillon Lake and the 127 year history of Breckenridge (saloons and live theater) and you will understand genuine Colorado.

## BRECKENRIDGE

English Tudor style house with beautiful mountain view, private entrance. One queen-size bedroom and bath suite. One twin bedroom and private attached bath. Third bedroom with twin beds could be used for two children or good friends. Large common sitting room with TV and stereo. Full breakfast. It is 1 1/2 miles to base of ski area and free shuttle bus to all Four Summit County ski areas. Own transportation required. Hosts are congenial retired couple. Host is interested in tennis, skiing, and public relations; hostess enjoys cooking and is a semiprofessional photographer. One outside CAT lives here. Sailboat and bikes available. Children of all ages welcome.
**Rates:** S $40, D $55-$58 DAILY.
**Reservations:** (303) 630-3433 MONDAY THROUGH FRIDAY, 9:00 - 6:00 SUMMER; MONDAY THROUGH FRIDAY, 1:00 - 6:00 NONSUMMER.

Cross-country ski from the front door of this beautiful passive solar, newly built home! Upstairs private bedroom with king-sized bed and private bath with attached shower. Hosts live on first floor. Located 8 miles from Breckenridge at foot of Hoosier Pass. Enjoy the lovely scenery. Home is nestled in valley with spectacular view of Northstar Mountain. HOT TUB is shared with guests. Full breakfast is served. Hosts are retired, enthusiastic, and active people. They enjoy golfing, hiking, and skiing and built their beautiful home. No babies or very small CHILDREN. SMOKING outside only.
**Rates:** S $35, D $50 DAILY.
**Reservations:** (303) 630-3433 MONDAY THROUGH FRIDAY, 9:00 - 6:00 SUMMER; MONDAY THROUGH FRIDAY, 1:00 - 6:00 NONSUMMER.

## DILLON

Guest bedrooms on lower level, Recently redecorated, double bed, share family room pool table and cozy woodburning stove in winter. Private

attached shower, huge walk-in closet. Two resident CATS and one DOG. It is 2 miles from the resort of Keystone/North Peak, and near Lake Dillon for boating and fishing, and near free shuttle for 4 major ski areas. Refrigerator available, coffee or tea any time. Full breakfast weekends, continental during week. Host is a former forest ranger. The hosts and their two teenaged children have lived in some of our country's most fabulous national parks for the past 15 years. They love the outdoors, skiing, camping, and fishing. PLAYER PIANO. NO CHILDREN. NO SMOKING.
**Rates:** S $35-$40, D $45-$50 DAILY. WEEKLY 7TH NIGHT FREE.
**Reservations:** (303) 630-3433 MONDAY THROUGH FRIDAY, 9:00 - 6:00 SUMMER; MONDAY THROUGH FRIDAY, 1:00 - 6:00 NONSUMMER.

## FRISCO

Country home with beautiful mountain view from large, open living room and wraparound deck. Two bedrooms downstairs and bath form a suite. Located in the heart of Summit County, transportation can be furnished to and from ski shuttle stop three-fourths of a mile away. Amenities include a HOT TUB on outside deck, video with an elaborate library of movies for your enjoyment, antique PUMP ORGAN for group sings (or solo for the brave), living room moss rock fireplace. Gaze while the snow gently prepares tomorrow's powder. Full, hearty breakfast. Hosts know and can share intimate knowledge of ski areas (six within half hour drive) and countless cross-country ski trails. Host is a professional photographer; hostess enjoys skiing and needlework. Children of all ages welcome.
**Rates:** S $40, D $57-$67 DAILY. ADDITIONAL ADULT $20 EACH, ADDITIONAL CHILDREN $10-$15 EACH DAILY.
**Reservations:** (303) 630-3433 MONDAY THROUGH FRIDAY, 9:00 - 6:00 SUMMER; MONDAY THROUGH FRIDAY, 1:00 - 6:00 NONSUMMER.

## VAIL VALLEY
### EDWARDS
### LAKE CREEK

WEST LAKE CREEK ROAD — Situated in beautiful Lake Creek Valley at the base of the scenic New York Mountain Range sits this house with West Lake Creek running through the front yard and towering 80 feet blue spruce. This is truly a peaceful location for the traveler who wants to get away from it all. The athelete will find plenty to do, with 5 golf courses in a 17 mile range, the closest only 10 minutes away. Downhill and cross-country skiing at Beaver Creek, 15 minutes away. Host travels throughout the world, including the Soviet Union and is an accomplished photographer; hostess has a small baking company. Both have lived in this area over 16 years. They live on the second floor. A first floor suite is available with one twin-bedded bedroom, living room, VCR (no TV hook up), and private bath. This is a new home that the owner built with a moss rock first floor and log second floor. It is filled with antiques, stained glass, plants, and beautiful photographs.

**Rates:** S $40, D $45; SUMMER (JUNE JULY AUGUST) S $35, D $40 DAILY.

**Reservations:** (303) 949-1212 WINTER DAILY 9 A.M. TO 6 P.M. SUMMER MONDAY THROUGH FRIDAY 12 - 5 P.M.

## WESTERN COLORADO
### SALIDA

King, queen, and twin beds available. Lovely inn, recently restored by an act of love by innkeepers (previously from California). On State Historical Register. Restored inn with beautiful Victorian furnishings including toilets with elevated flush tanks and pull chains. Resident menagerie (all outside) include two ducks, two POODLES, one peacock, one CAT, and one SIBERIAN HUSKY. Located approximately 2 hours west of Colorado Springs, 1 1/2 miles from Salida, 25 minutes from Monarch ski area. Amenities include: recently added co-ed dorm, excellent river rafting in summer, good skiing at Monarch. Host is a carpenter who enjoys sports; hostess also enjoys sports. Hosts enjoy outdoor recreation. Full breakfast for guests in private rooms; continental breakfast in dorm rooms. Bikes available. Children of all ages welcome.

**Rates:** WINTER S $29, D $39-$49 AND CO-ED DORM $14 DAILY.

**Reservations:** (303) 630-3433 MONDAY THROUGH FRIDAY, 9:00 - 6:00 SUMMER; MONDAY THROUGH FRIDAY, 1:00 - 6:00 NONSUMMER.

# MONTANA

## KALISPELL

Lovely two story Colonial home in the country with magnificent view in all directions. Manicured lawn with wildflowers and old-fashioned roses, large porch overlooking meadow and creek. Accommodations include four bedrooms: A) four poster bed; B) queen-sized bed; C) queen waterbed; and D) twin beds. They are all attractively decorated. All rooms share two bathrooms in home. Fireplace to share with host family, refrigerator shelf available. An 18 year old son lives here. WELSH CORGI DOG and CALICO CAT in residence. Near Glacier National Park. Flowers in summer. Pickup from airport available. Full breakfast. Hostess enjoys roses, Arabian horses, New England, reading, and quilting. Horses can be boarded nearby. CHILDREN over 8 welcome. NO SMOKING.
**Rates:** S OR D A) $45; B) $40; AND C & D) $35 DAILY. S $200, D $250 WEEKLY.
**Reservations:** (303) 630-3433 MONDAY THROUGH FRIDAY, 9:00 - 6:00 SUMMER; MONDAY THROUGH FRIDAY, 1:00 - 6:00 NONSUMMER.

## ROCKY MOUNTAINS
### BILLINGS

Nicely decorated, restored home. Four charming bedrooms, double beds, second story, hardwood floors, shared bath, sink in rooms. Located within walking distance to downtown and medical corridor. Cadillac limo for airport transportation can be arranged, as can lunches, dinners, private parties, seminars, and the like. Comfortable living room and TV to share. Interesting history of home and owner's ties to it. Continental breakfast with homemade muffins. Hostess reminds one of the type of aunt you always wished you had had.
**Rates:** S $24-$36, D $28-$36 DAILY. ADDITIONAL PERSON $5 DAILY.
**Reservations:** (303) 630-3433 MONDAY THROUGH FRIDAY, 9:00 - 6:00 SUMMER; MONDAY THROUGH FRIDAY, 1:00 - 6:00 NONSUMMER.

## BOZEMAN

A most unusual experience for Montana! Old Victorian mansion, furnished with antiques (most are for sale including Buffalo's Bill's gloves and Calamity Jane's antique brass bed), Oriental rugs, and plants. Collection of antique lamps are especially fascinating. It is rumored that a ghost, Michael, visits here (maybe lives here). Accommodates only six to nine guests. A suite is available. Flyfishing (blue ribbon package available). Host is a restorations consultant; hostess is a Ph.D. candidate in chemistry who enjoys piano and books. Two children, a daughter, aged 10, and a son, aged 12, are in residence. Pool table, picnic area, and bikes available. Children of all ages welcome. NO SMOKING.

**Rates:** S OR D $45 DAILY.

**Reservations:** (303) 630-3433 MONDAY THROUGH FRIDAY, 9:00 - 6:00 SUMMER; MONDAY THROUGH FRIDAY, 1:00 - 6:00 NONSUMMER.

## NEAR MISSOULA

Working cattle ranch nestled in the Bitterroot Valley. Deer and elk graze on ranch. Bald eagle nest. Great for those who appreciate the outdoors and wildlife. Double accommodation in two rooms available. Private bath. Cribs available. Located in western Montana, 20 miles south of Missoula at the end of a dirt road. Call hosts from Missoula for escort, or if you are challenged by directions, go for it! Resident BLACK LABRADOR, GOLDEN RETRIEVER, assorted CATS and kittens, and horses and foals (depending on time of year, over 500 cattle). Amenities include: HOT TUB, satellite TV, and ranch tour at no extra charge. Fishing on property. Orchard harvest in fall. Calving in spring. Excellent hiking in Bitterroots. Continental breakfasts and dinners available at extra charge with advanced notice. Both hosts love animals and the outdoors, gardening, and horseback riding. Ask host about previous generations homesteading here. It is suggested that guests eat in town on night of arrival and to schedule arrival between 6 and 8 P.M. Year old child and nanny live here. No SMOKING indoors.

**Rates:** S $28, D $38 DAILY. IN SECOND ROOM ADDITIONAL ADULTS $10 EACH, ADDITIONAL CHILDREN $5 EACH DAILY.

**Reservations:** (303) 630-3433 MONDAY THROUGH FRIDAY, 9:00 - 6:00 SUMMER; MONDAY THROUGH FRIDAY, 1:00 - 6:00 NONSUMMER.

# NEW MEXICO

## ALBUQUERQUE

Home away from home in this Southern Colonial "guest suite" with a private entrance into your own living room and kitchen. Great for a family! Upstairs are the bathroom and the two tastefully decorated bedrooms. Accommodations include: A) two twin-beds and B) double bed. View of the city lights and the mountains. Located northeast quadrant of the city, 2 1/2 miles from Interstate 40. Amenities include: residential area, privacy, near mountains and park for hikes, golf course, tennis courts, and the cable car ride to the 10,000 foot mountain top restaurant. It is 1 block to bus stop to Old Town, within walking distance to numerous restaurants. Your choice of continental, fix your own, or the special full breakfast. Hosts are a professional couple who have lived abroad, traveled widely (B&B included), and enjoy meeting people. Both are self-employed. Host is in business forms; hostess is a former international airline flight attendant who is in fashion design and loves to cook. Spanish is spoken here. One DOG, Sandy, is in residence. NO SMOKING.
**Rates:** S $40, D $60, T OR Q $75 DAILY. WEEKLY NEGOTIABLE.
**Reservations:** (303) 630-3433 MONDAY THROUGH FRIDAY, 9:00 - 6:00 SUMMER; MONDAY THROUGH FRIDAY, 1:00 - 6:00 NONSUMMER.

## NORTH CENTRAL
## ALBUQUERQUE

A touch of England delivered by your British hostess. Queen bed, private bath, SWIMMING POOL, enclosed JACUZZI, and fluffy hot tub towels provided. Can accommodate second couple in second small, modest bedroom. Located in the northeast section of the city near Tramway. Need own transportation. Amenities include: nearby to mountains, stables, golf, hiking, and tennis. A real full English breakfast. A comfortable home package full of interesting English furnishings and other eclectic pieces awaits. COLLIE, Laddie, is in residence. Host is a sales representative who likes to bowl and play golf. Young boys live here. Ranch style home. NO CHILDREN.
**Rates:** S $35, D $45 DAILY. ADDITIONAL ADULTS $15 EACH DAILY. 7TH NIGHT FREE.
**Reservations:** (303) 630-3433 MONDAY THROUGH FRIDAY, 9:00 - 6:00 SUMMER: MONDAY THROUGH FRIDAY, 1:00 - 6:00 NONSUMMER.

## NORTHEAST
## LAS VEGAS

Three story restored Victorian. Lone traveler or small groups will relish the cozy comfort of antique furnished rooms and puffy comforters. Two resident children. Seven Victorian decor bedrooms share 3 1/2 baths. Cots are available. Living room and dining room for guests. Intimate amd friendly. Located 64 miles from Santa Fe on Interstate 25 (toward Colorado). Large country breakfast. Hostess has renovated this large home and is now a resident innkeeper. She is an antique dealer (hence the charming pieces gracing the inn). Spanish and French are spoken here. Two young daughters live here. VCR and bikes available. Children welcome. SMOKING permitted in some rooms.
**Rates:** S $34, D $39 DAILY.
**Reservations:** (303) 630-3433 MONDAY THROUGH FRIDAY, 9:00 - 6:00 SUMMER; MONDAY THROUGH FRIDAY, 1:00 - 6:00 NONSUMMER.

## ROCKY MOUNTAINS
## TAOS

Accommodations include: A) truly unique second story suite with two bedrooms and queen sleeper sofa and B) suite on first floor has queen bed. Located 1 block from plaza. Amenities include: HOT TUB in larger suite, TV, FIREPLACE. Continental breakfast buffet style. Hostess is daughter of a well-known Indian trader, writer, artist, and craftsman of early days of Taos. Hostess smokes. Host is in real estate; hostess is an artist. One female GERMAN SHEPHERD lives here. CHILDREN over 12 welcome.
**Rates:** A) S $65, D $65, EACH ADDITIONAL PERSON $20 AND B) S $40, D $40, EACH ADDITIONAL PERSON $10 DAILY.
**Reservations:** (303) 630-3433 MONDAY THROUGH FRIDAY, 9:00 - 6:00 SUMMER; MONDAY THROUGH FRIDAY, 1:00 - 6:00 NONSUMMER.

Adobe style home. Two rooms adjoining the main house, bath between rooms. "Gallery East" room with FIREPLACE. Mexican tiled bathroom. Cribs and cots are available. Immaculately clean. Use and enjoy the main house with wood beamed ceilings, fireplace, and courtyard. Located 1 mile from center of Taos, 20 minutes from ski basin. Amenities include: full view of Taos mountain, outside HOT TUB (SPA) on deck. Walls are full of works by local, regional, and national artists. Individual thermostats. Private backyard. Full gourmet or New York experience breakfast. Host, a retired high school principal, knows history and art of Taos, also enjoys fishing, hiking, and skiing; hostess is a retired private school director. VCR. HANDICAPPED ACCESSIBLE. NO SMOKING.

**Rates:** S $55, D $60, WITH PRIVATE BATH $70 DAILY.
**Reservations:** (303) 630-3433 MONDAY THROUGH FRIDAY, 9:00 - 6:00 SUMMER; MONDAY THROUGH FRIDAY, 1:00 - 6:00 NONSUMMER.

1 MILE FROM PLAZA — The land of enchantment with a delightful dry climate year-round, cool summer days and nights, and a graceful mingling of Indian, Spanish, and Anglo cultures has much to interest the artist, outdoor person, and the history student. This is a 150 year old hacienda, pueblo adobe with thick walls, fireplaces, and JACUZZI. Indian chants and dances when requested. Sangria served on the Placita or before the fire. In the midst of art galleries, museums, churches, historic spots, and ski areas. Delicious breakfasts include homemade bread. Five rooms that can be arranged as single, double, or a suite for as many as six people. HANDICAPPED ACCESSIBLE.
**Rates:** A) S $33, D $53; B) S $45, D $65; AND C & D) D $83 DAILY. $5 OFF EACH NIGHT FOR STAYS OF TWO OR MORE NIGHTS. 6TH DAY FREE.
**Reservations:** (504) 346-1928 SEVEN DAYS 8 A.M. TO 8 P.M.

# UTAH

## ROCKY MOUNTAINS
### MONROE
### LITTLE GREEN VALLEY

In the heart of "the Little Green Valley" of Sevier County. An excellent halfway point between Los Angeles and Denver. Just 3 miles off US 89, the direct route to Bryce and Zion National Parks. Monroe is also near the Capitol Reef National Park, said to be the best kept secret in Utah. It has more color and diversity than either, according to local information. Near new Fremont Indian State Park, too. The home is a combination of old and new. The original home (now encased in a modern structure) is about 100 years old. Country inside and out. Host (formerly with Disneyland as head of painting and paperhanging) is retired, he enjoys people and his garden; hostess is a newspaperwoman working as editor for more than 30 years on the Daily Press in southern California, she is currently part of the Utah Travel Council, working with Panoramaland, one of the nine travel regions where she helps host familiarizing tours for Europeans, travel agencies, and the media. She enjoys cooking and has done three cookbooks. Swimming and tennis nearby. Also golf, fishing, and hunting. Accommodations include: two rooms with king beds and a single room. A suite can be made out of these rooms. One has a private bath. The other two share a bath. A 12 year old BEAGLE BASSETHOUND and stray CAT live lovingly here. Excellent Belgian Macademia Nut waffles, Dutch oven pancakes or a Mexican breakfast dish bring raves. There is cable TV, a private entrance, parking, and grassy yard. Behaved CHILDREN welcome. NO SMOKING.
**Rates:** S $25, D $35, SUITE $70 DAILY.
**Reservations:** (602) 990-0682 8 A.M. TO 8 P.M. DAILY, MOUNTAIN TIME.

### PARK CITY

Historic inn built in 1893. Suites available with rollaways. Seven rooms charming, delightful from king to twin private and shared baths. Feather pillows, down quilts in cozy, antique filled rooms. Perfect for small ski groups or seminars. Located in one of Utah's best ski areas only 30 miles from Salt Lake City. It is 1 hour (daily bus) to four of the best ski areas! Amenities include: no car needed here, fly to Salt Lake City, public transportation to Park City, free shuttle for skiers in town, ski lift 100 yards from your doorway (and you can ski back to the inn at the end of the day). HOT TUB, laundry, and kitchen available. Den/living room with fireplace, excellent value for a best yet inn. Five golf courses nearby, two reservoirs, and all water sports. Full breakfast. Four DOGS live here, too, ORGAN. Hosts are a trio of happy people making their dream come true. Children of all ages welcome. SMOKING in living room only. NO CIGARS.

**Rates:** S OR D A) $40-$70; B) $45-$80; C) $50-$90; D) $70-$115; E) $60-$100; F) $80-$135; AND G) $75-$125. RATES ARE SEASONAL AND DAILY. HOLIDAY PERIODS SLIGHTLY HIGHER. ADDITIONAL PERSON $15. TAXES NOT INCLUDED. DOUBLE OCCUPANCY.

**Reservations:** (303) 630-3433 MONDAY THROUGH FRIDAY, 9:00 - 6:00 SUMMER; MONDAY THROUGH FRIDAY, 1:00 - 6:00 NONSUMMER.

# WYOMING

## ROCKY MOUNTAINS
### LARAMIE

Beautifully restored old three story Post Victorian Queen Anne style. Six guestrooms, shared baths. Spacious living room/dining room. Charming, well landscaped. Interesting. House CATS in residence. Located across from University of Wyoming. Continental breakfast plus. Amenities include: light "Florida" room filled with plants, sundeck on third floor for relaxing. Hosts are enthusiastic entrepreneurs, who own a travel agency and restaurant in town. PIANO. Bikes available. Very young CHILDREN discouraged. No SMOKING in bedrooms.

**Rates:** S $33-$43, D $40-$50 DAILY.

**Reservations:** (303) 630-3433 MONDAY THROUGH FRIDAY, 9:00 - 6:00 SUMMER; MONDAY THROUGH FRIDAY, 1:00 - 6:00 NONSUMMER.

# 9

**Pacific**

- [ ] Alaska
- [ ] California
- [ ] Hawaii
- [ ] Nevada
- [ ] Oregon
- [ ] Washington

# ALASKA

## ELIAS NATONAL PARK
### MCCARTHY

SHUSHANA AVENUE — In the heart of the 12.5 million acre Wrangell/ Saint Elias National Park—a spectacular drive east of Anchorage. Road information available. Guests may stay in the Mother Lode Power House, on the National Historic Register, or in the Territorial Commissioner's House. These old-fashioned accommodations have a log sauna, wood heated HOT TUB, and shared outdoor facilities. Fresh spring water is provided for drinking and cooking. Kitchen privileges. Private cabin with kitchen sleeps six, UNHOSTED. Hostess serves a large Alaskan breakfast that includes homebaked treats. Bikes available. The local Museum is just 5 minutes away. Hiking to the Erie and Bonanza mines, or out to the Root Glacier easily accessible. Good berry picking nearby. Hosts operate Saint Elias Alpine Guides that offers sightseeing of the historic copper mining "ghost town" Kennicott, whitewater rafting, and glacier hiking. Children of all ages welcome. SMOKING not permitted inside due to fire hazards.

**Rates:** MAY THROUGH SEPTEMBER SEASON S $45, D $50 DAILY. S $275, D $300 WEEKLY. WHOLE PRIVATE CABIN THAT SLEEPS SIX WITH KITCHEN $150 DAILY. $900 WEEKLY.

**Reservations:** (907) 344-4006 MAY - SEPTEMBER 9 A.M. TO 9 P.M., OCTOBER - APRIL 9 A.M. TO 12 NOON.

## KACHEMAK BAY
### HOMER
### SKYLINE DRIVE

MARY LANE AND SANFORD — Private modern cabin with wood stove, double and single bed, simple cabin furniture. Bank of windows exposes spectacular view of Kachemak Bay, glaciers, and range of snowcapped peaks, Homer islands, and coves. Extra sleeping space for two or three children available in unheated playhouse near cabin. Located in middle of hundreds of sparsely populated acres available for hiking, cross-country skiing, and viewing of dozens of varieties of wildflowers. Moose are often seen in yard. Separate entrance to main house for complete and private bathroom facilities. Hostess will serve gourmet continental breakfast in dining room of main house. She is a retired teacher who has lived in Alaska for 35 years and operates a small ceramic business.

**Rates:** D $50, $5 EACH FOR EXTRA FAMILY MEMBERS, $10 EACH FOR EXTRA ADULTS DAILY.

**Reservations:** (907) 344-4006 MAY - SEPTEMBER 9 A.M. TO 9 P.M., OCTOBER - APRIL 9 A.M. TO 12 NOON.

# KENAI PENINSULA
## SOLDOTNA
### RURAL

STERLING HIGHWAY MILE 93 — Originally part of the Old Heath Homestead. This home is set back from the highway it overlooks Loren Lake. Newly redecorated and furnished, much of the original homestead of flair remains. Located on approximately 2 acres, surrounded by lawn and flowers, visited frequently by local moose, rabbits, eagles, and various water fowl. The ever flowering window boxes add a touch of New England in summer. Hosts' past experience includes psychology, psychiatry, nursing, and they are presently involved in real estate and oil field work. This is a flexible home that can fit up to 12 guests. Accommodations include four bedrooms with shared bath. Full breakfasts are highlighted with fresh baked breads and local game when available. Local airport courtesy service—charters. Alaskan stories and fishing tales available on request! Tourist must be willing to arrive as guest and depart as friend. Brochure available. One DOG. VCR.
**Rates:** S $50, D $60 DAILY PLUS 5% TAX.
**Reservations:** (907) 344-4006 MAY - SEPTEMBER 9 A.M. TO 9 P.M., OCTOBER - APRIL 9 A.M. TO 12 NOON.

## MAT-SU VALLEY
### WILLOW

A small lodge with a well-stocked bar and package store and a short menu that is available. Attractive, clean, and very friendly atmosphere. If one wishes to meet local residents, this is the place. Willow is in the heart of good fishing, hiking, sightseeing, and viewing Mount McKinley. Accommodations include: four cabins each with two rooms with central bathhouse. One DOG and one CAT. A PIANO and pool table.
**Rates:** D $45, $6 FOR EACH ADDITIONAL PERSON DAILY.
**Reservations:** (907) 344-4006 MAY - SEPTEMBER 9 A.M. TO 9 P.M., OCTOBER - APRIL 9 A.M. TO 12 NOON.

## MATANUSKA VALLEY
### PALMER
#### OLD NEWBY FARM NEAR PALMER

GERSHMEL LOOP AND DECAMP — Clean, comfortable, and restful guestrooms. Modern Alaskan home. Across from Colonist Barn. Remarkable view of Pioneer Peak. Two story solar room. Host is a data technician; hostess has own art studio, loves to pamper guests. Close to everything you could imagine. Accommodations include: A) queen-sized bed; B & C) two rooms each with twin-bedded room; and D) queen-sized hide-a-bed. Two baths are shared. Cable TV. CHILDREN in teens welcome.

**Rates:** S $35, D $45 DAILY. S $200, D $250 WEEKLY.
**Reservations:** (907) 344-4006 MAY - SEPTEMBER 9 A.M. TO 9 P.M.,
OCTOBER - APRIL 9 A.M. TO 12 NOON.

# SOUTH CENTRAL
## ANCHORAGE
### BROADMOOR ESTATES

BALCHEN DRIVE — Nice Split Level home in pleasant well-kept
residential area. Close to airport with pickup on request. Hosts, both
originally Dutch, are well-traveled and internationally oriented. Hosted
continental breakfast. Accommodations on separate lower level include:
A) queen-sized bed and B) double bed. Full bath and lounge area with
TV. Walking distance to restaurants, convenience stores, and bus stops.
Close to Lake Hood where charter flights for fishing and hunting originate.
VCR.
**Rates:** S $40, D $50, T $75, $10 EACH ADDITIONAL PERSON DAILY.
WINTER RATES $5 LESS.
**Reservations:** (907) 344-4006 MAY - SEPTEMBER 9 A.M. TO 9 P.M.,
OCTOBER - APRIL 9 A.M. TO 12-NOON.

### COLLEGE VILLAGE

PURDUE STREET — Hostess, an English teacher, has been an Alaskan
resident for 33 years. She enjoys people with diverse backgrounds, as
well as running, traveling, and playing the bagpipes. The home is located
in an elegant, well-groomed residential area near hospitals, universities,
and shopping centers. Bus stops are within walking distance. The decor
is country with antiques. Accommodations include: A) large queen-bedded
room; B) cozy room with trundle beds; and C) double bed. All share the
family bath. Laundry facilities are accessible. CHILDREN over 12
welcome. A friendly DOG, Peaches, welcomes guests.
**Rates:** S $35, D $45 DAILY. S $200, D $280 WEEKLY.
**Reservations:** (907) 344-4006 MAY - SEPTEMBER 9 A.M. TO 9 P.M.,
OCTOBER - APRIL 9 A.M. TO 12 NOON.

STANFORD — Large Contemporary home with two guestrooms that
share a guest bath. For Japanese visitors only. Close to universities and
hospitals. Host is retired and enjoys fishing, cooking, and gardening;
hostess is in real estate. She enjoys tennis, skiing, and Japanese culture.
Both speak Japanese. Pool table. Double accommodations available. NO
CHILDREN.
**Rates:** S $40, D $50 DAILY.
**Reservations:** (907) 344-4006 MAY - SEPTEMBER 9 A.M. TO 9 P.M.,
OCTOBER - APRIL 9 A.M. TO 12 NOON.

## DOWNTOWN

CORDOVA STREET — B&B high in a mountain cabin. Amazing Anchorage, stay downtown, under the marquee of the "Anchorage Sheraton." Two bedroom apartment, lots of privacy. Accommodations include: A) queen-sized bed and B) single. Both with full kitchen. Additional bedroom in the family quarters if needed. PETS WELCOME. Breakfast includes blueberry muffins, the speciality. Also, Camp David, Alaska style. It is 100 miles from Anchorage. Furnished transportation from Anchorage and a 3 mile all terrain vehicle ride to a mountain lake. Side trips into a big valley and a trappers' cabin. Wild game usually in the area. Includes three meals, sauna, and bed. Three to four people required: CABIN UNHOSTED.
**Rates:** A) S $50, D $65; AND B) S $40 DAILY. FOR CABIN PRICE, ASK RESERVATION SERVICE.
**Reservations:** (907) 344-4006 MAY - SEPTEMBER 9 A.M. TO 9 P.M., OCTOBER - APRIL 9 A.M. TO 12 NOON.

M STREET NEAR WEST 5TH AVENUE — A large Contemporary home overlooking a small park and knik arm with a majestic mountain view. Although within several blocks of busy downtown business distict, the immediate area is quiet and peaceful. Host is a mining engineer; hostess is a gardener. Both are long-time Alaskans. One teenage daughter lives at home. Many restaurants and tourist attractions nearby. Accommodations include: A) queen bed and B) two twin. Both share a bath and adjoining sitting room with phone. Pets welcome. Street level accommodations. Close to both city bus depot and Alaskan railroad station. Convenient transportation to the airport. TV. HANDICAPPED ACCESSIBLE. Older children welcome. NONSMOKERS only.
**Rates:** S $45, D $55 DAILY.
**Reservations:** (907) 344-4006 MAY - SEPTEMBER 9 A.M. TO 9 P.M., OCTOBER - APRIL 9 A.M. TO 12 NOON.

"N" STREET NEAR 5TH STREET — An attractive 17 room Contemporary, WATERFRONT house. Large decks extend on the south and west sides of the house. The decks, along with the sunroom, afford visitors a magnificent view of Cook Inlet, Mount Susitna, and the Alaska Range. Host is a consultant in planning and land management. Host is also an avid boating enthuslast who has been able to bring home fresh fish, king crab, and shrimp from nearby Prince William Sound for guests to sample on occasion; hostess is a legal secretary for a large downtown law firm, her hobbies include gourmet cooking and traveling. Accommodations include: one suite with bedroom (two twin beds), adjoining sitting or TV viewing room with private bath. The household includes two lovable black Labrador DOGS and one CAT. The home has a downtown location with

restaurants, stores, and museums within easy walking distance. Hosts will be happy to pick up guests from railway depot and downtown hotels. VCR. CHILDREN over 10 years of age welcome. SMOKING is not allowed inside.
**Rates:** S $50, D $65 DAILY.
**Reservations:** (907) 344-4006 MAY - SEPTEMBER 9 A.M. TO 9 P.M., OCTOBER - APRIL 9 A.M. TO 12 NOON.

O STREET — Quiet downtown neighborhood. Country antiques and Alaskan collectibles add to the charm of this well-kept home. Two bedrooms, "Granny's room and Westwind room" each have a double bed and share a guest bath and sauna. These rooms can be combined to form a suite. A spacious, sunlit, upper level suite catches the morning sunrise over the Chugach range. Skylights in this lovely room facilitate sleeping under the midnight sun. Suite includes queen-sized sleeper sofa and two twin beds, with separate entrance, woodstove, sundeck, private bath, and kitchenette. A great place for a small family or two compatible couples. For the stay at guesthome, there is a quiet nook for reading and an antique player PIANO. Close to the scenic coastal bike trail (bikes available), and an easy walk to downtown restaurants and entertainment. Hearty continental breakfast. SMOKING allowed in designated areas.
**Rates:** S $40, D $45, SUITE $60, $10 FOR AN ADDITIONAL PERSON DAILY. ADD $5 ON ONE NIGHT STAYS.
**Reservations:** (907) 258-1717 MONDAY THROUGH FRIDAY 9 A.M. - 5 P.M.

11TH AVENUE — Quiet neighborhood offers historic home with separate apartment for the guest wishing to have perfect privacy. Wonderful place for two couples traveling together or small family. There is a bedroom with double bed and a sleeper sofa in the living room. The hostess will leave breakfast provisions in the suite kitchen for you to prepare at your leisure. You can walk to downtown restaurants, gift shops, and Anchorage Art and History Museum. The home is a few blocks from the Coastal Bike Trail. Downtown convenience with B&B prices. Host is an attorney; hostess has a picture framing business. NONSMOKERS only.
**Rates:** S $50, D $55, Q PERSONS $75 DAILY. ADD $5 FOR ONE NIGHT STAYS.
**Reservations:** (907) 258-1717 MONDAY THROUGH FRIDAY 9 A.M. - 5 P.M.

## EASTSIDE LOCATION

HAMPTON DRIVE — Very comfortable townhouse in quiet setting overlooking natural park area with great view of mountains. On occasion moose can be sighted. Pleasant nature path leads to small lake where

waterfowl nest. Near University of Alaska, Anchorage; Anchorage Community College; and Alaska Pacific University. Easy access to major streets and highways. It is 40 minutes to Alaska ski resort by car. Accommodations include: upstairs twin-bedded room with private bath across the hall. Bus stop few yards from home. NO PETS. PIANO. NONSMOKERS PREFERRED. NO CHILDREN.
**Rates:** S $40, D $50 DAILY.
**Reservations:** (907) 344-4006 MAY - SEPTEMBER 9 A.M. TO 9 P.M., OCTOBER - APRIL 9 A.M. TO 12 NOON.

## HILLSIDE AREA

HANLEY CIRCLE — Log cottage with a Mount Denali view in secluded, wooded surroundings. Cottage is furnished with antiques, fireplace, and claw-foot bathtub. Kitchen comes complete with all amenities including microwave oven. Watch the Northern Lights and an occasional moose as you soak in the outdoor redwood HOT TUB. Host is a physician; hostess speaks French. There are three children, a 9 year old daughter and two sons 6 and 3. Cottage is an easy walk to Alaska Zoo and new 18 hole golf course. It is 5 minutes from cross-country skiing, local downhill ski area, cranberry and blueberry picking, equestrian center, and scenic alpine hiking. Convenient to all Anchorage sites (10 minutes), but automobile is recommended. Cottage is detached from host's log home. Hostess provides homemade banana bread and and all breakfast fixings for a full breakfast you cook for yourself at your leisure. Bikes are available. Accommodations include: room with two double beds. Can sleep up to four persons.
**Rates:** S $60 D $70 DAILY. S $325, D $395 WEEKLY.
**Reservations:** (907) 344-4006 MAY - SEPTEMBER 9 A.M. TO 9 P.M., OCTOBER - APRIL 9 A.M. TO 12 NOON.

## HILLCREST AREA

22ND STREET OFF FIREWOOD — Contemporary home in midtown Anchorage. Efficiency apartment with separate entrance. Queen-sized foldaway. Rollaway available for third person. Kitchenette with stove and refrigerator included. Dishes are in cabinets. Beautiful perennial garden in the back as well as vegetable gardens. Lots of trees, very quiet and private. On deadend street. Mount McKinley, city, and mountains can be seen from hosts' living quarters, to which guests are invited at any time. Private bath with SAUNA and JACUZZI for guests. Laundry facilities available in house. Very convenient to businesses, shops, and downtown, including museum and other sightseeing spots. Excellent restaurants within walking distance (Chinese, Mexican, steaks, fish, you name it). A perfect place many people have enjoyed over past summers and like to come back to. One DOG. NO SMOKING.
**Rates:** JUNE, JULY, AND AUGUST S $45, D $50, T $60 DAILY.

**Reservations:** (907) 344-4006 MAY - SEPTEMBER 9 A.M. TO 9 P.M., OCTOBER - APRIL 9 A.M. TO 12 NOON.

## MIDTOWN

A large private two bedroom apartment, 1 1/2 bath, Fully equipped kitchen, two queen-sized beds, stereo, color TV. Nicely furnished. Large picture windows give you view of city lights. One block to city bus. Airport and railroad pickup. UNHOSTED. VCR.
**Rates:** JULY, AUGUST, AND SEPTEMBER S $45, D $55, T $75, $10 EACH ADDITIONAL PERSON DAILY.
**Reservations:** (907) 344-4006 MAY    SEPTEMBER 9 A.M. TO 9 P.M., OCTOBER - APRIL 9 A.M. TO 12 NOON.

WEST 20TH NEAR ARCTIC — Northern hospitality. A comfortable home and a friendly family with a private one bedroom apartment with separate entry. A full kitchen, completely equipped, a washer and dryer, hide-a-bed in living room, and rollaway can comfortably accommodate up to six persons. Breakfast is served in the apartment. Centrally located near parks and bike path only minutes from downtown in a quiet neighborhood. Host family, 20 year Alaskans, enjoy sharing their knowledge of the last frontier. Extra amenities include: a HOT TUB, SAUNA, VCR, and picnic area. A CAT, DOG, and ferret reside here.
**Rates:** S $50, D $60, $10 EACH ADDITIONAL GUEST DAILY.
**Reservations:** (907) 344-4006 MAY - SEPTEMBER 9 A.M. TO 9 P.M., OCTOBER - APRIL 9 A.M. TO 12 NOON.

## ROMIG HILL SUBDIVISION

HILLCREST PLACE — A two story residence on a corner lot that is convenient to downtown, shopping, and restaurants, yet tucked into a quiet residential area. Summers here are free of the humidity, and stifling heat. Winters boast snow, skiing opportunities, and February sled dog races. Accommodations include: A) single room with private bath B) queen-sized double room with adjoining bathroom. Guests share dining room with host, hostess, and teenaged son. Host is a realtor and retired union carpenter; hostess is employed as an editorial assistant. Home has fireplaces, SAUNA, and large game room. NO YOUNG CHILDREN. NO SMOKERS. NO PETS. Transportation from airport or train station may be arranged. PIANO, VCR, and pool table.
**Rates:** A) S $35, B) S OR D $45 DAILY.
**Reservations:** (907) 344-4006 MAY - SEPTEMBER 9 A.M. TO 9 P.M., OCTOBER - APRIL 9 A.M. TO 12 NOON.

## SAND LANE

CHIVIGNEY — Close to the airport, high on a hill overlooking the city. Gracious hostess has three wonderful rooms, each with private bath: A) two twin beds, fireplace (can accommodate a rollaway for a child or third person) and B & C) two rooms each with queen-sized bed. Lovely patio to enjoy the long Alaskan evenings. Hostess will store suitcases while returning guests tour other areas. Ironing board and freezer space available. Hostess is an enthusiastic Alaskan who makes her guests feel welcome. Full breakfast is served. Convenient location close to bus stop. NONSMOKERS only.
**Rates:** S $45, D $50 DAILY. ADD $5 FOR ONE NIGHT STAYS.
**Reservations:** (907) 258-1717 MONDAY THROUGH FRIDAY 9 A.M. - 5 P.M.

## SOUTH ANCHORAGE HILLSIDE

This spacious, custom country home is located 7 miles (15 minutes) south of downtown Anchorage and convenient to airport. Walk out the front door to municipal parkland; take a nature walk through the forest inhabited by flowers and fauna native to area; bike, run, hike, cross-country ski on maintained trails nearby. Close to public golf course and riding stables. Home is beautifully furnished with antiques. Accommodations include an elegant master suite with sitting room, woodburning stove, spacious queen-sized bedroom, bath with dual headed shower, skylight, in Colonial decor. Outdoor HOT TUB to soak your weary bones. Gourmet continental breakfast served. Convenient to major highways to famous glaciers, panoramic mountains, trophy fishing, and sightseeing areas. Hosts offer advice on recreation, sightseeing, eateries, and activities based on 12 years of living, working, and traveling in Alaska. Two DOGS, PIANO and VCR. SMOKING RESTRICTED.
**Rates:** S $65, D $75, T $95 DAILY. RATES MINUS $10 IN WINTER.
**Reservations:** (907) 344-4006 MAY - SEPTEMBER 9 A.M. TO 9 P.M., OCTOBER - APRIL 9 A.M. TO 12 NOON.

## WEST SIDE

OFF NORTHERN LIGHTS BOULEVARD — Three level modern cedar townhouse. Comfortable and convenient. It is 5 minutes from International Airport, 10 minutes to downtown. Anchorage is the gateway to Kenai Peninsula south and Denali National Park north. Host is in construction; hostess is in education. They have two daughters aged 13 and 16. Accommodations include: A) suite with two twin beds, queen-sized hide-a-bed, private bath, color TV, phone and B) two single twin bed bedrooms, share bath. NO PETS. Courtesy pickup, drop off, laundry, bikes available. Full Alaska style breakfast or continental. All children welcome. NO SMOKERS.

**Rates:** A) S $40, D $50 AND B) S $35; $10 EACH ADDITIONAL PERSON DAILY.
**Reservations:** (907) 344-4006 MAY - SEPTEMBER 9 A.M. TO 9 P.M., OCTOBER - APRIL 9 A.M. TO 12 NOON.

## TALKEETNA

Located in a picturesque mining town 115 miles north of Anchorage, this cozy log cottage offers two bedrooms and shared bath; A) two twin beds and B) double bed. There is a woodstove in the living room. Talkeetna is the staging area for mountaineers preparing to climb Mount McKinley. During the long summer days the 375 residents are often outnumbered by guides and packers from all over the world. July is the month for the annual "Moose Dropping" festival. Fishing is good in surrounding lakes and streams. Flightseeing tours of Mount Denali is another popular activity. This is a wonderful stopping place if you are driving to Denali National Park. Breakfast delivered to this UNHOSTED home by the hostess. NONSMOKERS, only.
**Rates:** S OR D $50 DAILY. ADD $5 FOR ONE NIGHT STAYS.
**Reservations:** (907) 258-1717 MONDAY THROUGH FRIDAY 9 A.M. - 5 P.M.

# CALIFORNIA

## BANDERAS BAY AREA
### PUERTO VALLARTA
**OLD TOWN (SUR DE LA PUENTE)**

BASILIO BADILIC — A compact Spanish Colonial villa located in the Old Town section of Puerto Vallarta. It offers four spacious double bedrooms with large private bathrooms that feature sunken tubs. A two bedroom apartment is also available on a weekly basis with service. The villa surrounds a tropical garden, inground POOL, aviary, and fountain. The furnishings are comfortable Colonial with the accent on relaxation. Host was a Caribbean correspondent, now writing fiction; hostess is a Swiss business administrator. English, Spanish, French, German, and Swiss dialect are spoken. There are three servants, a friendly DOBERMAN, and an intelligent guacamaya parrot. A continental breakfast is served at private tables or in group. There is a sunset champagne libation for all guests. It is 1 block from beach, shops, dining, and dancing. A 61 foot SCHOONER is available for day charters. HANDICAPPED ACCESSIBLE. CHILDREN over 12 years welcome. NONSMOKERS PREFERRED.
**Rates:** $65 DAILY; $50 DAILY FOR MORE THAN 6 DAYS.
**Reservations:** (818) 344-7878 MONDAY THROUGH FRIDAY, 7 A.M. - 4 P.M. PACIFIC TIME; MACHINE SERVICE.

## CENTRAL CALIFORNIA
### CAMBRIA
**RESIDENTIAL**

Spacious Contemporary home surrounded by pine and oak trees, with a view of the ocean. Near Hearst Castle, San Simeon, and the Sea Otter Preserve. Hosts are retired and enjoy hosting travelers from around the world. Accommodations include: A) double bed and B) twin double bed. Both have private baths. Families with CHILDREN over 12 welcome.
**Rates:** S $64, D $64 DAILY.
**Reservations:**

## CENTRAL COAST
### PEBBLE BEACH
**CARMEL**

Very private king-sized bedroom, private bath, couch, TV, desk, private refrigerator. House with view of ocean on 2 acres, famous golf courses nearby. Ideal for runners or walking. Quiet, prestigious area. Bikes available. German is spoken here. NO CHILDREN. NO SMOKING.
**Rates:** S OR D $100 DAILY.
**Reservations:** (213) 699-8427 7 A.M. TO 7 P.M. MONDAY THROUGH FRIDAY.

# CENTRAL VALLEY
## TAFT
## TAFT HEIGHTS

PHILIPPINE — Custom built, split level home in foothills with citrus trees and inground POOL. Poolside room with pool table and fireplace. A living room with fireplace. Sundeck with million dollar view. A mixed POODLE/TERRIER is in residence. Complimentary wine, crackers, chocolate dipped reception sticks, and pillow mints. Hostess performs manicures, pedicures, and foot reflexology from business on premises for a reasonable fee. No pets. Accommodations include: three rooms with double accommodations, one with private bath and two that share a bath. HANDICAPPED ACCESSIBLE. Air conditioned. NO CHILDERN. Limited SMOKING.
**Rates:** S $30, D $40 DAILY. S $175, D $245 WEEKLY.
**Reservations:** (213) 699-8427 7 A.M. TO 7 P.M. MONDAY THROUGH FRIDAY.

# CONTRA COSTA
## WALNUT CREEK

CUTTING STREET/HIGHWAY 680 — Contemporary home on half acre, with a swimming POOL and grape arbor. Business relocations to Contra Costa County make this the fastest growing community in California. Accommodations include: A) queen-sized bed and B) single bed. Share one private guest bath. Room B rented to members of the same party only, shares bath. Car preferable. Air conditioning. Both Kosher and vegetarian meals are possible, as well as limited kitchen privileges. Ample street parking; buses to downtown and San Francisco nearby. One DOG lives here. CHILDREN must be swimmers. SMOKERS may smoke on the porch.
**Rates:** A) S $40, D $46 AND B) S $40 DAILY.
**Reservations:** (415) 525-4569. OPEN 9 A.M. - 5 P.M.

# DEL NORTE COUNTY
## CRESCENT CITY
## OFF PEBBLE BEACH DRIVE

Located in Crescent City where the redwoods meet the sea. The town is built close to the OCEAN. Home is steps away from the scenic Pebble Beach Drive and the sea. Accommodations include: A) room where you can watch the sunset and B) room where you can watch sunrise. Both offer privacy in the upstairs level. These rooms share a bath. Host is a contract and charter pilot; hostess is a former teacher. Breakfast includes French toast with sour cream and strawberries or eggs benedict. Both are served with fresh pineapple flown in from Hawaii and orange juice.

Activities include visiting Redwood National Park and Museum Lighthouse. PIANO. CHILDREN over 12 welcome.
**Rates:** S OR D A) $65 AND B) $55 DAILY.
**Reservations:** (503) 245-0642 8:00 TO 5:00.

## DESERT AREA
## PALM SPRINGS

FARREL DRIVE NEAR RACQUET — B&B JAPANESE STYLE in this spacious (3,500 square foot) custom designed home. Minutes from the famous Palm Springs tramway, airport, shopping, hiking, biking, boating, fishing, horseback riding, tennis, and over 50 golf courses. Enjoy a little bit of Japan in the desert. Accommodations include: A) two twin beds and a sofa that opens into a double futon and B) king-sized futon. Both have sliding doors that open out to the POOL and a great mountain view. Each room is Japanese in decor, with TV, private bath, and walk-in closet. Guests are furnished kimonos and slippers. Japanese video movies on VCR, Host is a professional musician who has performed in Japan and is very enthusiastic about Japan and its culture; hostess is Japanese, an artist, designer, and a hostess at a Japanese restaurant. She loves to prepare delicious American or Japanese breakfasts while Japanese music plays softly in the background. Dinners are sometimes available. Her 2 1/2 year old daughter entertains guests. Both have studied shiatsu (massage). Leave your shoes at the door and relax in the Rising Sun, in your kimono, sip saki and listen to the wind blowing from Mount Fuji in the evening. HANDICAPPED ACCESSIBLE. NO SMOKING.
**Rates:** OCTOBER THROUGH JUNE S $45, D $55 DAILY. $275-$300 WEEKLY.
**Reservations:** (213) 684-4426 MONDAY - SATURDAY 9 A.M. TO 5 P.M. PACIFIC TIME.

## HIGH SIERRAS/YOSEMITE
## GROVELAND

An expanded chalet home with open beam cathedral ceiling. Home is furnished with many original art pieces, PIANO, and accordian. Meals are served either on large deck with view of Yosemite National Park Mountains in background, or inn dining room with view of private manmade lake below. Home is located on top of a large wooded hill with panoramic views. Located in Mother Lode Gold country, near other gold rush towns and serves as the gateway to Yosemite National Park. Hostess is a native of Mexico and speaks fluent Spanish. She delights in gourmet cooking. Hosts are semiretired and can spend extra time providing attention to their guests. It is 30 minutes to Columbia College. Accommodations include: A) 10 foot queen bed, private bath and B) two rooms each with double beds, shared bath. A CAT is in residence. Children welcome.

**Rates:** A) LOFT S $35, D $45; B) S $30, D $40; CHILD $10 EXTRA DAILY. S OR D $225 WEEKLY.

**Reservations:** (213) 684-4426 MONDAY - SATURDAY 9 A.M. TO 5 P.M. PACIFIC TIME.

## TRUCKEE

SPRING AND HIGH STREETS — This 1870 Victorian home furnished with antiques and quilts. The living room has a picture window with a view of the mountains and downtown. It also has a woodburning stove. Host is a psychologist; hostess runs the inn. They have a 1 year old daughter and a 5 year old son. Accommodations include: A) double room, private bath; B) five rooms, shared bath; and C) two room suite with bath. Hosts enjoy hiking and skiing. Children welcome in suite. Baby equipment available. Bikes and river raft equipment as well as hiking and skiing information available. Small DOG in private quarters. Within walking distance to restaurants and shops. It is 10 minutes from major ski resorts, Donner Lake, and hiking; 20 to 30 minutes to Lake Tahoe, horseback riding, and numerous other summer and winter sports; 40 minutes to Reno Airport; and 2 blocks away is Amtrak train. Full breakfast and wine and cheese in evening. NO SMOKING.

**Rates:** D $45-$65 DAILY.

**Reservations:** (213) 699-8427 7 A.M. TO 7 P.M. MONDAY THROUGH FRIDAY.

## MONTEREY PENINSULA
## CARMEL

HIGH MEADOW LANE — Contemporary house close to all the attractions of the Monterey Peninsula, with SWIMMING POOL and TENNIS COURT available for guests. The host is a writer; hostess is an artist. Both are avid bridge players. Beautifully decorated guestroom has queen double bed, en suite bath. Room offers privacy. Easy parking. CHILDREN over 12 welcome.

**Rates:** S $50, D $58 DAILY.

**Reservations:** (415) 525-4569. OPEN 9 A.M. - 5 P.M.

## CARMEL VALLEY

This rustic, all redwood home located in the beautiful Carmel Valley is just a few steps from the Carmel River and framed by the lovely Santa Lucia Mountains. By the giant sycamore tree in front of this home is a mini farm and if the chickens are not nesting you might fetch a few eggs for your breakfast. Tennis, golf, and horseback riding are all available nearby. Side trips to Steinback's famous Cannery Row, Big Sur, Hearst

Castle, the 17 Mile Drive, the famous Monterey Aquarium, Carmel Mission founded by Father Serra, and many more historic sites are practically at your feet. This two bedroom, two bath home is UNHOSTED but is completely furnished for your every need. A double bed and twin beds are available. PETS WELCOME.
**Rates:** D $100, T OR Q $135 DAILY.
**Reservations:** (213) 684-4426 MONDAY - SATURDAY 9 A.M. TO 5 P.M. PACIFIC TIME.

## PEBBLE BEACH

Delightful home located in most prestigious area in and around Monterey. Walk to golf course and beach. Lodge guest quarters are very private. King-sized bed, private bath, refrigerator, and TV. European hostess, who speaks German, is an avid golfer. Two DOGS are on the premises. Lovely grounds and atmosphere. Bikes available. NO CHILDREN. NO SMOKING.
**Rates:** S $100; D $110 DAILY.
**Reservations:** (818) 344-7878 MONDAY THROUGH FRIDAY, 7 A.M. - 4 P.M. PACIFIC TIME; MACHINE SERVICE.

## NAPA SONOMA COUNTRIES
### NEAR CLOVERDALE
### A RANCH

Ranch house with SWIMMING POOL and vineyard. The ranch has Black Angus cattle, sheep, quarter horses, chickens, a DOG, CATS, and peacocks. The host, who raises llamas, is a lighting manufacturer; hostess is a physician. Accommodations include: A) twin double bed and B) single double bed. Guests share bath in hall. The start of Russian River canoeing is nearby the ranch. Hiking trails. Many fine wineries within 30 minute drive. CHILDREN who swim welcome. SMOKING outside on patio.
**Rates:** S $60, D $66 DAILY.
**Reservations:** (415) 525-4569. OPEN 9 A.M. - 5 P.M.

## NORTH COAST
### EUREKA

One hour's drive from Eureka in the mountains. All wood Bavarian Swiss chalet on a mountaintop, with a distant view of the Pacific Ocean. It is complete with yodeling mountaineer to serve as your host and his Belgian wife to serve the best French cooking this side of a Swiss farmhouse. Enjoy the old world charm and graciousness that is offered. Accommodations include: A) queen-sized bed and B) double bed. Both share a large bath. All meals are included—breakfast, lunch, hors d'oeuvre, open bar, and dinner by candlelight. The sunset from the deck,

soft music for dancing or relaxing, a large library, and lots of outdoor activities make you want to return again and again. Hiking boots, fishing rods, swim suits, and camera are recommended equipment, unless you just want to snooze in the warm mountain air. Two day minimum. One outside CAT. NO SMOKING.
**Rates:** D $170 DAILY. INCLUDES ALL MEALS, DRINKS, OPEN BAR.
**Reservations:** (503) 245-0642 8:00 TO 5:00.

## KNEELAND

BRIDGEVILLE ROAD — A Swiss Bavarian chalet of carved cedar and redwood on a mountaintop overlooking the Pacific Ocean and Humboldt Bay. Chalet is surrounded by 400,000 acres of ranch and timber preserve, with hiking trails, woods, meadows, wildlife, star gazing; and gourmet dining with excellent California wines and classic sunsets. It is 30 miles from the nearest town (Eureka), with a 1 1/2 mile private drive behind locked gates and panoramic 25 mile views. The chalet is especially suited for writers, painters, honeymoon couples, and others looking for serenity, solitude, and quiet elegance, in a pristine and glorious natural setting far from civilization. Hosts speak French, Dutch, and English. This exclusive European hideaway accepts only one or two couples. No pets. Accommodations include: A) queen-sized bed and B) double bed. Both share bath that has a claw-footed tub. Host is a writer and actor; hostess is in real estate. Bikes available. NO CHILDREN. NO SMOKERS.
**Rates:** D $170 INCLUDES ALL MEALS, WINES, DRINKS, AND HORS D'OEUVRES.
**Reservations:** (213) 699-8427 7 A.M. TO 7 P.M. MONDAY THROUGH FRIDAY.

# NORTH OF LOS ANGELES

Heading north from Los Angeles, you pass the delightful Malibu area with great beaches, restaurants, and fishing. Be sure to visit the J. Paul Getty Museum with its replica of an ancient Roman Villa, priceless statuary, and paintings. Santa Barbara is a city of obvious beauty with its Spanish style tile roofs, bell towers and love of color. Visit the Mission, the Botanic Gardens, Zoological Gardens, and the many miles of beaches. Stretch your visit up the coast to include the University of California, Santa Barbara, at Goleta. Futher along is Pismo Beach (clam capital) and the unbelievable Hearst Castle at San Simeon.

## CAMARILLO
### CAMARILLO HEIGHTS

MESA DRIVE OFF WEST LOOP — English country farmhouse set in a forest of avocado and other fruit trees situated in the hills above the town

of Camarillo with the blue Pacific on the horizon. On the spacious grounds are located a picnic area, small pond, barnyard animals, delightful HOT TUB, and the Beach, a unique full operation TV studio with live programming going out to the surrounding community daily. Hosts, who are well traveled, retired schoolteachers, have two young children, Kim and Andrew, who enjoy serving and providing for the needs of the travelers and helping them enjoy the local attractions and recreation of this quiet area in busy southern California. The two story house has many bedrooms, a large rustic attic, and living room with a baby grand PIANO, antique furniture, ORGAN, massive fireplace, and bay window. Best fresh food on the coast and lots of room and activities for guests and their children; bikes, boats, swimming, inground trampoline, archery, and library. NO SMOKERS. Accommodations include: A) double hide-a-bed and B) twin-bedded double. Rooms share family bath.
**Rates:** S OR D $33 DAILY. D $225 WEEKLY.
**Reservations:** (818) 889-8870 OR (818) 889-7325. MONDAY THROUGH FRIDAY, 9:00 TO 5:00.

## LOS OSOS
### OVERLOOKING BAY, MOUNTAINS

BAY OAKS DRIVE — Your Dutch born, Indonesian raised hostess who speaks Dutch, Indonesian, some German, French, Spanish, and Japanese, welcomes you. A full breakfast is served. Home is located 5 miles south of Morro Bay, 10 miles west of San Louis Obispo, 34 miles south of Hearst Castle, 5 miles east of state park. Accommodations include: A) twin-bedded double, private bath; B) twin double, shared bath; and C) king-sized bed, shared bath. PETS WELCOME. CHILDREN WELCOME. NO SMOKING.
**Rates:** A & B) S OR D $35 AND C) S OR D $40 DAILY.
**Reservations:** (818) 889-8870 OR (818) 889-7325. MONDAY THROUGH FRIDAY, 9:00 TO 5:00.

## MALIBU

RAMBLA PACIFICO — A new two story wooden home with a fantastic 180 degree view of white water ocean and coastline. Large decks. Second story is A) a suite with king-sized bed in master bedroom with loft sitting room and bath. Bedroom has balcony with view of mountains and ocean sunrises. House is surrounded by hillside of flowers and trees. Downstairs bedrooms include: B) double bed and C) twin beds. Hosts are teachers who have traveled widely and who enjoy collecting art and folk art. A CAT shares the home. A car is essential. Santa Monica is 9 miles (20 minutes), downtown Los Angeles is 20 miles (40 minutes), Universal Studio (1 hour), Santa Barbara (1 3/4 hours), 4 miles from Pepperdine University. Close to several state parks with good hiking.

**Rates:** A) (SUITE) D $50; B & C) D $40 DAILY.
**Reservations:** (818) 889-8870 OR (818) 889-7325. MONDAY THROUGH
FRIDAY, 9:00 TO 5:00.

WINDING WAY — Guesthouse. Enter down a path from the driveway
to this new addition. A) Living room with TV and double hide-a-bed. B)
Bedroom with queen-sized bed, private bath, full kitchen. Balcony looking
out through the canyon to the water. Car essential. UNHOSTED.
**Rates:** A) D $50, EXTRA PERSON $10 AND B) D $50, EXTRA
PERSON $10 DAILY.
**Reservations:** (818) 889-8870 OR (818) 889-7325. MONDAY THROUGH
FRIDAY, 9:00 TO 5:00.

## PISMO BEACH
### SAN SIMEON/ AVILA BEACH

A large, OCEAN FRONT home located 3 miles north of Pismo Beach
and 10 miles south of San Luis Obisbo. Beautiful views and sunsets.
Great fishing, clam digging, and sailing nearby. Launching facilities at
Avila Beach if you have your own boat. Accommodations include; A)
two twin beds, private entrance, private bath and B) double bed, private
bath. Both share a small refrigerator. Other rooms can be made available
for up to 10 guests for a family reunion. Guests select breakfast from a
gourmet list of choices. A small silver Cock-a-poo lives here. PETS
WELCOME ($25 deposit in case of damage by your pet, returned at end
of stay if no damage). Children welcome. SMOKING, outdoors only.
**Rates:** S $45, D $50. CHILD UNDER 6 IN SAME ROOM $10 EXTRA,
6-12 IN SUNROOM $25. ADULT GUESTS USING EXTRA
ACCOMMODATION IN SUNROOM $40 DAILY.
**Reservations:** (213) 684-4426 MONDAY - SATURDAY 9 A.M. TO 5
P.M. PACIFIC TIME.

## SANTA BARBARA

BATH STREET NEAR MISSION STREET — Inn and cottages.
California bungalow style main house with four cottages. Eight guestrooms.
Six with private bath, two share bath. FIREPLACES in some bedrooms;
also double accommodations in bedrooms. Located in quiet residential
neighborhood close to shopping, historic sites, galleries, fine restaurants,
beaches, mountains, wine tasting, and antique shops. University of
California at Santa Barbara, Santa Barbara Community College, Westmont
College, and Brooks Institute of Photography all within 15 minute drive.
Sansum Medical Clinic is 3 blocks away. Two charming COCKER
SPANIELS in residence. Bikes available as well as picnic lunches.
Delightful country atmosphere. CHILDREN over 12 welcome.
**Rates:** WINTER S $49, D $80 DAILY; SUMMER S $65, D $90 DAILY.

**Reservations:** (818) 889-8870 OR (818) 889-7325. MONDAY THROUGH FRIDAY, 9:00 TO 5:00.

SIERRA MADRE ROAD — Spacious Contemporary home with all rooms opening onto patios and views of the ocean and Santa Inez Mountains. Host is an educational research consultant; hostess is a technical writer. Accommodations include: A) double bed, private bath, private powder room with washbasin and toilet, rented only to members of the same party; and B) twin double bed. Car desirable. It is 10 minutes to beach, tourist attractions. Children welcome. SMOKERS use patio. **Rates:** S $42, D $46 + ONE IN FAMILY $10 DAILY. **Reservations:** (415) 525-4569. OPEN 9 A.M. - 5 P.M.

## MISSION CANYON

MISSION CANYON ROAD — Revel amidst the timeless vibrations of Maestro Padarewski's genius; imagine that enchanted evening when he filled this Italian villa's 20 foot ceilings with entralling music. Accommodations include: A) queen-sized bed, private bath and B) king-sized bed, private bath. A massive fireplace, GRAND PIANO, stunning antiques, giant projection TV system, VCR, stereo, and 14 foot mullioned windows overlooking splendid gardens are some of the amenities that await you. The guestrooms have special touches such as fresh flowers, telephones, oversized plush towels, alarm clocks and so on. Your "chefette" is a talented gourmet cook who lovingly creates gastronomic feasts for her delighted breakfast guests. Explore Santa Barbara from a unique hideaway that is located near the "Queen of the Missions," 5 minutes from miles of uncrowded beaches yet adjacent to the foothills of the beautiful Santa Ynez mountains. Host is a retired diplomat; hostess enjoys cooking, horticulture, and interior designing. There is an inground POOL and the villa is HANDICAPPED ACCESSIBLE. JACUZZI. SMOKING permitted in designated areas only. **Rates:** S OR D $125-$150 DAILY. **Reservations:** (818) 344-7878 MONDAY THROUGH FRIDAY, 7 A.M. - 4 P.M. PACIFIC TIME; MACHINE SERVICE.

Dramatic windows in the guestroom look out on lovely oaks, all located in a rural environment on a quiet street, yet 2 blocks from Santa Barbara's famous mission, and 5 minutes from shopping and the BEACH; 30 minutes to Solvang, a Danish community, where fine local wines are enjoyed. Home is Contemporary wood and plaster, set on half an acre, furnished with antiques. Host creates wonderful breakfasts, served on an oak-shaded deck. Three CATS reside here. The guestroom is upstairs, totally private with double bed and private bath. Special arrangements can be made to host more than two people. Hosts are both teachers.

Host loves to meet people and share the beauty of the area. Guests enjoy local beaches. Older CHILDREN welcome. NO SMOKERS.
**Rates:** S $40, D $50 DAILY.
**Reservations:** (213) 684-4426 MONDAY - SATURDAY 9 A.M. TO 5 P.M. PACIFIC TIME.

## MONTECITO FOOTHILLS

NORTH SIERRA VISTA — This Contemporary home in the Montecito foothills is a beauty inside and out. Its ambiance of tranquility and comfort will soothe even the most frazzled nerves. There is a variety of places to relax outdoors—a spacious patio with lounge chairs, a porch swing, or a deck with a view of the mountains. In the evening, it is a pleasure to sit in the living room around the grand PIANO and fireplace. Soft colored fabrics, rich carpeting, and professional decorating enhance the charming decor. Full gourmet breakfasts are served in bed, on the patio, or by the fireplace in the dining room. Fresh fruits and vegetables from the garden in season. Just 3 miles from downtown Santa Barbara and 1/2 block to bus. Pickup available from airport. "Practice hospitality" is a biblical teaching that your hosts take seriously. You will be a stranger here but once! Accommodations include: A) queen-sized bed, private attached bath with sunken tub and B) double bed, private bath in hall, outside entrance. Two night minimum. One CAT outside. OUTSIDE PETS WELCOME. HANDICAPPED ACCESSIBLE.
**Rates:** A) S $70, D $75 AND B) S $60, D $65 DAILY. $5 EACH NIGHT FOR STAY OF TWO OR MORE DAYS. A) D $345 AND B) D $315 WEEKLY.
**Reservations:** (714) 738-8361 MONDAY THROUGH FRIDAY 7 A.M. TO 6 P.M. PACIFIC TIME.

## THOUSAND OAKS
### NORTHWOOD

SAFFRON CIRCLE — Southern California retirement at its best! Hosts are retired educators who will share their attractive condominium. Decorated with elegant, traditional furnishings and featuring a shaded patio with a view of the hills. A small enclosed planted atrium off the guestroom provides a perfect place for relaxation. House privileges include use of a TV in the den. Extensive recreational facilities: POOL, SPA, hiking trails, bikes. Located 18 miles from Pacific Ocean, 1 hour from Los Angeles and Santa Barbara. Car is essential. Accommodations include: A) double bed and B) hide-a-bed in den for additional members of party. Guestroom has a private bath. One DOG resides here. ORGAN.
**Rates:** D $40, $15 FOR EACH EXTRA PERSON DAILY.
**Reservations:** (818) 889-8870 OR (818) 889-7325. MONDAY THROUGH FRIDAY, 9:00 TO 5:00.

# SAN BERNARDINO MOUNTAINS
## GREEN VALLEY LAKE

BOLSA CHICA — An exclusive and secluded health retreat and B&B on a private 10 acre gated estate in the California mountains with vistas from the desert to the sea. Offers a stress management program incorporating mother nature. Activities include trail hiking, rock climbing, biking, boating, fishing, horseback riding, ice skating, and cross-country and downhill skiing. Therapeutic massage, group mediation, Tai Chi, exercise, and nutritional counseling are available. Hostess, a writer/producer, is a veteran in the media and has studied Eastern philosophy, stress management, life extension, alternative lifestyles, healing arts, and metaphysics. Green Valley Lake is a picturesque lakeside village only a few miles from the major commercial resorts of Lake Arrowhead and Big Bear Lake. Only 1 hour, 45 minutes from Los Angeles. The lodge is rustic cedar Oriental Contemporary. The decor is rustic elegance. It features viewing decks, skylighted art gallery (local artists), JACUZZI tub, workout room, solarium, and large fully equipped country kitchen. Accommodations include four guestrooms with private baths and double occupancy. One DOG resides here. NO SMOKING.
**Rates:** S OR D $100-$125 DAILY.
**Reservations:** (213) 699-8427 7 A.M. TO 7 P.M. MONDAY THROUGH FRIDAY.

# SAN FERNANDO VALLEY
## NORTHRIDGE
### URBAN

MELVIN AVENUE — A large Ranch style home on 1 1/4 acres in a wooded setting. Flowers and fruit trees add to the atmosphere. Many antiques, leaded windows, and stained glass add to the country charm. A used brick fireplace, and paneled den add to guests' comfort. One CALICO CAT resides here. Host is an engineer; hostess is a therapist and painter. Accommodations include: A) large double bed, private bath down hall, country furnishings and B) attached studio apartment completely furnished, queen-sized bed and single bed, small private patio. Hostess serves meals in dining room, patio, or in bed. Convenient to shopping and restaurants. Friends of guests welcome for meals at extra charge. Bikes available. CHILDREN over 10 welcome. SMOKING outside only.
**Rates:** A) D $55 DAILY AND B) $550 AVAILABLE MONTHLY ONLY.
**Reservations:** (818) 344-7878 MONDAY THROUGH FRIDAY, 7 A.M. - 4 P.M. PACIFIC TIME; MACHINE SERVICE.

# SAN FRANCISCO BAY AREA

The San Francisco Bay Area is known for its hospitality, sheer beauty, and interesting cultures. Sample several of its many excellent restaurants, visit museums, shops, and dazzling nightlife. Enjoy a romantic cruise around the harbor and do not miss a thrilling cable car ride up and down the steep San Francisco hills.

## BERKELEY
### CAMPUS

FULTON — University of California, Berkeley campus is a short walk from this brown shingle, two family house, furnished in antiques and collectibles. Host is a caterer and clothing designer who speaks Italian and Spanish. Guestroom has a double bed, with a private bath across the hall. There is a CAT, Rocky. Guests may keep snacks in the refrigerator. A deck overlooks the large backyard. Street parking, buses nearby. Children are welcome. SMOKING in backyard.
**Rates:** S $38, D $44 DAILY. 10% DISCOUNT WEEKLY.
**Reservations:** (415) 525-4569. OPEN 9 A.M. - 5 P.M.

### NORTH BERKELEY HILLS

BETWEEN ARLINGTON AND SPRUCE — A spacious, modified English Tudor with spectacular view of San Francisco and Mount Tamalpais. A large private deck overlooks the view. Guest is guaranteed a room with a view and private bath. Guests can use the VCR, PIANO, easel, extensive library of books, sheet music, video films, exercise equipment, kitchen, and laundry facilities. It is 5 minutes from a small neighborhood park, large regional park, and University of California, Berkeley campus; 30 minutes from horseback riding and downtown San Fransisco; direct bus to BART; health club with daily rate, swimming, tennis, golf, fishing running track, hiking and biking trails, boating, gourmet restaurants, and specialty shops within 10 minutes. One CAT is in residence. No heavy users of ALCOHOL. Accommodations include: A) double bed, private bath and B) twin beds, private bath. CHILDREN over 10 welcome. No heavy users of CIGARETTES.
**Rates:** S $40, D $50 DAILY. S $150, D $200 WEEKLY. ADDITIONAL GUEST IN SAME PARTY $10 DAILY.
**Reservations:** (213) 684-4426 MONDAY - SATURDAY 9 A.M. TO 5 P.M. PACIFIC TIME.

## MARINA

BAY STREET — Beautiful marina flat furnished with antiques; it is light and sunny. Guests have a suite (double brass bedroom and sunroom/ sitting room over an Italian garden) and share bath with single owner.

Host is a school psychologist who has lived in other countries and welcomes guests from all over the world. Home is located on most traveled by tourists bus line, convenient to all major areas of interest, 2 blocks from the Palace of Fine Arts and San Francisco Bay near the Golden Gate Bridge. Union Street shops and restaurant are nearby as well as the St. Francis Yacht Club. NO CHILDREN. NO SMOKERS.
**Rates:** S $60 D $65 DAILY.
**Reservations:** (415) 931-3083 MONDAY THROUGH FRIDAY 9 A.M. TO 5 P.M.

## MUIR BEACH

Just 17 miles north of San Francisco stands this spectacular California redwood house on an acre of meadow with the Pacific Ocean at its foot. The two room guest suite has its own bath and balcony, a FIREPLACE, picture windows, a refrigerator, its own entrance, and three comfortable single-beds. Host is an attorney. Breakfast can be served in the sunny kitchen or on deck. Muir Beach is a tiny community reached by a winding road, so guests must have a car. Hiking trails abound. Within walking distance is an excellent restaurant and a beautiful BEACH. Just "over the hill" is Mill Valley for browsing, shopping, horseback riding, and movies; San Francisco Airport is less than an hour away. A DOG in residence. HANDICAPPED ACCESSIBLE.
**Rates:** S OR D $95, T $100 DAILY.
**Reservations:** (415) 931-3083 MONDAY THROUGH FRIDAY 9 A.M. TO 5 P.M.

## SAN FRANCISCO

This "country cottage" offers a cozy country style B&B stay in the heart of San Francisco. The three guestrooms available in double or queen beds, each with private entrance, are comfortably furnished in antiques and brass and oak beds, share two baths. The house is located at the end of a quiet street away from the city noise. It is like being in the country. There is a small patio with trees and birds for the guests to enjoy. The hosts are San Francisco experts and enjoy helping the guests get to know San Francisco. Excellent public transportation to Fisherman's Wharf, Golden Gate Park, and Chinatown is only 1 block away. A full breakfast is served in the sunny kitchen each morning and complimentary wine is alway available for the guests. German is spoken here. Hosts enjoy sailing and biking. A parakeet lives here. CHILDREN over 8 welcome.
**Rates:** S $45, D $55 DAILY.
**Reservations:** (415) 931-3083 MONDAY THROUGH FRIDAY 9 AM. TO 5 P.M.

Built in 1923 this inn has oak wood paneling throughout. A large living room, dining room, and two kitchens are for guests' use. Washer/dryer

available. Conveniently located 1 block from Golden Gate Park, museums, and public transportation. Close to Pacific Ocean and University of California Medical Center. Accommodations include: A) large room with double bed (extra twin bed available); B) sunny spacious double bed, balcony; C) double bed with antique dresser; D) two twin beds; E) small single with Dutch paintings; F) canopy double bed, balcony; G) double bed; H) single bed; I) two twin beds; and J) large double bedroom (extra twin bed or crib available). Two bedrooms have private baths. Others share private guest baths. All rooms have TV. A full breakfast is served. Hosts speak Dutch, French, German, and Danish. A public telephone is in the hallway. One room is available with telephone for businesspeople. Children of all ages welcome.
**Rates:** S $36, D $42 DAILY.
**Reservations:** (503) 245-0642 8:00 TO 5:00.

## ALAMO SQUARE

A restored 18 room Victorian inn that was built in the late 1800s. It is conveniently located, close to all public transportation and the San Francisco Cultural Center. Accommodations include: A) 8 rooms, private baths and B) 10 rooms, shared baths, two rooms to a bath. A variety of king, queen, and twin bedrooms are available. Two suites are available for families with children up to a group of five. Sightseeing and shuttle to the airport can be arranged. Community kitchen and laundry facilities are available for guests. Two 10 speed bikes are available.
**Rates:** A) $55 AND B) $35 DAILY.
**Reservations:** (213) 684-4426 MONDAY - SATURDAY 9 A.M. TO 5 P.M. PACIFIC TIME.

## ASHBURY HEIGHTS

ASHBURY — A stately, hillside Edwardian home built in 1917. Constructed as the private residence of a San Francisco judge, the house has been restored to its original warmth and dignity. Hardwood floors, stained glass windows, and a marble fireplace contribute to an atmosphere of stability and elegance. Breakfast is served in a beam ceiling dining room with walls and ceiling graced with the designs of William Morris, noted nineteenth Century British designer. Guests enjoy a view of the atrium and formal garden from the dining room. A two room suite has views of the ocean and Golden Gate Bridge. The bedroom is furnished with a brass double bed and other fine antiques. A handmade quilt and frieze stenciling add to the comfort and charm. An adjoining room features a comfortable sofabed that converts to a queen-sized bed; wing chair with ottoman and handpainted desk are also in room. Both rooms are lighted with antique wall scones. They access a private half bath. Your host will arrange fresh flowers for your room and light a fire in season for your arrival. Off-street parking is available for guests. Host is an attorney; hostess is an executive. Bikes are available. Children welcome. **Rates:** S OR D $65, T $95 DAILY. **Reservations:** (415) 931-3083 MONDAY THROUGH FRIDAY 9 A.M. TO 5 P.M.

## FISHERMAN'S WHARF

BAY STREET NEAR HYDE — Spacious 1920s California/Mediterranean home at Fisherman's Wharf. Host is a culinary authority and teacher, trained at the Cordon Bleu. Superb breakfasts. Speaks German, French, and Italian. Accommodations include: A) king double bed, private bath; B) twin double bed, private bath; and C) two queen double beds, private bath. Complimentary gourmet pension pot luck on Wednesdays. West Highland "Scottie" DOG in residence. Located at the foot of Russian Hill, close to cable car and ferry boats, with buses to all points of interest. Parking for Rooms A and C. CHILDREN over 12 welcome. **Rates:** A & C) S $70, D $76 AND B) S $60, D $66 DAILY. **Reservations:** (415) 525-4569. OPEN 9 A.M. - 5 P.M.

## HAIGHT

HAIGHT AND BAKER — Beautiful 1885 Queen Anne San Francisco Victorian mansion in historical area of the city. Stained glass faceted crystals, marble steps, handcarved oak, sculptured and guilded lyncresta, vaulted ceiling, filled with antiques and soft furnishings from London. Close to Golden Gate Park and across street from Buena Vista Park. Public transportation across street. Host is a pilot and wine merchant; hostess is a copper cookware importer. Two DOGS and one CAT reside here. Accommodations include: A) queen bed, private bath; B) double bed, shared bath; C) double bed, private bath; D) double bed, shared bath; E) double bed, shared bath; and F) king bed, private bath. NO CHILDREN. NO SMOKING. A little French is spoken here. **Rates:** S OR D $75-$125 DAILY. **Reservations:** (415) 931-3083 MONDAY THROUGH FRIDAY 9 A.M. TO 5 P.M.

Beautifully restored 1895 Queen Anne Victorian across the street from Buena Vista Park and 8 blocks from Golden Gate Park. Public transportation across the street. Six rooms full of antiques with featherbeds, duvets and down pillows, and beautiful linens. Breakfast is served in oak paneled dining room by Singaporian chef. Padded walls, elegant china and crystal, beveled and stained glass windows. Totally authentic. Accommodations include: A) queen-sized bed, shared bath; B-E) queen-sized bed, private bath; and F) king-sized bed, private bath. Host is an airline pilot and wine importer; hostess is an importer of French copper

cookware. A little French is spoken. Two dogs are in residence. NO CHILDREN. NO SMOKING.
**Rates:** D $75-$125; S $5 LESS DAILY.
**Reservations:** (818) 344-7878 MONDAY THROUGH FRIDAY, 7 A.M. - 4 P.M. PACIFIC TIME; MACHINE SERVICE.

## HAIGHT-ASHBURY

MASONIC AT FREDERICK — This 1904 spacious family home, in the historic Haight-Ashbury district is on a street of Victorian "Painted Ladies." Hostess is a physical therapist interested in remodeling and renovating her home. She speaks some French, German, and Spanish. Accommodations include: A) king double bed, washbasin; B) twin double bed; and C) double bed. Rooms share one bathroom, two water closets. Generally used for members of the same party. Near Golden Gate Park and University of California Medical Center, the former abode of the "Flower Children" has become an upscale neighborhood with interesting shops and restaurants. Attractive back deck, PIANO, antiques. There are 21 steps to the front porch, 17 to second floor. DOG and CAT. Limited kitchen privileges. Tight street parking. Bus on corner takes 10 minutes to Union Square. Children welcome. SMOKING only on deck.
**Rates:** S $42, D $48 DAILY. 10% DISCOUNT WEEKLY.
**Reservations:** (415) 525-4569. OPEN 9 A.M. - 5 P.M.

## NOB HILL

DAWSON PLACE — A cozy pink and white Victorian cottage in a quiet, sleepy mews just half a block from two famous hotels and all their entertainment, the Fairmont and Mark Hopkins, with the cable cars running between them. Small private garden in back with old brick terrace and wall, chairs and table for wine on warm evenings. Hostess is a retired interior decorator and the house is filled with antiques and collectibles, fireplace for cool nights in study. Accommodations include: A) double room furnished with antique white wicker and has some bay view and B) twin double bedroom has twin chintz beds, antiques and Oriental rug, windows on garden. All firm mattresses and boards. Shared bath. Hostess travels a lot, speaks some French and Spanish. She belongs to ballroom dance club, glad to share. Extremely central in city location on exclusive Nob Hill. Walking distance to Chinatown (3 blocks), downtown stores (4 blocks), and theater (5 blocks). Cable car to Fisherman's Wharf, good transportation everywhere. Difficult parking for private car. Taxi from air terminal in downtown San Francisco $2.50. Famous restaurants closeby. No pets. NO CHILDREN.
**Rates:** S $45, D $55 DAILY.
**Reservations:** (415) 931-3083 MONDAY THROUGH FRIDAY 9 A.M. TO 5 P.M.

## NOE VALLEY

NOE STREET NEAR 18TH — This host enjoys nothing more than delighting and pleasing his guests. His experience as a restauranteur in the Canadian province of Quebec, waiter in France, maitre'd in San Francisco, and delicatessen operator in California's Marin County culminates in the breakfast he prepares and serves. You know you are the special guest from the elegant china and crystal table setting in either the formal dining room of the 1902 Edwardian house or the glass enclosed deck by the redwood HOT TUB. Fresh orange juice, fresh fruits, an omelet, croissants, homemade jam or preserves, and coffee brewed from freshly ground coffee beans is a typical menu. His omelets are inspired. The ingredients change each day depending on what is growing in his garden and what produce is the best at the Farmer's Market. Accommodations include three rooms each with double bed. They share two baths. French is spoken here. CHILDREN over 10 welcome.
**Rates:** S $55, D $60 DAILY.
**Reservations:** (415) 931-3083 MONDAY THROUGH FRIDAY 9 A.M. TO 5 P.M.

## PACIFIC HEIGHTS

OCTAVIA — Centennial (1876) Victorian, on San Francisco Victorian House Tour, saved from earthquake because owners had a water tank and covered the roof with wet rugs. Furnished in museum quality antiques that hosts have used as models for the miniatures that they manufacture. To gild the lily, this 22 room mansion contains their collection of miniatures, one of the largest in the world. Guestroom has queen-sized bed and sink in room. Share bath (two water closets) with hosts only. Host also has charming double bed apartment. Host collects classic movies; hostess is a pianist. Grand PIANO. Parking garage nearby; 2 hour street parking on work days or get guest parking permit. Easy bus transport to all points. Walk to cable car, opera. Children welcome.
**Rates:** S $72, D $78 DAILY. APARTMENT $92 DAILY. 10% DISCOUNT WEEKLY.
**Reservations:** (415) 525-4569. OPEN 9 A.M. - 5 P.M.

## RUSSIAN HILL

LEAVENWORTH NEAR UNION — A flat is a shingled Victorian building in the Russian Hill neighborhood. The home is furnished with American antiques. It has a large country kitchen where breakfast is served. The guestroom has FIREPLACE and twin beds or king with shared bath. Hostess sells real estate, enjoys gourmet cooking and travel. Eli, the CAT, is on hand to welcome guests. Walking distance to cable car, Fisherman's Wharf, Chinatown, North Beach; Union Square closeby.

NO CHILDREN. SMOKING is allowed in room or on large outside deck. No pipe or cigar smoking allowed.
**Rates:** S $50, D $55 DAILY.
**Reservations:** (415) 931-3083 MONDAY THROUGH FRIDAY 9 A.M. TO 5 P.M.

## SUNSET HEIGHTS

Gracious surroundings and an inviting atmosphere describe this home located close to Golden Gate Park and the University of California Medical Center. Easy access to downtown via public transportation. Double accommodations in four rooms with private baths. Coffee and tea served all day. Hors d'oeuvres and sherry available for gatherings in living room for reading and conversation. Laundry facilities available for small fee. Host is Dutch and Danish girls make breakfast and clean the rooms. French and German are spoken here. Children welcome.
**Rates:** S OR D $70 DAILY.
**Reservations:** (213) 684-4426 MONDAY - SATURDAY 9 A.M. TO 5 P.M. PACIFIC TIME.

Charming house on a level street in the hills with a view of the ocean, the Golden Gate Bridge, and the mountains of Marin County. The home is very clean and well maintained and attractively furnished. Host is a retired teacher; hostess is a homemaker and runs a small gift and jewelry business out of her home. Hosts have European background, speak several European languages fluently. A very friendly and clean Welsh Corgi is in residence. The house is within easy access to Golden Gate Park with its museums, Natural Science Museum, and so on. There is excellent public transportation within easy walking distance and ample parking for guests who come by car. The University of California Medical Center is nearby as well as San Francisco State University and the Conservatory. Hosts request no food in the room in order to maintain the high standard of cleanliness of the house. NO SMOKERS.
**Rates:** S $45, D $55 DAILY.
**Reservations:** (503) 245-0642 8:00 TO 5:00.

SLOAT BOULEVARD — Gracious Mission Style home, in the Sunset District—a quiet residential area with wide lawns and palm trees, near the ocean. This is the area of choice for drivers because you do not have to go through the hills and traffic of downtown. Quality furnishings, Oriental rugs. Host is European born, speaks fluent German and French. Guestroom has double bed, garden view. Private water closet, share full bath. Easy parking. Walk to San Francisco State University, the beach, or Stern Grove. It is 15 minutes by car to Union Square; 40 minutes by bus. Children welcome.

**Rates:** S $36, D $42 DAILY. 10% DISCOUNT WEEKLY.
**Reservations:** (415) 525-4569. OPEN 9 A.M. - 5 P.M.

## TELEGRAPH HILL

KEARNY — This is a Telegraph Hill 1907 apartment building, restored to single family home. Semiretired hostess is interested in music, art, and travel. Accommodations include: A) double bed, double sofabed in sitting room; and B) double bed; Room A can have a private bath or share with Room B; and C) complete one bedroom apartment available in adjacent building as B&B or weekly rental. Located just below the famous Coit Tower, one can walk to the North Beach Italian neighborhood, Chinatown, Fisherman's Wharf, or the Financial District. Two hour parking only, except Sundays; parking garage nearby. CHILDREN welcome.
**Rates:** A) S $48-$72, D $54-$78; B) S OR D $50 AND C) S OR D $72 DAILY. 10% DISCOUNT WEEKLY.
**Reservations:** (415) 525-4569. OPEN 9 A.M. - 5 P.M.

## TWIN PEAKS/DIAMOND HEIGHTS

Large modern townhouse (architectural award winning) with panoramic view of the city and bay. It is located in a quiet residential neighborhood just south of the top of Market Street. Easy access to all of the city. Easy parking nearby. Host is a university professor and author; hostess is a retired businesswoman who is very knowledgeable about the city. Accommodations include: A) two rooms each with double bed and B) two twin beds. All guestrooms share a guest bath. Port-a-crib and highchair available. Host smokes. PIANO, VCR, and bikes available. Gourmet continental breakfast served.
**Rates:** S $35, D $45 DAILY.
**Reservations:** (213) 684-4426 MONDAY - SATURDAY 9 A.M. TO 5 P.M. PACIFIC TIME.

NEAR GOLDEN GATE PARK — UNHOSTED, detached cottage in a secluded area not far from Golden Gate Park. Guests have a peek at the bay from the kitchen. There are two twin beds, a FIREPLACE, separate bath, and kitchen. A continental breakfast is in the stocked refrigerator. Hosts live in the main house with their BULL TERRIER, Tinkerbell, who will come out to greet you. Long time residents of San Francisco, hosts enjoy sharing recommendations to restaurants and local places of interest.
**Rates:** S OR D $65 DAILY. TWO NIGHT MINIMUM.
**Reservations:** (213) 684-4426 MONDAY - SATURDAY 9 A.M. TO 5 P.M. PACIFIC TIME.

## SAUSALITO
### HOUSE BOATS

The picturesque HOUSE BOAT community is a world apart, where seals come up to gaze back at you with curiousity, yet San Francisco is a short distance by car or ferry boat. Hostess is a writer and owns a management consulting firm. High quality boat, with large, beautifully furnished guestroom, with queen double bed, connecting private bath. House boats move gently. Private parking, gourmet restaurants and boutiques nearby. NO CHILDREN. SMOKING on upper sundeck only.
**Rates:** S $76, D $82 DAILY.
**Reservations:** (415) 525-4569. OPEN 9 A.M. - 5 P.M.

## TIBURON

Owner, architect, designed home overlooking San Francisco Bay with panoramic view of Bay Bridge, San Francisco, and Sausalito. Widowed hostess loves pampering guests. Uses her sterling silver, linens, and crystal to serve full breakfast. Accommodations include: A) queen bed, private bath and B) two rooms each with single bed, shared bath. All rooms have full view of San Francisco Bay. Large garden surrounds this hillside home. It is 25 minutes from downtown San Francisco by car or ferry. Rarely rented to more than one group at a time. VCR. NONSMOKERS ONLY.
**Rates:** S $45, D $75 DAILY.
**Reservations:** (415) 931-3083 MONDAY THROUGH FRIDAY 9 A.M. TO 5 P.M.

## SAN GABRIEL MOUNTAINS
### LAKE ARROWHEAD
### THE WOODS

SANDALWOOD DRIVE — Two story mountain home, large sundeck amidst oaks and pines across rear. House nominated for annual Showcase House of the year. Many antiques, large stone fireplace, country English. Hosts enjoy antiquing, birdwatching, and decorating. Hostess serves breakfast on sundeck in summer, and in winter the keeping room in front of fireplace. Accommodations include: A) Victorian room, queen-sized bed, private bath and deck; B) Federalist room, twin beds, with sitting alcove or doubles as single bed for third person; and C) cozy Americana room, double brass bed, bath in between. CAT, Figero, in residence. It is 2 miles to private beach; 4 miles to boating, water skiing, and Swisslike village; 15 miles to ski slopes; and 75 miles to Los Angeles area. No pets. CHILDREN over 10 welcome. SMOKING on deck only. Closed Friday. Open Saturday 6:00 P.M. through Thursday.
**Rates:** A) D $65 AND B & C) D $60 DAILY.

**Reservations:** (818) 344-7878 MONDAY THROUGH FRIDAY; 7 A.M. - 4 P.M. PACIFIC TIME; MACHINE SERVICE.

## SAN GABRIEL VALLEY

CALIFORNIA AND LOS ROBLES — Comfortable craftsman frame home within walking distance to the Convention Center, Rose Parade route, Fuller Seminary, restaurants, and good shopping. Huntington Library and Rose Bowl nearby. Host family has lived abroad several years in both Sweden and England. Accommodations include: A) two rooms each with queen-bedded rooms; and B) twin bed. All guestrooms share two baths. PIANO. Children welcome. NONSMOKERS only. **Rates:** A) S $35, D $50 B) $30 DAILY. A) S $175, D $250 AND B) $140 WEEKLY. **Reservations:** (213) 684-4426 MONDAY - SATURDAY 9 A.M. to 5 P.M. PACIFIC TIME.

ORANGE GROVE BOULEVARD — Located along Pasadena's "Scenic Tour Drive," this gracious Spanish home is set in a lovely garden with orange and lemon trees and inground POOL. The home is cheerfully furnished and filled with flowers from the garden. Accommodations include: A) two twin beds, sitting area, private bath and B) private sitting room with mountain views, king-sized bed, private bath. Hostess loves to spoil guests with an elegant breakfast served on the terrace or in the sunfilled dining room. Visit Pasadena's fine museums and sites or venture to Universal Studios, the mountains, or the sites of Los Angeles. One CAT is in residence. Hosts are European and speak fluent German. Host is a civil engineer; hostess enjoys reading, the theater, and hiking, PIANO. Bikes available. NONSMOKERS only. **Rates:** A) S $35, D $40 AND B) S OR D $50 DAILY. **Reservations:** (213) 684-4426 MONDAY - SATURDAY 9 A.M. TO 5 P.M. PACIFIC TIME.

## ALTADENA
## EAST ALTADENA

PINECREST NEAR ALTADENA — A large Contemporary home at 1,500 foot elevation. Backyard is Angeles National Forest, near Mount Wilson Toll Road. Excellent hiking and nature trails. Swimming POOL, large deck overlooking pool for continental or full breakfasts in good weather. Two fireplaces, cable TV, old world wine cellar. Hostess enjoys travel, tennis, skiing, adventure, gourmet cooking, and people from all over the world. Accommodations include: A) two twin beds, private attached bath; and B) king bed, private bath. If your timing is right, you may be able to join a wine class or attend a five course gourmet dinner complete with wines for approximately $40. PIANO, NO SMOKING.

**Rates:** S $45, D $50 DAILY.
**Reservations:** (213) 684-4426 MONDAY - SATURDAY 9 A.M. TO 5 P.M. PACIFIC TIME.

## FOOTHILLS

Beautiful, stately Spanish style home in a lovely residential area just north of Pasadena. Accommodations include two rooms each with double bed, shared bath. Enjoy a continental breakfast near the fountain in the lushly landscaped walled garden area or in the family dining room overlooking the gardens. Host, an avid amateur astronomer, enjoys sharing his rooftop telescope with guests; hostess, a writer and movement teacher, teaches yoga. Museums and several colleges are nearby. Extras include: PIANO, VCR, and lots of antiques. NONSMOKERS only.
**Rates:** S $45, D $50 DAILY. S OR D $280 WEEKLY.
**Reservations:** (213) 684-4426 MONDAY - SATURDAY 9 A.M. TO 5 P.M. PACIFIC TIME.

Contemporary home on quiet cul-de-sac across from golf course has a one room guesthouse with private bath, small kitchen, and queen-sized hide-a-bed. Continental breakfast served by the POOL or in the dining room. Hosts love to travel and read when not working as an insurance agent and librarian. It is 20 minutes to Los Angeles and easy access to all southern California tourist attractions. One DOG lives here. PIANO. Bikes available. NO CHILDREN. NO SMOKING.
**Rates:** S $30, D $35 DAILY. S $175, D $200 WEEKLY.
**Reservations:** (213) 684-4426 MONDAY - SATURDAY 9 A.M. TO 5 P.M. PACIFIC TIME.

## ALTADENA/PASADENA

Unique 1926 French Normandy two story home accentuated with antiques. Located near the Angles Forest in lovely residential area. Hostess is an art teacher who enjoys travel and meeting people. Accomodations include: A) newly decorated second floor guestroom, king bed, windows overlooking the front garden, private bath and B) double bed, shared bath. Bikes, TV, VCR available. A small dog lives here. NONSMOKERS ONLY.
**Rates:** A) S $45, D $50 AND B) S $35, D $40 DAILY. S OR D $275 WEEKLY.
**Reservations:** (213) 684-4426 MONDAY - SATURDAY 9 A.M. TO 5 P.M. PACIFIC TIME.

## SAN GABRIEL

PALM AVENUE NEAR INTERSTATE 90 — Located 10 miles east of downtown Los Angeles on half an acre. This home has trees, roses, and a 36 foot POOL shaded by an avocado tree. Hosts are retired teachers

and avid square dancers. Hostess can speak some Spanish. Located 40 to 50 minutes from Disneyland or Universal Studios. Easy access to Los Angeles. Two CATS are in residence. Interstate 10 is closeby as are Pasadena, shopping malls, Chinatown, Little Tokyo, University of Southern California, Cal Tech, and Cal State University. Accommodations include: double bed, shared bath. There is a couch for third person in party. NO SMOKERS due to an allergy to smoke.
**Rates:** D $30, $15 EXTRA PERSON DAILY.
**Reservations:** (818) 889-8870 OR (818) 889-7325 MONDAY THROUGH FRIDAY, 9:00 TO 5:00.

## SANTA CRUZ BEACH
### SANTA CRUZ
### SCOTTS VALLEY

HACIENDA DRIVE RIDGE — This house in the Santa Cruz Mountains blends with the natural environment as it pays tribute to its famous architect John Taggart, a protege of the late Frank Lloyd Wright. You will enjoy a fully equipped kitchen in the round, with complimentary wine, an ever present basket of teas, and a sumptuous breakfast as you wake to the mountain morning. Avail yourself of the blazing HOT TUB and the entertainment possibilities in the lounge. Remote control color cable TV, cassette stereo, and, if you would rather do it yourself, a PIANO. There are two cozy bedrooms, each with private bath and all the comfort your relaxed body could ask for. A walk out the back of the house and you are on the halfround deck with the world spread out at your feet over 20,000 acres of redwood valley. Legendary redwoods tower above as their branches whisper hushed messages of grandeur against the counterpoint of running water in the circulating pond on the property. Valley view offers complete seclusion only 2 minutes from State Highway 17 and another 10 minutes to the beaches of Santa Cruz. Accommodations include: A) king-sized bed and B) queen-sized bed. No pets. HANDICAPPED ACCESSIBLE. NO CHILDREN. SMOKING only outdoors on the deck.
**Rates:** S OR D $85 DAILY. $500 WEEKLY.
**Reservations:** (415) 931-3083 MONDAY THROUGH FRIDAY 9 A.M. TO 5 P.M.

## SIERRA NEVADA FOOTHILLS
### THREE RIVERS

PO BOX 245 — Hidden in the small village of Three Rivers, you will find this private guest cottage, minutes away from Sequoia National Park. The cottage fits snugly into the Sierra foothills and has a panoramic view of mountain and sky. You can enjoy the fresh country air on the deck or wander down the wildflower path to the cool ferns along Salt Creek.

Continental breakfast is served daily, along with extras' for your own preparation in the complete kitchen facility. The cottage, which is adjacent to main house, has two double beds and a full bath. Both the cottage and main house were designed and built by the host. Host is an architect and artist; hostess is a registered nurse and a photographer. One hour drive from Giant Forest, home of the General Sherman tree. Air conditioned. SMOKING on deck outside only. Children welcome.
**Rates:** D $60, $5 EACH ADDITIONAL PERSON DAILY.
**Reservations:** (818) 889-8870 OR (818) 889-7325 MONDAY THROUGH FRIDAY, 9:00 TO 5:00.

## SIERRA NEVADA MOUNTAINS
### OAKHURST
#### YOSEMITE

EAST OAK LANE — Mountain home with swimming POOL, alongside a stream, in the closest residential area to the south gate to Yosemite. Retired hosts are interested in travel. Accommodations include: A) twin-bedded double, private bath; B) double bed, private bath; and C) hide-a-bed for members of the same party. TV, fireplace, pool table. It is 20 minutes to Yosemite, Mariposa redwoods; 5 minutes to Bass Lake. Children welcome.
**Rates:** S $42, D $48, FAMILY + 1 $10 EXTRA, FAMILY + 2 $15 EXTRA DAILY.
**Reservations:** (415) 525-4569. OPEN 9 A.M. - 5 P.M.

## SILICON VALLEY
### PALO ALTO
#### RESIDENTIAL

COWPER AND WEBSTER STREET — A Victorian inn built in 1895 offers a combination of forgotten elegance and a touch of European grace. Restaurants and shops are 1 block away. There are five guestrooms, each room with a sitting parlor, a queen- or king-sized bed, and private bath. Host is a consultant; hostess collects art and plays the violin. CHILDREN over 15 welcome. NO SMOKERS.
**Rates:** 2 ROOMS S OR D $90; 5 ROOMS $110; 3 ROOMS $120 DAILY.
**Reservations:** (818) 344-7878 MONDAY THROUGH FRIDAY, 7 A.M. - 4 P.M. PACIFIC TIME; MACHINE SERVICE.

## SONOMA COUNTY
### HEALDSBURG
#### DRY CREEK VALLEY

MILL CREEK — A large country home located in the heart of the Sonoma County wine country. The custom Colonial home is on 17 view acres overlooking Mount St. Helena, the Geysers, and Dry Creek Valley.

The three double-bedded guestrooms are separate from the house. Each has a private bath and a small kitchen area with coffee maker, refrigerator, toaster, dishes, and seating area. Cot and crib available. Guests are served breakfast in the large country kitchen overlooking the valley and the garden. Numerous wildlife is on the property and guests usually can see a flock of wild turkeys which come each morning. All guestrooms are furnished with antiques. Guests are welcome to join the hosts in the large beamed living room with fireplace. Hosts will provide maps, guidebooks, and suggest restaurants. There are several excellent restaurants within a 5 to 15 minute drive as well as over 50 wineries with tasting rooms. Three CATS reside here. Host is a self-employed businessman who enjoys sailing and cars; hostess is a teacher who enjoys gardening, folk arts, and cooking. Spanish and French are spoken here. SMALL DOG WELCOME.
**Rates:** D $75 DAILY.
**Reservations:** (415) 931-3083 MONDAY THROUGH FRIDAY 9 A.M. TO 5 P.M.

## SOUTH BAY

### HERMOSA BEACH

19TH STREET — Spectacularly located ultra modern home right on the BEACH. Decor is all white, red, and blue, with lots of stained glass, sunken living room and multileveled bedrooms and terraces with ocean view. Host is an engineer. Hosts will make guests feel very much at home. Accommodations include a queen-sized bed, private bath. One CAT in residence. NO SMOKING.
**Rates:** S $70, D $75 DAILY.
**Reservations:** (818) 344-7878 MONDAY THROUGH FRIDAY, 7 A.M. - 4 P.M. PACIFIC TIME; MACHINE SERVICE.

## SOUTH OF LOS ANGELES
### SEAL BEACH
#### OCEANFRONT

Large villa situated right on the sand. Indulge in all the WATER SPORTS; swimming, boating, sunning, surfing, fishing, and windsurfing steps away. The hosts are professional people who have traveled extensively and love meeting other travelers. Your host home features three beautifully decorated rooms with choice of A-C) king or two twin beds, each with private bath and a JACUZZI for guests. Full breakfast often includes home grown melons, strawberries, and raspberries in addition to the hostess' special pastries. Gardeners will marvel at the abundance and variety of vegetation grown in this waterfront paradise. Los Angeles with famous sites is 30 minutes away. Closer still are Disneyland, Knott's Berry Farm, Spruce Goose, and the Queen Mary. Tennis and racquetball within 2 blocks. Village shops and restaurants within walking distance. NO CHILDREN. SMOKING outside only.

**Rates:** A & B) $75 AND C) $60 EXTRA BED IN A OR B $15 EXTRA DAILY. WEEKLY RATES CAN BE ARRANGED.
**Reservations:** (213) 684-4426 MONDAY - SATURDAY 9 A.M. TO 5 P.M. PACIFIC TIME.

## OLD TOWN

Very private townhouse in Old Town. Only a few blocks to quaint Main Street shops and restaurants, excellent swimming and surfing BEACH, and sport fishing pier. Also eight ethnic restaurants only 2 blocks from house; TENNIS COURTS 1 block away; convenient to San Diego Freeway, Rockwell International Corporation, Long Beach State and Long Beach Marina; 15 minutes to Long Beach Airport, Queen Mary, and Spruce Goose; and 30 minutes to Disneyland. Accommodations include a garden patio between Mexican decor double room and smaller room with trundle beds. Adjoining sitting room with TV. Private bath for guestrooms. Kitchen and laundry room privileges. Willing to meet guests who arrive by limousine bus at Long Beach Airport from Los Angeles International Airport. Children welcome.
**Rates:** S $50, D $55 DAILY. S $225, D $275 WEEKLY.
**Reservations:** (818) 344-7878 MONDAY THROUGH FRIDAY, 7 A.M. - 4 P.M. PACIFIC TIME; MACHINE SERVICE.

## UNSPOILED VILLAGE

CORNER FIFTH AND CENTRAL — Elegant, full service B&B country inn with brick courtyard, blue canopies, fountains, stately streetlights, and glorious gardens. Exquisite accommodations, all rooms and suites individually appointed with genuine antique furnishings. All private baths, most with kitchens and sitting areas. Rates include lavish complimentary breakfast, including croissants, fresh inn made pastries, fresh seasonal fruits and fruit juice, inn made granola, cheese, freshly ground coffee, and inn's own jams and jellies. It is 1 block from the OCEAN. Located in quiet residential area, within walking distance to excellent restaurants and the Long Beach Marina. One of the most delightful and unique inns in the state, the spiritual enjoyment here comes from a sincerely caring staff. Guests are thrilled with an unexpected luxurious country inn experience. Prefer not to have CHILDREN. NO SMOKING.
**Rates:** D A) $78, B) $88, C) $110, AND D) $135 DAILY.
**Reservations:** (818) 889-8870 OR (818) 889-7325 MONDAY THROUGH FRIDAY, 9:00 TO 5:00.

## WATERFRONT

Winding walk with antique streetlights lead you from the courtyard and flowers everywhere to some of southern California's last dunes and wide beaches stretching out to the Pacific Ocean. Enjoy home grown fruits and homemade pastries at breakfast as you feast your eyes on the wide expanse of the ocean with Catalina on the horizon. Your hosts are well traveled and enjoy meeting travelers from around the world. They are very knowledgeable about points of interest. Tennis and racquetball are 2 blocks away; quaint shops and restaurants are within walking distance; most southern California attractions are less than 30 minutes away; and ferries to Catalina Island are 10 minutes away. The local pier beckons the fisherman and fishing boat trips are available daily. A warm JACUZZI awaits you after a day of sightseeing. Accommodations include: A) two large rooms with king or twins and a rollaway, private baths and B) small room with king or twins, private bath. Hosts are professional couple. One CAT in residence. Contemporary WATERFRONT home. VCR. NO CHILDREN. SMOKING OUTSIDE ONLY.

**Rates:** A) D $75 AND B) D $60; EXTRA BED IN A OR B $15 DAILY. WEEKLY QUOTE ON REQUEST.

**Reservations:** (818) 344-7878 MONDAY THROUGH FRIDAY, 7 A.M. - 4 P.M. PACIFIC TIME; MACHINE SERVICE.

## SOUTHERN CALIFORNIA

South of Los Angeles is Long Beach, a major port, manufacturing center, and resort area. Here the Queen Mary reigns, a popular attraction open for tours, dining or you can sleep on board in staterooms run as a hotel. Nearby is the famous Spruce Goose of Howard Hughes. Catalina Island, an offshore island resort, can be reached by boat or plane from the ports at Long Beach. Orange county, home of Disneyland and Knotts's Berry Farm, also has many other specialty attractions. Here is the great Golden Coast extending from Long Beach through Huntington Beach, Newport, Balboa, and the art colony of Laguna Beach. Among the rolling hills on the former Irvine Ranch is the University of California campus, part of a dynamic master planned community. You will also find remains of mission days at San Juan Capistrano, where the famed swallows return annually to visit.

Over the Santa Monica Mountains is the San Fernando Valley and a world of entertainment. Universal Studios offers elaborate tours through the studio's 420 acre lot. Studios in Burbank and NBC offer intimate views of movies and TV. Write for tickets in advance. Famous landmarks of history have been preserved in and near the valley. The original San Fernando Valley Mission, famous stage stops, and the location where the Portola party stopped some 200 years ago are all still here to be visited. Magic Mountain near Valencia features "white Knuckler" thrill rides and top name entertainment. Do not miss a drive through the Santa Monica Mountains, Mulholland Drive, providing vistas of canyons and cities along its 55 mile length. (See Los Angeles for more B&Bs in this area.)

Beautiful Contemporary home in lush southern California valley. Close to ocean. Home filled with tasteful art work and books. Home cooked food. Rose gardens. Fruit orchard on premises. Quiet and peaceful surroundings. NO pets. Accommodations include: A) double bed, shared bath and B) twin-bedded double, shared bath. HANDICAPPED ACCESSIBLE. NO CHILDREN. NO SMOKING.
**Rates:** D $65 DAILY WEEKDAYS. D $70 DAILY WEEKENDS.
**Reservations:** (818) 344-7878 MONDAY THROUGH FRIDAY, 7 A.M. - 4 P.M. PACIFIC TIME; MACHINE SERVICE.

Greater Los Angeles is a special place with something of everything— ocean to the west, mountains to the north, desert to the east, and Orange County to the south. It includes Beverly Hills, the Rose Bowl, El Pueblo de Los Angeles, Universal Studios, University of Southern California, University of California Los Angeles, Westwood, the Coliseum, and Hollywood. Stay at a B&B and get a closer look at one or more areas with suggestions about what to see and do and how to get there.

## ANAHEIM
## DISNEYLAND

HICKORY STREET NEAR BALL — A Ranch style home in a residential section, less than a mile from Disneyland and the Convention Center. You can get there easily from anywhere and can visit most of southern California by tour bus. Hosts are of European background and have traveled extensively. German, Swedish, Norwegian, Danish, and some French are spoken. Hostess is a long time resident of Anaheim. She knows the area intimately and can give you a real insider's view. The family room has a cozy fireplace and air conditioning. It overlooks the backyard. Snacks are sometimes served on the spacious patio and in summer, fireworks from Disneyland can be viewed from the backyard nightly. Breakfasts are generous. Accommodations include: A) double bed and B) two twin beds. Both rooms share a guest bath and overlook the backyard. Guestrooms cannot accommodate more than two people. Children welcome. NO SMOKING indoors.
**Rates:** A & B) S $25, D $35 DAILY. S $150, D $200 WEEKLY. 8% BED TAX.
**Reservations:** (213) 684-4426 MONDAY - SATURDAY 9 A.M. TO 5 P.M. PACIFIC TIME.

## SUBURBAN RESIDENTIAL

HICKORY STREET — A California Ranch style home in a quiet residential section, less than a mile from Disneyland and the Convention Center. You can get there easily from anywhere and it is an ideal

headquarters to visit other southern California attractions by tour buses. Host speaks all Scandinavian languages fluently and some French; hostess who is a long time resident of Anaheim and knows the area intimately, speaks German. Host will pick up guests from the airport terminal at Disneyland, if necessary. The home has a large family room with fireplace, lit in winter, and air conditioning in summer. The patio is spacious and the backyard gives a splendid view of nightly fireworks from Disneyland during the summer. Breakfast is generous, European and American style, according to taste. Accommodations include: A) twin beds; B) double bed: and C) single bed. Guestrooms overlooking the backyard share a bath in the hall. Guestrooms cannot accommodate more than two people. Children welcome. NO SMOKING inside home.
**Rates:** S $25, D $35 DAILY. PLUS 8% CITY TAX.
**Reservations:** (818) 889-8870 OR (818) 889-7325 MONDAY THROUGH FRIDAY, 9:00 TO 5:00.

WALNUT — This large, beautiful Princess Anne home was built in 1910 by John Cook, prominent landowner and former mayor of Anaheim. The inn is graced by beveled, leaded glass windows and charming turn-of-the-century country furnishings. Comfortable Victorian living room, airy porches and a garden with avocado trees. Start the new day off with a hearty breakfast in the sunny, country dining room. Fine restaurants nearby. HOT TUB, JACUZZI, and ORGAN on premises. Accommodations include: second floor—A) large room with queen-sized bed, adjoining the oversized family bathroom; B) room with balcony has a queen-sized bed and shared bath; C) twin beds, shared bath; D) corner room with double bed, can be used with sunroom to form a suite, shared bath; and E) single bed, shared bath. Downtairs accommodations are: F) double spool bed, old-fashioned sewing machine, shared bath; G) corner room with a nautical theme, brass and iron double bed, shared bath; H) high ceilinged pretty room with a white, iron double bed, shared bath; and I) spacious room with private outside entrance to the garden, queen-sized bed and double bed, private bath. Bikes available, SMOKING on outside porches only.
**Rates:** S $32; D $50 & $65; PRIVATE BATH $75 DAILY. 8% BED TAX.
**Reservations:** (818) 344-7878 MONDAY THROUGH FRIDAY, 7 A.M. - 4 P.M. PACIFIC TIME; MACHINE SERVICE.

## ARCADIA

Comfortable Ranch style home with POOL on a quiet cul-de-sac. Hostess is a medical technologist who enjoys gardening, hiking, and travel. Ready access to the Rose Bowl, Santa Anita Race Track, the Arboritum, the Huntington Library, many golf courses, and the beautiful San Gabriel

Mountains. Comfortable guestroom has a double bed. A second room is available with one twin bed. Both rooms share family bath, One DOG lives here. HANDICAPPED ACCESSIBLE. Children of any age welcome. **Rates:** S $35, D $50 DAILY. S $100, D $175 WEEKLY. **Reservations:** (213) 684-4426 MONDAY - SATURDAY 9 A.M. TO 5 P.M. PACIFIC TIME.

## BEVERLY HILLS
### THE FLATS

NORTH BEDFORD DRIVE — European furnishings throughout this unusual residence in Beverly Hills flats. Has a lovely garden and POOL. Accommodations include: A) queen-sized bed, private bath and B) double bed, shared bath with family. Dutch country antiques and fine art throughout. Cosmopolitan host will make guests welcome, no matter where they are from. He, who is a technical consultant, speaks German, French, Dutch, and Maylaysian. DOG resides here. Bikes available. NO CHILDREN. NO SMOKERS. **Rates:** S $50, D $55 DAILY. **Reservations:** (818) 344-7878 MONDAY THROUGH FRIDAY, 7 A.M. - 4 P.M. PACIFIC TIME; MACHINE SERVICE.

## BUENA PARK
### LOS COYOTES COUNTRY CLUB

CANDLEWOOD WAY — Bright and airy condominium in lovely Los Coyotes Country Club residential area. Condo is adjacent to swimming POOL and a 5 minute drive to TENNIS COURTS, a jogger can get there in 10 minutes. Home is convenient to the great entertainment areas of the southern California area: Disneyland, Fullerton College, Buena Park Convention Center 15 minutes; Knott's Berry Farm, 10 minutes; Anaheim Convention Center, 20 minutes; beautiful beaches and Los Angeles, 45 minutes. Host is an insurance salesman and enjoys golf; hostess is a marriage family therapist and interested in wine collecting, music, and theater. Two story condo and bedrooms are upstairs. The accommodations are comfortable for only two people. Bath is shared with two adults though there are two baths. Breakfast served in lovely open nook or on patio. HOT TUB. PIANO. VCR. Bikes available. CHILDREN over 12 welcome. **Rates:** S $35, D $43 DAILY. TAKE $5 OFF ON STAYS OF TWO OR MORE DAYS. S $160, D $200 WEEKLY. **Reservations:** (714) 738-8361 MONDAY THROUGH FRIDAY 7 A.M. TO 6 P.M. PACIFIC TIME.

## CONOGA PARK

RESCO AT DESATO — Beautiful home with living room and a formal dining room, furnished with contemporary furniture and a PIANO. There is a fireplace and patio with hanging plants. SPA is available at any time. Accommodations include: A) king-sized bed, shared bath, TV and B) double bed, shared bath, TV. Continental breakfast can be served on patio with tropical fruits and melons of season and a fresh flower from the yard. Dinner can be served. There is a beautiful BIRD DOG in yard. Home is close to public transportation, markets, shopping centers, colleges, and fine restaurants. Points of interest are Universal Studios, Dodger Stadium, Sports Arena, museums, Music Center, and much more. Approximately 20 minutes from ocean and 35 minutes to mountains. Hosts invite guests to join in neighborhood activities. Very friendly block. CHILDREN from 9 to 18 welcome.
**Rates:** S $50, D $55 DAILY.
**Reservations:** (818) 344-7878 MONDAY THROUGH FRIDAY, 7 A.M. - 4 P.M. PACIFIC TIME; MACHINE SERVICE.

## ENCINO

VALLEY MEADOW ROAD — Designed by Paul Sterling Hoag, this Contemporary home in the Royal Oaks section of Encino is spacious with the airiness that only glass walls can give. The exposed ceiling beams and the magnificent coloring and decor add up to the California "luxury look" that the world admires. POOL, TENNIS COURT, and SAUNA are available. Host is a Renaissance man, writer, sculptor, actor, inventor; hostess is a silversmith, whose studio is on the grounds. Chinese couple are in residence to serve breakfast either poolside or indoors. This home is within 25 minutes to University of Southern California; University of California, Los Angeles; and Beverly Hills, 20 minutes to Burbank Airport, 10 minutes to Van Nuys Airport, and 30 minutes to Los Angeles Airport. These accommodations are particularly attractive to businesspeople who prefer luxurious private surroundings to a hotel. Accommodations include: two single or double bed, private bath. Affectionate COCKER SPANIEL in residence. PIANO and pool table. NO SMOKERS.
**Rates:** S $95, D $110 DAILY.
**Reservations:** (818) 344-7878 MONDAY THROUGH FRIDAY, 7 A.M. - 4 P.M. PACIFIC TIME; MACHINE SERVICE.

## FOUNTAIN VALLEY

PLACER RIVER CIRCLE — Elegant California Ranch style home. Full gourmet breakfast served. Beautifully decorated, patio, wet bar. JACUZZI. Accommodations include: A) two rooms each with king-sized bed; B) queen-sized bed; and C) twin beds. All rooms have private baths. Inground POOL. VCR. PIANO. NO CHILDREN. NO SMOKERS.

**Rates:** D $50 DAILY. CHILDREN'S RATES BY ARRANGEMENT.
**Reservations:** (818) 889-8870 OR (818) 889-7325 MONDAY THROUGH
FRIDAY, 9:00 TO 5:00.

## FULLERTON

EAST GROVE NEAR ACADIA — A typical California tract house with
a large family room added. Guests are welcome in all living areas. Host
is a retired electronic engineer and speaks some Spanish; hostess is a
teacher specializing in English as a second language. She speaks some
French, German, and Spanish. JACUZZI in patio, guest TV, PIANO.
Full breakfast to guest's order including fresh orange juice, cereal, eggs,
bacon or sausage, and homemade bread or muffins. Afternoon tea on
request; dinners available. It is a 20 minute drive to Disneyland or Knott's
Berry Farm, 30 minutes to ocean beaches and Laguna Beach art galleries,
1 to 2 hours to mountain hiking and skiing in season. Local bus
transportation available. Host will meet airport bus at Disneyland on
request. Double accommodations in guestrooms. Air conditioned. NO
CHILDREN. SMOKING—cigarettes only and not in bedrooms.
**Rates:** S $25, D $33 DAILY. S $150, D $200 WEEKLY. TAKE $5 OFF
FOR STAYS OF TWO OR MORE DAYS.
**Reservations:** (714) 738-8361 MONDAY THROUGH FRIDAY 7 A.M.
TO 6 P.M. PACIFIC TIME.

SMOKEWOOD AVENUE — An attractive, Contemporary home with
many personal appointments including PIANO, fireplace, TV, VCR, nice
furnishings, and central air conditioning. The home is located in a quiet,
residential neighborhood with mature trees and rolling terrain. Host is a
life insurance underwriter; hostess enjoys travel, entertaining, and quilting.
Accommodations include: A) one double room with twin beds, shared
bathroom and B) single room, shared bathroom. Laundry facilities
available. The home is conveniently located near all Orange County
attractions. NONSMOKERS only.
**Rates:** S $35, D $45 DAILY. TAKE $5 OFF EACH DAY ON STAYS
OF TWO OR MORE DAYS. S $200, D $280 WEEKLY.
**Reservations:** (714) 738-8361 MONDAY THROUGH FRIDAY 7 A.M.
TO 6 P.M. PACIFIC TIME.

## GLENDALE
### ADAMS SQUARE

PARK AVENUE — This is a 1920s Spanish style home featuring 1930s
mahogany and walnut furnishings, original works of art, and collector
plates. A large attractive rear garden contains many fruit trees. Host and
hostess are a semiretired couple in their 50s with many interests including
travel, art, and the movies. Amenities include central heating and cooling,

a writing shelf, portable refrigerator, and TV in living room. Accommodations include a double bed, shared bath. Children welcome.
**Rates:** S $30, D $35 DAILY. S $180, D $210 WEEKLY.
**Reservations:** (213) 684-4426 MONDAY - SATURDAY 9 A.M. TO 5 P.M. PACIFIC TIME.

## LAGUNA BEACH
## MYSTIC HILLS

TAHITI AT PARK — A cozy, quiet seaside home with magnificent ocean and canyon views. Similar to a warm climate Swiss village. Victorian, Queen Anne, and oak antiques abound in all rooms. Hosts are international counselors in the medical field. Accommodations include: A) large double bed, Victorian antiques; B) large double bed, oak antiques; C) large antique iron twin bed, antiques; and D) large iron/brass king-sized bed, French antiques, private bath. Rooms A through C share a bath (private, however, if no other guests). All beds have fluffy comforters and quilts. Crib and cot available. Beautiful deck overlooks OCEAN view. Can take breakfast of homemade quiche, muffins, and fresh fruit on deck or in cozy antique dining area. On those cool days, cozy up in front of the fireplace with its antique mantel, have a glass of sherry, and watch the ocean toss or the birds soar in the canyon. Hiking at your doorstep, all beach sports, cultural events (Pageant of the Masters, Festival of Arts), unique shopping, tennis, golf, and much more. Laguna Transit picks you up at door; 5 minute ride to all events or hosts will make special arrangements. PIANO. HANDICAPPED ACCESSIBLE. Bikes available. NONSMOKERS preferred.
**Rates:** S $45, D $55 DAILY. TAKE $5 OFF ON STAYS OF TWO OR MORE DAYS. S $240, D $300 WEEKLY.
**Reservations:** (714) 738-8361 MONDAY THROUGH FRIDAY 7 A.M. TO 6 P.M. PACIFIC TIME.

## PORTO FINO

QUIVERA — Spanish style custom built home with 180 degree view of the OCEAN, looking up the coast toward Newport Beach and south toward Dana Point. Close to beach and city of Laguna Beach, famous as an artist colony. Full breakfast served. Host is practicing attorney; hostess sews and paints. Their interests are travel and the arts. Accommodations include: A) twin-bedded double, private hall bath; B) double bed, Oriental motif, private hall bath; C) queen hide-a-bed, pool table, 180 degree view of ocean, private attached bath; and D) double hide-a-bed, shared bath. HOT TUB. Children welcome.
**Rates:** S $50, D $60 DAILY. TAKE $5 OFF ON STAYS OF TWO OR MORE DAYS. ALL RATES $10 HIGHER DURING JULY AND AUGUST.

**Reservations:** (714) 738-8361 MONDAY THROUGH FRIDAY 7 A.M. TO 6 P.M. PACIFIC TIME.

## LA VERNE

PEYTON ROAD — A modern Ranch style residence in quiet neighborhood. The living room is furnished with some antiques, PIANO, and fireplace. Off the sunny patio is a large yard with many fruit trees. Host is an insurance salesman; hostess is a registered nurse. Accommodations include: A) double bed and B) two twin beds. Both share a hall bath. CHILDREN over 12 welcome. NONSMOKERS only.
**Rates:** S $30, D $35 DAILY. S $180, D $200 WEEKLY.
**Reservations:** (213) 684-4426 MONDAY - SATURDAY 9 A.M. TO 5 P.M. PACIFIC TIME.

## LONG BEACH

REDONDO AVENUE — Large early 1930s home, with antiques/collectibles. Host is a stevedore; hostess is a teacher. Both enjoy traveling and camping. Three small POODLES are in residence. PETS WELCOME. Located midway between Los Angeles and Orange County, and 1 mile from beach and airport. Accommodations include: A) two single beds, shower and B) king-sized bed, private bath. Both with complete house privileges, breakfast included. C) one bedroom apartment, two single beds and D) studio apartment, two single beds. Entire house is also available. CHILDREN WELCOME.
**Rates:** S OR D $40 DAILY. S $175, D $225 WEEKLY. EXTRA ROLLAWAY $5.
**Reservations:** (818) 889-8870 OR (818) 889-7325 MONDAY THROUGH FRIDAY, 9:00 TO 5:00.

Built in the early 1930s, this is a typical California bungalow which has been carefully restored. The furnishings can best be described as eclectic. There is an amazing assemblage of antiques, collectibles, artifacts, and memorabilia from all over the world. Every room is filled with an interesting assortment of antiques, paintings, and other curiosities. The whole house resembles a museum. The studio apartments are in a separate building that is located just a few steps from the main house. They have just been repainted and have new carpeting. The bedroom in each apartment is small and contains only one twin bed. There is a small, pullout bed in the living room. The bathrooms are large, well lighted, and contain a tub and shower. The kitchens are well equipped with stove, refrigerator, microwave oven, toaster, cooking utensils, and dishes. The closets are large. These apartments are not at all luxurious, but they are clean and comfortable. Accommodations included in main house are: A) two single beds, shower and B) king-sized bed, bath. Complete house privileges. Breakfast included. Host is a crane driver; hostess is a teacher. Three POODLES reside here. Air conditioned. Located midway between Los Angeles and Orange County; 1 mile from BEACH and airport. Children welcome. **Rates:** S $25, D $33 DAILY. TAKE $5 OFF PER DAY ON STAYS OF TWO OR MORE DAYS. **Reservations:** (714) 738-8361 MONDAY THROUGH FRIDAY 7 A.M. TO 6 P.M. PACIFIC TIME.

## LOS ANGELES

Major points of interest include the historic Pueblo de Los Angeles which marks the beginning of the Mexican and Spanish town. Just a few blocks away are Chinatown and Little Tokyo. The cultural heart of the city is the Music Center which houses the Dorothy Chandler Pavillion, the Mark Taper Forum, and the Ahmanson Theater. Four celebrity boulevards tie downtown to the beaches: Sunset Boulevard, Santa Monica Boulevard, Wilshire Boulevard (with its Miracle Mile), and Hollywood Boulevard. There is Hancock Park with the Pleistocene-era animals trapped in tar, the large Los Angeles County Museum of Art, and Hollywood with its Chinese Theater with footprints of stars and their signatures cast into cement. Visit the gigantic Farmer's Market complex or see a major Broadway production. In Beverly Hills you can drive past homes of the stars or shop and dine in fabulous surroundings. Westwood Village, at the foot of the University of California, Los Angeles, is a mecca for college students and a quaint village of recreation, riding, hiking, and sightseeing. Griffith Observatory and the Greek Theater is also located here. The Hollywood Bowl is noted for its Summer series featuring the Los Angeles Philharmonic Orchestra. There are 20 miles of sandy beaches. South and west of Los Angeles is Exposition Park, the Sports Arena, the Forum, and the Memorial Coliseum, site of the Olympic Games of 1932 and 1984.

## ANGELINO HEIGHTS

NEAR HOLLYWOOD FREEWAY — A romantic Victorian built in 1887. Hosts have carefully authenticated the Eastlake style, and all the rooms are decorated and furnished true to the period, with appropriate colors, wall decorations, and Oriental carpets. Even the bathrooms are period pieces with antique fixtures, claw-footed tubs, brass trappings, and wainscotting. Some of the windows are topped with ruby red etched glass called Flashed Glass, unique to the area. The inn is on a hillside overlooking downtown Los Angeles, in a historic residential district frequently used as a backdrop in movies and commercials. Accommodations include: A) single bed; B) double bed; C) large double bed; and D) queen-sized bed. There are four baths for six rooms. Host is a management

consultant; hostess is an English teacher. French is spoken here. NO SMOKING.
**Rates:** A) S $45; B) D $55; C & D) D $70; E) D $75; F & G) D $90; AND H) D $125 DAILY.
**Reservations:** (818) 344-7878 MONDAY THROUGH FRIDAY, 7 A.M. - 4 P.M. PACIFIC TIME; MACHINE SERVICE.

## BEVERLYWOOD

CANFIELD AVENUE — Centrally located air conditioned Contemporary home. It is 1 mile from Beverly Hills and Ranch Park Golf Course and 7 miles from ocean. Close to Universal Studios, Disneyland, museums, and universities. It is 15 minutes from LAX, a few minutes to freeways (Interstates 10 and 405). Host is the repairman to the stars and is also a radio and TV personality; hostess does TV and movie background work. Accommodations include: A) queen Murphy bed, color TV, refrigerator, hot plate, share bath; B) queen-sized bed, TV, shared bath and C) second floor unhosted suite, queen-sized bed, sitting room, kitchen, private bath, private entrance. Sundeck available. DOG and two CATS reside in home. Accessible by public transportation. VCR. Children of all ages welcome. Baby equipment available. NO SMOKING.
**Rates:** A & B) S $50, D $55 AND C) S $80, D $85 DAILY. A & B) S $250, D $275 AND C) S $340, D $375 WEEKLY. C) S $850, D $900 MONTHLY.
**Reservations:** (818) 344-7878 MONDAY THROUGH FRIDAY, 7 A.M. - 4 P.M. PACIFIC TIME; MACHINE SERVICE.

## CENTRAL

ANCHOR AVE/MOTOR AVENUE — Modern Ranch style home in exclusive neighborhood near Century City, a good central location. Host is an educator; hostess is a professional artist with a studio in the house. Their interests include hiking, biking, and golf. Guestroom has twin double bed, convertible to a king, with a private bath. A single sofabed in the den is available for CHILDREN over 12. Guests may use washer and dryer and keep snacks in refrigerator. Good parking.
**Rates:** S OR D $56 DAILY.
**Reservations:** (415) 525-4569. OPEN 9 A.M. - 5 P.M.

## DOWNTOWN

ALVARADO TERRACE — Nestled in the midst of modern, downtown Los Angeles, is one of several turn-of-the-century homes surrounding a park. All are officially registered as historical landmarks. Built in 1902, the inn contains its original stained and leaded glass windows, paneled walls, hardwood floors, and an Ionic columned fireplace with a built-in clock that still chimes on cue. There are period furnishings, unusual

collectibles, and the walls are a gallery of art work. Your stay includes a hearty breakfast of fruit in season, an entree such as French toast, fritatta, quiche, or omelet, and juice, coffee, or tea. Breakfast is served in the dining room or on the patio between 7:30-9:00 A.M. unless otherwise requested. In late afternoon guests are invited to gather in the parlor or library for an informal social hour with complimentary wine and a light repast. Accommodations include: A) single waterbed, TV, private bath; B) queen-sized waterbed, TV, shared bath; C) corner room with twin beds, TV, shared bath; D) sun room with king-sized bed, TV, shared bath; and E) suite with trundle beds. A little Spanish is spoken. The inn is also available for small parties and meetings. CHILDREN over 12 welcome. SMOKING on porch or on patio only.
**Rates:** A) D $55; B) D $65; C) D $75; D) D $85; AND E) D $85 DAILY.
**Reservations:** (818) 344-7878 MONDAY THROUGH FRIDAY, 7 A.M. - 4 P.M. PACIFIC TIME; MACHINE SERVICE.

This is a 1902 National Historic Landmark. Stained glass windows, rare oak paneling, antiques, art work and collectibles are in this house. Hearty gourmet breakfasts, afternoon wine, and refreshments. Near Convention Center, University of Southern California, and theaters. Guest passes available to famed Magic Castle in Hollywood. Accommodations include: A) two rooms each with double bed and twin beds, private bath. These two rooms can be made into a suite; B) king-sized bed, private bath; C) double bed, private bath; and D) queen-sized bed, private bath. CHILDREN over 12 only. Outside SMOKING only.
**Rates:** S $55, D $85 DAILY.
**Reservations:** (818) 889-8870 OR (818) 889-7325 MONDAY THROUGH FRIDAY, 9:00 TO 5:00.

## NEAR DOWNTOWN

RICHELIEU TERRACE — Less than 10 minutes to Center City businesses, financial district, theater, and restaurants. Comfortable, unusually quiet, safe, and close to all freeways. Accommodations include: A) twin beds, shared bath and B) two cots in living room, big closet, shared full bath. Veritable farm in the city: fruit trees, berries, and vegetables. Enormous kitchen and family room with fireplace usable by all residents. Hostess is a teacher who prepares continental breakfasts and enjoys meeting new people. One CAT resides here. Children of all ages welcome.
**Rates:** SEPTEMBER THROUGH JUNE S $40, D $45 DAILY. D $175 WEEKLY.
**Reservations:** (818) 344-7878 MONDAY THROUGH FRIDAY, 7 A.M. - 4 P.M. PACIFIC TIME; MACHINE SERVICE.

## GRANADA HILLS

NANETTE STREET — Modern hilltop home on the 14th fairway of the Knollwood Golf Course. Besides a 38 foot inground POOL with separate SPA, the home enjoys a 180 degree view of the San Fernando Valley to the south and the Santa Susanna Mountains to the north. Host is an engineer; hostess is a retired social worker who operates a craft boutique. Both love to travel. Small DOG and three CATS are in residence. Located in a separate wing, accommodations include: A) queen-sized bed, shared bath; B) two twin beds, shared bath. An additional 1/2 bath is near the entry. Easy access to three freeways (Interstates 118, 5, 405); 20 minutes to Universal Studios, Hollywood, Los Angeles 300, 1 hour to Disneyland, Queen Mary, and beaches. Amenities include air conditioning and bikes. CHILDREN over 12 welcome. Considerate SMOKERS accepted, but no cigars.
**Rates:** A) S $55, D $60 AND B) S $60, D $65 DAILY.
**Reservations:** (818) 344-7878 MONDAY THROUGH FRIDAY, 7 A.M. - 4 P.M. PACIFIC TIME; MACHINE SERVICE.

## HOLLYWOOD

NORTH SIERRA BONITA AVENUE — Spacious 1910 California bungalow on quiet, palm tree-lined residential street in Hollywood close to many of the major attractions. Accommodations include: A) guestroom on the second floor with two twin beds, private bath, and sundeck. Hosts' two sons, aged 10 and 6, live here also. Host speaks numerous languages and is a high school teacher; hostess speaks French and some Italian and Hebrew and works from home doing transcriptions. There is a playful IRISH SETTER DOG in residence and a white CAT who spends most of its time outside. Air conditioning available. Children of all ages welcome.
**Rates:** S $50, D $55 DAILY. S OR D $175 WEEKLY. S OR D $550 MONTHLY.
**Reservations:** (818) 344-7878 MONDAY THROUGH FRIDAY, 7 A.M. - 4 P.M. PACIFIC TIME; MACHINE SERVICE.

Spacious California bungalow on quiet, palm-tree-lined street in the heart of Hollywood, close to many of the tourist attractions, shops, and restaurants. Located between Sunset and Hollywood Boulevards with frequent buses on both of these streets. Host is a high school teacher who speaks a number of languages; hostess is English born and works from home. There are two sons, aged 8 and 6, an Irish Setter DOG, and a white CAT. The house itself was built in 1910 and still retains many of its original features. The guestroom has double accommodations, its own en suite bathroom and sundeck. It is the only room on the second floor so it is very private. Air conditioned. Children of all ages welcome.

**Rates:** S $30, D $35 DAILY.
**Reservations:** (818) 889-8870 OR (818) 889-7325 MONDAY THROUGH FRIDAY, 9:00 TO 5:00.

SIERRA BONITA AVENUE — A bungalow on quiet palm tree-lined street close to many of Hollywood's most well-known attractions. The house is very spacious and retains many of its original features. The guestroom, with double accommodations, is the only room on the second floor and has its own bathroom en suite. Crib and cot are available. Host is a high school teacher who dabbles in journalism; hostess works from home. Children are 7 and 5. The home is well situated for public transportation and there is plenty of street parking for guests with cars. Hebrew, French, German, Italian, Spanish, and Russian are spoken here. Air conditioned. Children welcome.
**Rates:** S $35, D $40, PLUS $5 FOR 3RD PERSON DAILY. S $175, D $210 WEEKLY.
**Reservations:** (213) 684-4426 MONDAY - SATURDAY 9 A.M. TO 5 P.M. PACIFIC TIME.

## HOLLYWOOD/MID-WILSHIRE

Convenient location near Hollywood and public transportation. This home is a duplex, so guests have their own fully equipped kitchen, laundry, dining room with PIANO, and living room with fireplace. Hostess is a biochemist who enjoys folk dancing and sewing. She speaks some German. Accommodations include: A) double bed and B) two twin beds with balcony overlooking the garden. Both share 1 1/2 baths. Cot available for an extra person. Interesting shops and excellent restaurants are nearby. Two outside CATS live here. Children of all ages welcome. NONSMOKERS only.
**Rates:** S $30, D $35 DAILY. S $160, D $200 WEEKLY.
**Reservations:** (213) 684-4426 MONDAY - SATURDAY 9 A.M. TO 5 P.M. PACIFIC TIME.

## CENTRAL LOS ANGELES

NEAR MELROSE AND VINE — Convenient location close to the center of Los Angeles (near Hollywood) and near public transportation. The house is a duplex, so guests have their own fully equipped kitchen, laundry, dining room with PIANO, and living room with a fireplace. Hostess is a biochemist who enjoys folk dancing and sewing and speaks some German. Interesting shops and excellent restaurants are nearby. Accommodations include: A) double bed and B) twin-bedded double with balcony overlooking the garden. The two rooms share 1 1/2 baths. A cot is available for an extra person. Children of all ages welcome. NONSMOKERS only.

**Rates:** S $30, D $35 DAILY. S $160, D $200 WEEKLY. CHILDREN OVER TWO $5 DAILY. ENTIRE SECOND STORY TWO BEDROOM HOUSE $65 DAILY OR $375 WEEKLY FOR FOUR PEOPLE. **Reservations:** (818) 889-8870 OR (818) 889-7325 MONDAY THROUGH FRIDAY, 9:00 TO 5:00.

## MAR VISTA

CULVER BOULEVARD — A rustic townhouse with wood beam ceiling, gas fireplace, and small patio. Accommodations include one guestroom with double bed and shared bath. Host is a programmer; hostess a social worker. Hosts enjoy cooking original and ethnic meals on request. They are two friendly musicians who play and sing traditional American music. Both are nonsmokers. The house is shared with a CAT named Macky. The exterior includes security gates, a garden setting, and patio picnic area. It is 15 minutes from prime beach areas including Venice and Santa Monica and from Los Angeles International Airport; 20 minutes to Hollywood, Westwood, downtown Los Angeles, and museums. Bike rentals are near scenic bike paths. Mountain hiking trails are nearby. Close to public transportation. SMOKING restricted to the patio. **Rates:** S $32, D $38 DAILY. S $200, D $240 WEEKLY. **Reservations:** (213) 684-4426 MONDAY - SATURDAY 9 A.M. TO 5 P.M. PACIFIC TIME.

## PACIFIC PALISADES

A beautiful, rustic townhouse located in a wonderful canyon setting with mountain views and only 2 minutes from Santa Monica Beach and the J. Paul Getty Museum. Close to Malibu, Beverly Hills, Hollywood, and University of California, Los Angeles. Amenities include: fireplace, PIANO, TENNIS COURTS, POOL, HOT TUB, and hiking trails. Host is an attorney practicing in nearby Marina Del Rey. He speaks a little French and German. Accommodations include: master suite with king bed, Chinese rugs, private bath, TV, VCR, and great view. NONSMOKERS only. **Rates:** S OR D $60 DAILY. **Reservations:** (213) 684-4426 MONDAY - SATURDAY 9 A.M. TO 5 P.M. PACIFIC TIME.

## RANCHO PALOS VERDES—QUIET RESIDENTIAL SUBURB

PALOS VERDES DRIVE SOUTH — Cozy OCEAN FRONT home. Private beach club across the road. Fully stocked beach car provided. Surf fishing. Generous full breakfast served on patio, front porch, or dining room. Both common rooms have fireplace. Home is 10 minutes to busy, working Los Angeles harbor with lovely shops and restaurants.

Close by Queen Mary and Spruce Goose, museums, art galleries, Disneyland, Knott's Berry Farm, Marineland, Universal Studios, and much more. Nearby are tennis courts and riding stables. Teatime or cocktail hour if convenient for guests. Accommodations include: A) double bed, private bath and B) twin beds, private bath. Crib, cot, rollaway available. Hostess speaks some Spanish and enjoys paddle tennis, travel, and swimming. Children welcome. Babysitting can be arranged. **Rates:** A) S $35, D $50 AND B) S $35, D $50 DAILY. SPECIAL RATES FOR CHILDREN. 10% SENIOR CITIZEN DISCOUNT. **Reservations:** (818) 889-8870 OR (818) 889-7325 MONDAY THROUGH FRIDAY, 9:00 TO 5:00.

## SAN FERNANDO VALLEY

VENTURA BOULEVARD — Cozy, charmingly furnished home located in woodsy area of east San Fernando Valley. Lovely gardens and barbecue in yard. Fireplace in living room. Accommodations include: A) king-sized bed with TV, private 3/4 bath and B) den room with queen-sized sofabed, TV, and full private bath. Host is in property management. PETS are in residence. NO CHILDREN. **Rates:** A) S $50, D $55 AND B) S $40, D $45 DAILY. **Reservations:** (818) 344-7878 MONDAY THROUGH FRIDAY, 7 A.M. - 4 P.M. PACIFIC TIME; MACHINE SERVICE.

## SILVER LAKE

ELEVADO — Private, deluxe, fully furnished apartment in Spanish style, two story duplex. Quiet residential area in picturesque Silverlake area of downtown Los Angeles. Secure. Dinette set and breakfast bar. Kitchenette has dishes, cookware, and everything necessary for short or long visit. All carpeted including bathroom, which has both tub and shower. View of mountains and civic center. Hostess owns a bakery and will provide Danish, bread, eggs, juice, and fruit for first week or longer if desired. Her retired parents are also on premises. Well-lighted outside entrance. Off-street parking included or garage available for $5 per night extra. Private apartment. Accommodations include: A) king-sized bed in large bedroom with two chests, desk, and large wardrobe closet and B) two 6 foot couches suitable for sleeping in large living room. Children welcome. **Rates:** S OR D $55 2-7 NIGHTS; $45 8-14 NIGHTS; $35 25-21 NIGHTS; $27 22-30+; $800/MONTH. T OR Q ADD $10 PER NIGHT. **Reservations:** (818) 889-8870 OR (818) 889-7325 MONDAY THROUGH FRIDAY, 9:00 TO 5:00.

## STUDIO CITY

Eclectic California living. Comes complete with the inground swimming POOL, gazebo with barbecue facilities, beautifully landscaped backyard. Evening PIANO concerts are performed by local pianist. Close to all major Los Angeles attractions, 3 minutes to Universal Studios, tennis, and racquetball; 10 minutes to three golf courses. Bikes available. Accommodations include: A) large bedroom/sitting room will sleep three persons, outside entrance, private bath in hall, light housekeeping and B) queen-sized bed, private bath in hall. Host is a broker contractor; hostess enjoys paddle tennis and gardening. One DOG and two CATS are in residence. FRIENDLY PETS WELCOME. JACUZZI. Children of all ages welcome.
**Rates:** A) S $50, D $55 AND B) S $60 D $65 T $70 DAILY.
**Reservations:** (818) 344-7878 MONDAY THROUGH FRIDAY, 7 A.M. - 4 P.M. PACIFIC TIME; MACHINE SERVICE.

BELLAIRE AVENUE — A tranquil oasis within 10 minutes of most major Los Angeles attractions including Beverly Hills, Hollywood, Burbank studios, and Ventura and San Diego freeways. Antique filled and comfortable. Host is an actor/lecturer; hostess is a writer/publisher/ television production coordinator. Several adult children in residence, an active family. Within walking distance of park, library, free tennis, golf. It is a charming village with movies, famous restaurants, and public transportation. NO pets though family has CATS and a DOG. Some Spanish spoken. A large, inground swimming POOL is available during the summer months. Fruit trees and brick patio for outdoor dining in peaceful surroundings. Extended continental breakfast can be served in your room. Handmade quilts, central air conditioning, TV, dressing room in a king-sized bedroom. Accommodations include: A) king-sized bed, private bath and B) twin beds, share bathroom. CHILDREN over 14 welcome. NO SMOKING.
**Rates:** A) S $40, D $50 AND B) S $35, D $45 DAILY. A) S $250, D $325 AND B) S $225, D $300 WEEKLY.
**Reservations:** (818) 889-8870 OR (818) 889-7325 MONDAY THROUGH FRIDAY, 9:00 TO 5:00.

A rambling country style home with inground POOL and numerous fruit trees, furnished with Victorian and oak antiques reflecting the hosts' eclectic taste. Host is an actor/lecturer. Hostess is a writer/publisher/TV production coordinator. Adult children are in and out. Within walking distance of free tennis, a small golf course, gourmet restaurants, minutes from the Ventura and Hollywood freeways, and 5 minutes from Universal Studios. Convenient to Beverly Hills, Hollywood, and Westwood and just 30 minutes to Santa Monica beaches and major airport. Public bus to downtown and Hollywood 7 blocks away, but car advised for any Los

Angeles traveler. Extended continental breakfast served in the sunlit dining area, on the patio or in your room. Some Spanish is spoken. Resident DOG and two CATS. Accommodations include: A) king-sized bed, private bath, TV. CHILDREN 14 and older welcome. **Rates:** S $50, D $55 DAILY. S $275, D $300 WEEKLY. **Reservations:** (818) 344-7878 MONDAY THROUGH FRIDAY, 7 A.M. - 4 P.M. PACIFIC TIME; MACHINE SERVICE.

BELLAIRE NEAR VENTURA — A large Ranch style with inground POOL, sports court, fruit trees. Furnished with antiques. Used in many TV commercials and movies. Host is an actor/teacher; hostess is a writer and TV production coordinator, publisher/editor of *Bed & Breakfast Update Newsletter* and author of two books on B&B. Host can speak a little French; hostess speaks some Spanish. CHILDREN over 12 welcome. Family has a DOG and two CATS. Bikes are available. Home is convenient to Burbank Airport (10 minutes), LAX (1/2 hour), within walking distance to golf and free tennis courts, gourmet restaurants, and movies. Universal Studios tour is 5 minutes by car; Burbank, NBC, Disney Studios, Hollywood, and Beverly Hills—10 minutes; downtown Los Angeles and UCLA—20 minutes; beaches and Santa Monica—30 minutes. Hobbies include travel, theater, decorating, and remodeling. Extended continental breakfast in room, patio, or dining area. Large king-sized bedroom with dressing room, private bath across the hall. This is a NONSMOKING home. **Rates:** S $40, D $50 DAILY. S $250, D $325 WEEKLY. **Reservations:** (213) 699-8427 7 A.M. TO 7 P.M. MONDAY THROUGH FRIDAY.

RHODES AVENUE — Charming small home in the Laurel Canyon Area, conveniently located to studios and freeways and within walking distance to shops. Accommodations include: A) twin-bedded room, private bath/shower, air conditioning. POOL, quiet tree-lined street with good parking. Approximately 10 miles to Burbank Airport and 25 miles to Los Angeles Airport. Two day minimum stay. A little French, German, and Greek are spoken here. Host is a technical director of network TV sports; hostess is a former nurse/stewardess. CHILDREN over 12 welcome. NONSMOKERS ONLY. **Rates:** A) S $60, D $65 DAILY. S $265, D $295 WEEKLY. **Reservations:** (818) 344-7878 MONDAY THROUGH FRIDAY, 7 A.M. - 4 P.M. PACIFIC TIME; MACHINE SERVICE.

## SUNSET AREA, PACIFIC PALISADES

CASALE — Magnificent ocean view from balcony and all rooms of lovely host home in most prestigious area. Very spacious bedroom and library with fireplace and small dining area with refrigerator and private

entrance, plus private bath comprise this exceptional and very private suite on its own lower floor. Delightful hosts inhabit upper floor. Host is a life insurance agent; hostess is a professor emeritus, University of Southern California. NO CHILDREN. NO SMOKERS.
**Rates:** D $85 DAILY.
**Reservations:** (818) 344-7878 MONDAY THROUGH FRIDAY, 7 A.M. - 4 P.M. PACIFIC TIME; MACHINE SERVICE.

## WEST LOS ANGELES

McCONNEL DRIVE — Colonial home in exclusive Cheviot Hills, Los Angeles, furnished in French and Italian antiques. A patio of beige cement surrounds an inground POOL. Decorative umbrellas and iron furniture enhance the garden. Host is a retired merchant interested in senior citizen clubs, home, and travel; hostess enjoys women's clubs and philanthropic, social, and cultural activities. Accommodations include: A) king-sized bed, gold and white furniture, blue carpet, private bath; B) twin beds, white Colonial ensemble with red Oriental carpet, hall bath; and C) double bed, blue room with antique silver French furniture and blue Oriental carpet, hall bath. Breakfast of delicious, generous food in dining room or patio beside pool. Kitchen privileges. Nearby attractions include: 60 minutes to Disneyland, Knotts Berry Farm, Wax Museum, Spruce Goose, Queen Mary, Rose Parade, and art museums; 30 minutes to Music Center, zoo, Chinatown, Mexican Village, Farmer's Market, TV stations, Getty Museum; 15 minutes to beaches, fishing piers, and yacht harbor; and 20 minutes to 10 fine shopping centers. CHILDREN over 12 welcome. SMOKERS NOT WELCOME.
**Rates:** A) S $60, D $65; B) S $50, D $55; AND C) S $40, D $45, DAILY.
**Reservations:** (818) 344-7878 MONDAY THROUGH FRIDAY, 7 A.M. - 4 P.M. PACIFIC TIME; MACHINE SERVICE.

BELFORD — Located near Los Angeles International Airport and the beaches of west Los Angeles. This home is on a quiet residential street with a bus line only 2 blocks away. TV is shared in the large family room with fireplace and PIANO. There are two teenagers in residence. A friendly, comfortable home away from home. Accommodations include: A) two rooms each with double bed, shared bath; B) twin beds, shared bath; and C) king-sized bed, shared bath. NO SMOKING.
**Rates:** A) S $35 D $40; B) S $40, D $45; AND C) S $40, D $45 DAILY.
**Reservations:** (818) 889-8870 OR (818) 889-7325 MONDAY THROUGH FRIDAY, 9:00 TO 5:00.

## WOODLAND HILLS

Wide open California style home with lots of warmth and very congenial hosts. Perfect backyard for children, safety fenced. Inground POOL with

slide and diving board. Lovely covered patio for relaxing. Will accept only one party at a time. Accommodations include: A) double bed, private bath and B) two twin beds, shared bath. Antique furniture. Host is an engineer who enjoys model ship building, travel, and photography; hostess is a homemaker who enjoys cooking and travel. They have a 1 year old son. One outside DOG resides here.
**Rates:** S $50, D $55 DAILY.
**Reservations:** (818) 344-7878 MONDAY THROUGH FRIDAY, 7 A.M. - 4 P.M. PACIFIC TIME; MACHINE SERVICE.

## NEWPORT BEACH

· Stunning large Contemporary home on water's edge. Accommodations include: A) queen bedroom and B) two twin beds. Both rooms with private baths. The guest den where a continental breakfast is served has a retractable roof, lounge chairs, and refrigerator. The grassy yard on the bay is lovely for sunbathing. Take the free shuttle bus to local shopping, restaurants, and beach areas. Hostess is an avid golfer and is interested in dance. Cable TV and bikes available.
**Rates:** S OR D $80 ONE OR TWO NIGHTS, $75 IF 3 OR MORE NIGHTS. (RATE PER NIGHT).
**Reservations:** (213) 684-4426 MONDAY - SATURDAY 9 A.M. TO 5 P.M, PACIFIC TIME.

Second story OCEAN FRONT, nicely decorated UNHOSTED apartment. Accommodations include two bedrooms with queen and double beds, living room, dining area, kitchen, den with sofabed, wet bar, and fireplace located on Balboa Peninsula at Newport Beach. Walk or take the shuttle to good restaurants and shopping. Watch the magnificent sunsets from the deck. This beach area is one of the most sought after in southern California. Children welcome. VCR.
**Rates:** S OR D WINTER $770, SUMMER $1,200 WEEKLY.
**Reservations:** (213) 684-4426 MONDAY - SATURDAY 9 A.M. TO 5 P.M. PACIFIC TIME.

## BALBOA

EAST OCEAN BOULEVARD BETWEEN L&M — Stained glass and lots of wood add up to a beautiful home just minutes from the BEACH. Accommodations include: A) guestroom in loft overlooking the living room has queen bed that can convert into two queen beds, private bath and stairs lead up to roof deck with kitchenette, more steps to the crow's nest with spectacular views and B) downstairs, double bed, bath shared with hosts. TV in living room. Two CATS reside here. Two day minimum on weekends. Hostess smokes. CHILDREN over six welcome.
**Rates:** A) S OR D $50 AND B) S OR D $50 DAILY.

**Reservations:** (818) 889-8870 OR (818) 889-7325 MONDAY THROUGH FRIDAY, 9:00 TO 5:00.

## OJAI

Handsome Contemporary home with 53 good works of art on walls. In quiet residential area overlooking the Los Padros Mountains. Homemade food. Oranges from host orchard. Enclosed patio and rose garden. Accommodations include two rooms each with double beds. Both rooms share a private guest bath. Cot available. CHILDREN over 8 welcome. **Rates:** D $65 WEEKDAYS, $70 WEEKENDS. **Reservations:** (213) 684-4426 MONDAY - SATURDAY 9 A.M. TO 5 P.M. PACIFIC TIME.

Contemporary home located in southern California. Hostess, who speaks Yiddish and French, enjoys reading, music, and tennis. Two guestrooms with double accommodations, both with private baths in hall. A cot is also available. HANDICAPPED ACCESSIBLE. NO CHILDREN. NO SMOKING. **Rates:** D $65-$75 DAILY. **Reservations:** (213) 699-8427 7 A.M. TO 7 P.M. MONDAY THROUGH FRIDAY.

## ORANGE
### MISSION VIEJO

Beautiful home tastefully furnished in this most delightful area of Orange County, just 11 miles to Laguna Beach, 25 miles to Disneyland. TV in nearby den shared with the family. Accommodations include: A) guestroom king-sized bed, private bath in hall and B) master bedroom, double size room with king-sized bed, sitting area, balcony, private bath, and TV. Car essential. **Rates:** A) D $45 AND B) D $50 DAILY. **Reservations:** (818) 889-8870 OR (818) 889-7325 MONDAY THROUGH FRIDAY, 9:00 TO 5:00.

MACKENZIE STREET — A private entrance leads up the stairs to the two guestrooms sharing a balcony and overlooking the Pool of this two story home. Accommodations include: A) king bed and B) twin (other beds can be added). Both share a bath in the private hallway. SPA and POOL for guests' use. French and Italian spoken. Host is an engineer. One toy POODLE lives here. CHILDREN over 16 welcome. SMOKING on balcony, only. **Rates:** A) S $30, D $40 AND B) S $30, D $40, Q $50 DAILY. **Reservations:** (818) 889-8870 OR (818) 889-7325 MONDAY THROUGH FRIDAY, 9:00 TO 5:00.

## ORANGE PARK ACRES

VALENCIA AT SANTIAGO — Country style in a quiet residential area called Orange Park Acres. A large glass and wood home on a quarter acre decorated for hosts' comfort and pleasure. Accommodations include: A) king bed; B) queen bed; C) two twin beds; and D) queen bed, private bath. Rooms A-C share two baths. Relax in the living room with floor to ceiling fireplace, family room with VCR and many popular movies, and spacious grounds. Bikes available. Swim in the 35 foot inground POOL. SPA. HANDICAPPED ACCESSIBLE with adaptive equipment. Hosts enjoy gourmet cooking, gardening, biking, and hiking. Near all Los Angeles attractions. Air conditioned. Children welcome. SMOKING outside.
**Rates:** A-C) S $45, D $50 DAILY. 10% DISCOUNT WEEKLY.
**Reservations:** (213) 684-4426 MONDAY - SATURDAY 9 A.M. TO 5 P.M. PACIFIC TIME.

Country style hospitality in a quiet, residential neighborhood called Orange Park Acres. Guests will find this large glass and wood home on a quarter acre decorated for their comfort and pleasure. Accommodations include three rooms with two shared baths, all beautifully furnished. Delicious farm style breakfast that satisfies the heartiest of appetites! You are welcome to relax in the living room with floor to ceiling fireplace, the family room with VCR and many popular movies or on spacious grounds. Bikes are available. A guest weary from a day of sightseeing or Disneyland will find the inground POOL and SPA just the spot to relax. For the person with special needs, this home is HANDICAPPED ACCESSIBLE with adaptive equipment. Hosts enjoy gourmet cooking, gardening, biking, and hiking in the nearby hills. Knott's Berry Farm and the BEACH are within minutes. Los Angeles, the Queen Mary, the Spruce Goose, and Universal and NBC Studios are available by nearby bus lines. Host is a business owner; hostess is a psychotherapist. CONTACT HOSTS FOR APPROVAL REGARDING PETS. PIANO. Children welcome. SMOKING is permitted outside.
**Rates:** S $60, D $65 DAILY. $5 OFF EACH NIGHT FOR STAY OF TWO OR MORE NIGHTS. WEEKLY TAKE 10% DAILY RATE.
**Reservations:** (714) 738-8361 MONDAY THROUGH FRIDAY 7 A.M. TO 6 P.M. PACIFIC TIME.

This inn offers guests country style hospitality in a quiet residential neighborhood called Orange Park Acres. Guests will find the large glass and wood home on a quarter acre decorated for their comfort and pleasure. A farm style breakfast that satisfies the heartiest of appetites is served here. You are welcome to relax in the living room with floor to ceiling fireplace, the family room with VCR and many popular movies or on the spacious grounds. Bikes are available for a closer look at the local

attractions. A guest weary from a day of sightseeing or Disneyland will find the 35 foot inground POOL and SPA just the spot to relax. For the person with speclal needs, inn is HANDICAPPED ACCESSIBLE with adaptive equipment. Hosts enjoy gourmet cooking, gardening, biking, and hiking in the nearby hills. Disneyland, Knott's Berry Farm, and the beach are within minutes. Los Angeles, the Queen Mary, the Spruce Goose, Universal and NBC Studios are available by nearby bus lines. Accommodations include: A) king-sized bed and B) two rooms each with queen-sized bed. Guestrooms share two baths and are all beautifully furnished.
**Rates:** D $45 DAILY. 10% DISCOUNT WEEKLY.
**Reservations:** (818) 889-8870 OR (818) 889-7325 MONDAY THROUGH FRIDAY, 9:00 TO 5:00.

## PACIFIC PALISADES

California Ranch style home, close to ocean, with view of Santa Monica mountains. Home is attractively furnished with art objects collected from travels. Patio and lovely garden face canyon. Home is in one of the most beautiful beach towns of southern California. Hostess is a retired secondary school teacher. Spanish and French are spoken here. Accommodations include a double bed, share bath with family. Bikes available. Accessible by public transportation. One CAT is in residence. NONSMOKERS ONLY.
**Rates:** S $50, D $55 DAILY.
**Reservations:** (818) 344-7878 MONDAY THROUGH FRIDAY, 7 A.M. - 4 P.M. PACIFIC TIME; MACHINE SERVICE.

## PASADENA

Enjoy your stay in southern California from the charm and privacy of your own quiet two room hilltop guest cottage, complete with flower filled, well-furnished sundeck overlooking panoramic view of valley and mountains. Between trips via nearby freeway system to tourist and cultural attractions, you can relax, sunbath, birdwatch on your deck, or enjoy nearby riding stables, handball, tennis, or golf. Luxury accommodations include comfortable sitting areas and excellent beds, A) three singles; B) one king-sized, electric blankets, down pillows, and designer sheets and towels. There is a radio alarm clock and color TV in each room. Also there is a refrigerator and hospitality coffee-tea center. Air conditioning or heat are at your control. Select your own time for and preference of delicious breakfast fare and enjoy the meal on the terrace or by the bay window in the country kitchen. Between the well-traveled hosts and charming Dutch Indonesian caretaker couple. French, German, Dutch Maylasian, and even Japanese are spoken. Host is a retired engineer;

hostess is a painter and musician. Children welcome. SMOKING on sundeck only!
**Rates:** A OR B) S $60, D $70, T $80 DAILY. BOTH ROOMS S $85, T $90, Q PERSONS $95, 5 $105 DAILY.
**Reservations:** (818) 344-7878 MONDAY THROUGH FRIDAY, 7 A.M. - 4 P.M. PACIFIC TIME; MACHINE SERVICE.

## MADISON HEIGHTS

OAKLAND/GLENARM — California bungalow in a lovely tree-lined neighborhood of gracious older homes. Accommodations include two rooms each with double bed, private bath. A HOT TUB is available on the patio. Home is close to the celebrated sites of Los Angeles. Hosts are retired and enjoy having guests when they are not traveling themselves. Bikes available. HANDICAPPED ACCESSIBLE. VCR. Children welcome.
**Rates:** S $45, D $50 DAILY.
**Reservations:** (213) 684-4426 MONDAY - SATURDAY 9 A.M. TO 5 P.M. PACIFIC TIME.

SOUTH LOS ROBLES — A sprawling, ranch type home in Colonial style, on a half acre, well back from the street. Spacious, rolling lawns, colorful planting areas, and fine trees abound. Adjoins both Oak Knoll and San Marino with many stately mansions and large properties in the immediate area. Accommodations include: A) queen-sized bed, shared bath and B) twin beds, shared bath. Guests are welcome in the large living room or book lined library, both with fireplaces. There is a sunny patio and large, formal dining room. Hostess offers a full range of gourmet repasts by special arrangement at reasonable prices. Host, a concert pianist, organist, and harpsichordist, teaches at a local college, speaks a little French and German. Tiger is resident, outside CAT. Convenient to a wide range of activities: downtown Los Angeles, Colliseum, Convention Center within 18 minutes driving, Pasadena shopping, convention and civic center, restaurants within walking distance, Huntington Library, gardens, and galleries close by. Accessible to public transportation. Air conditioning, PIANO, VCR, picnic area. HANDICAPPED ACCESSIBLE. SMOKING permitted outside.
**Rates:** S $50, D $55 DAILY. TWO DAY MINIMUM. S OR D WEEKLY.
**Reservations:** (818) 344-7878 MONDAY THROUGH FRIDAY, 7 A.M. - 4 P.M. PACIFIC TIME; MACHINE SERVICE.

Situated on a quiet tree-lined residential street in historic Pasadena, four upstairs bedrooms share two baths. Accommodations include: A) double bed; B) two twins; C) king bed; D) queen bed; and E) trundle bed. The single downstairs room has trundle beds, private entrance, and private bath. Cot available. Delightful antiques, lace, and leaded glass windows

provide a cozy and romantic atmosphere. Gazebo, SPA, and picnic area to read. Extras include: VCR, HOT TUB, gourmet continental breakfast. Two outside CATS here. CHILDREN over 12 welcome. NONSMOKERS only.
**Rates:** A) S $55, D $60; B & D) S $55, D $65; C) S $65, D $75; AND E) S $40, D $50 DAILY. 7TH DAY FREE.
**Reservations:** (818) 889-8870 OR (818) 889-7325 MONDAY THROUGH FRIDAY, 9:00 TO 5:00.

Two room hilltop cottage with well-furnished sundeck, panoramic view of valley and mountains. The cottage has one king bed and three twins, electric blankets, down pillows, designer sheets and towels, radio alarm clock, and TV. Refrigerator, coffee-tea center, and air conditioning are available. Hosts live on the property and speak many languages including French, German, Dutch, Maylasian, and some Japanese. FIREPLACE in bedroom. VCR. Children welcome.
**Rates:** S $45, D $50, EXTRA PERSON $10 DAILY.
**Reservations:** (213) 684-4426 MONDAY - SATURDAY 9 A.M. TO 5 P.M. PACIFIC TIME.

## SAN RAFAEL HILLS

Beautiful hillside home with spectacular panoramic view of Los Angeles and surrounding communities. It is 3 miles to the Rose Bowl, 8 miles to downtown Los Angeles, 11 miles to Universal Studios, and 20 miles to the Pacific Ocean. One guestroom with two twin beds and private bath is available. The guestroom is on a separate level from hosts for additional privacy. The comfortable living room, dining room, and year-round deck are available for guests' use. Hosts are a professional couple who enjoy making guests feel at home. VCR and bikes available. CHILDREN over 12 welcome. NONSMOKERS only.
**Rates:** S $38, D $42 DAILY. S $210, D $245 WEEKLY.
**Reservations:** (213) 684-4426 MONDAY - SATURDAY 9 A.M. TO 5 P.M. PACIFIC TIME.

## SAN DIEGO

Enjoy all that San Diego has to offer from its beautiful beaches, lush landscapes, world famous zoo, Sea World, theaters, and restaurants to star gazing at Palomar Observatory. A B&B stay will make you feel a part of the lovely San Diego experience.

In the northern part of San Diego, across the street from La Jolla, near Scripps Clinic (3 miles), and Salk Institute and the VA Hospital (1 mile), Torrey Pines Golf Course, and two large and lovely shopping centers (lots

of movies, shops, and restaurants). Within 15 minutes to Sea World, the San Diego Zoo, and Mission Bay. Hostess is a travel consultant. This townhouse has one guestroom with double bed and private bath. A delicious continental breakfast is served on the patio. Swimming POOL and JACUZZI available. NONSMOKERS only.
**Rates:** S $38, D $45 DAILY.
**Reservations:** (213) 684-4426 MONDAY - SATURDAY 9 A.M. TO 5 P.M. PACIFIC TIME.

## BALBOA PARK

PARK BOULEVARD — Built in 1915 for the first San Diego World's Fair which then developed into the city's 1,500 acre park, consists of four Colonial Spanish buildings located across from the north entrance of the park creating a corner effect whereby guests can enjoy courtyards and terrace. The inn has 25 unique and charming rooms and suites, each with a personality and personalized theme. For example, Tara from Gone with the Wind, Nouveau Ritz which sets the mood of New York in the 1940s, Paris in the 1930s, Las Palomas (Mexican doves), and so on. Some with FIREPLACES, JACUZZI WHIRLPOOL TUBS, wet bars, private patios, balconies, and so forth. Suites sleep from two to eight persons. Every suite and room has a private bathroom and the larger two bedroom suites have two baths. Sixteen of the suites have kitchens and complete cooking utensils are provided for a minimum charge. Complimentary continental breakfast is served to guests, along with the morning paper to one's room. Optionally they offer romantic candlelight dinners or picnics. Located just 10 minutes from the airport, 5 minutes from Amtrak. San Diego buses, San Diego zoo, golf course, tennis courts, and swimming pool nearby. Reservations a must. Catering available. Reception facilities. Complimentary laundromat as well as complimentary local dialing. HBO, color TV in all rooms.
**Rates:** D FROM $60, SUITES $75-$175 AND CAN ACCOMMODATE FROM TWO UP TO EIGHT PERSONS DAILY.
**Reservations:** (818) 889-8870 OR (818) 889-7325 MONDAY THROUGH FRIDAY, 9:00 TO 5:00.

## BEACH

SOUTH MISSION BEACH — This manor house and cottages offer you a delightful self-catered holiday in one or two bedroom apartments with queen-sized beds on the OCEAN FRONT or in quaint cottages with double beds only a short stroll from the ocean or bay. All include a fully equipped kitchen with the refrigerator stocked with breakfast provisions as requested by guests. Each suite has a private bath. Additional sleeping accommodations are provided by double or queen-sized hide-a-beds in the living rooms. Antiques, combined with country prints, offer a warm and

cozy feeling of English charm and hospitality. The broad, sandy beach is only steps away. Shops and restaurants are within walking distance and all San Diego attractions are 5 to 20 minutes away. Children of all ages welcome.
**Rates:** S OR D $60-$72 DAILY. RATES VARY WITH SEASON. AVAILABLE WEEKLY JULY 4 THROUGH LABOR DAY D $600 WEEK.
**Reservations:** (213) 684-4426 MONDAY - SATURDAY 9 A.M. TO 5 P.M. PACIFIC TIME.

## CLAIREMONT

GRANDVIEW/JULY — View of Mission Bay and the ocean. Breakfast served on garden patio. Hostess is a free-lance legal assistant, interested in restoring antiques, gardening, and sewing, with a special interest in history. Guestroom has a double queen bed and private bath. Guest may keep snacks in refrigerator and use laundry facilities. Restaurants within walking distance, easy parking, bus transportation available. One CAT. CHILDREN over 12 welcome. SMOKERS must use patio.
**Rates:** S $44, D $50 DAILY.
**Reservations:** (415) 525-4569. OPEN 9 A.M. - 5 P.M.

## DULZURA

MARRON VALLEY ROAD — Spacious country farmhouse, circa 1928 is in a small, quiet community just 10 miles from Tecate, Mexico and 35 minutes from San Diego. Gigantic oaks shade the terraced yard leading to the stream that races behind the house and stone barn. The hosts have used their talents in refurbishing the old farmhouse and restored antiques, made stained glass windows, handwoven rugs and a quilt for each of the seven guestrooms, with double accommodations and shared baths, giving each a personality of its own. One guestroom HANDICAPPED ACCESSIBLE. One cabin with private bath. A full farm breakfast is served in the fireside dining room and dinners (offered on weekends and holidays for $15 per person) are prepared by the host/chef. He also teaches a cooking school one weekend each month. Goats, chickens, pigs, and geese are in the barnyard and a young orchard and vineyard are developing. The large garden is always providing something for the breakfast or dinner table. NO CHILDREN. NO CIGARS. NO pets. CATS reside here. JACUZZI. PIANO.
**Rates:** GUESTROOMS IN HOUSE D $45 AND CABIN $65 DAILY.
**Reservations:** (213) 699-8427 7 A.M. TO 7 P.M. MONDAY THROUGH FRIDAY.

## ENCINITAS—OCEAN VIEW RESIDENTIAL

NEPTUNE AVENUE — One story redwood BEACH home with traditional furnishing. Guests welcome to use living room with oak manteled fireplace and TV and VCR room, as well as enclosed patio of sunbathing. Accommodations include: A) queen-sized bed and B) twin beds. Cot and crib on request. Home on cliff facing Pacific with steps down to beach. It is 3 blocks from public transportation. Host is an employment counselor; hostess is a social worker. They have been area residents for 40 years and are active in community, civic, and cultural activities. They are also gourmet cooks and will provide update information on countryside facilities and events. Gourmet full breakfast is served in the garden room. Children and teenagers welcome. DOG and CAT in residence. There is a PIANO. Home is HANDICAPPED ACCESSIBLE. NONSMOKING PREFERRED.
**Rates:** S $50, D $55 DAILY. S $250, D $275 WEEKLY.
**Reservations:** (818) 344-7878 MONDAY THROUGH FRIDAY, 7 A.M. - 4 P.M. PACIFIC TIME; MACHINE SERVICE.

## ESCONDIDO

CITRUS AVENUE — The hacienda is a large, adobe Ranch house that the hosts built themselves in the 1950s. It is furnished with many Colonial antiques and early California artifacts. The view, from the knoll on which it is situated, is of surrounding valley and hills. PIANO and ORGAN here. Accommodations include: A) queen-sized bed; B) double bed, with antiques and a comfortable brass; and C) two single beds. Continental breakfast is served indoors or on the patio. Escondido is the shopping hub of North San Diego County. Lake Hodges, Dixon Lake, and Lake Wolford are nearby, as is the San Diego Wild Animal Park. There is a 20 minute drive to the ocean and a 45 minute drive to San Diego. Host is a retired electrical engineer; hostess is a teacher. Some Spanish is spoken here. PETS WELCOME. There is an inground POOL and HOT TUB, as well as VCR. Bikes available. The house is HANDICAPPED ACCESSIBLE. Children welcome.
**Rates:** A) S $50, D $55; B) S $45, D $50; AND C) D $35 DAILY. RATES DROP AFTER FIRST DAY. A) $550 MONTH AND B & C) $500 MONTH.
**Reservations:** (818) 344-7878 MONDAY THROUGH FRIDAY, 7 A.M. - 4 P.M. PACIFIC TIME; MACHINE SERVICE.

## HILLCREST

ALBATROSS — Located in the uptown Hillcrest section of San Diego where old homes and canyons offer an unhurried, isolated atmosphere. This B&B offers an escape to the past. The turn-of-the-century furnishings

are reminiscent of a time long ago. Travel time to any part of San Diego is but a few minutes. The San Diego Zoo is 1 mile, Sea World is 2 miles, and beaches are 4 miles away. There are many restaurants and shops within 3 blocks of this home. Each morning you will be served a breakfast consisting of freshly baked bread, fruit of the season, and a beverage. Accommodations include: A) king-sized bed, private bath; B) king-sized bed, private bath share with C; and C) single bed in living room. Private entrance. PIANO. Host is a university professor who teaches sociology; hostess enjoys furniture restoration, gardening, and traveling.
**Rates:** A) S OR D $55 AND B & C) S OR D $45 DAILY.
**Reservations:** (818) 889-8870 OR (818) 889-7325 MONDAY THROUGH FRIDAY, 9:00 TO 5:00.

## LA JOLLA

TAFT/FORWARD — Lovingly landscaped with an arbored back patio, near the BEACH. The hostess has brought a home full of antiques from her native Ireland, as well as Irish style B&B. Guests can chat with her in Gaelic if they wish. Accommodations include: A) twin beds, private bath and B) garden cottage, ideal for HONEYMOONS, queen double bed, private bath, gas log FIREPLACE. Easy parking. Walk to the fine restaurants in La Jolla. CHILDREN over 12 welcome.
**Rates:** A) S $46, D $52 AND B) S $56, D $62; ADDITIONAL PERSON $15 DAILY.
**Reservations:** (415) 525-4569. OPEN 9 A.M. - 5 P.M.

## NORTH PARK

GRIM AVENUE — Historical site, built by the mayor of San Diego in 1904. Tastefully redecorated with furniture and antiques of the period. You will enjoy leisure conversation in the sitting room or lounging POOLSIDE, making new friends. Right next door to famous Balboa Park and the zoo. Easy access to freeways and 1 1/2 blocks from city bus lines. Complimentary continental breakfast. Complimentary wine and cheese served 4:30 to 6 P.M. A gracious, congenial social area with restored oak hardwood floors and Oriental carpets. Complimentary pickup from airport, Amtrak, or bus lines. Accommodations include: A) five rooms each with double beds and B) twin beds. Six rooms share two baths. CHILDREN over 16 years welcome.
**Rates:** S OR D $45 DAILY.
**Reservations:** (818) 889-8870 OR (818) 889-7325 MONDAY THROUGH FRIDAY, 9:00 TO 5:00.

## SCRIPPS RANCH

A large private home with newly decorated rooms. All rooms have a view of the forest. The backyard is beautiful with many varieties of plant

life and wildlife. Beyond the backyard is an open space with picnic tables and a barbecue. A very generous continental breakfast is served with all homebaked rolls and breads. Hostess is a former teacher who enjoys Bonsai gardening, people, travel, and sports. A small DOG is in residence. Accommodations include: A) queen bed, private bath; B) queen bed, shared bath; and C) double bed, shared bath. SMOKING permitted on patio only.
**Rates:** S OR D A) $37; B) $50; AND C) $55 DAILY.
**Reservations:** (213) 684-4426 MONDAY - SATURDAY 9 A.M. TO 5 P.M. PACIFIC TIME.

## SAN JUAN CAPISTRANO

AVENIDA AEROPUERTO — Two bedroom, two bath mobile home, spacious and sunny, in historical San Juan Capistrano. Sun patio, POOL, JACUZZI, Adjacent to picturesque shops and dining facilities. Minutes away from the BEACH, colorful Laguna Beach, Dana Point Marina, or shopping in Mission Viejo. One hour drive to San Diego, Wild Animal Kingdom, Del Mar Race Track, or Mission Bay. Emphasis on nutrition by hostess. Accommodations include: A) queen-sized bed, private bath and B) double bed, private bath. Can accommodate a child on additional bed. Amenities include: TV, kitchen privileges, microwave, PIANO, pool table.
**Rates:** A) S $45, D $55 FIRST NIGHT; S $40, D $50 SECOND NIGHT. B) S $35, D $43 FIRST NIGHT; S $30, D $38 SECOND NIGHT.
**Reservations:** (714) 738-8361 MONDAY THROUGH FRIDAY 7 A.M. TO 6 P.M. PACIFIC TIME.

## SANTA MONICA

MONTANA-SAN VICENTE — This house was built in 1945 and has a lovely garden and patio. The living room has a fireplace and lots of antiques. It is 18 blocks from Santa Monica beach and Palisades Park. Hosts have a small DOG, BUFFY, and two CATS, Sinbad and Tiger. Close to Westwood Village, Beverly Hills, University of California at Los Angeles, and within walking distance to shops and restaurants. Accommodations include: A) king bed, private bath and B) two twin beds, private bath. Polish is spoken here. PIANO, VCR, and HANDICAPPED ACCESSIBLE.
**Rates:** A) S $45, D $50 AND B) D $60 DAILY. A) $280 WEEKLY.
**Reservations:** (213) 684-4426 MONDAY - SATURDAY 9 A.M. TO 5 P.M. PACIFIC TIME.

### MONTANA AVENUE AREA

25TH NEAR MONTANA — This is a charming art filled Spanish style four bedroom house with large patio, PIANO, POOL, pool house, and

ping pong in a quiet residential area. It is 5 minutes to beach yet only 1/2 hour by freeway to most Los Angeles points of interest. Excellent restaurants, antique and boutique shops, galleries, tennis, and polo nearby. Good public transportation. Hostess is a widow, widely traveled, actress/writer, writes novels in home office and is born tour guide (1984 Olympic volunteer driver) who enjoys diversity of guests. Accommodations include: A) double bed, simple pleasant room, private full bath in hall; B) small pretty room, twin and double sofabeds can share hall bath or hostess 3/4 bath; and C) extra mattress and two twin beds in pool house for overflow if necessary. Living room, dining room, dinette, kitchen, garage, and yard are for all. A little French is spoken here. Children are welcome. NONSMOKING ONLY.
**Rates:** A) S $60, D $65; B) S $50, D $55; AND C) S $25, D $30 DAILY. $180-$250 WEEKLY.
**Reservations:** (818) 344-7878 MONDAY THROUGH FRIDAY, 7 A.M. - 4 P.M. PACIFIC TIME; MACHINE SERVICE.

STANFORD STREET — Ranch style home North of Wilshire Boulevard, on the bus line, close to shopping, University of California at Los Angeles, beach; 15 minutes from LAX, downtown Los Angeles. Accommodations include: room overlooking POOL and JACUZZI, queen-sized bed plus single waterbed, private bath. There is also a guesthouse with a single waterbed in the cottage and a private bath. Possible use of kitchen. PIANO. Host is a physician; hostess is a registered nurse and teacher. They have an 18 year old son and two daughters ages 16 and 12. Hobbies are music, reading, tennis, folk dancing, ethnic arts and crafts. Hosts speak French, Spanish, Hebrew, Rumanian, Hungarian, and some Russian. NO SMOKERS. One outside DOG resides here.
**Rates:** S $50, D $55 DAILY.
**Reservations:** (818) 344-7878 MONDAY THROUGH FRIDAY, 7 A.M. - 4 P.M. PACIFIC TIME; MACHINE SERVICE.

## SEAL BEACH
### WATERFRONT ON PACIFIC OCEAN

On the WATERFRONT, this is a large Spanish style home with huge gardens bursting with color year-round. Greenhouses and grape arbor in courtyard leading to the Pacific Ocean. Fishing pier within walking distance. Great beach for swimming, surfing, boating, windsurfing, and sunbathing. Restaurants and small shops in quaint village within short walk. Hosts are writers particularly interested in travel and meeting other travelers. JACUZZI available to guests. Near Queen Mary, Spruce Goose, Disneyland, Knott's Berry Farm, and launch to Catalina. Hosts well informed about local attractions and travel to assist you. Elaborate breakfast with homemade pastries is served with Pacific Ocean in full view. Tennis and racquetball courts 2 blocks away. Accommodations

include: A) large bedroom with king-sized bed, private hall bathroom; B) large bedroom with twin beds, private hall bathroom; C) small bedroom with king-sized bed, private hall bathroom; and D) small bedroom with twin beds, private hall bathroom. Rollaway bed available. SMOKING outside only.
**Rates:** A & B) S OR D $75; EXTRA BED IN ROOM $15; AND C) S OR D $60 DAILY. WEEKLY QUOTES ON REQUEST.
**Reservations:** (818) 889-8870 OR (818) 889-7325 MONDAY THROUGH FRIDAY, 9:00 TO 5:00.

## SHERMAN OAKS

VENTURA — Ranch style home. Host is a math professor; hostess is an office manager. Accommodations include: A) double bed, private bath; B) two rooms each with double bed, bath shared with other guests; and C) two rooms, each with double bed, bath shared with host family. AC. JACUZZI. PIANO. VCR. Inground POOL. CHILDREN over 8 welcome. NO SMOKING.
**Rates:** S $50, D $55 DAILY.
**Reservations:** (818) 344-7878 MONDAY THROUGH FRIDAY, 7 A.M. - 4 P.M. PACIFIC TIME; MACHINE SERVICE.

## SOLVANG

ALAMO PINTADO — Delightful estate in a charming Danish community close to Santa Barbara and the southern wine area. There is a POND where one can swim in the summer and the hosts raise llamas! The two cottages, which are separate from the main house, are furnished in country antiques and each has a queen-sized bed and private bath. Ideal for its total privacy and charm. Five CATS and three DOGS also live here. There is also a FIREPLACE in the bedroom. SMOKING OUTSIDE ONLY.
**Rates:** $95 DAILY; TWO DAY MINIMUM ON WEEKENDS.
**Reservations:** (818) 344-7878 MONDAY THROUGH FRIDAY, 7 A.M. - 4 P.M. PACIFIC TIME; MACHINE SERVICE.

## SOUTH PASADENA
### SMALL TOWN ATMOSPHERE

HERMOSA AND COLUMBIA — UNHOSTED redwood guesthouse approximately 430 square feet, fully carpeted with 3/4 bath, TV, cooking facilities and HOT TUB on large lot facing Arroyo Seco Nature Area. The Nature Area has two horse stables, a par 3 golf course, racquetball, and TENNIS COURTS all within walking distance. Less than a 10 minute drive are several nationally known attractions: the Rose Bowl, North Simon Art Museum, Huntington Library and Gardens, Santa Anita Race Track, and Dodger Stadium. Disneyland and Pacific Ocean beaches are

under an hour away. The host lives in a main house on the property. Two night minimum stay. Accommodations include a double hide-a-bed. NO CHILDREN. NO SMOKING.
**Rates:** D $55 DAILY. D $350 WEEKLY. CHILDREN OVER TWO $10 EACH PER NIGHT.
**Reservations:** (213) 684-4426 MONDAY - SATURDAY 9 A.M. TO 5 P.M. PACIFIC TIME.

## TARZANA

LINNET STREET — Half acre POOL, PADDLE TENNIS COURT WITH LIGHTS, fruit trees, vegetable, flower gardens. Home is furnished with some antiques. Has two fireplaces PIANO. Bikes available Host is a life insurance executive and big sports fan; hostess does many artistic endeavors, with catering and sewing professionally. A lovable AKITA is in residence along with a terrific outside CAT. Close to freeways. Easy to get to beach, Westwood, Hollywood downtown. Hostess loves to serve gourmet continental breakfast. The patio is used when it is warm. Everything is freshly baked and homemade. Accommodations include a twin beds, private bath down the hall. Accessible by public transportation. Contemporary style home. NO CHILDREN. NO SMOKING.
**Rates:** S $50, D $55 DAILY.
**Reservations:** (818) 344-7878 MONDAY THROUGH FRIDAY, 7 A.M. - 4 P.M. PACIFIC TIME; MACHINE SERVICE.

## TORRANCE

232ND STREET — A charming Contemporary B&B with a lovely courtyard entrance. The house has a light, open feeling created with glass motifs overlooking a planted atrium. Hostess enjoys gardening, traveling, and entertaining. Nearby attractions include: Marineland and Los Angeles; Disneyland and Knott's Berry Farm are a 45 minute ride. Accommodations include; A) queen bed and B) two twin beds. Both guestrooms share a guest bath. A full breakfast is served. HANDICAPPED ACCESSIBLE. Children welcome.
**Rates:** S $35, D $50 DAILY.
**Reservations:** (213) 684-4426 MONDAY - SATURDAY 9 A.M. TO 5 P.M. PACIFIC TIME.

## VENICE
## BEACH

NEAR LINCOLN-ROSE — Large, European style home with formal dining room, furnished with Hungarian antiques. Includes a spacious family room, fireplace, PIANO, and entertainment center. The patio and backyard are available to enjoy and to partake of the pleasant year-round southern California sunshine. Host works for the airlines and speaks

German; hostess is a homemaker and takes pride in her gourmet dinners which can be ordered in advance. This home is conveniently located to Venice Beach and downtown Santa Monica shopping center. Hosts welcome their guests with warm Christian hospitality. Pickup from and to airport, Los Angeles. City tours are available on advance notice. Accommodations include: two guestrooms, double occupancy, with private baths. Children of all ages welcome. NO SMOKERS. VCR.
**Rates:** S $35, D $45 DAILY. S $200, D $270 WEEKLY.
**Reservations:** (213) 699-8427 7 A.M. TO 7 P.M. MONDAY THROUGH FRIDAY.

## WHITTIER
## RIDEOUT HEIGHTS

SOUTH CIRCLE DRIVE — Come to the top of the hill and find your own quiet paradise. This home is located less than 5 minutes from Number 605 Freeway and is near No. 5 and No. 60 freeways, yet seems to be in a rural area. The quiet peacefulness is enhanced by the luxuriant patio where you may enjoy the sunshine along with a full breakfast prepared by your home economist hostess. She will direct you to nearby Disneyland, Knott's Berry Farm, and Queen Mary as well as other Los Angeles attractions. Accommodations include: A) large king bed with electric adjustment and extra large private bath, with private entrance; B) two extra long twin beds with private bath; C) double bed with private entrance and shared bath; and D) extra long adjustable twin bed with private bath. After your sightseeing, enjoy wine and cheese as the sun sets and the lights of the city flick on from below. The view from the deck is enchanting. You may dine here with previous arrangements. This home is near tennis, is excellent for jogging, and is 5 minutes to Whittier College; home is 30 minutes east of Los Angeles in a quiet, uncongested and historic Quaker town. Excellent hiking is found in the canyon nearby. Spanish is spoken here. Well-behaved CHILDREN over 12 welcome. SMOKING outside only.
**Rates:** A & B) S $40, D $50; C) S $20, D $30; AND D) S $35 DAILY. S $240, D $280 WEEKLY.
**Reservations:** (213) 699-8427 7 A.M. TO 7 P.M. MONDAY THROUGH FRIDAY.

## WOODLAND HILLS

MIRANDA STREET AT SHOUP — Sliding doors lead to the parklike yard with all kinds of fruit trees, swimming POOL, barbecue, and volleyball. Park across the street with many more facilities. Two guestrooms have single beds with a shared bath. The third guestroom has a queen hide-a-bed and shares a bath in the hall. Host, a teacher, enjoys children and can accommodate groups in the large family room. TV in family room or portable for guestroom. Bus line 2 blocks. CHILDREN welcome. NO SMOKING in house.

**Rates:** A-D) S $30, D $40, ADDITIONAL PERSON $15 DAILY.

**Reservations:** (818) 889-8870 OR (818) 889-7325 MONDAY THROUGH FRIDAY, 9:00 TO 5:00.

## WINE COUNTRY
## SONOMA

This architecturally designed home is in a planned community in California's idyllic wine country in beautiful Sonoma Valley, the heart of Jack London's storied Valley of the Moon. Cool summer evenings with low humidity make for a natural smog free climate. From the doorstep it is only a short distance to nearby golf, tennis, unique shops, art and craft centers, marvelous restaurants, and, of course, the many famous wineries and cheese factories. The town of Sonoma is richly endowed with much of California's history. It is here that the last of the California missions was founded and the only one of the missions to be established under Mexican rule. It would be hard not to enjoy and relax in this casual and beautiful setting. This home is UNHOSTED but completely furnished for your every need. There are two bedrooms with twin beds and two baths.

**Rates:** D $85, T OR Q $110 DAILY. THREE NIGHT MINIMUM.

**Reservations:** (213) 684-4426 MONDAY - SATURDAY 9 A.M. TO 5 P.M. PACIFIC TIME.

# HAWAII

## HAWAII (BIG ISLAND)
### HILO

KAHOA — Typical Hawaiian home, 500 yards from surfing BEACH, beautiful view of ocean and active volcano. Swimming POOL. Host is a former rancher, active in the Humane Society, golf, and swimming. Accommodations include A) king twin beds, private baths and B) twin double bed, private bath. Both rooms have a lanai. Two DOGS. TV, laundry facilities, use of refrigerator. Local bus, but car needed on island. Teahouse. NO CHILDREN. Smokers welcome.
**Rates:** S $36, D $44; FAMILY + 1 $15; + 2, $25 DAILY.
**Reservations:** (415) 525-4569. OPEN 9 A.M. - 5 P.M.

## KAUAI
### KOLOA
#### POIPU BEACH

Hawaiian style home near Poipu Beach, one of the best resorts in Hawaii, set on 35,000 square feet of land. Host is retired; hostess is a medical secretary. Both love to golf, bike, hike, jog, swim, and play tennis. They speak some Japanese. Guestroom has twin-double bed, private bath. Separate entrance, private patio, refrigerator. Car required. Children welcome.
**Rates:** S OR D $40 DAILY.
**Reservations:** (415) 525-4569. OPEN 9 A.M. - 5 P.M.

## MAUI-KAHULUI
### HULUI
#### MAKAWAO

KALUANUI ROAD — Century old Plantation home surrounded by pineapple fields, lovely ocean view, 15 minutes from the beautiful beach. Host is in real estate; hostess is a professional singer. Accommodations include: A) double bed and B) two twin-double beds. Rooms A and B have private baths. If occupied Room C shares with Room A and B. Refrigerator for guests' use. There is a 26 foot VESSEL available for charter. Two HORSES that guests can arrange to use. Outside DOGS and CATS. Nearby boating, fishing, snorkling, surfing, hiking. Car necessary. Hearty breakfasts. SMOKING outside only.
**Rates:** S $30, D $60 DAILY.
**Reservations:** (415) 525-4569. OPEN 9 A.M. - 5 P.M.

# OAHU-HONOLULU
## KANEOHE

HALEKOU ROAD — Spectacular Polynesian home in a jungle setting, 15 minute walk to beach, 30 minutes to downtown Honolulu. Host is president of a musical instrument company and the house is constructed of fine woods which he imports to manufacture ukeleles and other string instruments; hostess works part time helping him. They enjoy giving visitors an opportunity to experience real Hawaiian hospitality when their children are away at college. Accommodations include: A) twin-double bed and B) two single beds. Private bath shared by members of the same party only. Outside entrance to each room. PIANO, ORGAN, TV, stereo. Car necessary. Children welcome. SMOKERS may use patio.
**Rates:** A) S $40, D $50 AND B) S $34, D $44 DAILY.
**Reservations:** (415) 525-4569. OPEN 9 A.M. - 5 P.M.

## DESERT
### LAS VEGAS

TOPAZ (FLAMINGO) — Modern Ranch style home with large SWIMMING POOL. It is 3 miles from the strip. Hostess is a school librarian. Accommodations include A) double bed, private guest bath and B) twin double bed, members of same party only, share bath with A. Air conditioned. Three CATS. Car recommended. Bus possible, but slow. Children welcome.

**Rates:** S $38, D $44; FAMILY + 1 $10; + 2 $15 DAILY.
**Reservations:** (415) 525-4569. OPEN 9 A.M. - 5 P.M.

# OREGON

## CASCADE MOUNTAINS
### ASHLAND
### HISTORIC RAILROAD DISTRICT

OAK STREET — A lovingly restored 1890s Queen Anne in Ashland's historic railroad district. Beautiful yard, spacious front porch with swing and hammock, 1 1/2 blocks from Oregon Shakespearian Festival Theaters, downtown shopping, and restaurant district. Accommodations include A) double bed, B) double bed, shared bath. Gourmet breakfast and personal attention is a specialty. Air conditioned. CHILDREN over eight welcome. **Rates:** OCTOBER 15 THROUGH MARCH 15 A & B) D $55; $10 FOR EXTRA PERSON PLACED IN SMALLER SEPARATE ROOM DAILY. **Reservations:** (503) 245-0642 8:00 TO 5:00.

## CENTRAL OREGON

There are many lakes and rivers for fishing and boating in the Bend, La Pine, and Madras area. Mount Bachelor is world famous for its excellent skiing, almost year-round. It is a rock hound's paradise and the local Chamber of Commerce can give you directions to the digs. During the Fourth of July weekend, Madras has its annual Rock Hound Jamboree. There are many geological points of interest here, as the area was once a volcanic site. Pine Mountain Observatory, 30 miles South East of Bend, is the astronomical research facility for the University of Oregon. This is a year-round recreational center.

### BEND
### DRAKE PARK

CONGRESS AND LOUISIANA — Built in 1910 and recently renovated, this is one of Bend's finest homes. It is within walking distance of downtown restaurants and overlooks famous Drake Park and Mirror Pond. Accommodations include four large queen-bedded rooms as well as one with waterbed. Each has its own bath. Special features of this home are the fireplace, PIANO, solarium, HOT TUB, and SAUNA. Hostess manages a white water rafting company and includes a special package for all guests that are interested. She also enjoys skiing, biking, and other outdoor activities. A full gourmet breakfast is served. Children welcome. SMOKING is limited to bedrooms. **Rates:** S $45, D $50 DAILY. **Reservations:** (503) 245-0642 8:00 TO 5:00.

## PRINEVILLE

Lovingly restored to its original classic style both in decor and ambience, your stay reflects the rich history of this home and the land. All of the

448

bedrooms are on the second floor and are very large and airy. Accommodations include: A) double antique bed, TV, VCR, desk, table and chairs, comfortable couch, two easy chairs; B) inlaid antique bedroom set with marble tops, antique brass crib filled with doll collection, two comfortable chairs, walk-in closet that has sink and window, queen bed; and C) sunny room, Victorian lace curtains, double antique bed, FIREPLACE, gateleg table, antique dresser and chairs, large walkin closet, window and drawers. Host is a rancher and logger; hostess is a real estate broker. NO SMOKING.
**Rates:** S $54, D $60 DAILY. S OR D $240 WEEKLY.
**Reservations:** (503) 245-0642 8:00 TO 5:00.

## COLUMBIA RIVER
## THE DALLES

The pleasure of staying in a beautiful Victorian home is available to you. The home sits up and away from the street behind a wrought iron fence. Lawns and gardens surround the home with a natural arboretum extending on the westerly border to Mill Creek. The interior is furnished with a blend of Georgian and Victorian antiques with original oil paintings and early Oriental art. Three rooms are available. A) The master suite is on the main floor and has a sitting room with separate room with a four poster bed. The bath is furnished with original marbletop basin and a six foot claw-foot tub. B) The Georgian Room has a canopied four poster double bed, chaise lounge, period writing desk and highboy. A modern bath with tub and shower is shared with the East Room. Your own private balcony with chairs and table looks out over the Klickitat Hills. And C) East Room is furnished in the Victorian period and is equally as beautiful. It shares the bath with the Georgian Room. It has a separate balcony with two chairs and table overlooking the Klickitats to the north. Breakfast is served in a spacious dining room or, weather permitting, in the gazebo, surrounded by the garden and grove toward Mill Creek. A warm and inviting room with TV and fireplace with comfortable chairs is available. Air conditioned.
**Rates:** A) S $50, D $55; B & C) S $40, D $45 DAILY.
**Reservations:** (503) 245-0642 8:00 TO 5:00.

EAST 16TH PLACE — A Colonial home with PIANO, VCR, picnic area, and antiques. Guests have full breakfast, kitchen privileges, and can have breakfast in bed. HANDICAPPED ACCESSIBLE. Accommodations include: A) large room furnished with antiques, queen bed, TV, fresh flowers, fruits, overlooking oak trees and garden, private bath; and B) large room with double bed, private bath, antiques, view of Mount Adams. The home is at the sunny end of the Columbia River Gorge 5 minutes to fishing, boating, and sailboarding; 50 minutes to Mount Hood ski area. PIANO. CHILDREN over 6 welcome.

**Rates:** A) S $35, D $40; AND B) S $30, D $35; CHILD $10 DAILY.
**Reservations:** (503) 245-0642 8:00 TO 5:00.

# COOS COUNTY
## COOS BAY
### ALLEGANY

NEAR HIGHWAY 101 — Spacious cabin on the banks of the Mitticoma
River. Magnificent country setting. Furnished with country antiques and
quilts. Host has hydraulic business; hostess loves to garden and go
antiquing. Accommodations include a double bed, sleeping mats, kitchen,
private bath. Laundry facilities. The refrigerator is filled with fixings for
self-serve breakfast. Wood is supplied for FIREPLACE and woodcook
stove. A lovable SPRINGER SPANIEL is in host residence. Beaches and
State Parks are within 30 minutes. Four CATS and a lamb live here.
CHILDREN over 8 welcome. SMOKING is permitted outside.
**Rates:** D $50 DAILY.
**Reservations:** (503) 245-0642 8:00 TO 5:00.

## KLAMATH FALLS

Hosts invite guests to share their new home, built just two years ago by
Gil, with a beautiful view of the LAKE. Two bedrooms, one with a
private bath. Full breakfast. Use of canoe and paddle boat. Friendly,
family atmosphere. Year-round. VCR. One DOG resides here. Hosts
enjoy square dancing and sailing. Children welcome.
**Rates:** $30-$45 DAILY.
**Reservations:** (213) 699-8427 7 A.M. TO 7 P.M. MONDAY THROUGH
FRIDAY.

# MOUNT HOOD
## WELCHES
### LOLO PASS

An 8 year old log home on 40 acres surrounded by private forest land
and the Mount Hood National Forest. Two streams flow through the
property that is home to many birds and other wildlife. Secluded location
at the end of the road, yet near golf, skiing, swimming, fishing,
backpacking, and tennis. Some short trails on the property. Hostess is
retired from restaurant ownership and is now employed as a waitress.
Accommodations include: A) two rooms each with double bed, shared
bath and B) queen bed, woodstove, private bath. Hostess serves blueberry
muffins or pancakes, ham and eggs, fruit in dining room or on deck, both
with view of Mount Hood. Will try to accommodate special needs. Guests
may use kitchen and barbecue. Hosts are interested in birdwatching,
astronomy, painting, camping, and photography. Both are nonsmokers. A
GERMAN SHORTHAIR, "Ginger" and a mixed breed, "Tawney," are

in residence. Excellent Steelhead trout fishing within 15 minutes. VCR.
CHILDREN over 10 welcome.
**Rates:** A) S $40, D $45 AND B) S OR D $60 DAILY. A & B) $265
WEEKLY.
**Reservations:** (503) 245-0642 8:00 TO 5:00.

## OREGON COAST

Along the Oregon coast you will find many areas that provide hours of
beachcombing and tide pool discoveries. After a storm is the best time
for agate hunting. There are many pieces of driftwood that have been
sculptured by the wind and sand and are very interesting to collect. Also
available are charter deep sea fishing boats. In the spring and winter
months you can watch the whales migrate along the coast.

## BROOKINGS

NEAR AZALEA PARK — This is one of the community's classic homes,
built in 1917 by former mill manager, William Ward. Many antiques and
memorabilias. It is located a few blocks from the ocean as well as the
beautiful Azalea Park and the Chetco River. Host is a car dealer; hostess
is a nutrition and cosmetics consultant. One child 15 years old, daughter.
Norwegian is spoken. Accommodations include: A) large double bedroom
with great view and B) double bed with extra sitting area. TV and stereo
are available in the rooms. Shared bath. The parlor and dining room with
TV, video, and stereo are awaiting the guests, as well as a new spacious,
private spa including a HOT TUB and SAUNA. A full breakfast is served
in the dining room from 7 to 9 A.M. The menu includes eggs benedict
and Norwegian waffles with homemade jams. No pets. Refreshments
shared with your hosts at 6:00 P.M. CHILDREN over 14 welcome. No
SMOKING in the bedrooms.
**Rates:** A) S $35, D $42.50 AND B) S $42, D $47.50 DAILY. S $165, D
$235 WEEKLY.
**Reservations:** (503) 245-0642 8:00 TO 5:00.

HOLMES DRIVE — Located 2 miles north of Brookings, an interesting
small seacost town, nestled in the southwestern tip of the Oregon coast.
It is one of nature's wonderlands, a perfect place to relax completely and
get away from the busy city. The tastefully furnished 1965 coastal style
home and separate guest cottage, with queen bed, command a spectacular
ocean view. Meander down a winding trail to the private park near a
bubbly creek or continue on to the beach. The cottage plus two adjoining
rooms on the lower level in the house offer convenience, comfort, and
privacy. Private entry, bath, refrigerator, and TV are offered. A delicious
continental breakfast is served in the coziness of your room between 7
and 9:30 A.M. A small DOG called Punkin is in residence. Hosts enjoy
antiquing. No small CHILDREN. NO SMOKING.

**Rates:** S $52.50, D $57.50 DAILY. S $262.50, D $287.50 WEEKLY.
**Reservations:** (503) 245-0642 8:00 TO 5:00.

## CANNON BEACH
## HAYSTACK HEIGHTS

A two story Contemporary built in 1986 with large ocean view deck, private entrance, woodlands view to rear, large upstairs suite with sweeping view from living room, kitchenette with microwave and refrigerator. TV. One bedroom has king bed; the other has a queen and twin. Large hall bath in 1920s decor. Large farm breakfast. Town has art galleries, shopping galore, great beach, theater. Hostess is a retired English teacher. No CHILDREN under 14. SMOKING on deck only.
**Rates:** S $45, D $50 DAILY. S OR D $325 WEEKLY. TWO NIGHT MINIMUM WEEKENDS AND HOLIDAYS.
**Reservations:** (503) 245-0642 8:00 TO 5:00.

## EUGENE
## EAST SKINNER BUTTE HISTORIC

Quiet garden setting in the heart of East Skinner Butte Landmark Neighborhood. The Swiss bungalow style house was built in 1909. Offers privacy in independent apartments added on in the 1920s. Each has its own entrance, kitchen, bath, bedroom, with double bed and double fouton available, and sitting room furnished with antiques. Playpen available. Breakfast is continental served in the room. A short walk to the Hult Center for the Performing Arts, Fifth Street Market, Skinner Butte Park, Willamette River, downtown mall, bus route, greyhound and Amtrak. Bike and running path. No pets. HANDICAPPED ACCESSIBLE. Host is a marketing director; hostess is an athletic trainer. Children of all ages welcome. NO SMOKING allowed in apartments.
**Rates:** D $49 DAILY. $308.70 (10% DISCOUNT) WEEKLY.
**Reservations:** (503) 245-0642 8:00 TO 5:00.

## SOUTHWEST EUGENE

LORANE HIGHWAY — A turn-of-the-century home in a peaceful setting of 2 acres of fir and oak trees, rhododendron and azaleas. The highway is more like a country road much traveled by joggers and bikers. Suggestions for other routes are available from the resident jogger and bikers. Wildflowers abound in the spring, seeds are happily shared. The interior of the house features hardwood floors highlighted by Oriental rugs, fireplace, and antiques including a rosewood square grand PIANO. Accommodations include: A) Rainbow Room with a single bed, a sunny room adjoining a fully appointed bathroom with marble counter and tub enclosure, bathroom is shared with Lisa's room; B) furnished with a brass double bed and other antiques; and C) the Garden Room downstairs, furnished with a queen wrought iron bed, looks out onto a small garden and has a private bathroom. Hosts enjoy preparing a breakfast with Danish and German influences evident in the fruit, soups, and egg dishes featuring Oregon berries and cheeses. Guests have the choice of eating in a spacious formal dining room or on the front porch where birds and deer often frequent the scene. The porch swing also offers an opportunity to unwind. Host is a physician; hostess is a registered nurse. No CHILDREN under 12. NO SMOKING.

**Rates:** A) S $45; B) D $50; AND C) D $55 DAILY.

**Reservations:** (503) 245-0642 8:00 TO 5:00.

## 10 MILES SOUTHWEST OF EUGENE

**LORANE HIGHWAY** — An architecturally designed, award winning Passive Solar Home on 6 wooded acres, 20 minutes from Eugene. Guests enjoy exclusive use of a private suite, with two bedrooms, large sitting room, bath, sunroom, and deck. Furnished in contemporary comfort, with VCR and video movies. Vermont castings stove and upright PIANO. Ideal for families. Host is a graphic designer who paints and makes intaglio prints on his own press; hostess is an avid reader, interested in history. Both are active tennis players and travelers. Household includes two CATS who love people. Convenient to the beauties of the coast and mountains and to the varied cultural activities of a university town. Guests may choose a continental or full breakfast that is served in the sunroom or on the deck. Smoking outside only.

**Rates:** S $40-$45, D $45-$50 DAILY.

**Reservations:** (503) 245-0642 8:00 TO 5:00.

## GOLD BEACH

**HUNTER CREEK HEIGHTS** — This home 3 miles from Gold Beach 5 short miles from the mouth of the magnificent Rogue River. You will find here a tranquil haven set high in the foothills of the Siskiyous with a distant view of the ocean. Located on 5 acres of wooded trails will vie with a good library and woodstove for your attention, and a relaxing hot soak in the JACUZZI outside will leave you blissfully ready for your comfortable bed at night. Eclectically furnished with antiques and artifacts. Your host has spent a lifetime of traveling and collecting. Near Rogue River mail boats—trip reservations can be made on these mail boats. PIANO. Children welcome. NO SMOKING.

**Rates:** D $40, S $35 DAILY.

**Reservations:** (503) 245-0642 8:00 TO 5:00.

## GRESHAM
### CINNAMON RIDGE

A lovely professionally decorated two story home in Gresham, 30 minutes from Portland. It is environmentally safe, hypoallergenic for people with chemical sensitivities. Hostess has environmental illness and is acutely aware of the needs for this type of accommodation, Upstairs suite has a queen bed, en suite bath, FIREPLACE, TV, VCR, and a balcony with a view of Mount Hood to enjoy alfresco dining. Will cater to any dietary needs if given sufficient time and information. No pets. No heavy perfume. Transportation to and from the airport for a small fee. Hosts both enjoy jazz and classical music. NO CHILDREN. NO SMOKING.
**Rates:** S $55, D $55 DAILY.
**Reservations:** (503) 245-0642 8:00 TO 5:00.

## LAKESIDE
### SUNLAKE PARK

This B&B is clear of the coastal wind and fog, yet just a few minutes scenic drive from the coastal highway. This spacious scenic chalet style country home features a Great Room with fireplace and quiet music for listening or dancing. Accommodations include A) large queen bed and B) large room with two twin beds. Guests share bath. Outside are forest trails to explore, country lanes for hiking, a hammock for lounging and a charcoal grill and picnic table. Host is a retired naval aviator and stockbroker. He enjoys gardening, beach walking, reading, music, and plays. Friendly outside DOG. Lakeside is 7 miles away with fishing, boating, swimming, sailing, dining, and a light plane airport. Congenial hosts will help you plan your sightseeing and dining adventures to make your stay a memorable experience. Beaches, golf, and deep sea fishing nearby. Hearty breakfast. PIANO. CHILDREN over 12 welcome. NONSMOKERS welcome.
**Rates:** S $40, D $45 DAILY. S $250, D $280 WEEKLY.
**Reservations:** (503) 245-0642 8:00 TO 5:00.

## LINCOLN CITY
### TAFT AREA

SCHOONER CREEK ROAD — A separate suite overlooking Schooner Creek which flows into the Siletz Bay and the ocean. Within 3 blocks walking distance to the beach. Can accommodate group up to five. Suite includes a bedroom with double bed, TV, VCR, sitting room with double hide-a-bed, and private bathroom with tile tub and shower. It also has a large private deck and private entrance. A motor/row boat is available for rowing up the creek, or crabbing in the bay. Geese and ducks in the yard daily and wildlife abound including: deer, otter, heron, raccoon, and sometimes seals. Hostess enjoys serving elaborate breakfast on the deck, or even breakfast in bed. Close to excellent restaurants, golf course, and five star resort. Host is an insurance agent; hostess is an artist. Both enjoy white water rafting. Children welcome. SMOKING on deck only. **Rates:** S $35, D $45, EXTRA GUEST $8 DAILY. D $200 WEEKLY. **Reservations:** (503) 245-0642 8:00 TO 5:00.

## WEST DEVIL LAKE

A large ranch style home just steps away from Devil Lake. Includes: a large recreaction room with pool table, games and a bar, living room with fireplace, TV, VCR, and a PIANO for those who can play. Accommodations include: A) large airy bedroom with king waterbed, TV, en suite with private patio and separate entrance, and B) queen waterbed. TV. Both share a bath. A full breakfast is served in the bright dining area off the kitchen or in warm weather on the large deck. Another large deck (covered) is available for hot tubbing all year round. A boat launch is within walking distance from the house and you have your own dock to tie up to. You can swim, fish or wind surf. Near golf, racquetball, art galleries, dining, dancing, wine tasting, and the beach. Host enjoys painting and agate collecting. The is a small DOG. Host smokes. No CHILDREN.
**Rates:** A) $65, B) $55 DAILY.
**Reservations:** (503) 245-0642 8:00 TO 5:00.

## NEWBERG
## 25 MILES WEST OF PORTLAND

Secluded, owner designed and built country home. Ideal retreat in wooded setting for hiking, country walks, and visiting wineries. Antiques in each room. It is 20 minutes from McMinnville and 4 miles from Newberg. Convenient to George Fox College and Linfield College. About 1 hour from Lincoln City on the Oregon coast. Hosts' hobbies include stained glass, hunting, violin making, flower arranging, woodworking, gourmet cooking, gardening, and birdwatching. Involved with Audubon Society and the Blue Bird Trails nesting project. Large library. Hosts enjoy hosting international students. Accommodations include two rooms, A&B), each with double bed and use of decks. On request one large room with queen-sized bed. Antiques in beach room. PIANO. Children welcome. SMOKING on decks only.
**Rates:** A) S $37, D $42 AND B) S $30, D $35 DAILY.
**Reservations:** (503) 245-0642 8:00 TO 5:00.

## PORT ORFORD

A Contemporary two story, owner built home with dramatic ocean views from its two bedrooms. Each bedroom has a private bath and queen bed. A full breakfast is served. No pets. Guests will enjoy visiting the town's

harbor, where a unique fleet on wheels is launched daily by a huge hoist. Fine restaurants, shops, harbor, and beaches are only 1 to 2 blocks away. Hosts are long time residents, a schoolteacher and a carpenter. Their interests include computers and the fibre arts of handspinning and weaving. NO CHILDREN. NO SMOKING.
**Rates:** S $40, D $45 DAILY.
**Reservations:** (503) 245-0642 8:00 TO 5:00.

## SIUSLAW NATIONAL FOREST
### YACHATS

HIGHWAY 101 — Central Oregon coast surrounded by Siuslaw National Forest. Secluded private quiet inn on OCEAN front. Down the hill from Highway 101 on forested high sea cliffs. Large teak parquet floored B&B inn offers marvelous ocean views from wood beamed living and dining areas and ocean deck. Fireplace in center of the inn is focal point for relaxing evenings. Hostess is a psychologist. She has one 13 year old daughter. Accommodations include: A) large king with ocean views and large sunken tub, private bath; B) queen room with rose carpet and private bath; and C) garden (queen) room with private bath. Hosts encourage bonfires on the sandy beach at sunset. SMOKERS are allowed smoking on decks and covered patios.
**Rates:** D $46-$66 DAILY.
**Reservations:** (503) 245-0642 8:00 TO 5:00.

## ROGUE VALLEY
### MEDFORD
### OLDTOWN MEDFORD

4TH AND GRAPE — This one of a kind nineteenth-century Victorian cottage was built and owned by a local planning mill operator as a showplace for his craftsmanship. The beautiful woodwork throughout remains in its original state, including a carved archway. Cottage is rented as a private unit; one or two bedrooms. It is located near the heart of the city, historic town of Jacksonville, Shakespearean Ashland, Crater Lake and Oregon caves. Rafting, fishing, water slides, snow skiing, and the like are all less than 100 miles away, most within 25. PIANO. Host is a gold miner; hostess enjoys gardening and cooking. NO CHILDREN. SMOKING outside only.
**Rates:** D $65, T OR Q $75 PRIVACY OF ENTIRE COTTAGE FOR ALL RESERVATIONS DAILY.
**Reservations:** (503) 245-0642 8:00 TO 5:00.

# WESTERN OREGON
## PORTLAND

Some of the attractions in Portland that are not yet well known are the local wineries; tours and tasting available. Also, the free concerts in the summer at McCall Waterfront Park on the Willamette River and in Washington Park at the zoo. Price is admission to the zoo. Bring a "picnic dinner" and enjoy the music. The magnificent Columbia River Gorge, with its many waterfalls and dams, is right in the backyard. The 145 foot sternwheeler, Columbia Gorge, operates in Portland during the fall, early winter, and spring and in the Columbia River Gorge during the summer months as a charter and tourist vessel. There are many golf courses in and around the city, high-tech industries in Beaverton and Hillsboro (15 minutes from Portland). One hour's drive will take you to Mount Hood for skiing.

A large, handsome Tudor style home in an area of fine homes, furnished with antique pieces from France and England. Grand PIANO and fireplace in reception room. Fine selection of books in library. Accommodations include: A) exceptional bedroom with antique furnishings, soft down chaise lounge and bed fittings, cable TV, FIREPLACE, large bath en suite; B) airy double bedroom with wicker accessories, private bath, cable TV; and C) comfortable lower level room with twin beds, cable TV, private bath. A large game room with fireplace is also on lower level. A full breakfast is served. Home is very convenient to the airport and downtown entertainment area. Hostess is an interior designer who speaks a little French and Spanish. Children welcome. NONSMOKERS only.
**Rates:** S OR D A) $50 AND B & C) $40 DAILY.
**Reservations:** (503) 245-0642 8:00 TO 5:00.

## ALAMEDA

A comfortable, private apartment with outside entrances. Self-service breakfast in kitchen stocked with food, dishwasher, and laundry facilities. Near neighborhood groceries including excellent natural foods store, local restaurants and 2 miles from Lloyd Center Shopping Mall. Cozy living room with TV, stereo, fireplace, varied reading materials, and indirect lighting for a romantic evening. Use of JACUZZI HOT TUB on request, which is located in the privacy of the apartment. Queen bed in room opening onto private deck lined with flowers in season. Also single room with waterbed in family portion of the house that shares family bath. Hostess is a professional who enjoys photography, gardening, cooking, and travel. Ranch style house. CHILDREN OVER 12 welcome. NO SMOKING.
**Rates:** S OR D $55 DAILY. S OR D $300 WEEKLY.
**Reservations:** (503) 245-0642 8:00 TO 5:00.

## BULL MOUNTAIN, TIGARD

Country French with panoramic views of mountains and valley below. Landscaped setting with a rose walk, clipped hedges, flower bordered lawns, and quiet surroundings of orchards and vinyards. Private TENNIS COURT and solar heated POOL. Many continental furnishings and appointments. PIANO and harpsichord. Four fireplaces. One FIREPLACE in three room guest level suite. Second guest level room with queen waterbed available for additional members of same party. Host is corporate community affairs manager; hostess is a retired real estate broker who enjoys serving elaborate breakfasts featuring seasonal fruits grown on surrounding acreage. Household also includes well-mannered calico CAT. Six minutes from Interstate 5 exit south of Portland, 11 freeway miles from downtown Portland; 6 blocks from city bus stop. Some German is spoken here. No SMOKING in B&B suite.
**Rates:** D $40 DAILY. D $260 WEEKLY.
**Reservations:** (503) 245-0642 8:00 TO 5:00.

## COLONIAL HEIGHTS

NEAR 22 AND SOUTH EAST HAWTHORNE — The tantalizing aroma of fresh baked yeast rolls and fruited bran muffin grace the halls of this interesting late nineteenth century classic home. Five immaculate, newly decorated bedrooms share two attractive bathrooms. The large spacious living room boasts a few antiques and plenty of comfortable seating space. Host, a retired military man, is a garden enthusiast; hostess, a retired bank employee and Jill-of-All-Trades, makes you welcome. For antique buffs, Hawthorne Boulevard and the Sellwood District are closeby. Cable TV is free in the TV room. No pets. City buses within 1 block; Downtown and Interstate 5 Freeway, 10 minutes; airport 20 minutes. CHILDREN over 12 welcome. NO SMOKERS.
**Rates:** S $25, D $30-$40, T $40-$45 DAILY. S $125, D $185, T $225 WEEKLY.
**Reservations:** (503) 245-0642 8:00 TO 5:00.

## DUNTHORPE

This is a 1921 French Country Estate on 1 1/2 landscaped acres. It is furnished with traditional and antique decor. Accommodations include five large bedrooms with twin or queen beds and private baths on the second floor. A) king suite with fireplace, B) queen bed, private bath, C) double bed, D) twin beds. A large continental breakfast is served in the dining room or on the patio overlooking the gardens. Host likes to ski, play tennis, and travel. Two outside DOGS share this residence. Pool table.
**Rates:** A) S $70, D $75; B) S $55, D $60; C) S $50, D $55 AND D) S $55, D $60 DAILY.
**Reservations:** (503) 245-0642 8:00 TO 5:00.

## EAST COUNTY

SOUTH EAST MARKET STREET — A blue and white Cape Cod cottage set in an old-fashioned garden with white picket fence. A large rose garden, herb garden, and grape arbor provide a quiet spot for relaxing. The home is traditionally furnished with a fireplace and PIANO. Hostess is a Registered Nurse. Westhighland TERRIERS. Accommodations are in a separate guesthouse with a shared bath. They include: A) queen-sized bed and B) double and single bed. Local travel information, maps, books, magazines, and flowers fill the guest areas. Each breakfast is created to appeal to the eye as well as the taste. Located 15 minutes from Downtown Airport; near Interstate 205. PIANO. HANDICAPPED ACCESSIBLE. CHILDREN over 12 welcome. NO SMOKING.
**Rates:** A & B) S $40, AND D $45 AND B) T $50 DAILY.
**Reservations:** (503) 245-0642 8:00 TO 5:00.

## EAST MORELAND

Beautiful neighborhood in Portland near Reed College and Dwyer Community Hospital. Large two story home with one double bed and a private bath on the second floor. Continental breakfast served in the dining room or on the patio, weather permitting. Lovely garden, family room, TV, fireplace. Close to bus, golf, and Sellwoods' Antique Row. Cape Cod style home. CHILDREN over 16 welcome.
**Rates:** S $35, D $40 DAILY.
**Reservations:** (503) 245-0642 8:00 TO 5:00.

## IRVINGTON

Large three story Portland home built in 1910. Four large bedrooms two baths with claw-foot tubs. Antiques throughout with lace curtains, quilts, Laura Ashley and special linens. Sunroom and balcony on second floor. Although this home has four bedrooms, the hostess will rent only two of the four bedrooms, giving the guests their choice of rooms. Accommodations include: A) king bed; B) two rooms each with queen beds; and C) double bed and FIREPLACE. No pets. Hostess provides full breakfast, and coffee, tea, and hot chocolate are available anytime. Airport, Amtrak, or bus only 20 minutes away. City bus at doorstep. The hostess has been an innkeeper since 1979. CHILDREN welcome if they are well behaved and under parents' supervision at all times. NO SMOKING.
**Rates:** S $40-$45, D $45-$50 DAILY. S OR D $225 WEEKLY.
**Reservations:** (503) 245-0642 8:00 TO 5:00.

## LAIR HILL HISTORIC

SOUTHWEST BARBUR BOULEVARD — An elegant Victorian townhouse on a quiet, tree-lined street in a Historic District. This home combines the best of two centuries. Old Portland ambience and modern

amenities: air conditioning/filtration throughout, TV, cable, VCR, phone jacks in every bedroom. Delightful roofdeck affords a leafy refuge in which to sip a glass of wine while taking in a great city view. During winter guests are served wine and beer around woodstove. Hostess is a speech pathologist with wide-ranging interests that are reflected in art, book, and tape collections. Abyssinian CAT present. Home is adult oriented. Accommodations include: A) master bedroom with oversize king (or two twin beds), private skylit bath, private entry with direct access to roofdeck; B) queen bed, shared bath; and C) smaller room with daybed (opens to make an extremely comfortable double bed. Rooms B and C combine ideally to make a family or business suite with private bath. Continental breakfast served. CHILDREN over 13 welcome. SMOKING allowed on deck only.
**Rates:** A) S $61, D $66; B) S $50, D $55; AND C) S $45, D $50 DAILY. 20% DISCOUNT WEEKLY.
**Reservations:** (503) 245-0642 8:00 TO 5:00.

## MULTNOMAH

Older home decorated in contemporary taste with a touch of the old. Quiet neighborhood, comfortable setting, just minutes from downtown, major colleges, and law and medical schools. Walk to village area of antique and specialty shops, neighborhood cafes, art center, 90 acre park, and bus lines. Umbrellas provided. Two upstairs bedrooms, A) one queen with a loveseat that becomes a single bed for a child and B) the other a single bed. Both share bath. Full breakfast served. An apartment is sometimes available C) with double bed, sitting room, kitchen, private bath and entrance. Except for the apartment, accommodations are available weekends, holidays, and summers only as your hostess is a teacher. A CAT is in residence. SMOKING in the apartment only.
**Rates:** A) $40, CHILD $10, B) S $25, AND C) $50 WITHOUT BREAKFAST, $55 WITH BREAKFAST.
**Reservations:** (503) 245-0642 8:00 TO 5:00.

## NORTHWEST

CORNELL ROAD — Large four story home built in 1907 by Portland's first pediatrician. Overlooks the city and the Cascade Mountain peaks. Incredible views of Mount Saint Helens and Mount Hood. Home is shared by five professional adults with interest in folk dancing, vocal and piano music, white water rafting, skiing, and Oregon wine tasting. Occupations include a microbiologist, criminal justice worker, writer, professional piano player, and Hospice administrator. The B&B room has beautiful furnishings with double bed adjacent to shared bath. Elegant full breakfasts are served. Fantastic location only 5 minutes from downtown. Boutiques, bookstores, and gourmet restaurants within walking distance. Located on city bus route. Hosts invite guests to share evening meals.

NO pets. PIANO. NO SMOKING.
**Rates:** S $35 D $40 DAILY. S OR D $200 WEEKLY.
**Reservations:** (503) 245-0642 8:00 TO 5:00.

CORNELL ROAD—NORTHWEST — This is a 1905 vintage Portland mansion, featured in publications including the 1930 Compton Encyclopedia that cites it as typical turn-of-the-century northwest architecture. The house abounds with character and charm and is lovingly appointed with beautiful antiques. Oriental rugs and art and happy plants. Each bedroom has a spectacular view of city, rivers, mountains, and combines antique furnishings with luxurious new carpeting. Guests are welcome to enjoy the huge living room that features a 1927 Chickering PIANO, cozy fireplace and variety of books and periodicals. In additional to delicious breakfasts, treats are always available in the dining room. Hosts are both contractors and outdoor enthusiasts. The house is close to skiing, tennis, and a huge park offering miles of trails for walking or jogging. The area is abundant with quaint shops and restaurants, all within walking distance. City center is less than 10 minutes away. There is a resident CAT and DOG. Three double rooms available. VCR. Baby equipment available. Children welcome and enjoyed. NO SMOKING.
**Rates:** A) S $50, D $55 AND B & C) S $40, D $45 DAILY. A) S $240, D $270 AND B & C) S $300, D $330 WEEKLY.
**Reservations:** (503) 245-0642 8:00 TO 5:00.

## RESIDENTIAL

OFF 39th AND INTERSTATE 84 — English Tudor home is on a quiet tree-lined street near Interstate 84 and town. Close to the bus and shopping at Lloyd Center. The two bedrooms are on the second floor and share a bathroom. Hostess is an artist as well as painting teacher in her home. A small French POODLE is in residence. Continental breakfast served in the dining room and you are invited to share the living room fireplace with your hostess. She speaks German. CHILDREN over 3 welcome. NONSMOKERS only.
**Rates:** S $35, D $40 DAILY.
**Reservations:** (503) 245-0642 8:00 TO 5:00.

## WEST HILLS

Comfortable Ranch style house in a lovely residential area near top of hill. Views of the city, river, and mountains from the breakfast room. It is a 10 minute drive to city center with art museums, old town, government buildings, universities, coliseum, and shops; 90 minutes to Mount Hood skiing or to Pacific Coast; many wineries within an hour's drive; city bus 3 blocks; 15 minutes to town, bus or train station; and 30 minute drive to airport. Easy access to zoo, science museum, forest center, and arboretum, Pittock Mansion, rose gardens, riverfront activities,

and scenic drives. Host is retired chemical engineer who does old cars, toys, trains, and wood; hostess is retired elementary teacher who enjoys gourmet cooking, bridge, social activites, foreign travel, and conversation. The 2 1/2 room suite had private entrance, large living room, with a fireplace and queen hide-a-bed, private patio to relax on. Rooms are on the garden level. Twin beds are in the bedroom. Baby equipment available. Bikes and motor boat available. CHILDREN WELCOME.
**Rates:** S $35, D $40 DAILY.
**Reservations:** (503) 245-0642 8:00 TO 5:00.

MISSISSIPPI — This 1890 award winning landmark Victorian home is filled with quality antiques and Bradbury's hand silk screened papers. There is an 1860 Parlor Grand PIANO. Host is a speech therapist; hostess is a school counselor. They have a 16 year old daughter. One LHASA APSO in dungeon. One 88 year old grandmother, daughter of Oregon pioneers and hosts' pride and joy. Gourmet breakfast in fabulous formal dining room or veranda. Horse and 1875 carriage for touring. JACUZZI at annex. Accommodations include: A) three rooms with city view; B) double bed, shared bath in main house; C) two single beds; D) double bed; and E) single bed with shared bath in annex. It is 5 minutes from city center by car, 15 by bus. Speed boat and bikes available. CHILDREN over 14 welcome. NO SMOKING.
**Rates:** S $30, D $45, A) SUITE $65; PRIVATE BATH $95 DAILY. B-E) S $180, D $270 WEEKLY.
**Reservations:** (503) 245-0642 8:00 TO 5:00.

OFF FREEWAY 205 — This guest cottage has a large room with king or two twin beds, studio kitchenette, and a private bath. Your host lives next door and provides you with a self-serve breakfast, with everything in the refrigerator. A nice enclosed yard with a picnic table and barbecue for your use. Bus at door and a large shopping center near. Close to Interstates 84 and 205 and the airport. Your host is retired and likes to hike, garden, and work with stained glass. There are two small DOGS, but not in the guest cottage.
**Rates:** S $40, D $45 DAILY. S $175, D $210 WEEKLY.
**Reservations:** (503) 245-0642 8:00 TO 5:00.

PACIFIC HIGHWAY — This home borders a wooded, undeveloped park and open fields. The Ranch style home has three bedrooms with a shared bath on the garden level that can accommodate four guests. The large family room has a fireplace and pool table or you may join your hosts on the main floor. The full breakfast is served in the country kitchen. There is a baby grand PIANO in the living room; a deck and nice garden are also available for your enjoyment. Close to Interstate 5 (15 minutes to town) Washington Square Shopping Center and Multnomah Village for

antique shopping. Home has many antique furnishings. Accommodations include: A) queen bed and B) twin beds. Crib is available. Host is a retired salesman; hostess enjoys knitting, piano playing, and gardening. NONSMOKERS only.
**Rates:** A) S $30, D $35 AND B) S $20, D $40 DAILY.
**Reservations:** (503) 245-0642 8:00 TO 5:00.

A Cape Cod home 7 miles from town in a quiet, residential neighborhood. The home is furnished with many antiques and traditionals. The host is a retired mechanical engineer, his hobbies include rock hounding, making thunderegg clocks, bookends, and the like; and gardening; hostess runs a B&B reservation service, enjoys gardening and is a volunteer for the American Cancer Society. Accommodations include: A) double bed and B) two twins are on the second floor. The bath is shared between the two bedrooms, but there is another private bath on the garden level if someone wants a private bath when both bedrooms are full. Hostess serves a full or continental breakfast, whichever the guest prefers. There is a lovely flower garden where guests may relax with cool drinks or coffee and cookies. The front room is available or guests may join the hosts on the garden level to watch TV. Hosts have both traveled a bit and enjoy exchanging experiences with other travelers. A little French is spoken here. CHILDREN over 10 welcome. NONSMOKERS only.
**Rates:** A) S $25, D $35 AND B) S $30, D $40 DAILY. 10% DISCOUNT WEEKLY.
**Reservations:** (503) 245-0642 8:00 TO 5:00.

## SEAL ROCK

PACIFIC COAST HIGHWAY — A 1940s Cape Cod updated for guests. Private guest area and entrance. HOT TUB. Visit farm animals, explore nature trails on the 2 1/2 acres, or walk to the beaches and tide pools. Decorated in cozy country style, some antiques, breakfast prepared on old wood cookstove. Home shared with three children (separate part of house). No pets. Located near Newport and Sea Lion Caves. Host is a thoroughbred horse owner and trainer; hostess enjoys cooking and arts and crafts. Double accommodations are available. NO CHILDREN. NO SMOKING.
**Rates:** S $45, D $49 DAILY.
**Reservations:** (503) 245-0642 8:00 TO 5:00.

## SEASIDE

HOLLADAY DRIVE — This is charming inn on the Necanicum River near the center of the bustling resort town of Seaside on the north Oregon coast. Hosts offer the warmth and enchantment of grandmother's house, yet the private baths and entrances give each unit the privacy and

seclusion of a small, quaint hotel. Breakfast is served between 8:30 and 10:00 A.M. in the comfort of the parlor library, in the intimacy of the guest's own quarters, or on the riverfront deck when weather invites. The inn was built in 1907 and completely refurbished in 1982. The new annex was completed in June 1986 and offers four additional units with their own unique flavor and views of the river and Tillamook Head. All of the accommodations are furnished with a country flavor and a touch of antiquity. Each unit has its own special decor of lace curtains, flowers, quilts, plants, and framed prints. There are also periodicals, hardcover books, and plants in each unit. All have color TVs and some have fully equipped kitchens. Hosts enjoy cross-country skiing. Children welcome.
**Rates:** D $37-$65 DAILY.
**Reservations:** (503) 245-0642 8:00 TO 5:00.

PROM (PROMENADE) — Gracious ocean front home on Promenade within 4 blocks of downtown Seaside. The home's informal living room provides a panoramic view of the beautiful Pacific Ocean. Two double A & B) rooms decorated in country antiques, share bath. Perfect base for vacationer to north Oregon coast. Beachcomb, fly kites, windsurf, fish, hike, bicycle, golf. Visit gift shops, antique shops, galleries, museums, and historical sites. Over 40 restaurants serve fresh seafood. Live theater, concerts, and festivals are scheduled throughout the year. Watch the breakers spilling over the long sandy beach, during your leisurely breakfast or be served in the privacy of your room. Breakfasts are bountiful and feature a variety of specialties. Pool nearby and bikes available. Boats can be chartered nearby. Horse stall. Host is a longshoreman; hostess is a caterer and wedding consultant. Two black LABRADORS live here. Children welcome. NO SMOKING.
**Rates:** A) S OR D $35 AND B) S $35, D $40 DAILY. EXTRA CHILD $5; FAMILY BOTH ROOMS $65 DAILY.
**Reservations:** (503) 245-0642 8:00 TO 5:00.

# WILLAMETTE VALLEY
## LAKE OSWEGO

This charming Cape Cod home is in a parklike setting and at one time was a lake cabin. Since then it has been updated but still retains its charm. On the tower level there is a two room suite; queen bed, bath with a SAUNA, and a sitting room with a TV, VCR, stereo. A double sofabed in the sitting room for extra guests in the same party. Full or continental breakfast served in the dining room, patio or greenhouse. Lake privileges. Indoor HOT TUB. Resident CAT and DOG. Bus 1 block. Host is in agrichemical research; hostess is an interior designer. Both enjoy the outdoors and photography. CHILDREN over 8 welcome. NO SMOKING.

**Rates:** S $45, D $50, CHILD 8-16 $10, ADULT $20 EXTRA DAILY.
**Reservations:** (503) 245-0642 8:00 TO 5:00.

## WILSONVILLE
## RURAL FARM NEAR INTERSTATE 5

NEAR STAFFORD ROAD — This is a new home located in quiet, rolling farm country on two landscaped and wooded acres with stream. Guests enjoy a completely private suite including: private bath, private entrance, patio, sitting room, master bedroom with queen bed, and an adjoining room for CHILDREN over 6. A full country breakfast is served in the dining room or sunroom featuring fresh local fruit in season. Home is 20 minutes south of downtown Portland with nearby recreational, cultural, and historical activities. Hosts are interested and knowledgeable about local tourist points of interest. Air conditioned. Bikes available. NO SMOKING.
**Rates:** S $40, D $45, ADDITIONAL TWO MAXIMUM $10 EACH DAILY.
**Reservations:** (503) 245-0642 8:00 TO 5:00.

# WASHINGTON

## EASTERN WASHINGTON
### SPOKANE

HODIN DRIVE — A lovely Contemporary home located on the banks of the Spokane River in a parklike setting just 15 minutes from downtown Spokane. The two guestrooms share a bath. A private entrance for guests is available. A cozy sitting/TV room with a crackling woodstove is inviting in cool weather. The outdoor HOT TUB/JACUZZI that overlooks the river is a pleasant way to relax. After a quiet, refreshing rest guests will enjoy an elaborate breakfast on the patio overlooking the river in warm weather or in the dining room in the cooler weather. ALCOHOLIC BEVERAGES are not permitted on the premises. Spokane boasts a variety of activities. Some of the nicest golf courses in the northwest, water skiing on one of the 50 lakes within 50 miles, downhill skiing within 30 minutes. Excellent shopping and beautiful parks. A canoe or rowboat is available to guests. PIANO. Host is a doctor of optometry. NO SMOKING.
**Rates:** S $38, D $43 DAILY.
**Reservations:** (503) 245-0642 8:00 TO 5:00.

## PUGET SOUND
### BELLINGHAM

1/2 HOUR DRIVE TO INTERSTATE 5 — A working dairy farm with Jersey cattle, some timber, and nature trails with wildlife. It is 1 hour from the city of Vancouver, Canada; a 1 1/2 hour drive to ski area with many hiking trails through the summer. The home has an open area that includes living room, kitchen, and family room with fireplace and ORGAN. Lake and mountain views from large windows. Accommodations include: A) two rooms each with double bed, antiques and B) twin beds with antiques. All share bath. A farm style breakfast is served each morning. Children welcome. NO SMOKING.
**Rates:** S $30, D $38, $10 EACH EXTRA CHILD DAILY.
**Reservations:** (503) 245-0642 8:00 TO 5:00.

### BELLVILLE
#### MEYDENBAUER BAY

8TH STREET NEAR BELLEVUE WAY — This Contemporary home in a quiet wooded suburb of Seattle is a half mile from highway 405 and from shopping at Bellevue Square. B&B facilities are complete, separate, and private with large windows to enjoy view of mountains and city. Close to park on Lake Washington. Full breakfast, complimentary wine. Accommodations include: a suite of three rooms (two bedrooms and large living room), kitchen, cable TV, washer/dryer, phone. HANDICAPPED

ACCESSIBLE. Easy access to public transportation. Children welcome.
NONSMOKERS only.
**Rates:** S $35, D $45 DAILY. S $210, D $270 WEEKLY. WINTER S
$25, D $35 DAILY.
**Reservations:** (503) 245-0642 8:00 TO 5:00.

## SAN JUAN ISLANDS
### ORCAS

One large airy room with queen-sized bed in French country cottage in
the woods. The room is on the first floor with window seat. Private bath
with shower and tub. Keeping room included for use, with eighteenth
century French and English antiques and FIREPLACE. Private dining
room. Host has suite upstairs. Very private and romantic accommodation.
Full continental breakfast includes fresh fruit, juice, muffins, croissants,
cereal, coffee, tea, and so on. SMALL PETS WELCOME. Located on
Orcas Island; can be reached by ferry. Hosts have their own insurance
agency. Bikes available. NONSMOKERS only.
**Rates:** S $55, D $60 DAILY.
**Reservations:** (206) 784-0539 MONDAY THROUGH FRIDAY 9 A.M.
TO 5 P.M. PACIFIC TIME.

## SEATTLE
### LAKE CITY

Country seclusion 10 minutes from City Center, University of Washington.
Gourmet full breakfast. Host enthusiastic about guests and travel. Outdoor
DOG. Port-a-crib, highchair, toys, and books available for children.
Accommodations include: A) elegant quilted bird coverlet as theme for
prints and sculpture, queen room, garden overview. En suite: guest
bathroom, living Room, FIREPLACE, TV, library. B) Blue Room, white
shutters, eighteenth century furnishings, double bed, overlooks garden,
quilted block spread. En suite guest bathroom, living room, FIREPLACE,
TV, library. And C) twin beds, patchwork quilts, sink vanity in alcove.
En suite: guest bath, living room, FIREPLACE, TV, library. SMOKING
on patio only.
**Rates:** S $40, D $45, INFANTS $7.50 DAILY.
**Reservations:** (206) 784-0539 MONDAY THROUGH FRIDAY 9 A.M.
TO 5 P.M. PACIFIC TIME.

## WESTERN WASHINGTON
### SEATTLE
#### BALLARD

Here is a private apartment with everything. Double bed in bedroom, 19
inch color TV with cable, telephone, private bath (shower), private

entrance, living room comfortably furnished and a full kitchen stocked with staple foods. On bus line, be downtown in minutes; near beach, restaurants, the university, walk to grocery store. Daily maid service. Also some special touches like mints on the pillow, fresh flowers. No pets. Host is an artist and illustrator; hostess is a business owner who enjoys travel, antiques, and the arts. CHILDREN over 8 welcome. NONSMOKERS only.
**Rates:** S $32, D $38 DAILY. 10% DISCOUNT WEEKLY.
**Reservations:** (206) 784-0539 MONDAY THROUGH FRIDAY 9 A.M. TO 5 P.M. PACIFIC TIME.

UNHOSTED cottage with all the comforts of home with two bedrooms. One is furnished with a lovely bedroom set, double bed, from 1925, the vintage of the cottage. The second bedroom features twins beds. Color TV, free telephone, fireplace, oak furniture with brass accents in the living room. The cozy breakfast nook in the fully furnished kitchen, complete with fine china and crystal, is a most popular spot with guests. Small but quiet backyard. The location is handy. Close to grocery stores, restaurants, beaches, the University of Washington. Children welcome. NO SMOKERS.
**Rates:** S $45, D $55, $10 EACH ADDITIONAL PERSON DAILY.
**Reservations:** (206) 784-0539 MONDAY THROUGH FRIDAY 9 A.M. TO 5 P.M. PACIFIC TIME.

## CAPITOL HILL

Situated on Capitol Hill amongst stately mansions, this spacious family home built in 1904 has been completely renovated by the hosts, a charming mother and daughter team. The first floor public rooms, entry, library, living and dining rooms are light and airy with polished maple floors, Oriental carpets, leaded windows and French doors opening to a wraparound porch. The guestrooms, reached by an open stairway to the second floor, each have a different color scheme, furniture, and accessories. Accommodations include: A) Blue Room, a country atmosphere in beiges and blues featuring a queen-sized bed with down comforter. At the rear of the house overlooking the gardens. Quiet. B) Green Room, all white room enlivened with bright green comforters on twin beds and a view of 80 year old plum tree in the side yard. C) Rose Room, large elegant front room has a walk-in closet, window seat, antique furnishings, a down comforter on the queen-sized bed. And D) Lavender Room, airy white and lavender room has an inviting window seat, cheval mirror, armoire and bedside table in yellow and white and a queen-sized bed with down comforter. Two full bathrooms, each with tub and shower, are shared by the four guestrooms. The 6 foot claw-footed tub in the "new" bathroom is great for soaking. A generous continental breakfast is

served either in the dining room, the library, or in the rear garden. PIANO. SMOKING on porch only.
**Rates:** A & B) S $40, D $45 AND C & D) S $50, D $55 DAILY.
**Reservations:** (206) 784-0539 MONDAY THROUGH FRIDAY 9 A.M. TO 5 P.M. PACIFIC TIME.

Lovely brick house, furnished with marbletop tables, PIANO, antiques, Oriental rugs, and tapestries. Situated on a tree-lined street in a quiet and exclusive residential neighborhood. On two bus lines. Close to the University of Washington and downtown Seattle. All mountain and water sports. It is 3 to 4 hours from Victoria and Vancouver, Canada. The hostess is interested in world travel, the performing and visual arts, and needlepoint. She is retired from the University of Washington. Accommodations include: A) large, elegant master suite, private bath with tub and shower. Antique white Mediterranean furniture. king-sized bed; B) large, light and airy twin-bedded bedroom with dressing room and plum plush carpet, shared bath with tub and shower; and C) small, cozy and sunny double-bedded bedroom, plum plush carpet, shared bath with tub and shower. NONSMOKERS only.
**Rates:** A) S $40, D $45; B) S $30, D $40; AND C) S $30, D $35 DAILY.
**Reservations:** (206) 784-0539 MONDAY THROUGH FRIDAY 9 A.M. TO 5 P.M. PACIFIC TIME.

Handsome 1848 mansion close to town on Capitol Hill. Hospitable hosts are a university professor and a computer specialist. Some Spanish is spoken here. PIANO. Generous breakfast. Guest sitting room and balcony, super comfortable. Accommodations include: A) East Room, light and airy with private bath, mountain view, firm double four poster bed, extra pillows; and B) West Room, peaceful with neighborhood view, private bath/shower across the hall, firm double bed, extra pillows. Children of all ages welcome. NO SMOKING in house.
**Rates:** S $32.50, D $45.50 DAILY.
**Reservations:** (206) 784-0539 MONDAY THROUGH FRIDAY 9 A.M. TO 5 P.M. PACIFIC TIME.

Located in the prestigious Capitol Hill section of Seattle, close to downtown, 1 block from Volunteer Park on "Millionaire's Row." Within walking distance to the Broadway District with its fine restaurants and shops. It is also near the University of Washington Arboretum and Stadium, Japanese Gardens, the Cornish Institute, and the Fred Hutchinson Cancer Research Center. This home was built in 1912. The former owners entertained lavishly in this grand old mansion with its huge ballroom and pipe organ on the third floor. Hosts have restored the home to its former splendor. The second floor suites have the real old world charm and comfort, featuring many antiques, original tile baths and pedestal sinks

and showers. Pool table. Enjoy breakfast of croissants or sweet rolls in the solarium. Guestrooms have double beds, some with private bath, some with shared baths. Suites have sitting rooms with excellent views. Executive suites have antique double sleigh beds, private baths, and wet bars. Five PIANOS. Smoking permitted.
**Rates:** $45-$125 DAILY.
**Reservations:** (206) 784-0539 MONDAY THROUGH FRIDAY 9 A.M. TO 5 P.M. PACIFIC TIME.

### QUEEN ANNE

Queen Anne Victorian home built in 1906. Accommodations include: A) on second floor, room that has picture windows and padded window seats looking onto a territorial view of the Cascade Mountains, lace covered queen canopy bed, antiques, telephone, TV, shared bath and B) antique canopy converted rope bed that came across the country on a covered wagon, extra long double bed in cozy room also with padded window seats and picture windows, phone in room, shared bath. Continental breakfast is provided in the formal living room with fireplace or in the country kitchen. Oak porch swing and white wicker chairs available to watch the sunset over the mountains. Resident COCKER SPANIEL and professional couple are your hosts. Handmade quilts and antique prints decorate this home away from home. PIANO. Some French is spoken here. SMOKING in designated areas only.
**Rates:** A) S $40, D $45 AND B) S $30, D $35.
**Reservations:** (206) 784-0539 MONDAY THROUGH FRIDAY 9 A.M. TO 5 P.M. PACIFIC TIME.

### WEST SEATTLE

Magnificent view from this guesthome of the Seattle skyline, the Cascade Mountains, Mount Rainier and Mount Baker, and the blue waters of Puget Sound. Sit at night and sip a glass of wine in the solarium or have your fine breakfast there if you wish. It is all yours as a pampered guest in this very special guesthome. Accommodations include: A) round king bed, 6 remote control TV set, sliding glass doors to your own private deck, private bath across the hall and B) queen bed, private bath en suite. There is a HOT TUB. It is 10 minutes from Seattle and 20 minutes to the airport. The newest, most popular restaurant in town is located within walking distance. Hostess can make reservations for you and you will be seated right away. Other guests usually have to make reservations 1 to 2 weeks ahead of time. One DOG and one CAT reside here. WATERFRONT. Pool table. CHILDREN over 10 welcome. NO SMOKING.
**Rates:** S OR D $65 DAILY.
**Reservations:** (206) 784-0539 MONDAY THROUGH FRIDAY 9 A.M. TO 5 P.M. PACIFIC TIME.

## SNOHOMISH

Located 40 minutes from Seattle, this 28 room historically identified Victorian mansion is ideally situated within walking distance to antique shops, restaurants, and galleries. A complimentary riding tour is given to all guests of historic Snohomish with its displays of antiquity and diversity of architectural styling of the homes built at the turn of the century. Brass beds, Victorian furnishings. Even its own art gallery. Accommodations include: A) the Queen Anne Room offers relaxing comfort with queen-sized bed, FIREPLACE in room, wicker table and chairs, sitting area, private bath and B) the Floral Bouquet Room offers the comfort of two twin beds in a light airy room with white wicker couch and sitting area, private bath. Crib is available. Full breakfast. No resident pets. PIANO. Children of all ages welcome. NO SMOKING.
**Rates:** S $40, D $45 DAILY.
**Reservations:** (206) 784-0539 MONDAY THROUGH FRIDAY 9 A.M. TO 5 P.M. PACIFIC TIME.

## WESTPORT

The main house where guests may relax by the fire in the library or enjoy breakfast or afternoon tea in the dining room is furnished with antiques, many of them for sale. Accommodations include: A) second floor, five guestrooms with double accommodations and a small sitting room; B) adjoining the main house are three rooms with doors opening onto the HOT TUB deck; and C) four guest cottages can accommodate from 4 to 14 guests and have completely furnished kitchens. The largest has a private covered deck and fireplace; the smallest is a cozy studio apartment. On premises bakery will provide a "no host" breakfast on request or guests may have continental breakfast in the main dining room. Located 2 hours from Seattle, on the OCEAN on 8 secluded acres in the heart of Westport. Badminton, volleyball, and horseshoes. Wooded paths, picnic and barbecue facilities. HORSE and horse trailer facilities. Fish and clam cleaning stations. No pets in rooms. Within minutes of flocks of sand pipers, gray whale migrations, and parading pelicans. Miles of sandy beaches. Children welcome. SMOKERS are welcome in B rooms.
**Rates:** A & B) $45-$75 AND C) $45-$190.
**Reservations:** (206) 784-0539 MONDAY THROUGH FRIDAY 9 A.M. TO 5 P.M. PACIFIC TIME.

# 10

# Canada

☐ **Quebec**
☐ **British Columbia**

# QUEBEC

## LAURENTIAN MOUNTAINS
### SUITE ADELE AREA

This country home with high vaulted ceilings, walls of African walnut, floor to ceiling living room windows, fireplace, and rich indoor foliage is a LAKEFRONT property. It is a 15 minute drive to the village of Suite Adele for restaurants, shopping, galleries, and nightlife. Hostess is a former innkeeper of German heritage. A gourmet cook, she delights in offering guests their dinner meal at reasonable prices. Accommodations include: A) two rooms each with double beds, one with toilet and washbasin and the other with washbasin and B) twin beds. ONE DOG resides here. German and French are spoken here. CHILDREN over 6 welcome.
**Rates:** A) D $50 AND B) D $55 DAILY. CANADIAN DOLLARS.
**Reservations:** (514) 738-9410 MONDAY THROUGH FRIDAY 9 A.M. TO 7 P.M.; SUMMER MONTHS, MONDAY THROUGH SUNDAY 9 A.M. TO 7 P.M.

## GREATER MONTREAL
### MONTREAL
### DOWNTOWN

This seven room lower duplex features antique furniture, PIANO, and fireplace. Books, music, politics, and sports are subjects easily discussed with this host family. Hostess, French Canadian and fluent in English, heads the library at the city's largest TV station. One son, an avid cyclist, studies at the university. Their CAT completes this household. It is a half block from a subway station. Tennis courts on this street. PIANO. Bikes available.
**Rates:** S $35, D $50 DAILY. CANADIAN DOLLARS.
**Reservations:** (514) 738-9410 MONDAY THROUGH FRIDAY 9 A.M. TO 7 P.M.; SUMMER MONTHS, MONDAY THROUGH SUNDAY 9 A.M. TO 7 P.M.

OPPOSITE MOUNT ROYAL PARK — This luxury apartment compound, an architectural gem, lies opposite Mount Royal Park and offers a magnificent view of the city and river. Joggers have a beautiful run awaiting them. Hostess' large apartment offers the warmth of a crackling fireplace, fine furnishings, and much coziness. She is an importer who speaks French fluently and is an expert skier with a ski chalet where guests may also book a room. Accommodtions include a double bed with adjoining bathroom. Parking available on the compound's premises. Air conditioning available in the apartment. Location is accessible by public transportation.
**Rates:** D $65 DAILY. CANADIAN DOLLARS.

**Reservations:** (514) 738-9410 MONDAY THROUGH FRIDAY 9 A.M. TO 7 P.M.; SUMMER MONTHS, MONDAY THROUGH SUNDAY 9 A.M. TO 7 P.M.

## PLATEAU MONT ROYAL

NEAR ST. LOUIS SQUARE — An unusual, remodeled two story Victorian era greystone just steps from the lovely St. Louis Square. Spiral staircase in skylit (indoor) patio adjoining the double guestroom with private bathroom. Hostess a multitalented Montreal personality, actress, model, and writer; she enjoys entertaining regularly. Her flamboyant kitchen overflows with exotic utensils brought back from her worldwide travels. Two small DOGS will welcome you. St. Denis and Prince Arthur streets are a stone's throw away. Metro (subway), Sherbrooke. French is spoken here. Smoking is permitted, but not if other guests are sensitive. **Rates:** D $75 DAILY. CANADIAN DOLLARS.
**Reservations:** (514) 738-9410 MONDAY THROUGH FRIDAY 9 A.M. TO 7 P.M.; SUMMER MONTHS, MONDAY THROUGH SUNDAY 9 A.M. TO 7 P.M.

NEAR ST. LOUIS SQUARE — This completely renovated three story greystone overlooks St. Louis Square in Montreal's Latin Quarter district (Plateau Mont Royal). This home features fireplace, many Oriental rugs, large armchairs in chintz fabrics, and objects d'art from world travels. Accommodations include: A) double bed with private bathroom, antique furniture, brass headboard, quilt spread and B) room with sofabed can be used to accommodate third member of family. Hostess is of Polish origin and speaks Polish, German, French, and English fluently. Two DOGS (Spaniels) complete the household. Take in St. Denis and Prince Arthur Streets as well as St. Laurent Boulevard, all part of this neighborhood. Air conditioning. Accessible by public transportation. CHILDREN over 7 welcome.
**Rates:** A) D $65 DAILY. CANADIAN DOLLARS.
**Reservations:** (514) 738-9410 MONDAY THROUGH FRIDAY 9 A.M. TO 7 P.M.; SUMMER MONTHS, MONDAY THROUGH SUNDAY 9 A.M. TO 7 P.M.

## SNOWDON

VICTORIA — An eight room bright, high ceilinged Georgian style home. Some Victorian antiques and Canadian furniture. Hostess is a former music librarian turned coordinator of Montreal Bed & Breakfast. Accommodations include: A) single bed, shared bath; B) double bed, shared bath; and C) double and single bed, shared bath. Usually only two rooms are rented at one time. Close to subway system (downtown in 12 minutes). Metro (subway), Snowdon. Safe street parking available. St. Joseph's Oratory and the Wax Museum are within walking distance.

French is spoken here. CHILDREN over 5 welcome. NONSMOKERS ONLY.
**Rates:** S $40, D $55, T $75 DAILY. CANADIAN DOLLARS.
**Reservations:** (514) 738-9410 MONDAY THROUGH FRIDAY 9 A.M. TO 7 P.M.; SUMMER MONTHS, MONDAY THROUGH SUNDAY 9 A.M. TO 7 P.M.

Large, corner property, Georgian style home, filled with family treasures and a wonderful collection of Canadian art. Patio and attractive garden furniture can be used by the guests. Hostess is a former travel agent who now lets the world come to her. Accommodations include: A) single bed, shared bath; B) double bed, shared bath; and C) twin beds, shared bath. It is a 5 minute walk to Snowdon subway. On the street parking. English and French are spoken here. CHILDREN over 8 welcome.
**Rates:** A) S $35, B) D $55, C) D $50 DAILY. CANADIAN DOLLARS.
**Reservations:** (514) 738-9410 MONDAY THROUGH FRIDAY 9 A.M. TO 7 P.M.; SUMMER MONTHS, MONDAY THROUGH SUNDAY 9 A.M. TO 7 P.M.

# BRITISH COLUMBIA

## VANCOUVER ISLAND
### DUNCAN

Nineteenth century country manor house and 130 acres working sheep farm. Quiet, secluded valley, mountain stream, natural homegrown food including bread, butter, and eggs. Large rooms and log fires, all meals available as a package.

**Rates:** S $38, D $55, ADDITIONAL ADULT $38, CHILD $15 DAILY.
**Reservations:** (604)595-BEDS -595-2337. APRIL THROUGH SEPTEMBER 7 A.M. - 8 P.M. PACIFIC DAYLIGHT TIME, MONDAY THROUGH SATURDAY. OCTOBER THROUGH MARCH, REDUCED HOURS. MACHINE WILL ANSWER. YOUR CALL WILL BE RETURNED.

## VANCOUVER ISLAND

This old fishing lodge has four guest rooms which share two baths, all overlook the warm lake-fed river. Stroll the seven wooded and landscaped acres. Breakfast with fresh eggs, homemade jams, and rich coffee sitting on the wraparound veranda. Fish, play croquet and horseshoes. Walk the Cowichan River footpath or take an easy drive to the Chemainus murals and Forestry Museum. NO SMOKING.

**Rates:** S $35, D $45-$50, TWIN D $55 DAILY.
**Reservations:** (604)595-BEDS -595-2337. APRIL THROUGH SEPTEMBER 7 A.M. - 8 P.M. PACIFIC DAYLIGHT TIME, MONDAY THROUGH SATURDAY. OCTOBER THROUGH MARCH, REDUCED HOURS. MACHINE WILL ANSWER. YOUR CALL WILL BE RETURNED.

## MAYNE ISLAND
### CAMPBELL BAY

CAMPBELL BAY ROAD — A 1900 Victorian house, nestled high on the shore of Canpbell Bay, a sheltered pocket inlet on Mayne Island. The home is filled with antiques and each guestroom has its own features. Accommodations include: A) large double bed with French Provincial furnishings and woodburning heater, large French doors open onto grounds, private bath, view of meadow and bay; B) double bed with country antiques and grounds, view of meadow and bay; and C) twin bed with country antiques. B and C, two rooms share one bath. Fine dining in the evenings, featuring fresh farm produce and herbs picked from the garden to enhance any exotic dish. Docking and moorage facilities available. Close to excellent salmon fishing in Active Pass. Small airport on island for light planes. TENNIS COURT on grounds. Both sail and power boat available. Less than 90 minutes from both Vancouver or Victoria. Complimentary ferry pickup service. Host and hostess are

interested in racing pigeons, genetics, and gourmet cooking. CATS live here. CHILDREN over 12 welcome. NO SMOKING.
**Rates:** A) S $70, D $75, EXTRA ADULT $20; B) S $49, D $54; AND C) S $43, D $48 DAILY. CANADIAN DOLLARS.
**Reservations:** (604)595-BEDS -595-2337. APRIL THROUGH SEPTEMBER 7 A.M. - 8 P.M. PACIFIC DAYLIGHT TIME, MONDAY THROUGH SATURDAY. OCTOBER THROUGH MARCH, REDUCED HOURS. MACHINE WILL ANSWER. YOUR CALL WILL BE RETURNED.

## CAMPBELL RIVER

BIRCH STREET — Charming older home nestled in an acre of dogwood and pine trees. Centrally located, within walking distance of the beach, restaurants, downtown, swimming pool, tennis courts, and the neighborhood pub. In winter, skiing is only an hour away. Host is a teacher and offers fishing charters and guiding. Both hosts are interested in fishing, writing, hiking, painting, skiing, and beachcombing. Double accommodations. Two CATS. SMOKING in designated areas.
**Rates:** S $30, D $40, ADDITIONAL ADULT $10 DAILY. CANADIAN DOLLARS.
**Reservations:** (604)595-BEDS -595-2337. APRIL THROUGH SEPTEMBER 7 A.M. - 8 P.M. PACIFIC DAYLIGHT TIME, MONDAY THROUGH SATURDAY. OCTOBER THROUGH MARCH, REDUCED HOURS. MACHINE WILL ANSWER. YOUR CALL WILL BE RETURNED.

## COOMBS
### MAIN HIGHWAY

ALBERN HIGHWAY — Country home on 21 acres contains your own spacious living quarters. The ground floor entrance opening into the kitchen is supplied with choice of breakfast items that includes farm fresh eggs. Double accommodations available. The suite contains living room with fireplace, bedroom, bath, and recreation room with hide-a-bed. Two DOGS in residence and only PET DOGS welcome. This home is within a 15 minute drive to beaches, fishing, and most other recreational entertainment. HANDICAPPED ACCESSIBLE. Pool table and picnic area. CHILDREN over 12 welcome. NONSMOKERS only.
**Rates:** S $30, D $40 DAILY. CANADIAN DOLLARS.
**Reservations:** (604)595-BEDS -595-2337. APRIL THROUGH SEPTEMBER 7 A.M. - 8 P.M. PACIFIC DAYLIGHT TIME, MONDAY THROUGH SATURDAY. OCTOBER THROUGH MARCH, REDUCED HOURS. MACHINE WILL ANSWER. YOUR CALL WILL BE RETURNED.

## NANAIMAO
### DEPARTURE BAY

COSGROVE CRESCENT — This home is a 10 minute walk to the beach with an excellent golf course edging in the garden. Fireplace in the guest TV room. Accommodations include: A) double bed with private bath; B) queen bed with toilet and sink, shared shower; and C) bed/Chesterfield in TV room. Full breakfast; tea, coffee, and home baking in evenings. Laundry facilities. Controlled PETS welcome. Hosts are willing to pick up guests at ferry and bus depot. Boating, salmon fishing charter can be arranged; swimming, golfing, hiking all within a few minutes from home. Come and enjoy the Nanaimo Festival—"Shakespeare Plus" in summer. NONSMOKERS preferred. One CAT. CHILDREN over 2 welcome.
**Rates:** S $28, D $38 DAILY. FAMILY RATES. 10% DISCOUNT 4 DAYS OR MORE. CANADIAN DOLLARS.
**Reservations:** (604)595-BEDS -595-2337. APRIL THROUGH SEPTEMBER 7 A.M. - 8 P.M. PACIFIC DAYLIGHT TIME, MONDAY THROUGH SATURDAY. OCTOBER THROUGH MARCH, REDUCED HOURS. MACHINE WILL ANSWER. YOUR CALL WILL BE RETURNED.

### NANOOSE BAY

Modern bi-level home; secluded, serne. Stroll, swim, or relax on safe, sandy beach. Enjoy sunrises, sunsets, and sealife. One mile to marina, pub, cafe and dining room. Excellent salmon fishing. Accommodations include; self-contained suite with king bed, private bath, full kitchen, living room with log fireplace, TV, deck and water view. Cots, crib, and highchair available. SMOKING in designated areas only. Children and leashed pets welcome.
**Rates:** S $45, D $50, K $60 DAILY.
**Reservations:** (604)595-BEDS -595-2337. APRIL THROUGH SEPTEMBER 7 A.M. - 8 P.M. PACIFIC DAYLIGHT TIME, MONDAY THROUGH SATURDAY. OCTOBER THROUGH MARCH, REDUCED HOURS. MACHINE WILL ANSWER. YOUR CALL WILL BE RETURNED.

### PARKSVILLE

A modern home on a quiet cul-de-sac in a lovely treed setting. This attractive home offers a choice of three upstairs bedrooms, one with queen bed and private bath, others with double bed, shared bath. Enjoy the family room with fireplace, games, and patio. Walking distance to shopping, beach, tennis courts, and community park. Centrally located to Qualicum Beach, Cathedral Grove, Long Beach, Campbell River, and Nanaimo. English breakfast with homemade delectables served to 11 A.M.
**Rates:** S $25, D (SHARED BATH) $35, D (PRIVATE BATH) $40, CHILDREN $5 DAILY.

**Reservations:** (604)595-BEDS -595-2337. APRIL THROUGH SEPTEMBER 7 A.M. - 8 P.M. PACIFIC DAYLIGHT TIME, MONDAY THROUGH SATURDAY. OCTOBER THROUGH MARCH, REDUCED HOURS. MACHINE WILL ANSWER. YOUR CALL WILL BE RETURNED.

## PORT ALBERNI
### MCCOY LAKE AREA

STIRLINE ARM DRIVE — You are invited to enjoy a country home and farm. Eat breakfast on the sundeck and later take a walk to visit the calves and the garden. This home has an interesting 1899 genuine musical grandfather clock. From Port Alberni, you can take a trip on the M.V. Lady Rose to the west coast and Broken Islands and see the fish hatchery. Hostess is a reflexologist. Both hosts are interested in flying, hiking, skiing, and gardening. Double accommodations. One CAT and one DOG. NO SMOKING.
**Rates:** S $30, D $40, CHILDREN $15 DAILY. CANADIAN DOLLARS.
**Reservations:** (604)595-BEDS -595-2337. APRIL THROUGH SEPTEMBER 7 A.M. 8 P.M. PACIFIC DAYLIGHT TIME, MONDAY THROUGH SATURDAY. OCTOBER THROUGH MARCH, REDUCED HOURS. MACHINE WILL ANSWER. YOUR CALL WILL BE RETURNED.

## UCLUELET

Lovely waterfront home on a small island, accessible by causeway (drive over). A view from every window, large living room, fireplace, books, games, TV, recreation room with pool table. Use of rowboat by arrangement. Groceries supplied. Guests make breakfast at their leisure. Double rooms share guest bath. NO SMOKING.
**Rates:** S $30-$40, D $35-$45, ADDITIONAL PERSON $15 DAILY.
**Reservations:** (604)595-BEDS -595-2337. APRIL THROUGH SEPTEMBER 7 A.M. - 8 P.M. PACIFIC DAYLIGHT TIME, MONDAY THROUGH SATURDAY. OCTOBER THROUGH MARCH, REDUCED HOURS. MACHINE WILL ANSWER. YOUR CALL WILL BE RETURNED.

## VICTORIA

Period stucco house in parkland setting close to golf course and jogging paths, only minutes to downtown. Views Olympic Mountains in the dining room while enjoying gourmet breakfast; private parking off-street; and English gardens. Accommodations include: A) carpeted bedroom with exquisite double bed, burled walnut antique suite, roses wallpaper, beautiful antique vanity, private TV, shared bath with tub and shower and B) carpeted bedroom with double bed, floral wallpaper, shared bath with tub and shower. Hostess is English and also speaks French and German. Her hobbies include bridge, skiing, gardening, and walking. One resident CAT. Children of all ages welcome.

**Rates:** S $30, D $35 DAILY, U.S. DOLLARS.
**Reservations:** (206) 784-0539 MONDAY THROUGH FRIDAY 9 A.M.
TO 5 P.M. PACIFIC TIME.

Two queen bedrooms offered in this lovely home just 15 minutes from downtown. Hosts offer complimentary use of two bikes and salmon fishing on their boat at only $10 per hour with all gear supplied. Resident parrot and cockateel. Hearty breakfasts are served. Guestrooms have a shared bath; one bedroom is decorated with feminine touches, the other with a more masculine style. CHILDREN over 10 welcome. SMOKING permitted on sundeck with view of the Strait of Juan de Fuca.
**Rates:** S $35, D $40 DAILY. U.S. DOLLARS.
**Reservations:** (206) 784-0539 MONDAY THROUGH FRIDAY 9 A.M.
TO 5 P.M. PACIFIC TIME.

## ARBUTUS COVE

ARBUTUS ROAD — A unique nineteenth Century house, 2 acres of OCEAN FRONT, sandy cove, tall trees, garden, and wildlife. The house shares the property with another B&B house. Simply furnished with Canadian antiques, the cottage has two bedrooms upstairs with two double and single beds. Downstairs has complete kitchen, dining room, four piece bath, dressing room, and living room with woodburning stove and fireplace. Full breakfast served in host's home which is also furnished with antiques. Located on scenic Marine Drive in a lovely private residential area close to the University of Victoria. This house is for the private use of individual groups. Hosts are interested in sailing, cooking, music, theater, gardening, people, and pets. NO SMOKING.
**Rates:** D $70, ADDITIONAL ADULTS $15, CHILDREN AGES 1 THROUGH 6 $5, 7 THROUGH 11 $10 DAILY. CANADIAN DOLLARS.
**Reservations:** (604)595-BEDS -595-2337. APRIL THROUGH SEPTEMBER 7 A.M. - 8 P.M. PACIFIC DAYLIGHT TIME, MONDAY THROUGH SATURDAY. OCTOBER THROUGH MARCH, REDUCED HOURS. MACHINE WILL ANSWER. YOUR CALL WILL BE RETURNED.

## BRENTWOOD

BARBARA PLACE — A newer, spacious home near Butchart Gardens in Brentwood. Large English pub style recreation room with fireplace, bar, and games are for your use. Host is a chef and breakfast is quite an event (you may even have fresh garden grown strawberries when in season). If salmon fishing or golfing suits your taste, tours can be arranged. Ideal for families. Baby equipment available. Hosts are interested in bridge, cards, flower arranging, and gardening. They have one CAT. Double and queen beds. HANDICAPPED ACCESSIBLE.
**Rates:** S $30, D $45, QUEEN WITH EN SUITE $50, CHILDREN AGES 2 THROUGH 11 $10 DAILY. CANADIAN DOLLARS.

**Reservations:** (604)595-BEDS -595-2337. APRIL THROUGH SEPTEMBER 7 A.M. - 8 P.M. PACIFIC DAYLIGHT TIME, MONDAY THROUGH SATURDAY. OCTOBER THROUGH MARCH, REDUCED HOURS. MACHINE WILL ANSWER. YOUR CALL WILL BE RETURNED.

**CATHEDRAL HILL**

BURDETT AND BLANSHARD — Built in the early 1900s, this house is a restored guesthome with seven bedrooms. A delicious breakfast is served in the spacious dining room. This character home is ideal for guests who want to be within walking distance from downtown as parking is limited. It is only 7 1/2 blocks from the Seattle ferry and 4 blocks from the bus depot. Hosts are interested in art, music, and golf. They have one Siamese CAT. Accommodations include: A) single; B) double; C) queen; and D) twin beds. SMOKING allowed in designated areas. **Rates:** A) S $35; B) D $45; C) D $50; AND D) D $50, CHILDREN 1 THROUGH 6 $5 AND 7 THROUGH 11 $7.50 DAILY. CANADIAN DOLLARS.
**Reservations:** (604)595-BEDS -595-2337. APRIL THROUGH SEPTEMBER 7 A.M. - 8 P.M. PACIFIC DAYLIGHT TIME, MONDAY THROUGH SATURDAY. OCTOBER THROUGH MARCH, REDUCED HOURS. MACHINE WILL ANSWER. YOUR CALL WILL BE RETURNED.

**ELK LAKE**

PATRICIA BAY HIGHWAY (HIGHWAY 17) — This beautiful house is a delightful LAKESIDE B&B, just 15 minutes from beautiful downtown Victoria. They are situated on a small hobby farm across from lovely Elk Lake. The lake and its parks provide something for everyone from swimming and canoeing to hiking, windsurfing, and picnicing. Accommodations include four guestrooms, all with iron and brass double beds, decorated in old country fashion. The home also offers a parlor for the guests' use which includes a cozy fireplace, PIANO, TV, and stereo. There are two full bathrooms to share. Breakfast is a treat, a full country style meal featuring fresh fruit, baking, and homemade preserves. This home is conveniently located from downtown, Butchart Gardens. The airport and ferries are all less than 20 minutes away. Hosts enjoy bridge, karate, and needlework. Horses available. Children welcome. **Rates:** S $35-$45, D $40-$50, CHILDREN AGES 2 THROUGH 12 $5 EXTRA DAILY. CANADIAN DOLLARS.
**Reservations:** (604)595-BEDS -595-2337. APRIL THROUGH SEPTEMBER 7 A.M. - 8 P.M. PACIFIC DAYLIGHT TIME, MONDAY THROUGH SATURDAY. OCTOBER THROUGH MARCH, REDUCED HOURS. MACHINE WILL ANSWER. YOUR CALL WILL BE RETURNED.

## ESQUIMALT

A private suite in a WATERFRONT home with queen-sized brass bed, JACUZZI, living room, fireplace, and sunroom. The location affords superb views, immediate access to a rocky beach and garden. It is within walking distance to shops, parks, restaurants, and the Olde England Inn or take the bus conveniently located at the door for these attractions that are further away. The atmosphere is friendly and breakfast generous. Served at leisure in your sunroom off the bedroom. Hosts are interested in gardening and investments. NO CHILDREN. NONSMOKERS ONLY.
**Rates:** D $70 DAILY. CANADIAN DOLLARS.
**Reservations:** (604)595-BEDS -595-2337. APRIL THROUGH SEPTEMBER 7 A.M. - 8 P.M. PACIFIC DAYLIGHT TIME, MONDAY THROUGH SATURDAY. OCTOBER THROUGH MARCH, REDUCED HOURS. MACHINE WILL ANSWER. YOUR CALL WILL BE RETURNED.

## FAIRFIELD

CORNER COOK AND DALLAS ROAD — Enjoy the comfort and privacy of your own elegant suite in one of Victoria's traditional Tudor mansions. Gaze out your window at the Strait of Juan de Fuca and the United States' Olympic Mountains. If you are an early riser, you may see seals, killer whales, or sea otters frolicking offshore. Listen to the songbirds. Watch an eagle cruise by. Help yourself to breakfast from your private, well-stocked kitchen. You are minutes away from the attractions of downtown Victoria. Stroll there through the beautiful Beacon Hill Park. In the evenings, relax by your FIREPLACE. This home was built in 1912 on property once owned by Governor Sir James Douglas, purchased from the Hudson's Bay Company. Emily Carr painted many canvases of the area, including the BEACH and bluffs across the street from the mansion. One small DOG and one CAT reside here. SMALL DOGS WELCOME. There are 14 rooms with private baths and double accommodations available. Cots and cribs are also available. Hosts enjoy tennis, golf, and heritage conservation. NONSMOKERS preferred.
**Rates:** S $65, D $95 DAILY. CANADIAN DOLLARS.
**Reservations:** (604)595-BEDS -595-2337. APRIL THROUGH SEPTEMBER 7 A.M. - 8 P.M. PACIFIC DAYLIGHT TIME, MONDAY THROUGH SATURDAY. OCTOBER THROUGH MARCH, REDUCED HOURS. MACHINE WILL ANSWER. YOUR CALL WILL BE RETURNED.

LEONARD STREET — While visiting beautiful Victoria, stay at this 1911 Victorian style home, located in a desirable district. Beacon Hill Park and TENNIS COURT across the street. It is 2 blocks from BEACH and ocean walking paths, ideal for joggers. Walk through the park to city center, Empress Hotel (famous for their high tea), Provincial Museum, theaters, and shopping. Beautifully decorated bedrooms, with very

comfortable queen-sized beds and color TV. Two guestrooms share a bedroom. Sumptuous four course breakfast is cheerfully served on china and silverware. Secluded backyard. Other services provided: free pick up from downtown ferries and bus depot, free bikes available, off-street parking. Dutch and German spoken. Hosts are interested in gardening, music, and cooking. PIANO. NO SMOKING.
**Rates:** S $45, D $55 DAILY. CANADIAN DOLLARS.
**Reservations:** (604)595-BEDS -595-2337. APRIL THROUGH SEPTEMBER 7 A.M. - 8 P.M. PACIFIC DAYLIGHT TIME, MONDAY THROUGH SATURDAY. OCTOBER THROUGH MARCH, REDUCED HOURS. MACHINE WILL ANSWER. YOUR CALL WILL BE RETURNED.

PAKINGTON (NEAR COOK) — Charming, completely modern, 1930s home with a touch of class. On a delightful tree-lined residential street. Close to everything. Accommodations include two bedrooms with queen-sized beds. They are beautifully furnished. Guests share the bathroom. Hosts are professionals, teacher and nurse respectively, who really enjoy giving superb service. They are interested in gardening, cooking, and fishing. Guests have exclusive use of large, comfortable living room with cozy fireplace. Excellent shopping, banks and restaurants are only a few blocks away. Full breakfasts are served in the dining room by gourmet cook. Visit is guaranteed to be a memorable experience. One DOG in residence. NONSMOKERS PREFERRED.
**Rates:** S $40, D $55 DAILY. CANADIAN DOLLARS.
**Reservations:** (604)595-BEDS -595-2337. APRIL THROUGH SEPTEMBER 7 A.M. - 8 P.M. PACIFIC DAYLIGHT TIME, MONDAY THROUGH SATURDAY. OCTOBER THROUGH MARCH, REDUCED HOURS. MACHINE WILL ANSWER. YOUR CALL WILL BE RETURNED.

ROBERSTON — This B&B house nestled on Gonzales Bay (tidal saltwater) is in a character neighborhood. The home sits on a bluff overlooking a sandy BEACH. Hosts offer spacious, friendly, and affordable accommodations. They are semiretired and the B&B is their living. Hosts enjoy a friendly game of bridge. Their CAT's name is Vicky. Hostess is fluent in German. Accommodations include: A) two double rooms with private baths, separate entrances overlooking the ocean and B) small room with two single beds and shared bathroom. Cooked breakfast is included. CHILDREN over 12 welcome. NONSMOKERS PREFERRED.
**Rates:** A) D $65; B) D $55; AND C) D $40; SINGLE SUBTRACT $5 FOR EACH ROOM DAILY. CANADIAN DOLLARS.
**Reservations:** (604)595-BEDS -595-2337. APRIL THROUGH SEPTEMBER 7 A.M. - 8 P.M. PACIFIC DAYLIGHT TIME, MONDAY THROUGH SATURDAY. OCTOBER THROUGH MARCH, REDUCED HOURS. MACHINE WILL ANSWER. YOUR CALL WILL BE RETURNED.

## GONZALES BAY AREA

CRESCENT ROAD — Relax and enjoy your vacation in this beautiful, quiet home. Your suite has a separate entrance, a morning room where you will be served breakfast, a comfortable living room with fireplace, a bedroom with twin beds or "put together" king-sized bed, a bathroom with tub and shower, a patio area with spring or summer flowers, and direct yard access to a sandy BEACH. There are two CATS and one small DOG. Hosts are interested in boating gardening, and golfing. NO SMOKING.
**Rates:** S $40, D $55 DAILY. S $240, D $330 WEEKLY, 7TH NIGHT FREE. CANADIAN DOLLARS.
**Reservations:** (604)595-BEDS -595-2337. APRIL THROUGH SEPTEMBER 7 A.M. - 8 P.M. PACIFIC DAYLIGHT TIME, MONDAY THROUGH SATURDAY. OCTOBER THROUGH MARCH, REDUCED HOURS. MACHINE WILL ANSWER. YOUR CALL WILL BE RETURNED.

## JAMES BAY

ST. ANDREWS — This charming 1912 Heritage style home is conveniently located in the historical James Bay neighborhood, close to the home of the late famous West Coast artist and authoress, Emily Carr. It is a 15 minute walk to downtown, Parliament Building, Provincial Museum, restaurants, and tea rooms; 5 minute walk to ocean front and beaches. One block to beautiful Beacon Hill Park and the bus stop. Easy access to "Princess Marguerite" and "M.V. Coho" ferries to the state of Washington. Accommodations include: A) two rooms with twin beds and B) four poster double bed, FIREPLACE, and balcony. The three guestrooms are separate from the family quarters and share a guest bathroom. A fresh fruit basket and flowers are placed in the rooms. A full and hearty breakfast is served from 8 to 9 A.M. Hosts are interested in reading. the arts, gardening, and travel. PIANO. CHILDREN 16 and up. NONSMOKERS only.
**Rates:** S $40, A) TWIN $50, B) D $55 DAILY. S $200, A) TWIN $280, B) D $300 WEEKLY. CANADIAN DOLLARS.
**Reservations:** (604)595-BEDS -595-2337. APRIL THROUGH SEPTEMBER 7 A.M. 8 P.M. PACIFIC DAYLIGHT TIME, MONDAY THROUGH SATURDAY. OCTOBER THROUGH MARCH, REDUCED HOURS. MACHINE WILL ANSWER. YOUR CALL WILL BE RETURNED.

## LANGFORD

MILLSTREAM ROAD — An old English style country pub. Hosts offer you cozy accommodations. This guesthouse is separate from the main house. The bedroom features a canopy bed and a private bathroom with shower. Hide-a-bed is also available. The parlor is furnished with antiques and memorabilia. A full or continental breakfast is served from the main

house to your own tables. The home is approximately 11 miles from the city center, surrounded by beautiful forest. There is easy accessibility to good salmon fishing, golfing, and a recreational park. CHILDREN 17 and up welcome.
**Rates:** S $30, D $60, ADDITIONAL ADULT $15 DAILY. CANADIAN DOLLARS.
**Reservations:** (604)595-BEDS -595-2337. APRIL THROUGH SEPTEMBER 7 A.M. - 8 P.M. PACIFIC DAYLIGHT TIME, MONDAY THROUGH SATURDAY. OCTOBER THROUGH MARCH, REDUCED HOURS. MACHINE WILL ANSWER. YOUR CALL WILL BE RETURNED.

## OAK BAY BORDER

REDFERN OFF OAK BAY — An older home renovated with love and with a respect for the past, located close to Victoria's beautiful inner city. Hosts strive to live up to their name cultivating a casual and relaxed atmosphere. This semiretired couple are former entertainers and share an appreciation for fine cuisine, good music, and ready humor. Delectable breakfasts are served on the main floor overlooking a patio garden. Guests are encouraged to share the hosts' living room with cozy fireplace on cooler evenings and/or tinker on the baby grand PIANO. This residence has only two bedrooms (twin beds) reserved for guests. Both rooms are tasteful and privately located on the second floor along with the guest bathroom. The home is convenient to most tourist attractions; 1 mile to the ocean; 1 1/2 miles to downtown; 2 1/2 miles to the University of Victoria.
**Rates:** S $40, D $50 DAILY. CANADIAN DOLLARS.
**Reservations:** (604)595-BEDS -595-2337. APRIL THROUGH SEPTEMBER 7 A.M. - 8 P.M. PACIFIC DAYLIGHT TIME, MONDAY THROUGH SATURDAY. OCTOBER THROUGH MARCH, REDUCED HOURS. MACHINE WILL ANSWER. YOUR CALL WILL BE RETURNED.

## PORTAGE INLET

PORTAGE ROAD — A delightful WATERFRONT home, overlooking Portage Inlet, with an acre of garden. Each guest has a comfortable king-sized or twin room, one with private bathroom, two sharing a guest bathroom. Color TV in every room. Private entrance. Breakfast served between 8 and 9 A.M. Hosts specialize in organic home grown food such as their own fruits and juices, homemade jams, jellies, and ketchup. They also grind their own flour from wheat to make bread, scones, and pancakes. They heat with wood; solar panels heat the water in the summer. They do not spray with pesticides and have an abundance of wildlife that reside on their property such as swans, Canada Geese, pheasants, eagles, and ducks. Host are interested in flying, and bridge and chess playing. Two CATS. SMOKING in one room only.
**Rates:** S $40, D $55 DAILY. CANADIAN DOLLARS.

**Reservations:** (604)595-BEDS -595-2337. APRIL THROUGH SEPTEMBER 7 A.M. - 8 P.M. PACIFIC DAYLIGHT TIME, MONDAY THROUGH SATURDAY. OCTOBER THROUGH MARCH, REDUCED HOURS. MACHINE WILL ANSWER. YOUR CALL WILL BE RETURNED.

## ROCKLAND DISTRICT

PEMBERTON ROAD — An architecturally designed six bedroom, four bathroom home. It is 1 block from Government House and Craigdarroch Castle. Walking distance to city center, the beach, Oak Bay Recreation Centre, the Art Gallery, and antique stores. Quick bus transportation to downtown. Bikes rented at reasonable rates. Fenced in backyard with climbing frame, tire swing, and sandbox. Babysitting may be booked in advance. Hosts are interested in camping, kayaking, and international travel. Two CATS. Double accommodations, twin beds, and cribs available. SMOKING allowed except in bedrooms.
**Rates:** S $30, D $45, WITH PRIVATE BATHS $50, CHILDREN 1 THROUGH 6 $5 AND 7 THROUGH 11 $7.50, CRIBS $5 DAILY. CANADIAN DOLLARS.
**Reservations:** (604)595-BEDS -595-2337. APRIL THROUGH SEPTEMBER 7 A.M. - 8 P.M. PACIFIC DAYLIGHT TIME, MONDAY THROUGH SATURDAY. OCTOBER THROUGH MARCH, REDUCED HOURS. MACHINE WILL ANSWER. YOUR CALL WILL BE RETURNED.

## ROYAL OAK

CAREY ROAD — This guesthome is located just minutes away from parks, tennis courts, lakes, beaches, and shopping centers. Both single or double bedrooms with private or shared bathroom. Host offers to share the garden with barbecue, picnic table, or sundeck where you will enjoy the view of the Olympic Mountain. Recreation room with TV and stereo is also available, along with laundry facilities. Breakfast is served between 7 and 10 A.M. Pickup from airport or ferry terminals can be arranged. Dutch and German spoken. Hosts are interested in walking and swimming. HANDICAPPED ACCESSIBLE.
**Rates:** S $30, D $45, CHILDREN 1 THROUGH 6 $5, 7 THROUGH 11 $7.50, ADDITIONAL ADULT $20 DAILY. CANADIAN DOLLARS.
**Reservations:** (604)595-BEDS -595-2337. APRIL THROUGH SEPTEMBER 7 A.M. - 8 P.M. PACIFIC DAYLIGHT TIME, MONDAY THROUGH SATURDAY. OCTOBER THROUGH MARCH, REDUCED HOURS. MACHINE WILL ANSWER. YOUR CALL WILL BE RETURNED.

## SAANICH PENINSULA

EAST STELLY'S CROSS ROAD — This home is in a rural setting on beautiful Saanich Peninsula. It is a 10 minute drive from the internationally famous Butchart Gardens and nearby airport and ferries to Vancouver or several of the Gulf Islands. Golf, tennis, swimming, and horse riding are available nearby. For the salmon fisherman, boat and tackle rental on the sheltered Saanich inlet. Hosts invite guests to relax with a cup of coffee or tea in their living room and the delicious full English style breakfast is served in the adjoining dining room. Accommodations include twin and double beds, also a rollaway, shared bathroom. NONSMOKERS ONLY. **Rates:** S $35, D $45, COT $15 EXTRA DAILY. CANADIAN DOLLARS. **Reservations:** (604)595-BEDS -595-2337. APRIL THROUGH SEPTEMBER 7 A.M. - 8 P.M. PACIFIC DAYLIGHT TIME, MONDAY THROUGH SATURDAY. OCTOBER THROUGH MARCH, REDUCED HOURS. MACHINE WILL ANSWER. YOUR CALL WILL BE RETURNED.

TULIP AVENUE — There are two guestrooms in this modern home overlooking Colquitz River Park. Guests may feel free to use the large sundeck in a very private backyard. One room has double bed, the other has single bed and hide-a-bed (FIREPLACE also in this room). The bathroom is shared by the guests. Hosts welcome families and they find the arrangements very good as the children are in the next room thus giving the parents privacy. A small TV can be provided. Breakfast is served in spacious family dining room/kitchen. Full breakfast. Tea, coffee, and cookies in the room. Shopping centers and hospital located about 1 mile away and easy access to ferry terminal. Tennis and softball played in the park, childrens' playground and pleasant walking and jogging trails closeby. NONSMOKERS PREFERRED. One CAT. PIANO. **Rates:** S $35, D $45, ADDITIONAL ADULT $15, CHILDREN $7.50 DAILY. CANADIAN DOLLARS. **Reservations:** (604)595-BEDS -595-2337. APRIL THROUGH SEPTEMBER 7 A.M. - 8 P.M. PACIFIC DAYLIGHT TIME, MONDAY THROUGH SATURDAY. OCTOBER THROUGH MARCH, REDUCED HOURS. MACHINE WILL ANSWER. YOUR CALL WILL BE RETURNED.

## SAANICHTON

CENTRAL SAANICH ROAD — Large English Tudor home nestled in 4 acres on the Saanich Peninsula. Space to roam and relax. Close to airport, ferries and Butchart Gardens. Friendly family atmosphere. Discover B&B in this "little bit of Olde England." Private entrance, private bathrooms. Two large bed sitting rooms. Queen-sized bed and remote TV. Full and continental breakfast served. Two CATS and two DOGS. CHILDREN over 12 welcome. NONSMOKERS ONLY. **Rates:** D $65 DAILY. CANADIAN DOLLARS. **Reservations:** (604)595-BEDS -595-2337. APRIL THROUGH SEPTEMBER 7 A.M.-8 P.M. PACIFIC DAYLIGHT TIME, MONDAY THROUGH SATURDAY. OCTOBER THROUGH MARCH, REDUCED HOURS. MACHINE WILL ANSWER. YOUR CALL WILL BE RETURNED.

ADMIRALS ROAD — Situated on a cozy BAY on Portage Inlet, this home offers a large self-contained suite ideal for families. You can feed the swans, Canadian geese, and ducks from the water's edge. The suite has two bedrooms with one double bed, twin-double bed, and hide-a-bed in the living room. Private bathrooms. Fireplace in living room, kitchen and water view dining room are all for your enjoyment. One DOG. Rowboat.
**Rates:** D $55, CHILDREN 1 THROUGH 6 $5, 7 THROUGH 11 $7.50, ADDITIONAL ADULT $15 DAILY. CANADIAN DOLLARS.
**Reservations:** (604)595-BEDS -595-2337. APRIL THROUGH SEPTEMBER 7 A.M. - 8 P.M. PACIFIC DAYLIGHT TIME, MONDAY THROUGH SATURDAY. OCTOBER THROUGH MARCH, REDUCED HOURS. MACHINE WILL ANSWER. YOUR CALL WILL BE RETURNED.

BEACH DRIVE — A large home located in one of the most beautiful areas of the provincial capital city. Located close to those West Coast wonders of tennis in January, beach walks and year-round jogging. It is 10 minutes from an excellent theater, the Art Gallery, antiquing, or a day at the Provincial Museum. Victoria also has many fine restaurants to tease your palate. The home is bedecked in Laura Ashley and furnished in Quebec pine and English antiques. The top floor of the home is yours —a bedroom with twin beds, en suite bathroom, and sitting room stocked with books, skylights, and a teddy bear too! Say good morning, read the papers, and enjoy an individually prepared breakfast, in bed if you like. Hosts are well-traveled and enjoy a sherry with the guests. A young child is well-received and easily accommodated here, as are well-behaved PETS. This home may be just your cup of tea!
**Rates:** S $55, D $60, CHILDREN THROUGH 6 $5 DAILY. CANADIAN DOLLARS.
**Reservations:** (604)595-BEDS -595-2337. APRIL THROUGH SEPTEMBER 7 A.M. - 8 P.M. PACIFIC DAYLIGHT TIME, MONDAY THROUGH SATURDAY. OCTOBER THROUGH MARCH, REDUCED HOURS. MACHINE WILL ANSWER. YOUR CALL WILL BE RETURNED.

DENMAN STREET — A comfortable home with a deck to enjoy the morning sun and a hearty breakfast. A fireplace in the front room adds to the ambiance. Accommodations include: A) double hide-a-bed, matching chair, TV and books and B) single bed, comfortable rocker, and good lighting. Guests share a large bathroom, and a shower is also available. A 5 to 10 minute drive will take you to a large shopping center, a good recreational center, or ocean beaches. One CAT. Hosts are interested in golfing and painting.
**Rates:** S $35, D $40 DAILY. CANADIAN DOLLARS.
**Reservations:** (604)595-BEDS -595-2337. APRIL THROUGH SEPTEMBER 7 A.M. - 8 P.M. PACIFIC DAYLIGHT TIME, MONDAY THROUGH

SATURDAY. OCTOBER THROUGH MARCH, REDUCED HOURS. MACHINE WILL ANSWER. YOUR CALL WILL BE RETURNED.

NEAR EMPRESS' HOTEL — This is an 1895 Victorian house with PIANO, located within walking distance to everything in Victoria. It is 4 blocks behind the famous Empress Hotel. Accommodations include four comfortable double guestrooms, shared baths. Great breakfasts served in formal dining room. Hospitality at its finest. Bikes available. NONSMOKERS only.
**Rates:** S $5-$40, D $40-$45 DAILY. U.S. DOLLARS.
**Reservations:** (206) 784-0539 MONDAY THROUGH FRIDAY 9 A.M. TO 5 P.M. PACIFIC TIME.

FORT STREET AND FOUL BAY ROAD — This bungalow, with spacious gardens, is located a mile from the Hillside Shopping Center, Willows Beach, and Oak Bay Village. Bus stop at the door! Your hosts practice the "Old County" traditions of B&B. Comfortable rooms, warm friendship, and generous breakfast will make your visit a memorable event. Accommodations include ground floor suite, private bathroom, and private entrance with A) twin and B) double beds. Hosts are interested in cooking, travel, and entertaining. CHILDREN over 12 welcome. NO SMOKING.
**Rates:** A) S $30, D $45 and B) S $40, D $50; ADDITIONAL ADULT $10 DAILY. CANADIAN DOLLARS.
**Reservations:** (604)595-BEDS -595-2337. APRIL THROUGH SEPTEMBER 7 A.M. - 8 P.M. PACIFIC DAYLIGHT TIME, MONDAY THROUGH SATURDAY. OCTOBER THROUGH MARCH, REDUCED HOURS. MACHINE WILL ANSWER. YOUR CALL WILL BE RETURNED.

VANCOUVER STREET — This B&B house built in 1892 is a designated heritage Victorian Italianate offering the warmth and comforts of home. The rooms are furnished with antiques and decorated with charm and delicate taste. Accommodations include: A) queen bed and 3/4 mahogany Victorian wallbed; B) twin bedded double; and C) two rooms each with cast iron and brass double bed. The four rooms share two baths. A full gourmet breakfast is served in the dining room. Hosts have interests in antique collecting, quilting, and French. The home is on a city bus route and located withing easy walking distance of the Inner Harbor, U.S. Ferries, Empress Hotel, Art Gallery, Provincial Museum, and more. One tabby CAT. CHILDREN over 12 welcome. NO SMOKING.
**Rates:** A) S $40, D $60; B) $55; AND C) S $40, D $50. ADDITIONAL ADULTS $15 DAILY. CANADIAN DOLLARS.
**Reservations:** (604)595-BEDS -595-2337. APRIL THROUGH SEPTEMBER 7 A.M. - 8 P.M. PACIFIC DAYLIGHT TIME. MONDAY THROUGH SATURDAY. OCTOBER THROUGH MARCH, REDUCED HOURS. MACHINE WILL ANSWER. YOUR CALL WILL BE RETURNED.

This beautifully restored turn-of-the-century home is within walking distance from downtown, Beacon Hill Park, and the waterfront. You will enjoy a delicious breakfast served by your hostess and her family. Hosts are interested in nursing and sports. Single and double beds available.
**Rates:** D $45, S $35 DAILY. CANADIAN DOLLARS.
**Reservations:** (604)595-BEDS -595-2337, APRIL THROUGH SEPTEMBER 7 A.M. - 8 P.M. PACIFIC DAYLIGHT TIME, MONDAY THROUGH SATURDAY. OCTOBER THROUGH MARCH, REDUCED HOURS. MACHINE WILL ANSWER. YOUR CALL WILL BE RETURNED.

# Appendix A

---

# Reservation Services

Alaska Private Lodging
1236 W. 10th Avenue
Anchorage, Alaska 99501
(907) 258-1717
Monday through Friday 9 A.M. to 5 P.M.

All Season Bed & Breakfast Agency
Box 5511, Stnd. B
Victoria, British Columbia V8R 6S4
Maureen Vesey
(604) 595-BEDS
Monday through Saturday 7 A.M. to 8 P.M. Pacific Daylight Time;
April through September. Reduced hours machine will answer,
your call will be returned, October through March.

American Family Inn Bed & Breakfast
Box 349
San Francisco, California 94101
Richard & Susan Kreibech
(415) 931-3083
Monday through Friday 9 A.M. to 5 P.M.

Bed & Breakfast of Rhode Island
Box 3291
Newport, Rhode Island 02840-3291
Joy Meiser
(401) 849-1298
Monday through Friday 9:00 A.M. to 5:30 P.M.; Saturday 9:00 A.M.
to 12:00 P.M., in season. Monday through Friday 9:00 A.M. to 5:30
P.M., off season.

Bed & Biscuits
Box 19664
Raleigh, North Carolina 27619
Ginger Moore
(919) 787-2109
Monday through Friday 9 A.M. to 8 P.M.

Bed & Breakfast Accommodations—Oregon Plus Bed & Breakfast
Oregon
Plus 5733 S.W. Dickinson Street
Portland, Oregon 97219
Marcelle Tebo
(593) 245-0642
(8:00 to 5:00.)

Bed & Breakfast Host Homes of Tennessee
Box 110227
Nashville, Tennessee 37222-0227
Fredda Odom
(615) 331-5244
Monday through Friday 9 A.M. to 5 P.M. (answering machine other
times).

Bed & Breakfast in Memphis
Box 41621
Memphis, Tennessee 38174
Helen Denton
(901) 726-5920
Monday through Friday 8 A.M. to 6 P.M.; Saturday and Sunday 1
P.M. to 4 P.M.

Bed & Breakfast International
151 Admore Road
Kensington, California 94707
Jean Brown
(415) 525-4569
Open 9 A.M. to 5 P.M.

Bed & Breakfast Marblehead and North Shore
54 Amherst Road
Beverly, Massachusetts 01915
Helena M. Champion
(617) 921-1336
Seven days a week, 7:00 A.M. to 9:00 A.M., 12:00 noon to 9:00 P.M.

Bed & Breakfast Network of New York
134 W. 32nd Street, Room 602
New York City, New York 10001
Leslie Goldberg
(212) 645-8134
Monday through Friday 8 A.M. to 6 P.M.

Bed & Breakfast of Milwaukee, Inc.
320 East Buffalo Street
Milwaukee, Wisconsin 53202
Barbara Gardner
(414) 271-beds
Monday through Friday 9 A.M. to 6 P.M. Central Time.

Bed & Breakfast of New Jersey
103 Godwin Avenue, Suite 132
Midland Park, New Jersey 07432
Aster Mould
(201) 444-7409
Monday through Friday 9 A.M. to 4 P.M.

Bed & Breakfast of Philadelphia
Box 680
Devon, Pennsylvania 19333-0680
C. Yarrow & S. Fullerton
(215) 688-1633
Mondays through Fridays 9:00 A.M. to 5:00 P.M.

Bed & Breakfast of Rochester
Box 444
Fairport, New York 14450
Beth Kinsman
(716) 223-8877
Monday through Friday 12 P.M. to 5 P.M.

Bed & Breakfast of Southeast Pennsylvania
Box 278, Road 1
Baro, Pennsylvania 19054
Joyce Stevenson
(215) 845-3526
Monday through Friday 8:00 A.M. to 8:00 P.M. (answering machine at other times.)

Bed & Breakfast of Southern California
1943 Sunny Crest Drive
Fullerton, California 92635
Joyce Garrison
(714) 738-8361
Monday through Friday 7 A.M. to 6 P.M. Pacific Time.

Bed & Breakfast of the Arkansas Ozarks
White River Landing, Inc.
Box 38, Route 1
Calico Rock, Arkansas 72519
Christian & Carolyn Eck
(501) 297-8764
Monday through Friday 8:00 A.M. to 12:00 P.M.

Bed & Breakfast Rocky Mountains
Box 804
Colorado Springs, Colorado 80901
Kate Peterson
(303) 630-3433
Monday through Friday 9:00 A.M. to 6:00 P.M., summer; Monday
through Friday, 1:00 P.M. to 6:00 P.M., nonsummer.

Bed & Breakfast Society of Texas
921 Heights Boulevard
Houston, Texas 77008
Marguerite Swanson
(713) 868-4654
Monday through Friday 7:30 A.M. to 9:00 P.M.; Saturday and
Sunday 8:00 A.M. to 5:00 P.M.

Bed & Breakfast Texas Style
4224 W. Red Bird Lane
Dallas, Texas 75237
Ruth Wilson
(214) 298-8586

Bed & Breakfast U.S.A., Ltd.
Box 606
Croton-on-hudson, New York 10520
Barbara & George Klein
(914) 271-6228
Monday through Friday 10 A.M. to 4 P.M., April through October; 9
A.M. to 3 P.M., November through March.

Bed & Breakfast, Inc.
1360 Moss Street
New Orleans, Louisiana 70152-2257
Hazel Boyce
(504) 525-4640; (800) 228-9711
Monday through Friday 8:00 A.M. to 5:00 P.M.

Bed & Breakfast, Vail Valley
Box 491
Vail, Colorado 81658
Kathy Fagan
(303) 949-1212
Daily 9:00 A.M. to 6:00 P.M., Winter; Monday through Friday 12:00
P.M. to 5:00 P.M., summer.

Bed & Breakfast of Maine
32 Colonial Village
Falmouth, Maine 04105
Peg Tierney
(207) 781-4528
Evenings and Weekends.

Bed and Breakfast of Los Angeles
32127 Harborview Lane
Westlake Village, California 91361
A. Kobabe & P. Marshall
(818) 889-8870; (818) 889-7325
Monday through Friday, 9:00 A.M. to 5:00 P.M.

Bensonhouse
2036 Monument Avenue
Richmond, Virginia 23220
L.M. Benson
(804) 648-7560
Monday through Friday 11 A.M. to 6 P.M.

Betsy Ross Bed & Breakfast in Michigan
Box 1731
Dearborn, Michigan 48121
Diane Shields
(313) 561-6041
Monday through Friday 6:00 P.M. to 11:00 P.M.; Saturday and
Sunday 9:00 A.M. to 9:00 P.M.

Blue Ridge Bed & Breakfast
Rocks & Rills
Box 259, Route 2
Berryville, Virginia 22611
Rita Duncan
(703) 955-1246
Monday through Saturday 9 A.M. to 1 P.M. (answering machine at
other times.)

California House Guests International, Inc.
18653 Ventura Boulevard
Tarzana, California 91356
Trudy Alexi
(818) 344-7878
Mondays through Fridays 7:00 A.M. to 4:00 P.M. Pacific Time
(machine Service).

Cohost, America's Bed & Breakfast
Box 9302
Whittier, California 90608
Coleen Davis
(213) 699-8427
Monday through Friday 7 A.M. to 7 P.M.

Eye Openers Bed & Breakfast Reservations
Box 694
Altadena, California 91001
Ruth Judkins & Betty Cox
(213) 684-4428
Monday through Saturday 9 A.M. to 5 P.M. Pacific Time.

Greater Boston Hospitality
Box 1142
Brookline, Massachusetts 02146
Lauren Simonelli
(617) 277-5430
Monday through Friday 9 A.M. to 5 P.M.

Guesthouses, Inc.
Road 9
West Chester, Pennsylvania 19380
Janice
(215) 692-4575
Monday through Friday 12 P.M. to 4 P.M.

Historic Charleston Bed & Breakfast
43 Legare Street
Charleston, South Carolina 29401
Charlotte Fainey
(803) 722-6606
Mondays through Fridays 9:30 A.M. to 5:30 P.M.

Kansas City Bed and Breakfast
Box 14781
Lenexa, Kansas 66215
Diane Kuhn
(913) 268-4214
(usually) Monday through Friday 8 A.M. to 9 P.M.
(answering machine otherwise).

Kentucky Homes Bed & Breakfast, Inc.
1431 St. James Court
Louisville, Kentucky 40208
L. Marshall & J. Dillehay
(502) 635-7341
Monday through Fridays 8 A.M. to 11 A.M., 4 P.M. to 7 P.M.
(machine all other times).

Leatherstocking Bed & Breakfast
389 Brockway Road
Frankfort, New York 13340
Floranne Mccraith
(315) 733-0040

Lincoln Limited Bed & Breakfast Mississippi Reservation Service
Box 3479
Merridan, Mississippi 39303
Barbara Lincoln Hall
(601) 482-5483
Monday through Friday 8:30 A.M. to 4:30 P.M.

Mi Casa Su Casa
Box 950
Tempe, Arizona 85281
Ruth Young
(602) 990-0682
Daily 8 A.M. to 8 P.M. Mountain Time.

Montreal Bed & Breakfast
4912 Victoria
Montreal, Quebec H3w 2n1
Marian Kahn
(514) 738-9410
Monday through Friday 9:00 A.M. to 7:00 P.M.;
Summer Months Mondays through Sundays 9:00 A.M. to 7:00 P.M.

Nutmeg Bed & Breakfast
222 Girard Avenue
Hartford, Connecticut 06105
Maxine Kates
(203) 236-6698
Monday through Friday 9 A.M. to 5 P.M.

Ohio Valley Bed & Breakfast
6876 Taylor Mill Road
Independence, Kentucky 41051
N. Cully & S. Parker Lotz
(606) 356-7865
Monday through Saturday 8:00 A.M. to 9:00 P.M.
Sunday Calls Answered Depending on Availability.

Pacific Bed & Breakfast
701 N.W. 60th Street
Seattle, Washington 98107
Irmgard Castleberry
(206) 794-0539
Monday through Friday 9 A.M. to 5 P.M. Pacific Time.

Pittsburgh Bed and Breakfast
2190 Ben Franklin Drive
Pittsburgh, Pennsylvania 15237
Judy Antico
(412) 367-8080
Monday through Friday 9:00 A.M. to 5:00 P.M.

Rainbow Hospitality
9348 Hennepin Avenue
Niagara Falls, New York 14304
Schoenherr & Broderick
(716) 283-4794
Monday through Friday 9:00 A.M. to 6:00 P.M.